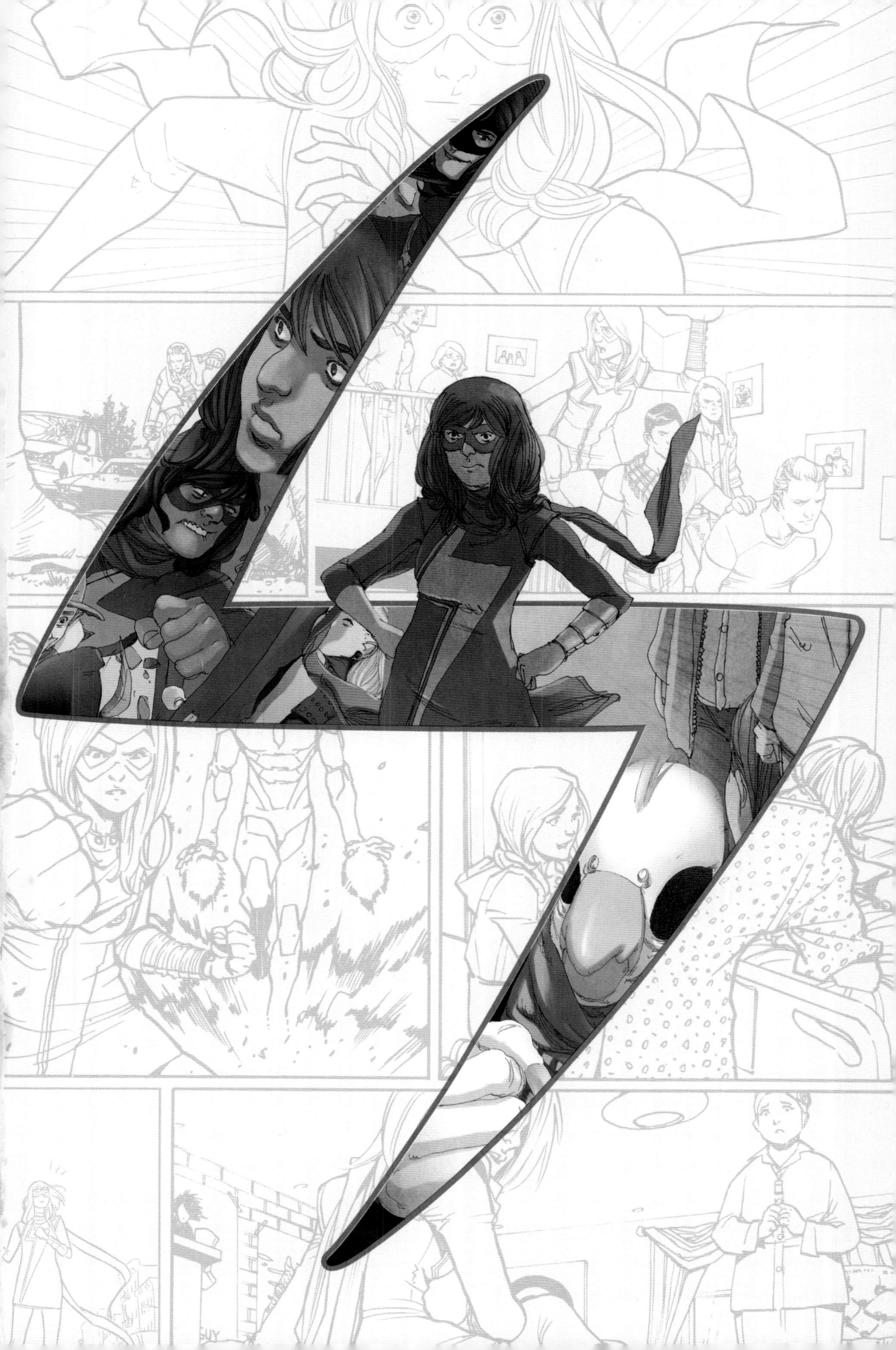

collection editor JENNIFER GRÜNWALD • assistant editor CAITLIN O'CONNELL
associate managing editor KATERI WOODY • editor, special projects MARK D. BEAZLEY
vp production & special projects JEFF YOUNGQUIST • svp print, sales & marketing DAVID GABRIEL

editor in chief AXEL ALONSO • chief creative officer JOE QUESADA
president DAN BUCKLEY • executive producer ALAN FINE

MS. MARVEL VOL. 3. Contains material originally published in magazine form as MS. MARVEL #1-12. First printing 2017. ISBN# 978-1-302-90361-9. Published by MARVEL WORLDWIDE, INC., a subsidiary of MARVEL ENTERTAINMENT, LLC. OFFICE OF PUBLICATION: 135 West 50th Street, New York, NY 10020. Copyright © 2017 MARVEL No similarity between any of the names, characters, persons, and/or institutions in this magazine with those of any living or dead person or institution is intended, and any such similarity which may exist is purely coincidental. Printed in China. DAN BUCKLEY, President, Marvel Entertainment; JOE QUESADA, Chief Creative Officer; TOM BREVOORT, SVP of Publishing; DAVID BOGART, SVP of Business Affairs & Operations, Publishing & Partnership; C.B. CEBULSKI, VP of Brand Management & Development, Asia; DAVID GABRIEL, SVP of Sales & Marketing, Publishing; JEFF YOUNGQUIST, VP of Production & Special Projects; DAN CARR, Executive Director of Publishing Technology; ALEX MORALES, Director of Publishing Operations; SUSAN CRESPI, Production Manager; STAN LEE, Chairman Emeritus. For information regarding advertising in Marvel Comics or on Marvel.com, please contact Vit DeBellis, Integrated Sales Manager, at vdebellis@marvel.com. For Marvel subscription inquiries, please call 888-511-5480. Manufactured between 2/10/2017 and 4/24/2017 by R.R. DONNELLEY ASIA PRINTING SOLUTIONS, CHINA.
10 9 8 7 6 5 4 3 2 1

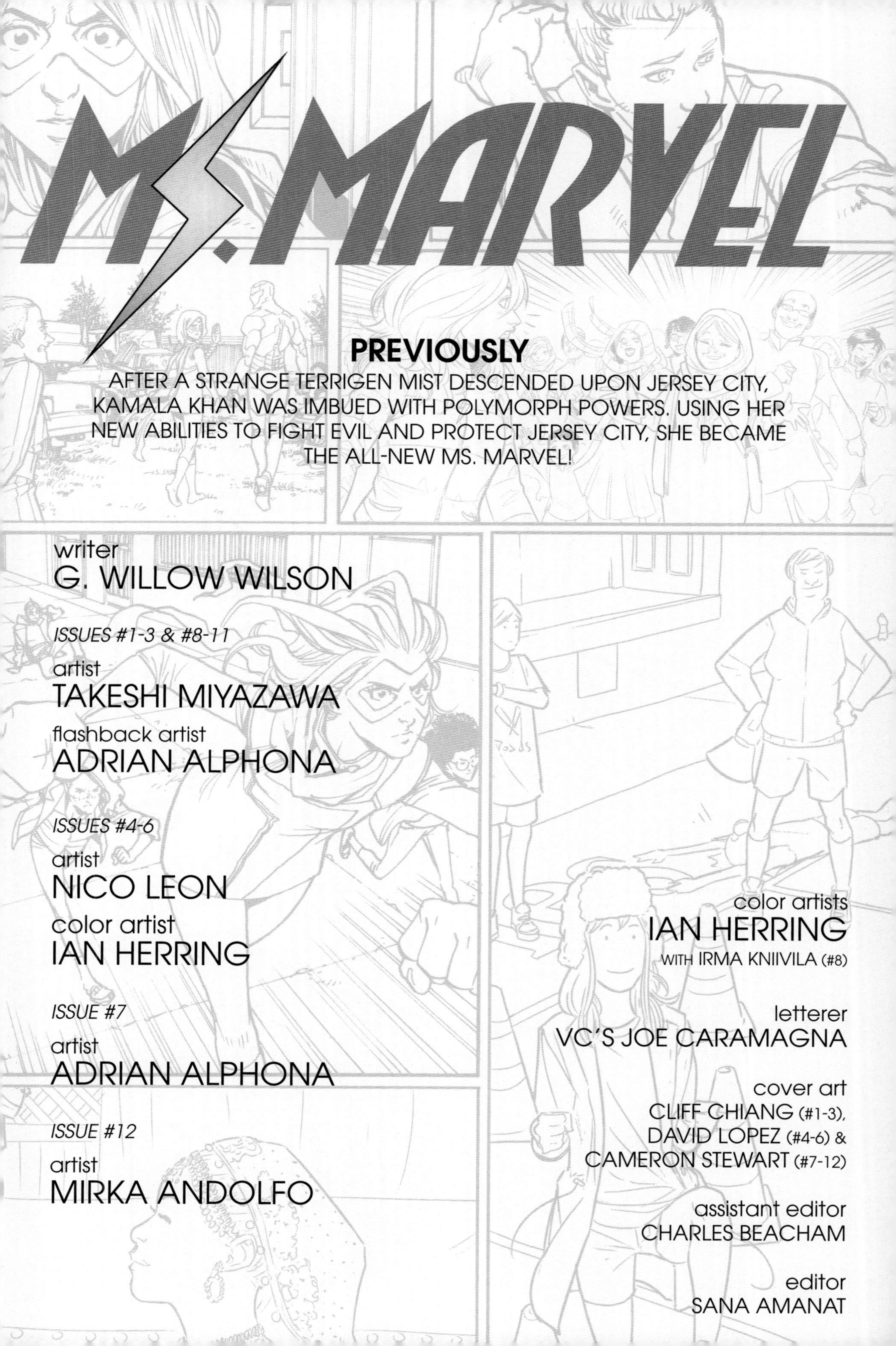

MS. MARVEL

PREVIOUSLY

AFTER A STRANGE TERRIGEN MIST DESCENDED UPON JERSEY CITY, KAMALA KHAN WAS IMBUED WITH POLYMORPH POWERS. USING HER NEW ABILITIES TO FIGHT EVIL AND PROTECT JERSEY CITY, SHE BECAME THE ALL-NEW MS. MARVEL!

writer
G. WILLOW WILSON

ISSUES #1-3 & #8-11

artist
TAKESHI MIYAZAWA

flashback artist
ADRIAN ALPHONA

ISSUES #4-6

artist
NICO LEON

color artist
IAN HERRING

ISSUE #7

artist
ADRIAN ALPHONA

ISSUE #12

artist
MIRKA ANDOLFO

color artists
IAN HERRING
WITH IRMA KNIIVILA (#8)

letterer
VC'S JOE CARAMAGNA

cover art
CLIFF CHIANG (#1-3),
DAVID LOPEZ (#4-6) &
CAMERON STEWART (#7-12)

assistant editor
CHARLES BEACHAM

editor
SANA AMANAT

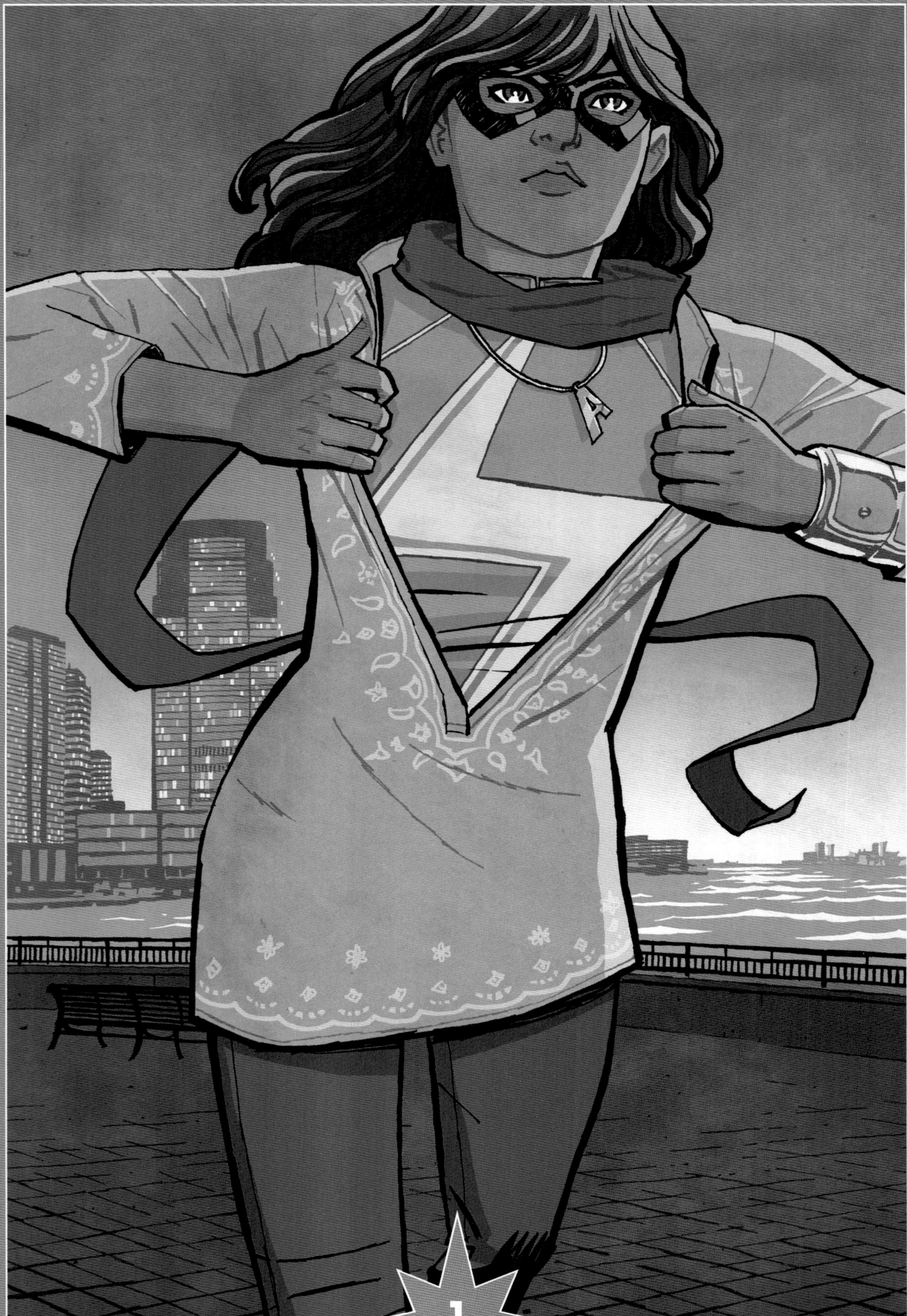
1

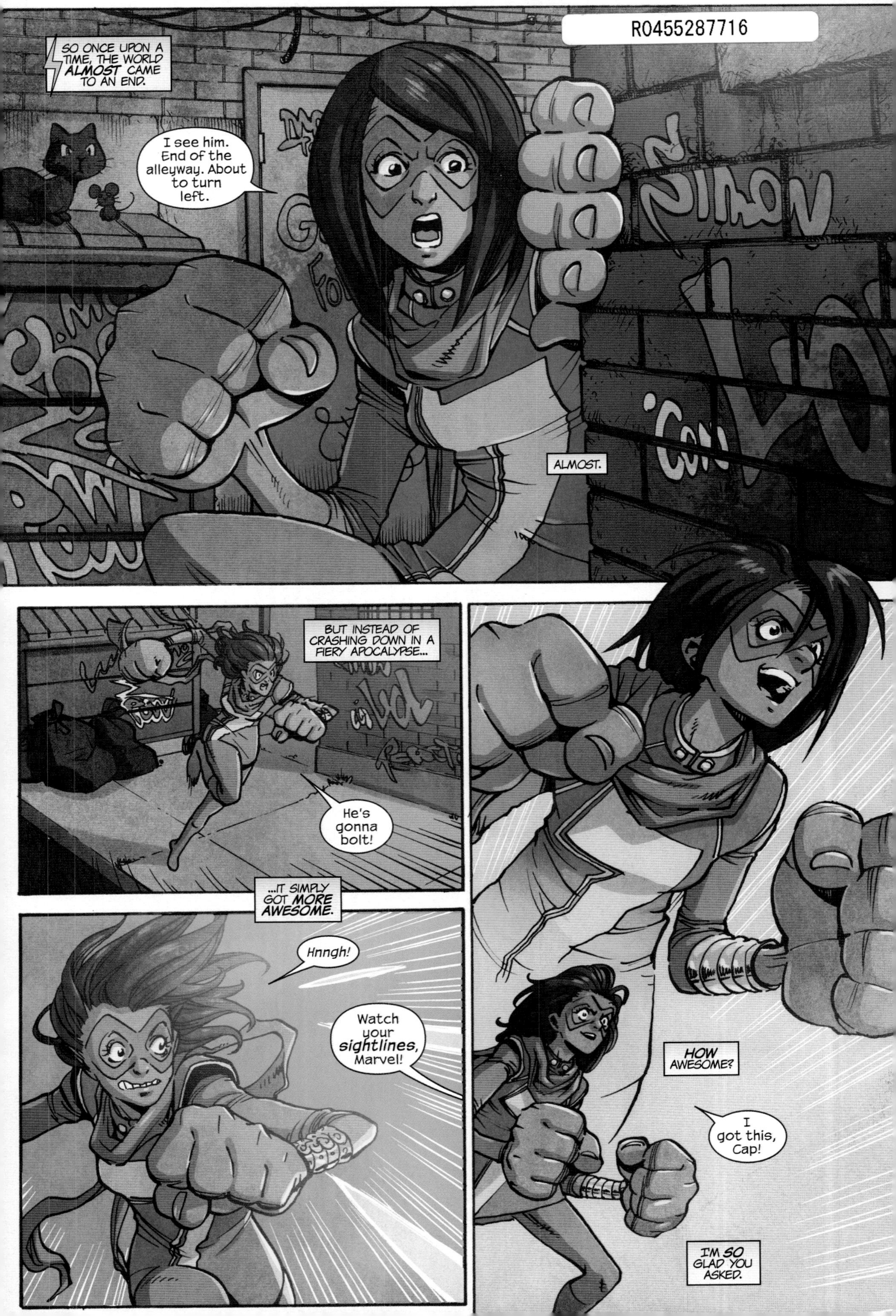
SO ONCE UPON A TIME, THE WORLD *ALMOST* CAME TO AN END.
I see him. End of the alleyway. About to turn left.
ALMOST.
BUT INSTEAD OF CRASHING DOWN IN A FIERY APOCALYPSE...
He's gonna bolt!
...IT SIMPLY GOT *MORE AWESOME*.
Hnngh!
Watch your *sightlines*, Marvel!
HOW AWESOME?
I got this, Cap!
I'M *SO* GLAD YOU ASKED.

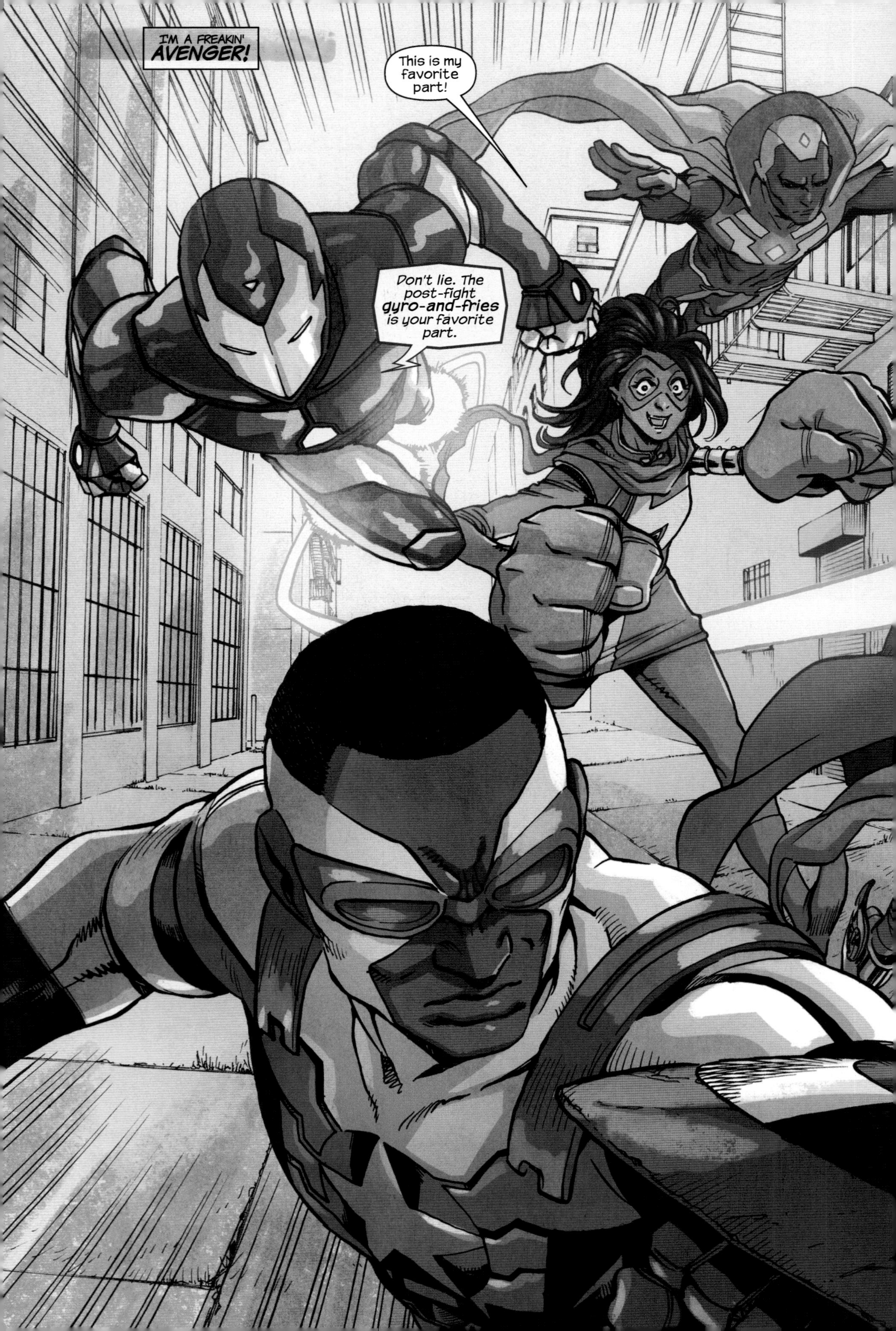
I'M A FREAKIN' AVENGER!
This is my favorite part!
Don't lie. The post-fight gyro-and-fries is your favorite part.

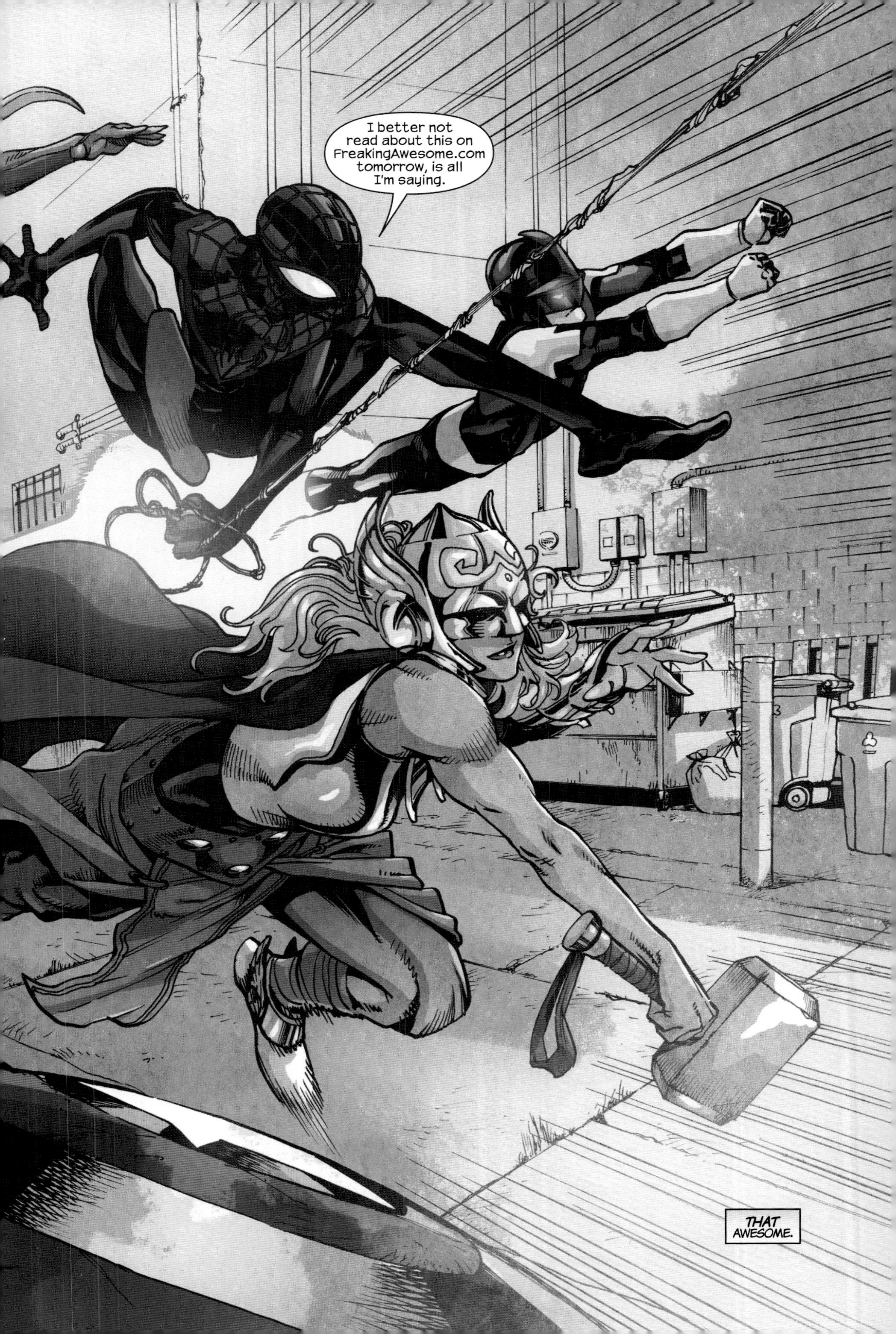
I better not read about this on FreakingAwesome.com tomorrow, is all I'm saying.
THAT AWESOME.

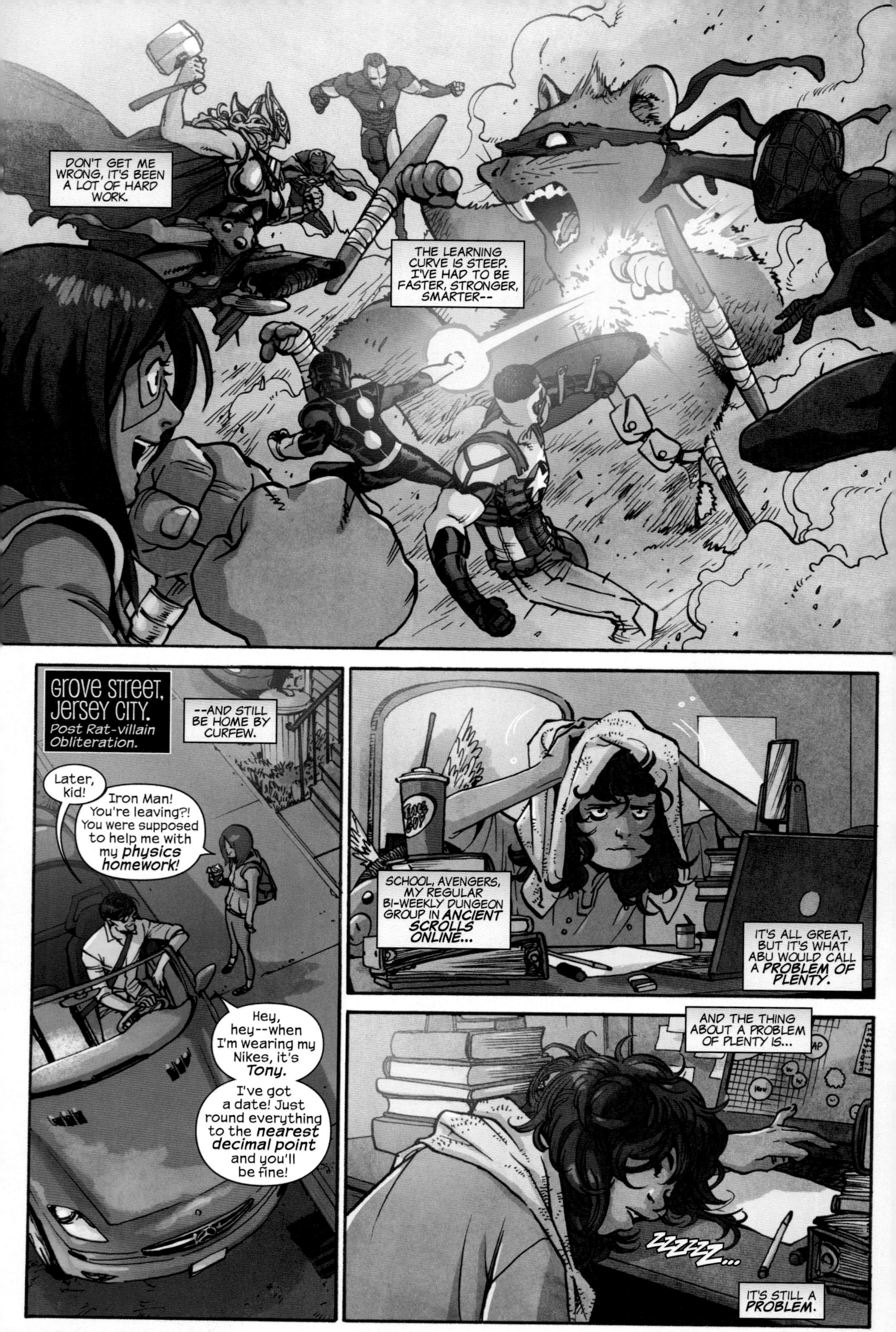

DON'T GET ME WRONG, IT'S BEEN A LOT OF HARD WORK.
THE LEARNING CURVE IS STEEP. I'VE HAD TO BE FASTER, STRONGER, SMARTER--
Grove Street, Jersey City. Post Rat-villain Obliteration.
--AND STILL BE HOME BY CURFEW.
Later, kid!
Iron Man! You're leaving?! You were supposed to help me with my physics homework!
Hey, hey--when I'm wearing my Nikes, it's Tony.
I've got a date! Just round everything to the nearest decimal point and you'll be fine!
SCHOOL, AVENGERS, MY REGULAR BI-WEEKLY DUNGEON GROUP IN ANCIENT SCROLLS ONLINE...
IT'S ALL GREAT, BUT IT'S WHAT ABU WOULD CALL A PROBLEM OF PLENTY.
AND THE THING ABOUT A PROBLEM OF PLENTY IS...
ZZZZZZ...
IT'S STILL A PROBLEM.

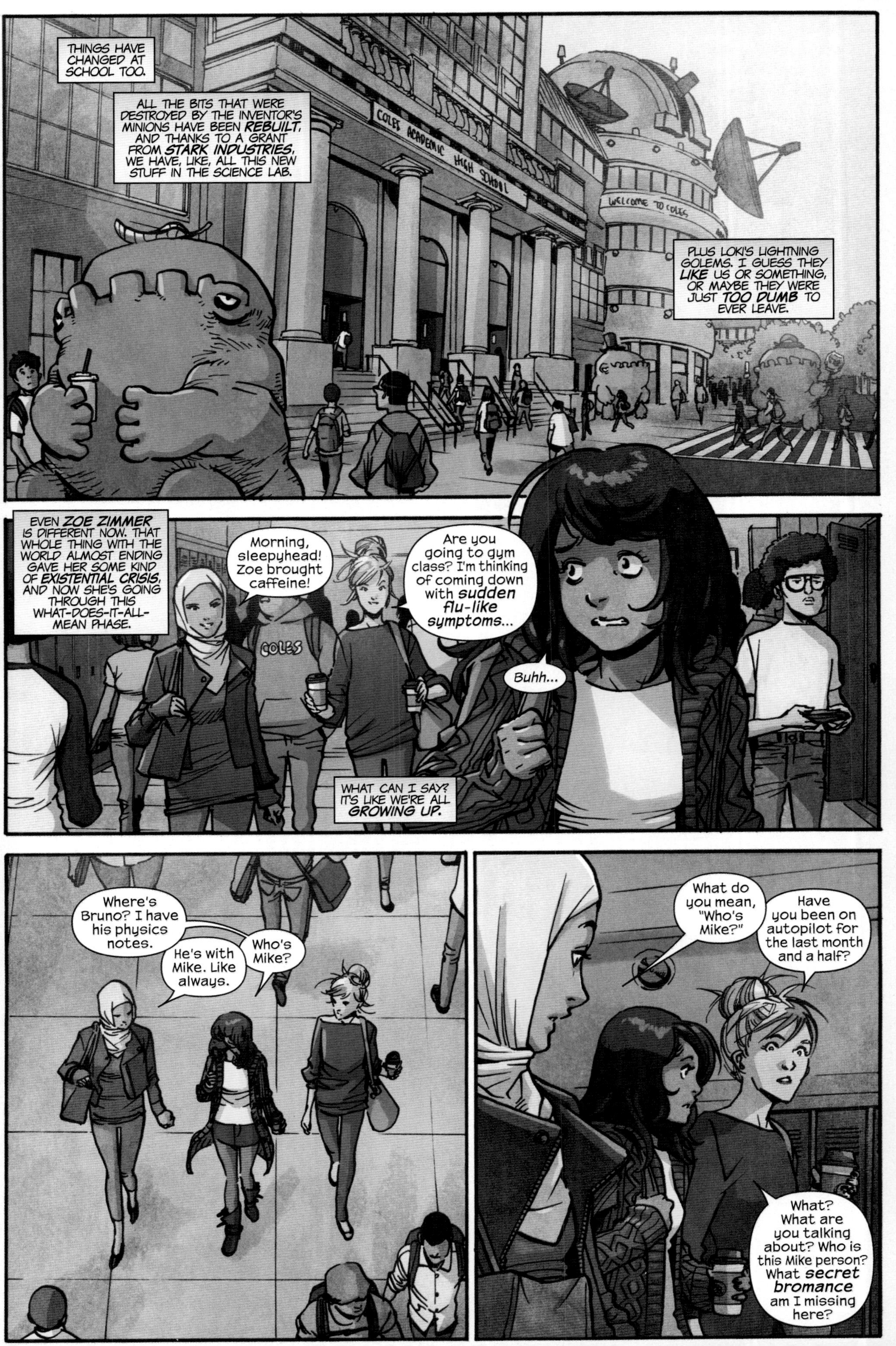
THINGS HAVE CHANGED AT SCHOOL TOO.
ALL THE BITS THAT WERE DESTROYED BY THE INVENTOR'S MINIONS HAVE BEEN REBUILT, AND THANKS TO A GRANT FROM STARK INDUSTRIES, WE HAVE, LIKE, ALL THIS NEW STUFF IN THE SCIENCE LAB.
COLES ACADEMIC HIGH SCHOOL
WELCOME TO COLES
PLUS LOKI'S LIGHTNING GOLEMS. I GUESS THEY LIKE US OR SOMETHING, OR MAYBE THEY WERE JUST TOO DUMB TO EVER LEAVE.
EVEN ZOE ZIMMER IS DIFFERENT NOW. THAT WHOLE THING WITH THE WORLD ALMOST ENDING GAVE HER SOME KIND OF EXISTENTIAL CRISIS, AND NOW SHE'S GOING THROUGH THIS WHAT-DOES-IT-ALL-MEAN PHASE.
Morning, sleepyhead! Zoe brought caffeine!
Are you going to gym class? I'm thinking of coming down with sudden flu-like symptoms...
COLES
Buhh...
WHAT CAN I SAY? IT'S LIKE WE'RE ALL GROWING UP.
Where's Bruno? I have his physics notes.
He's with Mike. Like always.
Who's Mike?
What do you mean, "Who's Mike?"
Have you been on autopilot for the last month and a half?
What? What are you talking about? Who is this Mike person? What secret bromance am I missing here?

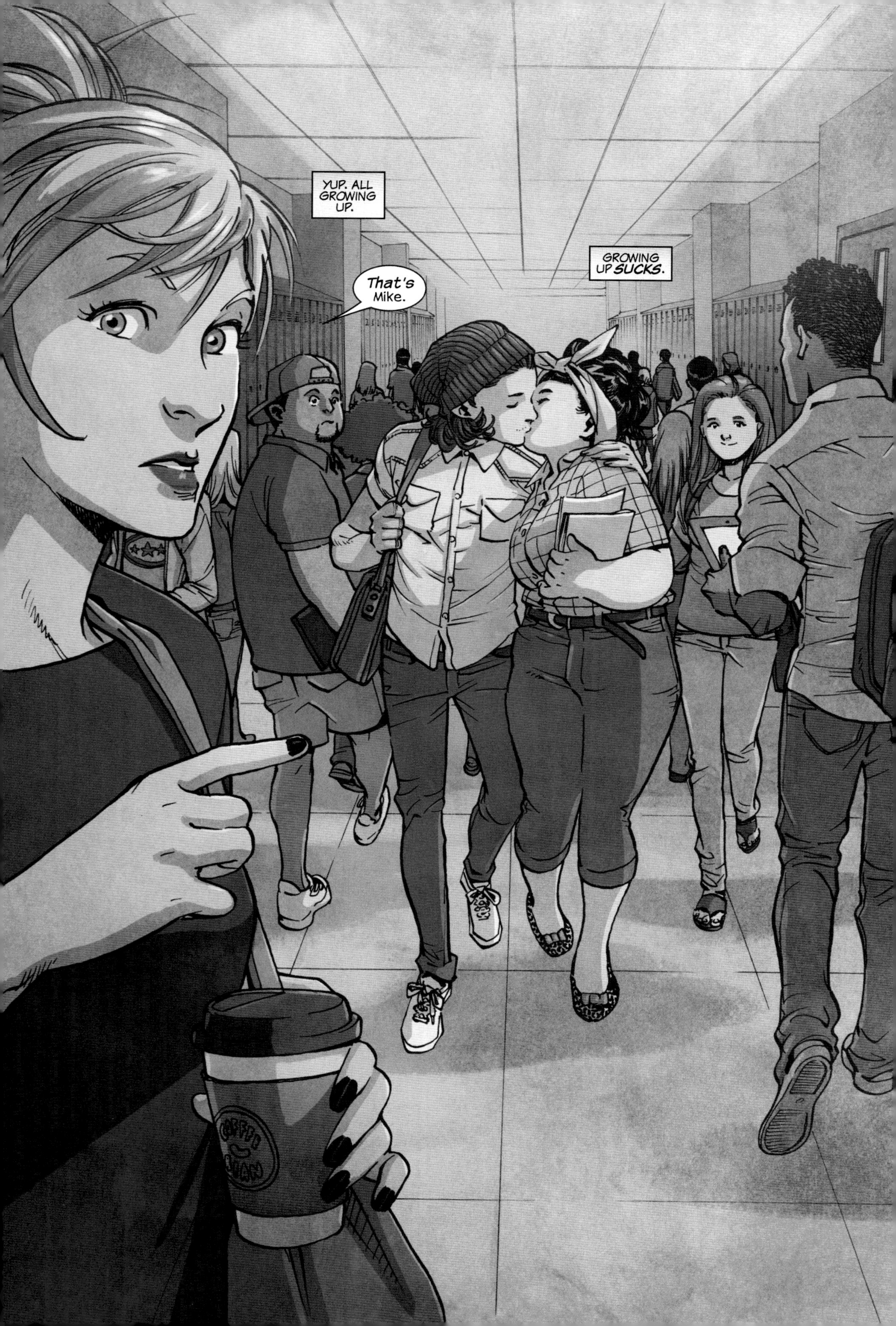

YUP. ALL GROWING UP.
That's Mike.
GROWING UP SUCKS.

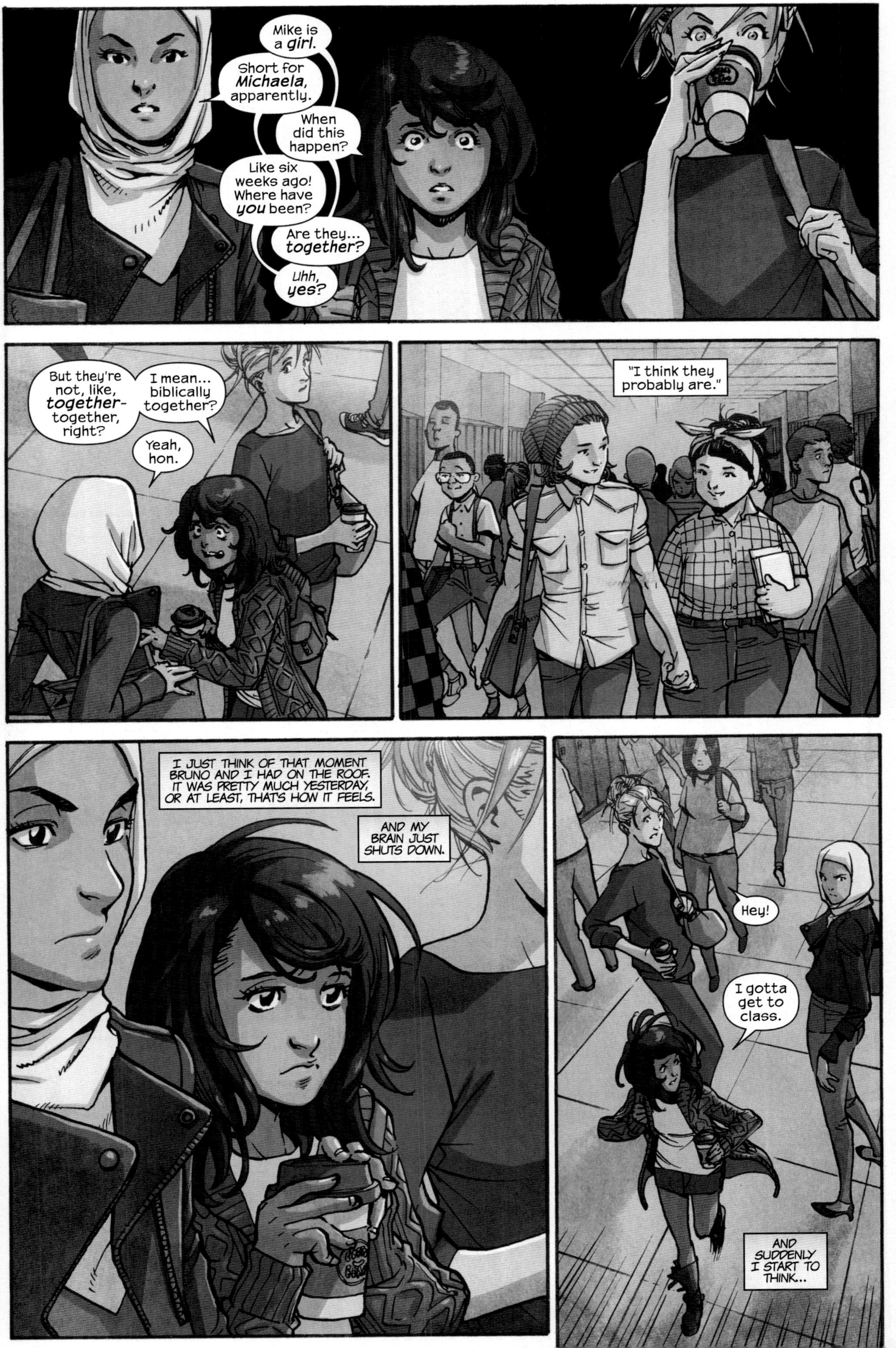
Mike is a *girl*.
Short for *Michaela*, apparently.
When did this happen?
Like six weeks ago! Where have *you* been?
Are they... *together*?
Uhh, *yes*?
But they're not, like, *together*-together, right?
I mean... biblically together?
Yeah, hon.
"I think they probably are."
I JUST THINK OF THAT MOMENT BRUNO AND I HAD ON THE ROOF. IT WAS PRETTY MUCH YESTERDAY, OR AT LEAST, THAT'S HOW IT FEELS.
AND MY BRAIN JUST SHUTS DOWN.
Hey!
I gotta get to class.
AND SUDDENLY I START TO THINK...

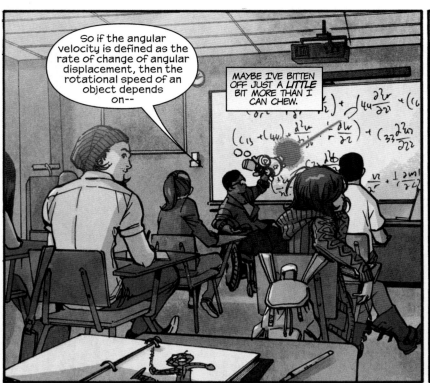

So if the angular velocity is defined as the rate of change of angular displacement, then the rotational speed of an object depends on--

MAYBE I'VE BITTEN OFF JUST A *LITTLE* BIT MORE THAN I CAN CHEW.

Hey--did you get the homework last night? I didn't understand the last part.

Gosh. That's too bad.

Why are you being *mean*? It was a totally innocent question!

Maybe you should ask your *girlfriend* instead.

Is *that* what this is about?! Mike?!

Yes, *Mike*. Mike who *everybody* knew about except *me*.

Kamala! Bruno! You know my policy. Drama gets left at the door. In here, we speak *science*.

Sorry, Ms. Norris.

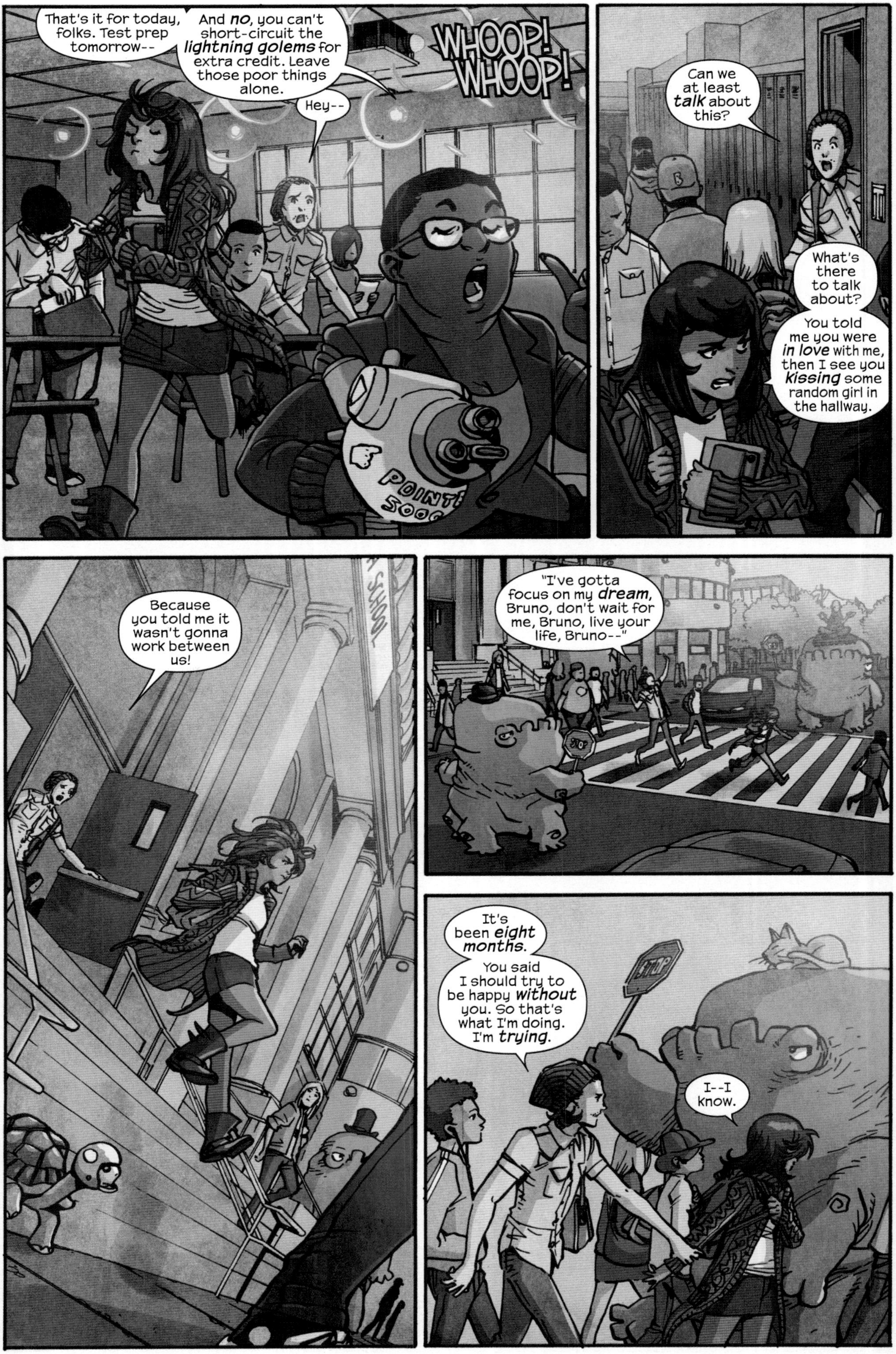

That's it for today, folks. Test prep tomorrow--
And **no**, you can't short-circuit the **lightning golems** for extra credit. Leave those poor things alone.
WHOOP! WHOOP!
Hey--
POINT 5000
Can we at least **talk** about this?
What's there to talk about?
You told me you were **in love** with me, then I see you **kissing** some random girl in the hallway.
Because you told me it wasn't gonna work between us!
"I've gotta focus on my **dream**, Bruno, don't wait for me, Bruno, live your life, Bruno--"
It's been **eight months**.
You said I should try to be happy **without** you. So that's what I'm doing. I'm **trying**.
I--I know.

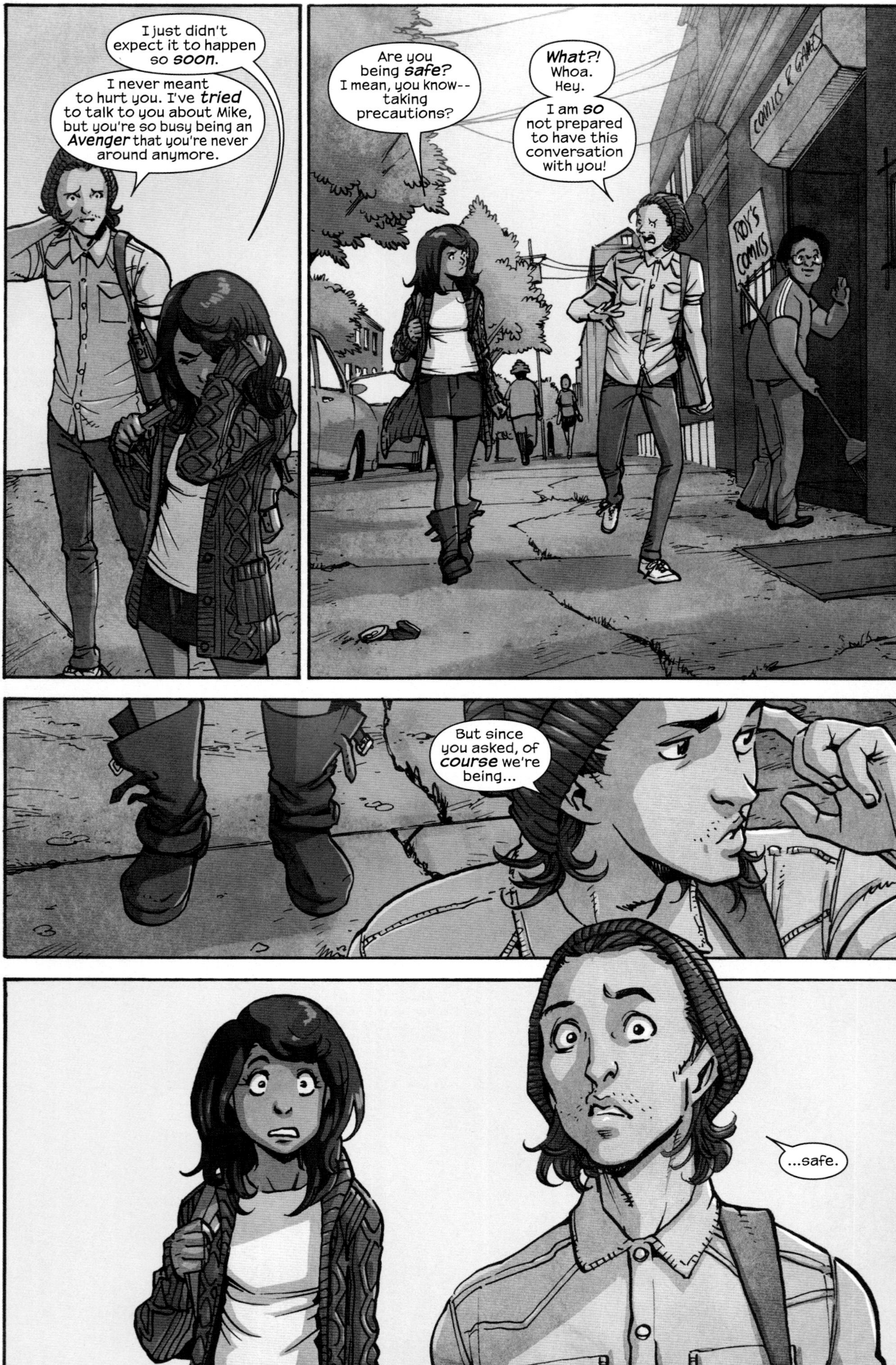

I just didn't expect it to happen so *soon*.
I never meant to hurt you. I've *tried* to talk to you about Mike, but you're so busy being an *Avenger* that you're never around anymore.
Are you being *safe*? I mean, you know-- taking precautions?
What?! Whoa. Hey.
I am *so* not prepared to have this conversation with you!
COMICS & GAMES
ROY'S COMICS
But since you asked, of *course* we're being...
...safe.

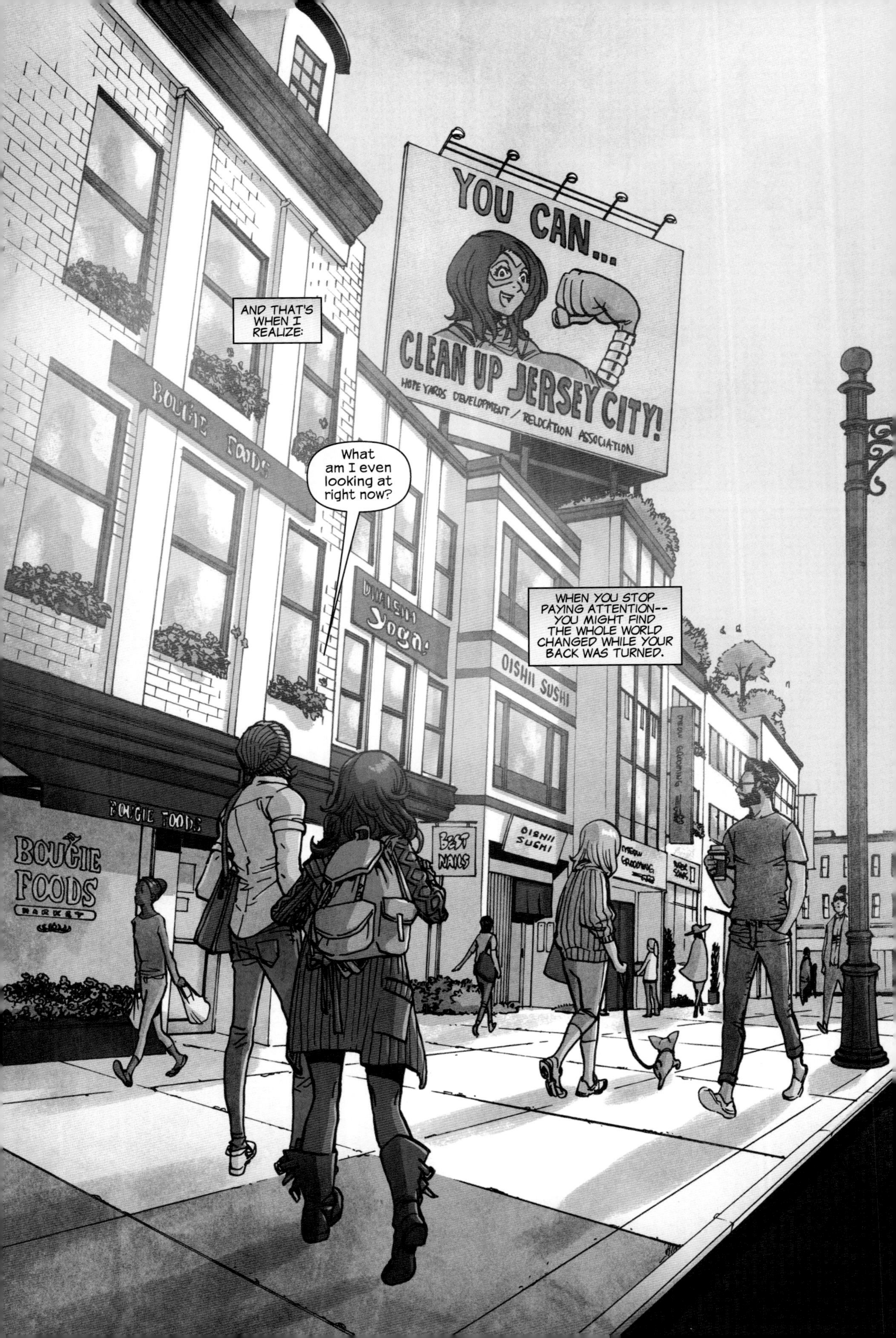
AND THAT'S WHEN I REALIZE:
YOU CAN...
CLEAN UP JERSEY CITY!
HOPE YARDS DEVELOPMENT / RELOCATION ASSOCIATION
What am I even looking at right now?
BOUGIE FOODS
Yoga!
WHEN YOU STOP PAYING ATTENTION-- YOU MIGHT FIND THE WHOLE WORLD CHANGED WHILE YOUR BACK WAS TURNED.
OISHII SUSHI
BOUGIE FOODS
BOUGIE FOODS MARKET
BEST NAILS
OISHII SUSHI

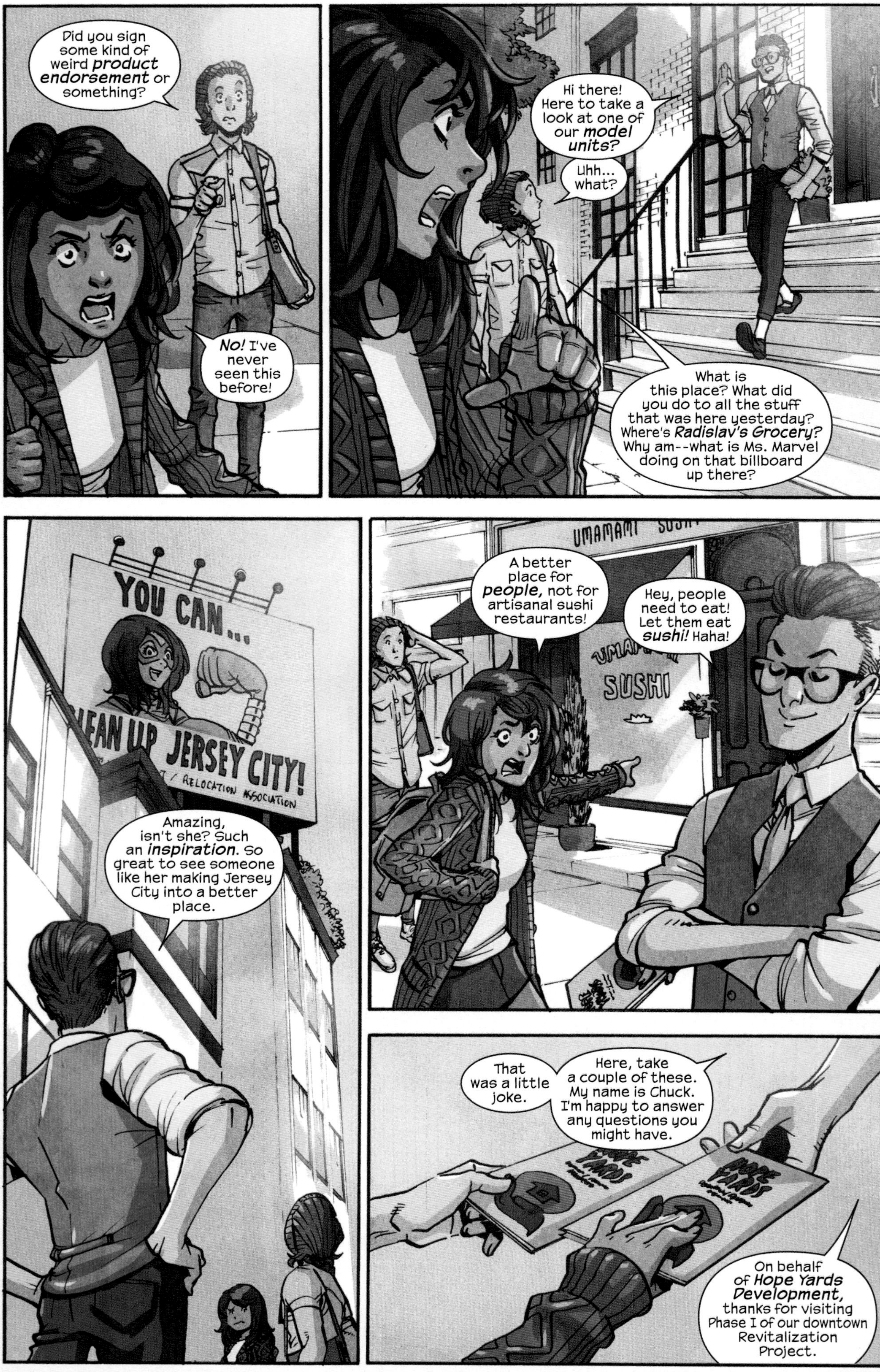

Did you sign some kind of weird *product endorsement* or something?
No! I've never seen this before!
Hi there! Here to take a look at one of our *model units?*
Uhh... what?
What is this place? What did you do to all the stuff that was here yesterday? Where's *Radislav's Grocery?* Why am--what is Ms. Marvel doing on that billboard up there?
YOU CAN...
JERSEY CITY!
RELOCATION ASSOCIATION
Amazing, isn't she? Such an *inspiration*. So great to see someone like her making Jersey City into a better place.
UMAMAMI
SUSHI
A better place for *people,* not for artisanal sushi restaurants!
Hey, people need to eat! Let them eat *sushi!* Haha!
That was a little joke.
Here, take a couple of these. My name is Chuck. I'm happy to answer any questions you might have.
HOPE YARDS
On behalf of *Hope Yards Development,* thanks for visiting Phase I of our downtown Revitalization Project.

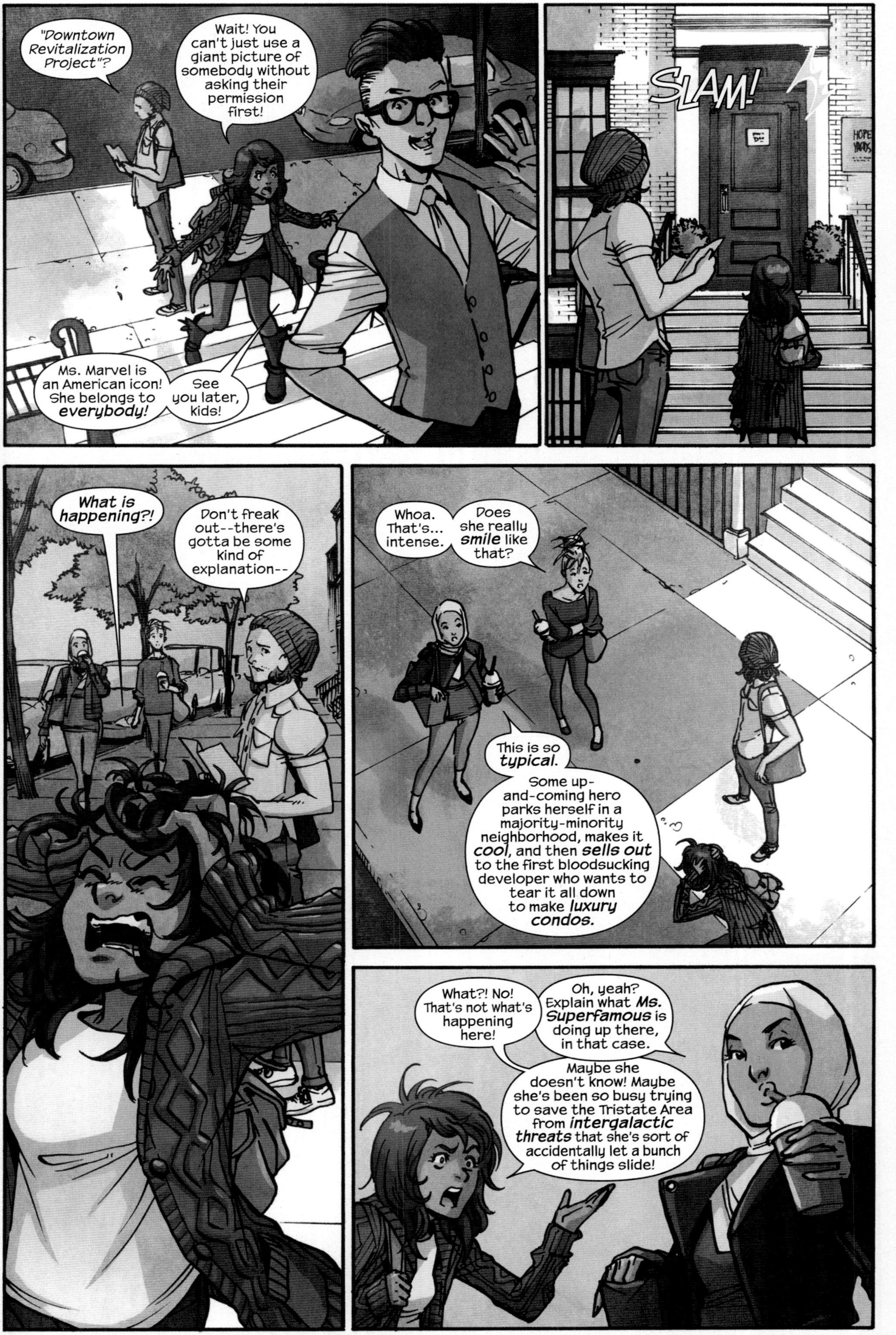
"Downtown Revitalization Project"?
Wait! You can't just use a giant picture of somebody without asking their permission first!
Ms. Marvel is an American icon! She belongs to *everybody!*
See you later, kids!
SLAM!
HOPE YARDS
What is happening?!
Don't freak out--there's gotta be some kind of explanation--
Whoa. That's... intense.
Does she really *smile* like that?
This is so *typical*.
Some up-and-coming hero parks herself in a majority-minority neighborhood, makes it *cool*, and then *sells out* to the first bloodsucking developer who wants to tear it all down to make *luxury condos.*
What?! No! That's not what's happening here!
Oh, yeah? Explain what *Ms. Superfamous* is doing up there, in that case.
Maybe she doesn't know! Maybe she's been so busy trying to save the Tristate Area from *intergalactic threats* that she's sort of accidentally let a bunch of things slide!

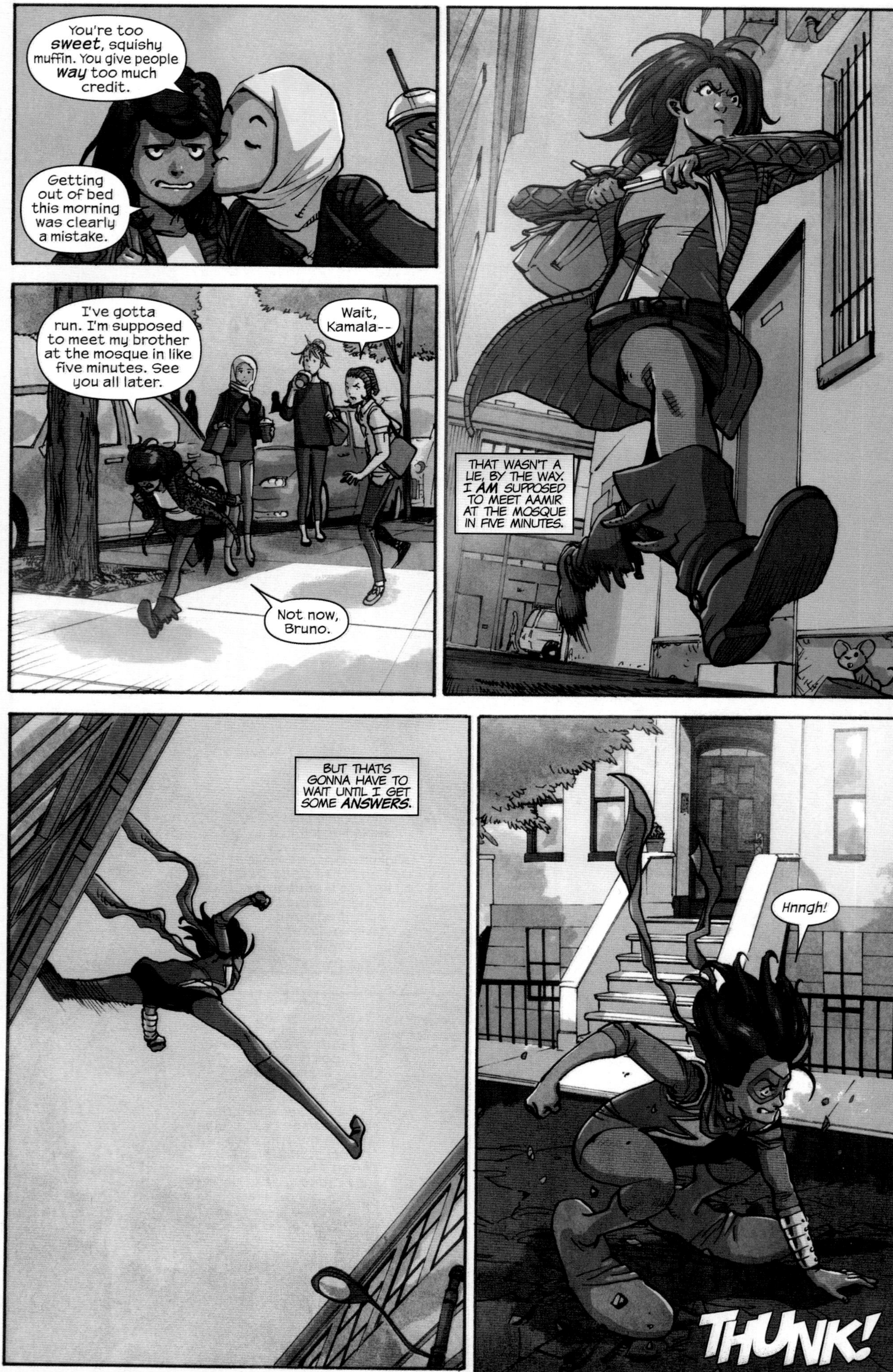
You're too sweet, squishy muffin. You give people way too much credit.
Getting out of bed this morning was clearly a mistake.
I've gotta run. I'm supposed to meet my brother at the mosque in like five minutes. See you all later.
Wait, Kamala--
Not now, Bruno.
THAT WASN'T A LIE, BY THE WAY. I AM SUPPOSED TO MEET AAMIR AT THE MOSQUE IN FIVE MINUTES.
BUT THAT'S GONNA HAVE TO WAIT UNTIL I GET SOME ANSWERS.
Hnngh!
THUNK!

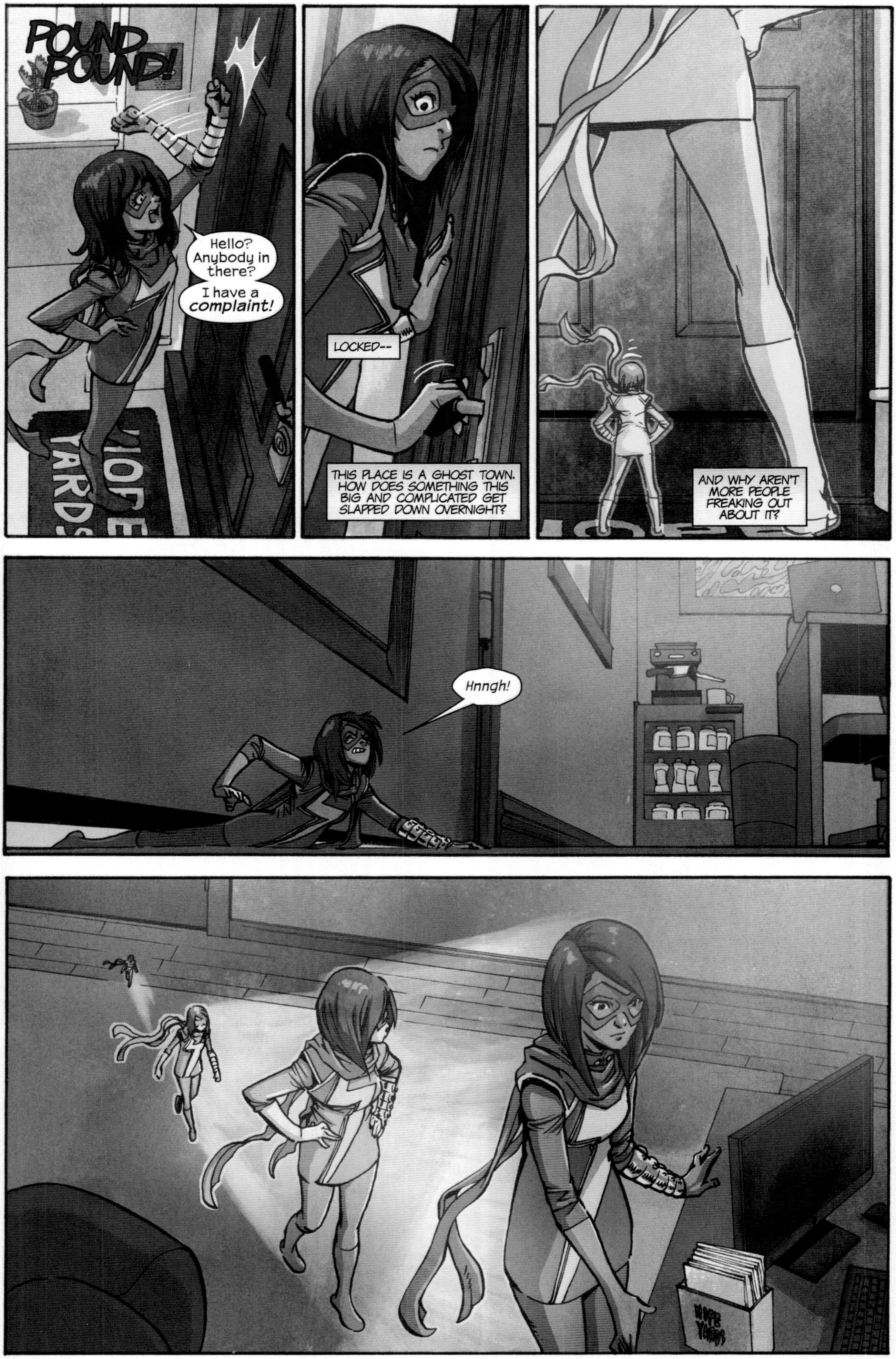
POUND POUND!
Hello? Anybody in there?
I have a complaint!
LOCKED--
THIS PLACE IS A GHOST TOWN. HOW DOES SOMETHING THIS BIG AND COMPLICATED GET SLAPPED DOWN OVERNIGHT?
AND WHY AREN'T MORE PEOPLE FREAKING OUT ABOUT IT?
Hnngh!

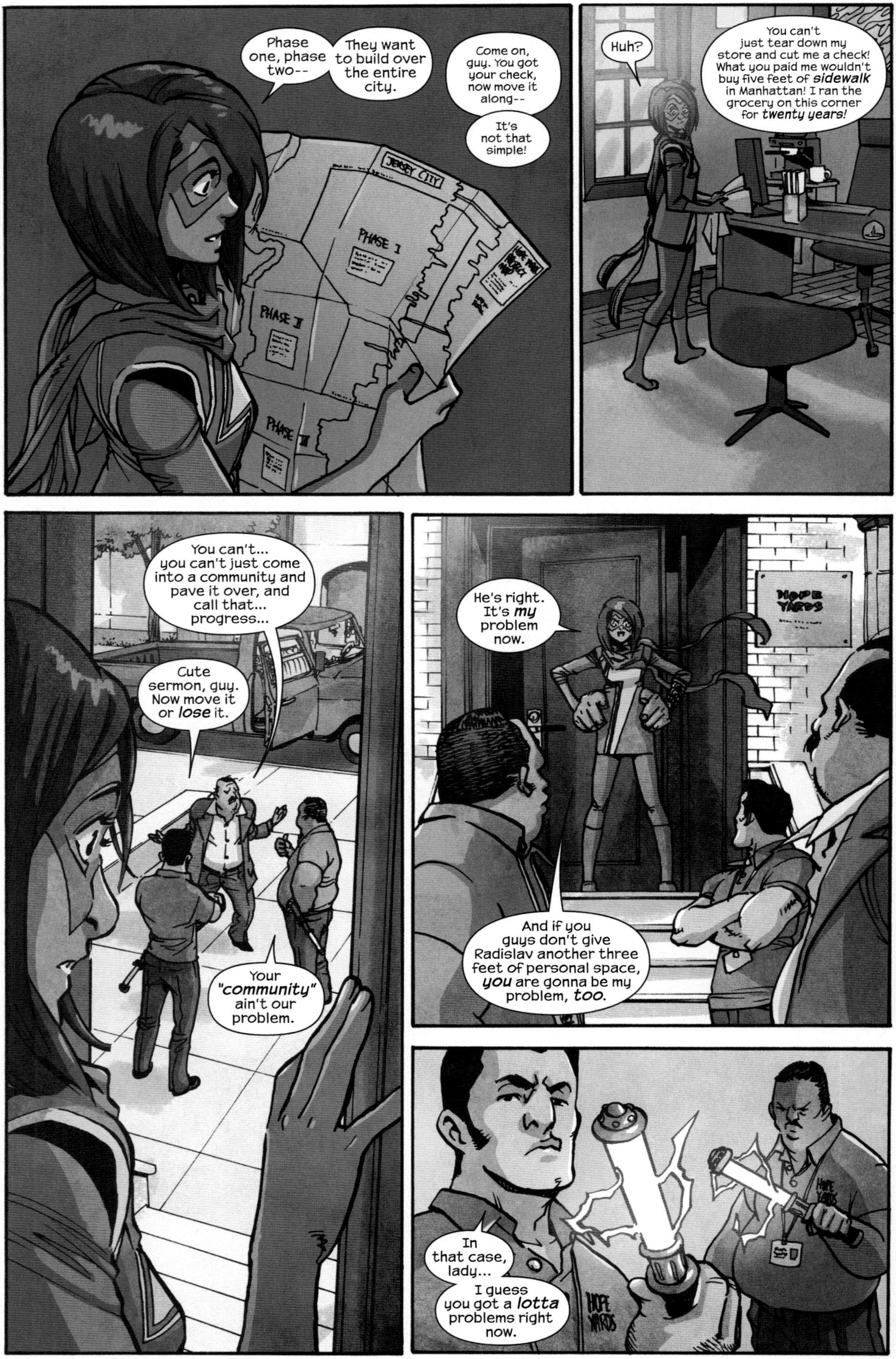
Phase one, phase two--
They want to build over the entire city.
Come on, guy. You got your check, now move it along--
It's not that simple!
JERSEY CITY
PHASE I
PHASE II
PHASE III
Huh?
You can't just tear down my store and cut me a check! What you paid me wouldn't buy five feet of sidewalk in Manhattan! I ran the grocery on this corner for twenty years!
You can't... you can't just come into a community and pave it over, and call that... progress...
Cute sermon, guy. Now move it or lose it.
Your "community" ain't our problem.
He's right. It's my problem now.
HOPE YARDS
And if you guys don't give Radislav another three feet of personal space, you are gonna be my problem, too.
In that case, lady...
I guess you got a lotta problems right now.
HOPE YARDS

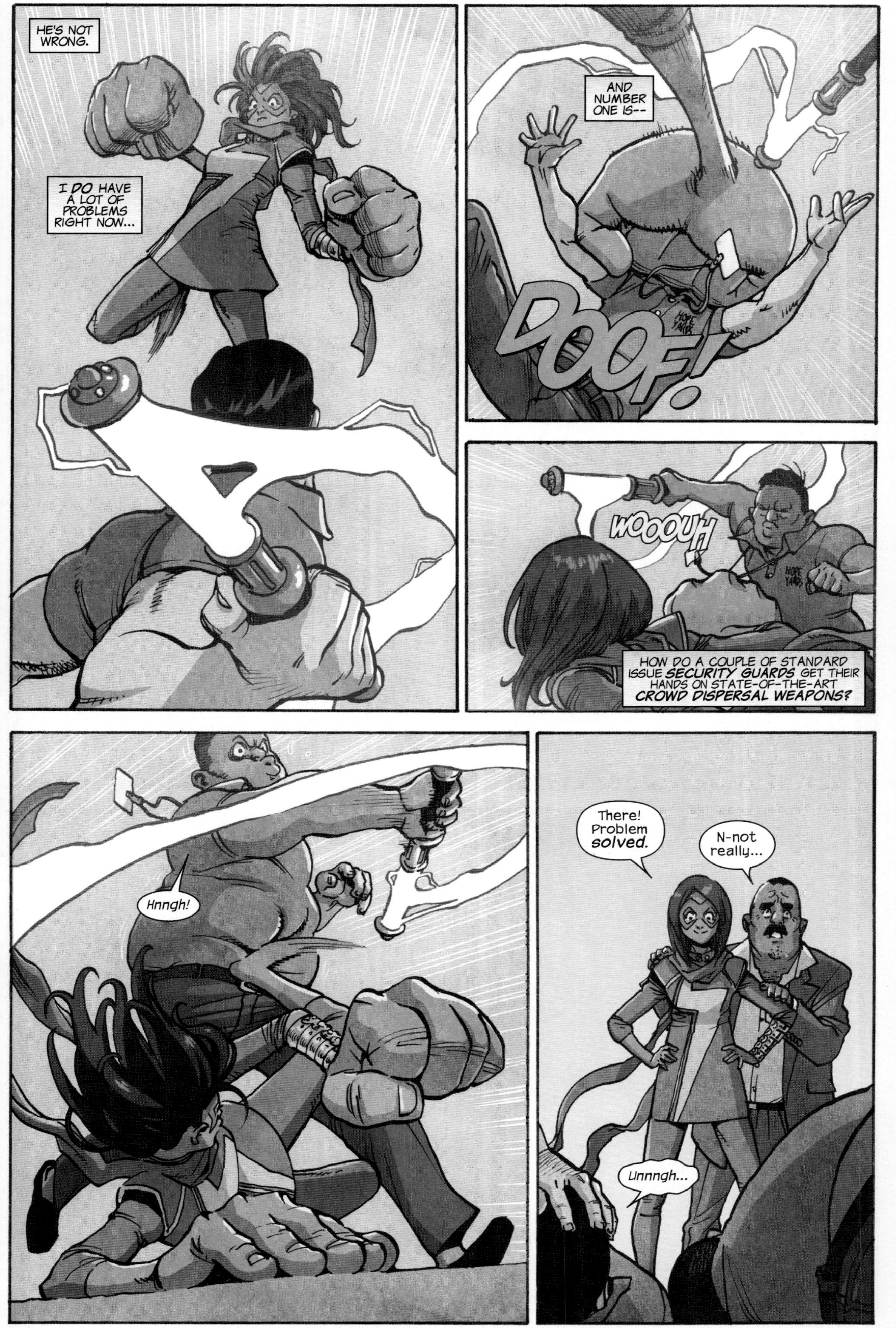
HE'S NOT WRONG.
I DO HAVE A LOT OF PROBLEMS RIGHT NOW...
AND NUMBER ONE IS--
DOOF!
WOOOUH
HOW DO A COUPLE OF STANDARD ISSUE SECURITY GUARDS GET THEIR HANDS ON STATE-OF-THE-ART CROWD DISPERSAL WEAPONS?
Hnngh!
There! Problem solved.
N-not really...
Unnngh...

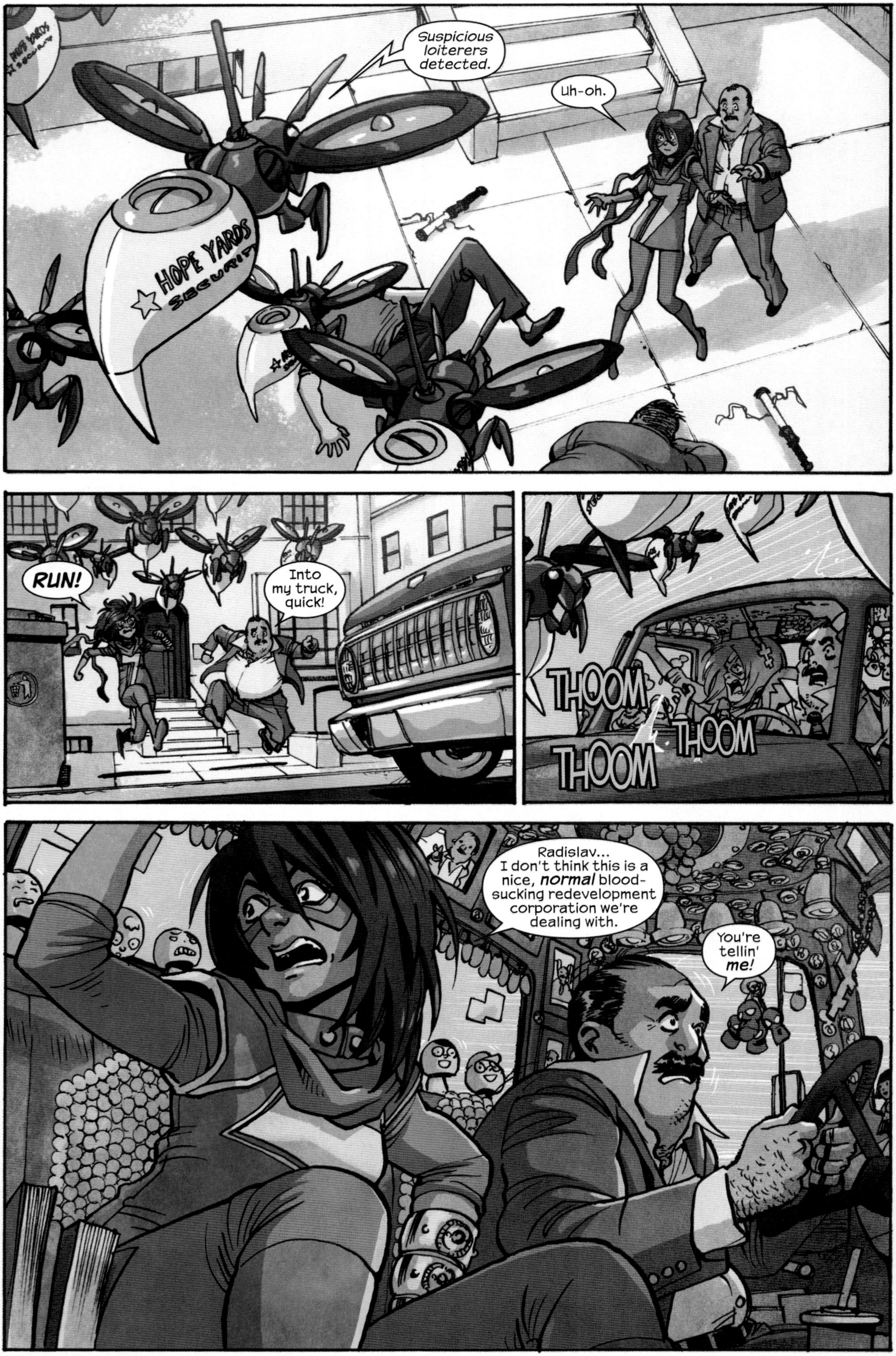
Suspicious loiterers detected.
Uh-oh.
HOPE YARDS SECURITY
RUN!
Into my truck, quick!
THOOM
THOOM
THOOM
Radislav... I don't think this is a nice, **normal** blood-sucking redevelopment corporation we're dealing with.
You're tellin' **me!**

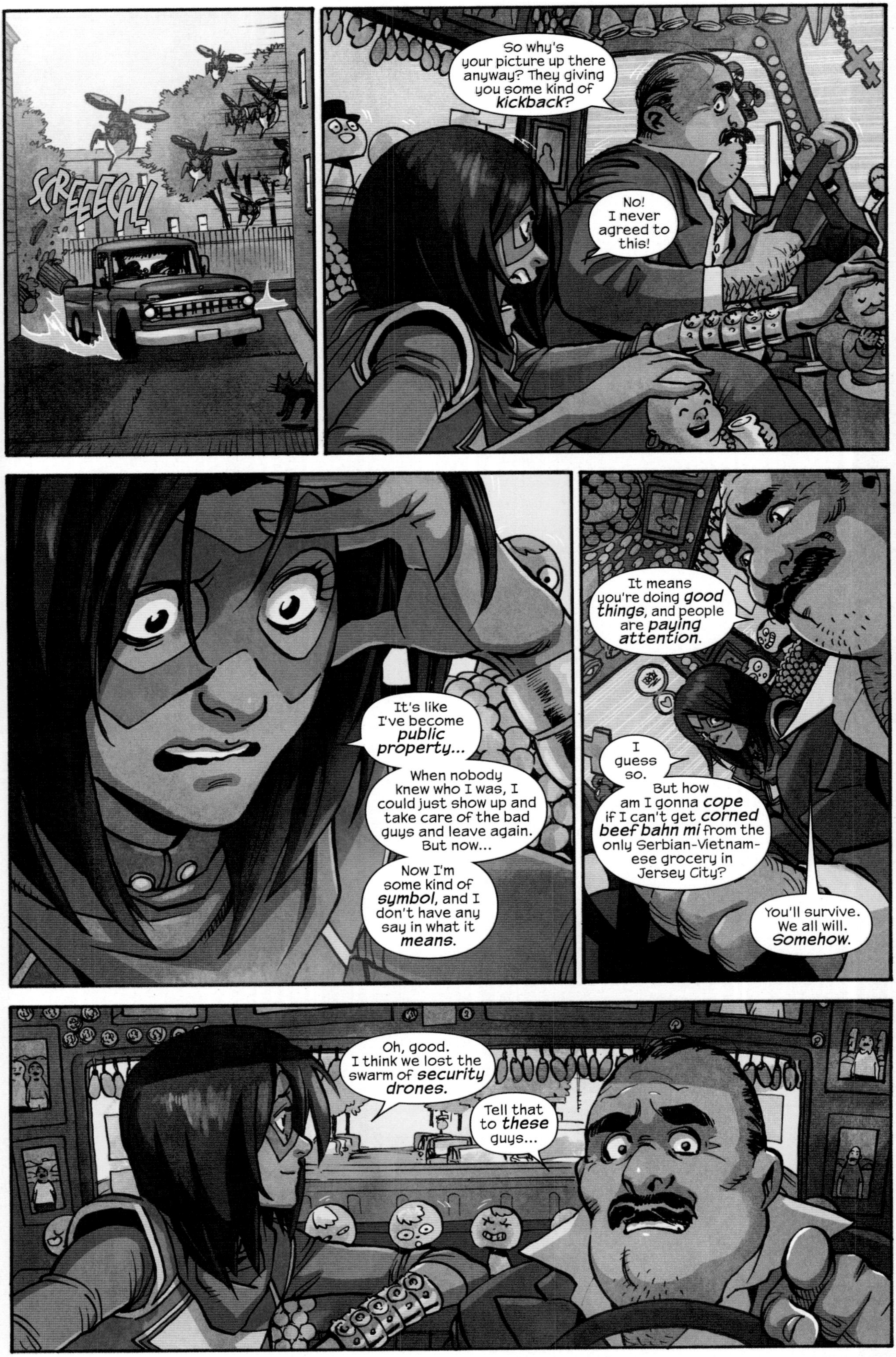
SCREEECH!
So why's your picture up there anyway? They giving you some kind of kickback?
No! I never agreed to this!
It's like I've become public property...
When nobody knew who I was, I could just show up and take care of the bad guys and leave again. But now...
Now I'm some kind of symbol, and I don't have any say in what it means.
It means you're doing good things, and people are paying attention.
I guess so.
But how am I gonna cope if I can't get corned beef bahn mi from the only Serbian-Vietnamese grocery in Jersey City?
You'll survive. We all will. Somehow.
Oh, good. I think we lost the swarm of security drones.
Tell that to these guys...

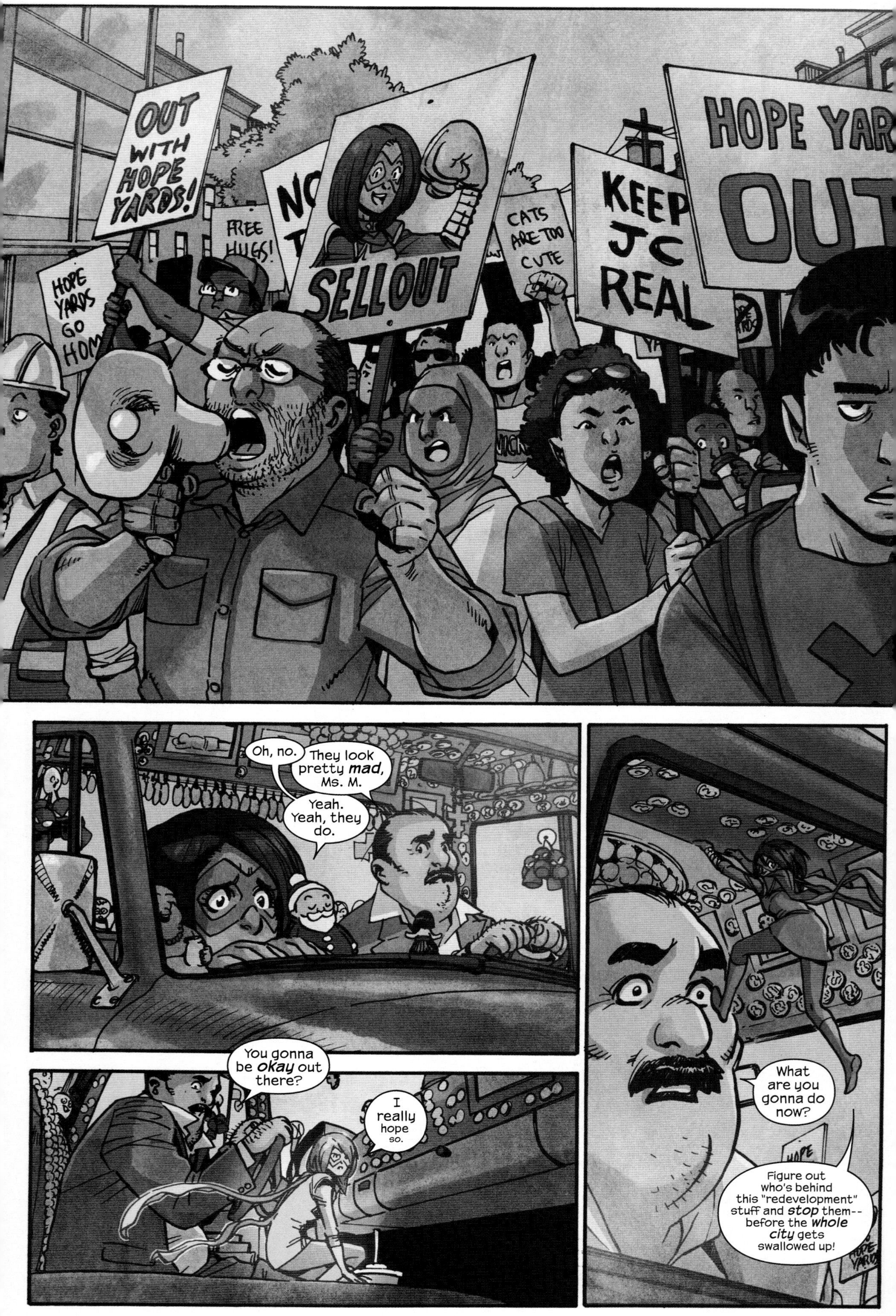
OUT WITH HOPE YARDS!
FREE HUGS!
HOPE YARDS GO HOM
SELLOUT
CATS ARE TOO CUTE
KEEP JC REAL
HOPE YAR
OUT
Oh, no.
They look pretty *mad*, Ms. M.
Yeah. Yeah, they do.
What are you gonna do now?
Figure out who's behind this "redevelopment" stuff and *stop* them-- before the *whole city* gets swallowed up!
You gonna be *okay* out there?
I really hope so.

I kind of hate *shrinking*...

No matter how many times I do it, it never gets less weird to see soda cans the size of *minivans*...

KAMALA? HELLLOOO?

I coulda sworn she went this way...

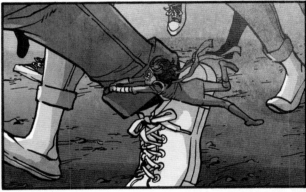

Huh?!

Just keep walking! Away!

Let's *never* do this again. Tiny Ms. Marvel is *terrifying*.

Fine by me! Since you're already spending 99% of your time with your *non-tiny* girlfriend!

Hey. I know you're *upset*, but that wasn't cool.

Don't be that guy. You're *not* that guy. Mike is *great* the way she is.

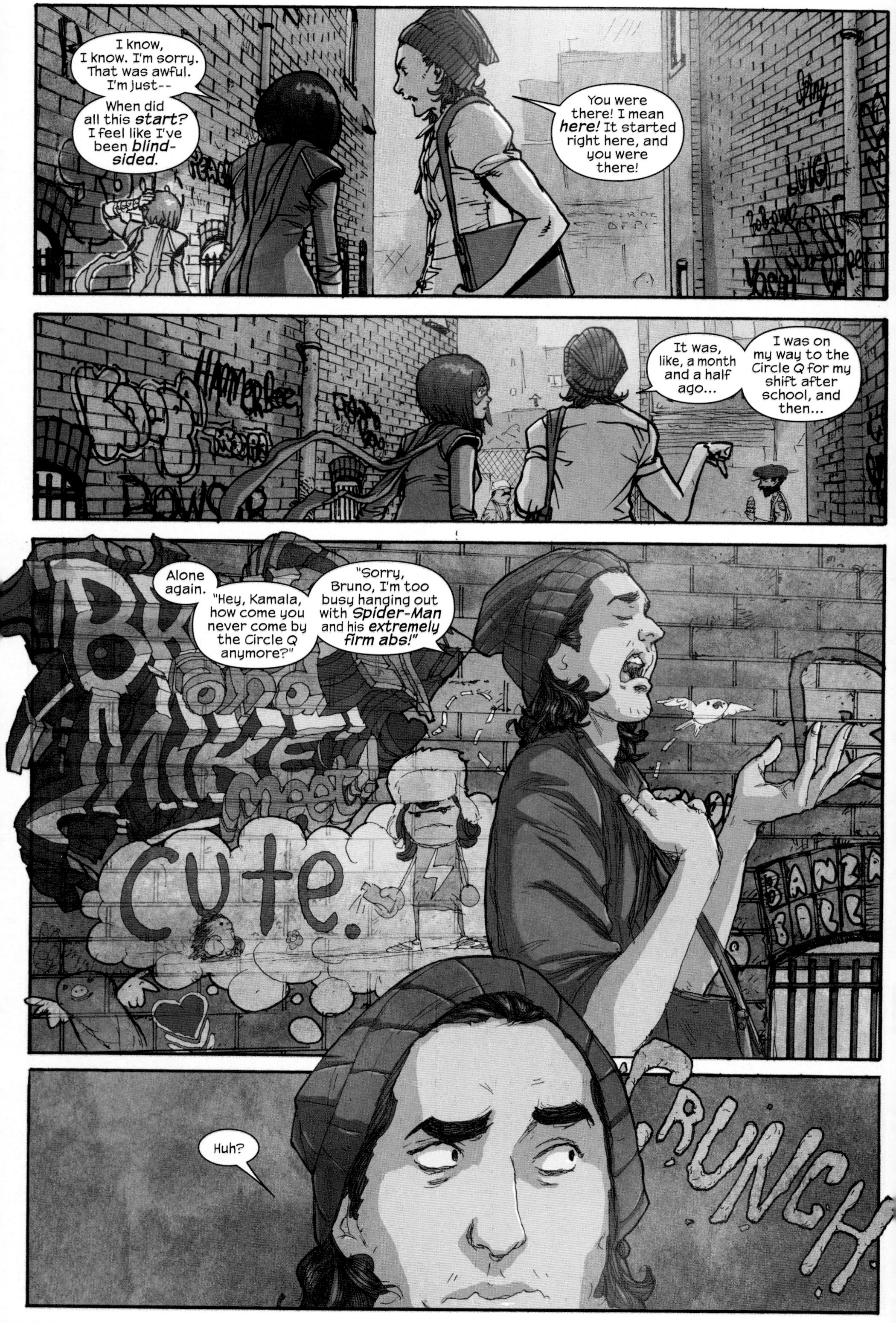
I know, I know. I'm sorry. That was awful. I'm just--
When did all this *start?* I feel like I've been *blind-sided.*
You were there! I mean *here!* It started right here, and you were there!
It was, like, a month and a half ago...
I was on my way to the Circle Q for my shift after school, and then...
Alone again.
"Hey, Kamala, how come you never come by the Circle Q anymore?"
"Sorry, Bruno, I'm too busy hanging out with *Spider-Man* and his *extremely firm abs!"*
Huh?
RUNCH

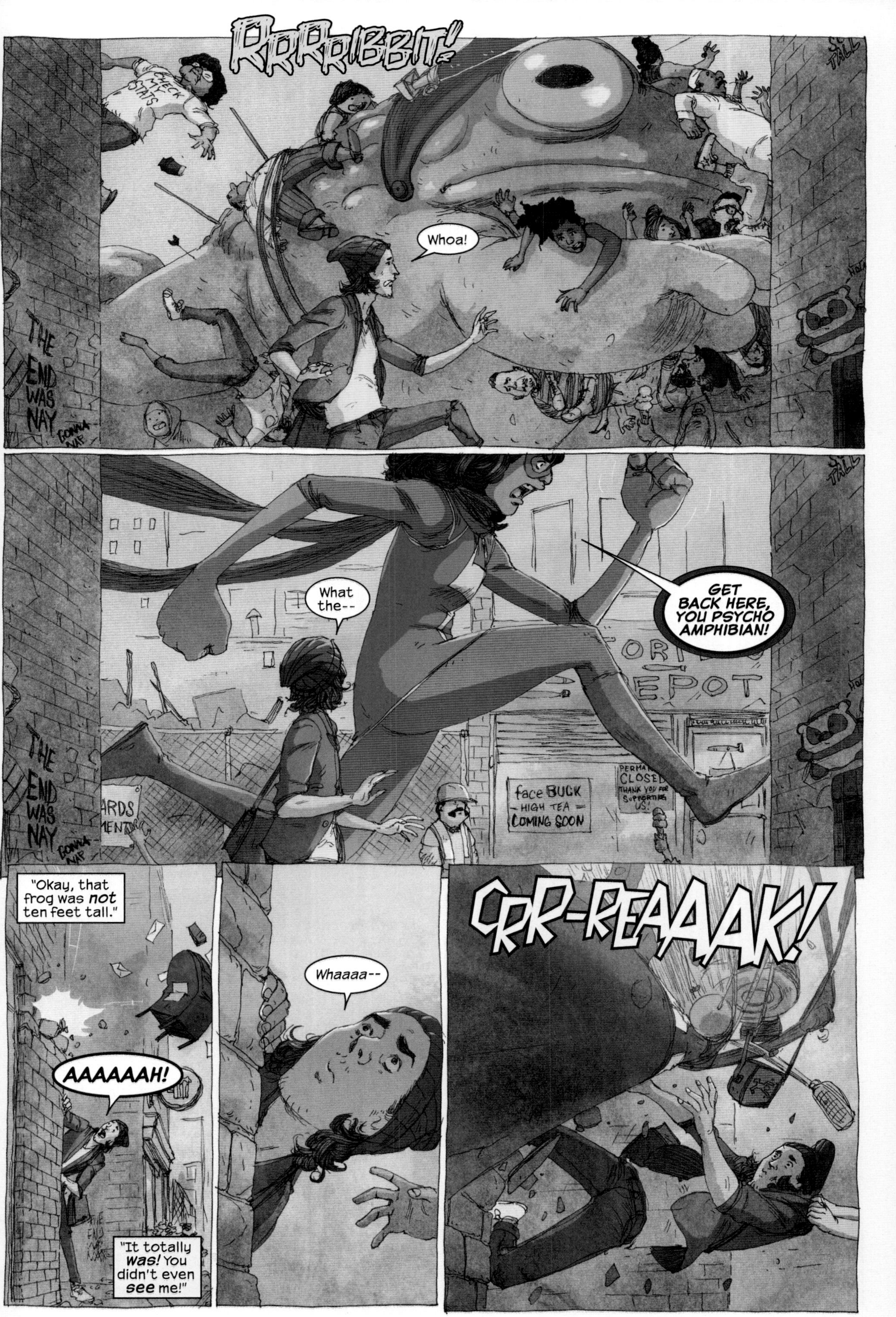
RRRRIBBIT!
CHECK MY STATS
Whoa!
THE END WAS NAY
GONNA NAP
What the--
GET BACK HERE, YOU PSYCHO AMPHIBIAN!
face BUCK
HIGH TEA
COMING SOON
CLOSED
THANK YOU FOR SUPPORTING US!
"Okay, that frog was *not* ten feet tall."
AAAAAAH!
"It totally *was!* You didn't even *see* me!"
Whaaaa--
CRR-REAAAAK!

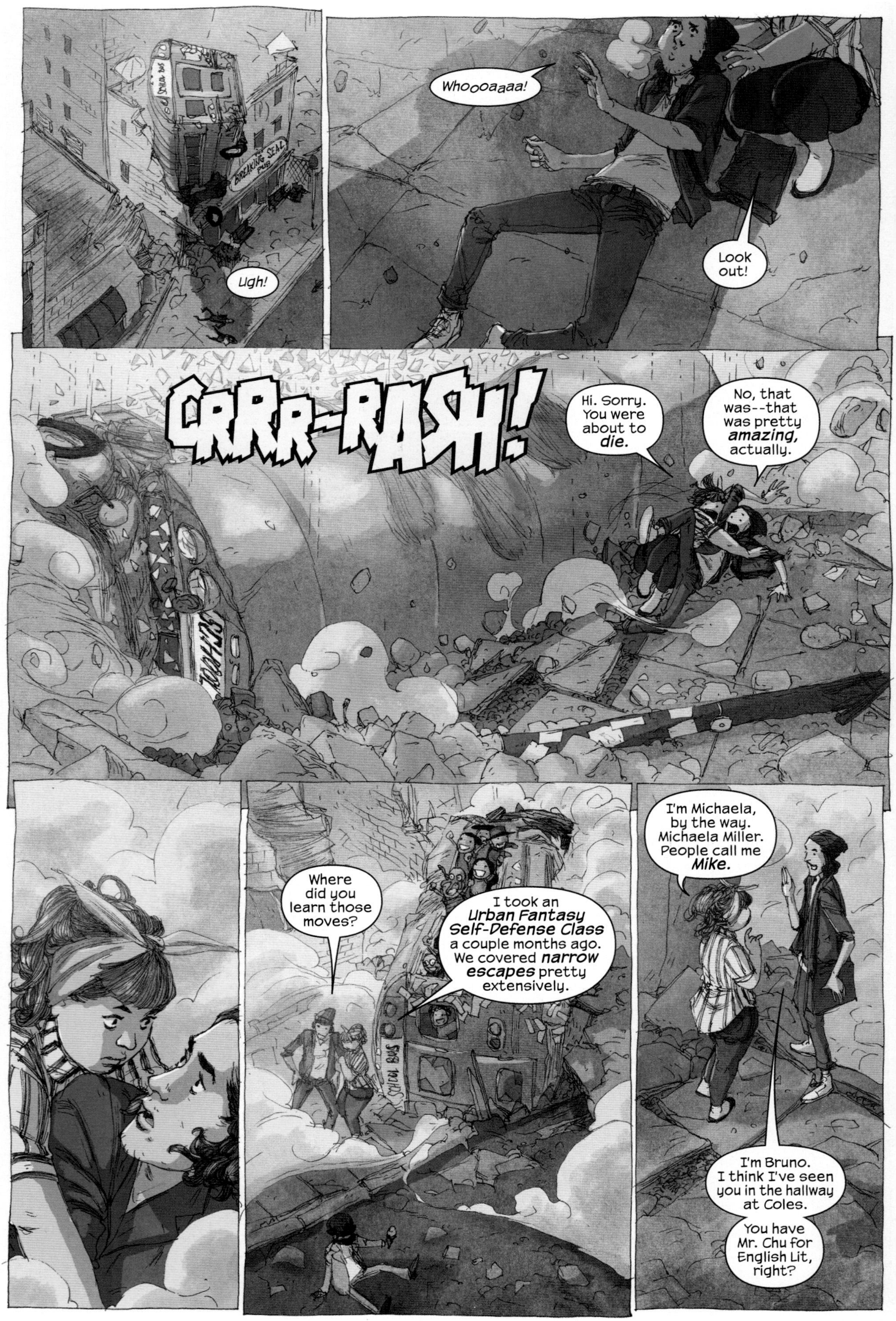
SCHOOL BUS
BREAKING SEAL PUB
Ugh!
Whoooaaaa!
Look out!
CRRR-RASH!
Hi. Sorry. You were about to **die.**
No, that was--that was pretty ***amazing,*** actually.
SCHOOL
Where did you learn those moves?
I took an ***Urban Fantasy Self-Defense Class*** a couple months ago. We covered ***narrow escapes*** pretty extensively.
SCHOOL BUS
I'm Michaela, by the way. Michaela Miller. People call me ***Mike.***
I'm Bruno. I think I've seen you in the hallway at Coles.
You have Mr. Chu for English Lit, right?

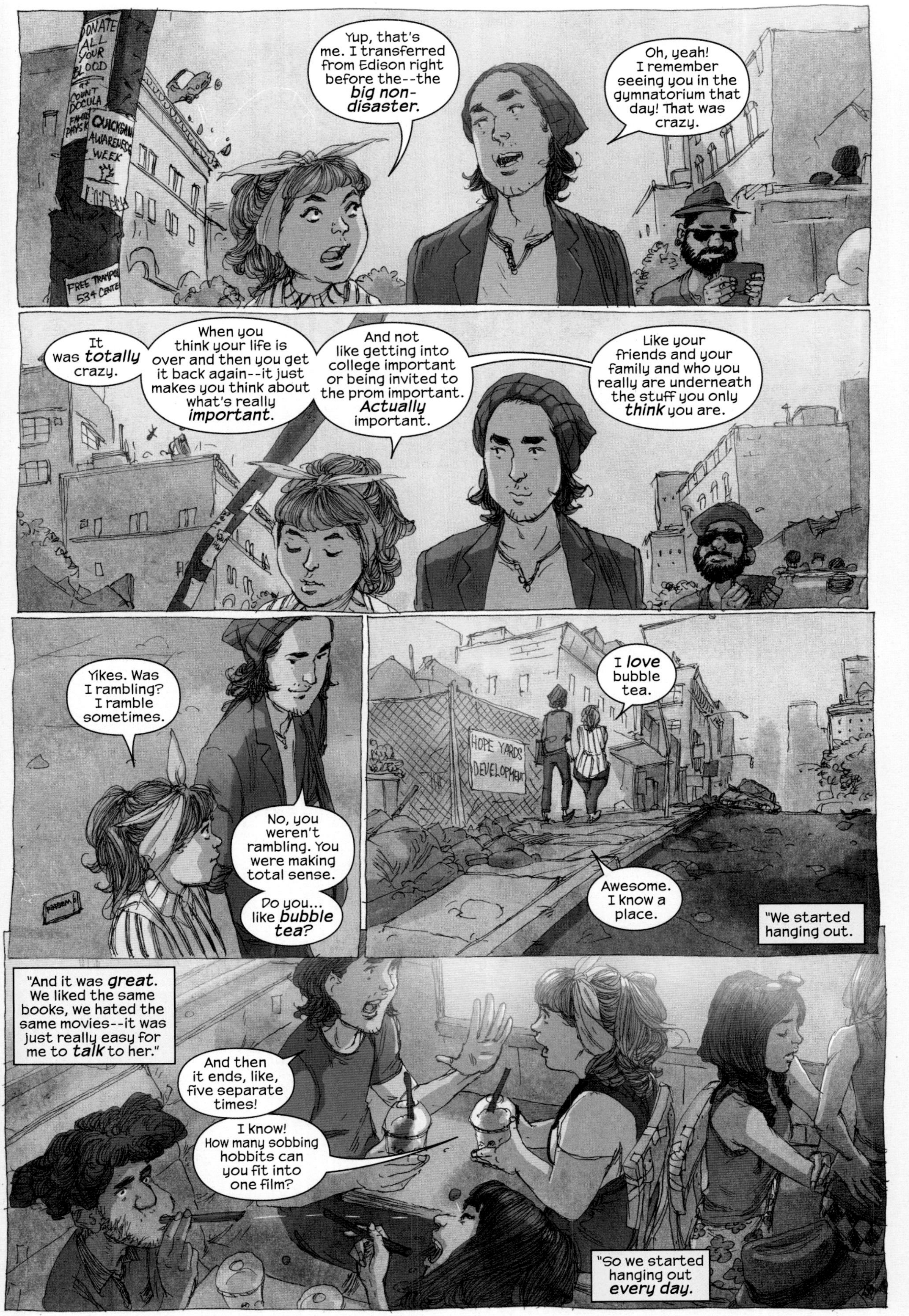
DONATE ALL YOUR BLOOD at COUNT DOCULA
QUICKSAND AWARENESS WEEK
FREE TRAMPO 534 CENTE
Yup, that's me. I transferred from Edison right before the--the *big non-disaster*.
Oh, yeah! I remember seeing you in the gymnatorium that day! That was crazy.
It was *totally* crazy.
When you think your life is over and then you get it back again--it just makes you think about what's really *important*.
And not like getting into college important or being invited to the prom important. *Actually* important.
Like your friends and your family and who you really are underneath the stuff you only *think* you are.
Yikes. Was I rambling? I ramble sometimes.
No, you weren't rambling. You were making total sense.
Do you... like *bubble tea?*
HOPE YARDS DEVELOPMENT
I *love* bubble tea.
Awesome. I know a place.
"We started hanging out.
"And it was *great*. We liked the same books, we hated the same movies--it was just really easy for me to *talk* to her."
And then it ends, like, five separate times!
I know! How many sobbing hobbits can you fit into one film?
"So we started hanging out *every day*.

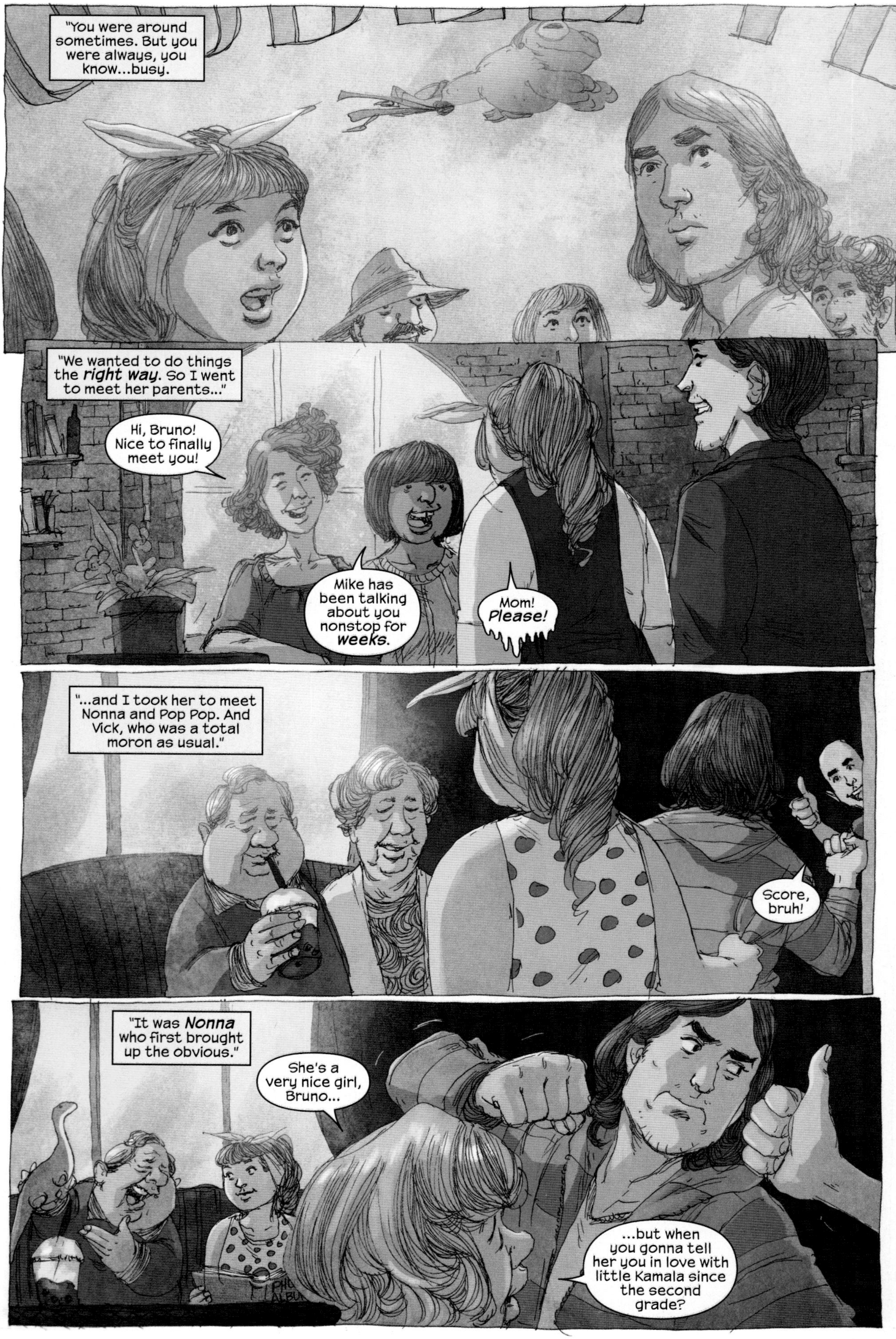
"You were around sometimes. But you were always, you know...busy.
"We wanted to do things the *right way*. So I went to meet her parents..."
Hi, Bruno! Nice to finally meet you!
Mike has been talking about you nonstop for *weeks*.
Mom! *Please!*
"...and I took her to meet Nonna and Pop Pop. And Vick, who was a total moron as usual."
Score, bruh!
"It was *Nonna* who first brought up the obvious."
She's a very nice girl, Bruno...
...but when you gonna tell her you in love with little Kamala since the second grade?

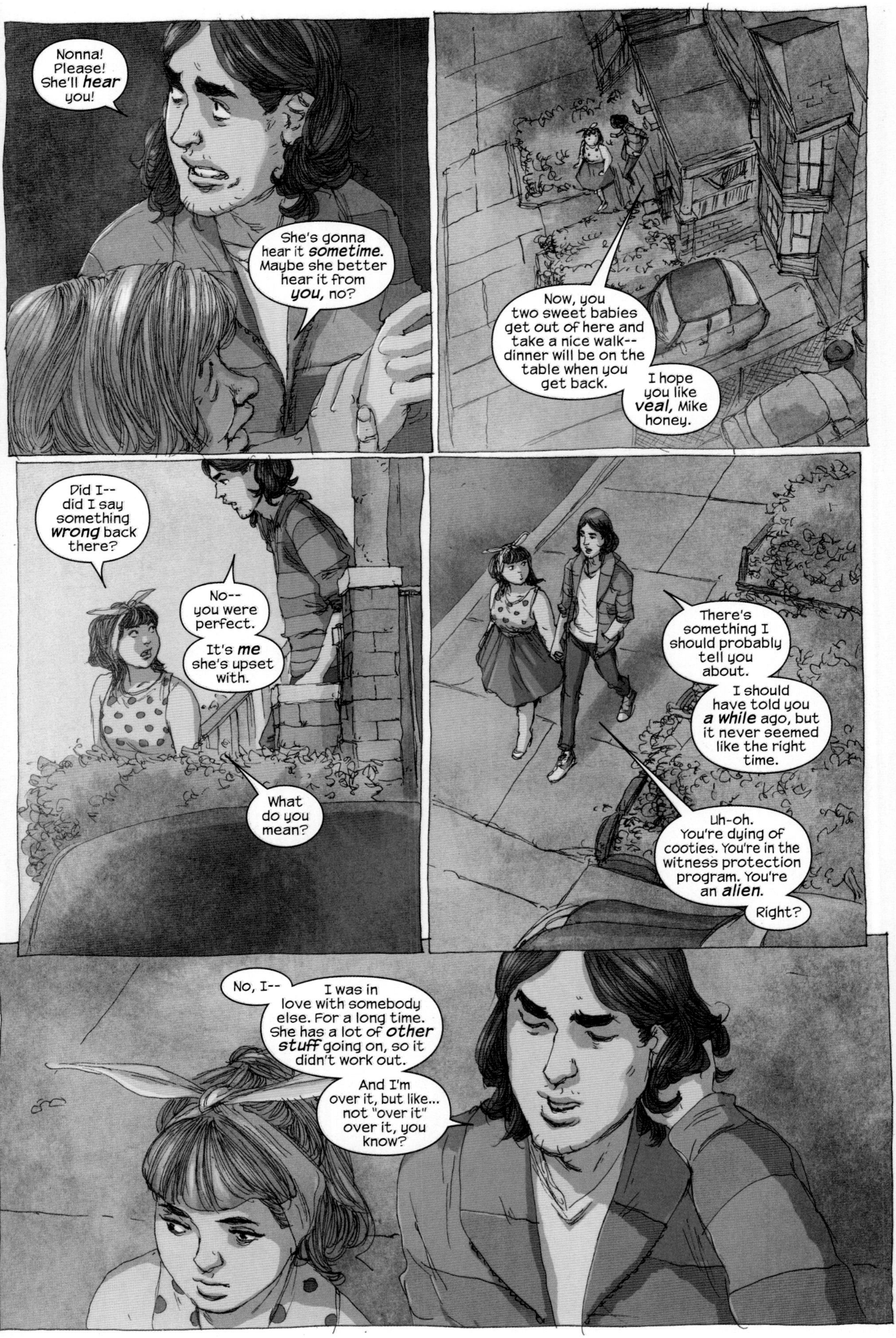
Nonna! Please! She'll *hear* you!
She's gonna hear it *sometime*. Maybe she better hear it from *you*, no?
Now, you two sweet babies get out of here and take a nice walk-- dinner will be on the table when you get back.
I hope you like *veal*, Mike honey.
Did I-- did I say something *wrong* back there?
No-- you were perfect.
It's *me* she's upset with.
What do you mean?
There's something I should probably tell you about.
I should have told you *a while* ago, but it never seemed like the right time.
Uh-oh. You're dying of cooties. You're in the witness protection program. You're an *alien*.
Right?
No, I--
I was in love with somebody else. For a long time. She has a lot of *other stuff* going on, so it didn't work out.
And I'm over it, but like... not "over it" over it, you know?

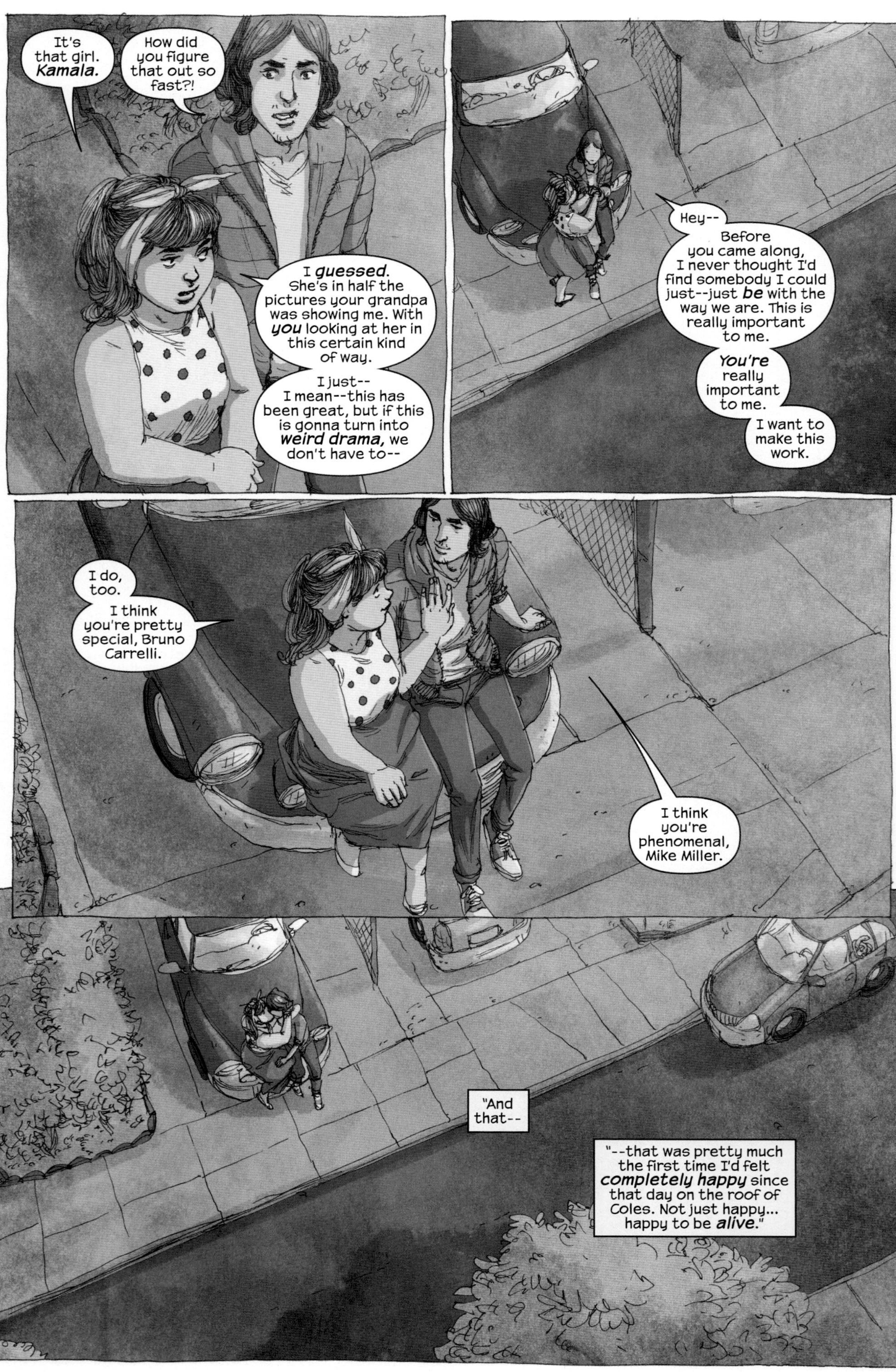
It's that girl. Kamala.
How did you figure that out so fast?!
I guessed. She's in half the pictures your grandpa was showing me. With you looking at her in this certain kind of way.
I just-- I mean--this has been great, but if this is gonna turn into weird drama, we don't have to--
Hey--
Before you came along, I never thought I'd find somebody I could just--just be with the way we are. This is really important to me.
You're really important to me.
I want to make this work.
I do, too.
I think you're pretty special, Bruno Carrelli.
I think you're phenomenal, Mike Miller.
"And that--
"--that was pretty much the first time I'd felt completely happy since that day on the roof of Coles. Not just happy... happy to be alive."

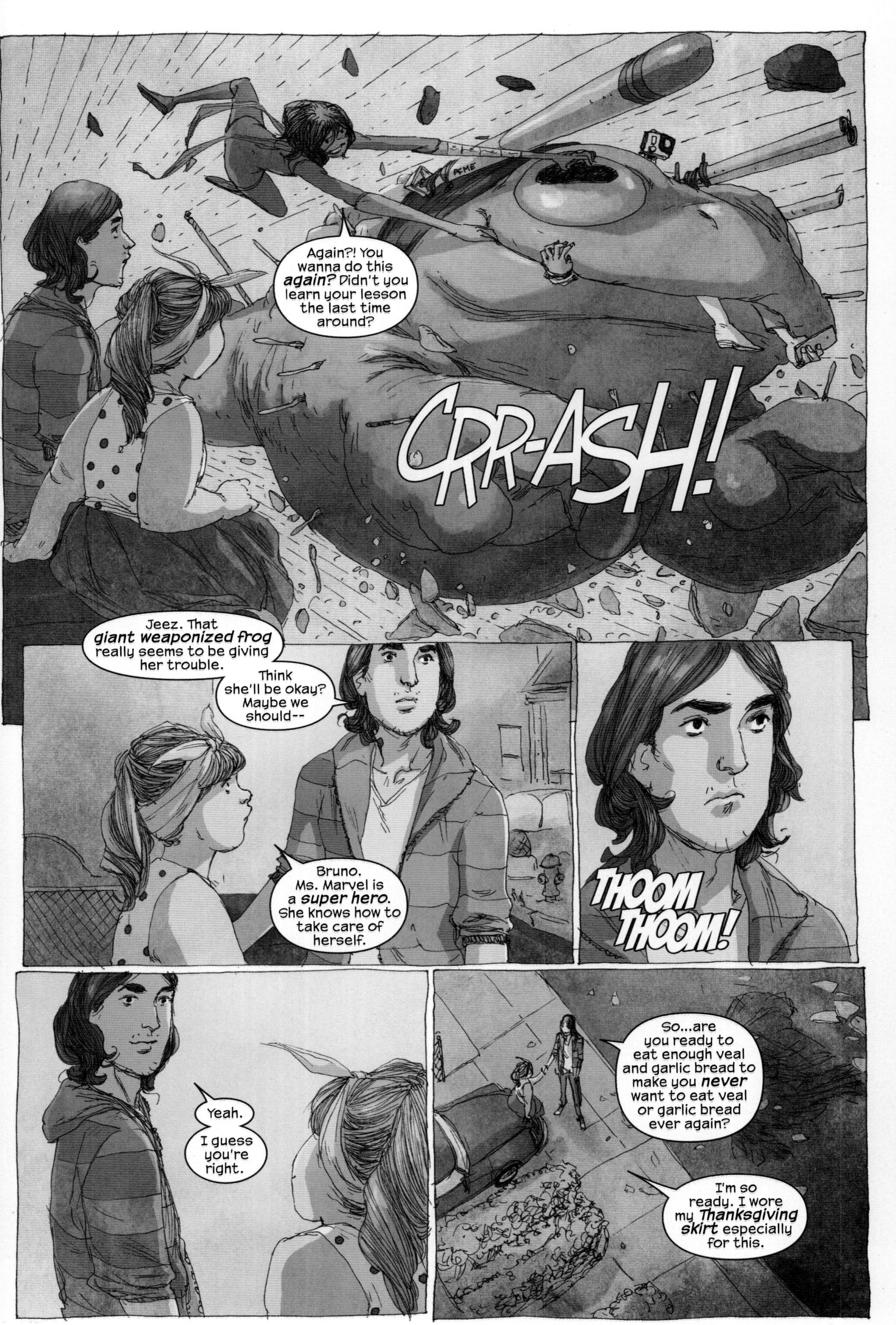
Again?! You wanna do this again? Didn't you learn your lesson the last time around?
CRR-ASH!!
Jeez. That giant weaponized frog really seems to be giving her trouble.
Think she'll be okay? Maybe we should--
Bruno. Ms. Marvel is a super hero. She knows how to take care of herself.
THOOM THOOM!
Yeah.
I guess you're right.
So...are you ready to eat enough veal and garlic bread to make you never want to eat veal or garlic bread ever again?
I'm so ready. I wore my Thanksgiving skirt especially for this.

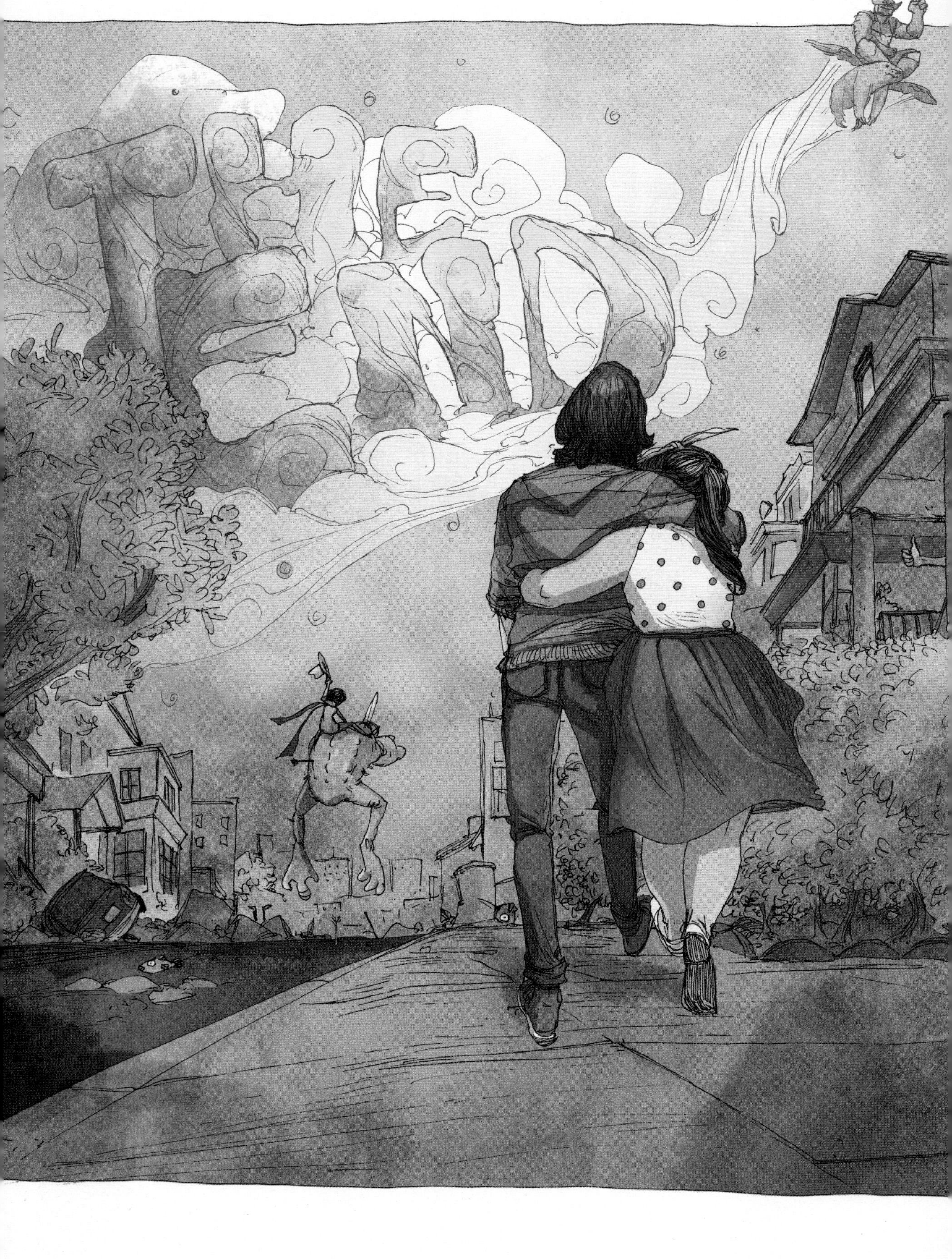
THE END

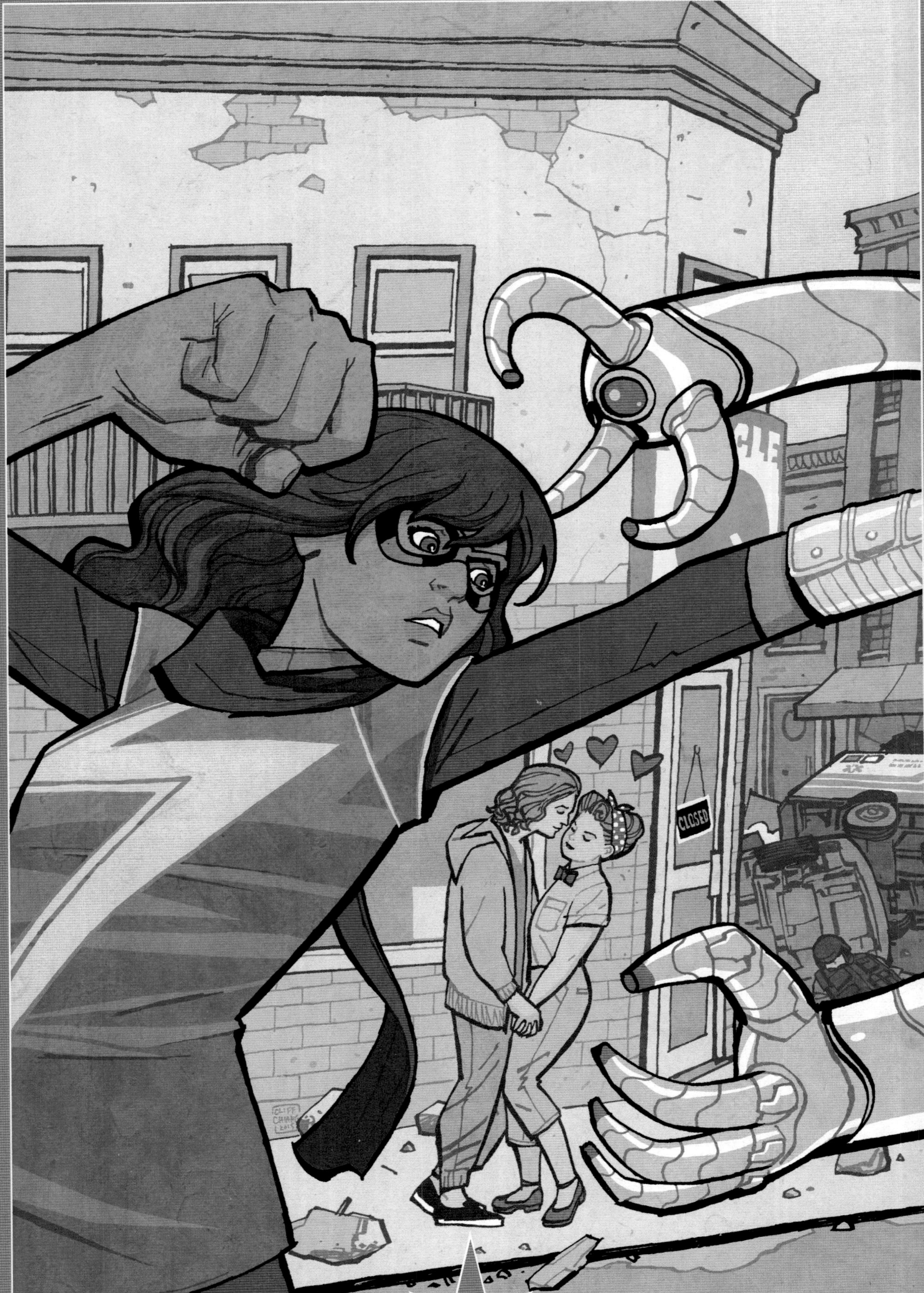
CLOSED

2

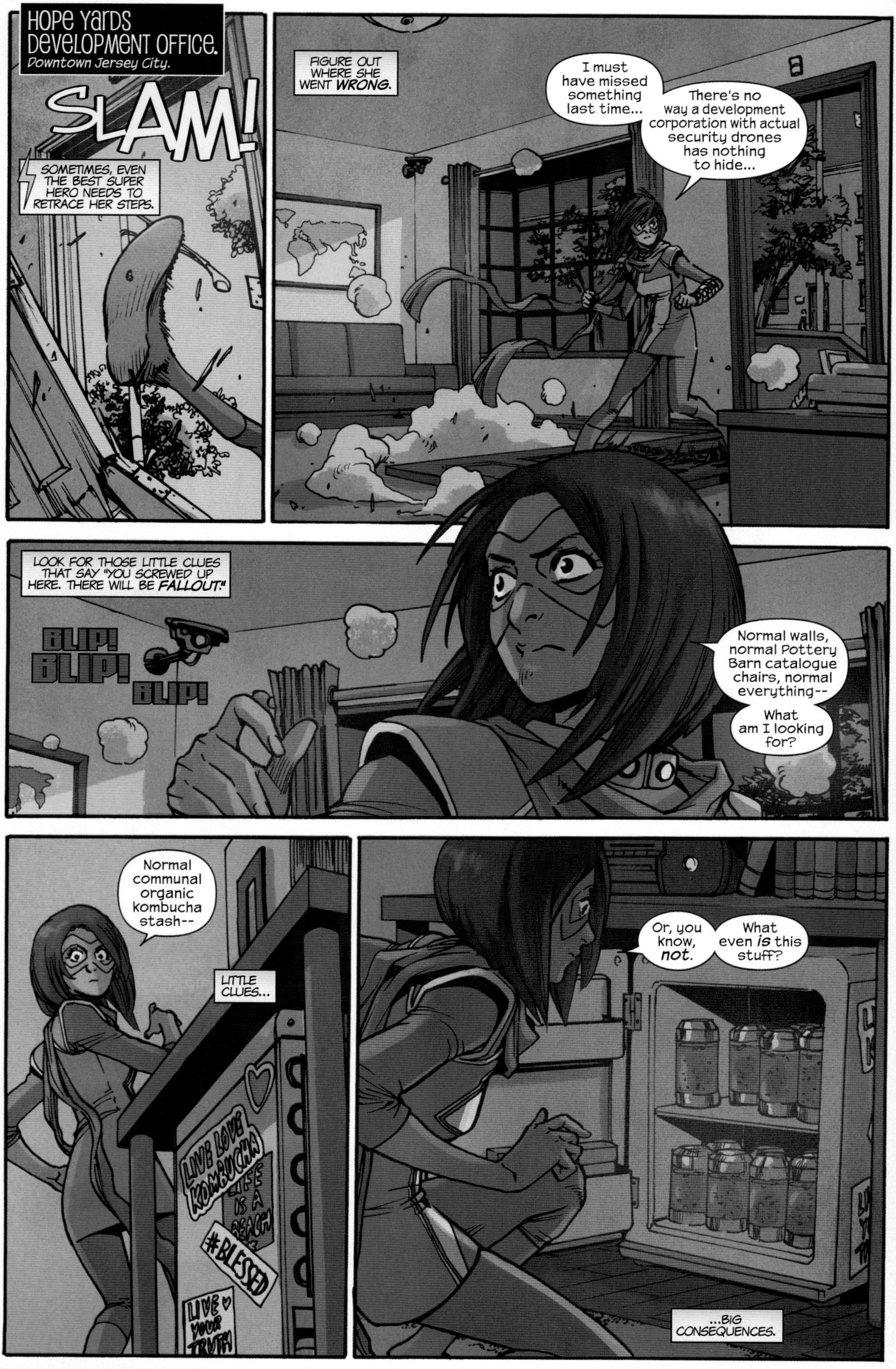

HOPE YARDS DEVELOPMENT OFFICE.
Downtown Jersey City.
SLAM!
SOMETIMES, EVEN THE BEST SUPER HERO NEEDS TO RETRACE HER STEPS.
FIGURE OUT WHERE SHE WENT WRONG.
I must have missed something last time...
There's no way a development corporation with actual security drones has nothing to hide...
LOOK FOR THOSE LITTLE CLUES THAT SAY "YOU SCREWED UP HERE. THERE WILL BE FALLOUT."
BLIP!
BLIP!
BLIP!
Normal walls, normal Pottery Barn catalogue chairs, normal everything--
What am I looking for?
Normal communal organic kombucha stash--
LITTLE CLUES...
LIVE LOVE KOMBUCHA
LIFE IS A BEACH
#BLESSED
LIVE YOUR TRUTH
Or, you know, not.
What even is this stuff?
...BIG CONSEQUENCES.

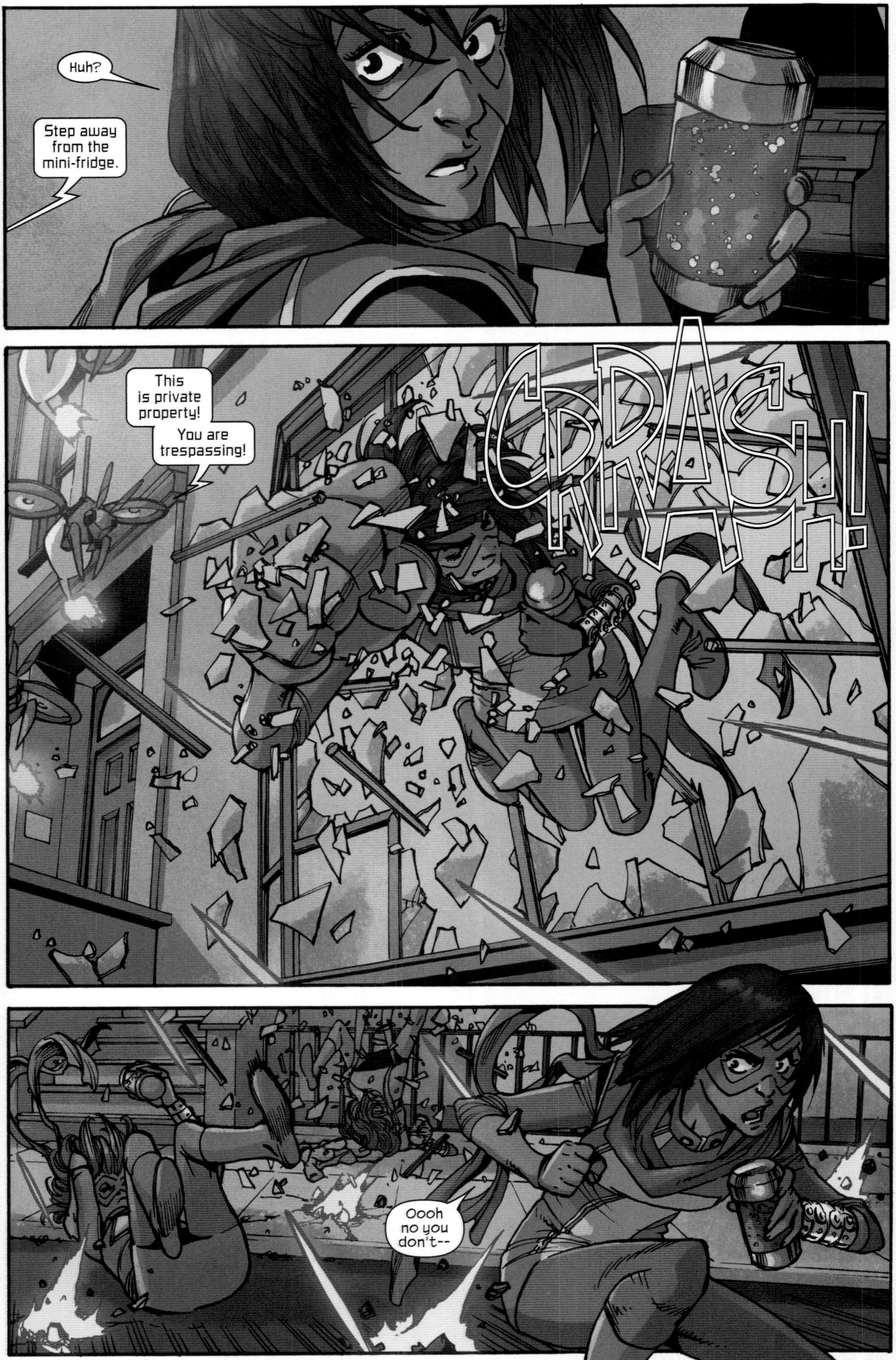

Huh?
Step away from the mini-fridge.
This is private property!
You are trespassing!
CRASH!
KRAASH!
Oooh no you don't--

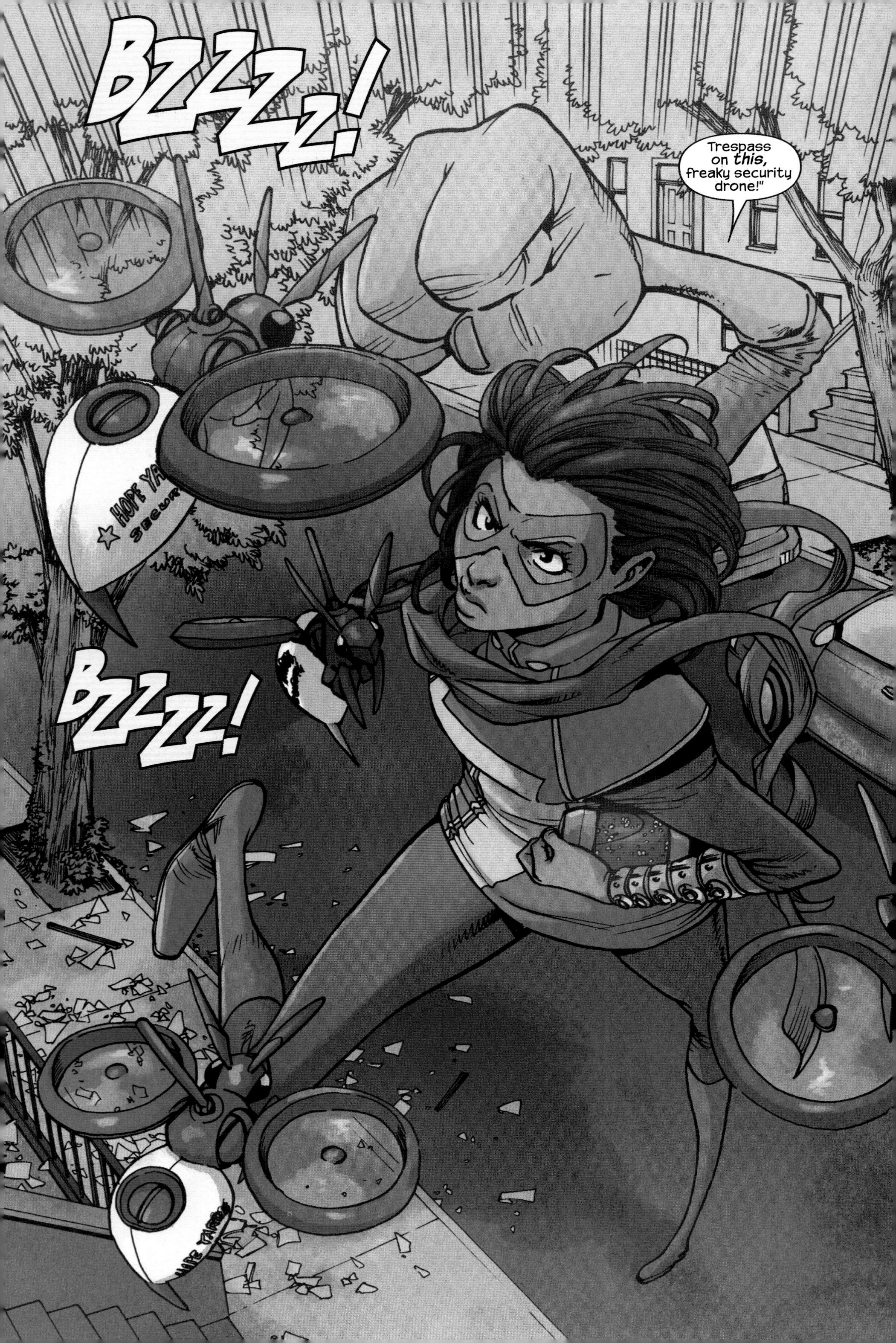
BZZZZz!
Trespass on *this,* freaky security drone!"
BZZZZ!

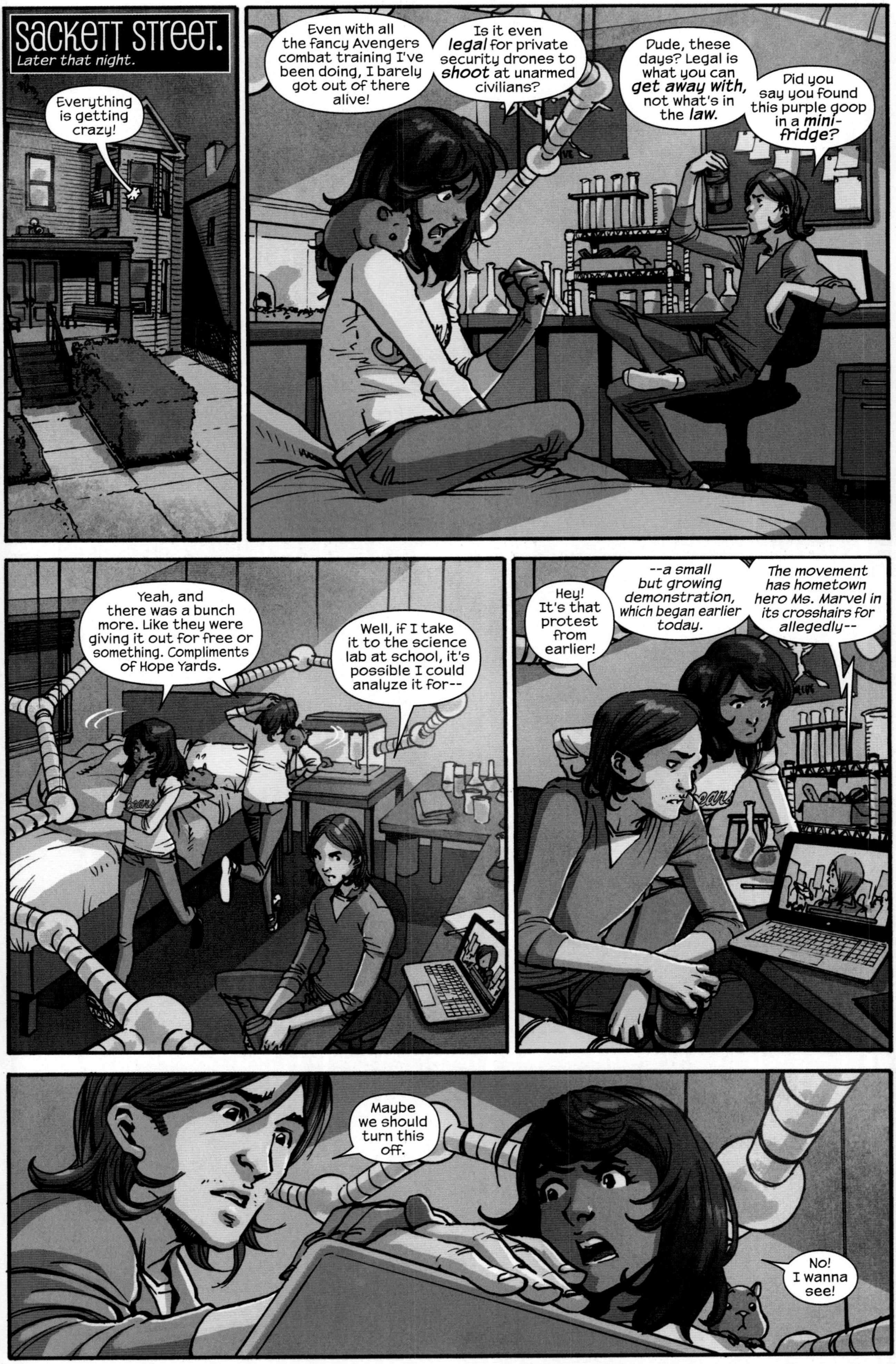
SACKETT STREET.
Later that night.
Everything is getting crazy!
Even with all the fancy Avengers combat training I've been doing, I barely got out of there alive!
Is it even legal for private security drones to shoot at unarmed civilians?
Dude, these days? Legal is what you can get away with, not what's in the law.
Did you say you found this purple goop in a mini-fridge?
Yeah, and there was a bunch more. Like they were giving it out for free or something. Compliments of Hope Yards.
Well, if I take it to the science lab at school, it's possible I could analyze it for--
Hey! It's that protest from earlier!
--a small but growing demonstration, which began earlier today.
The movement has hometown hero Ms. Marvel in its crosshairs for allegedly--
Maybe we should turn this off.
No! I wanna see!

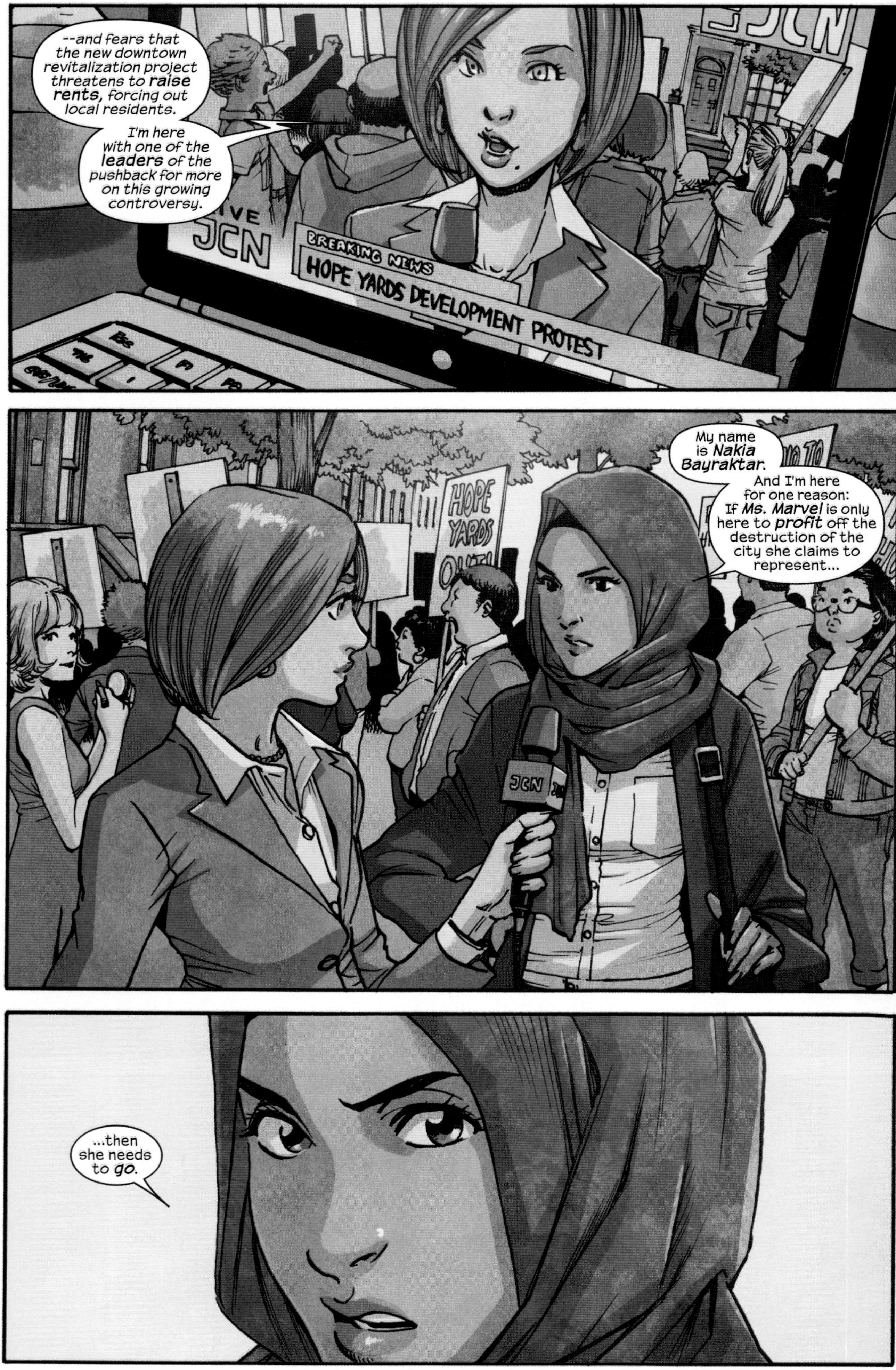
--and fears that the new downtown revitalization project threatens to **raise rents,** forcing out local residents.
I'm here with one of the **leaders** of the pushback for more on this growing controversy.
JCN
BREAKING NEWS
HOPE YARDS DEVELOPMENT PROTEST
HOPE YARDS
JCN
My name is *Nakia Bayraktar*.
And I'm here for one reason: If *Ms. Marvel* is only here to ***profit*** off the destruction of the city she claims to represent...
...then she needs to *go*.

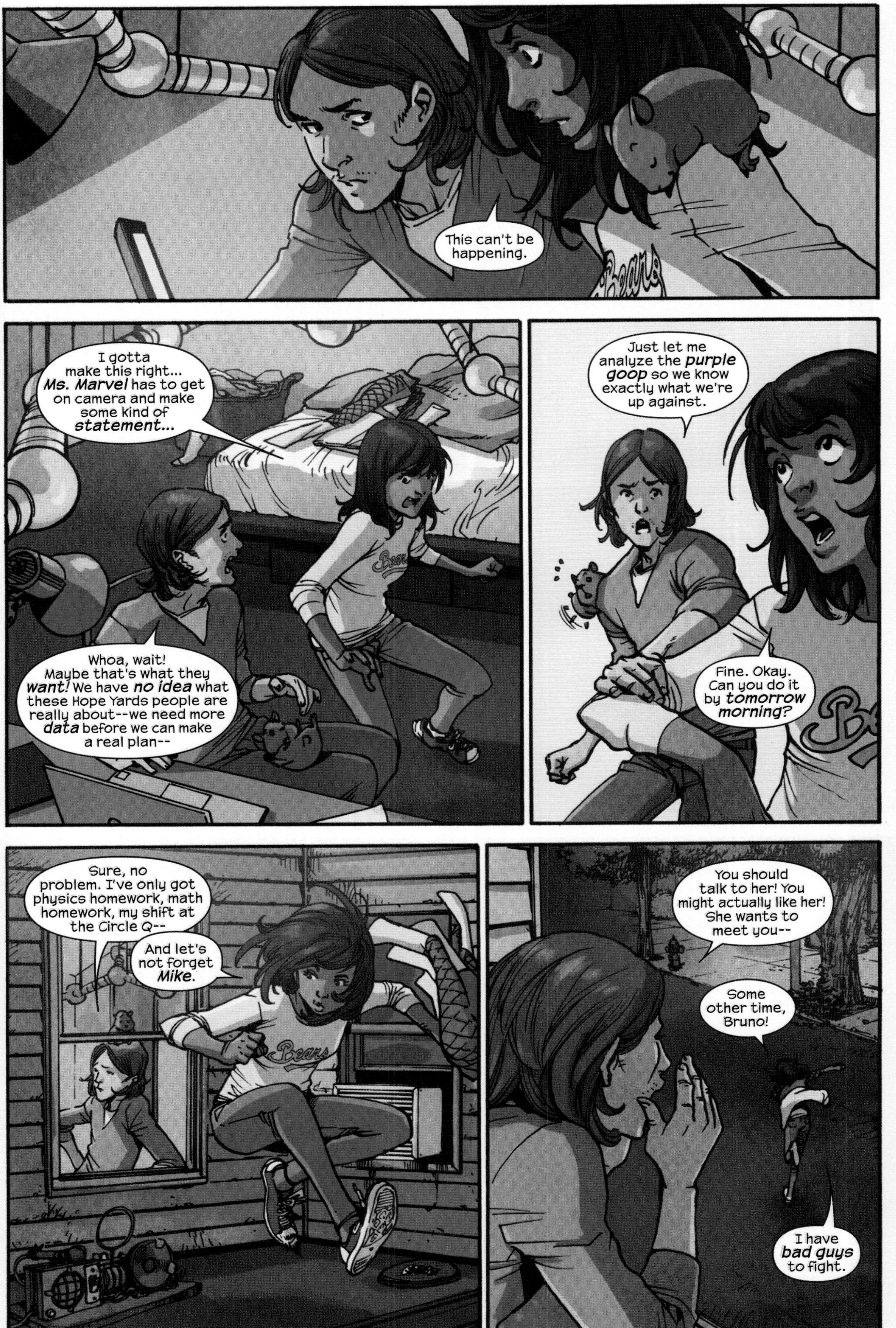
This can't be happening.
I gotta make this right... Ms. Marvel has to get on camera and make some kind of statement...
Whoa, wait! Maybe that's what they want! We have no idea what these Hope Yards people are really about--we need more data before we can make a real plan--
Just let me analyze the purple goop so we know exactly what we're up against.
Fine. Okay. Can you do it by tomorrow morning?
Sure, no problem. I've only got physics homework, math homework, my shift at the Circle Q--
And let's not forget Mike.
You should talk to her! You might actually like her! She wants to meet you--
Some other time, Bruno!
I have bad guys to fight.

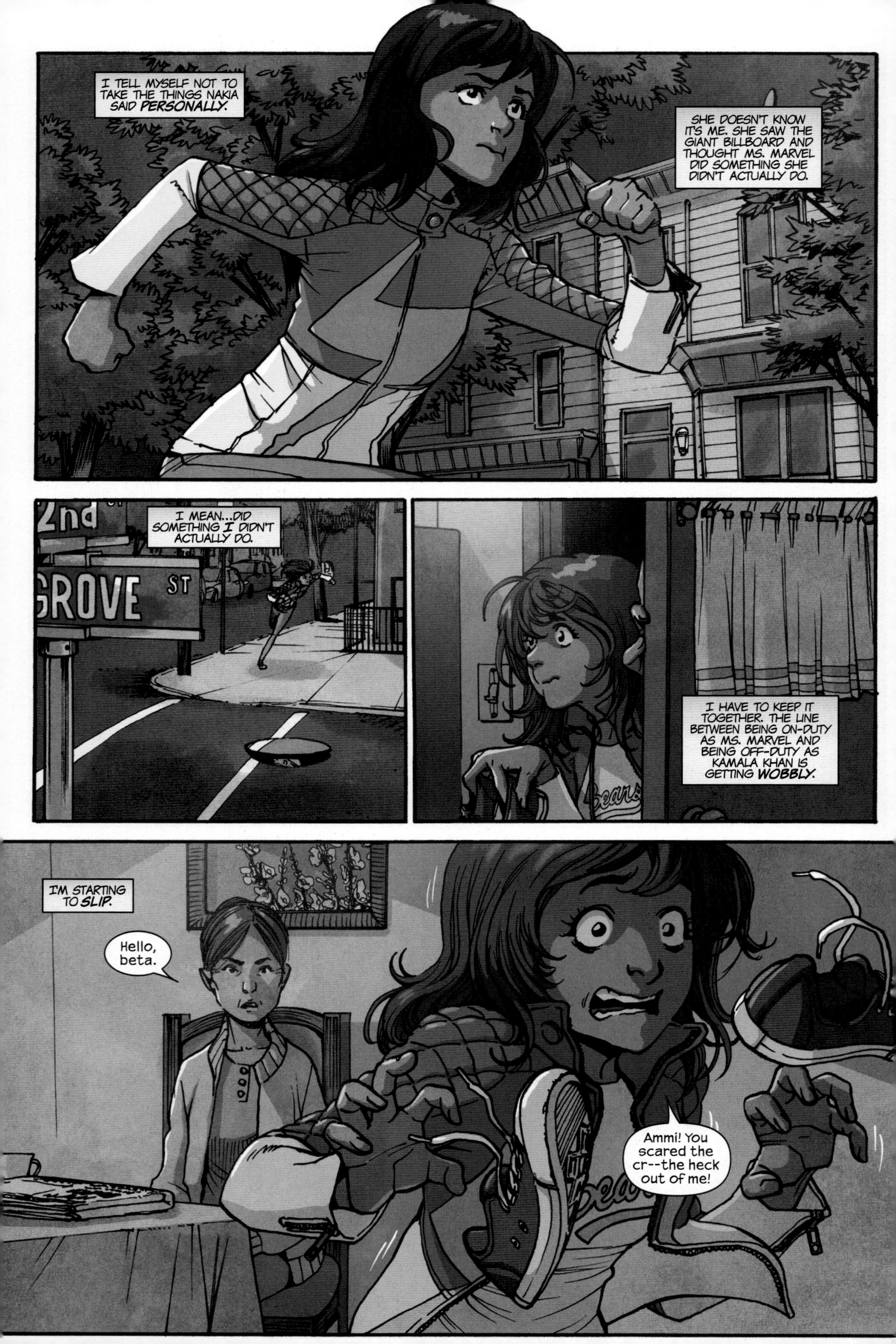
I TELL MYSELF NOT TO TAKE THE THINGS NAKIA SAID PERSONALLY.
SHE DOESN'T KNOW IT'S ME. SHE SAW THE GIANT BILLBOARD AND THOUGHT MS. MARVEL DID SOMETHING SHE DIDN'T ACTUALLY DO.
2nd
GROVE ST
I MEAN...DID SOMETHING I DIDN'T ACTUALLY DO.
I HAVE TO KEEP IT TOGETHER. THE LINE BETWEEN BEING ON-DUTY AS MS. MARVEL AND BEING OFF-DUTY AS KAMALA KHAN IS GETTING WOBBLY.
I'M STARTING TO SLIP.
Hello, beta.
Ammi! You scared the cr--the heck out of me!

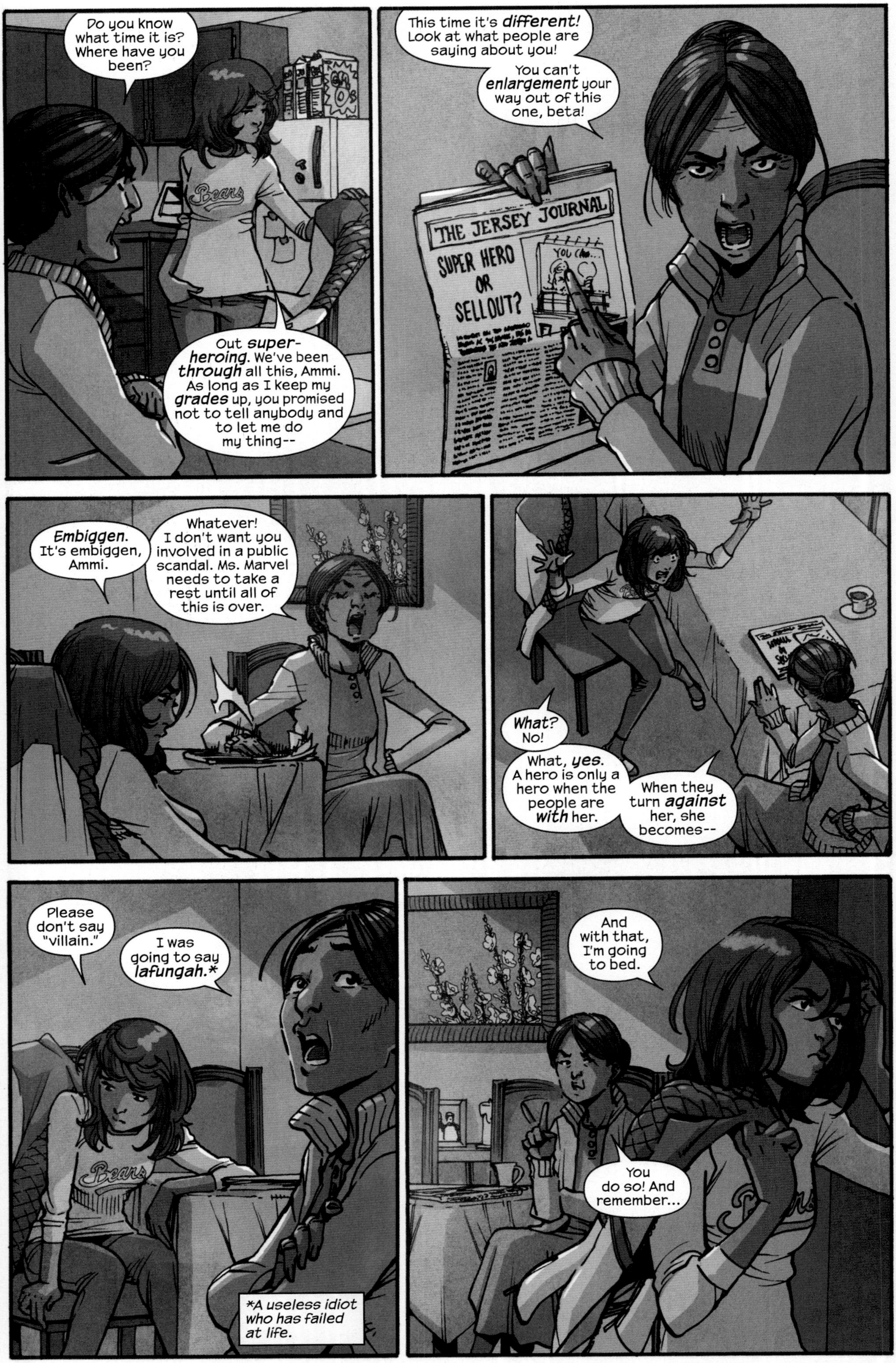
Do you know what time it is? Where have you been?
Out super-heroing. We've been through all this, Ammi. As long as I keep my grades up, you promised not to tell anybody and to let me do my thing--
This time it's different! Look at what people are saying about you!
You can't enlargement your way out of this one, beta!
THE JERSEY JOURNAL
SUPER HERO OR SELLOUT?
Embiggen. It's embiggen, Ammi.
Whatever! I don't want you involved in a public scandal. Ms. Marvel needs to take a rest until all of this is over.
What? No!
What, yes. A hero is only a hero when the people are with her.
When they turn against her, she becomes--
Please don't say "villain."
I was going to say lafungah.*
*A useless idiot who has failed at life.
And with that, I'm going to bed.
You do so! And remember...

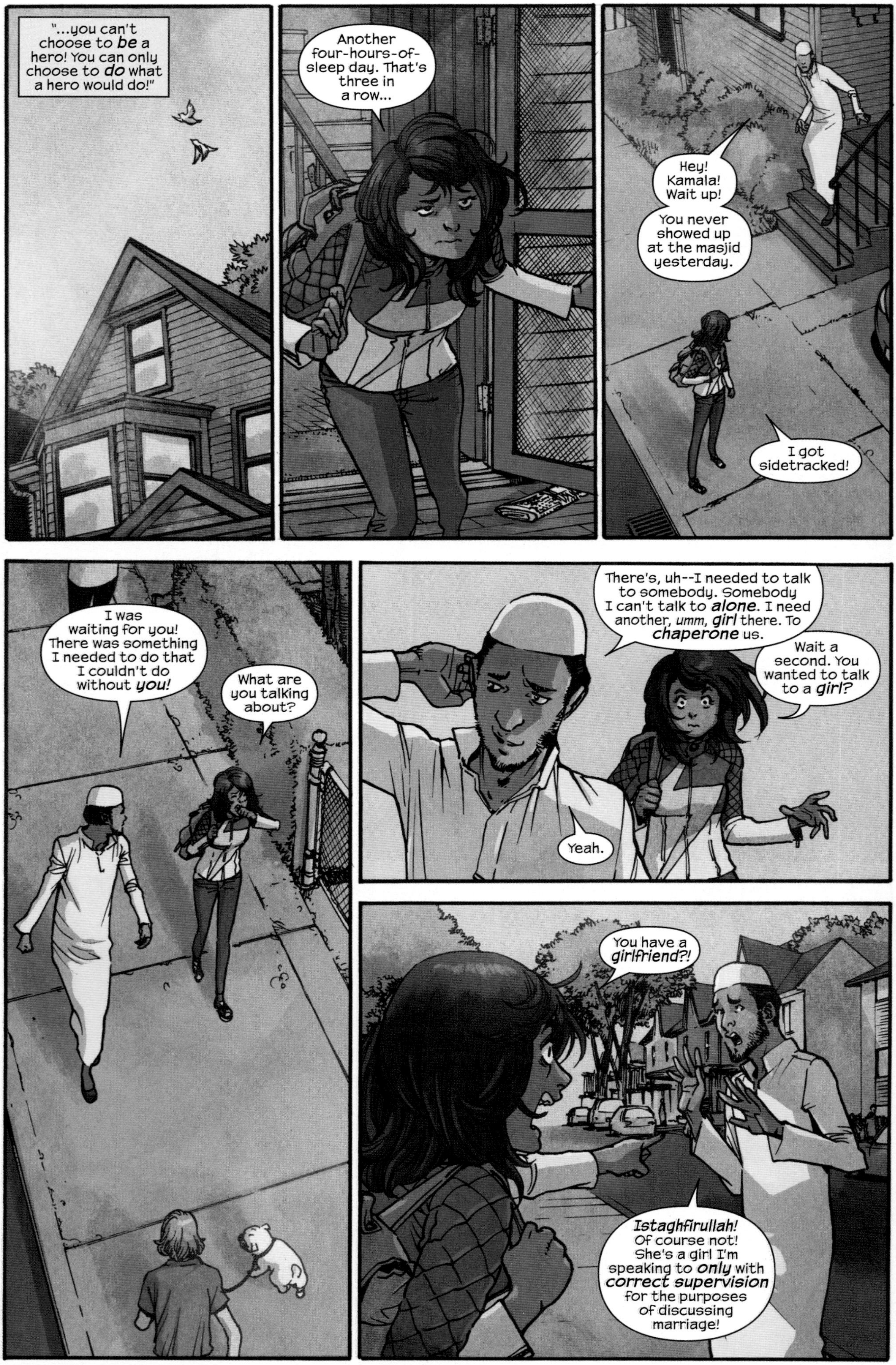
"...you can't choose to *be* a hero! You can only choose to *do* what a hero would do!"
Another four-hours-of-sleep day. That's three in a row...
Hey! Kamala! Wait up!
You never showed up at the masjid yesterday.
I got sidetracked!
I was waiting for you! There was something I needed to do that I couldn't do without *you!*
What are you talking about?
There's, uh--I needed to talk to somebody. Somebody I can't talk to *alone*. I need another, *umm*, *girl* there. To *chaperone* us.
Wait a second. You wanted to talk to a *girl?*
Yeah.
You have a *girlfriend?!*
Istaghfirullah! Of course not! She's a girl I'm speaking to *only* with *correct supervision* for the purposes of discussing marriage!

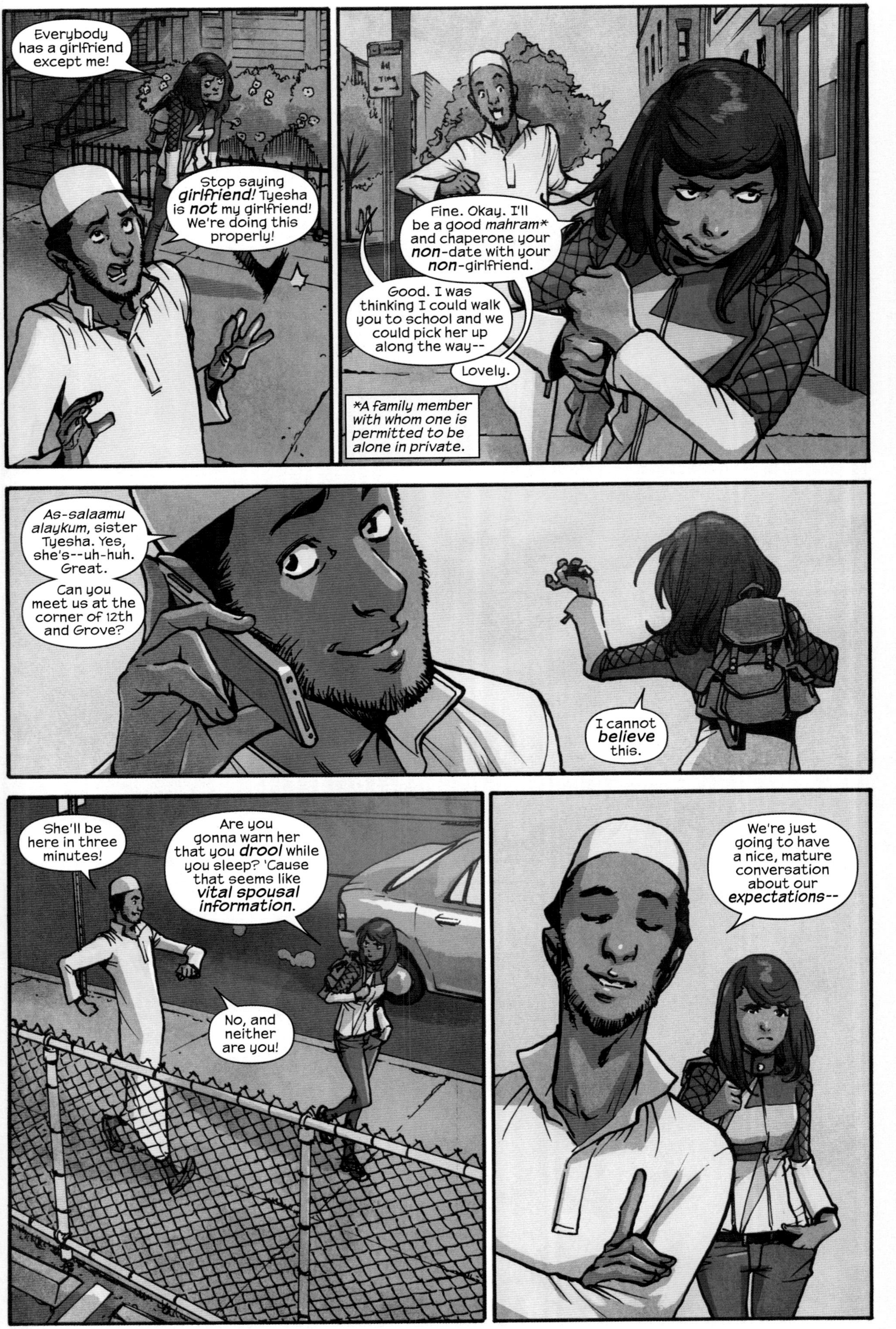
Everybody has a girlfriend except me!
Stop saying girlfriend! Tyesha is not my girlfriend! We're doing this properly!
Fine. Okay. I'll be a good mahram* and chaperone your non-date with your non-girlfriend.
Good. I was thinking I could walk you to school and we could pick her up along the way--
Lovely.
*A family member with whom one is permitted to be alone in private.
As-salaamu alaykum, sister Tyesha. Yes, she's--uh-huh. Great.
Can you meet us at the corner of 12th and Grove?
I cannot believe this.
She'll be here in three minutes!
Are you gonna warn her that you drool while you sleep? 'Cause that seems like vital spousal information.
No, and neither are you!
We're just going to have a nice, mature conversation about our expectations--

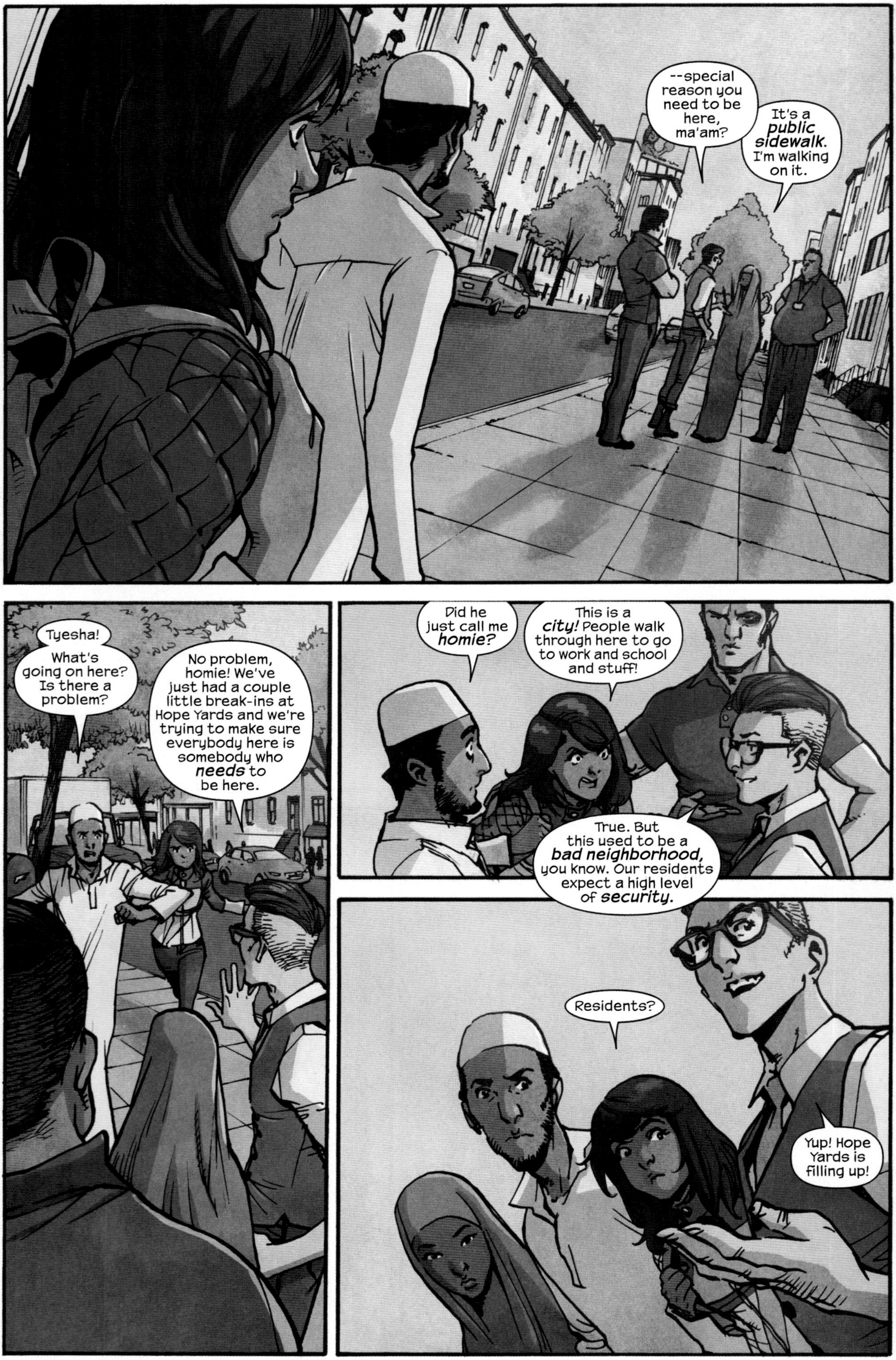
--special reason you need to be here, ma'am?
It's a *public sidewalk*. I'm walking on it.
Tyesha!
What's going on here? Is there a problem?
No problem, homie! We've just had a couple little break-ins at Hope Yards and we're trying to make sure everybody here is somebody who *needs* to be here.
Did he just call me *homie?*
This is a *city!* People walk through here to go to work and school and stuff!
True. But this used to be a *bad neighborhood,* you know. Our residents expect a high level of *security*.
Residents?
Yup! Hope Yards is filling up!

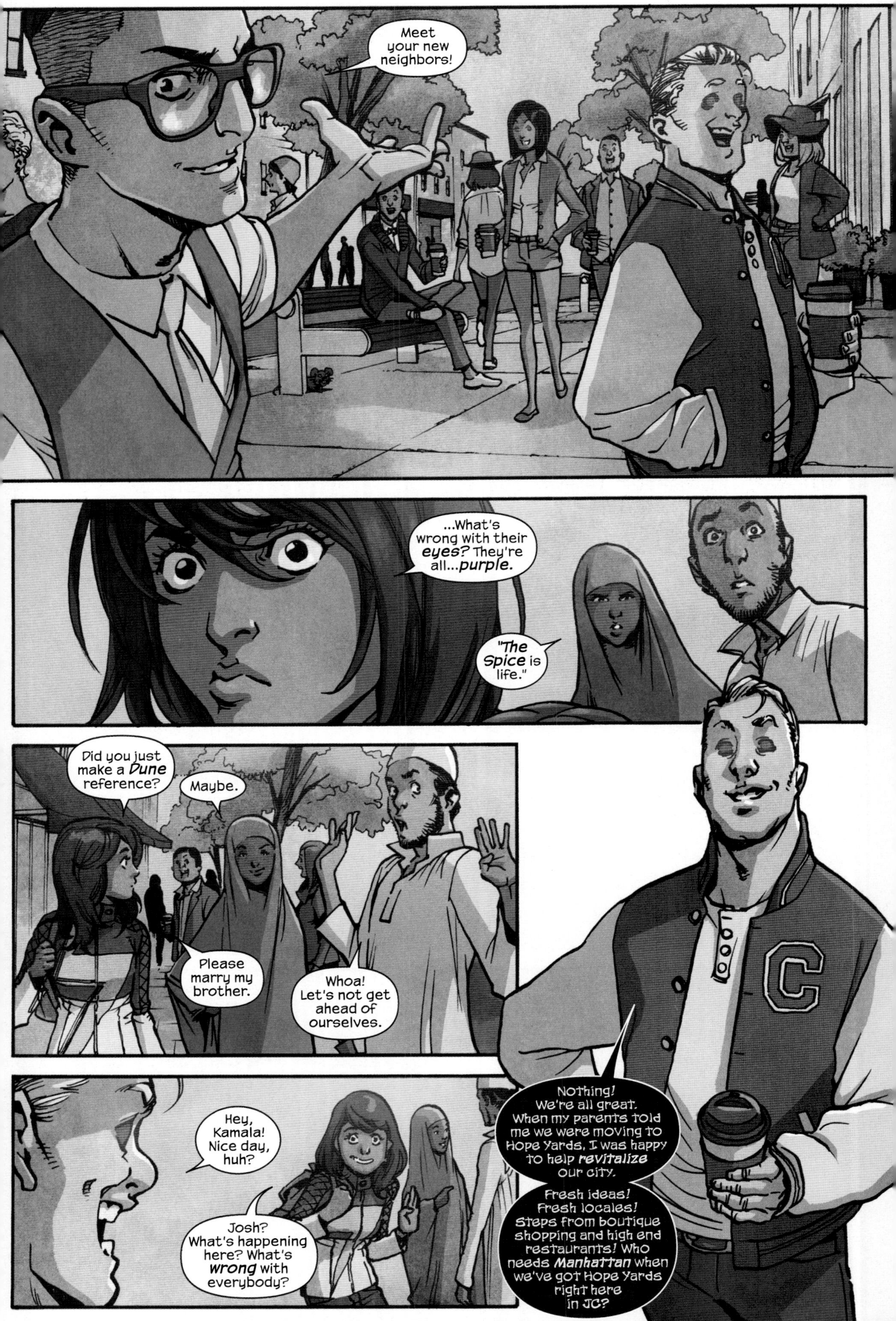
Meet your new neighbors!
...What's wrong with their *eyes?* They're all...*purple.*
"*The Spice* is life."
Did you just make a *Dune* reference?
Maybe.
Please marry my brother.
Whoa! Let's not get ahead of ourselves.
Hey, Kamala! Nice day, huh?
Josh? What's happening here? What's *wrong* with everybody?
Nothing! We're all great. When my parents told me we were moving to Hope Yards, I was happy to help *revitalize* our city.
Fresh ideas! Fresh locales! Steps from boutique shopping and high end restaurants! Who needs *Manhattan* when we've got Hope Yards right here in JC?

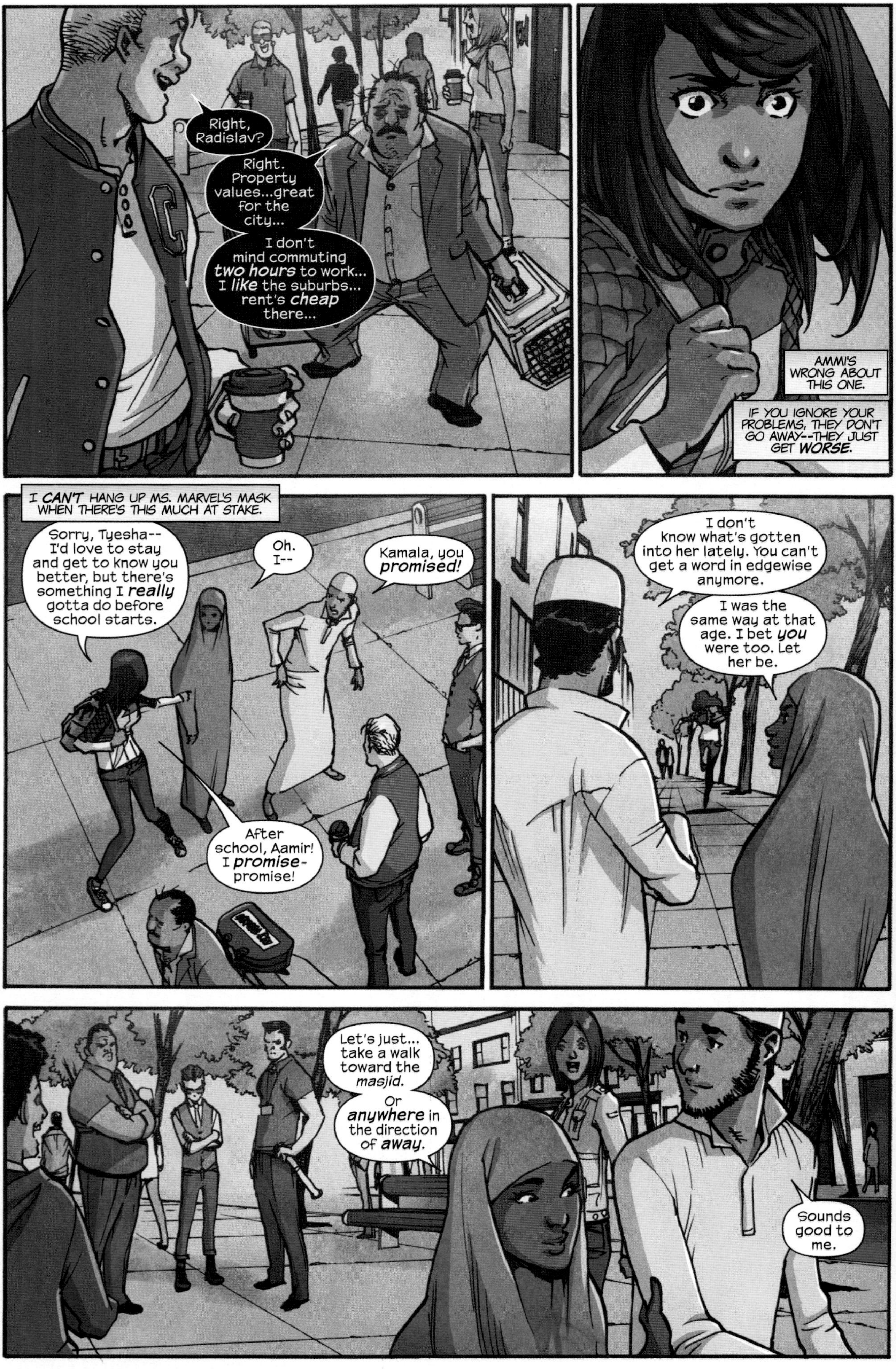
Right, Radislav?
Right. Property values...great for the city...
I don't mind commuting two hours to work... I like the suburbs... rent's cheap there...
AMMI'S WRONG ABOUT THIS ONE.
IF YOU IGNORE YOUR PROBLEMS, THEY DON'T GO AWAY--THEY JUST GET WORSE.
I CAN'T HANG UP MS. MARVEL'S MASK WHEN THERE'S THIS MUCH AT STAKE.
Sorry, Tyesha-- I'd love to stay and get to know you better, but there's something I really gotta do before school starts.
Oh. I--
Kamala, you promised!
After school, Aamir! I promise-promise!
I don't know what's gotten into her lately. You can't get a word in edgewise anymore.
I was the same way at that age. I bet you were too. Let her be.
Let's just... take a walk toward the masjid.
Or anywhere in the direction of away.
Sounds good to me.

SOMETHING TELLS ME I DON'T HAVE MUCH TIME.

Don't fail me now, Bruno...

Bruno? Hey--so we have a new problem.

I just saw Josh and Radislav and a bunch of other people wandering around Hope Yards like *zombies*. Like they'd been *brainwashed* by an *actual* evil overlord.

I'm not surprised.

You're not?!

Nope. I made a slide of that purple goop from the mini-fridge and looked at it under the high-powered microscope, and guess what I found--

"--*nanotech*. Anybody who drank that stuff has ingested *thousands* of little artificial viruses. They're being *reprogrammed*, neuron by neuron.

"They're probably crawling all over Josh's *frontal cortex* right this second."

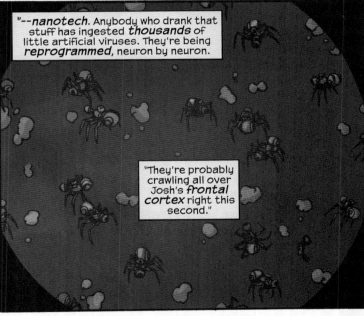

Crap. I'm gonna have to move *fast*, then.

Tell Ms. Norris I won't be in physics class today-- I'm going to see if I can follow one of these Hope Yards *catalog models* back to wherever their corporate headquarters is.

Sounds g-- oh no.

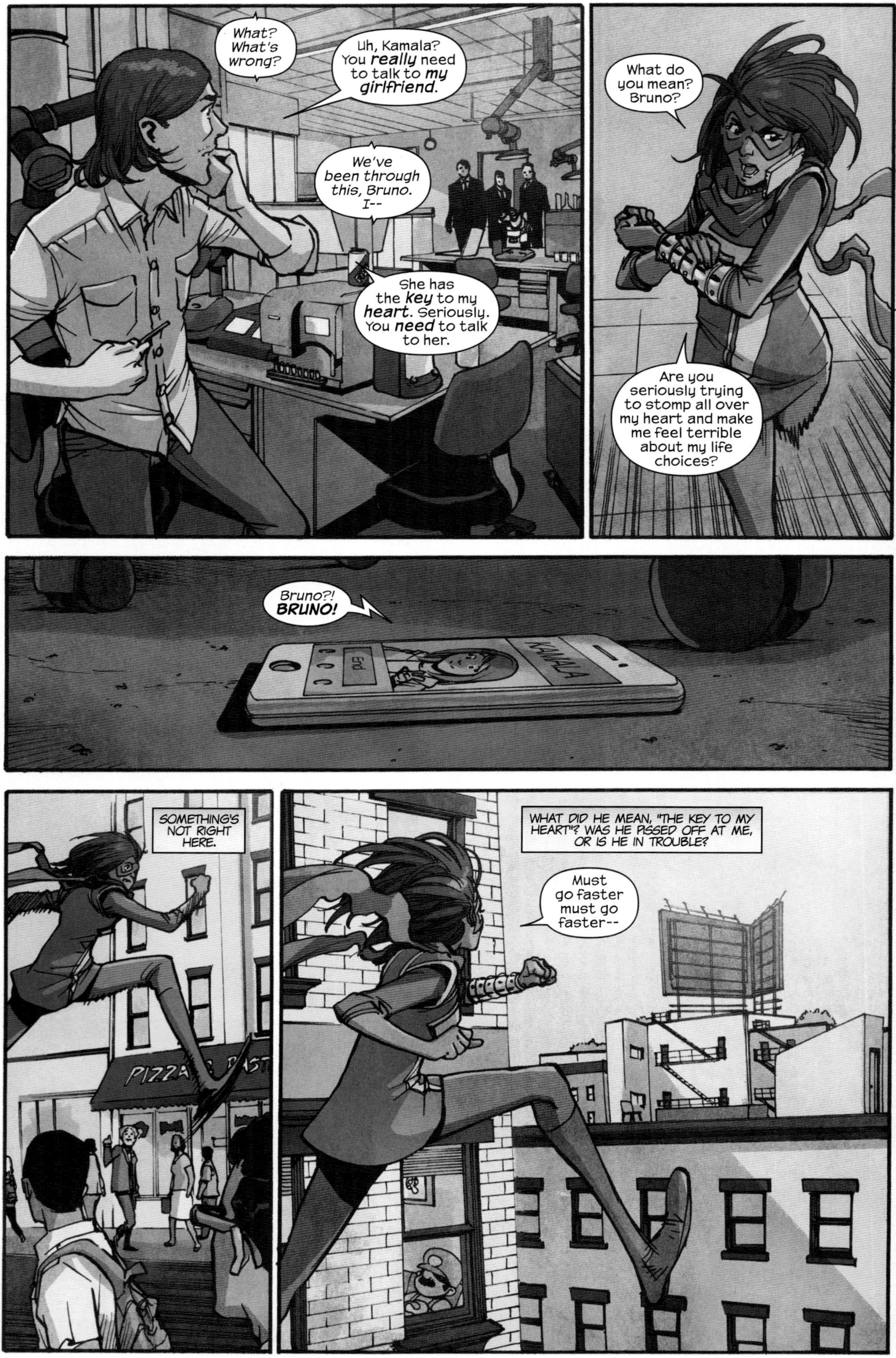
What? What's wrong?
Uh, Kamala? You **really** need to talk to **my girlfriend**.
We've been through this, Bruno. I--
She has the **key** to my **heart**. Seriously. You **need** to talk to her.
What do you mean? Bruno?
Are you seriously trying to stomp all over my heart and make me feel terrible about my life choices?
Bruno?! **BRUNO!**
End
KAMALA
SOMETHING'S NOT RIGHT HERE.
PIZZA
WHAT DID HE MEAN, "THE KEY TO MY HEART"? WAS HE PISSED OFF AT ME, OR IS HE IN TROUBLE?
Must go faster must go faster--

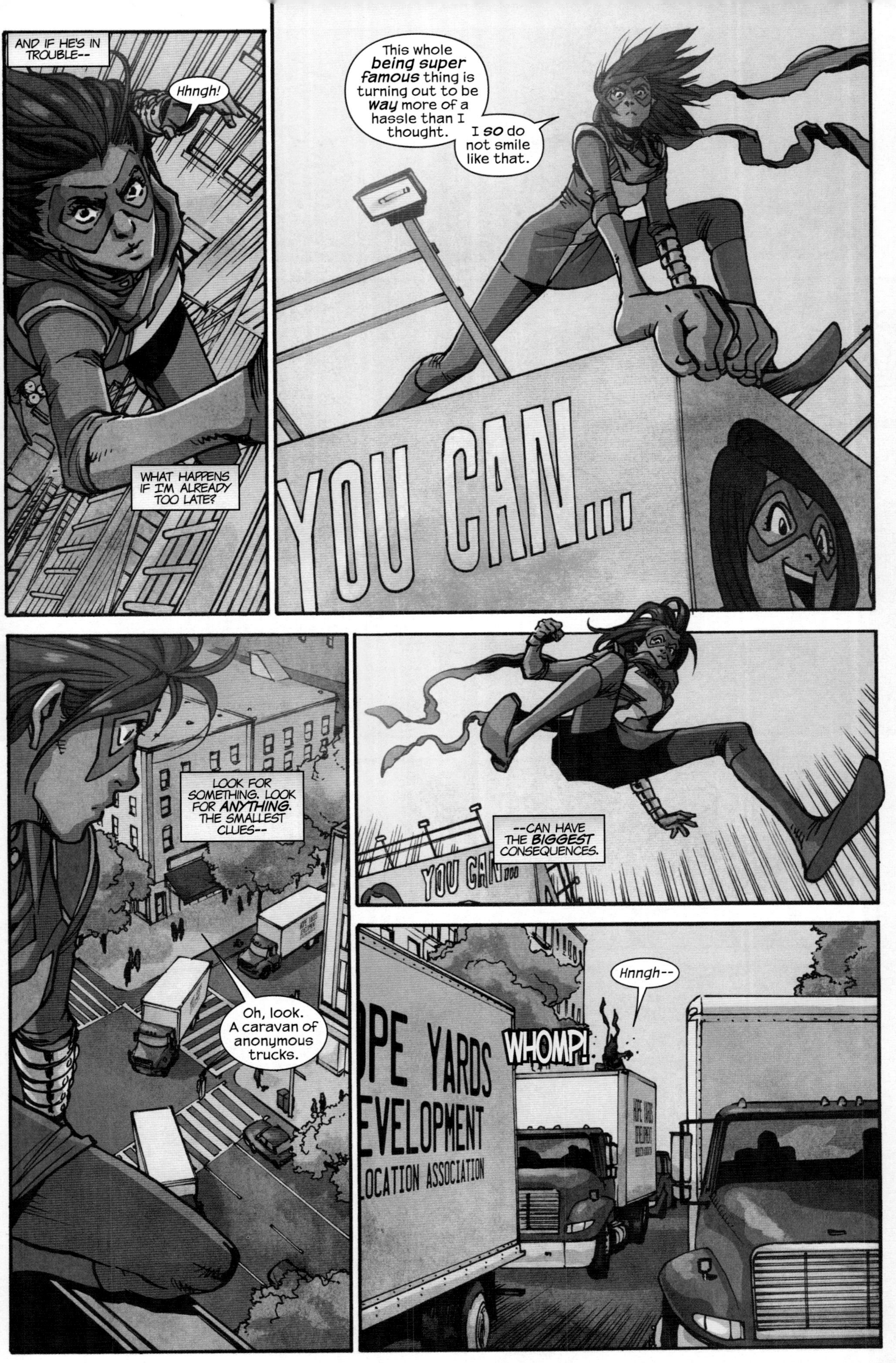
AND IF HE'S IN TROUBLE--
Hhngh!
WHAT HAPPENS IF I'M ALREADY TOO LATE?
This whole ***being super famous*** thing is turning out to be ***way*** more of a hassle than I thought.
I ***so*** do not smile like that.
YOU CAN...
LOOK FOR SOMETHING. LOOK FOR ***ANYTHING***. THE SMALLEST CLUES--
Oh, look. A caravan of anonymous trucks.
--CAN HAVE THE ***BIGGEST*** CONSEQUENCES.
YOU CAN...
Hnngh--
WHOMP!
OPE YARDS
EVELOPMENT
LOCATION ASSOCIATION

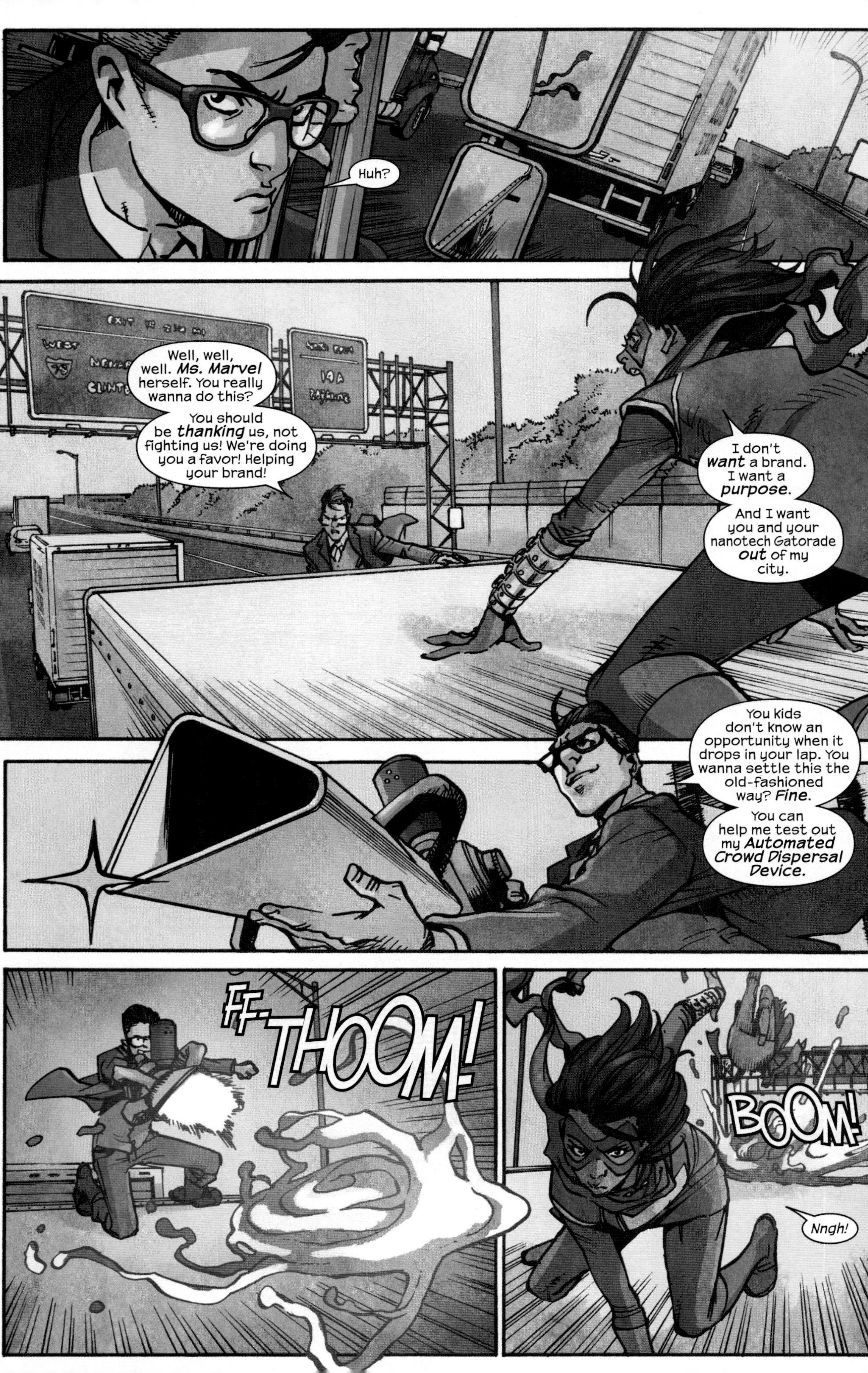

Huh?
Well, well, well. Ms. Marvel herself. You really wanna do this?
You should be thanking us, not fighting us! We're doing you a favor! Helping your brand!
I don't want a brand. I want a purpose.
And I want you and your nanotech Gatorade out of my city.
You kids don't know an opportunity when it drops in your lap. You wanna settle this the old-fashioned way? Fine.
You can help me test out my Automated Crowd Dispersal Device.
FF-THOOM!
BOOM!
Nngh!

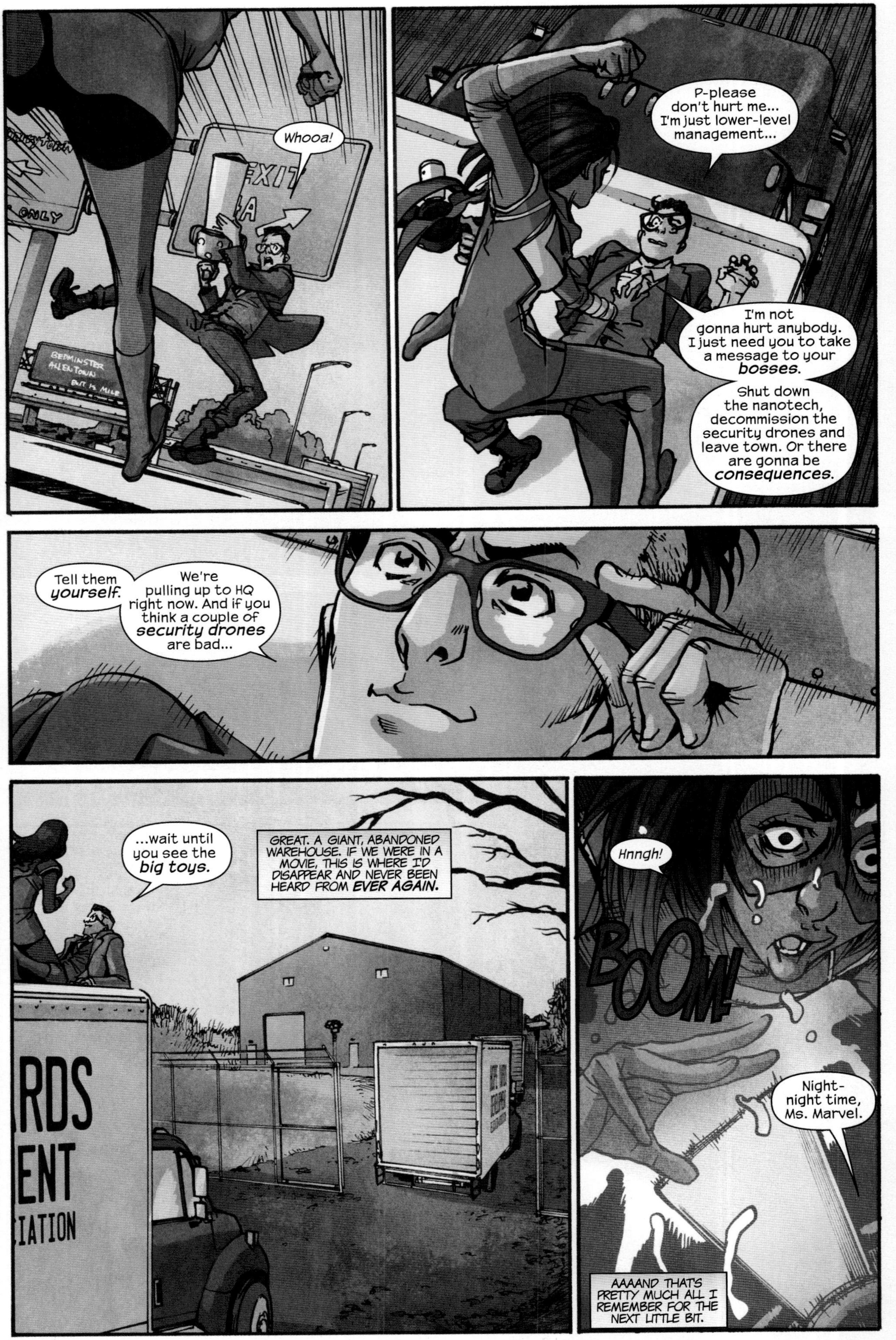
Whooa!
ONLY
EXIT
BEDMINSTER ALLENTOWN
P-please don't hurt me... I'm just lower-level management...
I'm not gonna hurt anybody. I just need you to take a message to your *bosses*.
Shut down the nanotech, decommission the security drones and leave town. Or there are gonna be *consequences*.
Tell them *yourself*.
We're pulling up to HQ right now. And if you think a couple of *security drones* are bad...
...wait until you see the *big toys*.
GREAT. A GIANT, ABANDONED WAREHOUSE. IF WE WERE IN A MOVIE, THIS IS WHERE I'D DISAPPEAR AND NEVER BEEN HEARD FROM *EVER AGAIN*.
ARDS
ENT
CIATION
Hnngh!
BOOM!
Night-night time, Ms. Marvel.
AAAAND THAT'S PRETTY MUCH ALL I REMEMBER FOR THE NEXT LITTLE BIT.

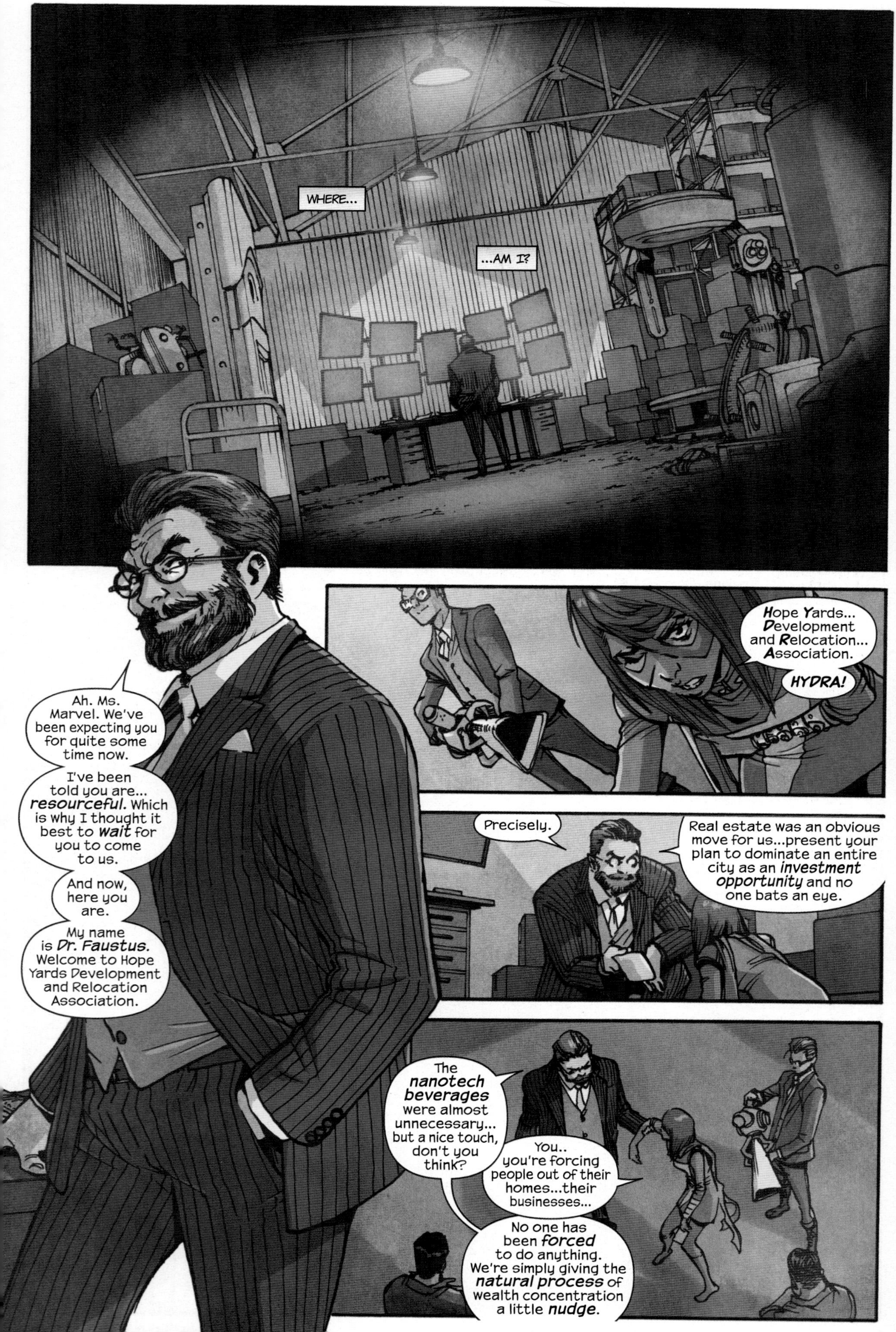
WHERE...
...AM I?
Ah. Ms. Marvel. We've been expecting you for quite some time now.
I've been told you are... resourceful. Which is why I thought it best to wait for you to come to us.
And now, here you are.
My name is Dr. Faustus. Welcome to Hope Yards Development and Relocation Association.
Hope Yards... Development and Relocation... Association.
HYDRA!
Precisely.
Real estate was an obvious move for us...present your plan to dominate an entire city as an investment opportunity and no one bats an eye.
The nanotech beverages were almost unnecessary... but a nice touch, don't you think?
You.. you're forcing people out of their homes...their businesses...
No one has been forced to do anything. We're simply giving the natural process of wealth concentration a little nudge.

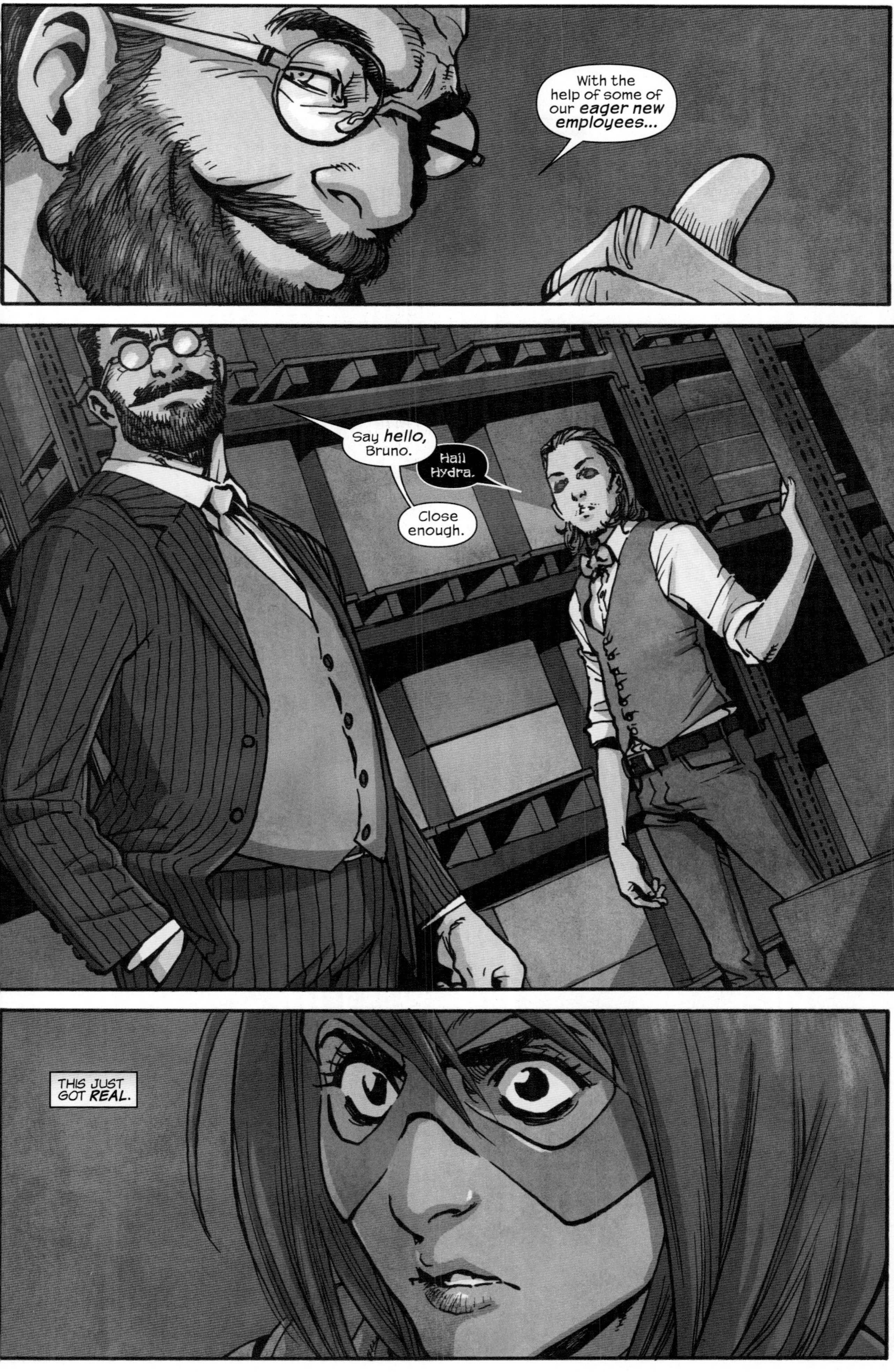

With the help of some of our eager new employees...
Say hello, Bruno.
Hail Hydra.
Close enough.
THIS JUST GOT REAL.

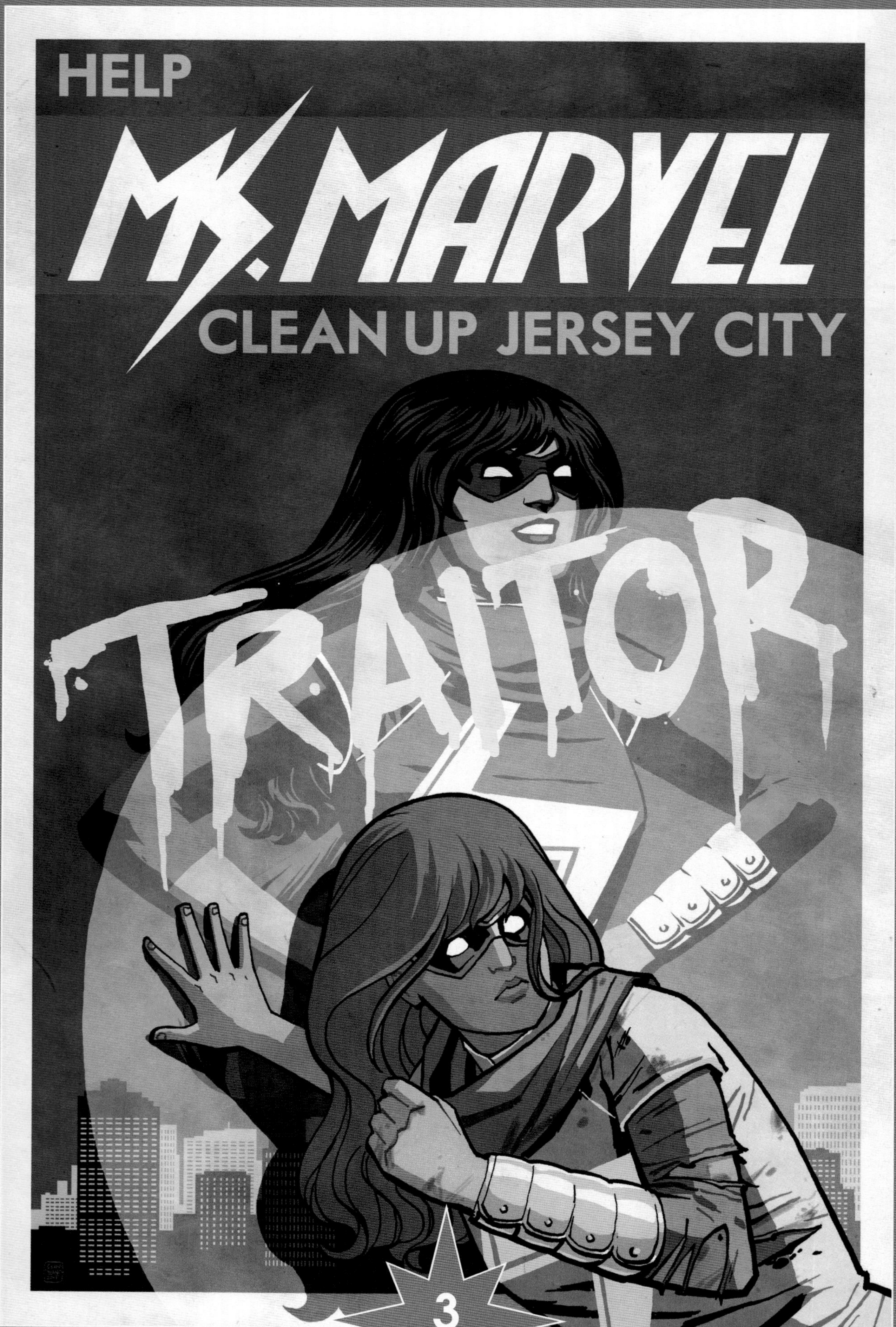

HELP
MS. MARVEL
CLEAN UP JERSEY CITY
TRAITOR
3

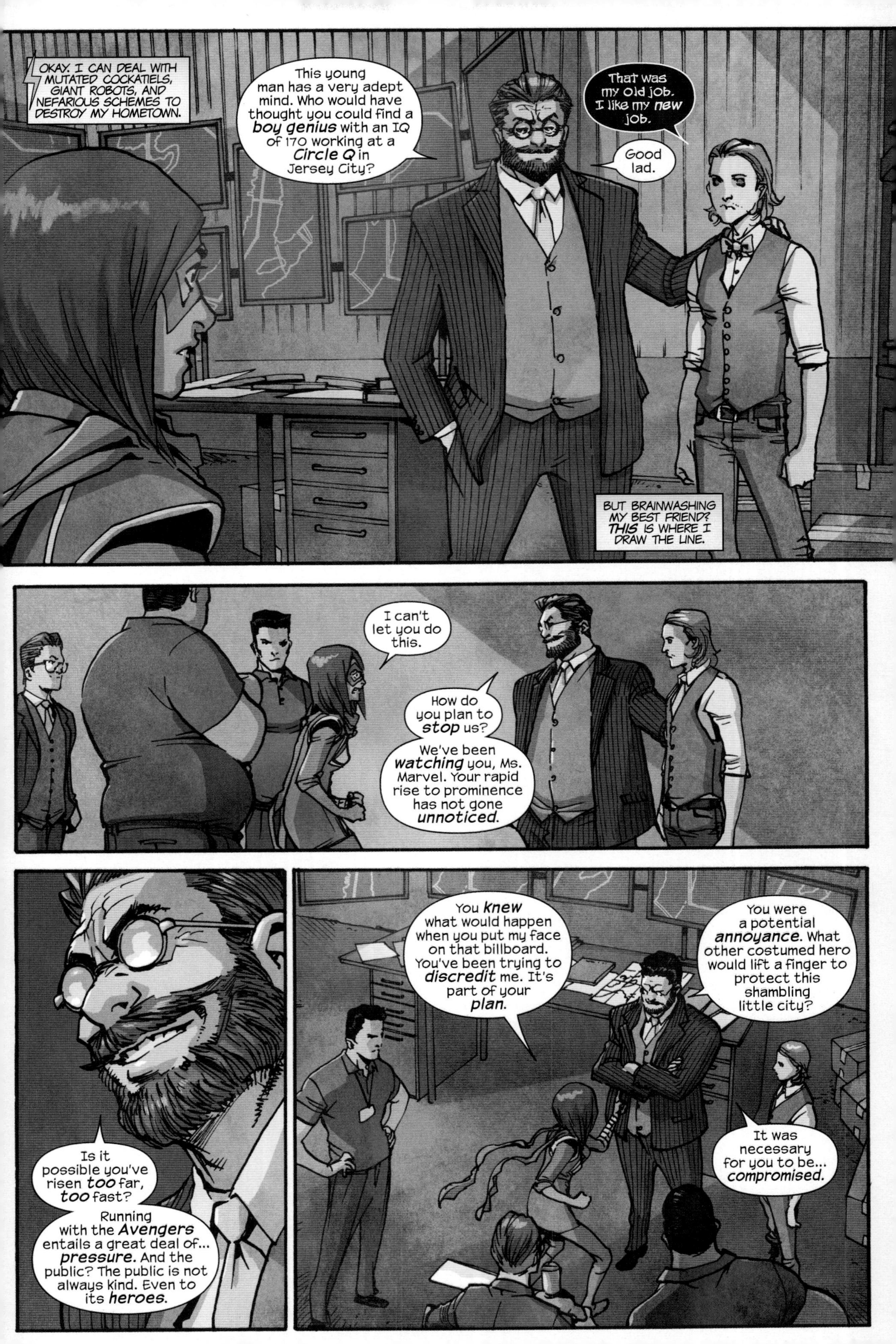
OKAY. I CAN DEAL WITH MUTATED COCKATIELS, GIANT ROBOTS, AND NEFARIOUS SCHEMES TO DESTROY MY HOMETOWN.
This young man has a very adept mind. Who would have thought you could find a boy genius with an IQ of 170 working at a Circle Q in Jersey City?
That was my old job. I like my new job.
Good lad.
BUT BRAINWASHING MY BEST FRIEND? THIS IS WHERE I DRAW THE LINE.
I can't let you do this.
How do you plan to stop us?
We've been watching you, Ms. Marvel. Your rapid rise to prominence has not gone unnoticed.
Is it possible you've risen too far, too fast?
Running with the Avengers entails a great deal of... pressure. And the public? The public is not always kind. Even to its heroes.
You knew what would happen when you put my face on that billboard. You've been trying to discredit me. It's part of your plan.
You were a potential annoyance. What other costumed hero would lift a finger to protect this shambling little city?
It was necessary for you to be... compromised.

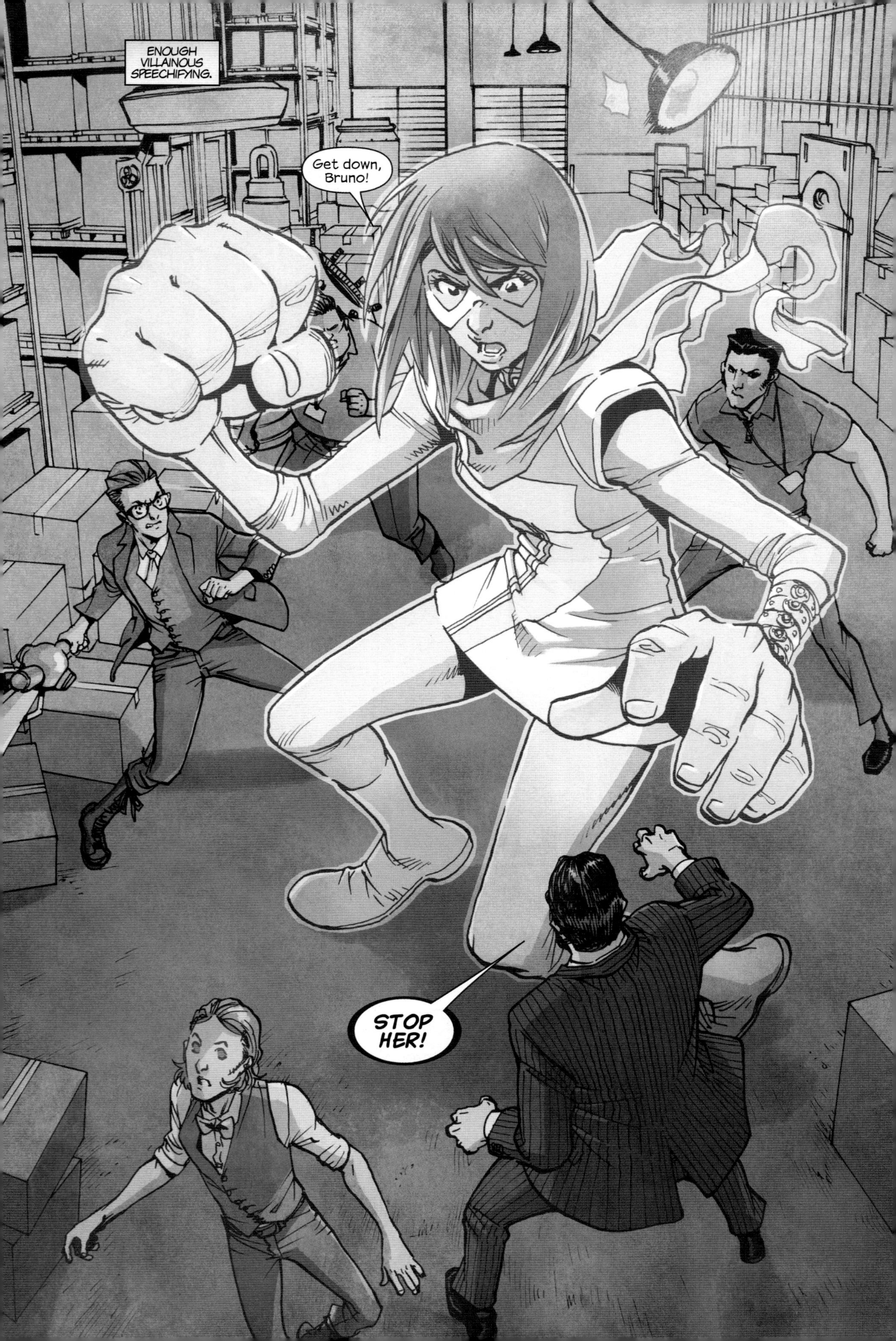
ENOUGH VILLAINOUS SPEECHIFYING.
Get down, Bruno!
STOP HER!

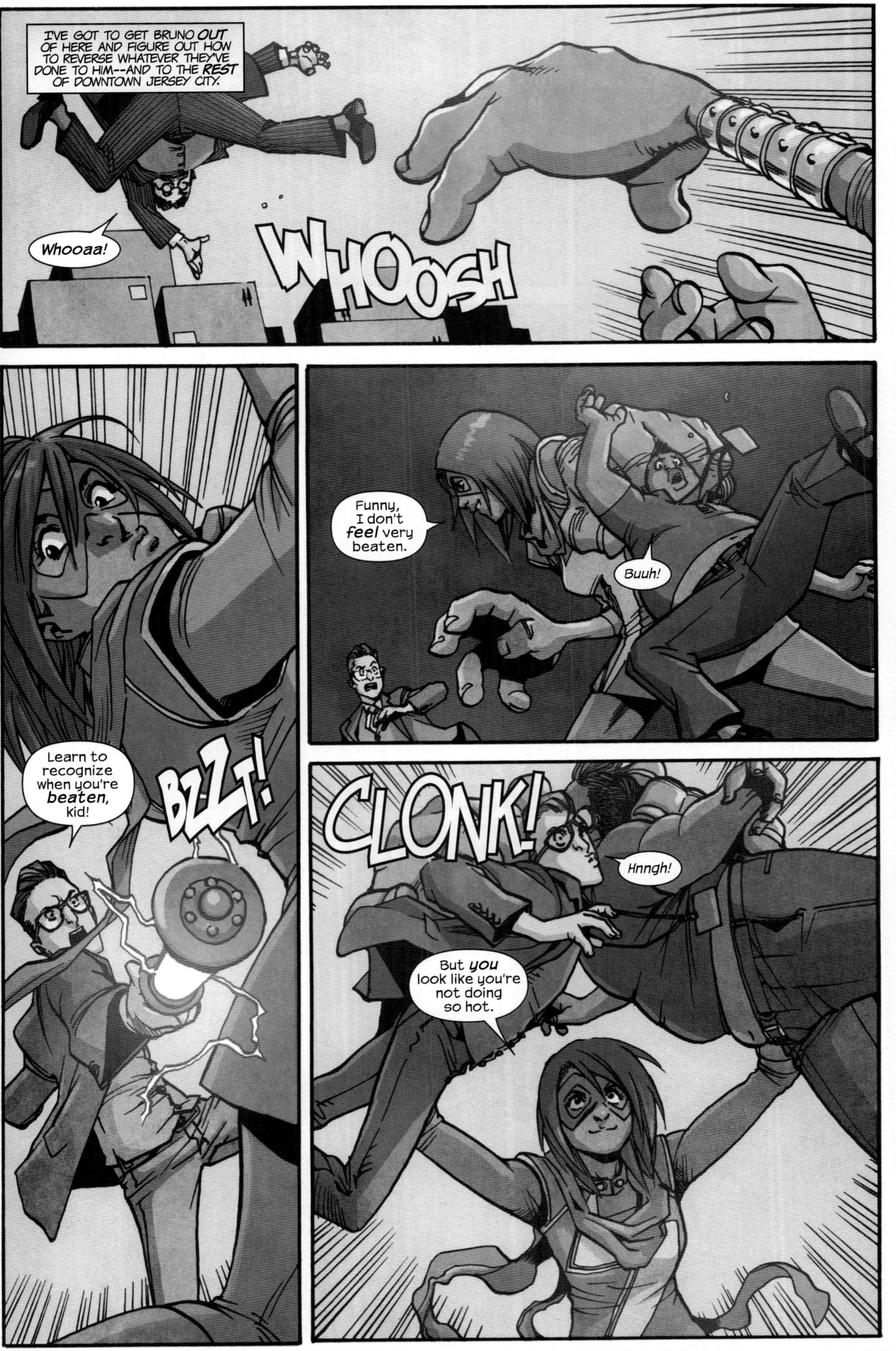
I'VE GOT TO GET BRUNO OUT OF HERE AND FIGURE OUT HOW TO REVERSE WHATEVER THEY'VE DONE TO HIM--AND TO THE REST OF DOWNTOWN JERSEY CITY.
Whooaa!
WHOOSH
Learn to recognize when you're beaten, kid!
BZZT!
Funny, I don't feel very beaten.
Buuh!
CLONK!
Hnngh!
But you look like you're not doing so hot.

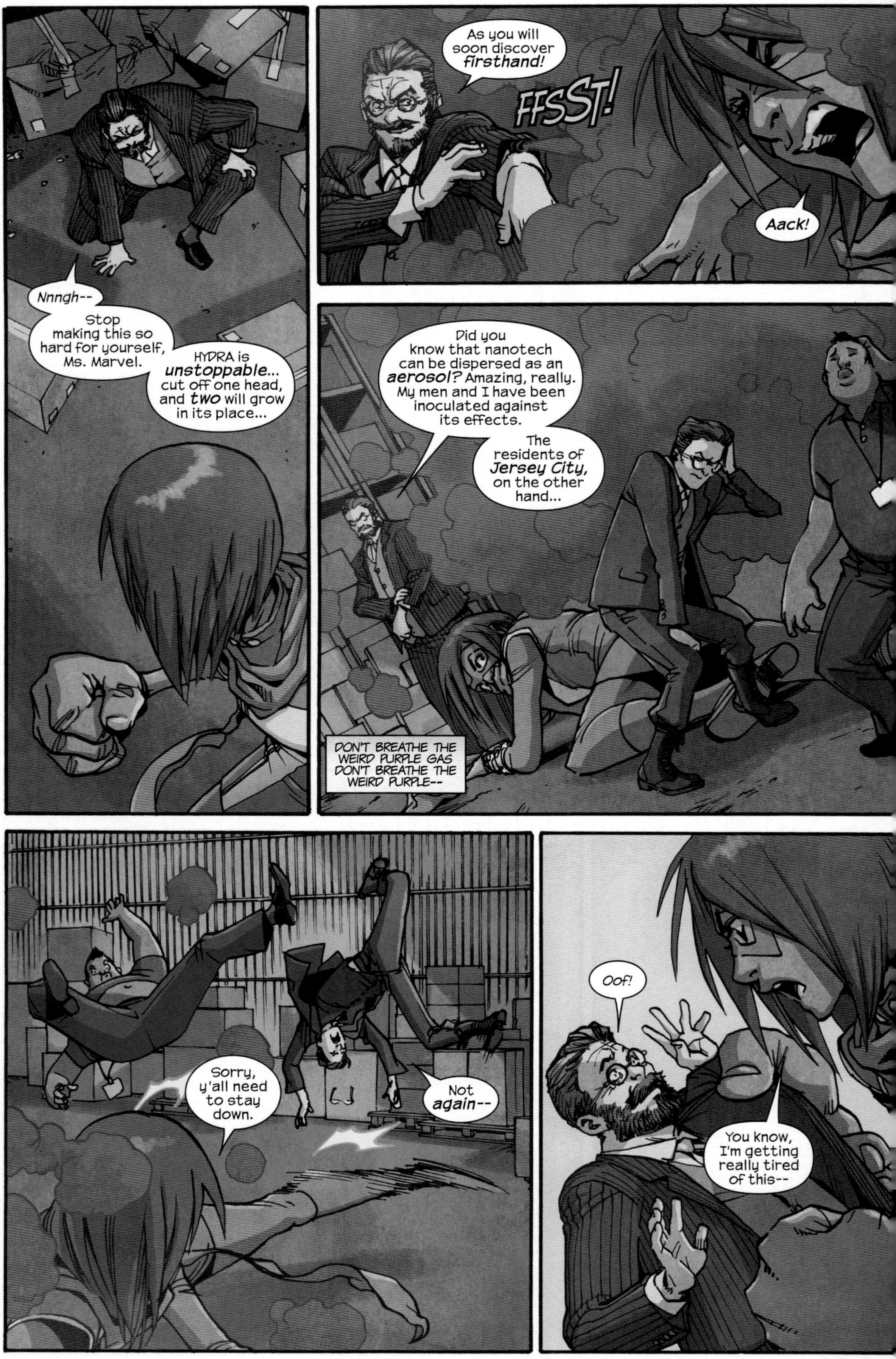
Nnngh--
Stop making this so hard for yourself, Ms. Marvel.
HYDRA is unstoppable... cut off one head, and two will grow in its place...
As you will soon discover firsthand!
FFSST!
Aack!
Did you know that nanotech can be dispersed as an aerosol? Amazing, really. My men and I have been inoculated against its effects.
The residents of Jersey City, on the other hand...
DON'T BREATHE THE WEIRD PURPLE GAS DON'T BREATHE THE WEIRD PURPLE--
Sorry, y'all need to stay down.
Not again--
Oof!
You know, I'm getting really tired of this--

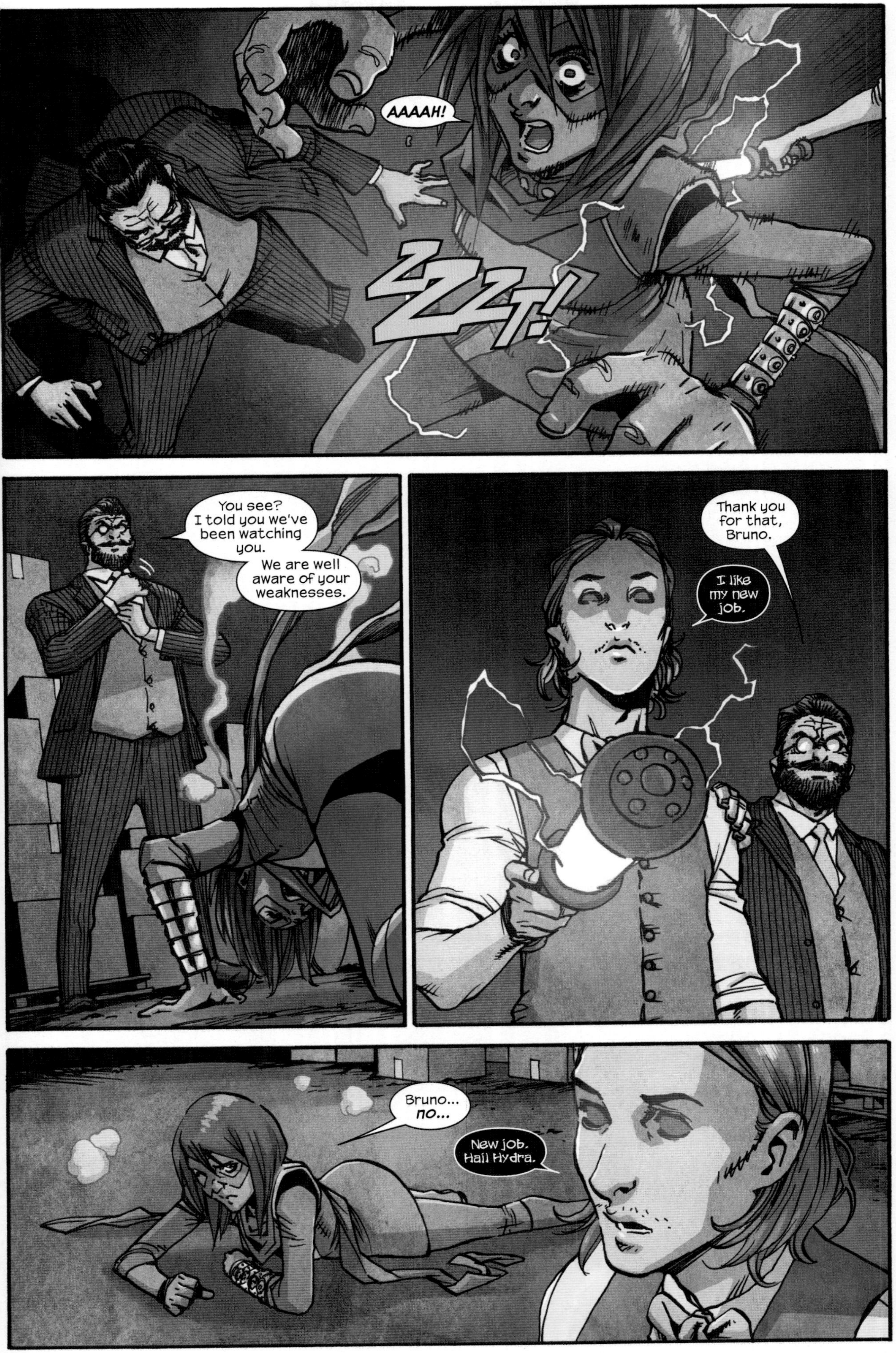
AAAAH!
ZZZT!
You see? I told you we've been watching you.
We are well aware of your weaknesses.
Thank you for that, Bruno.
I like my new job.
Bruno... no...
New job. Hail Hydra.

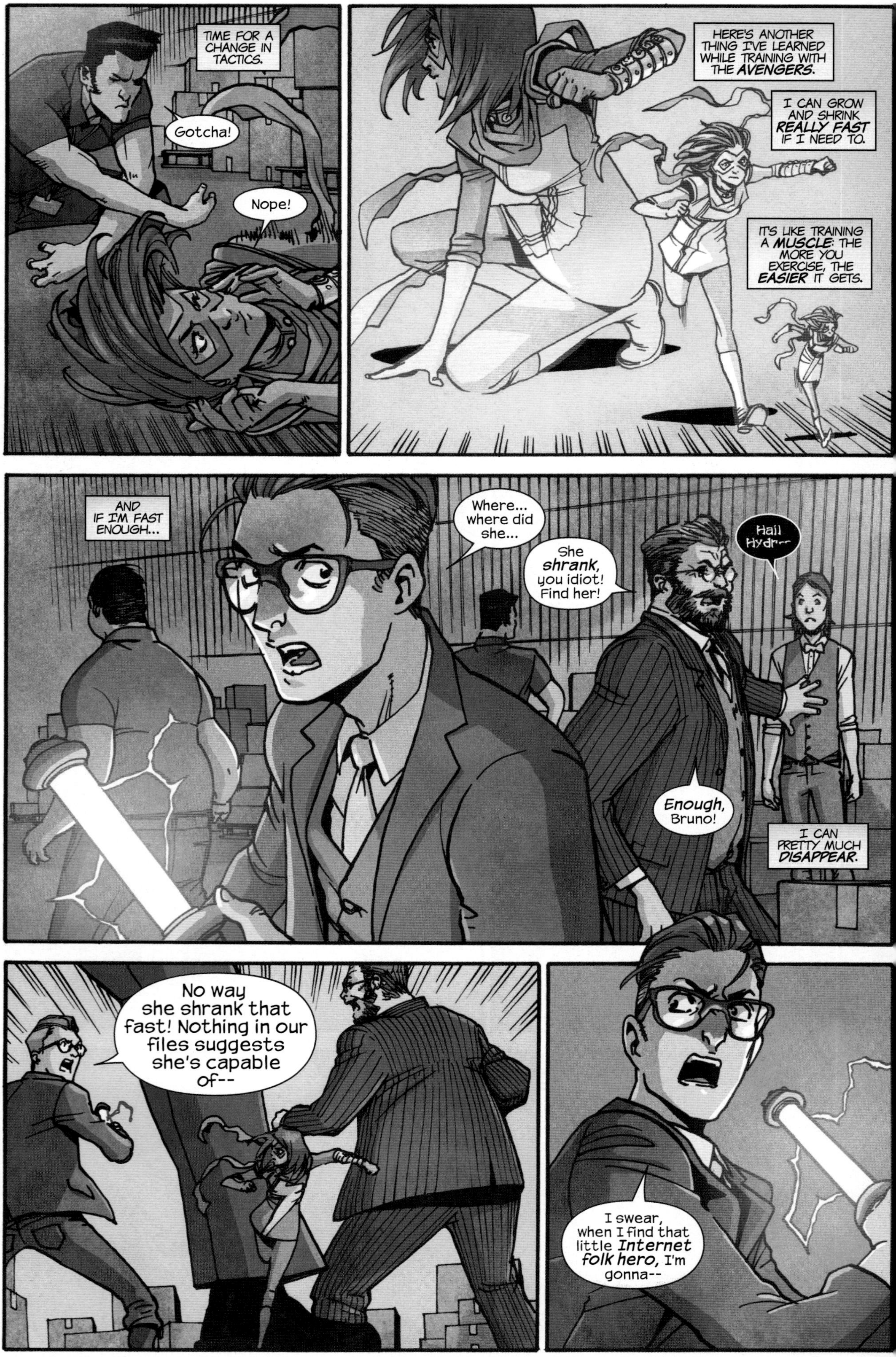

TIME FOR A CHANGE IN TACTICS.
Gotcha!
Nope!
HERE'S ANOTHER THING I'VE LEARNED WHILE TRAINING WITH THE AVENGERS.
I CAN GROW AND SHRINK REALLY FAST IF I NEED TO.
IT'S LIKE TRAINING A MUSCLE: THE MORE YOU EXERCISE, THE EASIER IT GETS.
AND IF I'M FAST ENOUGH...
Where... where did she...
She shrank, you idiot! Find her!
Hail Hydr--
Enough, Bruno!
I CAN PRETTY MUCH DISAPPEAR.
No way she shrank that fast! Nothing in our files suggests she's capable of--
I swear, when I find that little Internet folk hero, I'm gonna--

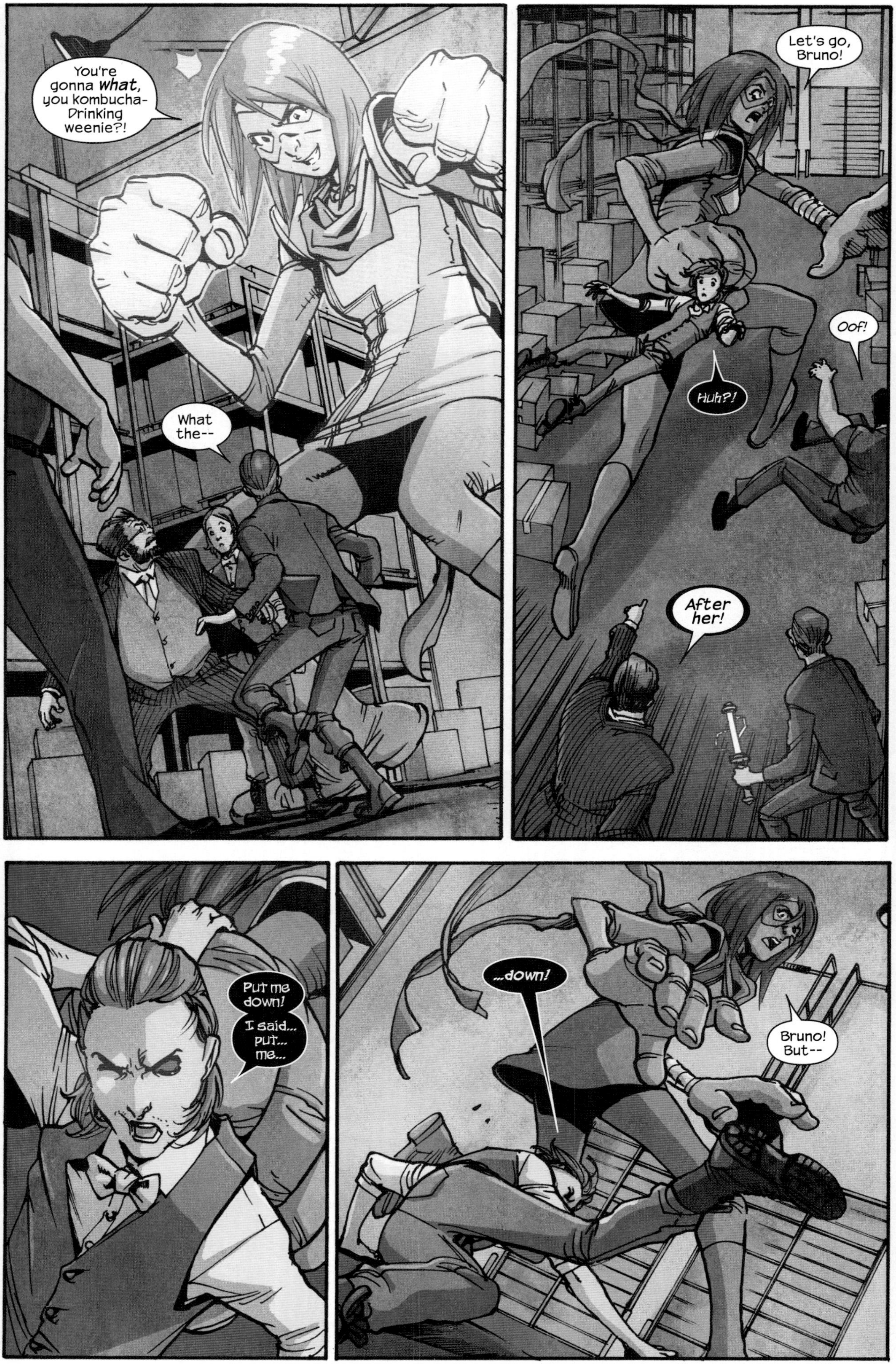
You're gonna *what*, you kombucha-Drinking weenie?!
What the--
Let's go, Bruno!
Huh?!
Oof!
After her!
Put me down!
I said... put... me...
...down!
Bruno! But--

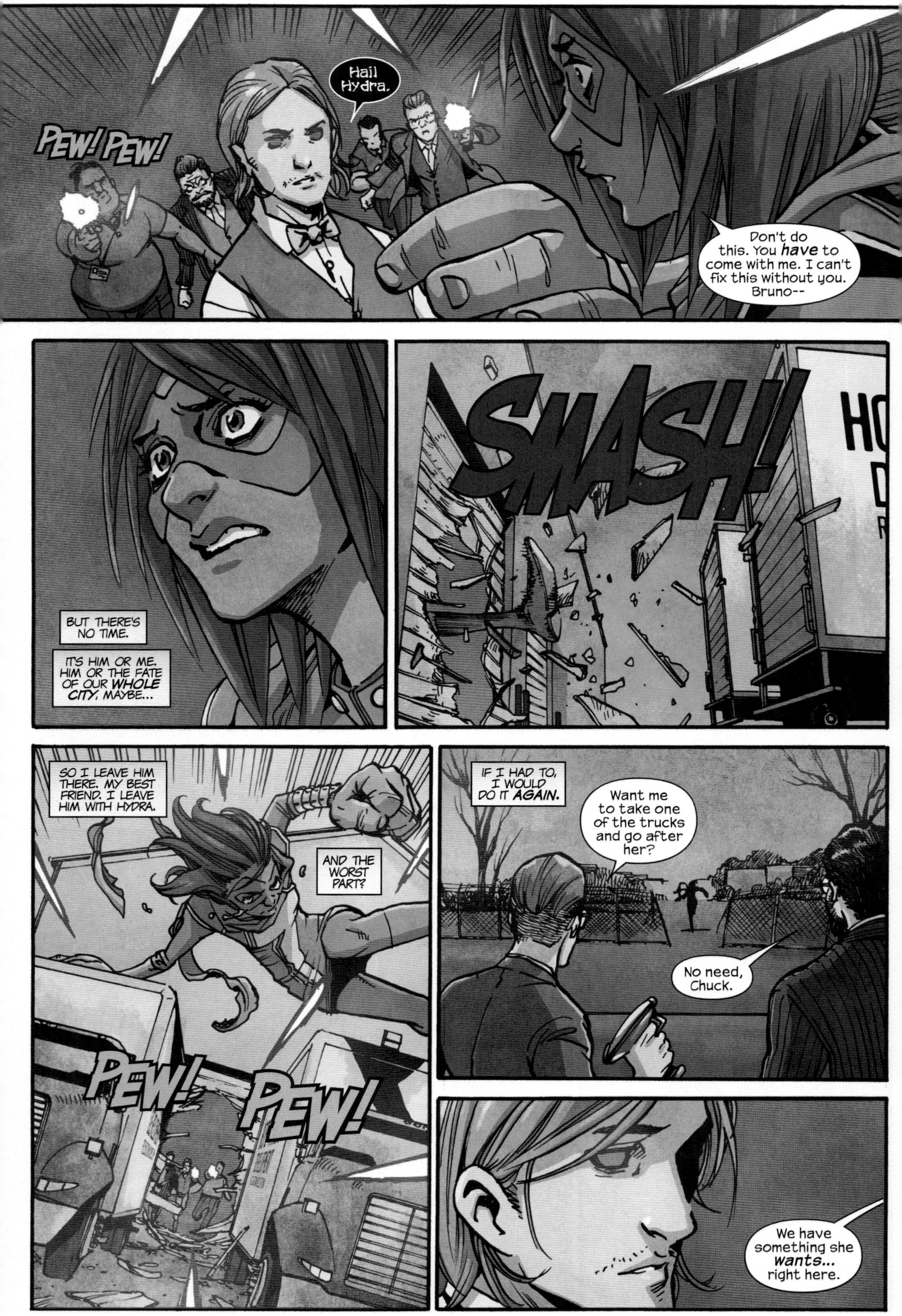
PEW! PEW!
Hail Hydra.
Don't do this. You have to come with me. I can't fix this without you. Bruno--
BUT THERE'S NO TIME.
IT'S HIM OR ME. HIM OR THE FATE OF OUR WHOLE CITY, MAYBE...
SMASH!
SO I LEAVE HIM THERE. MY BEST FRIEND. I LEAVE HIM WITH HYDRA.
AND THE WORST PART?
PEW! PEW!
IF I HAD TO, I WOULD DO IT AGAIN.
Want me to take one of the trucks and go after her?
No need, Chuck.
We have something she wants... right here.

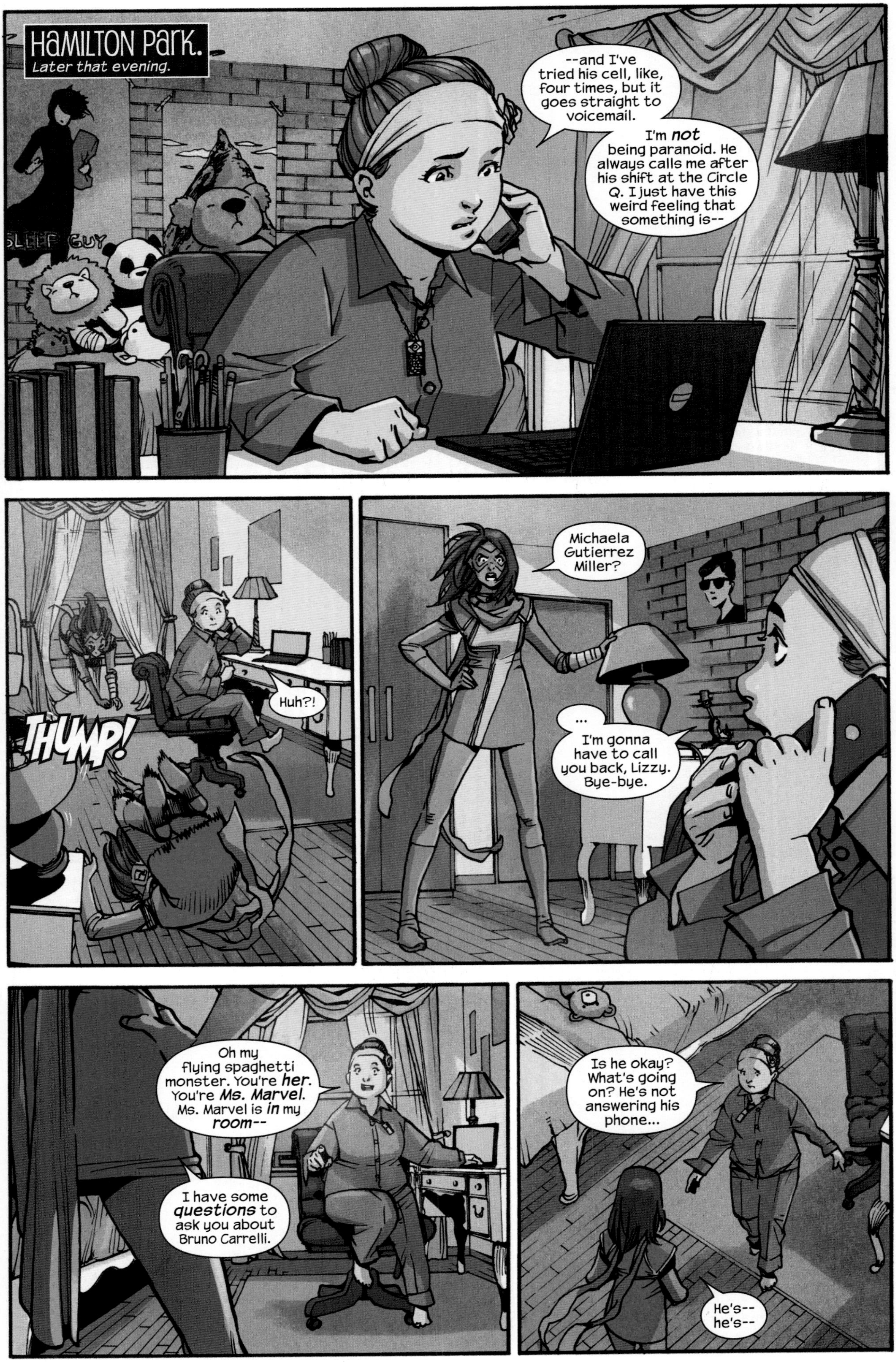
Hamilton Park.
Later that evening.
--and I've tried his cell, like, four times, but it goes straight to voicemail.
I'm *not* being paranoid. He always calls me after his shift at the Circle Q. I just have this weird feeling that something is--
SLEEP GUY
Huh?!
THUMP!
Michaela Gutierrez Miller?
...
I'm gonna have to call you back, Lizzy. Bye-bye.
Oh my flying spaghetti monster. You're *her*. You're *Ms. Marvel*. Ms. Marvel is *in* my *room*--
I have some *questions* to ask you about Bruno Carrelli.
Is he okay? What's going on? He's not answering his phone...
He's-- he's--

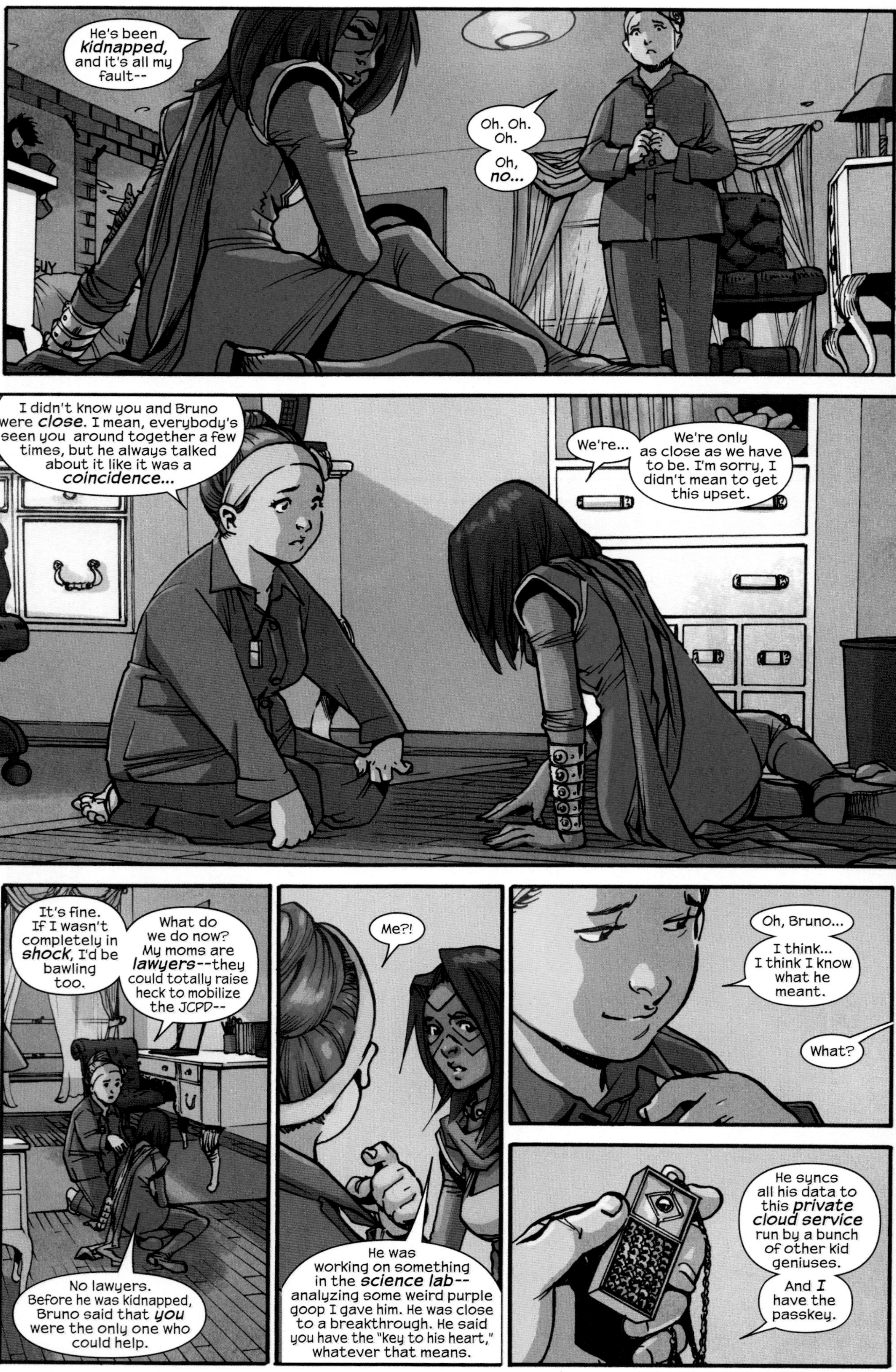
He's been *kidnapped,* and it's all my fault--
Oh. Oh. Oh.
Oh, *no...*
I didn't know you and Bruno were *close.* I mean, everybody's seen you around together a few times, but he always talked about it like it was a *coincidence...*
We're...
We're only as close as we have to be. I'm sorry, I didn't mean to get this upset.
It's fine. If I wasn't completely in *shock,* I'd be bawling too.
What do we do now? My moms are *lawyers*--they could totally raise heck to mobilize the JCPD--
No lawyers. Before he was kidnapped, Bruno said that *you* were the only one who could help.
Me?!
He was working on something in the *science lab*--analyzing some weird purple goop I gave him. He was close to a breakthrough. He said you have the "key to his heart," whatever that means.
Oh, Bruno...
I think... I think I know what he meant.
What?
He syncs all his data to this *private cloud service* run by a bunch of other kid geniuses.
And *I* have the passkey.

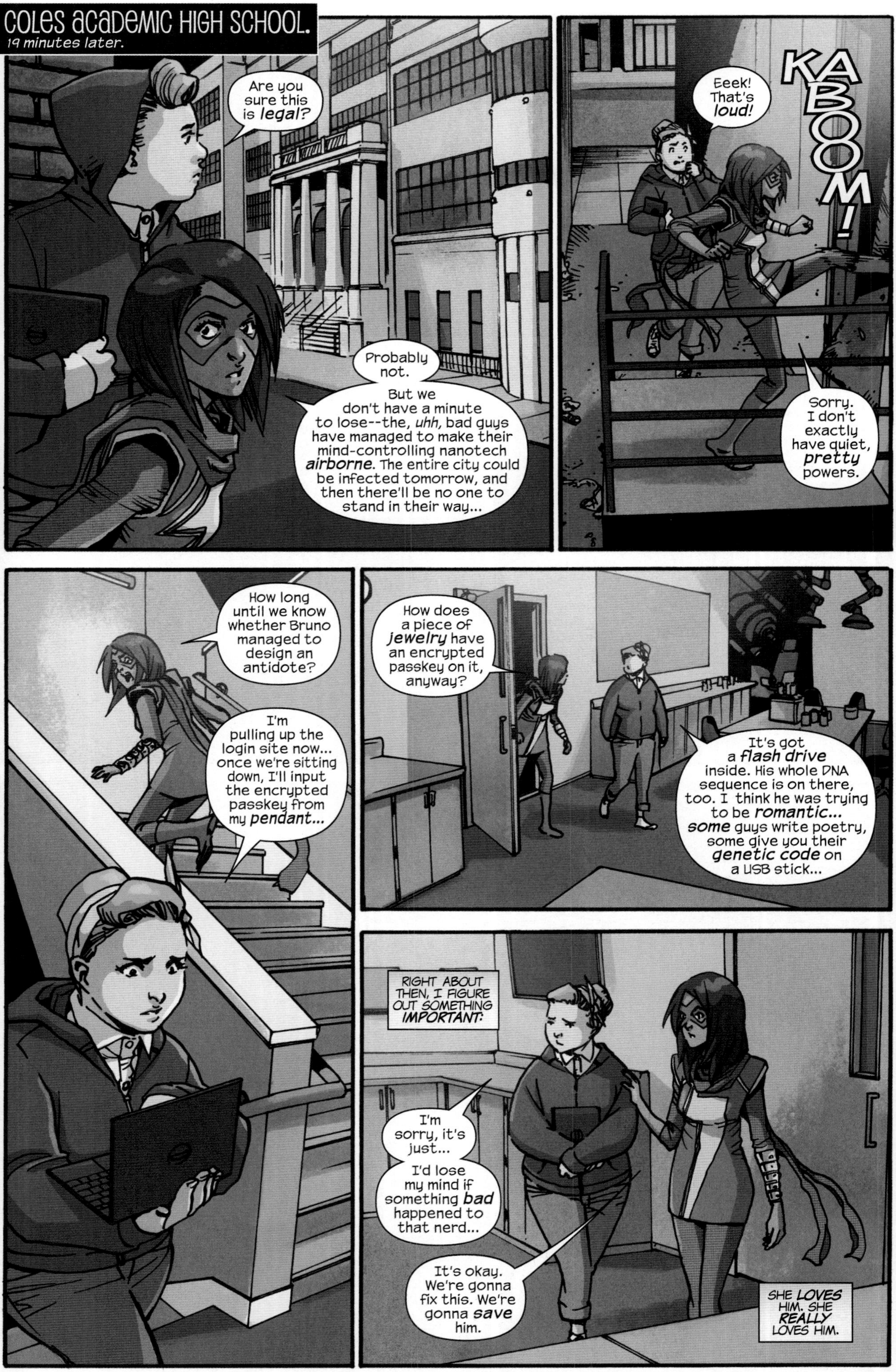
COLES ACADEMIC HIGH SCHOOL.
19 minutes later.
Are you sure this is *legal*?
Probably not.
But we don't have a minute to lose--the, *uhh,* bad guys have managed to make their mind-controlling nanotech ***airborne***. The entire city could be infected tomorrow, and then there'll be no one to stand in their way...
KABOOM!
Eeek! That's *loud!*
Sorry. I don't exactly have quiet, ***pretty*** powers.
How long until we know whether Bruno managed to design an antidote?
I'm pulling up the login site now... once we're sitting down, I'll input the encrypted passkey from my *pendant*...
How does a piece of ***jewelry*** have an encrypted passkey on it, anyway?
It's got a ***flash drive*** inside. His whole DNA sequence is on there, too. I think he was trying to be ***romantic... some*** guys write poetry, some give you their ***genetic code*** on a USB stick...
RIGHT ABOUT THEN, I FIGURE OUT SOMETHING ***IMPORTANT:***
I'm sorry, it's just...
I'd lose my mind if something ***bad*** happened to that nerd...
It's okay. We're gonna fix this. We're gonna ***save*** him.
SHE ***LOVES*** HIM. SHE ***REALLY*** LOVES HIM.

Are you going to be all right?

Yeah. Thanks. I'm *trying* to keep it together, only--

I know. It's hard sometimes. When the people you love best are in trouble, it's like you can't focus.

I'm gonna focus. If Bruno needs my help, I have to.

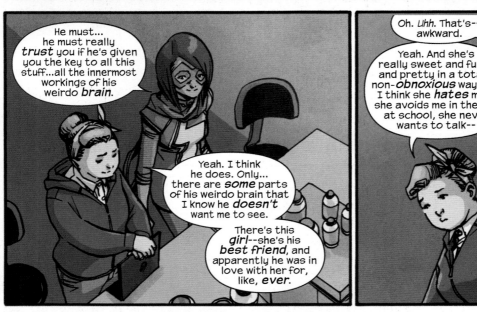

He must... he must really *trust* you if he's given you the key to all this stuff...all the innermost workings of his weirdo *brain*.

Yeah. I think he does. Only... there are *some* parts of his weirdo brain that I know he *doesn't* want me to see.

There's this *girl*--she's his *best friend*, and apparently he was in love with her for, like, *ever*.

Oh. *Uhh.* That's-- awkward.

Yeah. And she's really sweet and funny and pretty in a totally non-*obnoxious* way. But I think she *hates* me-- she avoids me in the hall at school, she never wants to talk--

Maybe she just needs time to *adjust*. Maybe the whole best-friend-dating-someone-else thing came as a *total shock* and she hasn't really wrapped her mind around it yet.

Maybe. I just wish I didn't feel so... *intimidated.*

We, *umm...* we should get back to work.

You're right, you're right.

Okay, here goes nothing...

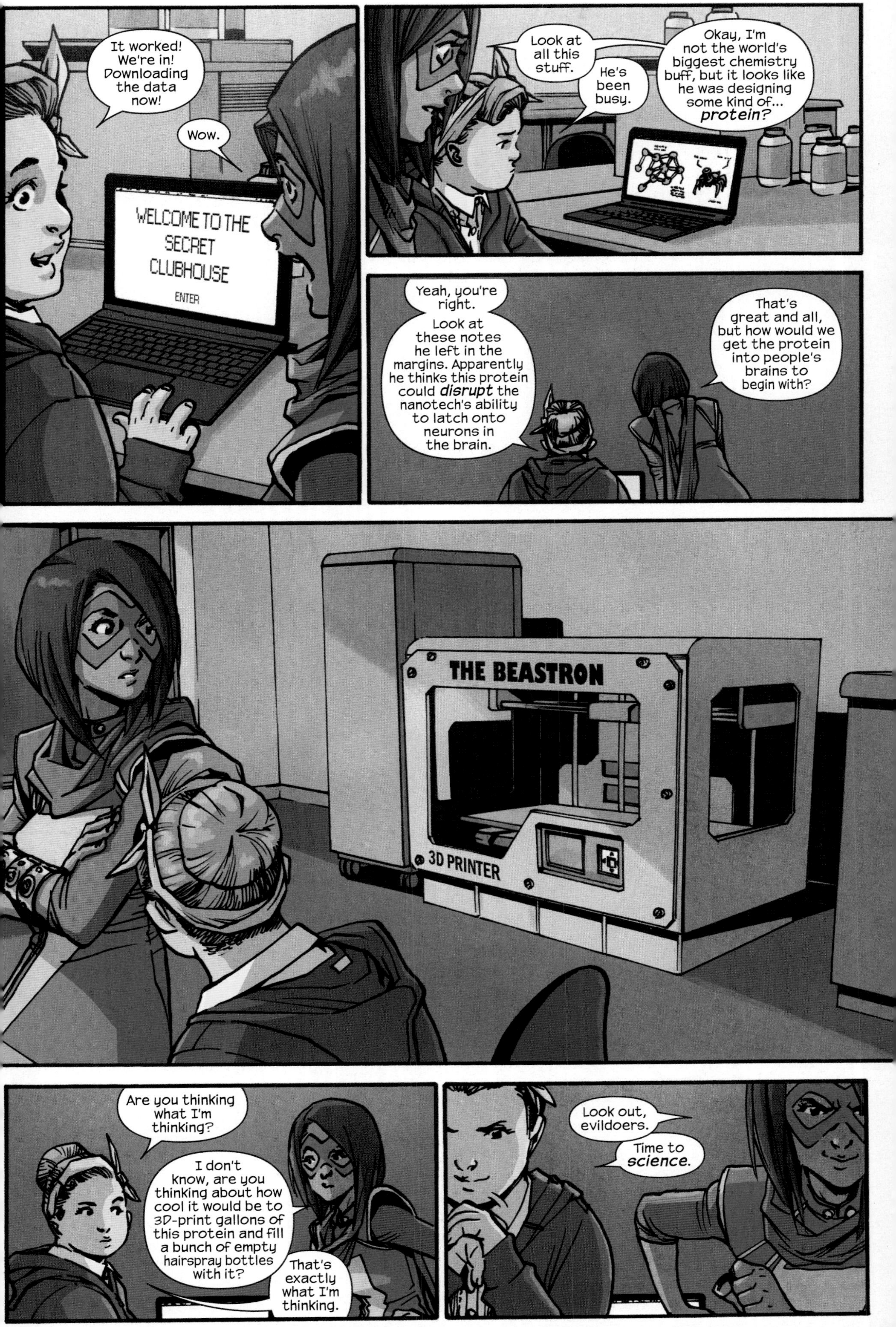
It worked! We're in! Downloading the data now!
Wow.
WELCOME TO THE SECRET CLUBHOUSE
ENTER
Look at all this stuff.
He's been busy.
Okay, I'm not the world's biggest chemistry buff, but it looks like he was designing some kind of... protein?
Yeah, you're right.
Look at these notes he left in the margins. Apparently he thinks this protein could disrupt the nanotech's ability to latch onto neurons in the brain.
That's great and all, but how would we get the protein into people's brains to begin with?
THE BEASTRON
3D PRINTER
Are you thinking what I'm thinking?
I don't know, are you thinking about how cool it would be to 3D-print gallons of this protein and fill a bunch of empty hairspray bottles with it?
That's exactly what I'm thinking.
Look out, evildoers.
Time to science.

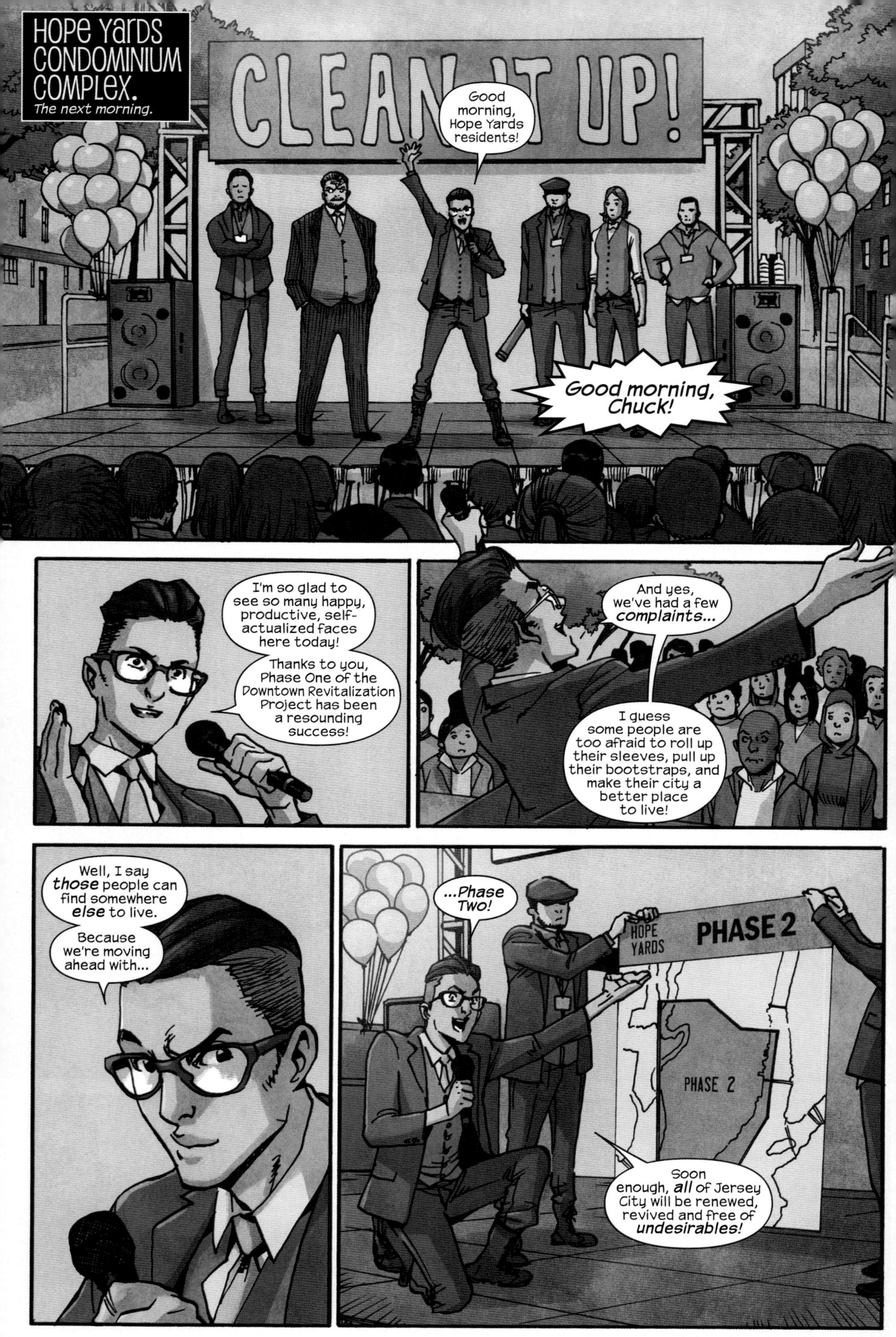
HOPE YARDS CONDOMINIUM COMPLEX.
The next morning.
CLEAN IT UP!
Good morning, Hope Yards residents!
Good morning, Chuck!
I'm so glad to see so many happy, productive, self-actualized faces here today!
Thanks to you, Phase One of the Downtown Revitalization Project has been a resounding success!
And yes, we've had a few *complaints...*
I guess some people are too afraid to roll up their sleeves, pull up their bootstraps, and make their city a better place to live!
Well, I say *those* people can find somewhere *else* to live.
Because we're moving ahead with...
...Phase Two!
HOPE YARDS
PHASE 2
PHASE 2
Soon enough, *all* of Jersey City will be renewed, revived and free of *undesirables!*

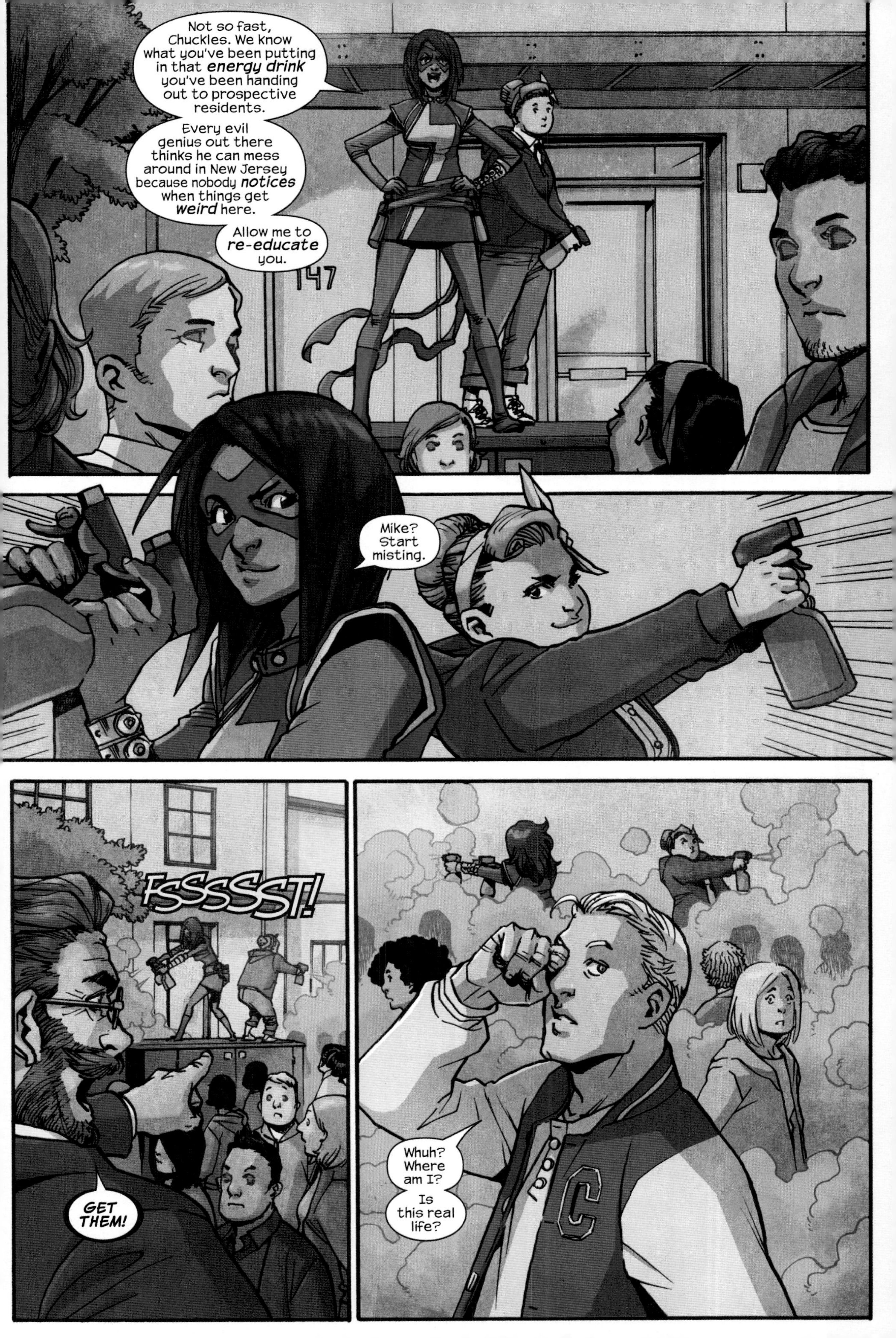

Not so fast, Chuckles. We know what you've been putting in that energy drink you've been handing out to prospective residents.
Every evil genius out there thinks he can mess around in New Jersey because nobody notices when things get weird here.
Allow me to re-educate you.
147
Mike? Start misting.
FSSSSST!
GET THEM!
Whuh? Where am I?
Is this real life?

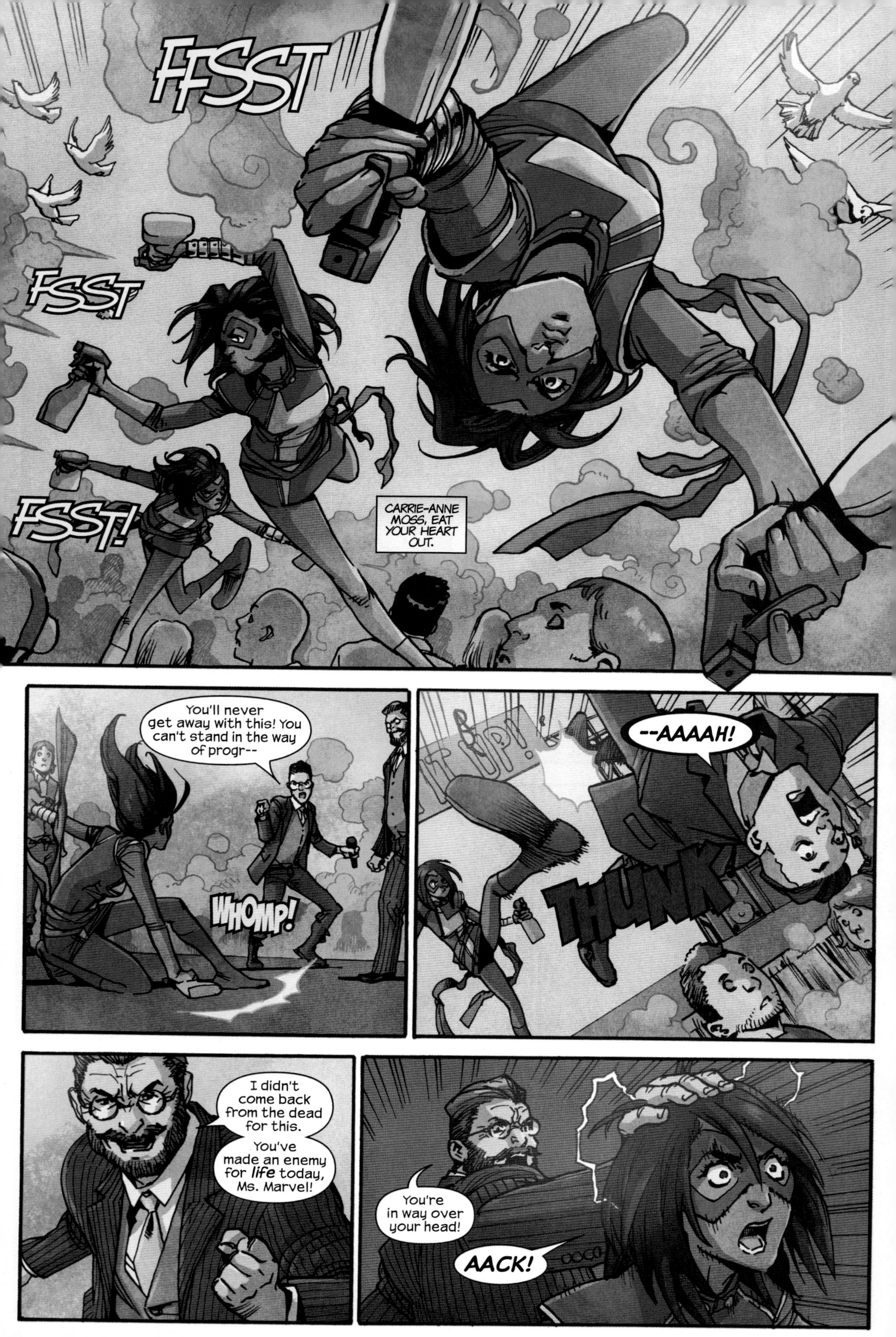
FFSST
FSST
FSST!
CARRIE-ANNE MOSS, EAT YOUR HEART OUT.
You'll never get away with this! You can't stand in the way of progr--
WHOMP!
--AAAAH!
THUNK
I didn't come back from the dead for this.
You've made an enemy for *life* today, Ms. Marvel!
You're in way over your head!
AACK!

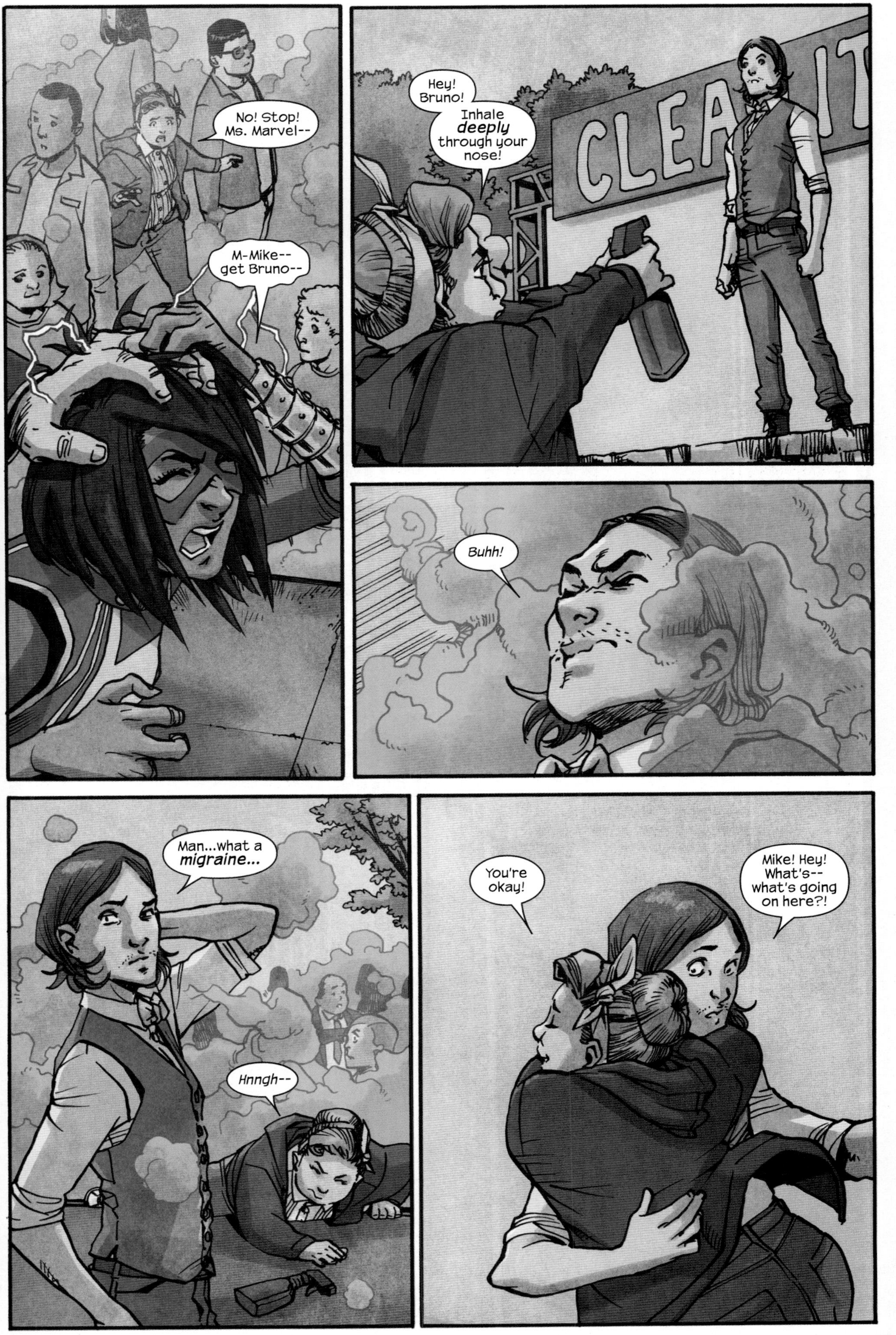
No! Stop! Ms. Marvel--
M-Mike-- get Bruno--
Hey! Bruno!
Inhale *deeply* through your nose!
CLEA IT
Buhh!
Man...what a *migraine...*
Hnngh--
You're okay!
Mike! Hey! What's-- what's going on here?!

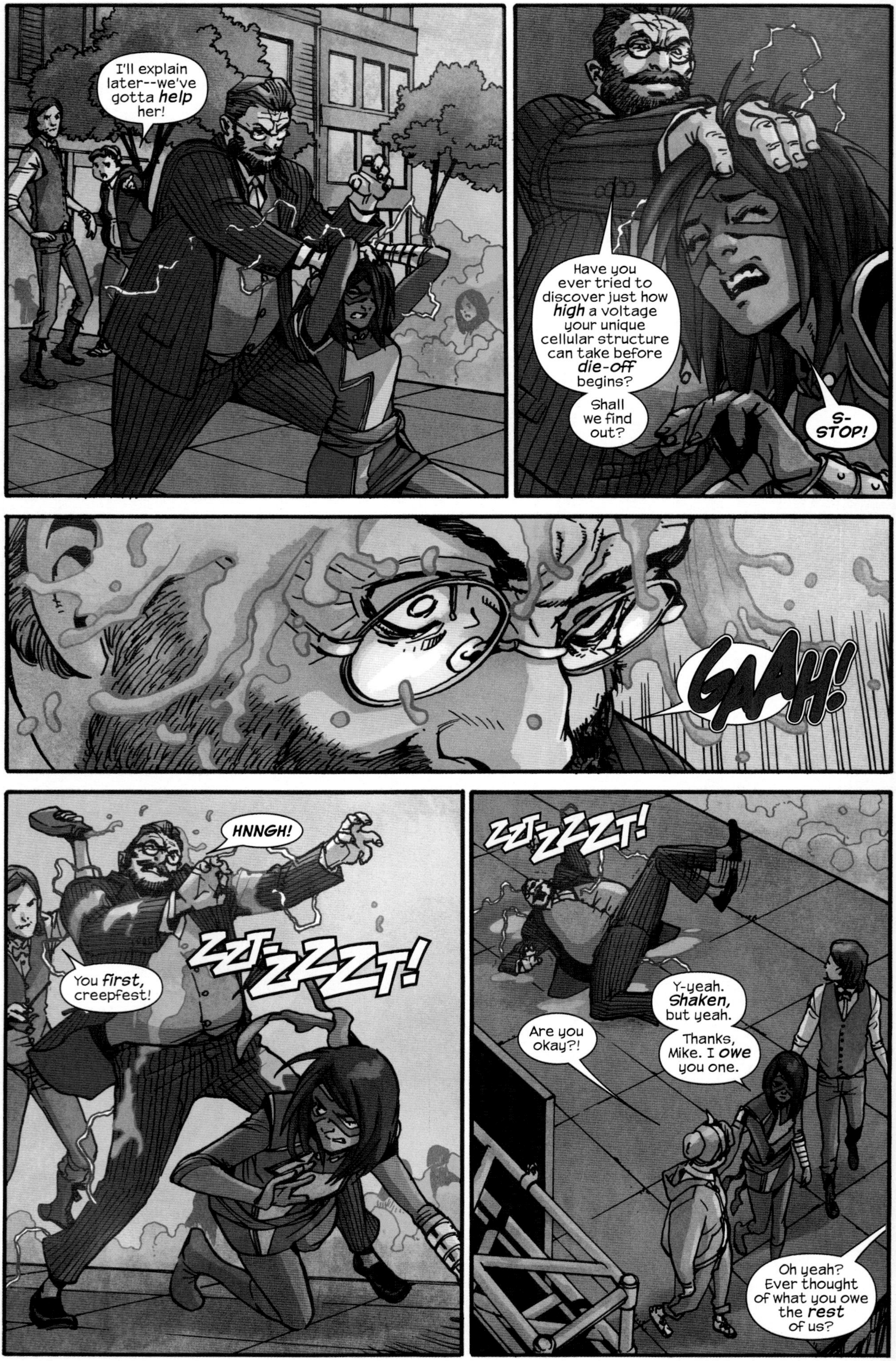
I'll explain later--we've gotta *help* her!
Have you ever tried to discover just how *high* a voltage your unique cellular structure can take before *die-off* begins?
Shall we find out?
S-STOP!
GAAH!
HNNGH!
You *first,* creepfest!
ZZT-ZZZZT!
ZZT-ZZZT!
Are you okay?!
Y-yeah. *Shaken,* but yeah.
Thanks, Mike. I *owe* you one.
Oh yeah? Ever thought of what you owe the *rest* of us?

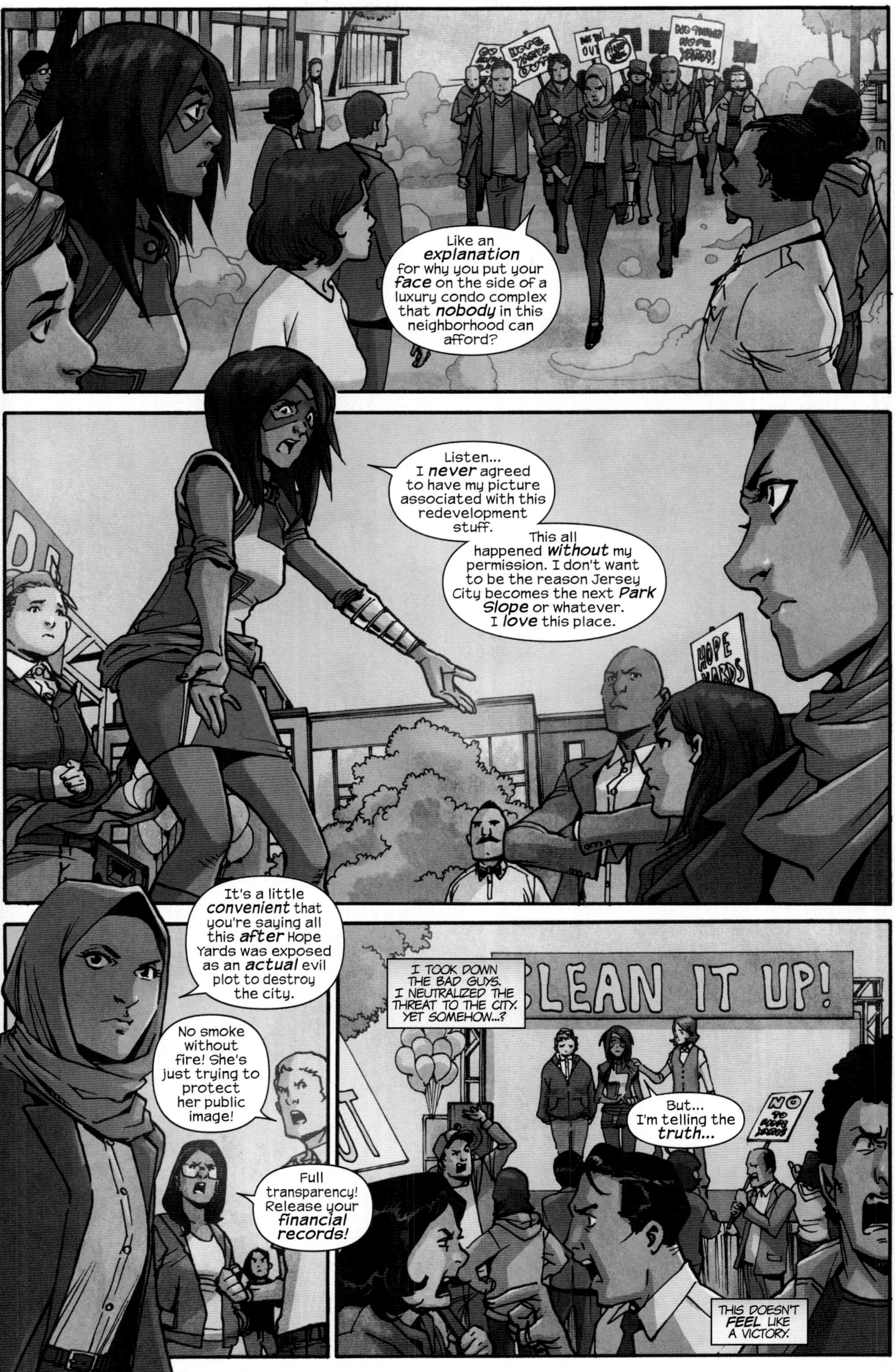
Like an *explanation* for why you put your *face* on the side of a luxury condo complex that *nobody* in this neighborhood can afford?
Listen... I *never* agreed to have my picture associated with this redevelopment stuff.
This all happened *without* my permission. I don't want to be the reason Jersey City becomes the next *Park Slope* or whatever. I *love* this place.
HOPE YARDS
It's a little *convenient* that you're saying all this *after* Hope Yards was exposed as an *actual* evil plot to destroy the city.
No smoke without fire! She's just trying to protect her public image!
Full transparency! Release your *financial records!*
I TOOK DOWN THE BAD GUYS. I NEUTRALIZED THE THREAT TO THE CITY. YET SOMEHOW...?
CLEAN IT UP!
But... I'm telling the *truth*...
THIS DOESN'T *FEEL* LIKE A VICTORY.

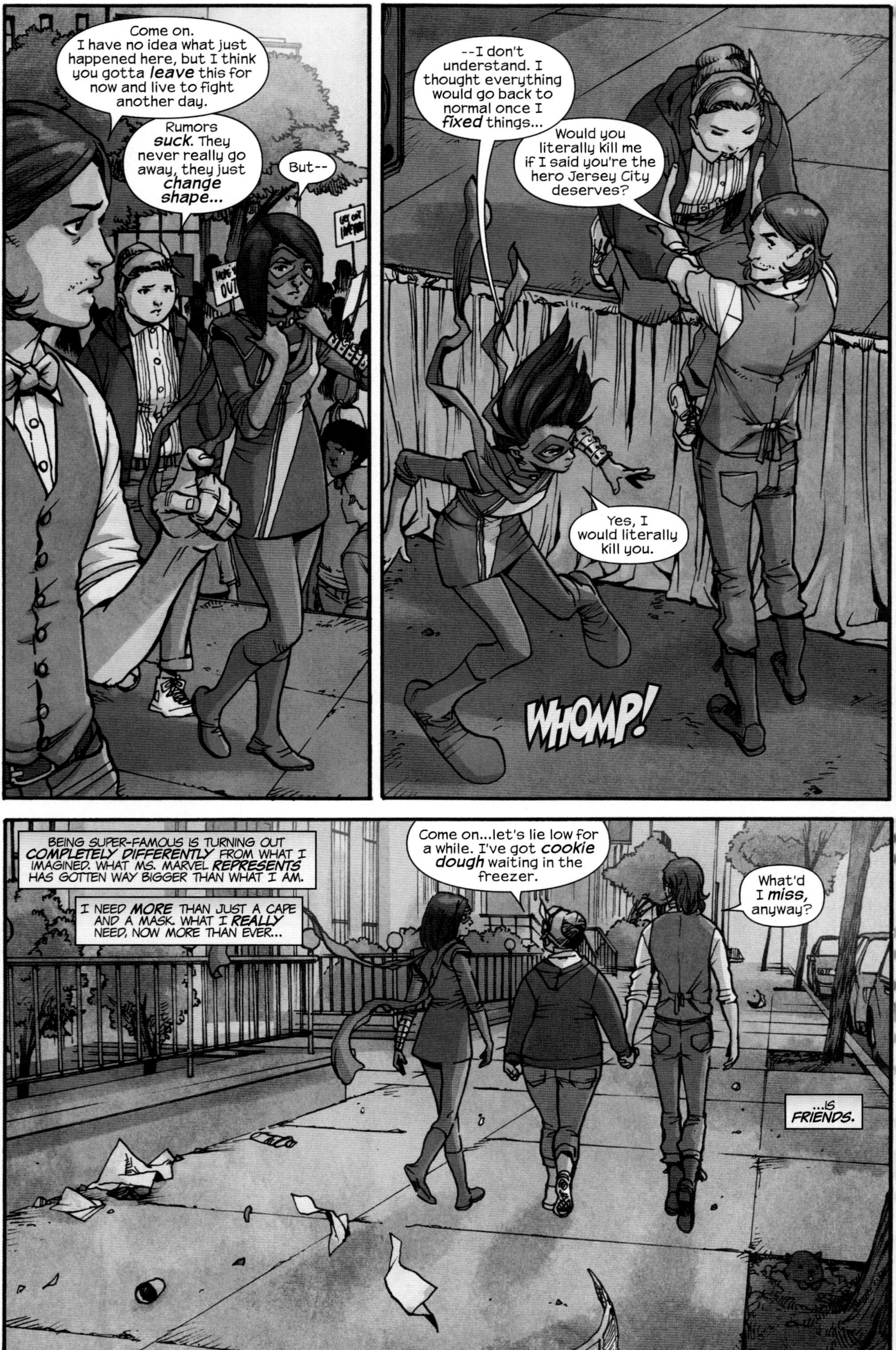
Come on. I have no idea what just happened here, but I think you gotta *leave* this for now and live to fight another day.
Rumors *suck*. They never really go away, they just *change shape*...
But--
--I don't understand. I thought everything would go back to normal once I *fixed* things...
Would you literally kill me if I said you're the hero Jersey City deserves?
Yes, I would literally kill you.
WHOMP!
BEING SUPER-FAMOUS IS TURNING OUT *COMPLETELY DIFFERENTLY* FROM WHAT I IMAGINED. WHAT MS. MARVEL *REPRESENTS* HAS GOTTEN WAY BIGGER THAN WHAT I AM.
I NEED *MORE* THAN JUST A CAPE AND A MASK. WHAT I *REALLY* NEED, NOW MORE THAN EVER...
Come on...let's lie low for a while. I've got *cookie dough* waiting in the freezer.
What'd I *miss*, anyway?
...IS *FRIENDS*.

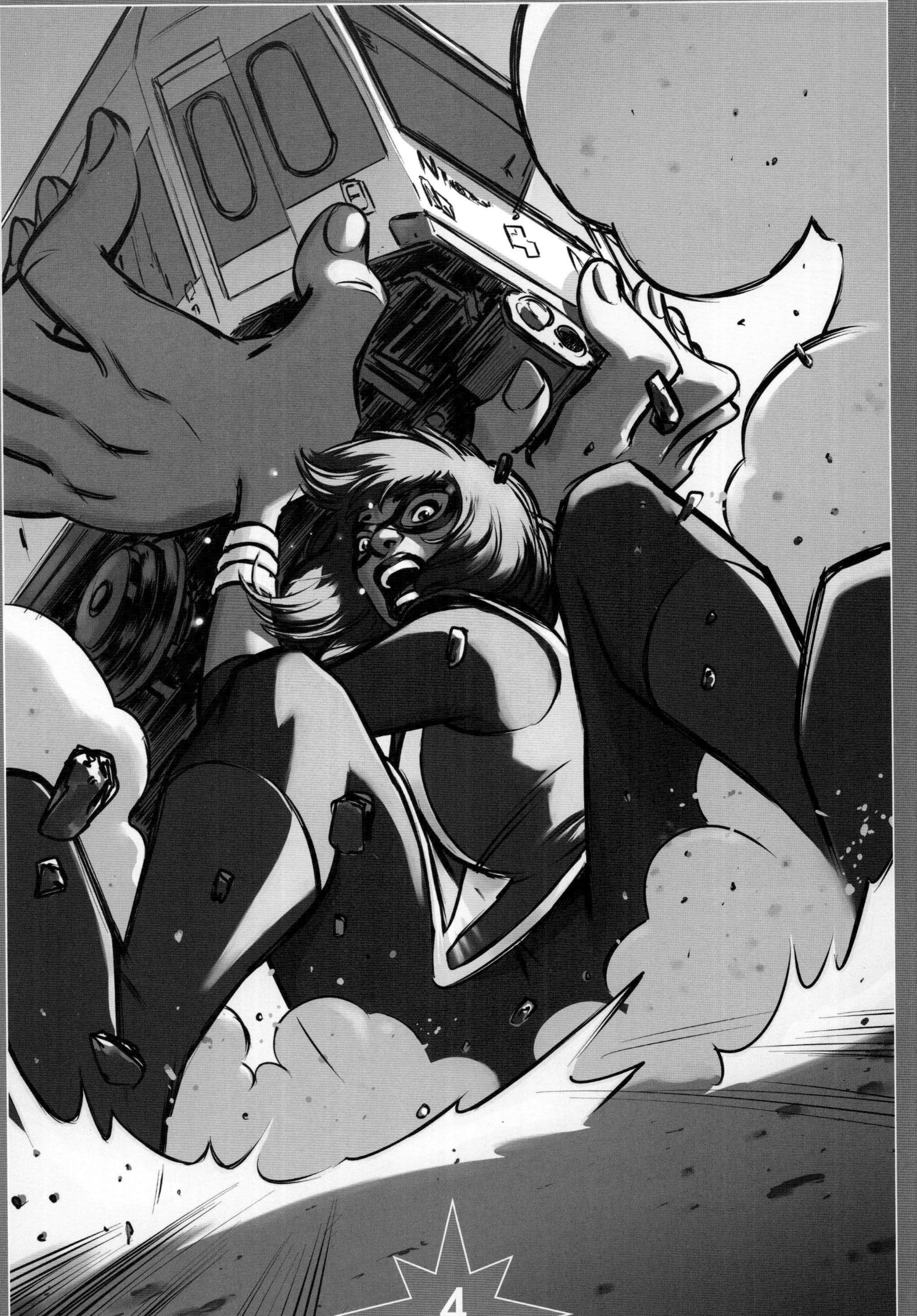

4

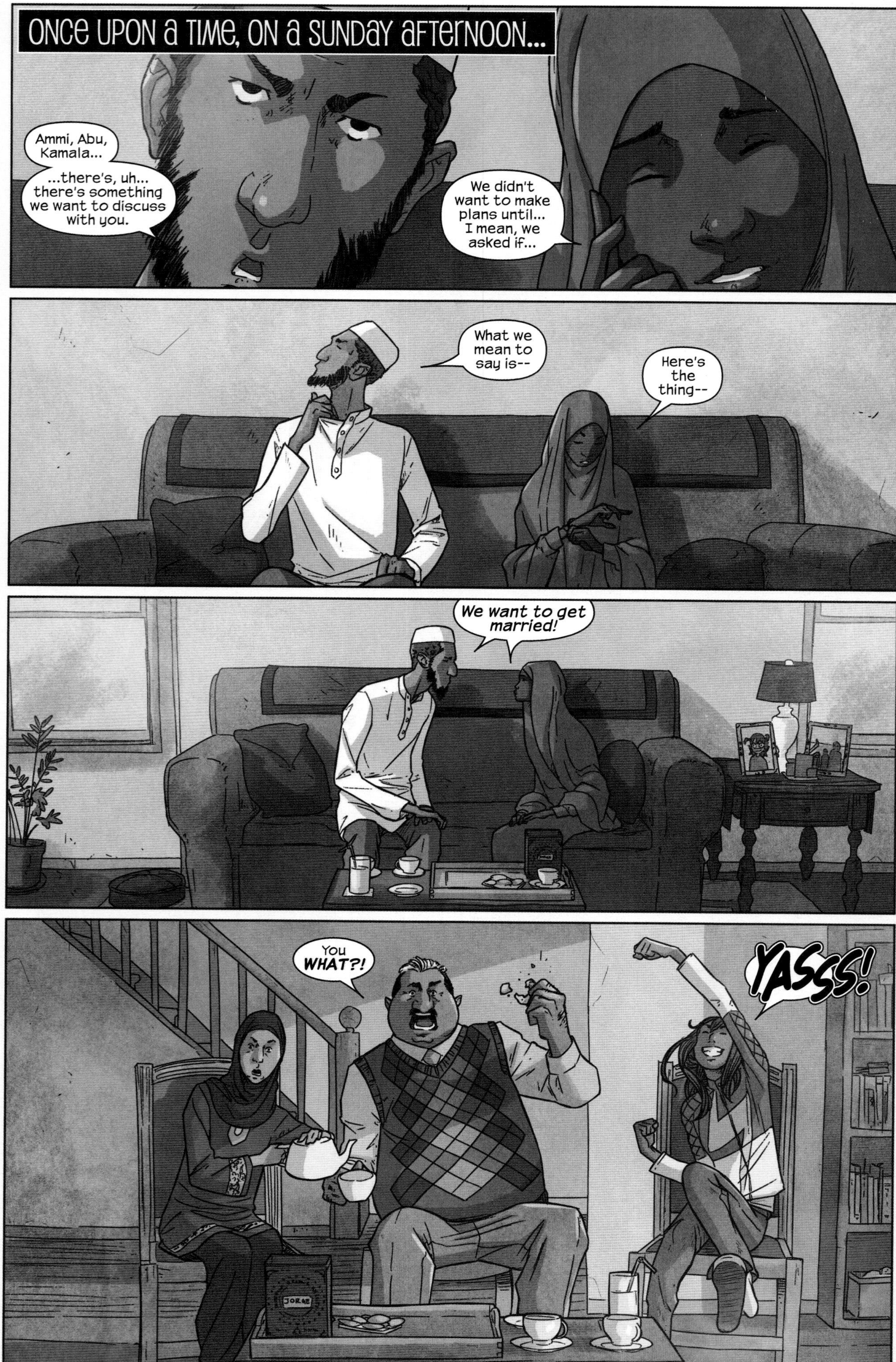

ONCE UPON A TIME, ON A SUNDAY AFTERNOON...
Ammi, Abu, Kamala...
...there's, uh... there's something we want to discuss with you.
We didn't want to make plans until... I mean, we asked if...
What we mean to say is--
Here's the thing--
We want to get married!
You WHAT?!
YASSS!
JORGE

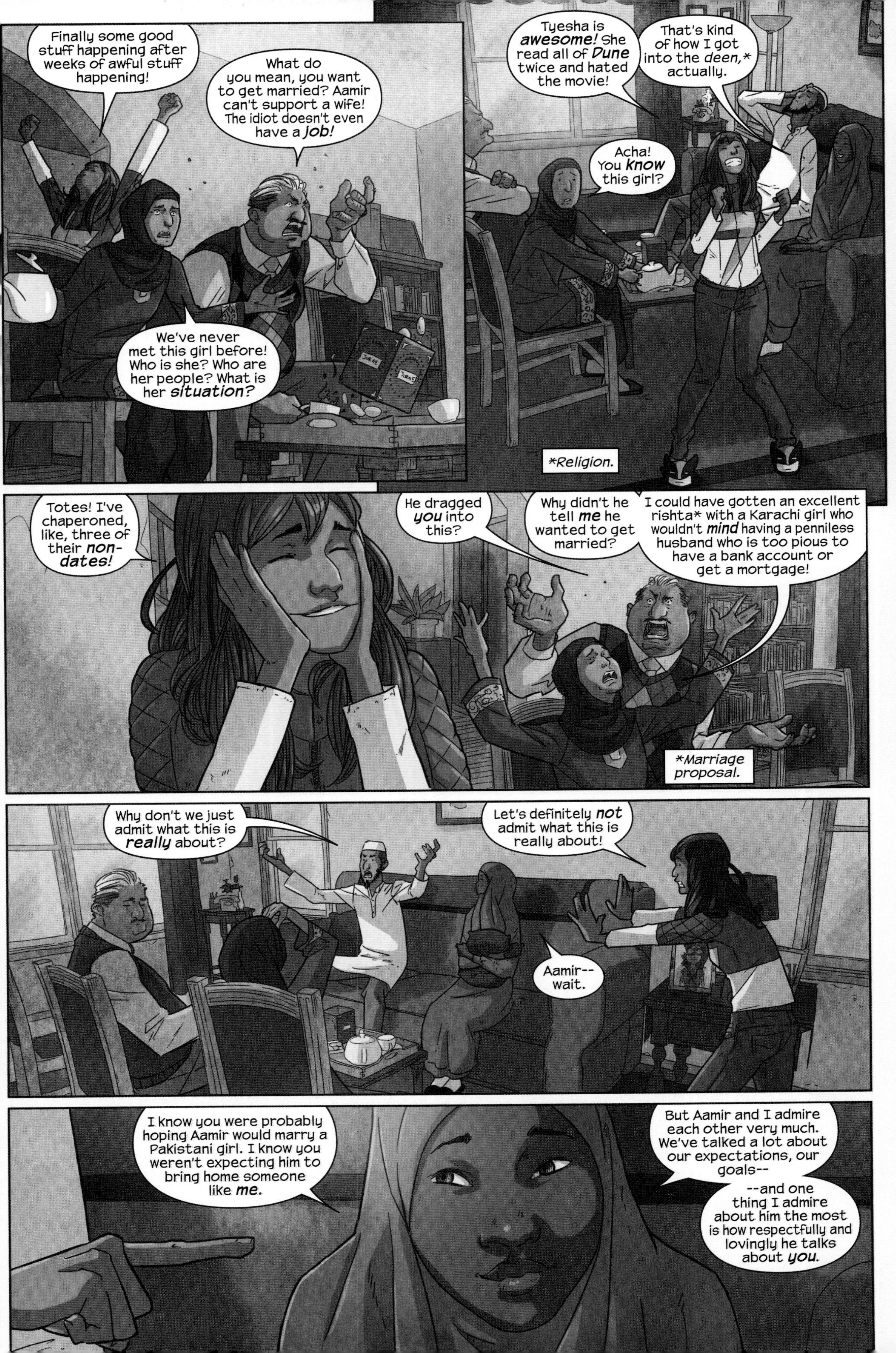

Finally some good stuff happening after weeks of awful stuff happening!
What do you mean, you want to get married? Aamir can't support a wife! The idiot doesn't even have a job!
We've never met this girl before! Who is she? Who are her people? What is her situation?
Tyesha is awesome! She read all of Dune twice and hated the movie!
That's kind of how I got into the deen,* actually.
Acha! You know this girl?
*Religion.
Totes! I've chaperoned, like, three of their non-dates!
He dragged you into this?
Why didn't he tell me he wanted to get married?
I could have gotten an excellent rishta* with a Karachi girl who wouldn't mind having a penniless husband who is too pious to have a bank account or get a mortgage!
*Marriage proposal.
Why don't we just admit what this is really about?
Let's definitely not admit what this is really about!
Aamir-- wait.
I know you were probably hoping Aamir would marry a Pakistani girl. I know you weren't expecting him to bring home someone like me.
But Aamir and I admire each other very much. We've talked a lot about our expectations, our goals--
--and one thing I admire about him the most is how respectfully and lovingly he talks about you.

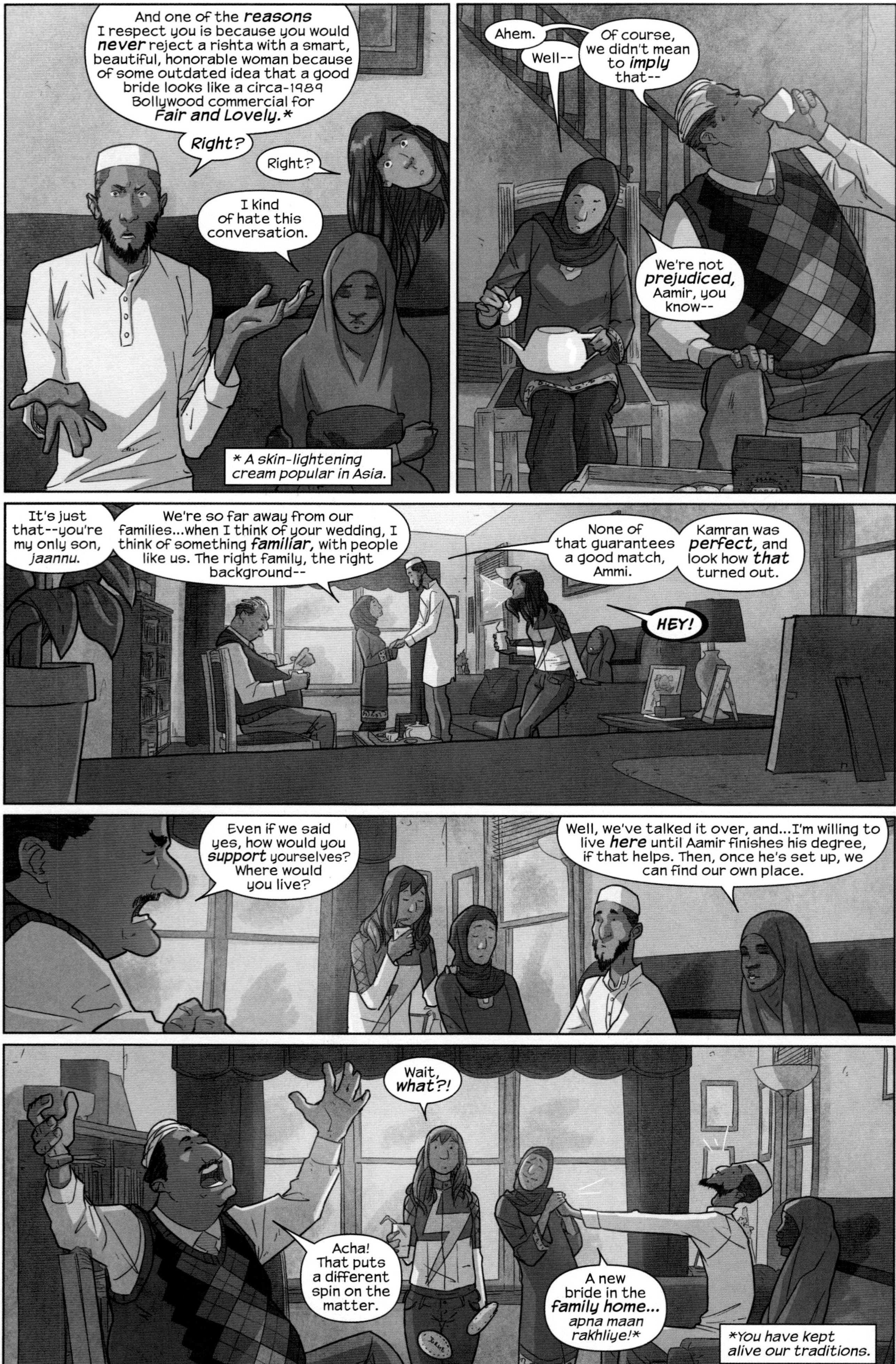

And one of the reasons I respect you is because you would never reject a rishta with a smart, beautiful, honorable woman because of some outdated idea that a good bride looks like a circa-1989 Bollywood commercial for Fair and Lovely.*
Right?
Right?
I kind of hate this conversation.
* A skin-lightening cream popular in Asia.
Ahem.
Well--
Of course, we didn't mean to imply that--
We're not prejudiced, Aamir, you know--
It's just that--you're my only son, jaannu.
We're so far away from our families...when I think of your wedding, I think of something familiar, with people like us. The right family, the right background--
None of that guarantees a good match, Ammi.
Kamran was perfect, and look how that turned out.
HEY!
Even if we said yes, how would you support yourselves? Where would you live?
Well, we've talked it over, and...I'm willing to live here until Aamir finishes his degree, if that helps. Then, once he's set up, we can find our own place.
Wait, what?!
Acha! That puts a different spin on the matter.
A new bride in the family home... apna maan rakhliye!*
*You have kept alive our traditions.

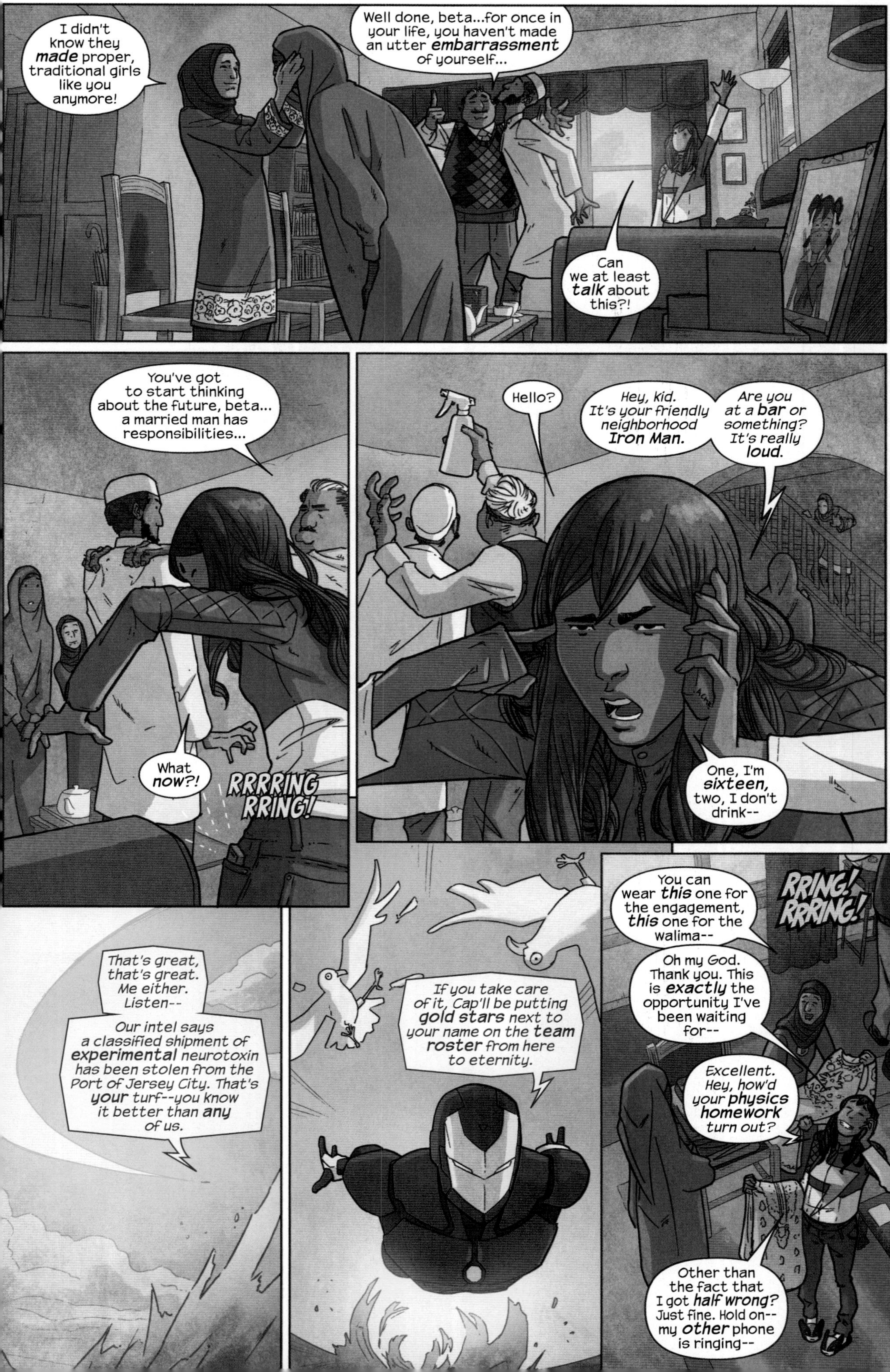
I didn't know they made proper, traditional girls like you anymore!
Well done, beta...for once in your life, you haven't made an utter embarrassment of yourself...
Can we at least talk about this?!
You've got to start thinking about the future, beta... a married man has responsibilities...
What now?!
RRRRING RRING!
Hello?
Hey, kid. It's your friendly neighborhood Iron Man.
Are you at a bar or something? It's really loud.
One, I'm sixteen, two, I don't drink--
That's great, that's great. Me either. Listen--
Our intel says a classified shipment of experimental neurotoxin has been stolen from the Port of Jersey City. That's your turf--you know it better than any of us.
If you take care of it, Cap'll be putting gold stars next to your name on the team roster from here to eternity.
You can wear this one for the engagement, this one for the walima--
RRING! RRRING!
Oh my God. Thank you. This is exactly the opportunity I've been waiting for--
Excellent. Hey, how'd your physics homework turn out?
Other than the fact that I got half wrong? Just fine. Hold on-- my other phone is ringing--

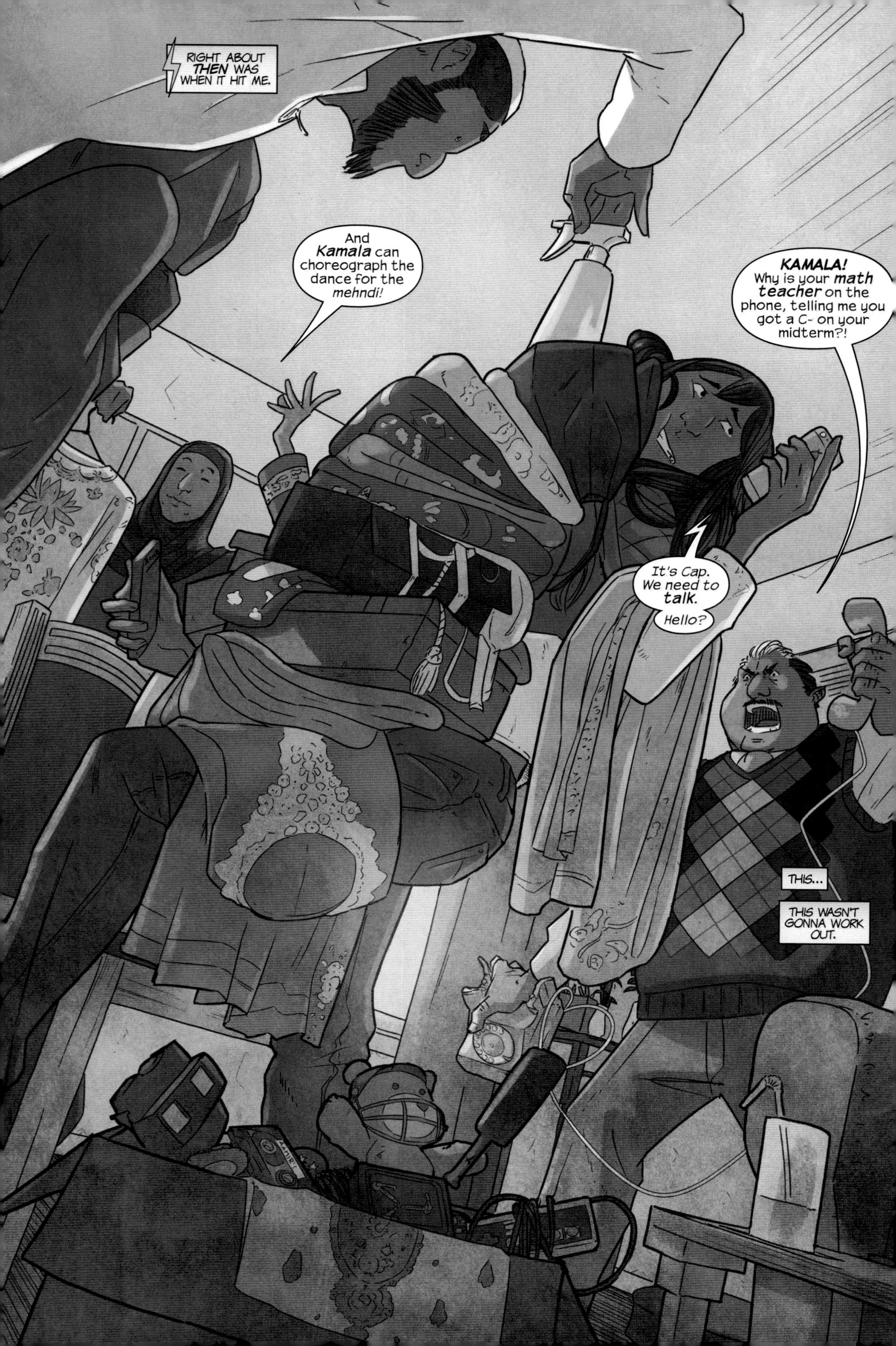
RIGHT ABOUT THEN WAS WHEN IT HIT ME.
And Kamala can choreograph the dance for the mehndi!
KAMALA! Why is your math teacher on the phone, telling me you got a C- on your midterm?!
It's Cap. We need to talk.
Hello?
THIS...
THIS WASN'T GONNA WORK OUT.

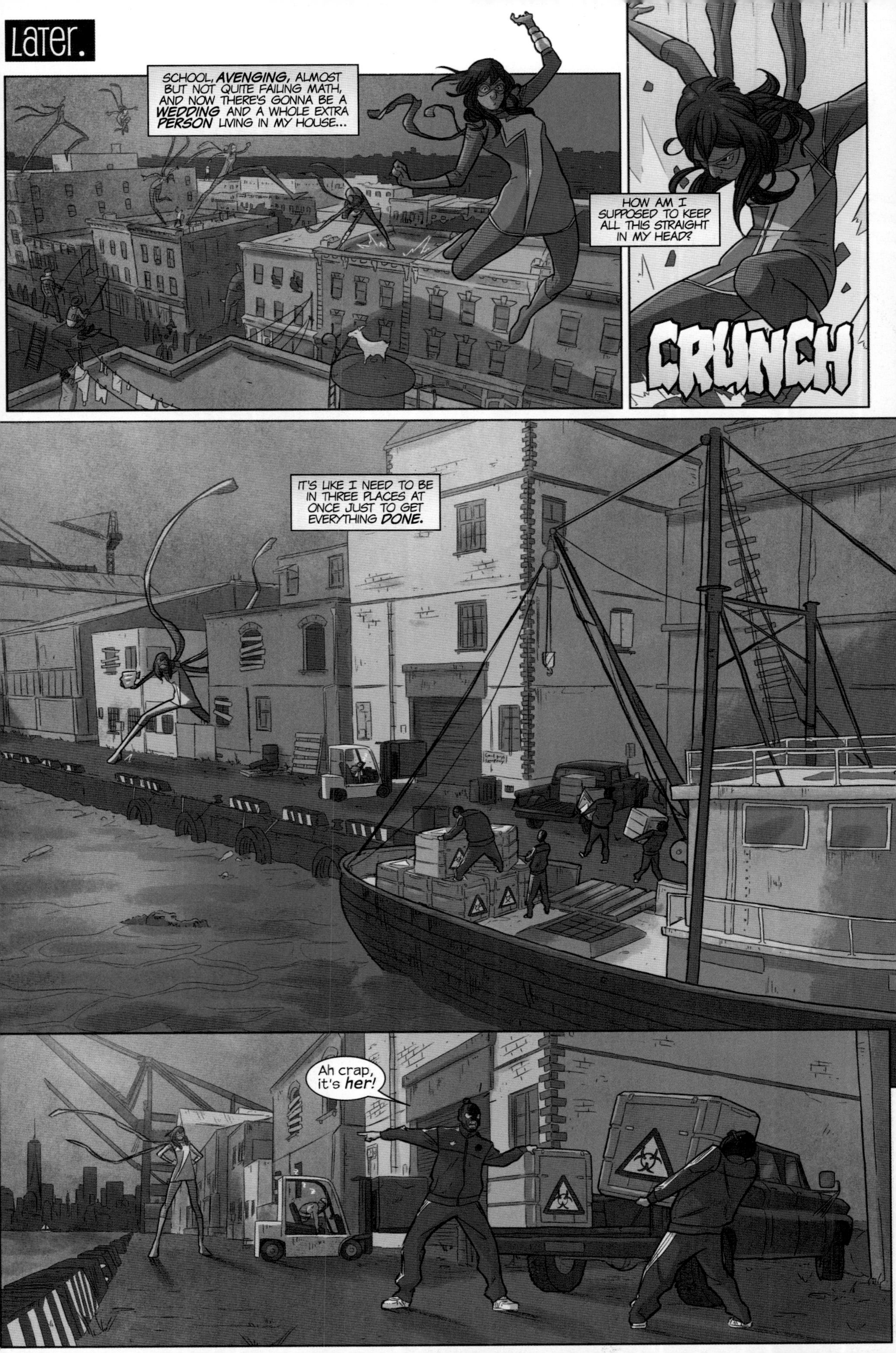
LATER.
SCHOOL, AVENGING, ALMOST BUT NOT QUITE FAILING MATH, AND NOW THERE'S GONNA BE A WEDDING AND A WHOLE EXTRA PERSON LIVING IN MY HOUSE...
HOW AM I SUPPOSED TO KEEP ALL THIS STRAIGHT IN MY HEAD?
CRUNCH
IT'S LIKE I NEED TO BE IN THREE PLACES AT ONCE JUST TO GET EVERYTHING DONE.
Ah crap, it's her!

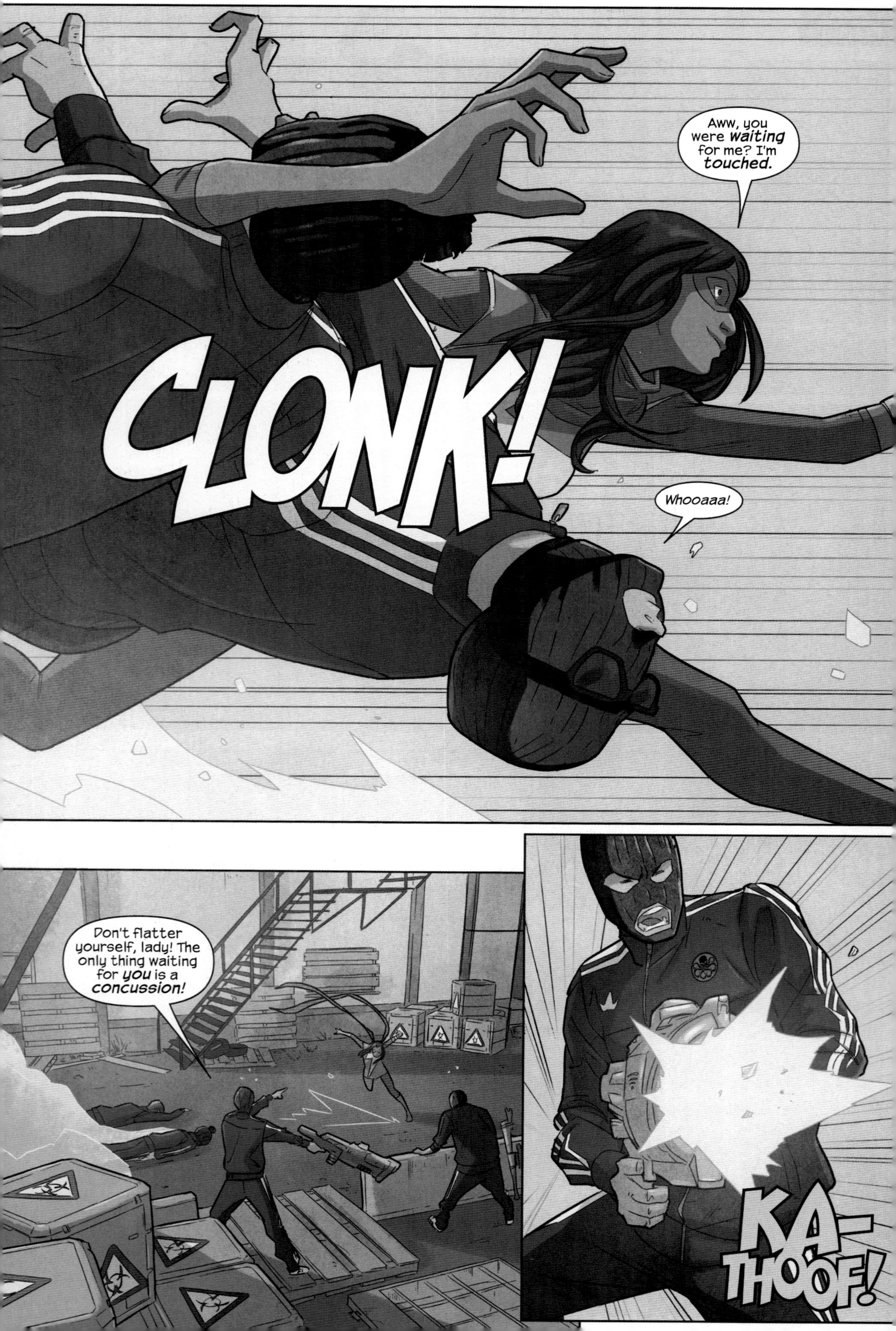
Aww, you were *waiting* for me? I'm *touched.*
CLONK!
Whooaaa!
Don't flatter yourself, lady! The only thing waiting for *you* is a *concussion!*
KA-THOOF!

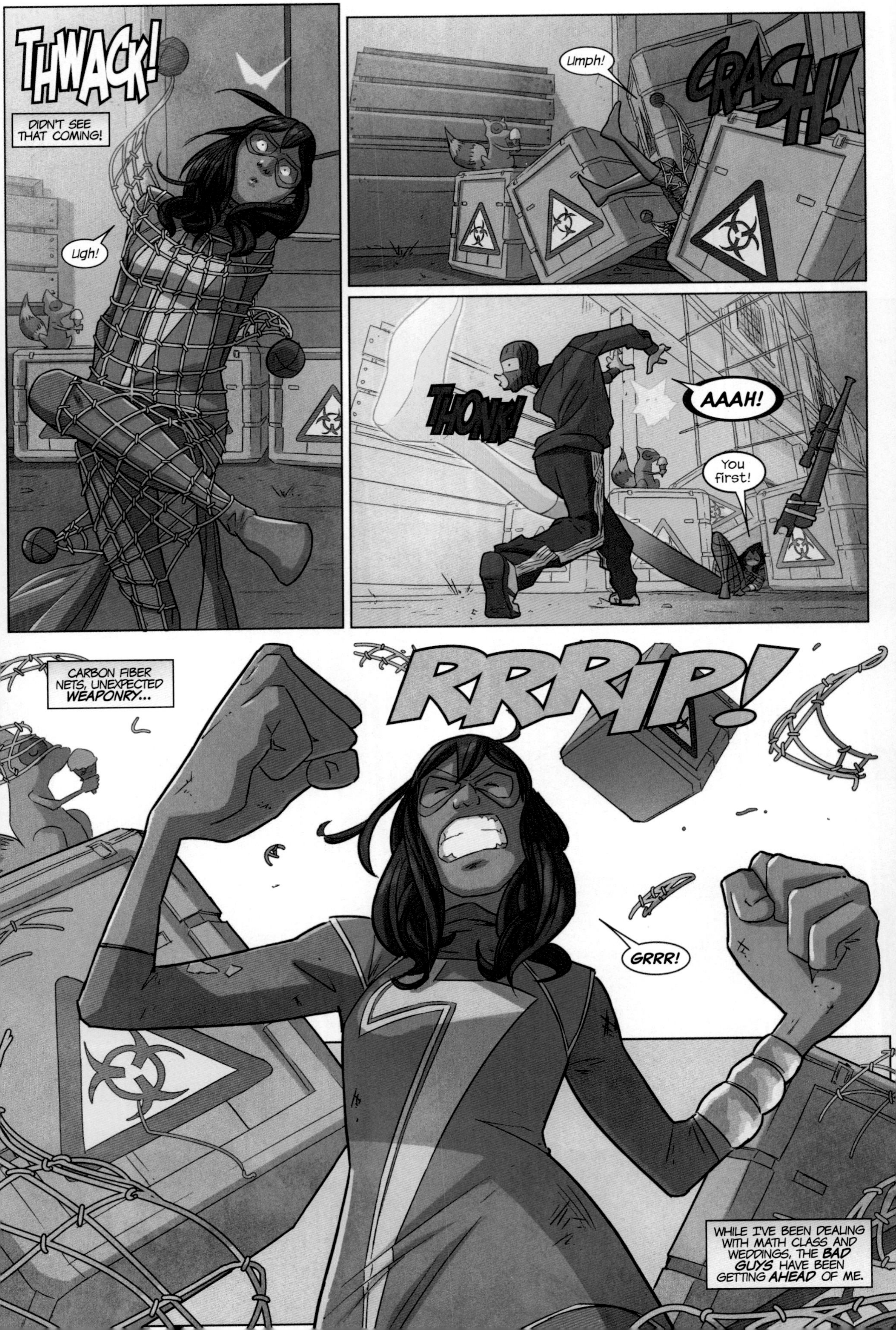
THWACK!
DIDN'T SEE THAT COMING!
Ugh!
Umph!
CRASH!
THONK!
AAAH!
You first!
CARBON FIBER NETS, UNEXPECTED WEAPONRY...
RRRRIP!
GRRR!
WHILE I'VE BEEN DEALING WITH MATH CLASS AND WEDDINGS, THE BAD GUYS HAVE BEEN GETTING AHEAD OF ME.

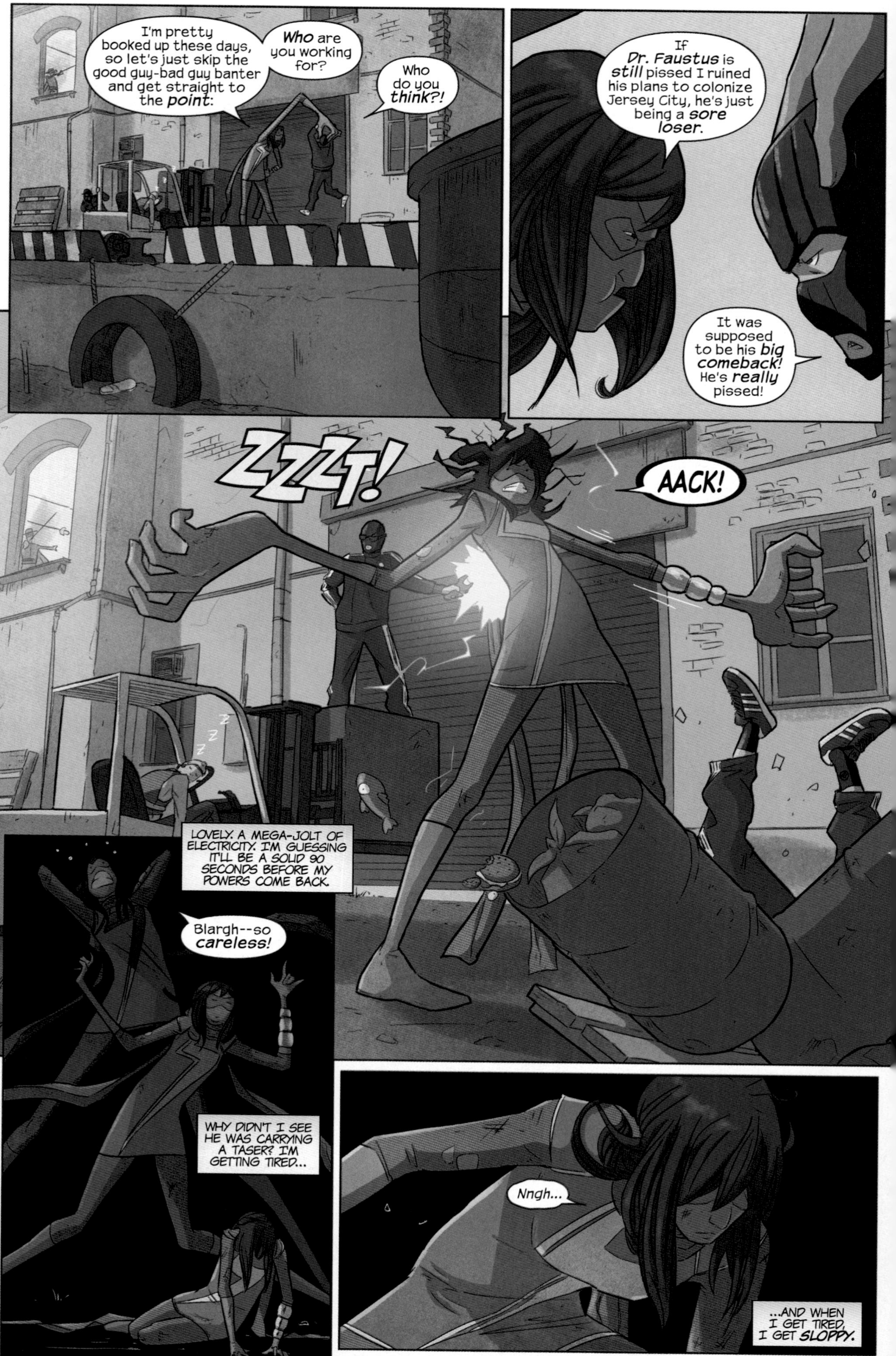

I'm pretty booked up these days, so let's just skip the good guy-bad guy banter and get straight to the point:
Who are you working for?
Who do you think?!
If Dr. Faustus is still pissed I ruined his plans to colonize Jersey City, he's just being a sore loser.
It was supposed to be his big comeback! He's really pissed!
ZZZZT!
AACK!
Z
Z
Z
LOVELY. A MEGA-JOLT OF ELECTRICITY. I'M GUESSING IT'LL BE A SOLID 90 SECONDS BEFORE MY POWERS COME BACK.
Blargh--so careless!
WHY DIDN'T I SEE HE WAS CARRYING A TASER? I'M GETTING TIRED...
Nngh...
...AND WHEN I GET TIRED, I GET SLOPPY.

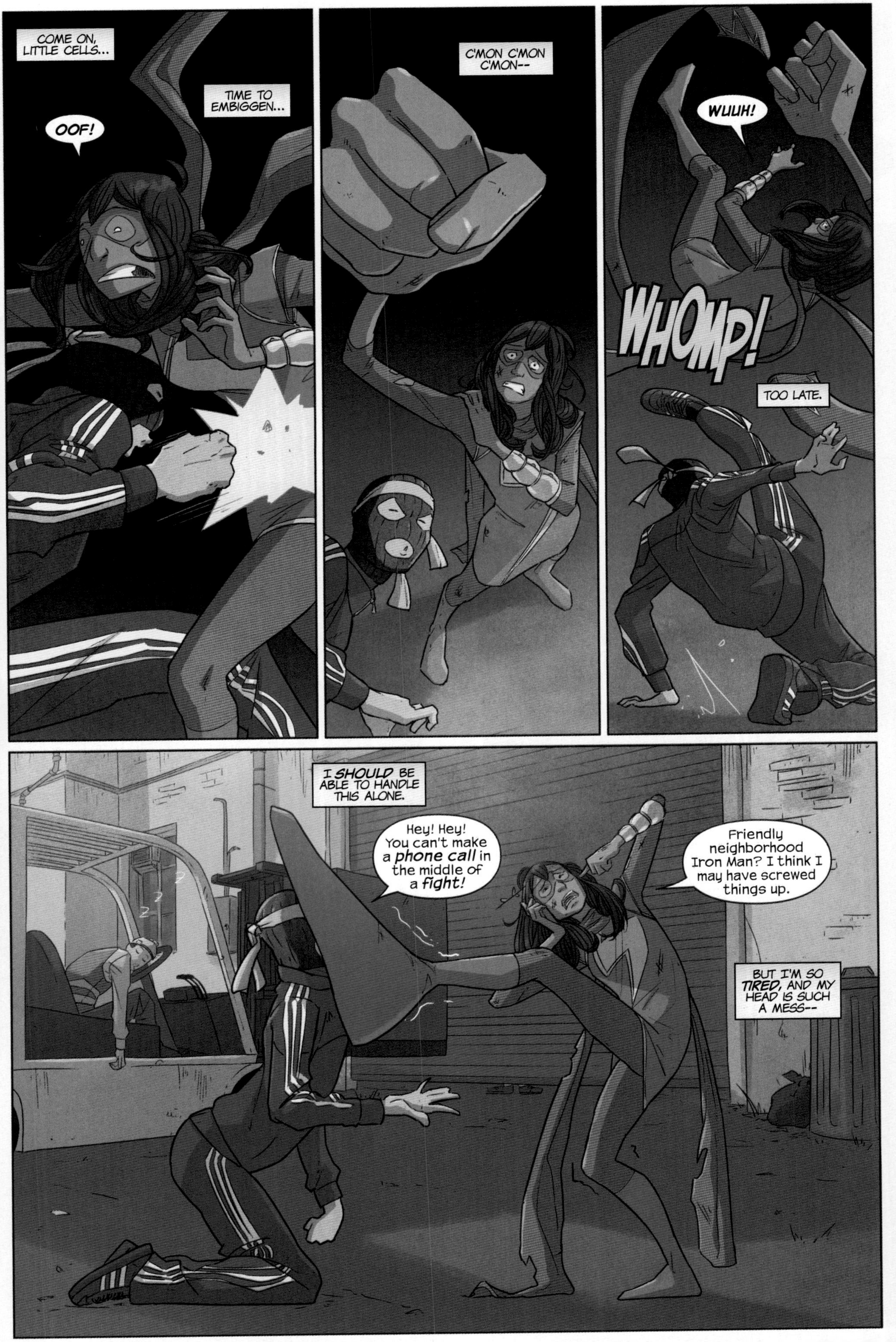

COME ON, LITTLE CELLS...
TIME TO EMBIGGEN...
OOF!
C'MON C'MON C'MON--
WUUH!
WHOMP!
TOO LATE.
I SHOULD BE ABLE TO HANDLE THIS ALONE.
Hey! Hey! You can't make a phone call in the middle of a fight!
Friendly neighborhood Iron Man? I think I may have screwed things up.
BUT I'M SO TIRED, AND MY HEAD IS SUCH A MESS--

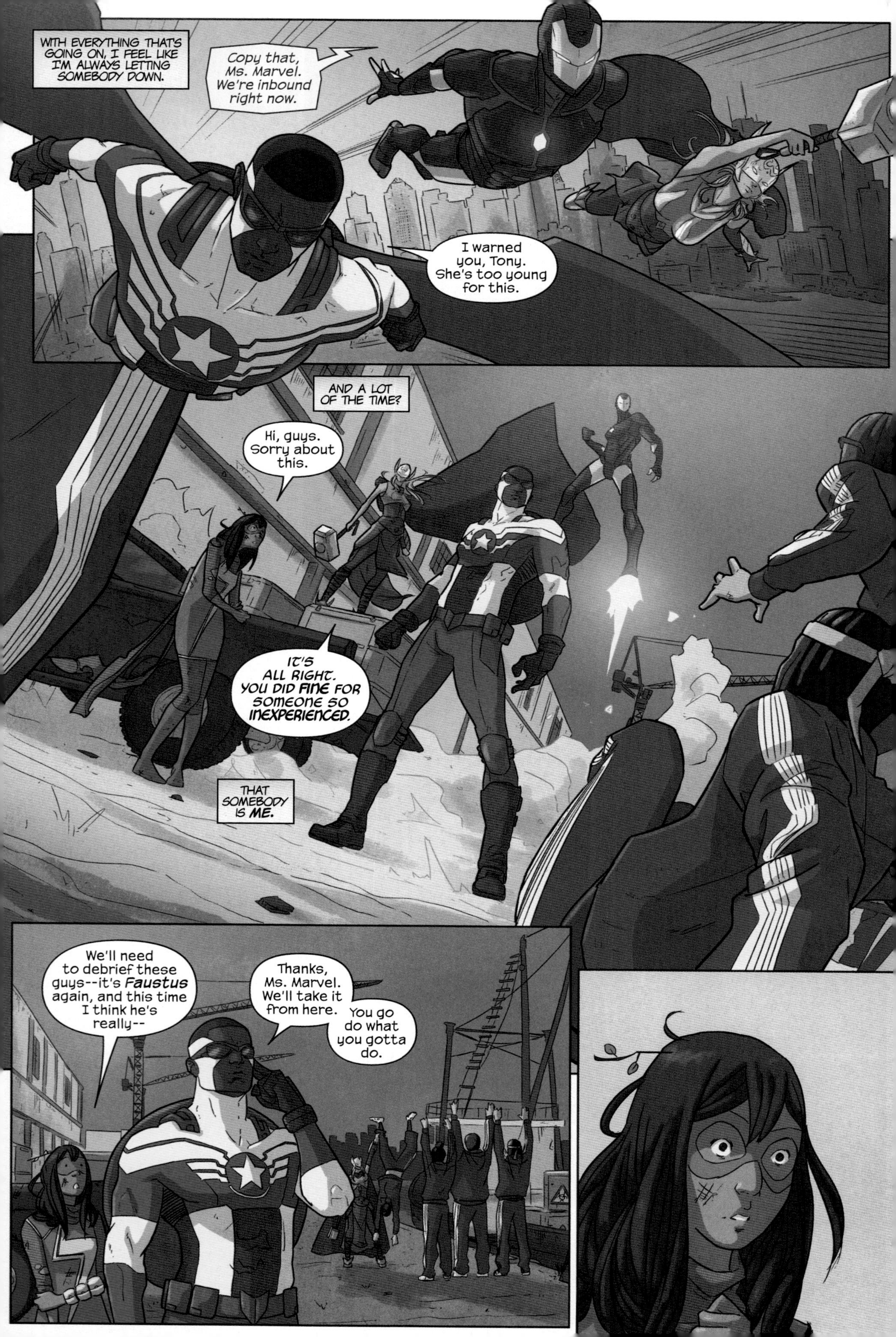
WITH EVERYTHING THAT'S GOING ON, I FEEL LIKE I'M ALWAYS LETTING SOMEBODY DOWN.
Copy that, Ms. Marvel. We're inbound right now.
I warned you, Tony. She's too young for this.
AND A LOT OF THE TIME?
Hi, guys. Sorry about this.
IT'S ALL RIGHT. YOU DID FINE FOR SOMEONE SO INEXPERIENCED.
THAT SOMEBODY IS ME.
We'll need to debrief these guys--it's Faustus again, and this time I think he's really--
Thanks, Ms. Marvel. We'll take it from here.
You go do what you gotta do.

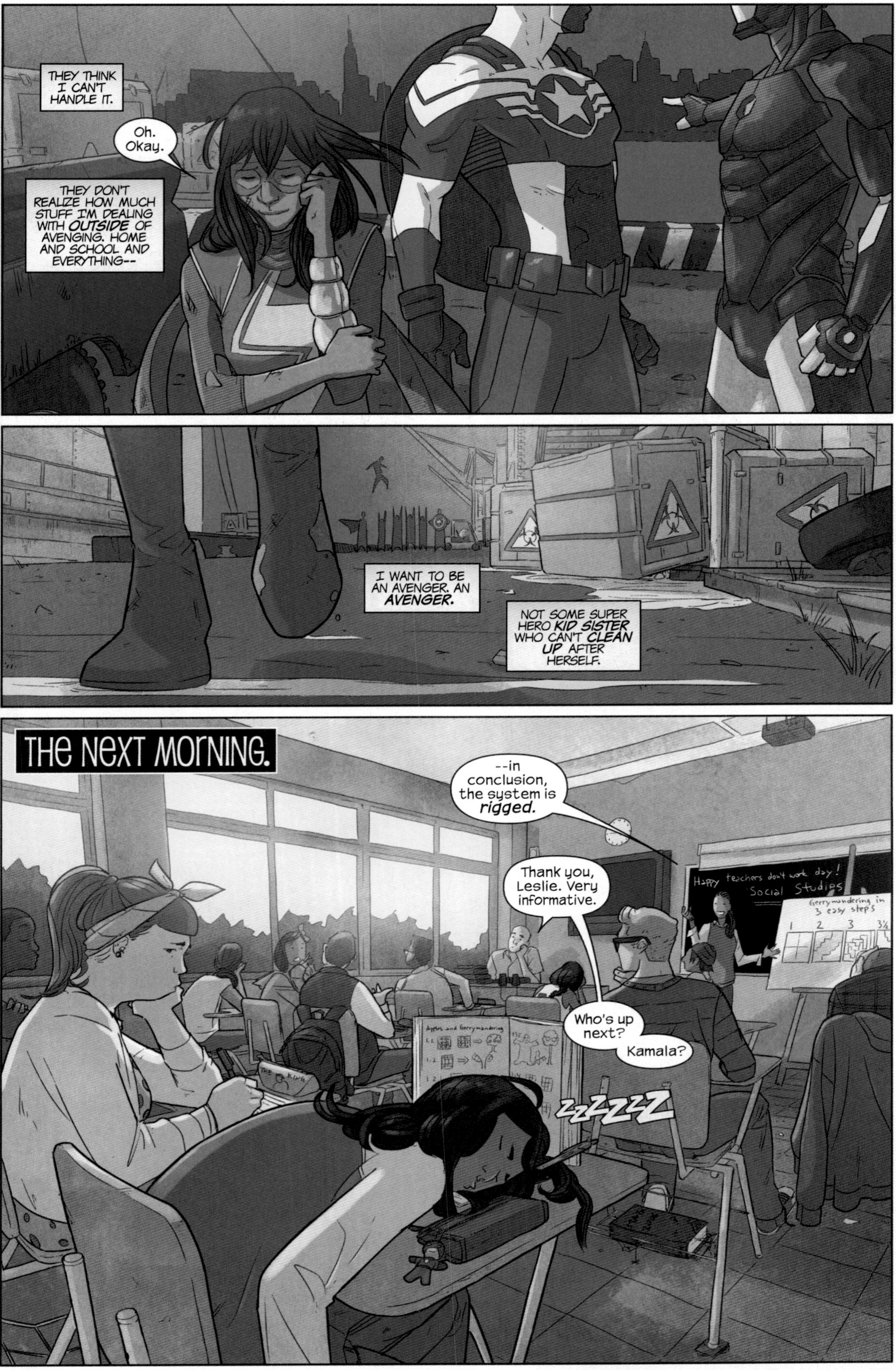
THEY THINK I CAN'T HANDLE IT.
Oh. Okay.
THEY DON'T REALIZE HOW MUCH STUFF I'M DEALING WITH OUTSIDE OF AVENGING. HOME AND SCHOOL AND EVERYTHING--
I WANT TO BE AN AVENGER. AN AVENGER.
NOT SOME SUPER HERO KID SISTER WHO CAN'T CLEAN UP AFTER HERSELF.
THE NEXT MORNING.
--in conclusion, the system is rigged.
Thank you, Leslie. Very informative.
Happy teachers don't work day!
Social Studies
Gerrymandering in 3 easy steps
1 2 3 3½
Apples and Gerrymandering
Who's up next?
Kamala?
ZZZZZZ

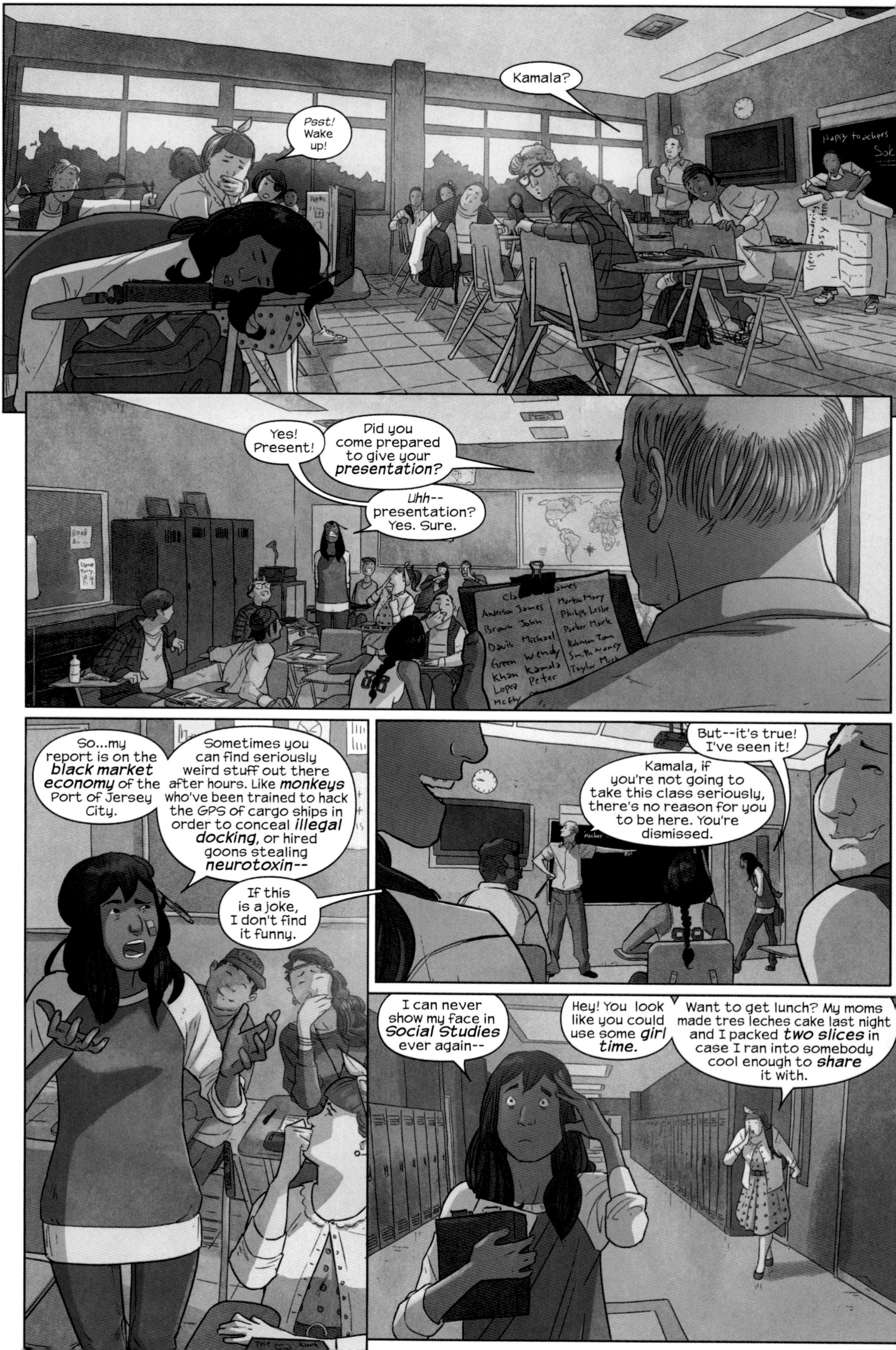

Psst! Wake up!
Kamala?
Yes! Present!
Did you come prepared to give your *presentation*?
Uhh-- presentation? Yes. Sure.
So...my report is on the ***black market economy*** of the Port of Jersey City.
Sometimes you can find seriously weird stuff out there after hours. Like ***monkeys*** who've been trained to hack the GPS of cargo ships in order to conceal ***illegal docking***, or hired goons stealing ***neurotoxin***--
If this is a joke, I don't find it funny.
Kamala, if you're not going to take this class seriously, there's no reason for you to be here. You're dismissed.
But--it's true! I've seen it!
I can never show my face in *Social Studies* ever again--
Hey! You look like you could use some *girl time.*
Want to get lunch? My moms made tres leches cake last night and I packed *two slices* in case I ran into somebody cool enough to *share* it with.

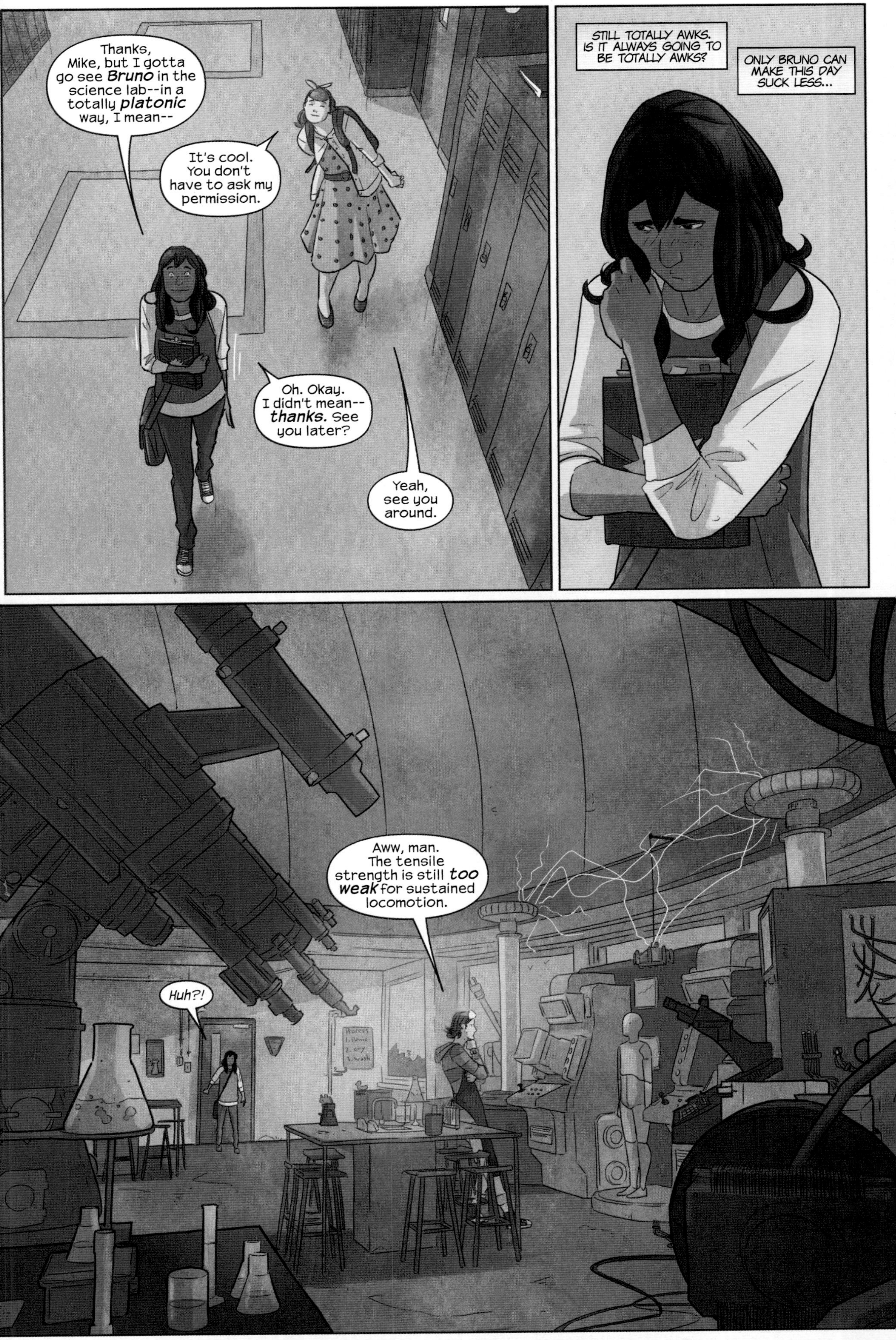
Thanks, Mike, but I gotta go see Bruno in the science lab--in a totally platonic way, I mean--
It's cool. You don't have to ask my permission.
Oh. Okay. I didn't mean-- thanks. See you later?
Yeah, see you around.
STILL TOTALLY AWKS. IS IT ALWAYS GOING TO BE TOTALLY AWKS?
ONLY BRUNO CAN MAKE THIS DAY SUCK LESS...
Aww, man. The tensile strength is still too weak for sustained locomotion.
Huh?!

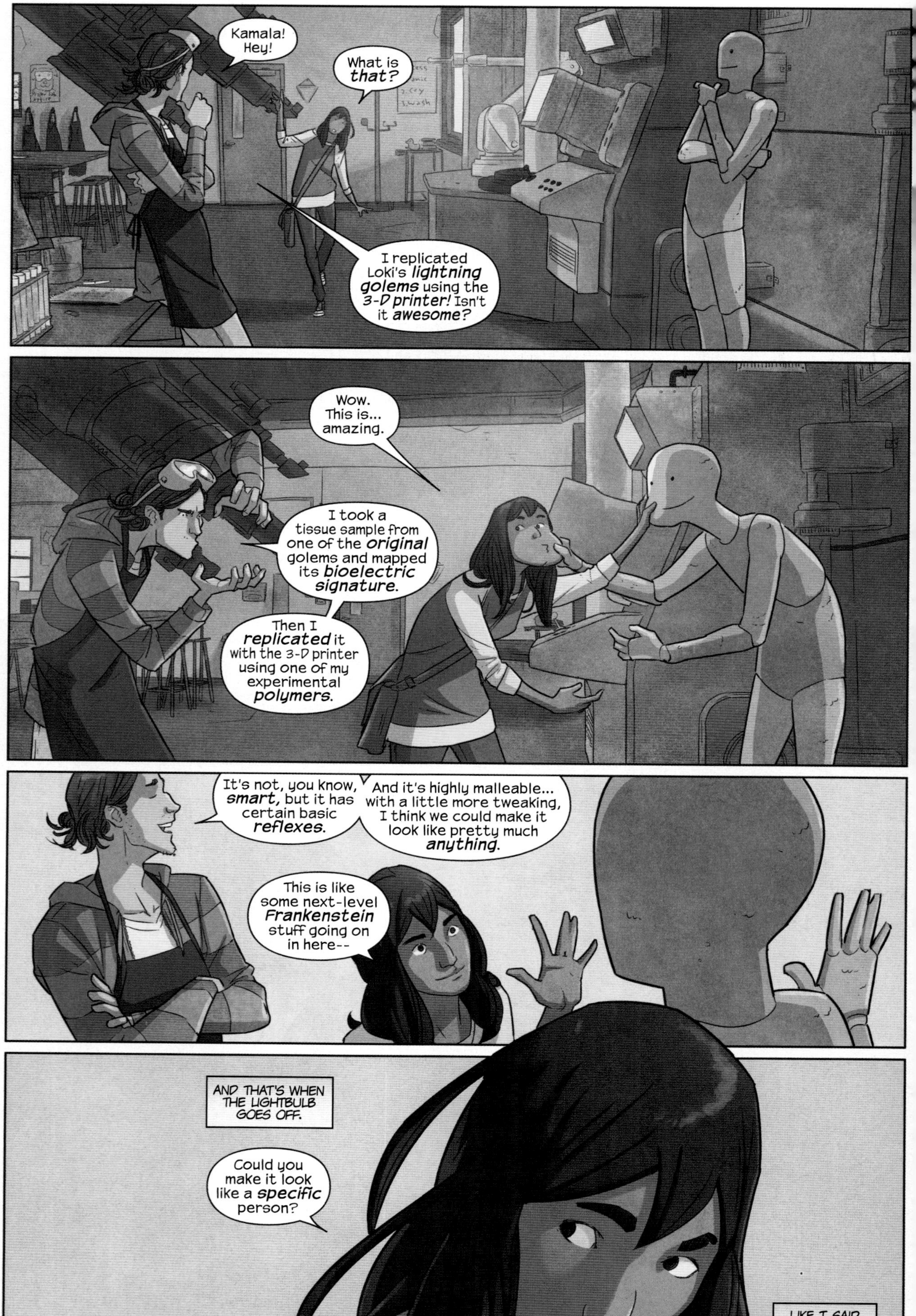
Kamala! Hey!
What is that?
I replicated Loki's lightning golems using the 3-D printer! Isn't it awesome?
Wow. This is... amazing.
I took a tissue sample from one of the original golems and mapped its bioelectric signature.
Then I replicated it with the 3-D printer using one of my experimental polymers.
It's not, you know, smart, but it has certain basic reflexes.
And it's highly malleable... with a little more tweaking, I think we could make it look like pretty much anything.
This is like some next-level Frankenstein stuff going on in here--
AND THAT'S WHEN THE LIGHTBULB GOES OFF.
Could you make it look like a specific person?
LIKE I SAID, I CAN'T BE IN THREE PLACES AT ONCE.

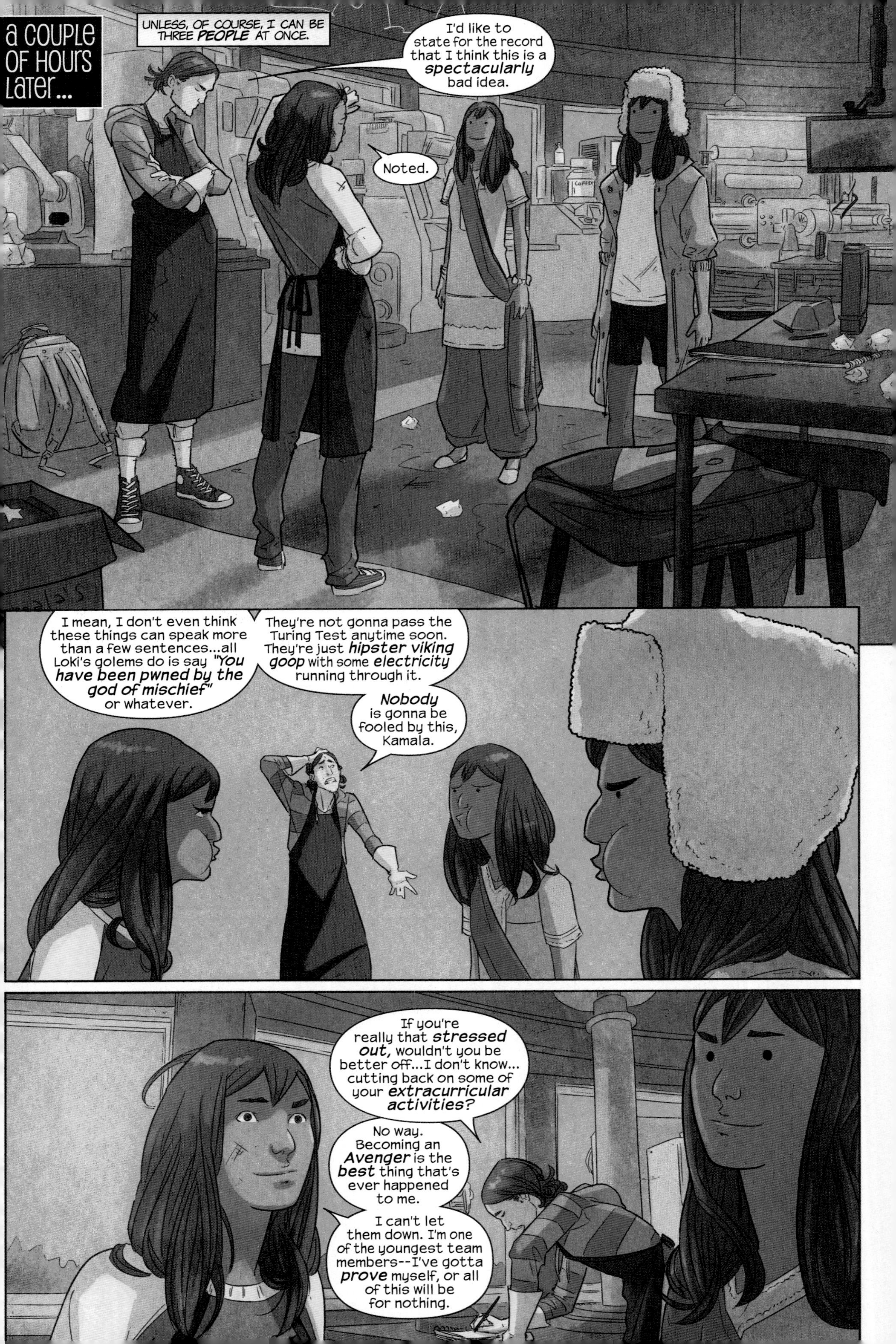

a COUPLE OF HOURS LaTer...
UNLESS, OF COURSE, I CAN BE THREE PEOPLE AT ONCE.
I'd like to state for the record that I think this is a spectacularly bad idea.
Noted.
I mean, I don't even think these things can speak more than a few sentences...all Loki's golems do is say "You have been pwned by the god of mischief" or whatever.
They're not gonna pass the Turing Test anytime soon. They're just hipster viking goop with some electricity running through it.
Nobody is gonna be fooled by this, Kamala.
If you're really that stressed out, wouldn't you be better off...I don't know... cutting back on some of your extracurricular activities?
No way. Becoming an Avenger is the best thing that's ever happened to me.
I can't let them down. I'm one of the youngest team members--I've gotta prove myself, or all of this will be for nothing.

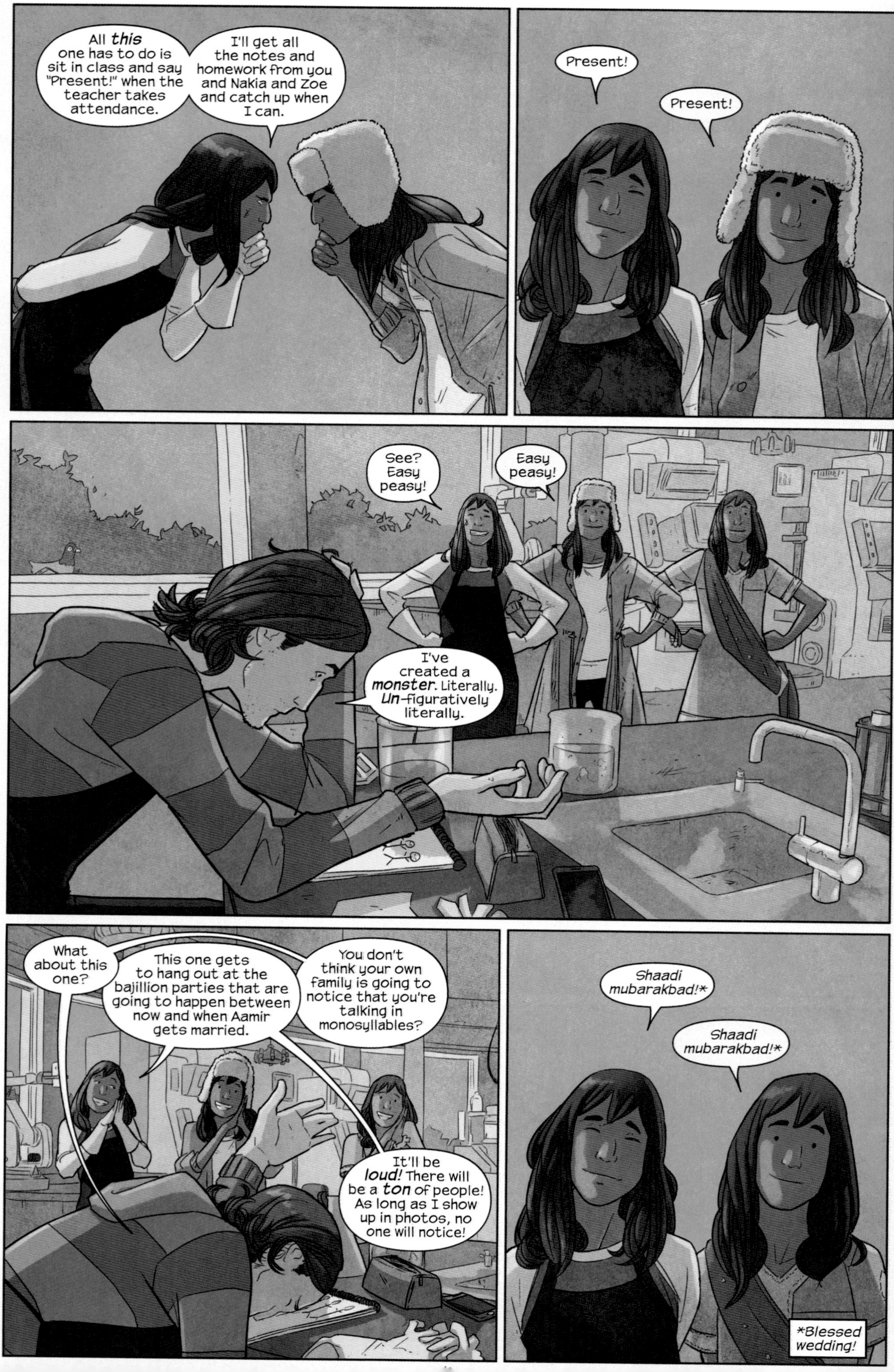
All *this* one has to do is sit in class and say "Present!" when the teacher takes attendance.
I'll get all the notes and homework from you and Nakia and Zoe and catch up when I can.
Present!
Present!
See? Easy peasy!
Easy peasy!
I've created a **monster**. Literally. *Un*-figuratively literally.
What about this one?
This one gets to hang out at the bajillion parties that are going to happen between now and when Aamir gets married.
You don't think your own family is going to notice that you're talking in monosyllables?
It'll be *loud!* There will be a *ton* of people! As long as I show up in photos, no one will notice!
*Shaadi mubarakbad!**
*Shaadi mubarakbad!**
**Blessed wedding!*

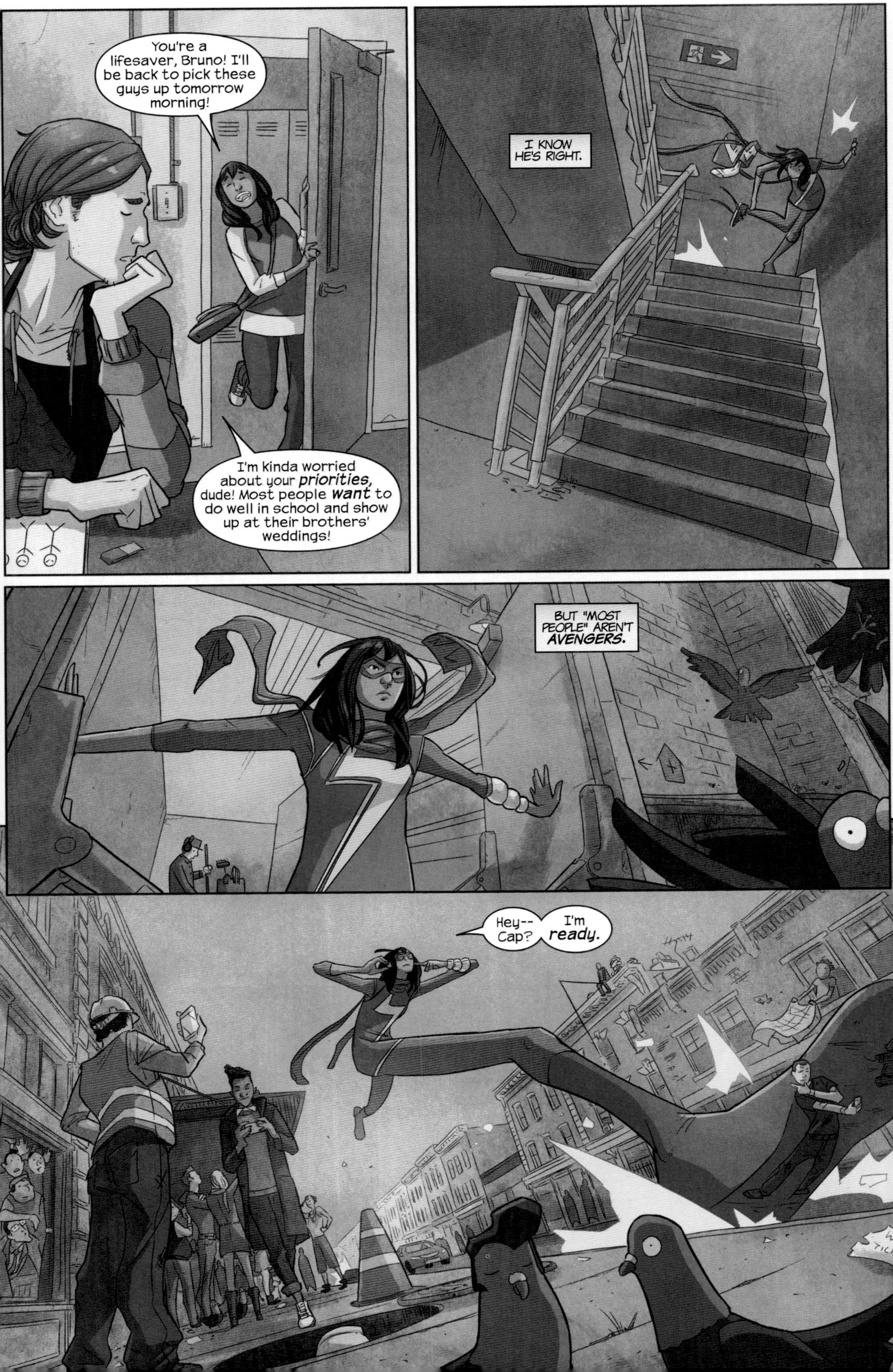

You're a lifesaver, Bruno! I'll be back to pick these guys up tomorrow morning!
I'm kinda worried about your priorities, dude! Most people want to do well in school and show up at their brothers' weddings!
I KNOW HE'S RIGHT.
BUT "MOST PEOPLE" AREN'T AVENGERS.
Hey-- Cap?
I'm ready.

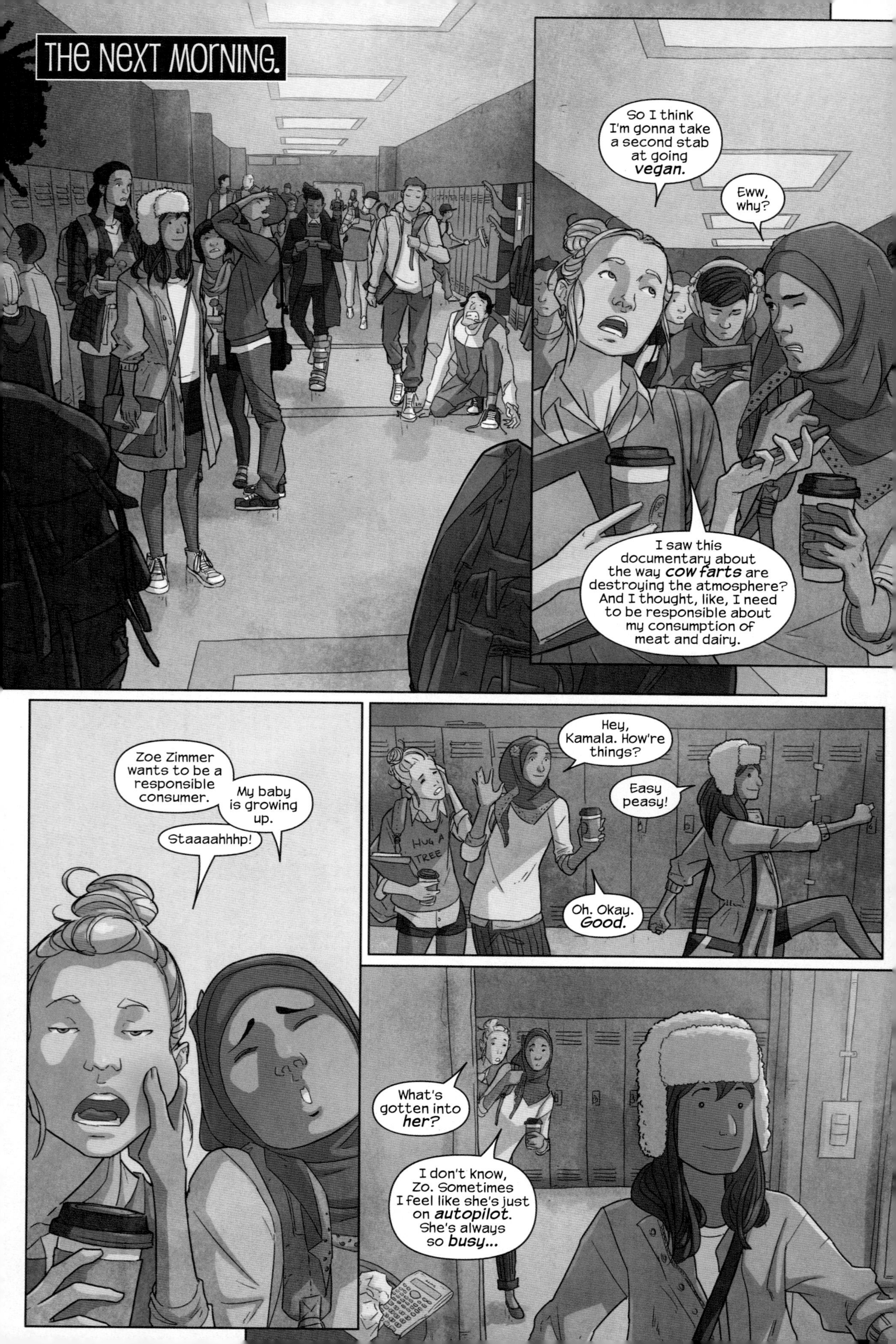
THE NEXT MORNING.
So I think I'm gonna take a second stab at going vegan.
Eww, why?
I saw this documentary about the way cow farts are destroying the atmosphere? And I thought, like, I need to be responsible about my consumption of meat and dairy.
Zoe Zimmer wants to be a responsible consumer.
My baby is growing up.
Staaaahhhp!
Hey, Kamala. How're things?
Easy peasy!
Oh. Okay. Good.
HUG A TREE
What's gotten into her?
I don't know, Zo. Sometimes I feel like she's just on autopilot. She's always so busy...

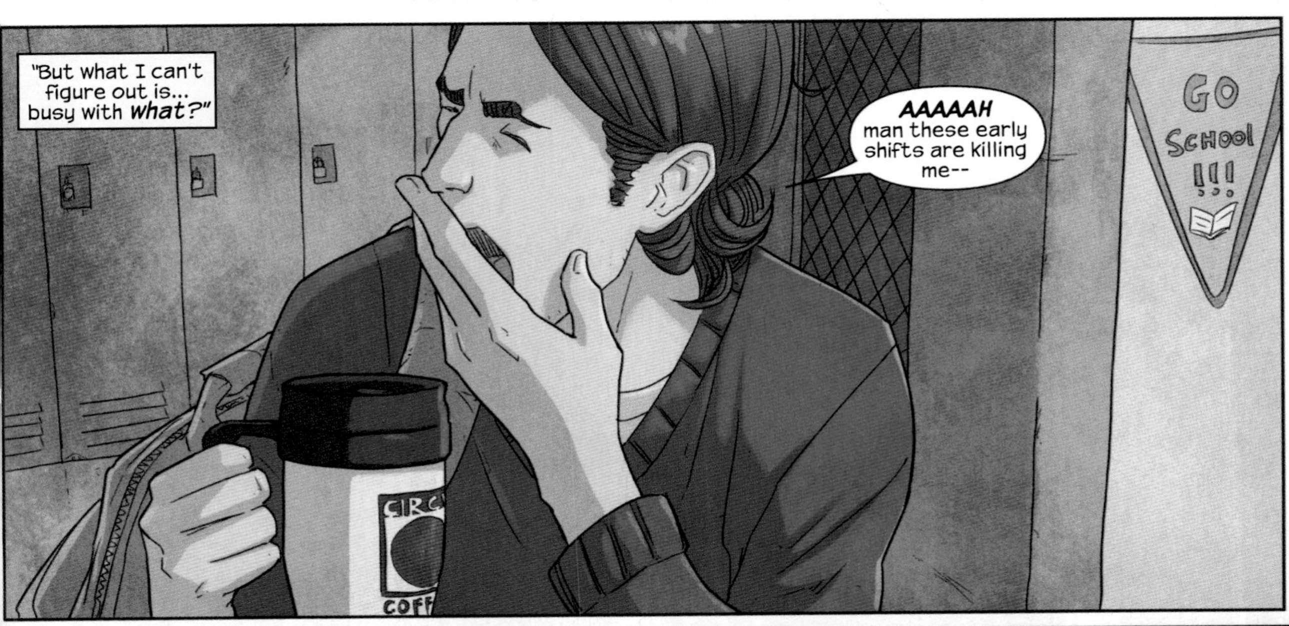
"But what I can't figure out is... busy with *what*?"
AAAAAH man these early shifts are killing me--
GO SCHOOL !!!
CIRC
COFF

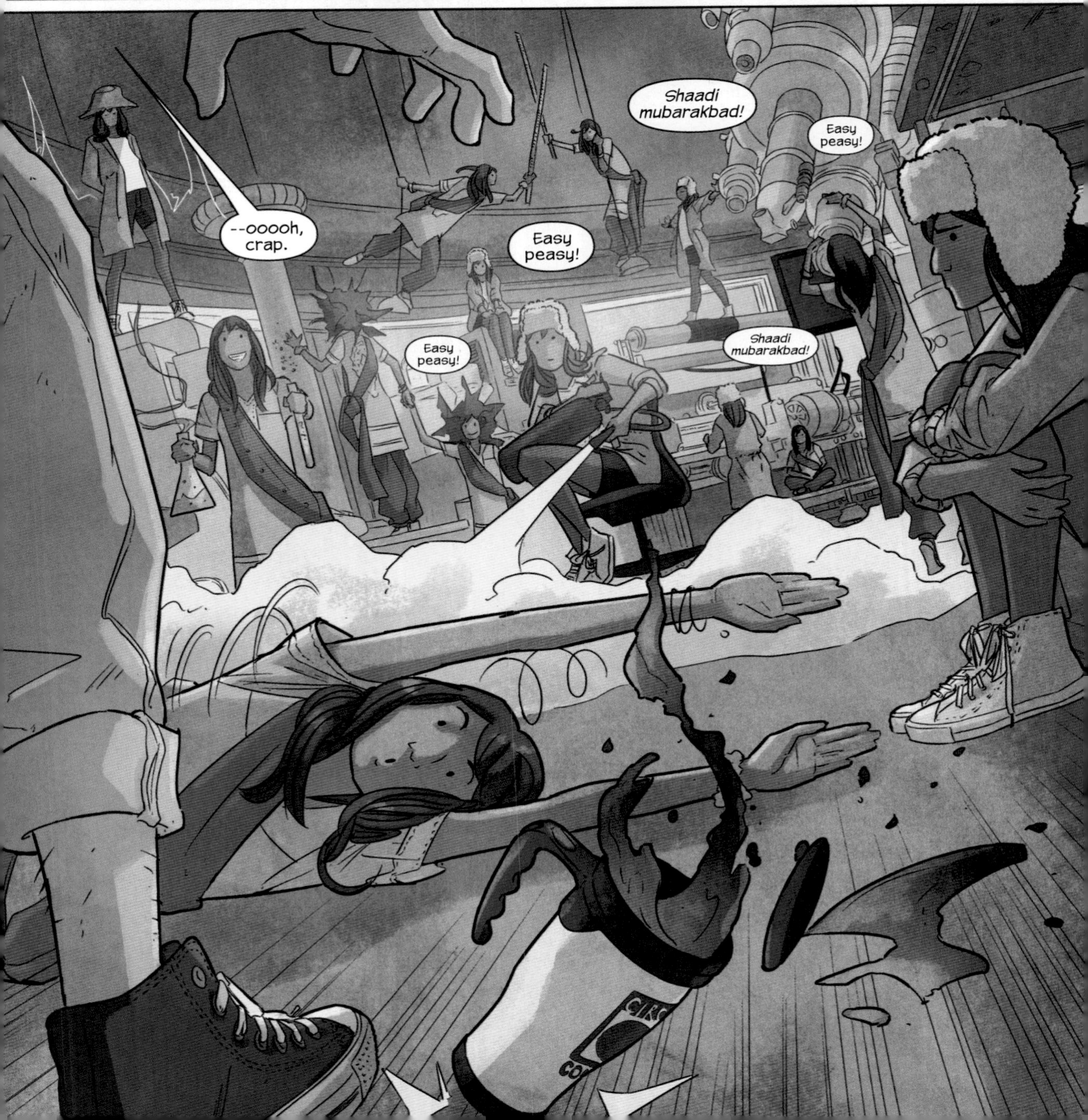
--ooooh, crap.
Shaadi mubarakbad!
Easy peasy!
Easy peasy!
Easy peasy!
Shaadi mubarakbad!
CIRC
CO

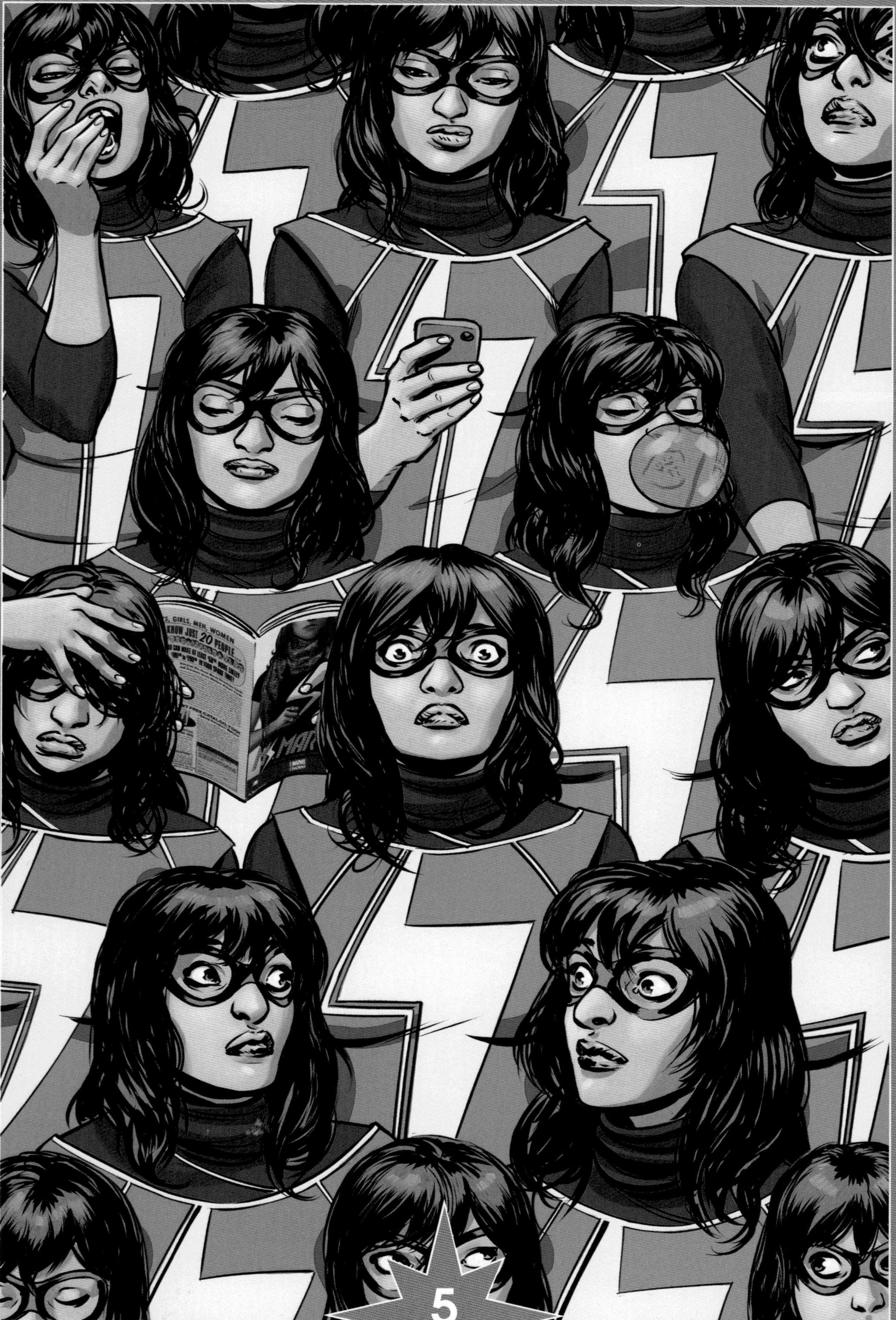
GIRLS, MEN, WOMEN
KNOW JUST 20 PEOPLE
5

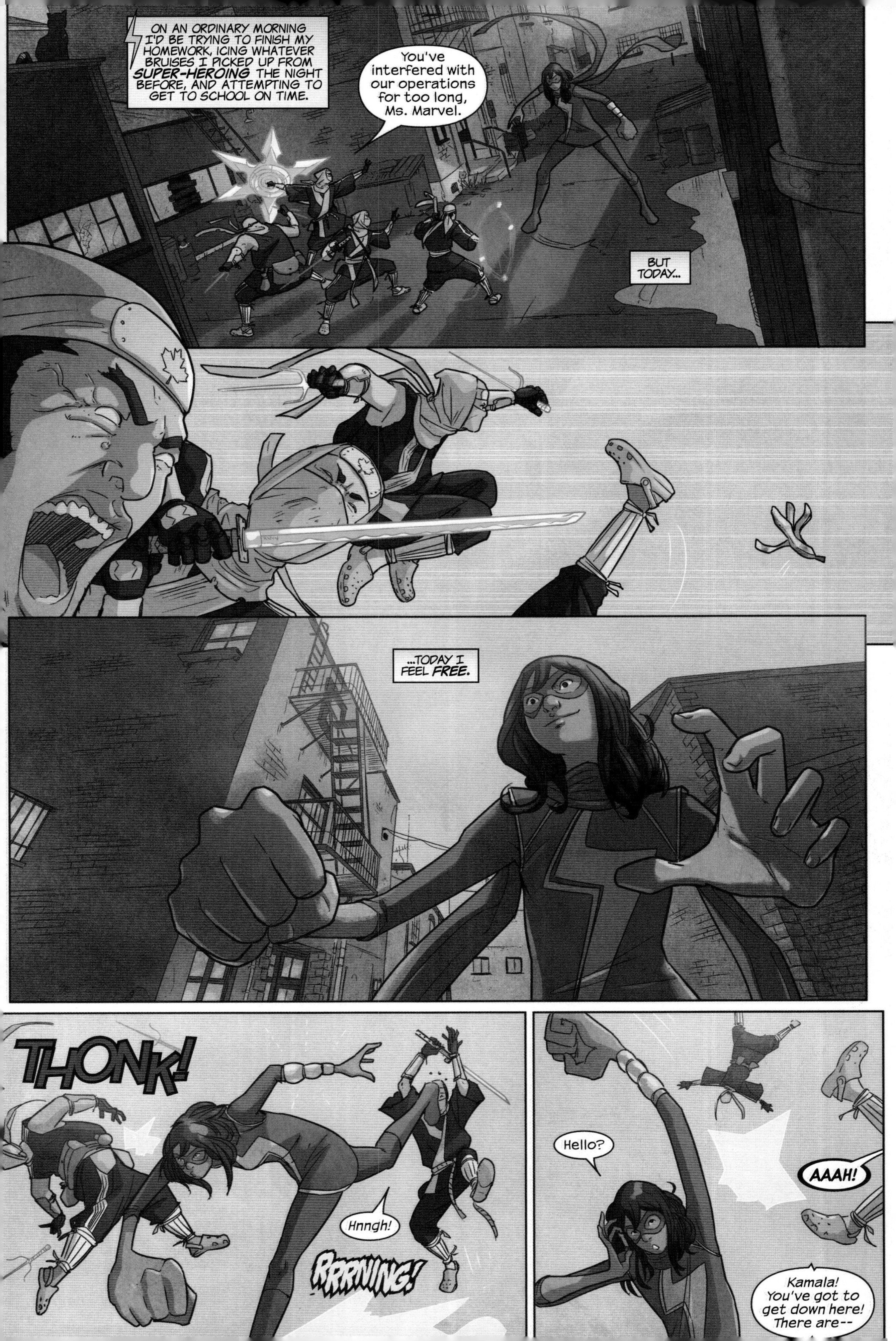
ON AN ORDINARY MORNING I'D BE TRYING TO FINISH MY HOMEWORK, ICING WHATEVER BRUISES I PICKED UP FROM SUPER-HEROING THE NIGHT BEFORE, AND ATTEMPTING TO GET TO SCHOOL ON TIME.
You've interfered with our operations for too long, Ms. Marvel.
BUT TODAY...
...TODAY I FEEL FREE.
THONK!
Hnngh!
RRRNING!
Hello?
AAAH!
Kamala! You've got to get down here! There are--

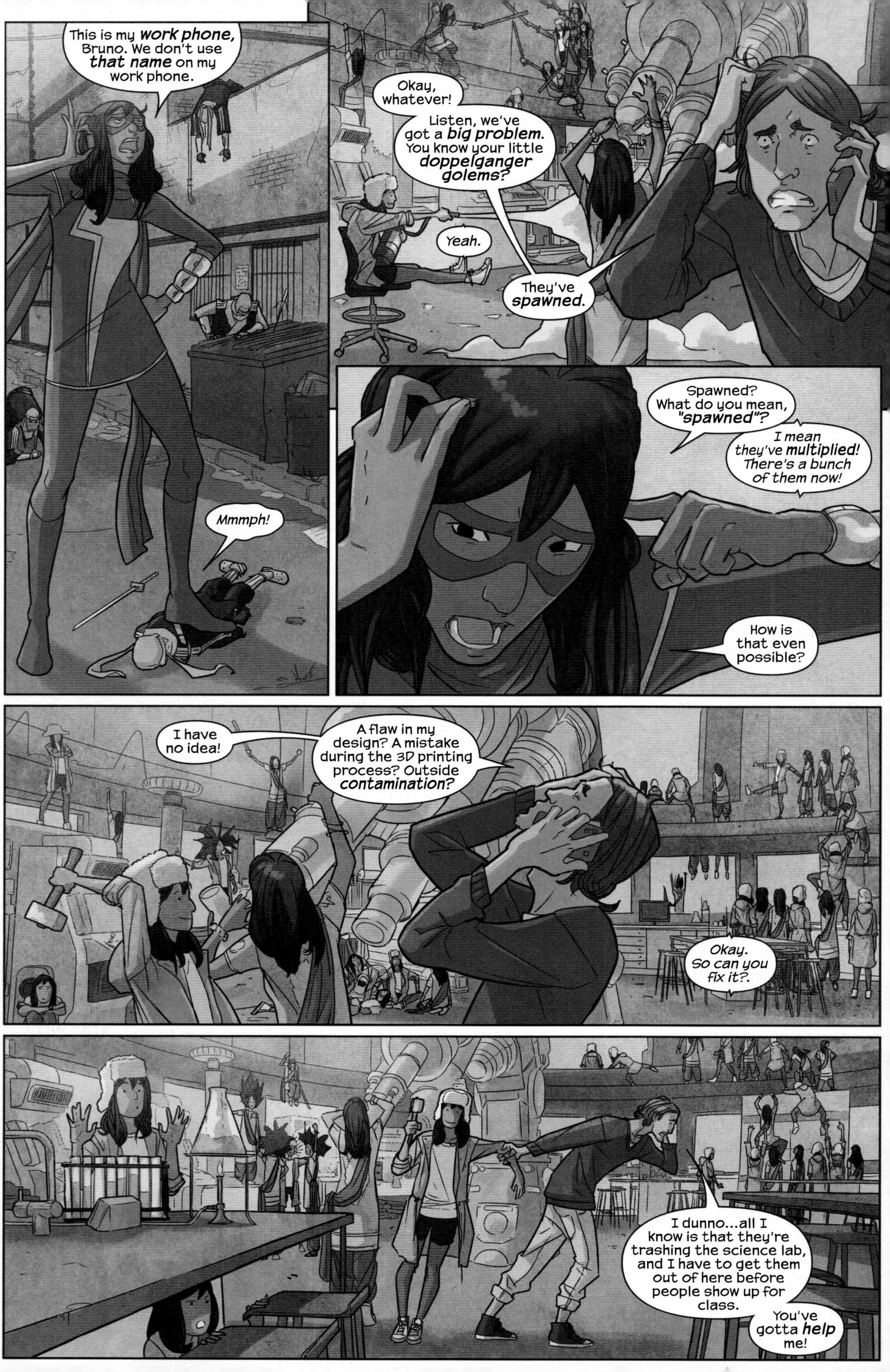
This is my work phone, Bruno. We don't use that name on my work phone.
Okay, whatever!
Listen, we've got a big problem. You know your little doppelganger golems?
Yeah.
They've spawned.
Mmmph!
Spawned? What do you mean, "spawned"?
I mean they've multiplied! There's a bunch of them now!
How is that even possible?
I have no idea!
A flaw in my design? A mistake during the 3D printing process? Outside contamination?
Okay. So can you fix it?.
I dunno...all I know is that they're trashing the science lab, and I have to get them out of here before people show up for class.
You've gotta help me!

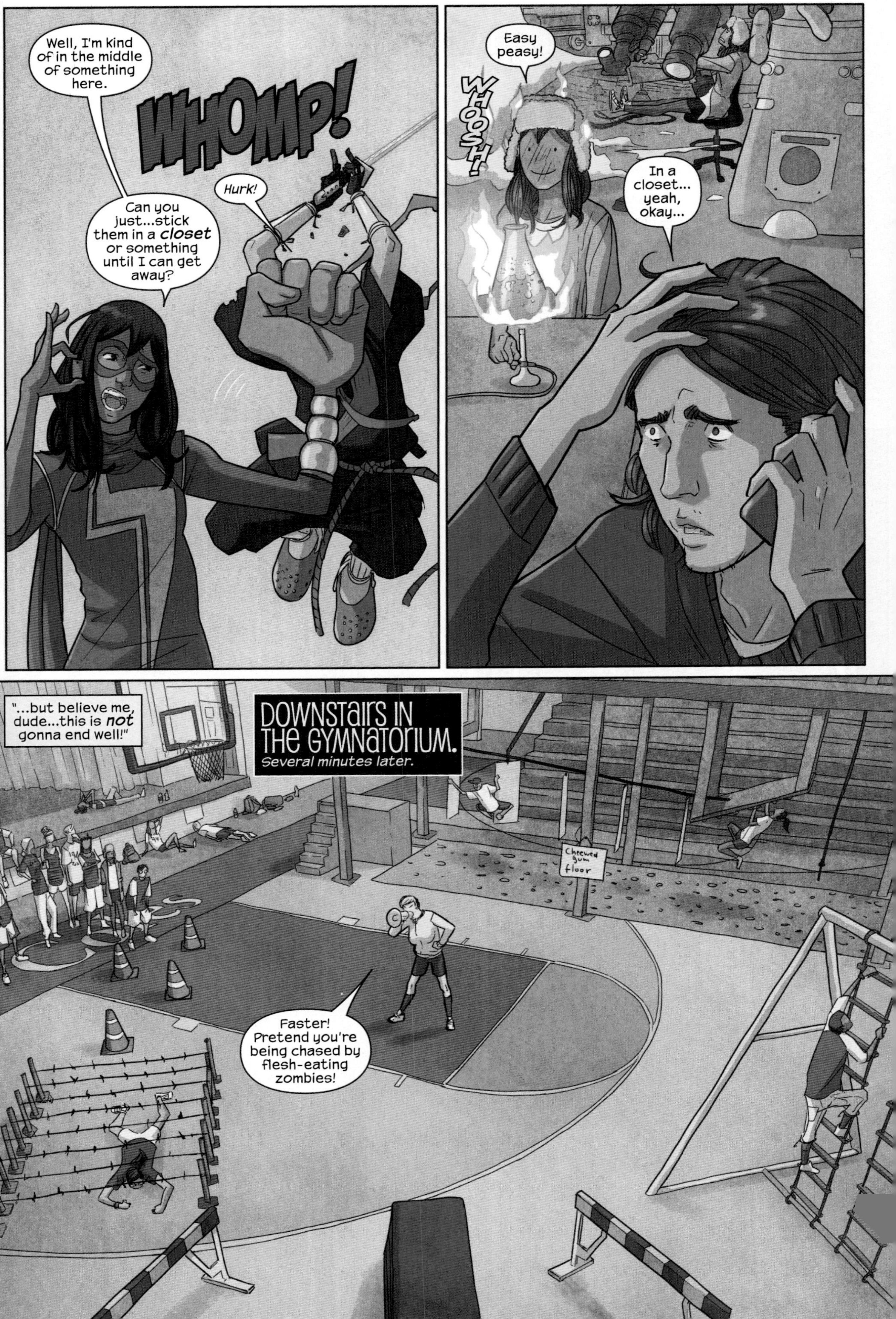

Well, I'm kind of in the middle of something here.
WHOMP!
Hurk!
Can you just...stick them in a *closet* or something until I can get away?
Easy peasy!
WHOOSH!
In a closet... yeah, okay...
"...but believe me, dude...this is *not* gonna end well!"
DOWNSTAIRS IN THE GYMNATORIUM.
Several minutes later.
Chewed gum floor
Faster! Pretend you're being chased by flesh-eating zombies!

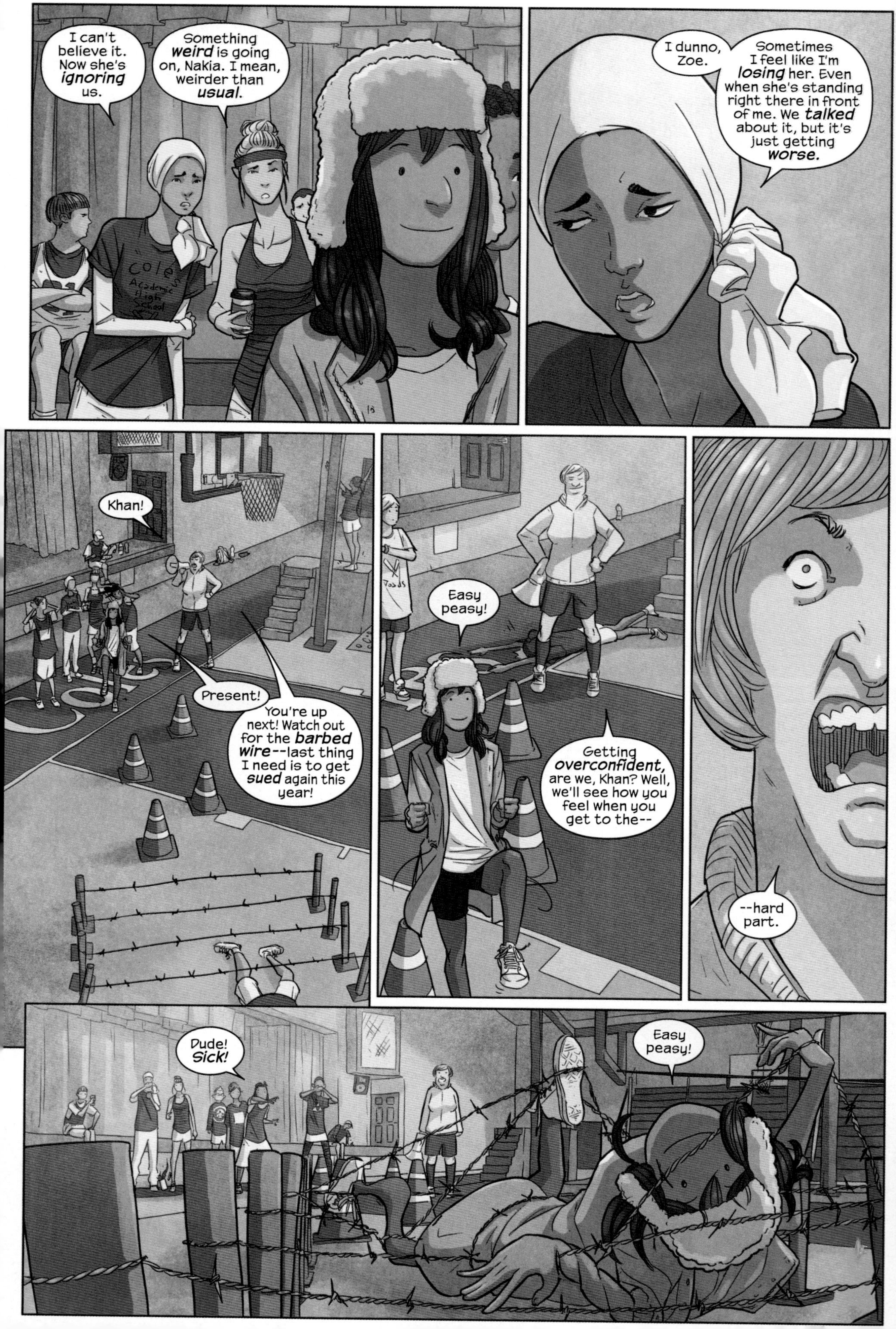

I can't believe it. Now she's *ignoring* us.
Something *weird* is going on, Nakia. I mean, weirder than *usual*.
I dunno, Zoe.
Sometimes I feel like I'm *losing* her. Even when she's standing right there in front of me. We *talked* about it, but it's just getting *worse.*
Khan!
Present!
You're up next! Watch out for the *barbed wire*--last thing I need is to get *sued* again this year!
Easy peasy!
Getting *overconfident,* are we, Khan? Well, we'll see how you feel when you get to the--
--hard part.
Dude! *Sick!*
Easy peasy!

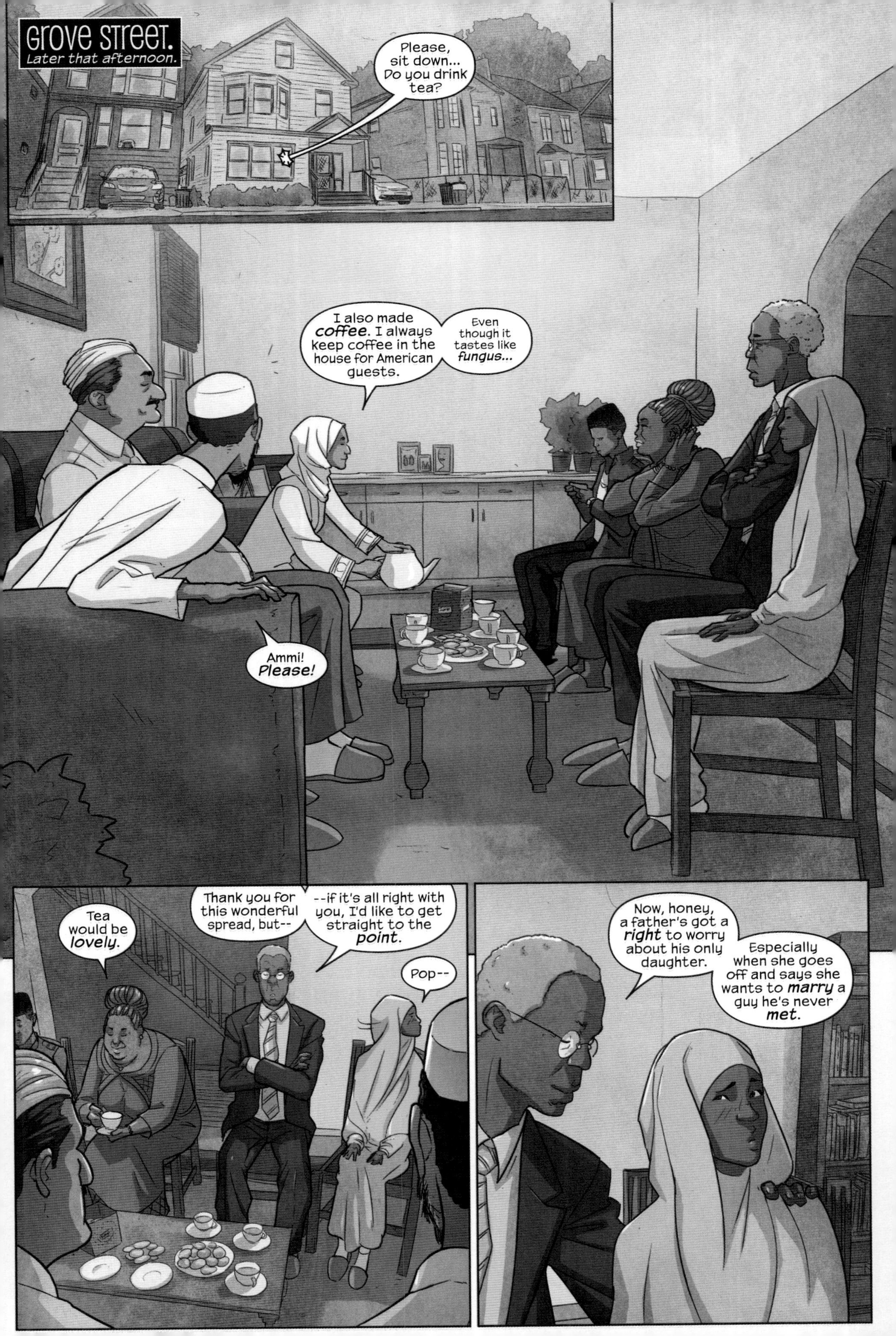
GROVE STREET.
Later that afternoon.
Please, sit down... Do you drink tea?
I also made coffee. I always keep coffee in the house for American guests.
Even though it tastes like fungus...
Ammi! Please!
Tea would be lovely.
Thank you for this wonderful spread, but--
--if it's all right with you, I'd like to get straight to the point.
Pop--
Now, honey, a father's got a right to worry about his only daughter.
Especially when she goes off and says she wants to marry a guy he's never met.

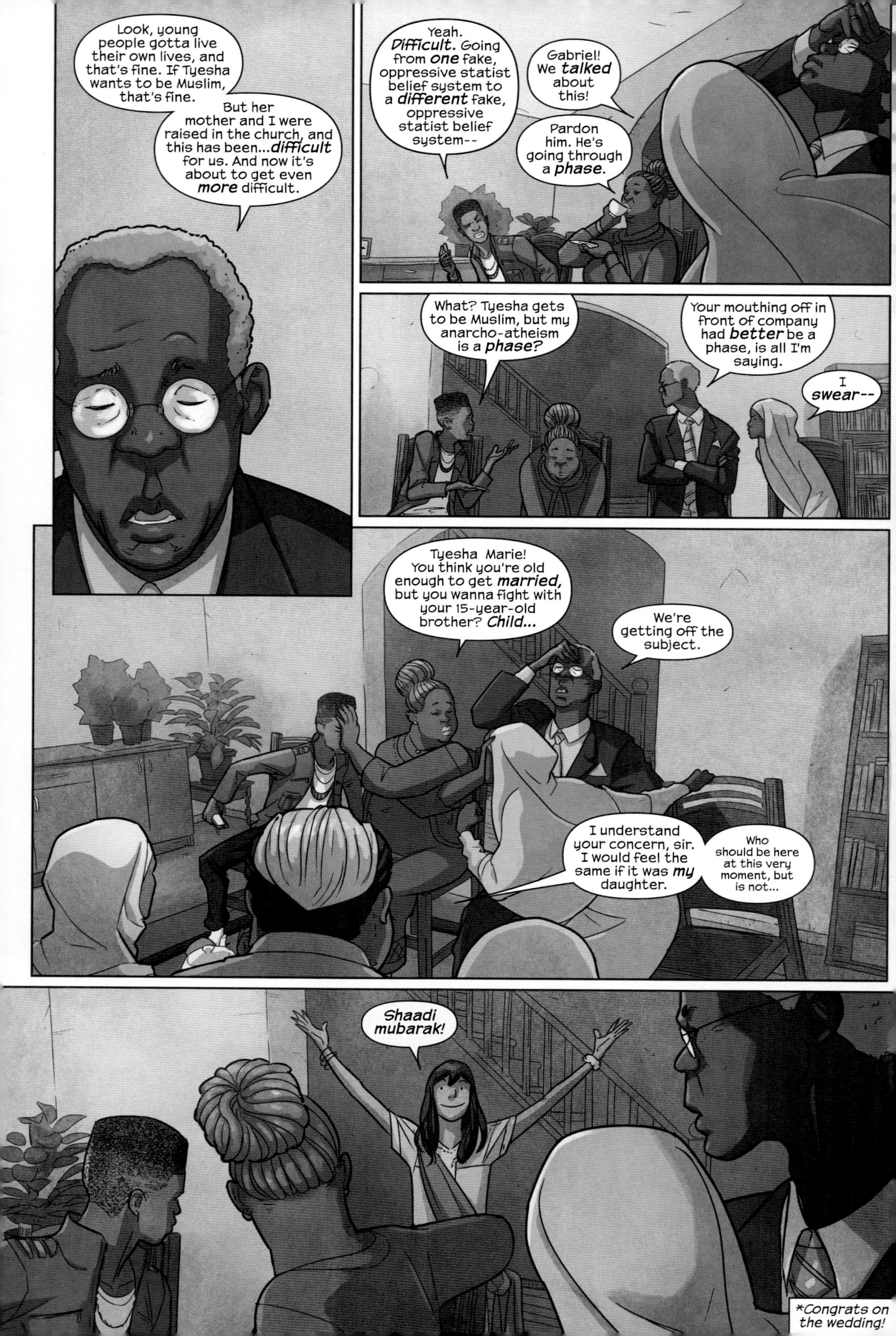
Look, young people gotta live their own lives, and that's fine. If Tyesha wants to be Muslim, that's fine.
But her mother and I were raised in the church, and this has been...difficult for us. And now it's about to get even more difficult.
Yeah. Difficult. Going from one fake, oppressive statist belief system to a different fake, oppressive statist belief system--
Gabriel! We talked about this!
Pardon him. He's going through a phase.
What? Tyesha gets to be Muslim, but my anarcho-atheism is a phase?
Your mouthing off in front of company had better be a phase, is all I'm saying.
I swear--
Tyesha Marie! You think you're old enough to get married, but you wanna fight with your 15-year-old brother? Child...
We're getting off the subject.
I understand your concern, sir. I would feel the same if it was my daughter.
Who should be here at this very moment, but is not...
Shaadi mubarak!
*Congrats on the wedding!

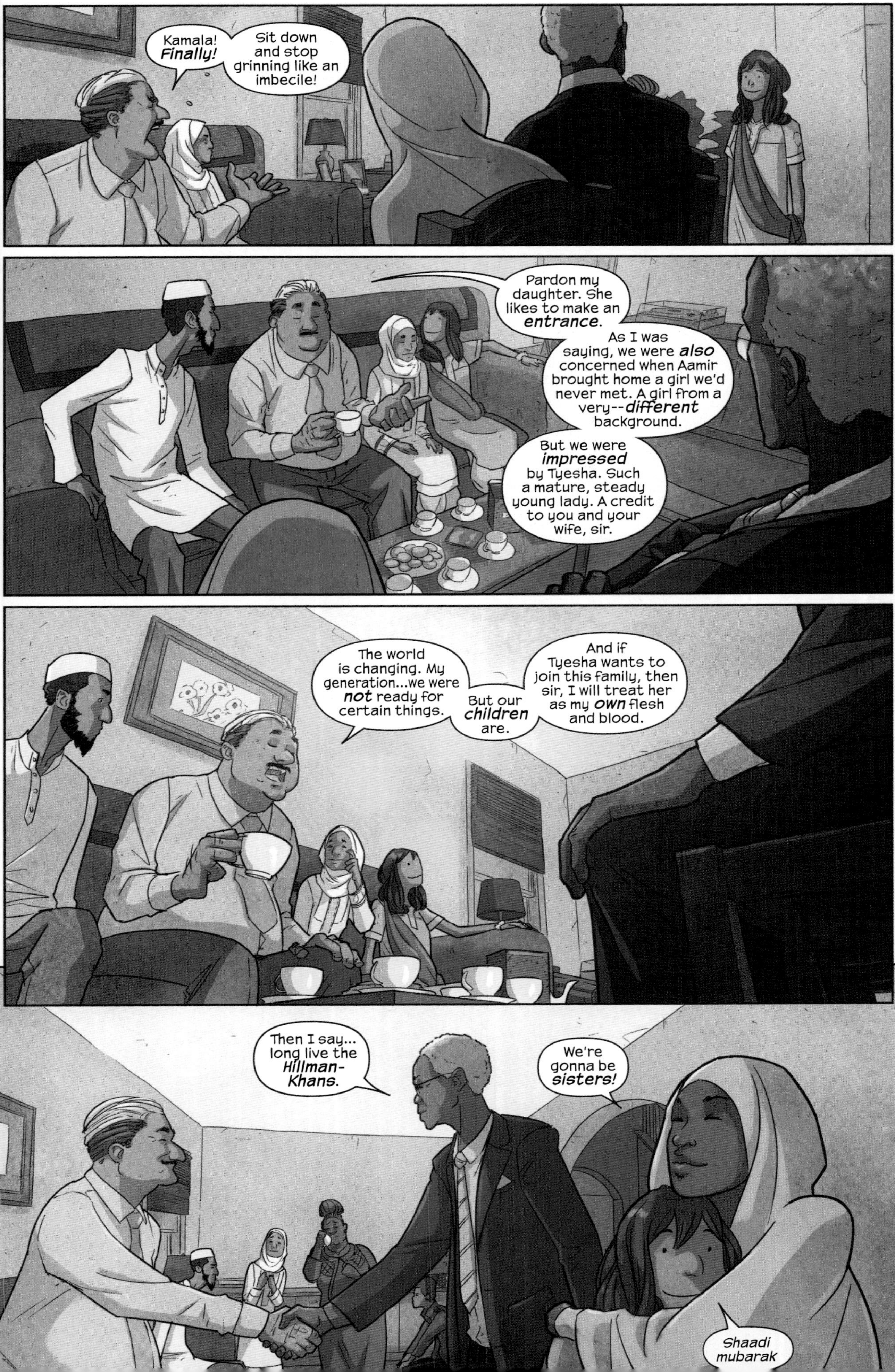
Kamala! *Finally!*
Sit down and stop grinning like an imbecile!
Pardon my daughter. She likes to make an *entrance*.
As I was saying, we were *also* concerned when Aamir brought home a girl we'd never met. A girl from a very--*different* background.
But we were *impressed* by Tyesha. Such a mature, steady young lady. A credit to you and your wife, sir.
The world is changing. My generation...we were *not* ready for certain things.
But our *children* are.
And if Tyesha wants to join this family, then sir, I will treat her as my *own* flesh and blood.
Then I say... long live the *Hillman-Khans*.
We're gonna be *sisters!*
Shaadi mubarak

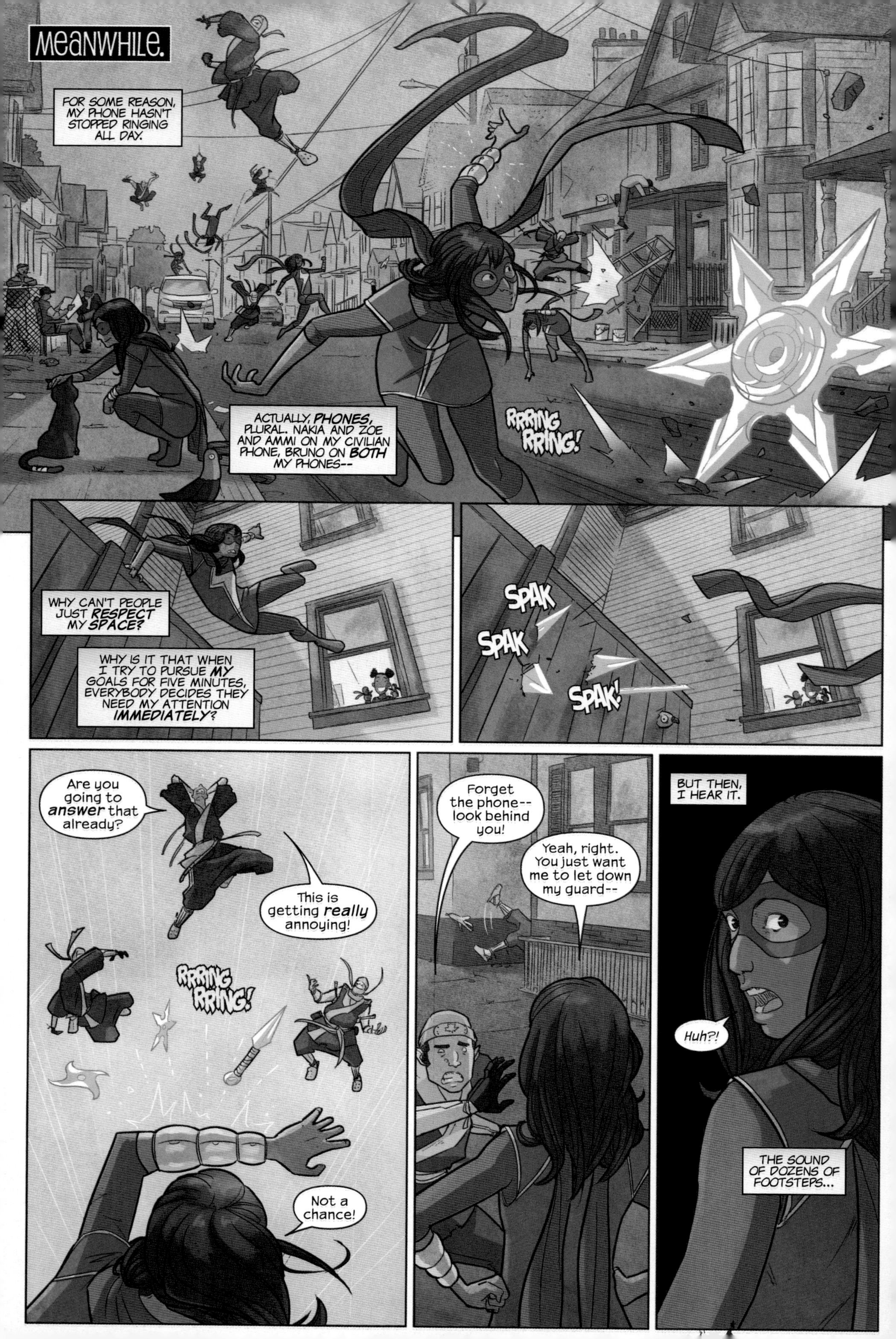
MEANWHILE.
FOR SOME REASON, MY PHONE HASN'T STOPPED RINGING ALL DAY.
ACTUALLY, PHONES, PLURAL. NAKIA AND ZOE AND AMMI ON MY CIVILIAN PHONE, BRUNO ON BOTH MY PHONES--
RRRING RRING!
WHY CAN'T PEOPLE JUST RESPECT MY SPACE?
WHY IS IT THAT WHEN I TRY TO PURSUE MY GOALS FOR FIVE MINUTES, EVERYBODY DECIDES THEY NEED MY ATTENTION IMMEDIATELY?
SPAK
SPAK
SPAK!
Are you going to answer that already?
This is getting really annoying!
RRRING RRING!
Not a chance!
Forget the phone-- look behind you!
Yeah, right. You just want me to let down my guard--
BUT THEN, I HEAR IT.
Huh?!
THE SOUND OF DOZENS OF FOOTSTEPS...

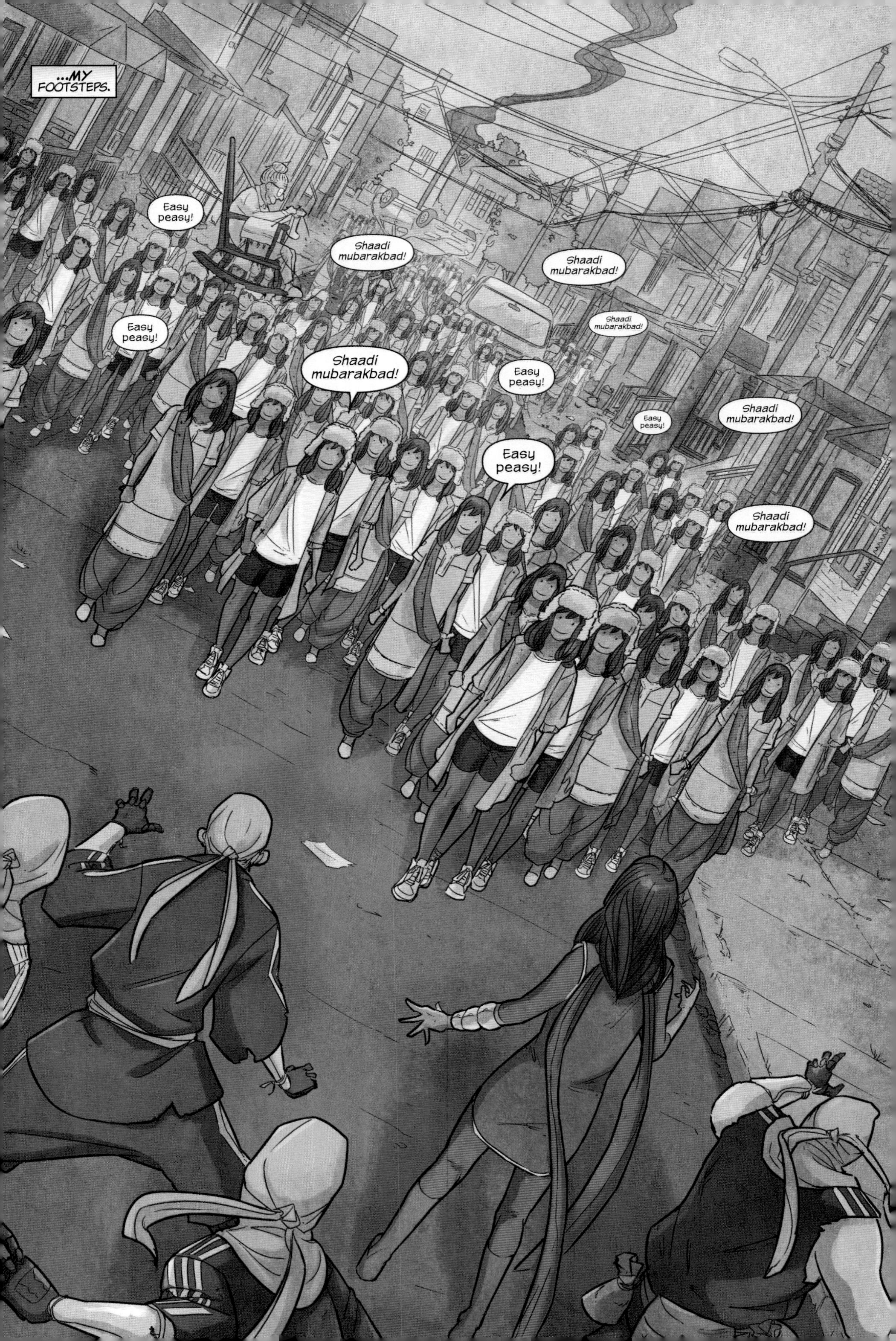
...MY FOOTSTEPS.
Easy peasy!
Easy peasy!
Shaadi mubarakbad!
Shaadi mubarakbad!
Shaadi mubarakbad!
Shaadi mubarakbad!
Easy peasy!
Easy peasy!
Shaadi mubarakbad!
Easy peasy!
Shaadi mubarakbad!

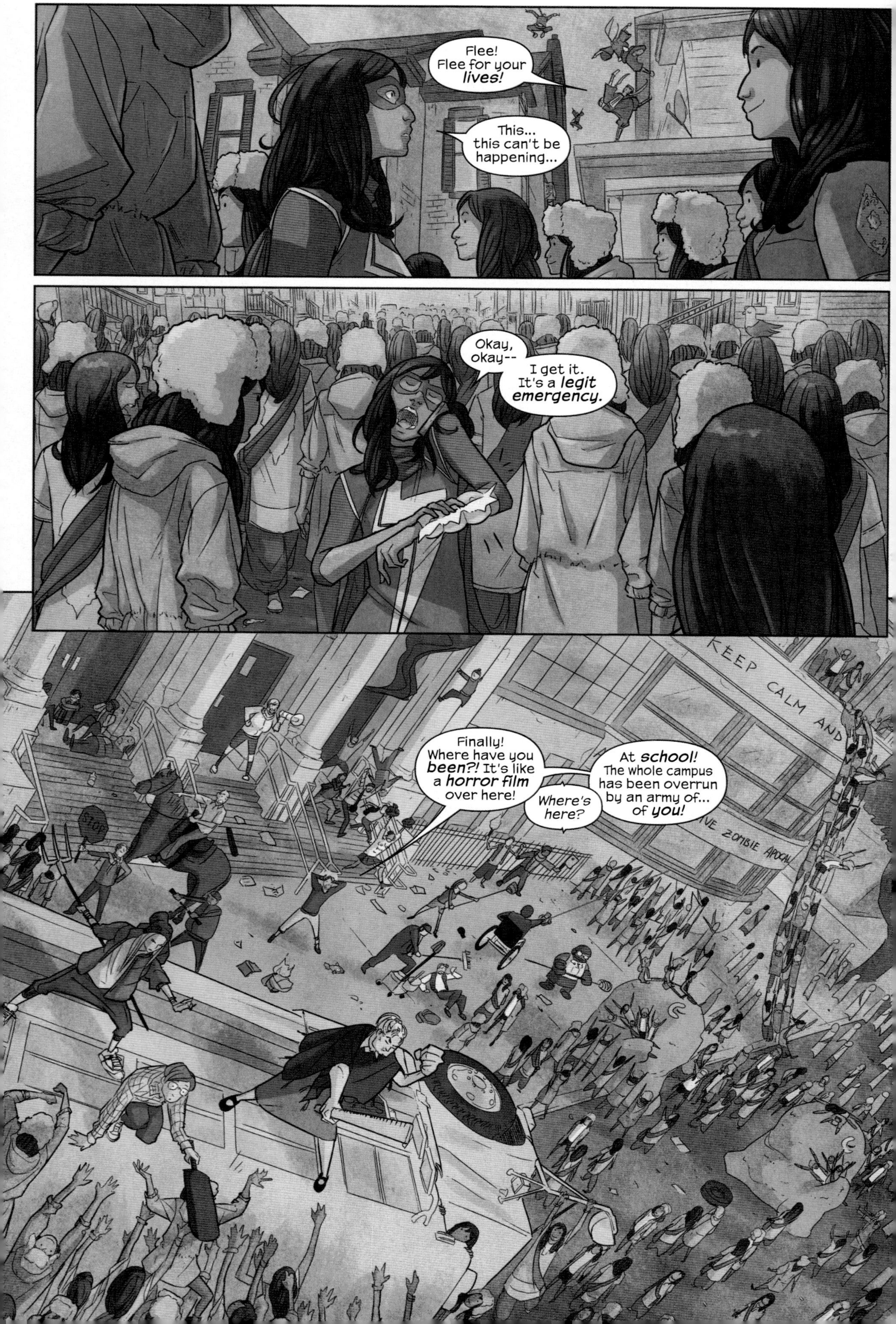
Flee! Flee for your *lives!*
This... this can't be happening...
Okay, okay--
I get it. It's a *legit emergency.*
KEEP CALM AND
Finally! Where have you *been?!* It's like a *horror film* over here!
Where's here?
At *school!* The whole campus has been overrun by an army of... of *you!*

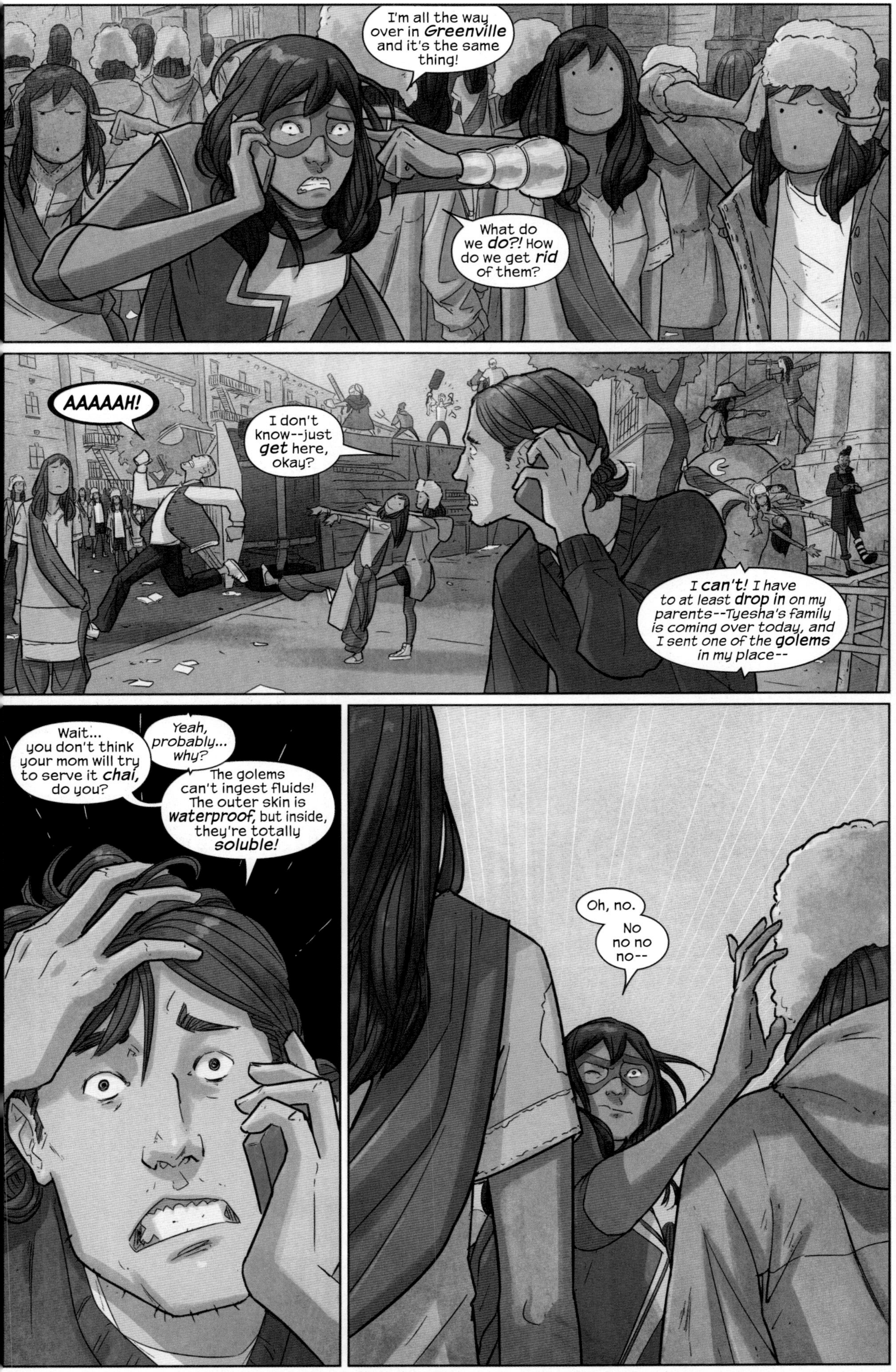
I'm all the way over in Greenville and it's the same thing!
What do we do?! How do we get rid of them?
AAAAAH!
I don't know--just get here, okay?
I can't! I have to at least drop in on my parents--Tyesha's family is coming over today, and I sent one of the golems in my place--
Wait... you don't think your mom will try to serve it chai, do you?
Yeah, probably... why?
The golems can't ingest fluids! The outer skin is waterproof, but inside, they're totally soluble!
Oh, no.
No no no no--

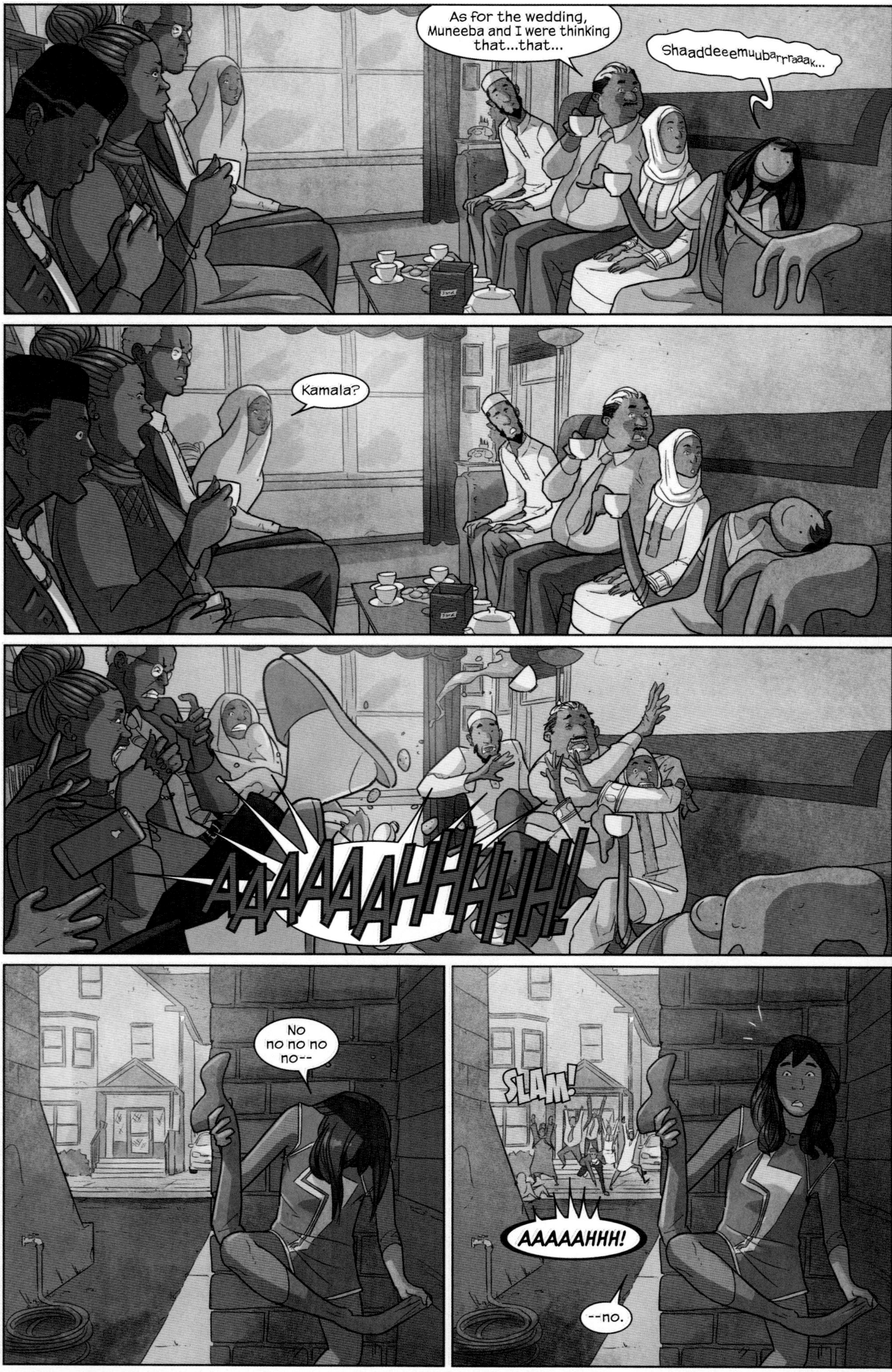
As for the wedding, Muneeba and I were thinking that...that...
Shaaddeeemuubarrraaak...
Kamala?
AAAAAAHHHHH!
No no no no no--
SLAM!
AAAAAHHH!
--no.

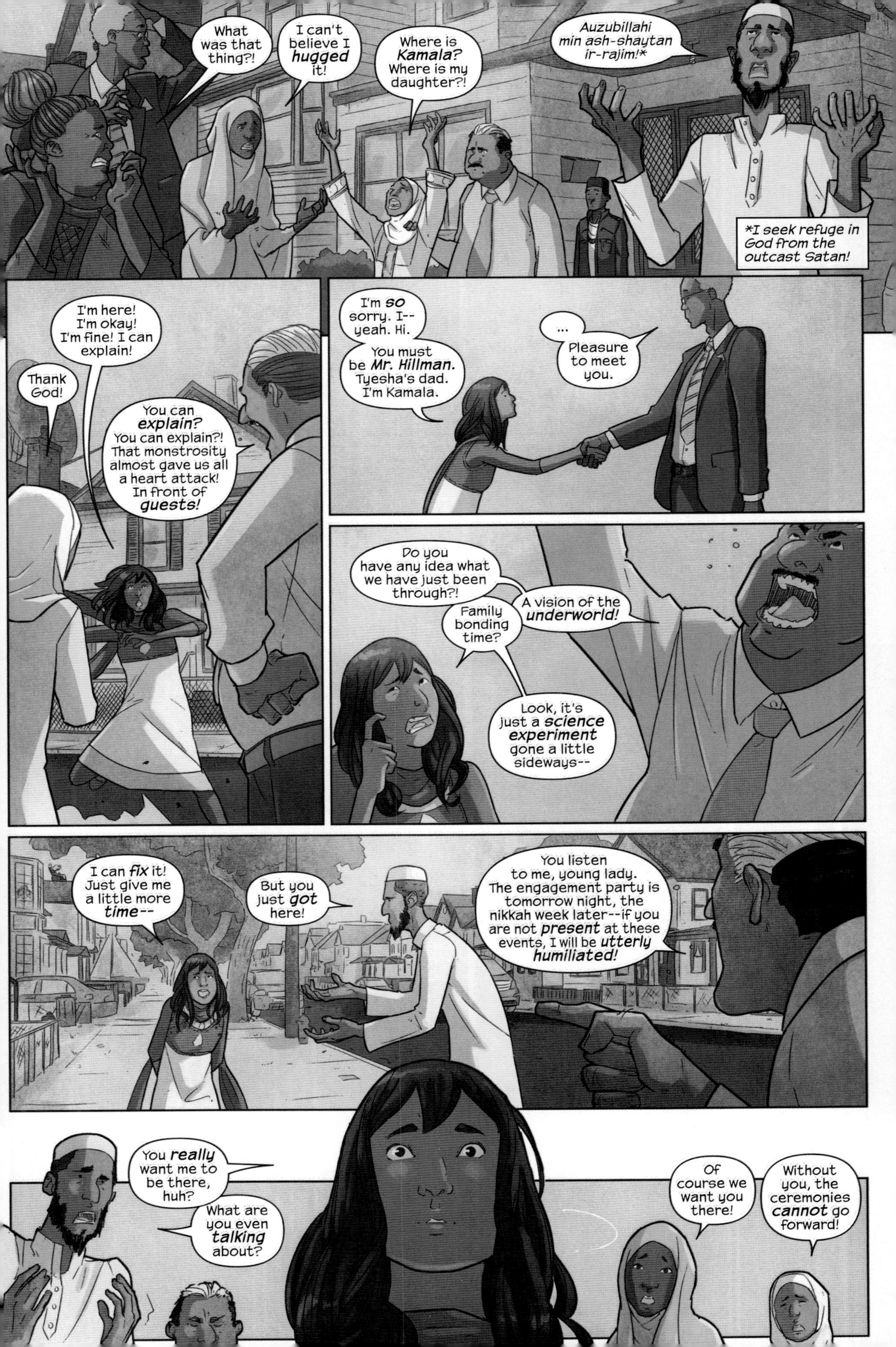

What was that thing?!
I can't believe I hugged it!
Where is Kamala? Where is my daughter?!
Auzubillahi min ash-shaytan ir-rajim!*
*I seek refuge in God from the outcast Satan!
I'm here! I'm okay! I'm fine! I can explain!
Thank God!
You can explain? You can explain?! That monstrosity almost gave us all a heart attack! In front of guests!
I'm so sorry. I-- yeah. Hi.
You must be Mr. Hillman. Tyesha's dad. I'm Kamala.
... Pleasure to meet you.
Do you have any idea what we have just been through?!
A vision of the underworld!
Family bonding time?
Look, it's just a science experiment gone a little sideways--
I can fix it! Just give me a little more time--
But you just got here!
You listen to me, young lady. The engagement party is tomorrow night, the nikkah week later--if you are not present at these events, I will be utterly humiliated!
You really want me to be there, huh?
What are you even talking about?
Of course we want you there!
Without you, the ceremonies cannot go forward!

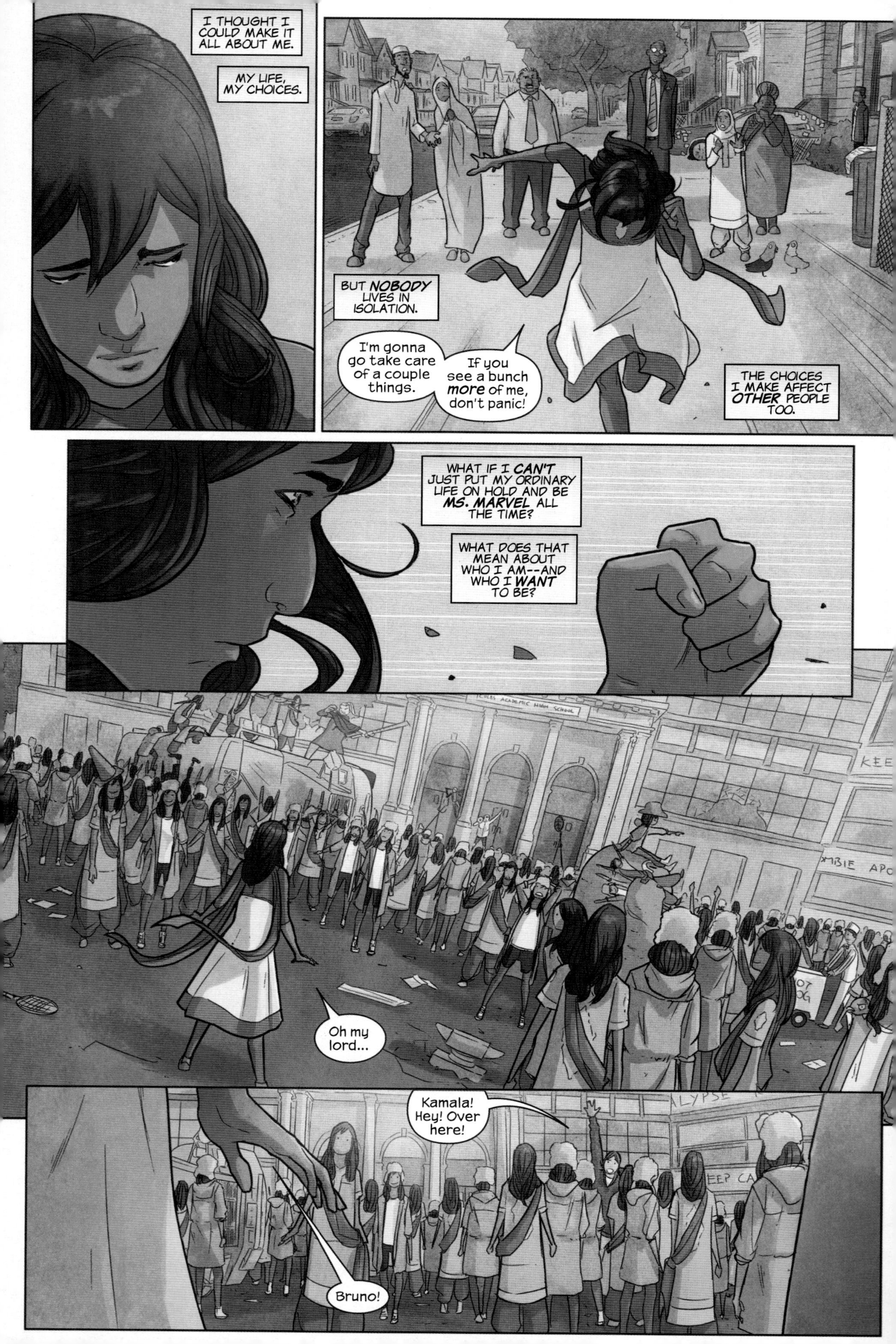

I THOUGHT I COULD MAKE IT ALL ABOUT ME.
MY LIFE, MY CHOICES.
BUT NOBODY LIVES IN ISOLATION.
I'm gonna go take care of a couple things.
If you see a bunch more of me, don't panic!
THE CHOICES I MAKE AFFECT OTHER PEOPLE TOO.
WHAT IF I CAN'T JUST PUT MY ORDINARY LIFE ON HOLD AND BE MS. MARVEL ALL THE TIME?
WHAT DOES THAT MEAN ABOUT WHO I AM--AND WHO I WANT TO BE?
Oh my lord...
Kamala! Hey! Over here!
Bruno!

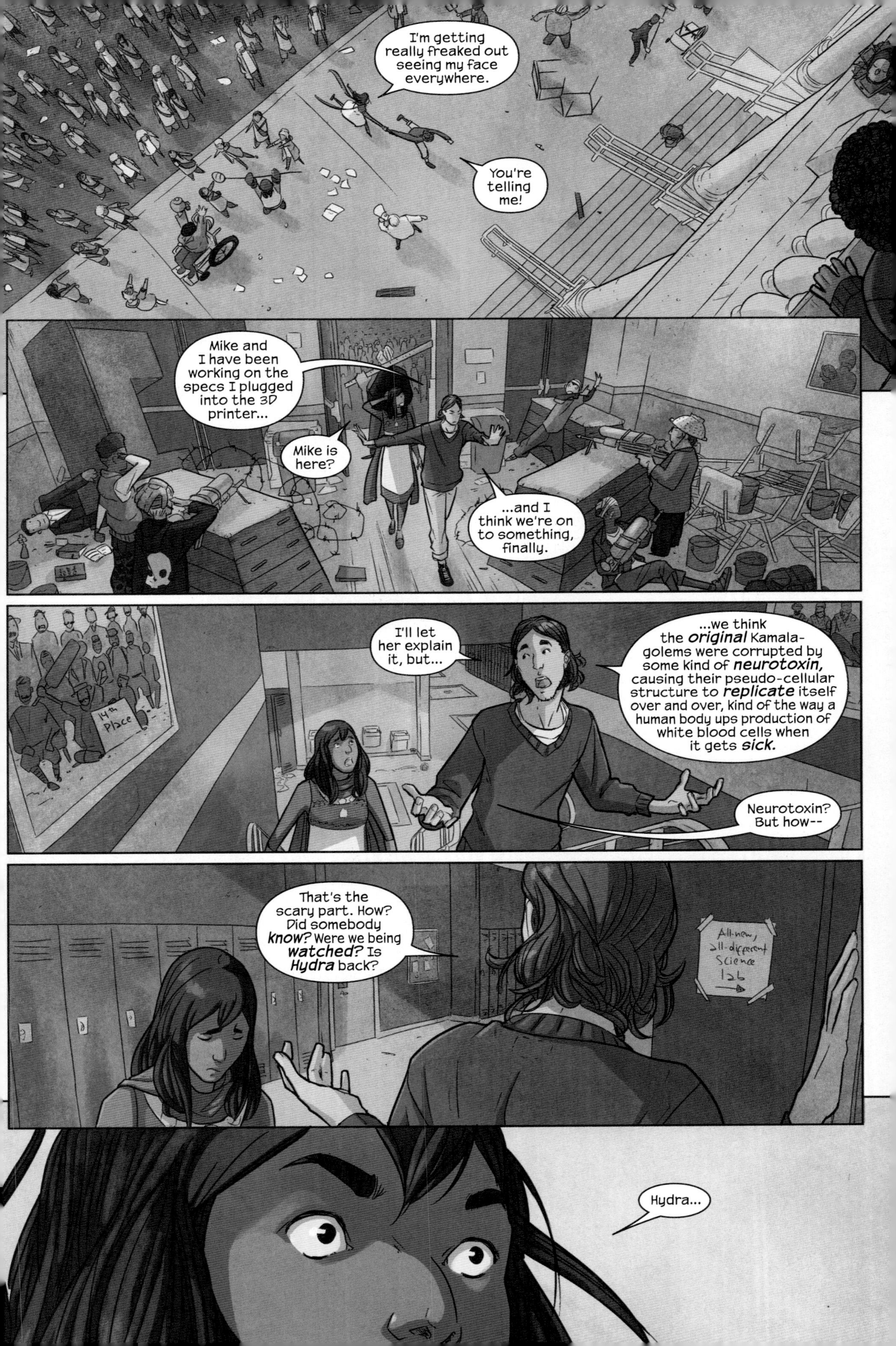

I'm getting really freaked out seeing my face everywhere.
You're telling me!
Mike and I have been working on the specs I plugged into the 3D printer...
Mike is here?
...and I think we're on to something, finally.
14th Place
I'll let her explain it, but...
...we think the *original* Kamala-golems were corrupted by some kind of *neurotoxin,* causing their pseudo-cellular structure to *replicate* itself over and over, kind of the way a human body ups production of white blood cells when it gets *sick.*
Neurotoxin? But how--
That's the scary part. How? Did somebody *know?* Were we being *watched?* Is *Hydra* back?
All-new, all-different Science lab
Hydra...

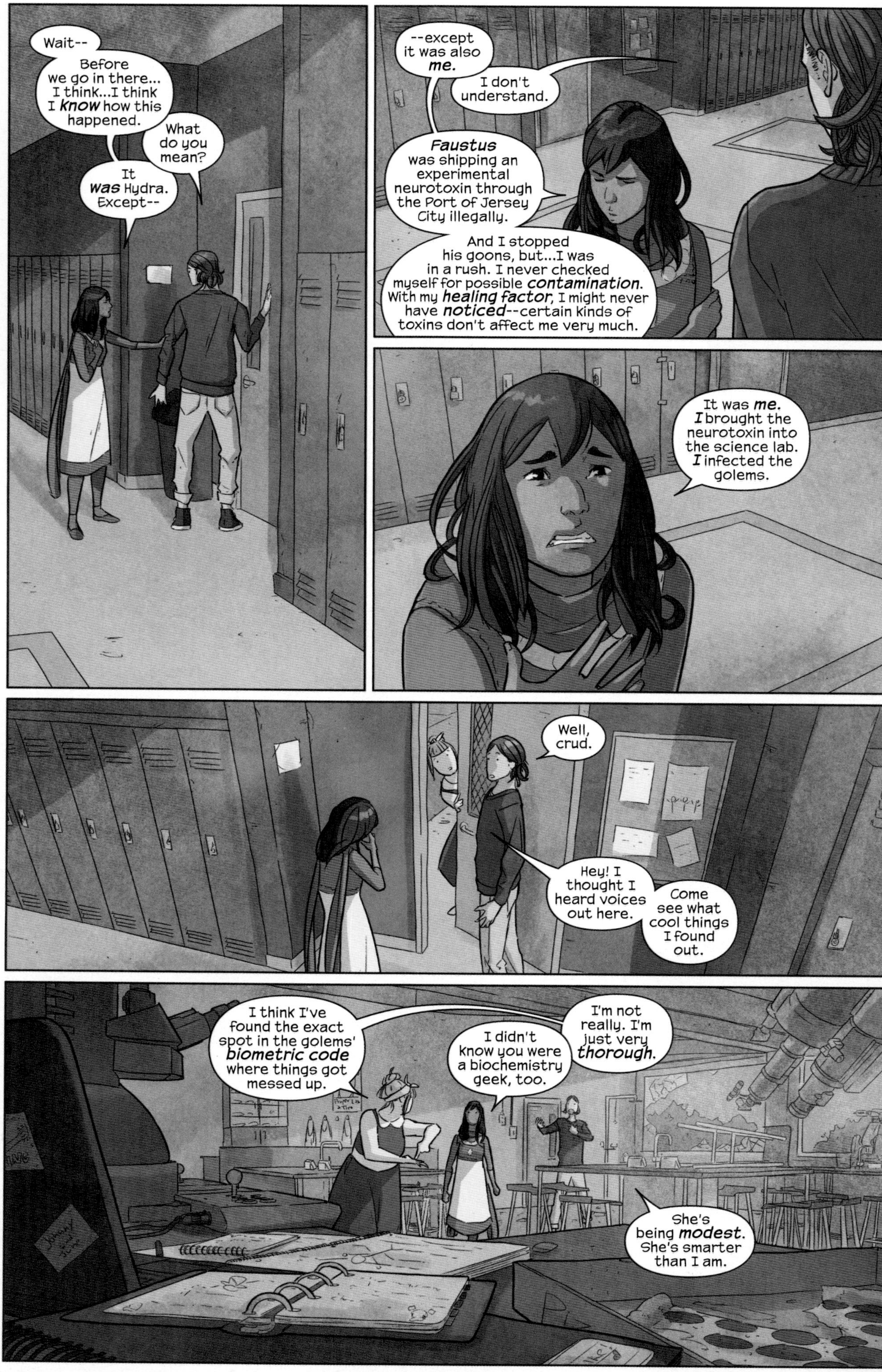
Wait--
Before we go in there... I think...I think I know how this happened.
What do you mean?
It was Hydra. Except--
--except it was also me.
I don't understand.
Faustus was shipping an experimental neurotoxin through the Port of Jersey City illegally.
And I stopped his goons, but...I was in a rush. I never checked myself for possible contamination. With my healing factor, I might never have noticed--certain kinds of toxins don't affect me very much.
It was me. I brought the neurotoxin into the science lab. I infected the golems.
Well, crud.
Hey! I thought I heard voices out here.
Come see what cool things I found out.
I think I've found the exact spot in the golems' biometric code where things got messed up.
I didn't know you were a biochemistry geek, too.
I'm not really. I'm just very thorough.
She's being modest. She's smarter than I am.

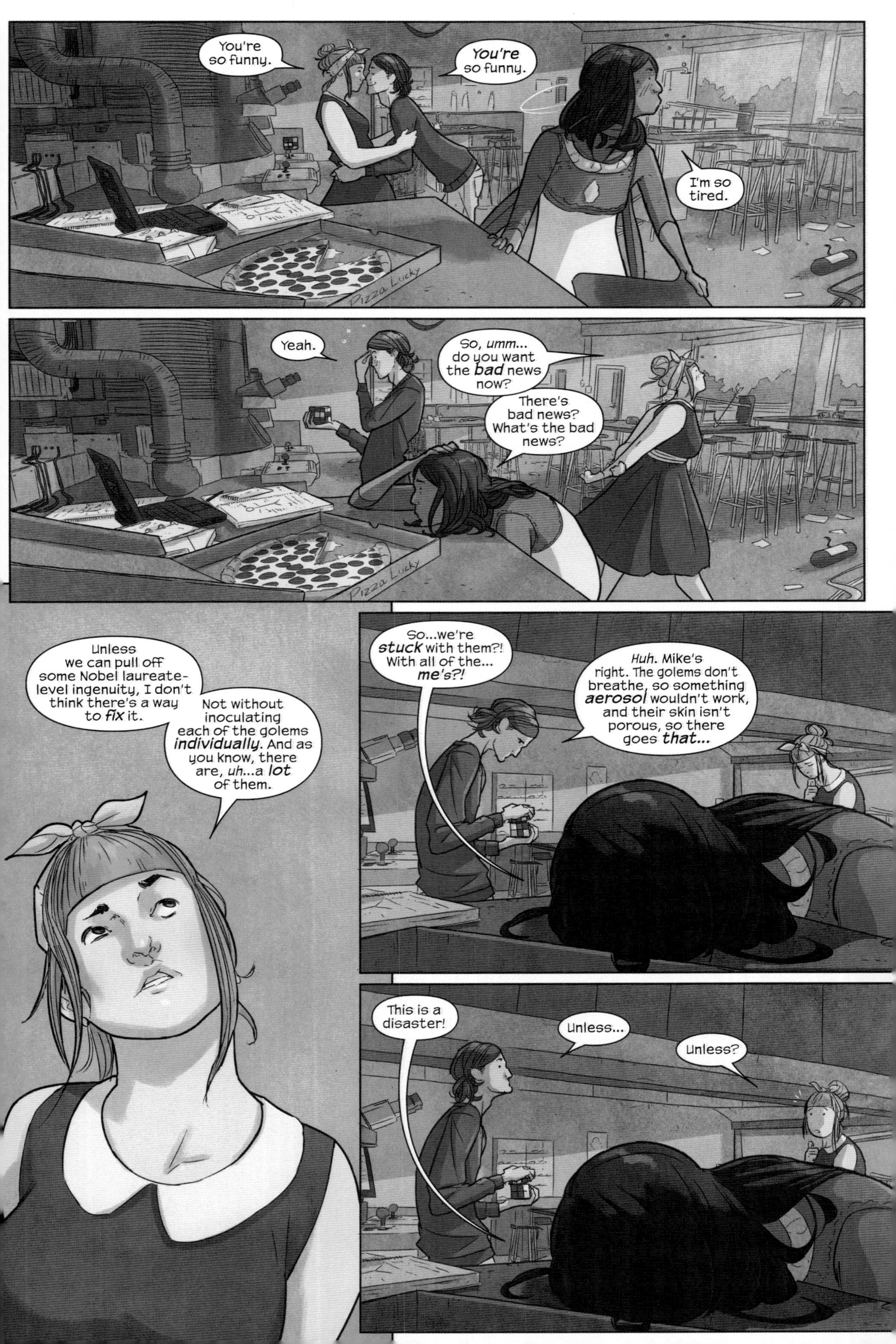

You're so funny.
You're so funny.
I'm so tired.
Pizza Lucky
Yeah.
So, umm... do you want the bad news now?
There's bad news? What's the bad news?
Pizza Lucky
Unless we can pull off some Nobel laureate-level ingenuity, I don't think there's a way to fix it.
Not without inoculating each of the golems individually. And as you know, there are, uh...a lot of them.
So...we're stuck with them?! With all of the... me's?!
Huh. Mike's right. The golems don't breathe, so something aerosol wouldn't work, and their skin isn't porous, so there goes that...
This is a disaster!
Unless...
Unless?

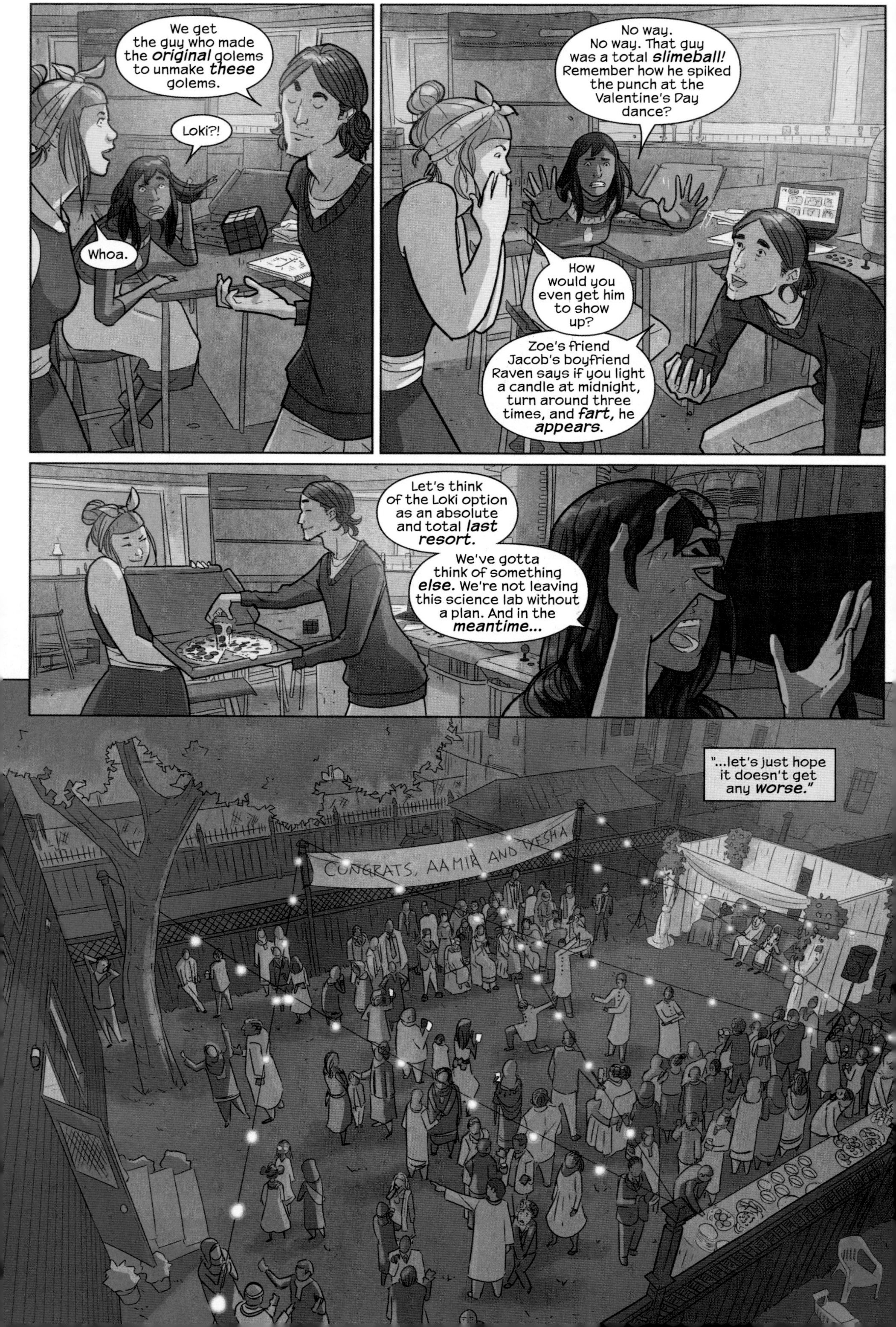
We get the guy who made the *original* golems to unmake *these* golems.
Loki?!
Whoa.
No way. No way. That guy was a total *slimeball!* Remember how he spiked the punch at the Valentine's Day dance?
How would you even get him to show up?
Zoe's friend Jacob's boyfriend Raven says if you light a candle at midnight, turn around three times, and *fart,* he *appears*.
Let's think of the Loki option as an absolute and total *last resort.*
We've gotta think of something *else.* We're not leaving this science lab without a plan. And in the *meantime...*
"...let's just hope it doesn't get any *worse.*"
CONGRATS, AAMIR AND TYESHA

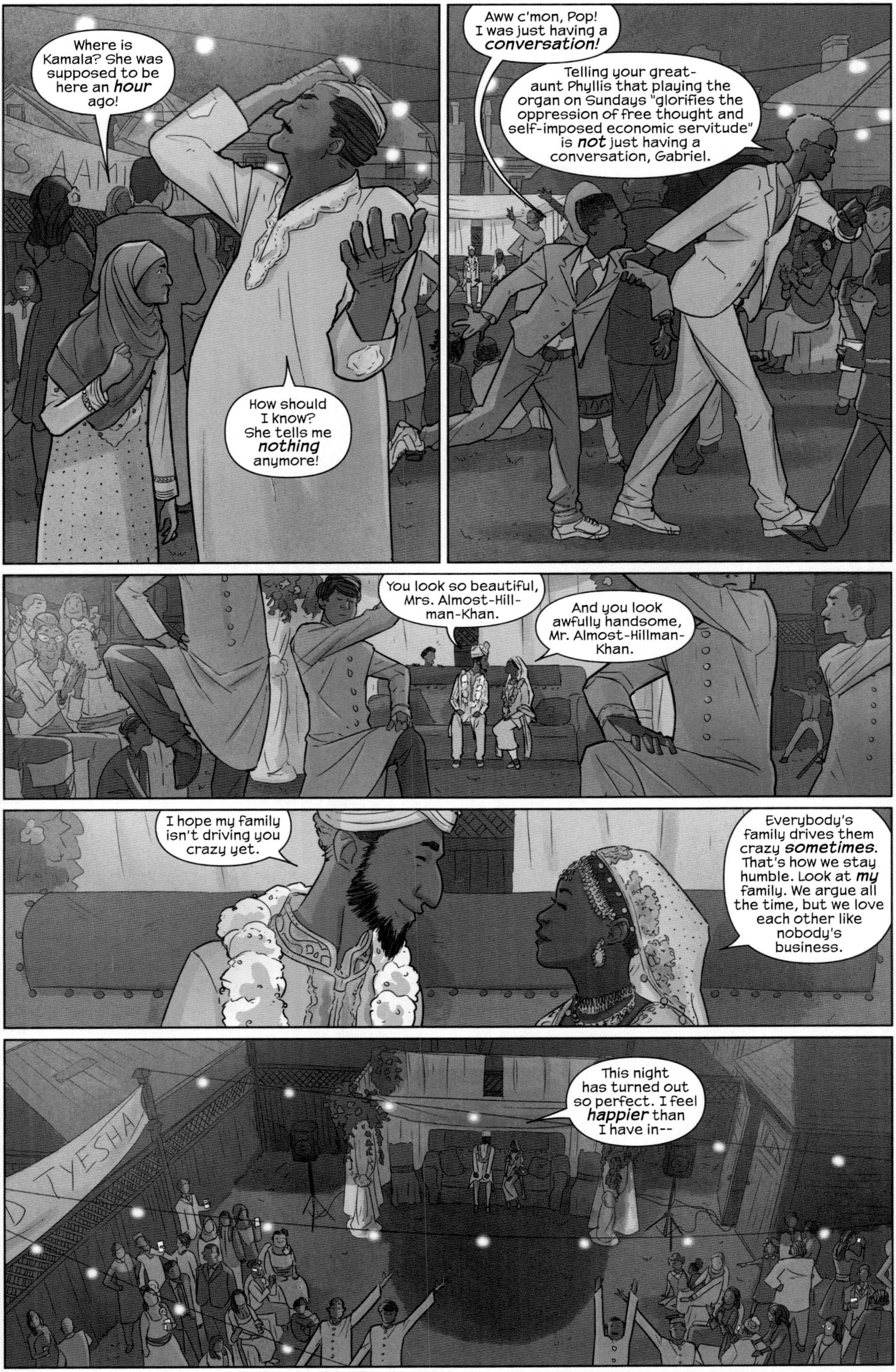

Where is Kamala? She was supposed to be here an *hour* ago!
How should I know? She tells me *nothing* anymore!
Aww c'mon, Pop! I was just having a *conversation!*
Telling your great-aunt Phyllis that playing the organ on Sundays "glorifies the oppression of free thought and self-imposed economic servitude" is *not* just having a conversation, Gabriel.
You look so beautiful, Mrs. Almost-Hill-man-Khan.
And you look awfully handsome, Mr. Almost-Hillman-Khan.
I hope my family isn't driving you crazy yet.
Everybody's family drives them crazy *sometimes*. That's how we stay humble. Look at *my* family. We argue all the time, but we love each other like nobody's business.
This night has turned out so perfect. I feel *happier* than I have in--

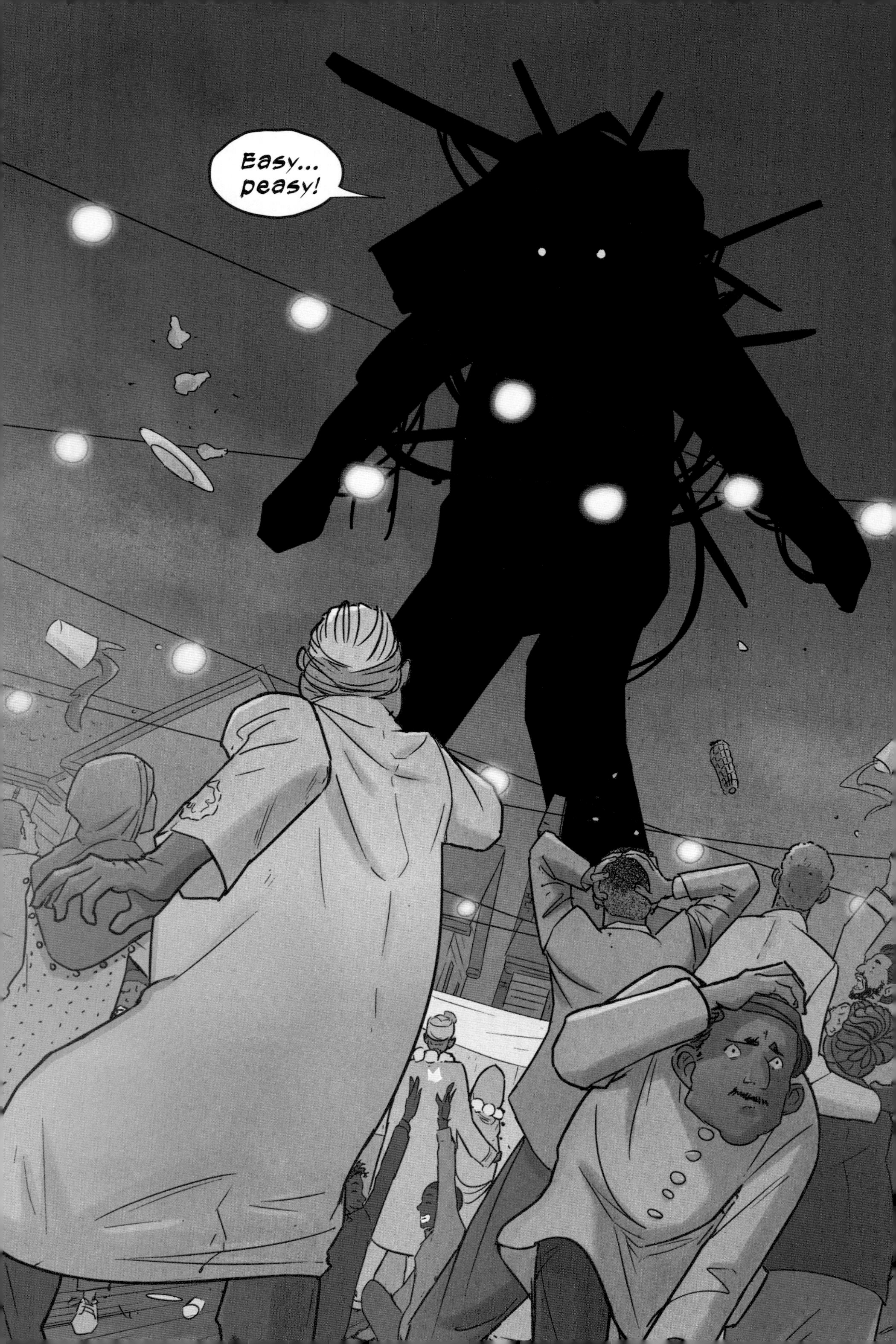
Easy... peasy!

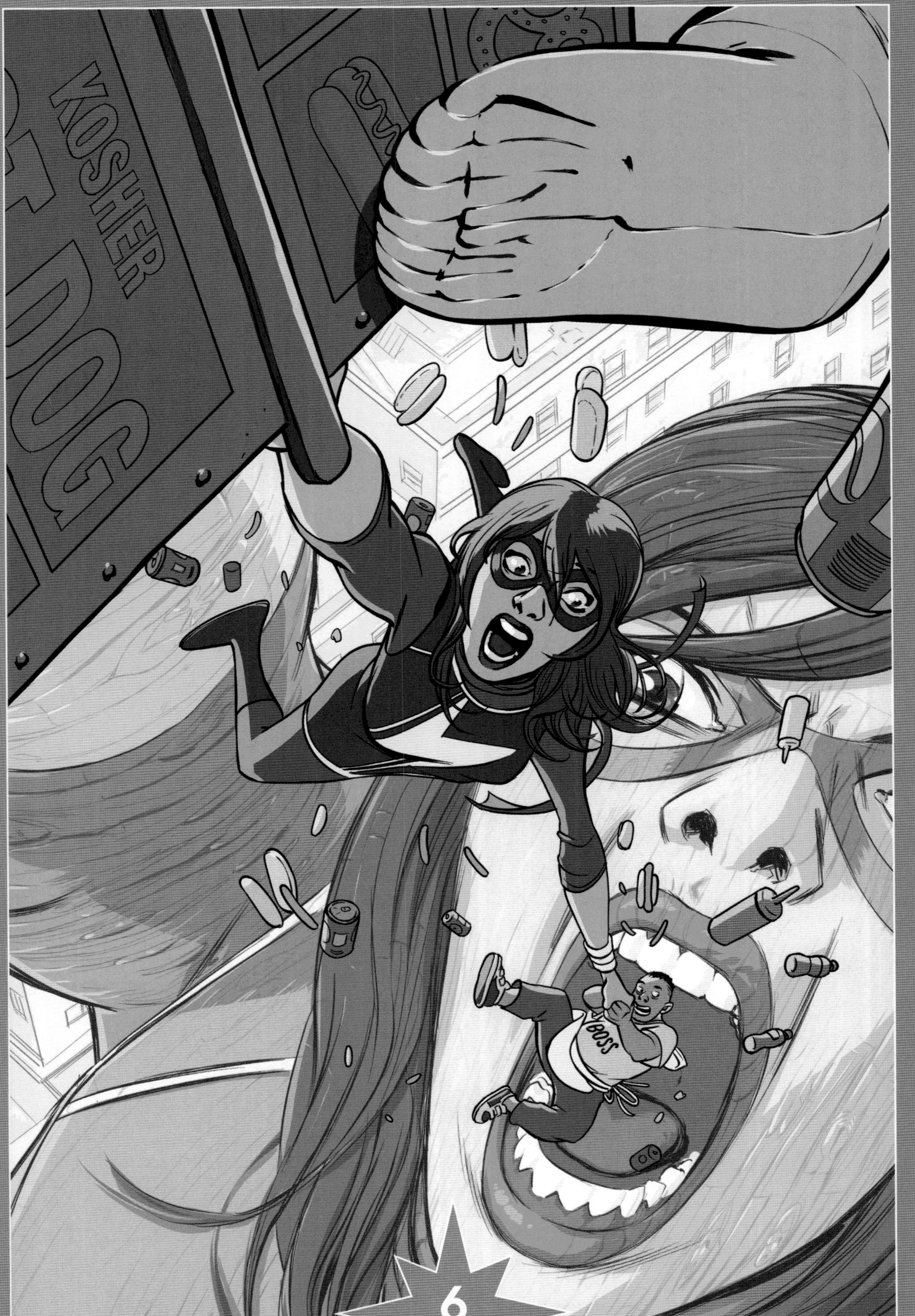
KOSHER
DOG
BOSS

6

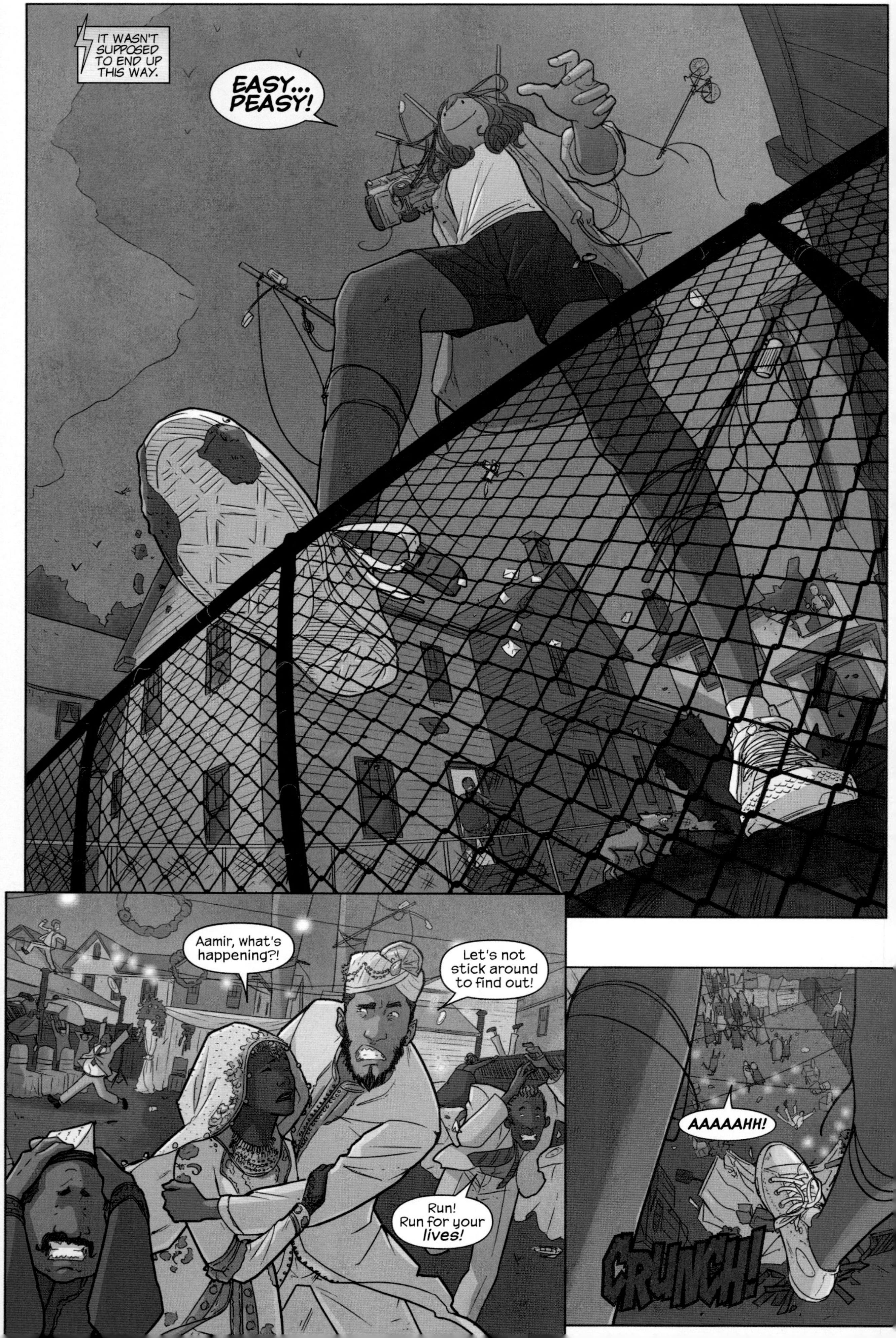
IT WASN'T SUPPOSED TO END UP THIS WAY.
EASY... PEASY!
Aamir, what's happening?!
Let's not stick around to find out!
Run! Run for your lives!
AAAAAHH!
CRUNCH!

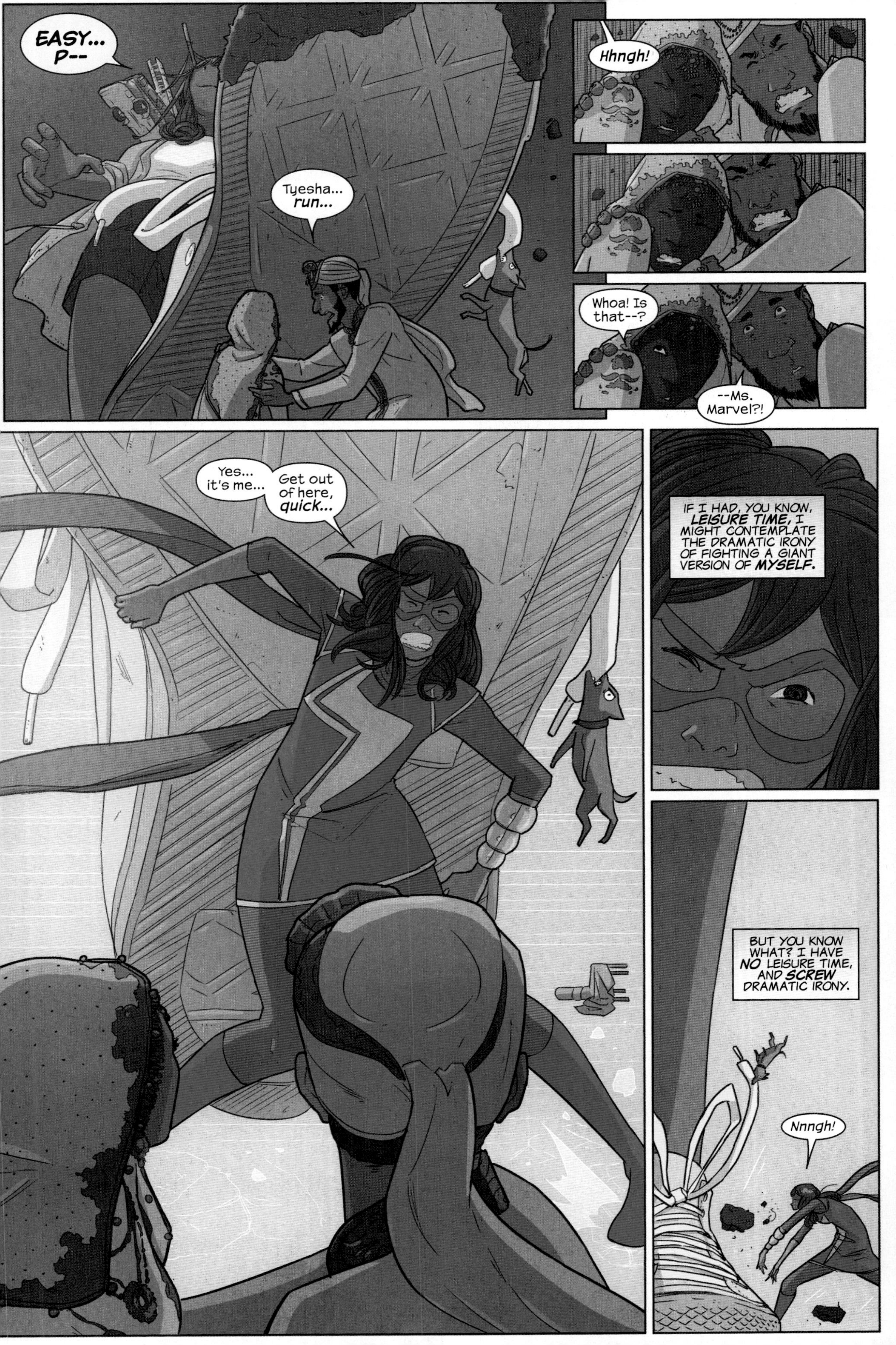
EASY... P--
Tyesha... run...
Hhngh!
Whoa! Is that--?
--Ms. Marvel?!
Yes... it's me...
Get out of here, quick...
IF I HAD, YOU KNOW, LEISURE TIME, I MIGHT CONTEMPLATE THE DRAMATIC IRONY OF FIGHTING A GIANT VERSION OF MYSELF.
BUT YOU KNOW WHAT? I HAVE NO LEISURE TIME, AND SCREW DRAMATIC IRONY.
Nnngh!

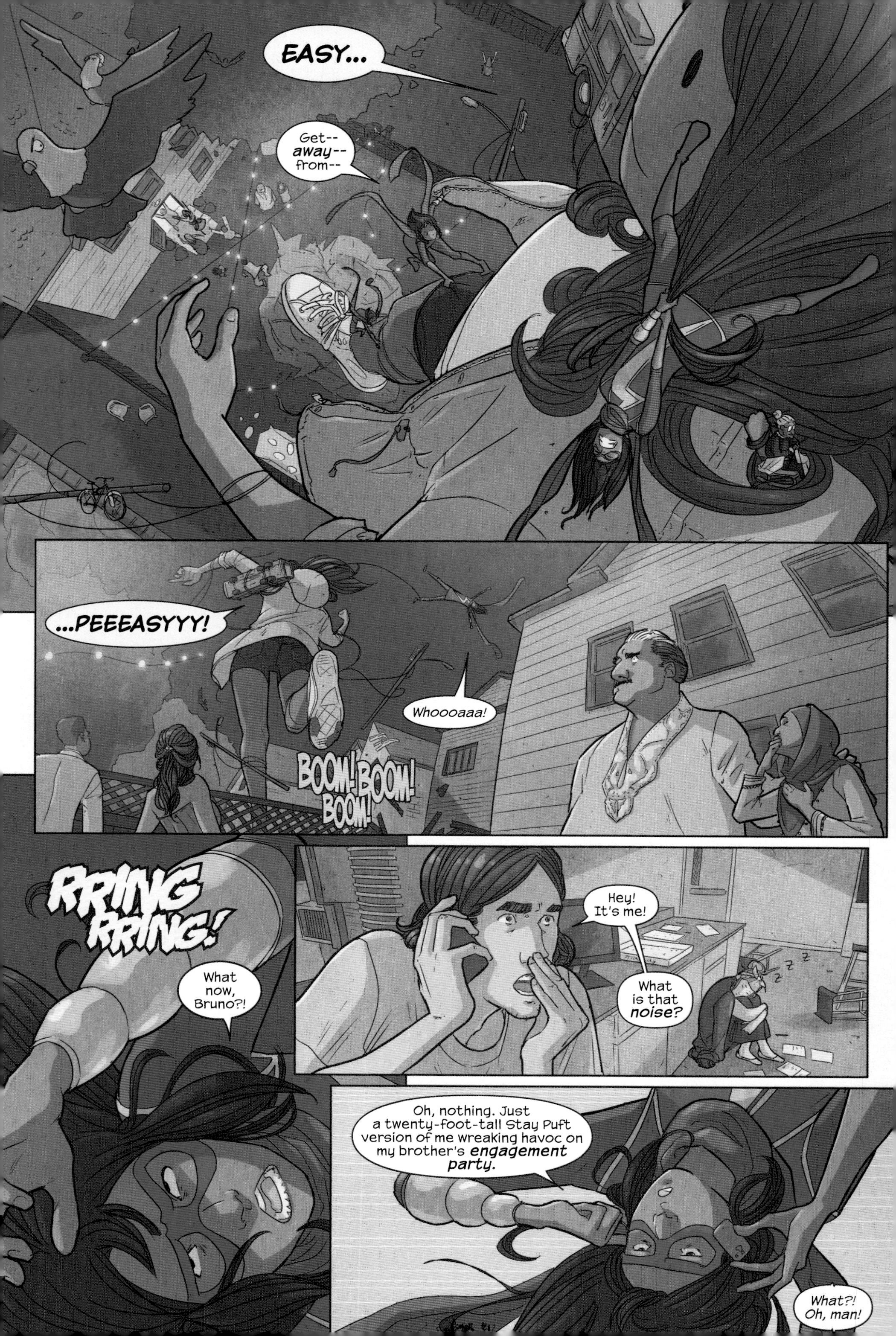
EASY...
Get-- away-- from--
...PEEEASYYY!
Whoooaaa!
BOOM! BOOM! BOOM!
RRING RRING!
What now, Bruno?!
Hey! It's me!
What is that noise?
Oh, nothing. Just a twenty-foot-tall Stay Puft version of me wreaking havoc on my brother's engagement party.
What?! Oh, man!

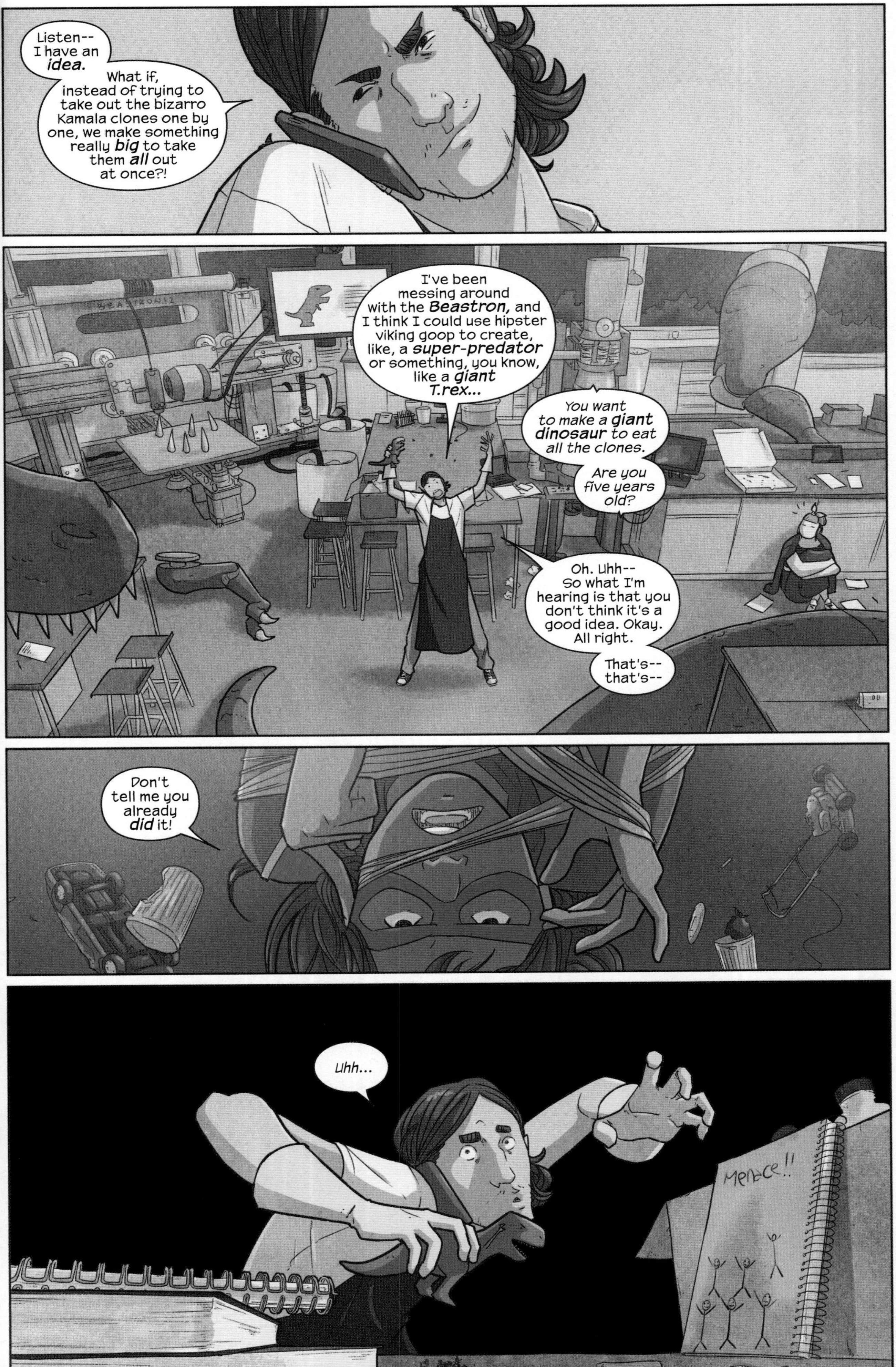
Listen-- I have an *idea.*
What if, instead of trying to take out the bizarro Kamala clones one by one, we make something really *big* to take them *all* out at once?!
I've been messing around with the *Beastron,* and I think I could use hipster viking goop to create, like, a *super-predator* or something, you know, like a *giant T.rex...*
You want to make a *giant dinosaur* to eat all the clones.
Are you five years old?
Oh. Uhh-- So what I'm hearing is that you don't think it's a good idea. Okay. All right.
That's-- that's--
Don't tell me you already *did* it!
Uhh...
Menace!!

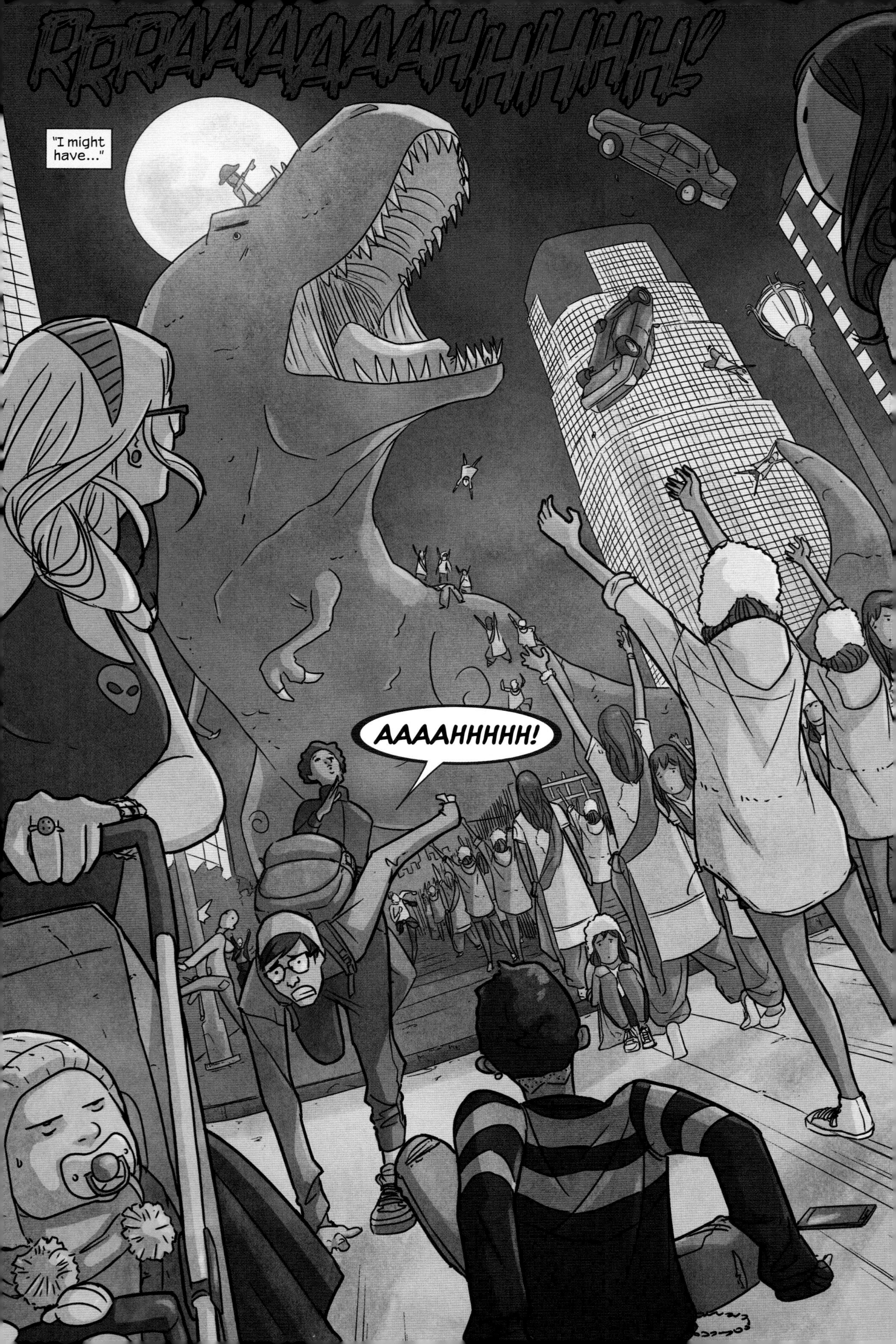
RRRAAAAAAHHHHH!
"I might have..."
AAAAHHHHH!

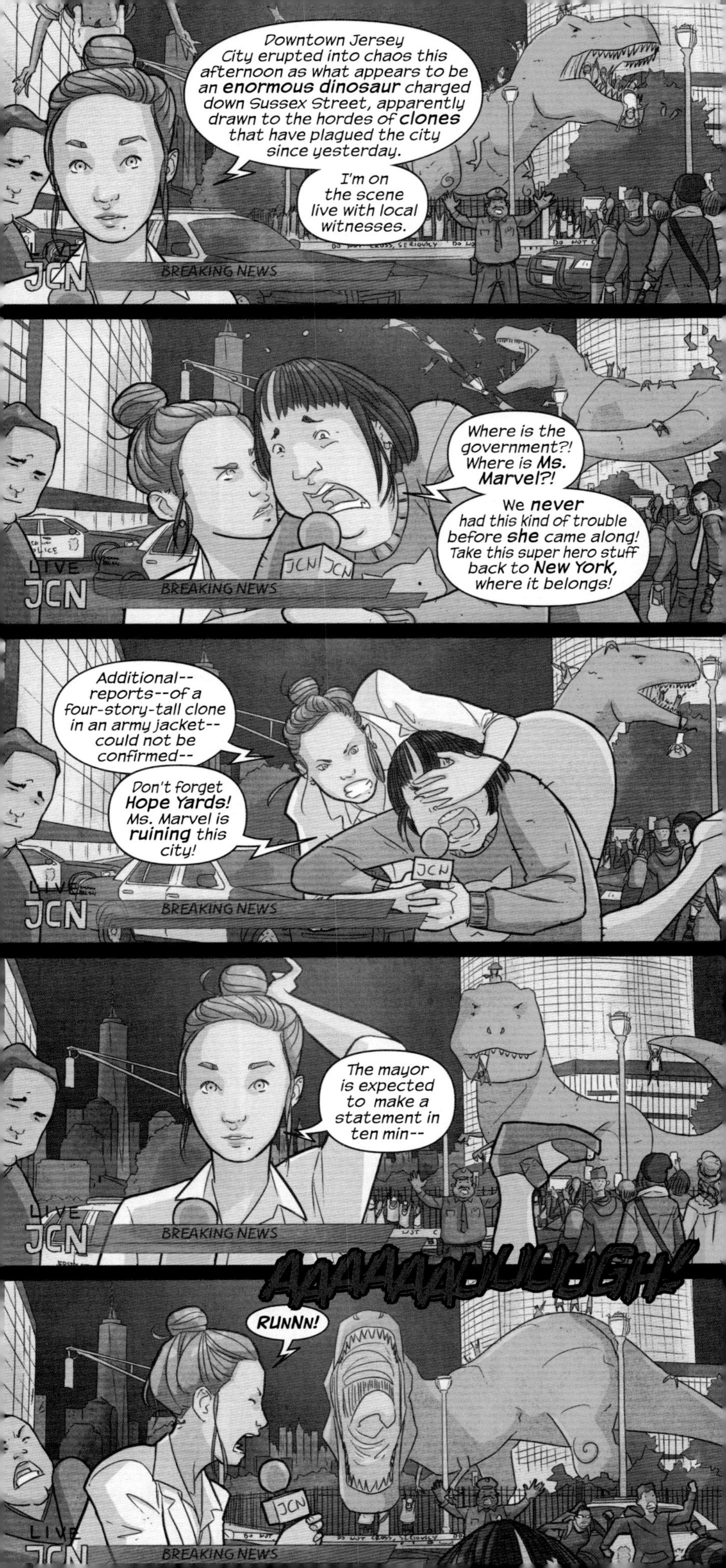
Downtown Jersey City erupted into chaos this afternoon as what appears to be an **enormous dinosaur** charged down Sussex Street, apparently drawn to the hordes of **clones** that have plagued the city since yesterday.
I'm on the scene live with local witnesses.
LIVE JCN
BREAKING NEWS
Where is the government?! Where is **Ms. Marvel**?!
We **never** had this kind of trouble before **she** came along! Take this super hero stuff back to **New York**, where it belongs!
LIVE JCN
BREAKING NEWS
Additional-- reports--of a four-story-tall clone in an army jacket-- could not be confirmed--
Don't forget **Hope Yards!** Ms. Marvel is **ruining** this city!
LIVE JCN
BREAKING NEWS
The mayor is expected to make a statement in ten min--
LIVE JCN
BREAKING NEWS
AAAAAAUUUUGH!
RUNNN!
LIVE JCN
BREAKING NEWS

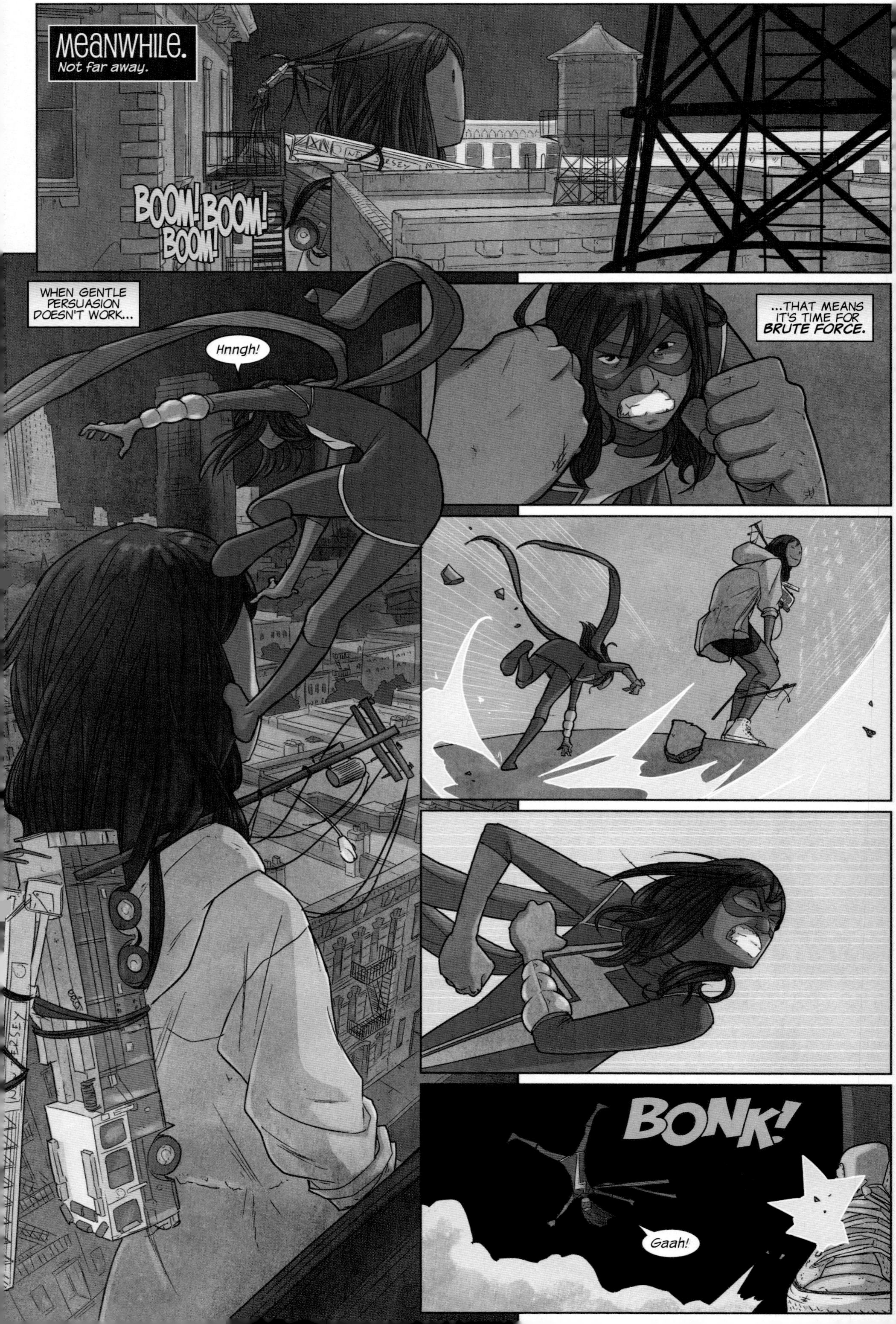
MEANWHILE.
Not far away.
BOOM! BOOM! BOOM!
WHEN GENTLE PERSUASION DOESN'T WORK...
Hnngh!
...THAT MEANS IT'S TIME FOR BRUTE FORCE.
BONK!
Gaah!

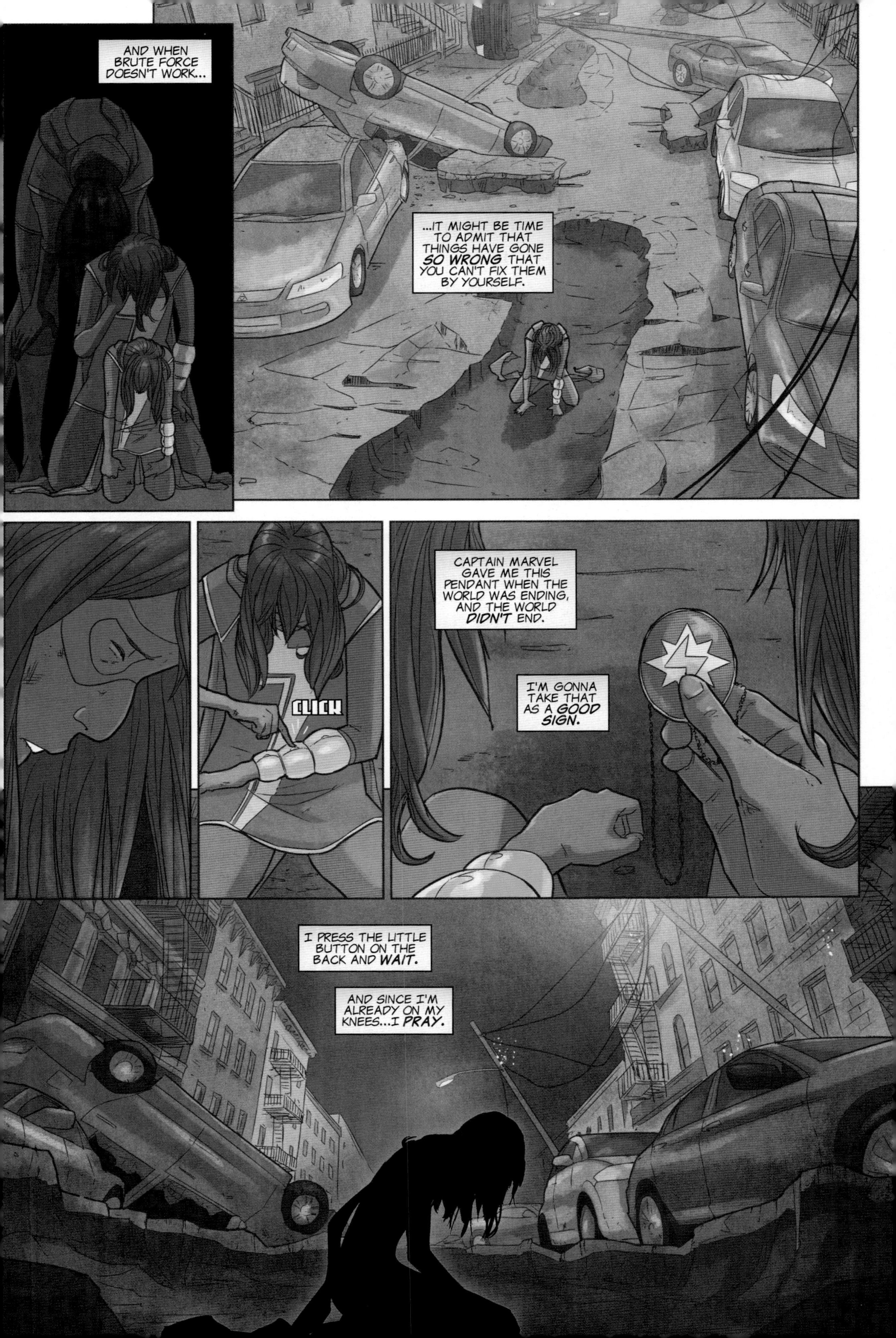
AND WHEN BRUTE FORCE DOESN'T WORK...
...IT MIGHT BE TIME TO ADMIT THAT THINGS HAVE GONE SO WRONG THAT YOU CAN'T FIX THEM BY YOURSELF.
CLICK
CAPTAIN MARVEL GAVE ME THIS PENDANT WHEN THE WORLD WAS ENDING, AND THE WORLD DIDN'T END.
I'M GONNA TAKE THAT AS A GOOD SIGN.
I PRESS THE LITTLE BUTTON ON THE BACK AND WAIT.
AND SINCE I'M ALREADY ON MY KNEES...I PRAY.

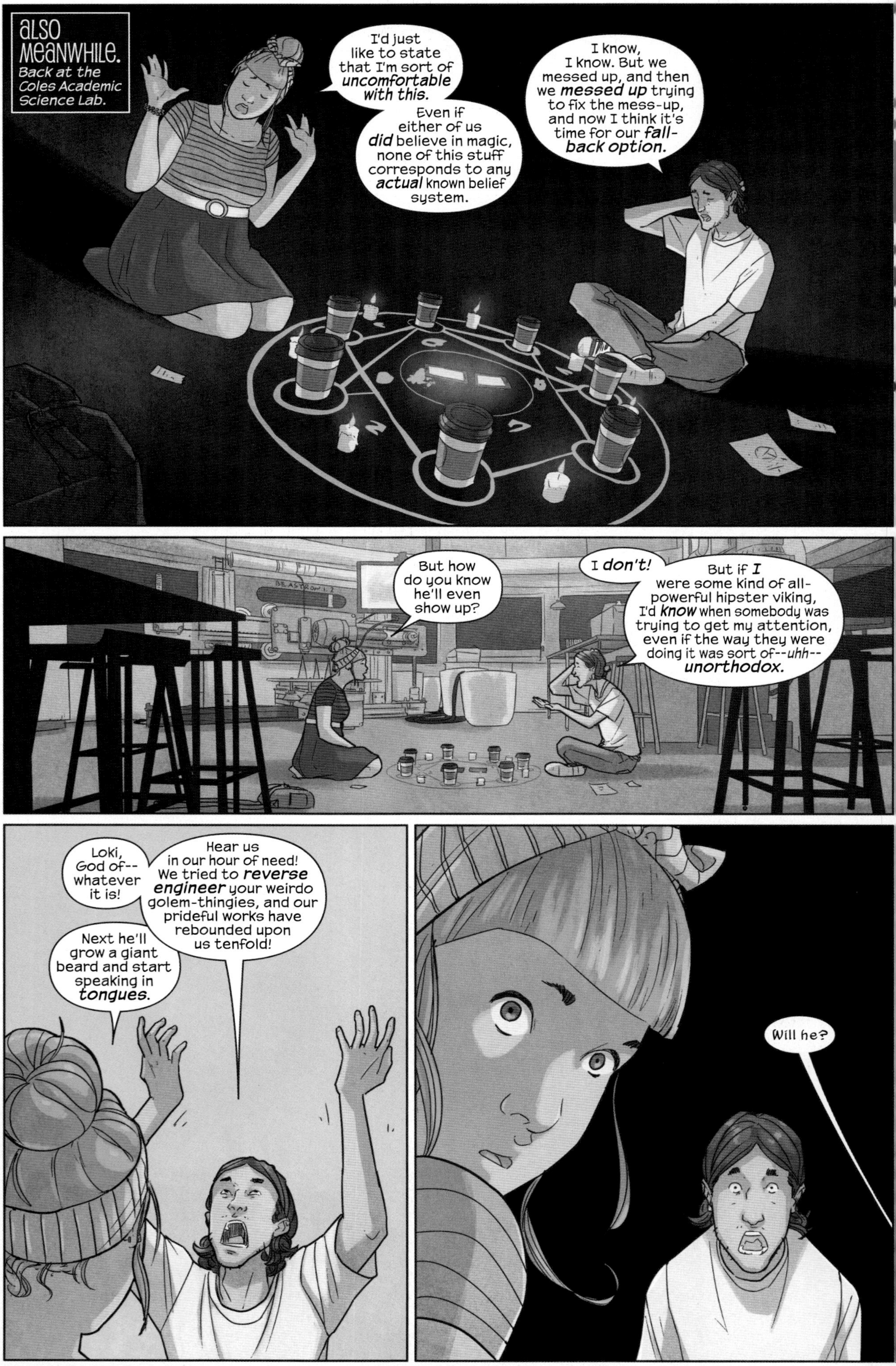
ALSO MEANWHILE. Back at the Coles Academic Science Lab.
I'd just like to state that I'm sort of *uncomfortable with this.*
Even if either of us *did* believe in magic, none of this stuff corresponds to any *actual* known belief system.
I know, I know. But we messed up, and then we *messed up* trying to fix the mess-up, and now I think it's time for our *fall-back option.*
But how do you know he'll even show up?
I *don't!*
But if *I* were some kind of all-powerful hipster viking, I'd *know* when somebody was trying to get my attention, even if the way they were doing it was sort of--*uhh*--*unorthodox.*
Loki, God of-- whatever it is!
Hear us in our hour of need! We tried to *reverse engineer* your weirdo golem-thingies, and our prideful works have rebounded upon us tenfold!
Next he'll grow a giant beard and start speaking in *tongues*.
Will he?

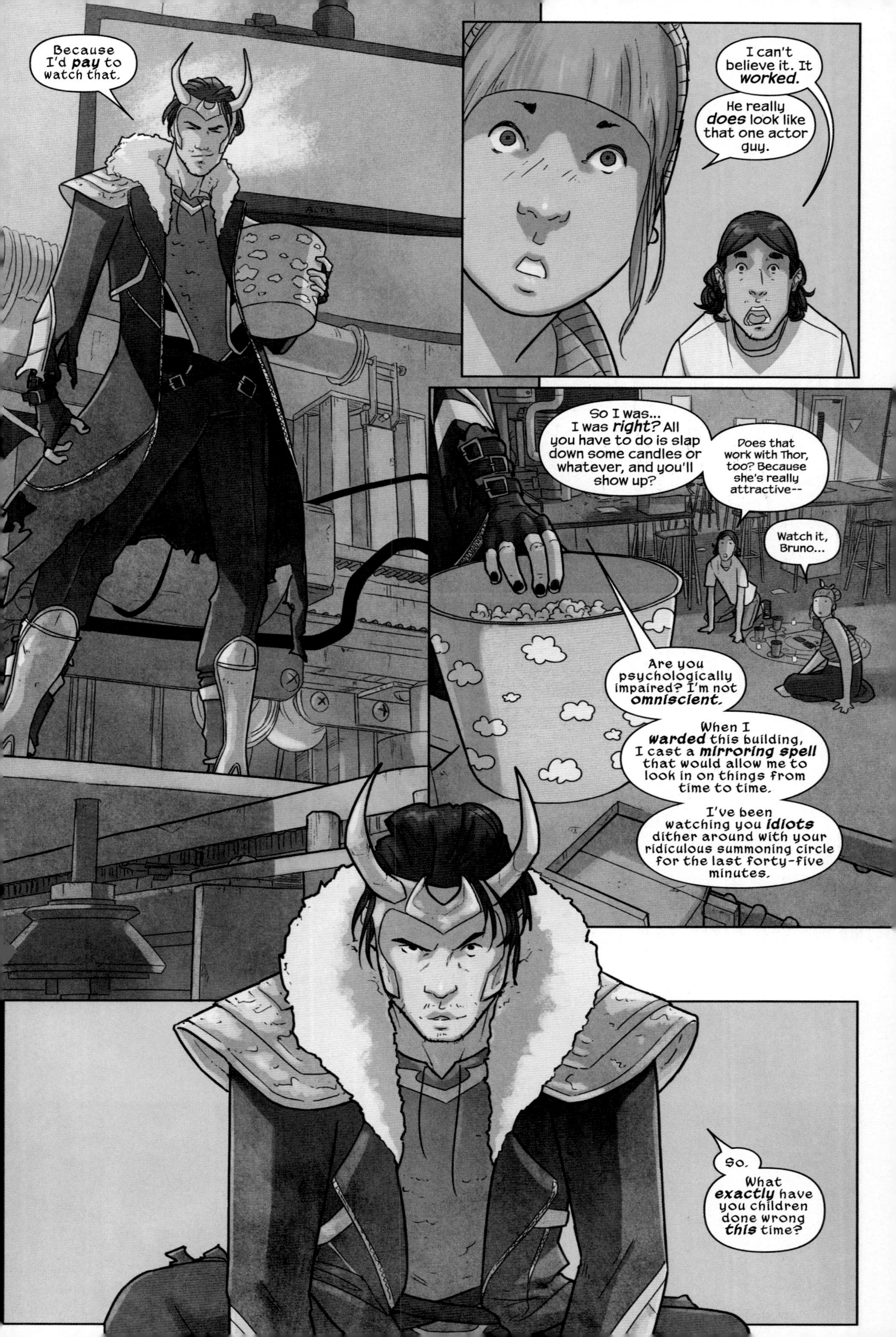
Because I'd **pay** to watch that.
I can't believe it. It **worked.**
He really **does** look like that one actor guy.
So I was... I was **right?** All you have to do is slap down some candles or whatever, and you'll show up?
Does that work with Thor, too? Because she's really attractive--
Watch it, Bruno...
Are you psychologically impaired? I'm not **omniscient.**
When I **warded** this building, I cast a **mirroring spell** that would allow me to look in on things from time to time.
I've been watching you **idiots** dither around with your ridiculous summoning circle for the last forty-five minutes.
So.
What **exactly** have you children done wrong **this** time?

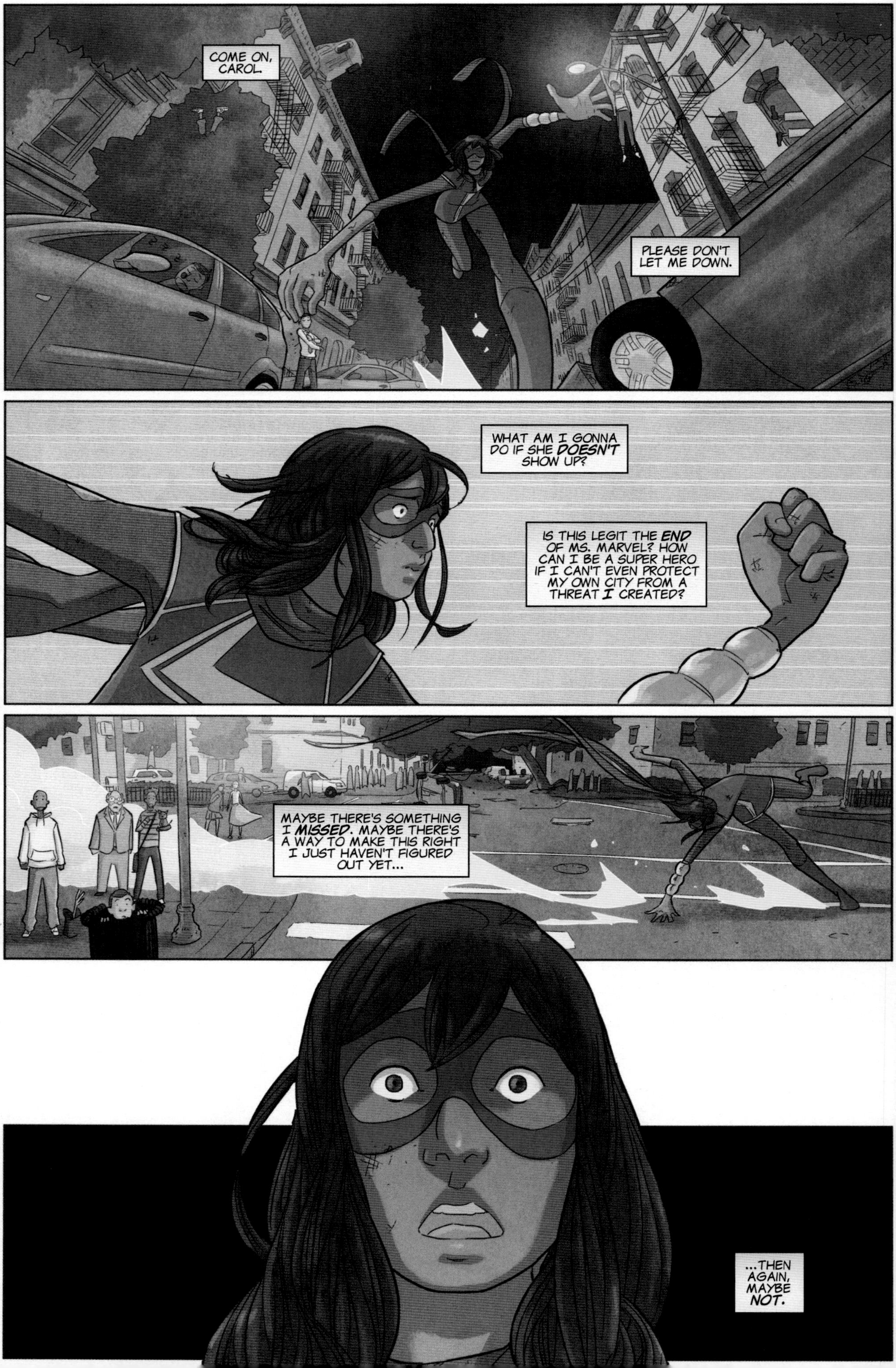
COME ON, CAROL.
PLEASE DON'T LET ME DOWN.
WHAT AM I GONNA DO IF SHE DOESN'T SHOW UP?
IS THIS LEGIT THE END OF MS. MARVEL? HOW CAN I BE A SUPER HERO IF I CAN'T EVEN PROTECT MY OWN CITY FROM A THREAT I CREATED?
MAYBE THERE'S SOMETHING I MISSED. MAYBE THERE'S A WAY TO MAKE THIS RIGHT I JUST HAVEN'T FIGURED OUT YET...
...THEN AGAIN, MAYBE NOT.

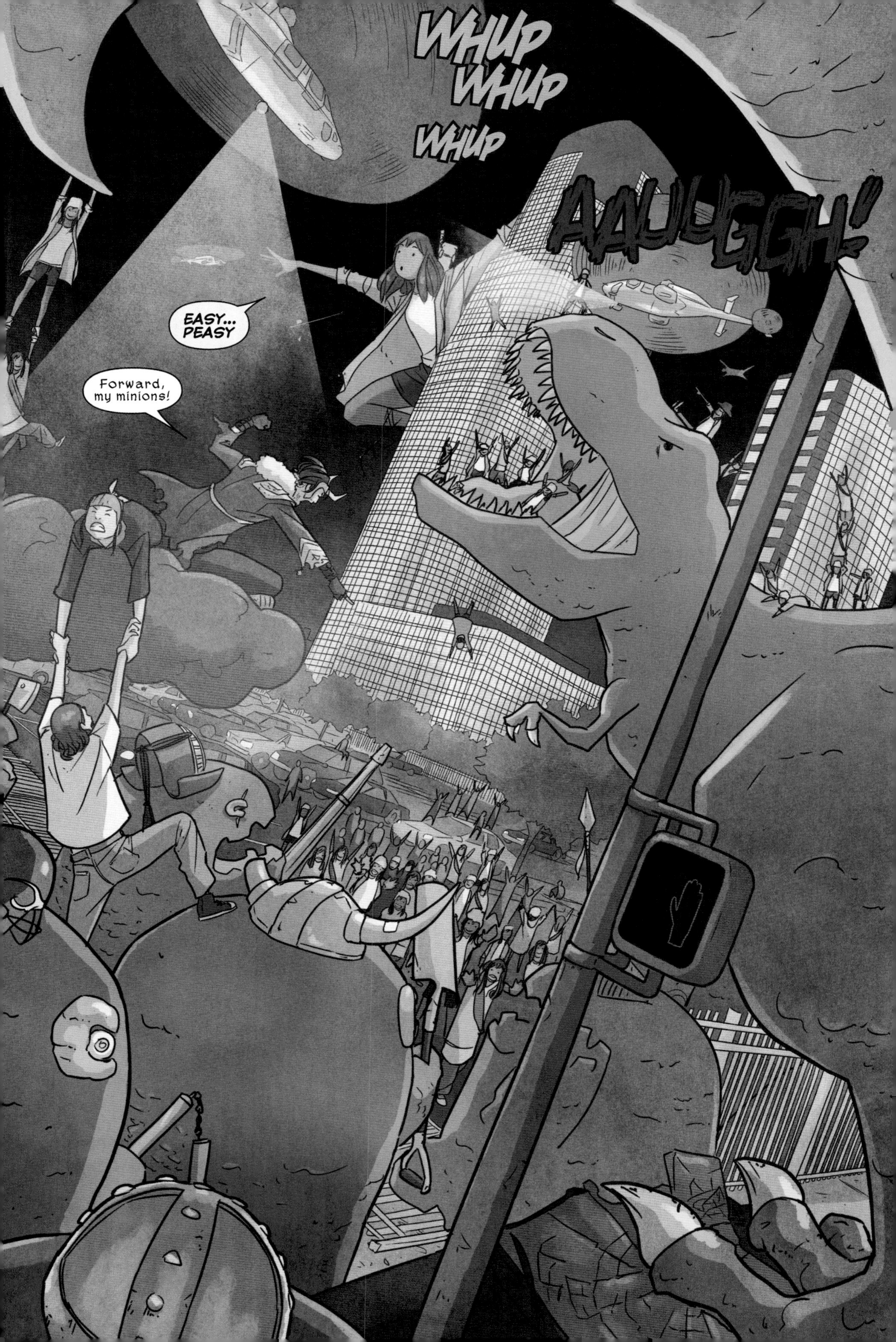
WHUP
WHUP
WHUP
AAUUGGH!
EASY... PEASY
Forward, my minions!

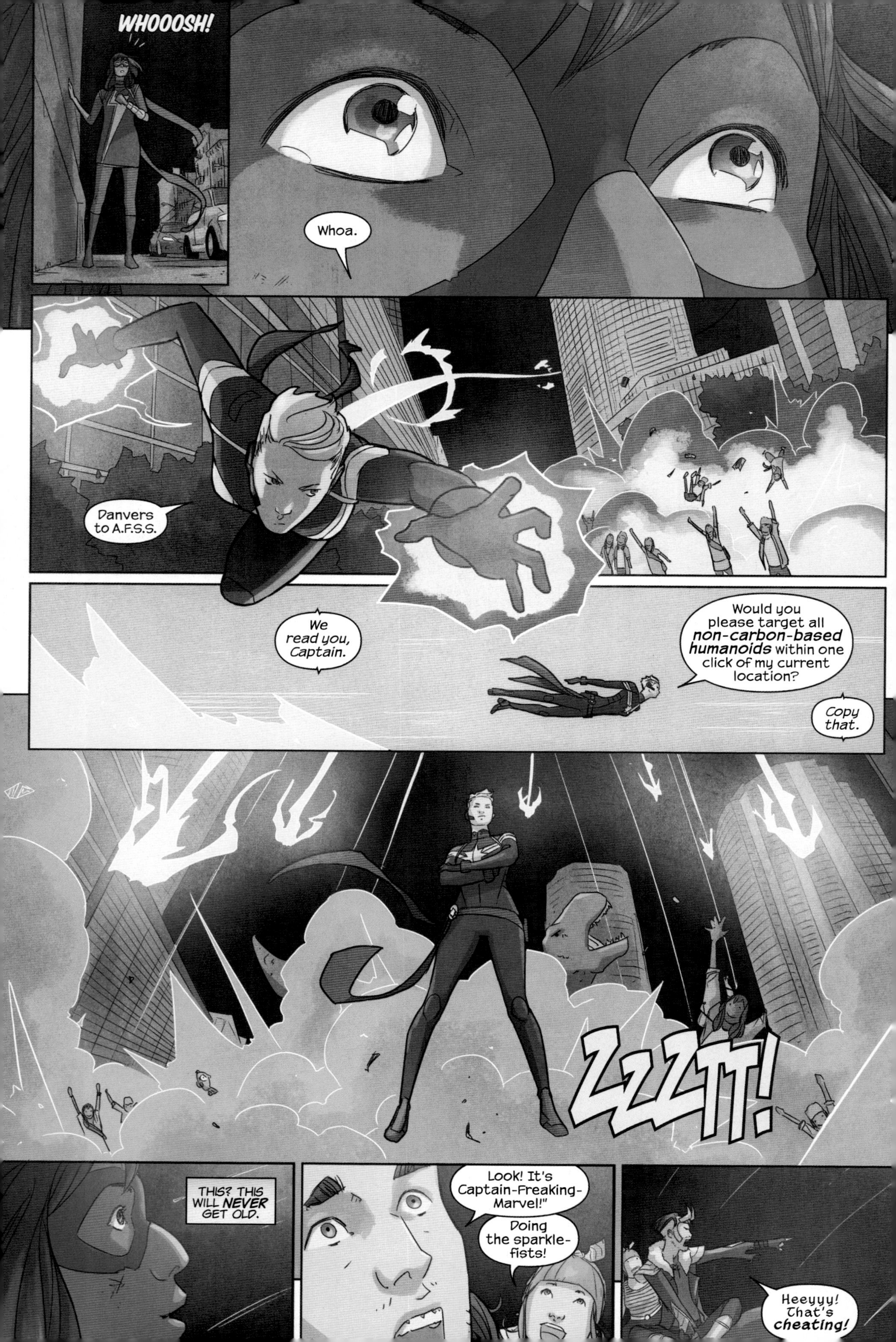
WHOOOSH!
Whoa.
Danvers to A.F.S.S.
We read you, Captain.
Would you please target all **non-carbon-based humanoids** within one click of my current location?
Copy that.
ZZZTT!
THIS? THIS WILL **NEVER** GET OLD.
Look! It's Captain-Freaking-Marvel!"
Doing the sparkle-fists!
Heeyyy! That's **cheating!**

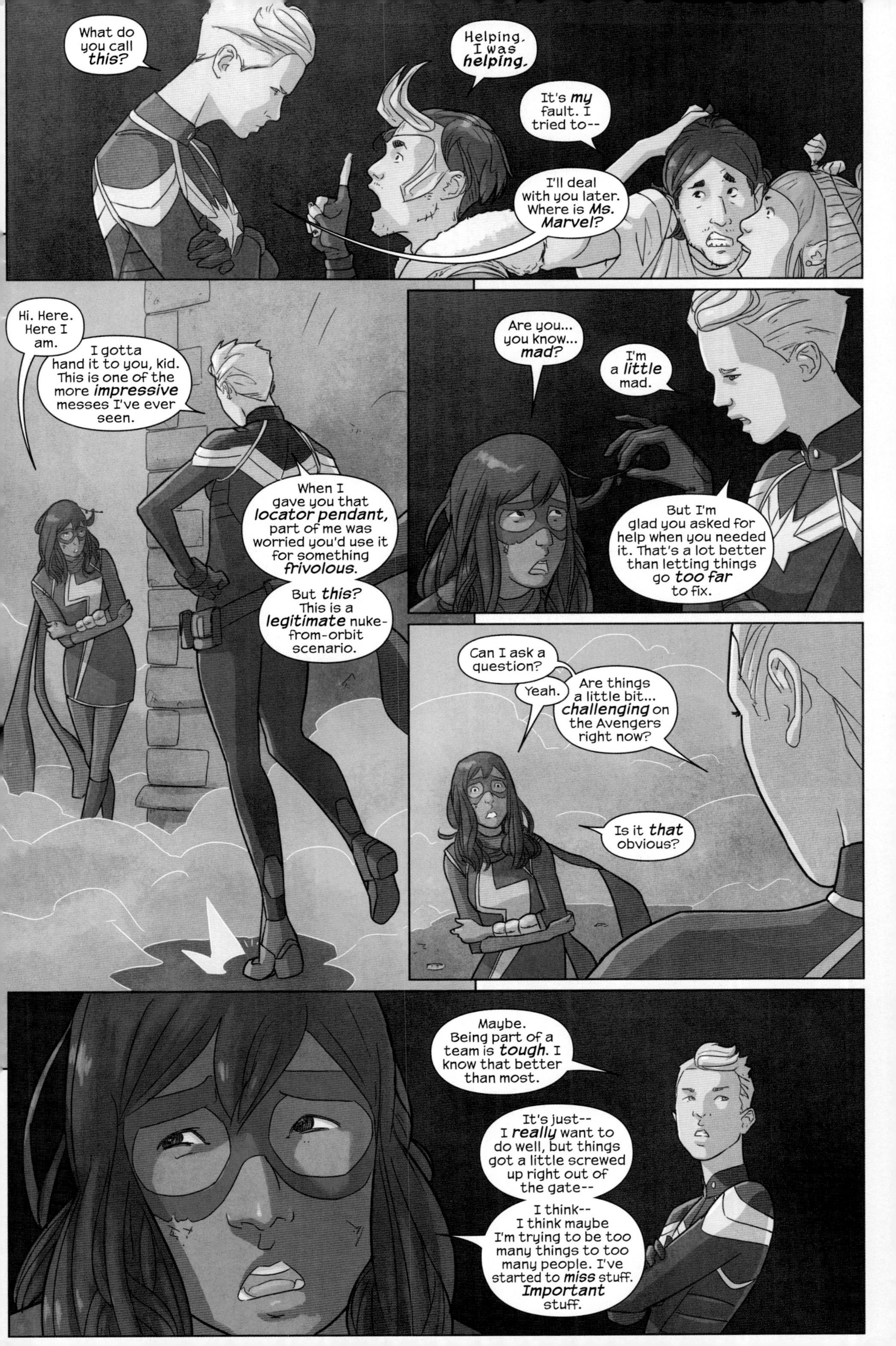
What do you call *this?*
Helping. I was *helping.*
It's *my* fault. I tried to--
I'll deal with you later. Where is *Ms. Marvel?*
Hi. Here. Here I am.
I gotta hand it to you, kid. This is one of the more *impressive* messes I've ever seen.
When I gave you that *locator pendant,* part of me was worried you'd use it for something *frivolous.*
But *this?* This is a *legitimate* nuke-from-orbit scenario.
Are you... you know... *mad?*
I'm a *little* mad.
But I'm glad you asked for help when you needed it. That's a lot better than letting things go *too far* to fix.
Can I ask a question?
Yeah.
Are things a little bit... *challenging* on the Avengers right now?
Is it *that* obvious?
Maybe. Being part of a team is *tough.* I know that better than most.
It's just-- I *really* want to do well, but things got a little screwed up right out of the gate--
I think-- I think maybe I'm trying to be too many things to too many people. I've started to *miss* stuff. *Important* stuff.

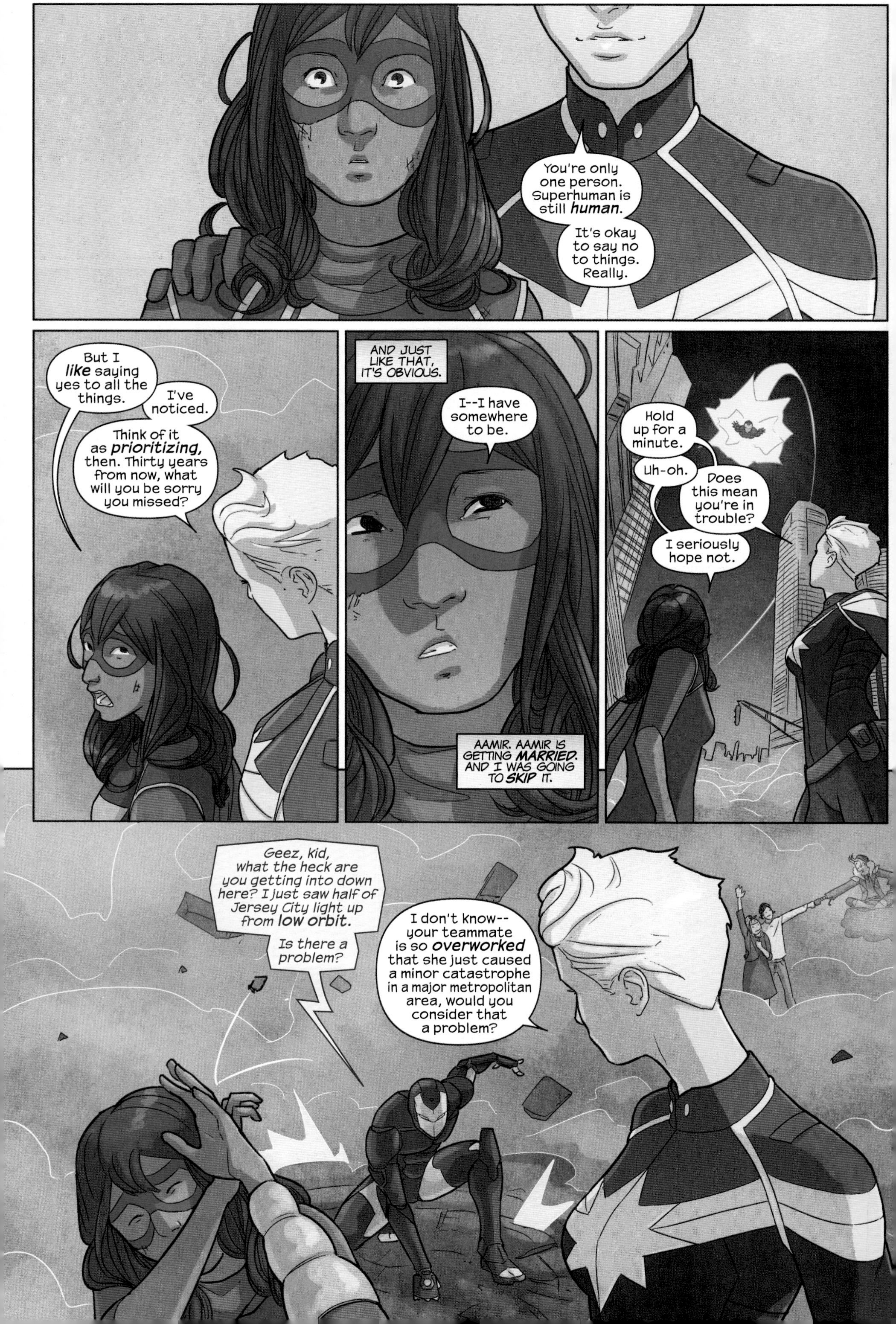
You're only one person. Superhuman is still *human*.
It's okay to say no to things. Really.
But I *like* saying yes to all the things.
I've noticed.
Think of it as *prioritizing,* then. Thirty years from now, what will you be sorry you missed?
AND JUST LIKE THAT, IT'S OBVIOUS.
I--I have somewhere to be.
AAMIR. AAMIR IS GETTING *MARRIED*. AND I WAS GOING TO *SKIP* IT.
Hold up for a minute.
Uh-oh.
Does this mean you're in trouble?
I seriously hope not.
Geez, kid, what the heck are you getting into down here? I just saw half of Jersey City light up from *low orbit*.
Is there a problem?
I don't know-- your teammate is so *overworked* that she just caused a minor catastrophe in a major metropolitan area, would you consider that a problem?

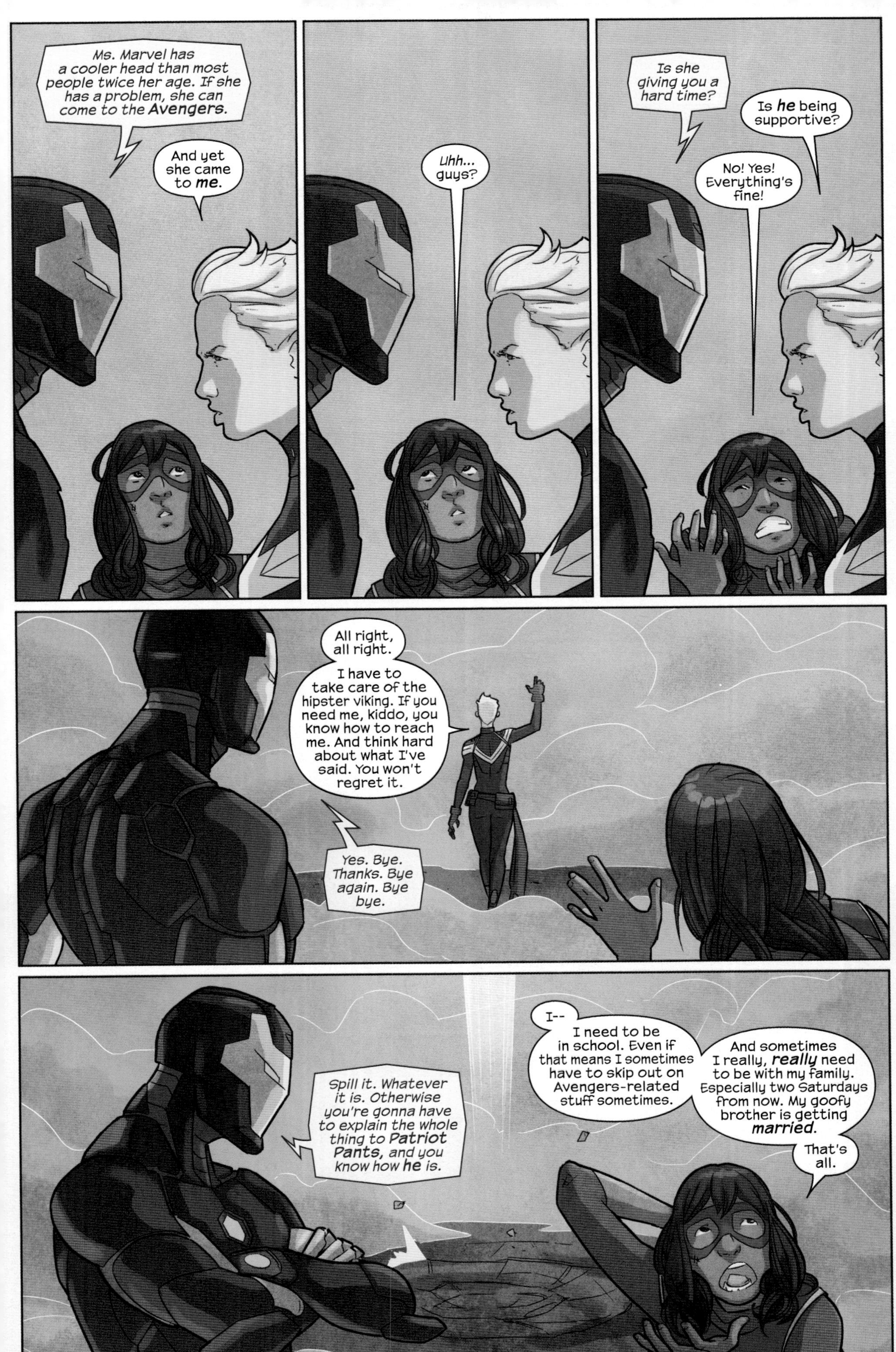

Ms. Marvel has a cooler head than most people twice her age. If she has a problem, she can come to the Avengers.
And yet she came to me.
Uhh... guys?
Is she giving you a hard time?
Is he being supportive?
No! Yes! Everything's fine!
All right, all right.
I have to take care of the hipster viking. If you need me, kiddo, you know how to reach me. And think hard about what I've said. You won't regret it.
Yes. Bye. Thanks. Bye again. Bye bye.
Spill it. Whatever it is. Otherwise you're gonna have to explain the whole thing to Patriot Pants, and you know how he is.
I--
I need to be in school. Even if that means I sometimes have to skip out on Avengers-related stuff sometimes.
And sometimes I really, really need to be with my family. Especially two Saturdays from now. My goofy brother is getting married.
That's all.

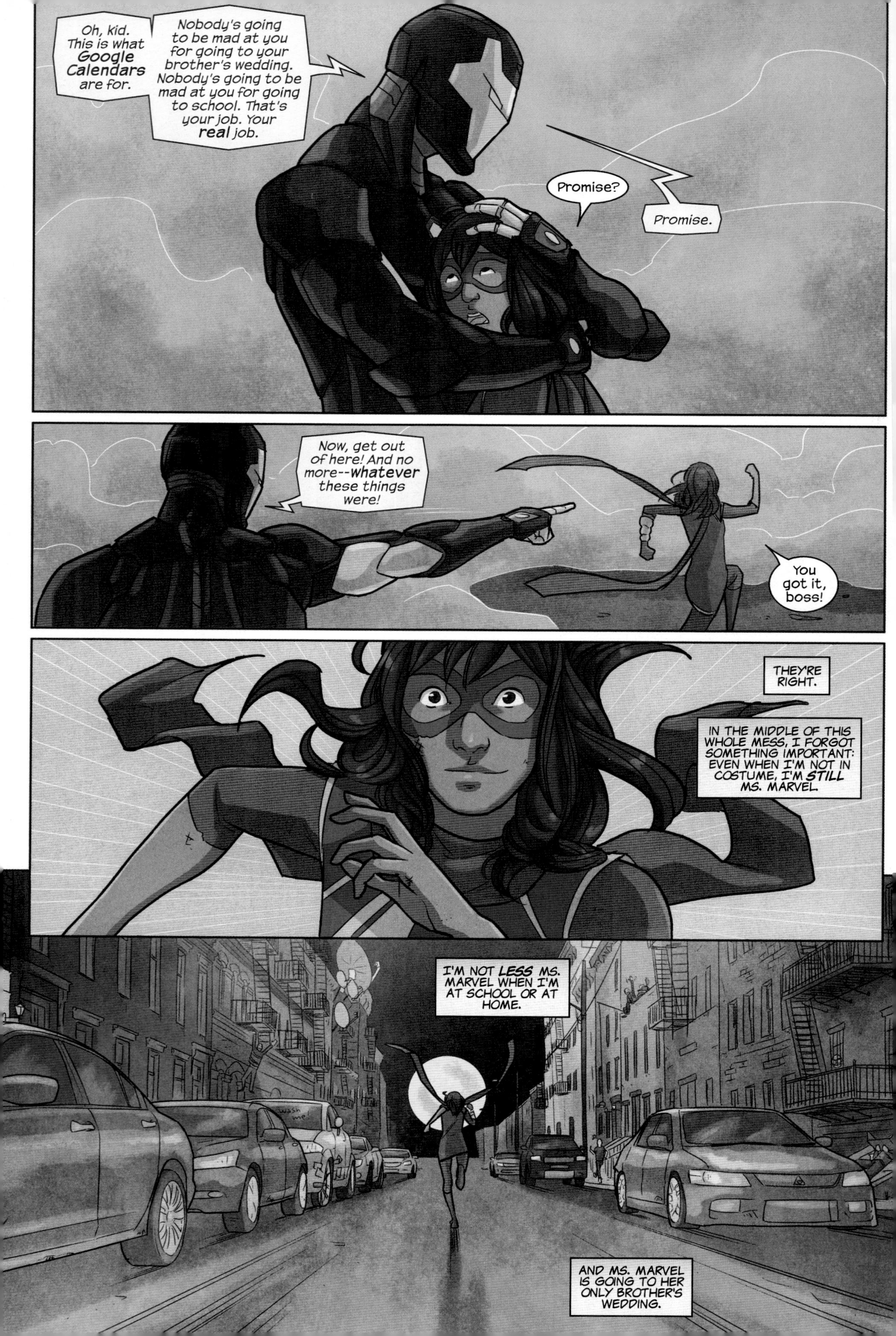
Oh, kid. This is what Google Calendars are for.
Nobody's going to be mad at you for going to your brother's wedding. Nobody's going to be mad at you for going to school. That's your job. Your real job.
Promise?
Promise.
Now, get out of here! And no more--whatever these things were!
You got it, boss!
THEY'RE RIGHT.
IN THE MIDDLE OF THIS WHOLE MESS, I FORGOT SOMETHING IMPORTANT: EVEN WHEN I'M NOT IN COSTUME, I'M STILL MS. MARVEL.
I'M NOT LESS MS. MARVEL WHEN I'M AT SCHOOL OR AT HOME.
AND MS. MARVEL IS GOING TO HER ONLY BROTHER'S WEDDING.

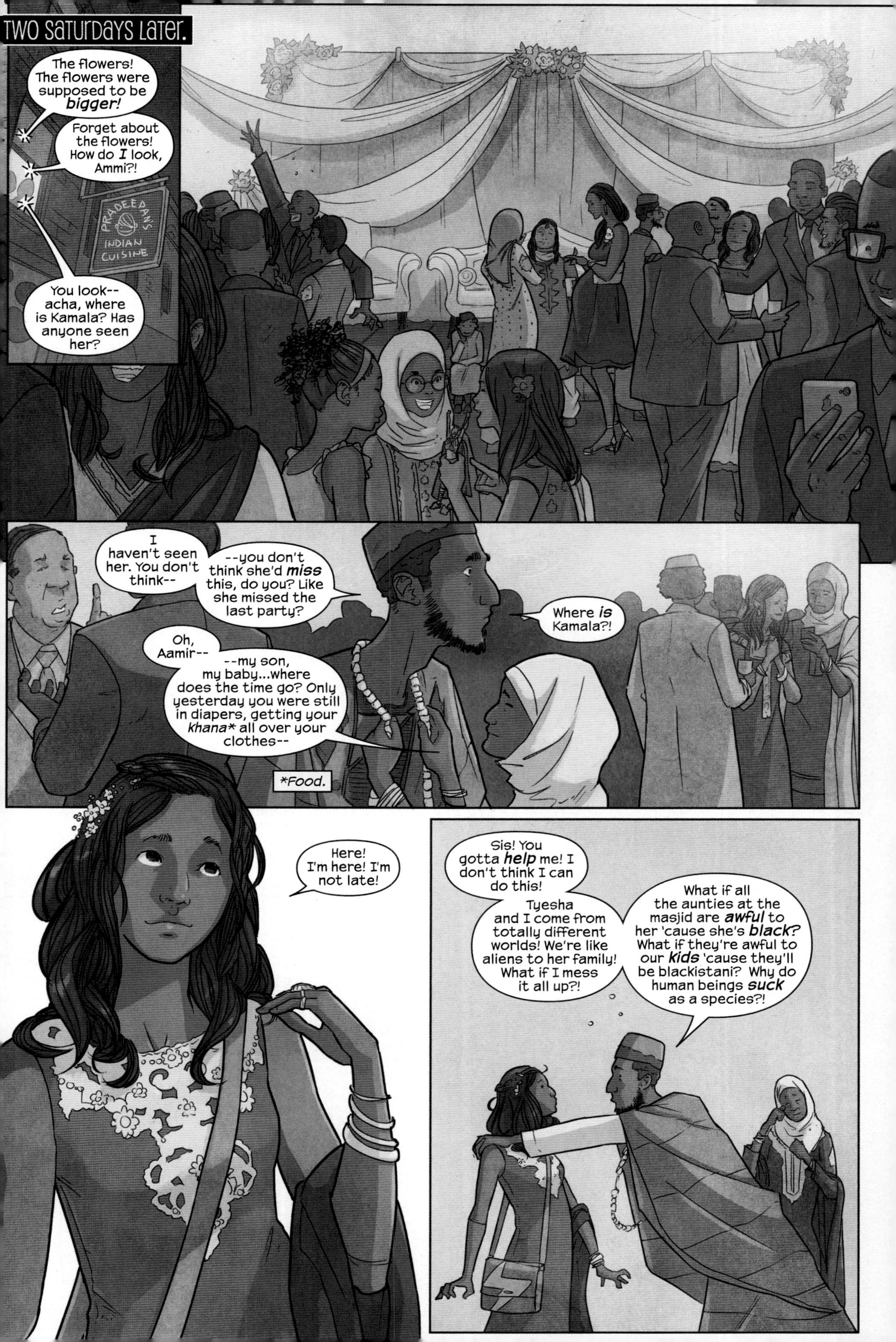
TWO SATURDAYS LATER.
The flowers! The flowers were supposed to be bigger!
Forget about the flowers! How do I look, Ammi?!
PRADEEPAN'S INDIAN CUISINE
You look--acha, where is Kamala? Has anyone seen her?
I haven't seen her. You don't think--
--you don't think she'd miss this, do you? Like she missed the last party?
Where is Kamala?!
Oh, Aamir--
--my son, my baby...where does the time go? Only yesterday you were still in diapers, getting your khana* all over your clothes--
*Food.
Here! I'm here! I'm not late!
Sis! You gotta help me! I don't think I can do this!
Tyesha and I come from totally different worlds! We're like aliens to her family! What if I mess it all up?!
What if all the aunties at the masjid are awful to her 'cause she's black? What if they're awful to our kids 'cause they'll be blackistani? Why do human beings suck as a species?!

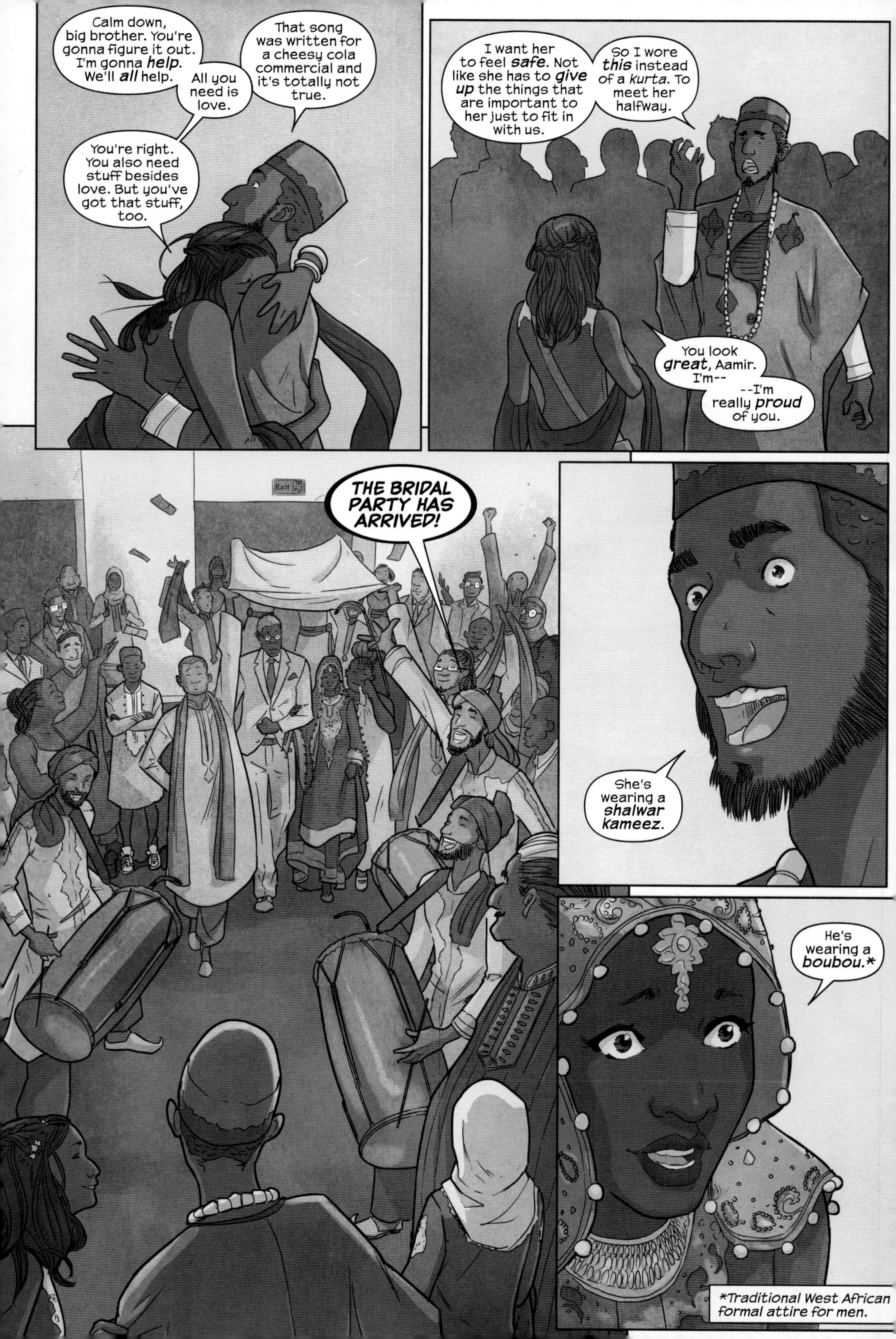
Calm down, big brother. You're gonna figure it out. I'm gonna *help*. We'll *all* help.
All you need is love.
That song was written for a cheesy cola commercial and it's totally not true.
You're right. You also need stuff besides love. But you've got that stuff, too.
I want her to feel *safe*. Not like she has to *give up* the things that are important to her just to fit in with us.
So I wore *this* instead of a *kurta*. To meet her halfway.
You look *great*, Aamir. I'm--
--I'm really *proud* of you.
THE BRIDAL PARTY HAS ARRIVED!
She's wearing a *shalwar kameez*.
He's wearing a *boubou*.*
*Traditional West African formal attire for men.

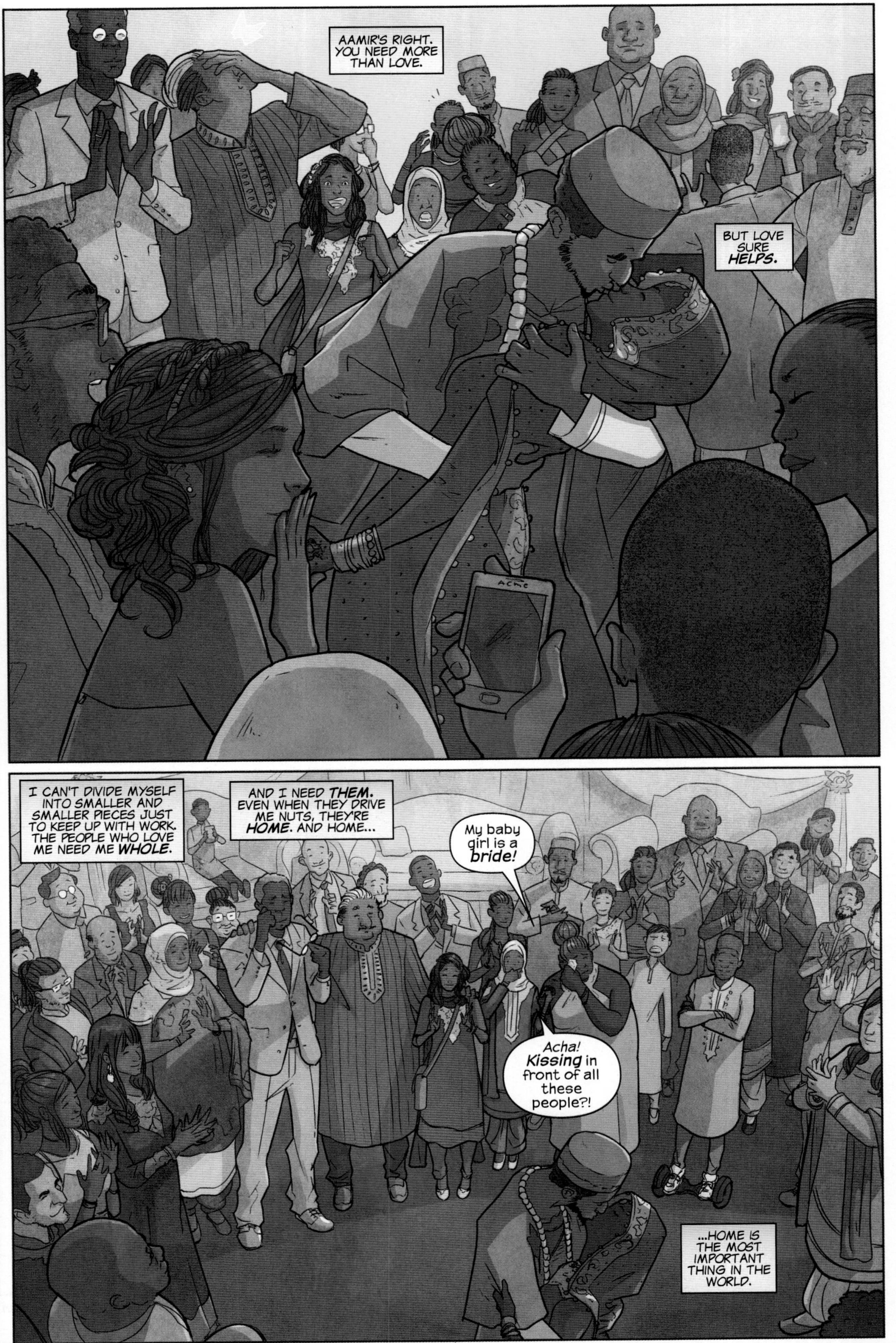
AAMIR'S RIGHT. YOU NEED MORE THAN LOVE.
BUT LOVE SURE *HELPS*.
I CAN'T DIVIDE MYSELF INTO SMALLER AND SMALLER PIECES JUST TO KEEP UP WITH WORK. THE PEOPLE WHO LOVE ME NEED ME *WHOLE*.
AND I NEED *THEM*. EVEN WHEN THEY DRIVE ME NUTS, THEY'RE *HOME*. AND HOME...
My baby girl is a *bride!*
Acha! **Kissing** in front of all these people?!
...HOME IS THE MOST IMPORTANT THING IN THE WORLD.

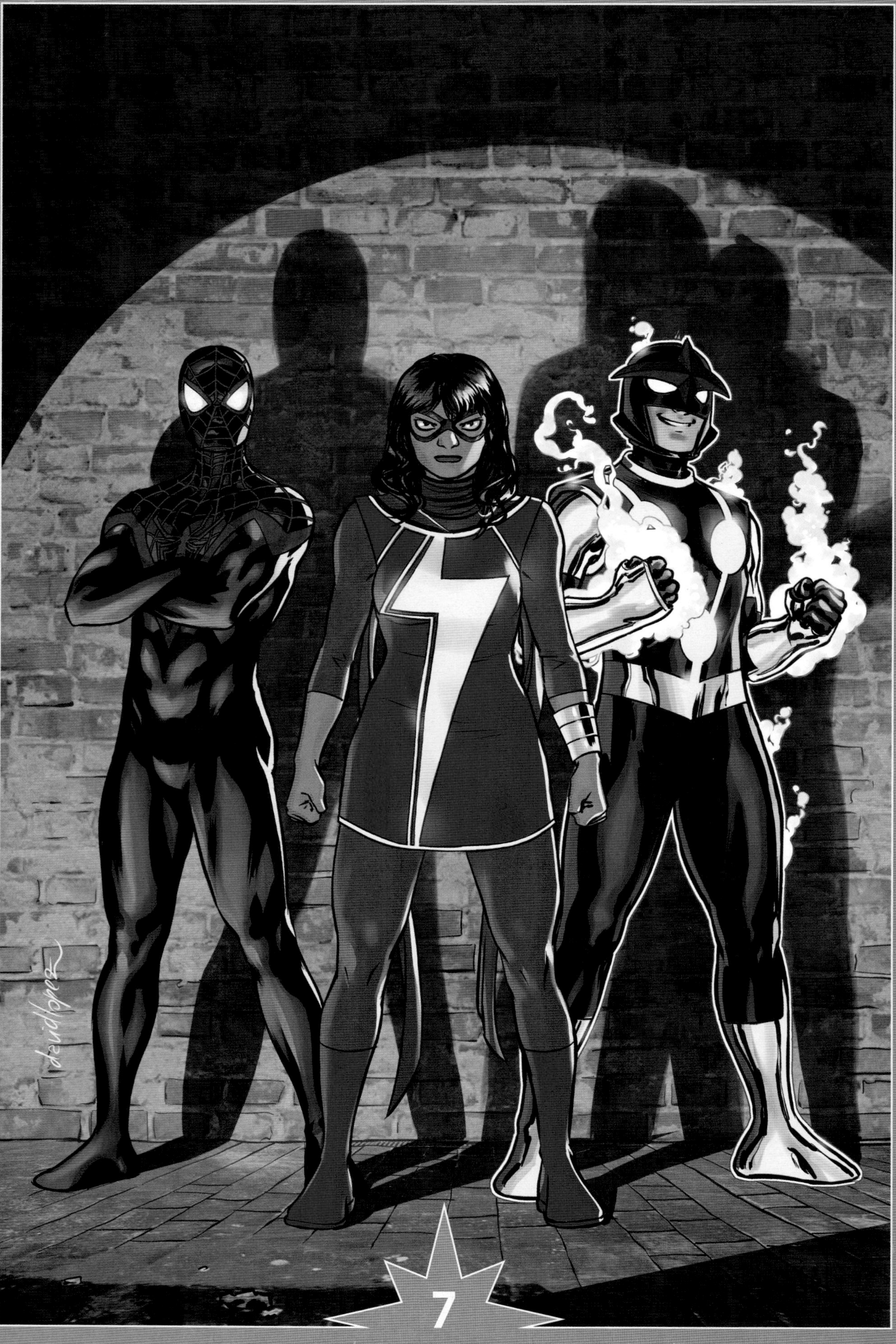

7

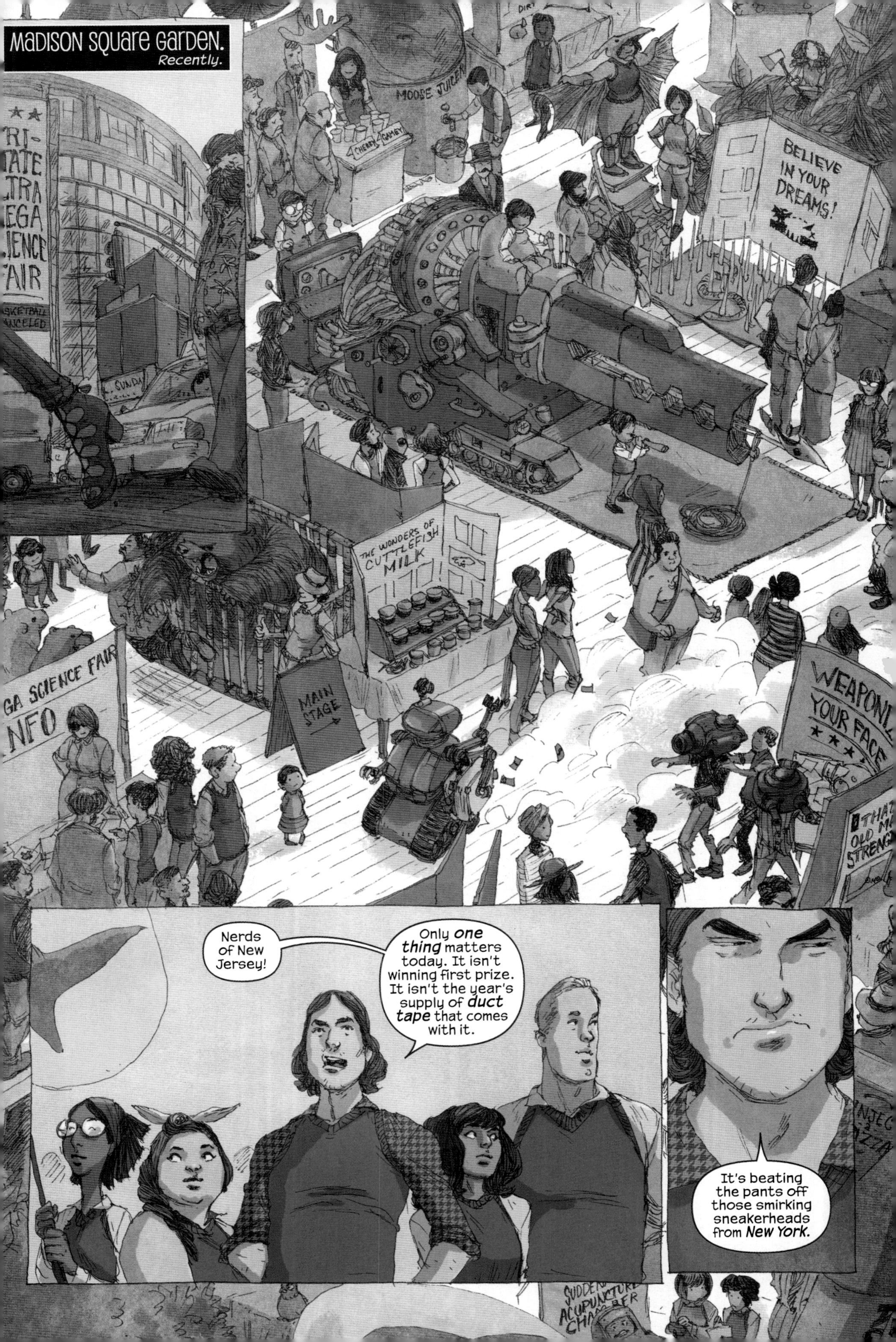
MADISON SQUARE GARDEN.
Recently.
MOOSE JUICER
CHERRY
GAMEY
BELIEVE IN YOUR DREAMS!
THE WONDERS OF CUTTLEFISH MILK
MAIN STAGE
Nerds of New Jersey!
Only one thing matters today. It isn't winning first prize. It isn't the year's supply of duct tape that comes with it.
It's beating the pants off those smirking sneakerheads from New York.

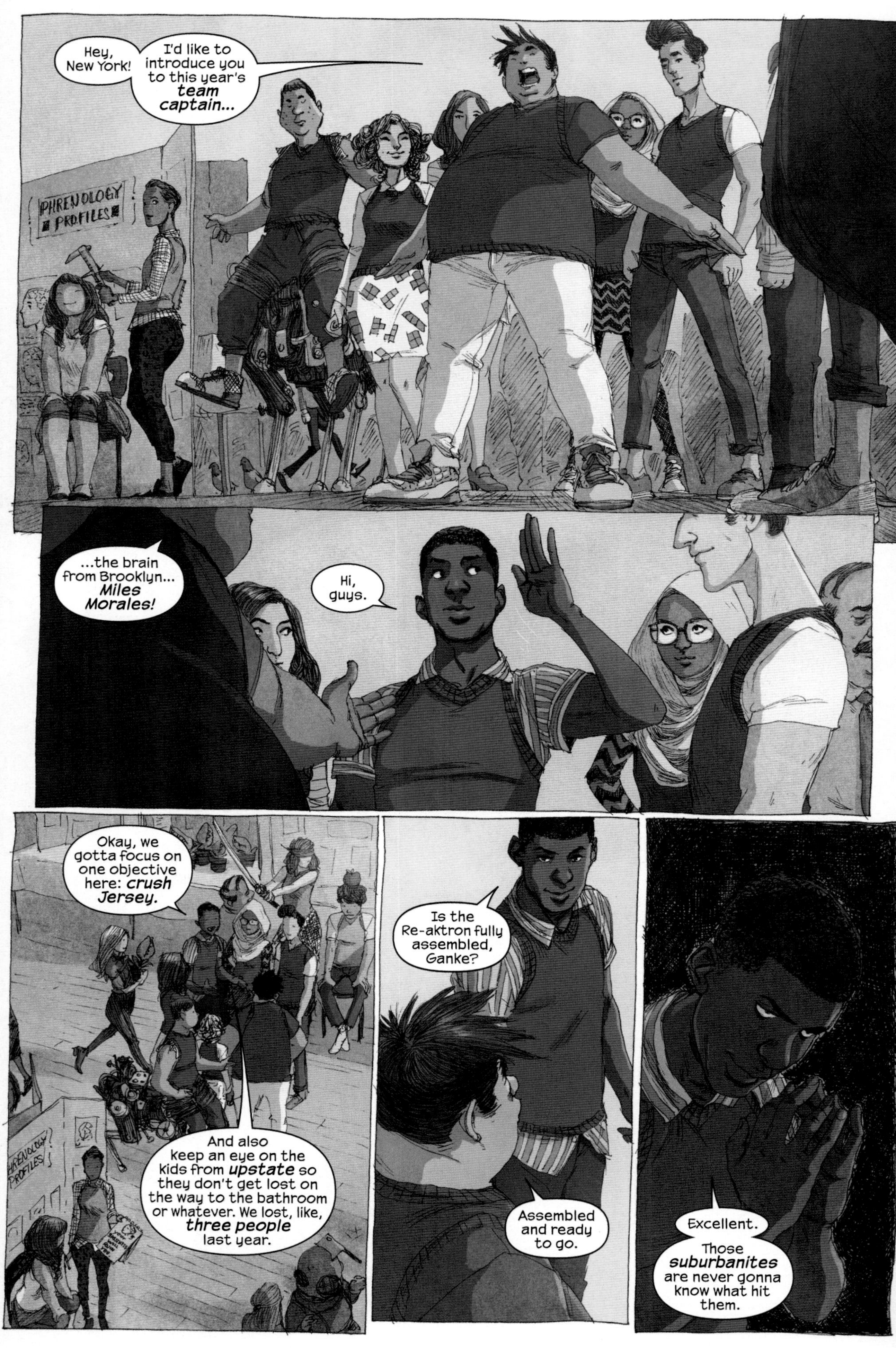
Hey, New York!
I'd like to introduce you to this year's *team captain...*
PHRENOLOGY PROFILES
...the brain from Brooklyn... *Miles Morales!*
Hi, guys.
Okay, we gotta focus on one objective here: *crush Jersey.*
And also keep an eye on the kids from *upstate* so they don't get lost on the way to the bathroom or whatever. We lost, like, *three people* last year.
Is the Re-aktron fully assembled, Ganke?
Assembled and ready to go.
Excellent.
Those *suburbanites* are never gonna know what hit them.

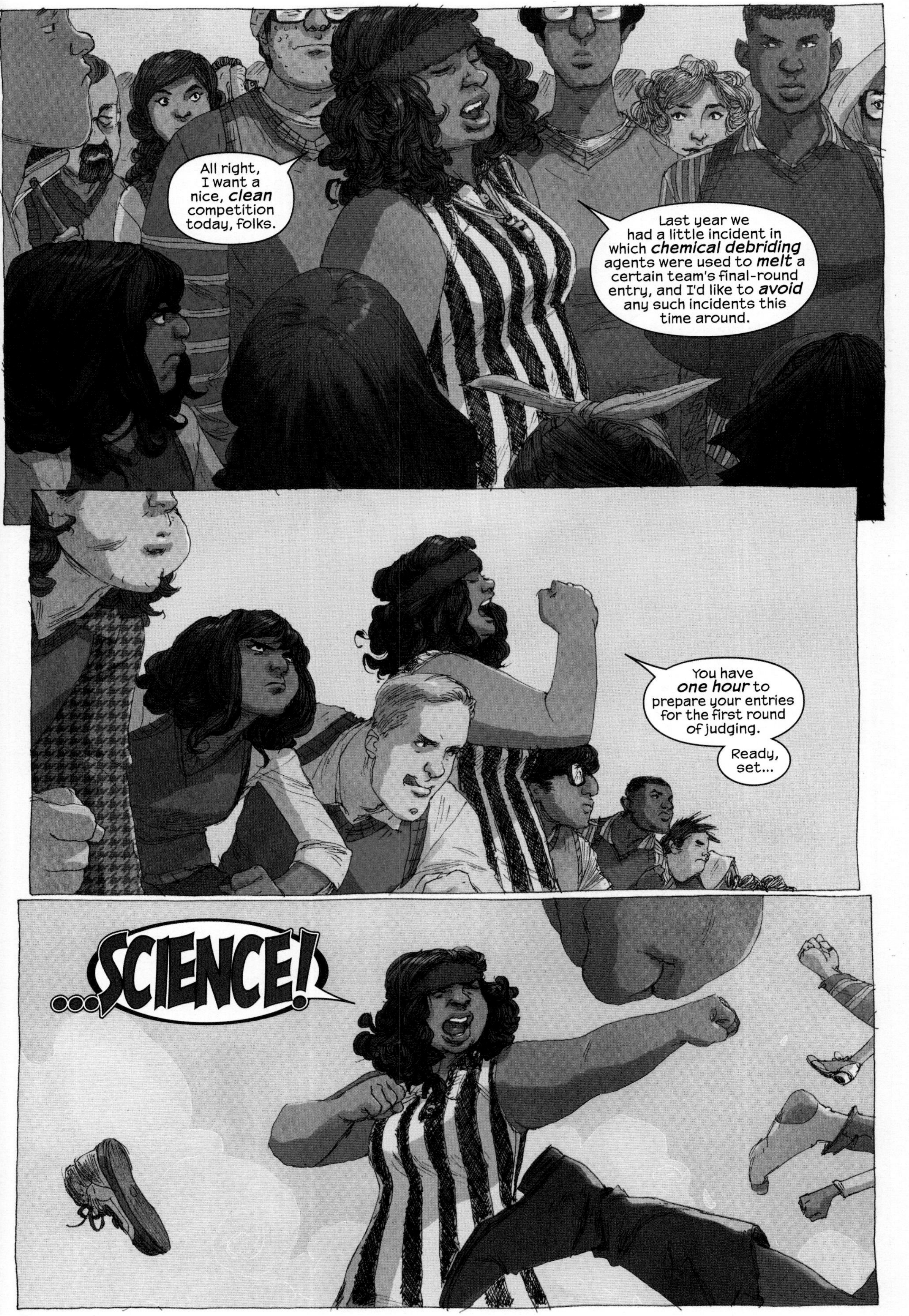
All right, I want a nice, clean competition today, folks.
Last year we had a little incident in which chemical debriding agents were used to melt a certain team's final-round entry, and I'd like to avoid any such incidents this time around.
You have one hour to prepare your entries for the first round of judging.
Ready, set...
...SCIENCE!

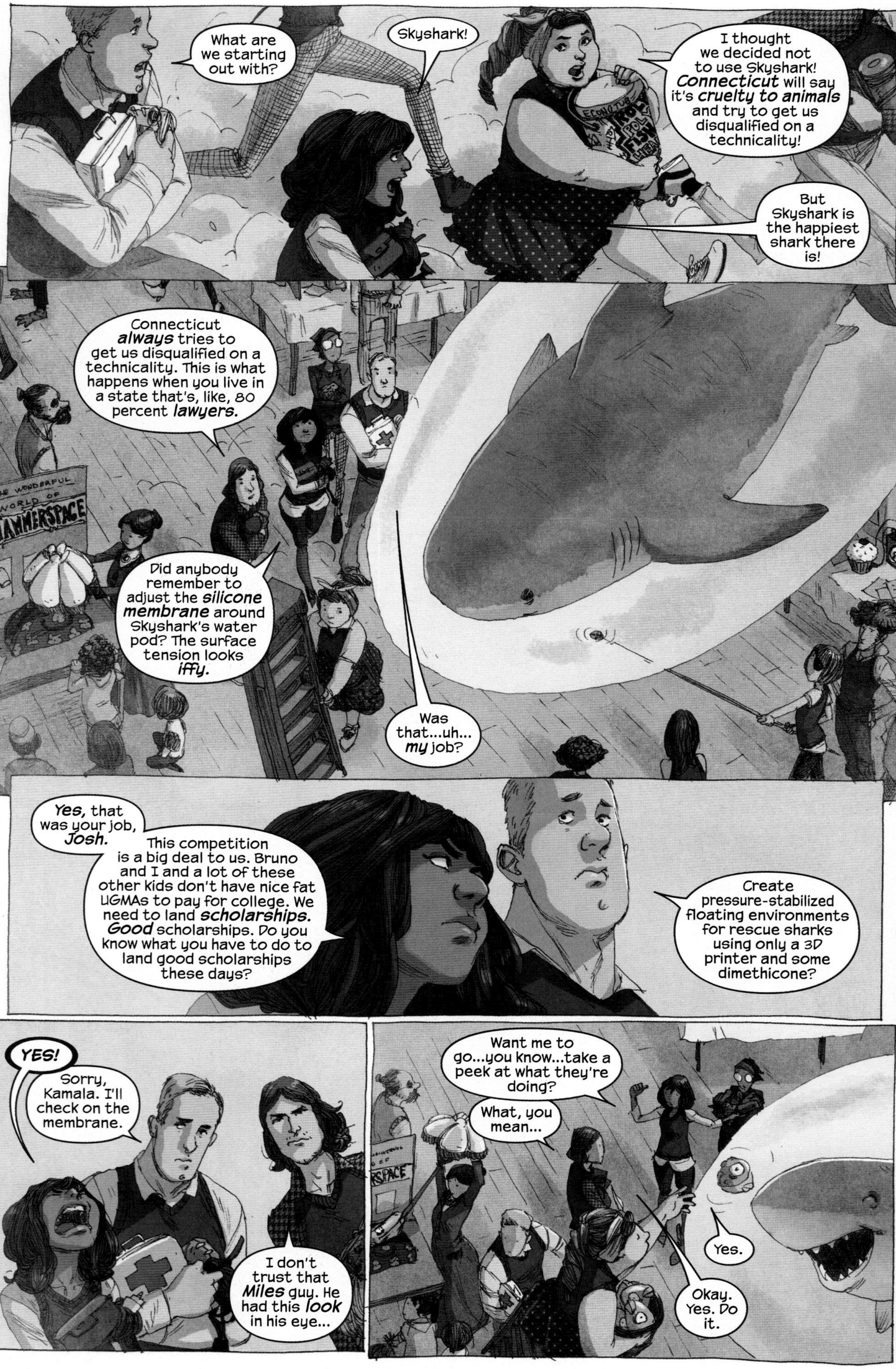
What are we starting out with?
Skyshark!
I thought we decided not to use Skyshark! Connecticut will say it's cruelty to animals and try to get us disqualified on a technicality!
But Skyshark is the happiest shark there is!
Connecticut always tries to get us disqualified on a technicality. This is what happens when you live in a state that's, like, 80 percent lawyers.
THE WONDERFUL WORLD OF HAMMERSPACE
Did anybody remember to adjust the silicone membrane around Skyshark's water pod? The surface tension looks iffy.
Was that...uh... my job?
Yes, that was your job, Josh.
This competition is a big deal to us. Bruno and I and a lot of these other kids don't have nice fat UGMAs to pay for college. We need to land scholarships. Good scholarships. Do you know what you have to do to land good scholarships these days?
Create pressure-stabilized floating environments for rescue sharks using only a 3D printer and some dimethicone?
YES!
Sorry, Kamala. I'll check on the membrane.
I don't trust that Miles guy. He had this look in his eye...
Want me to go...you know...take a peek at what they're doing?
What, you mean...
Yes.
Okay. Yes. Do it.

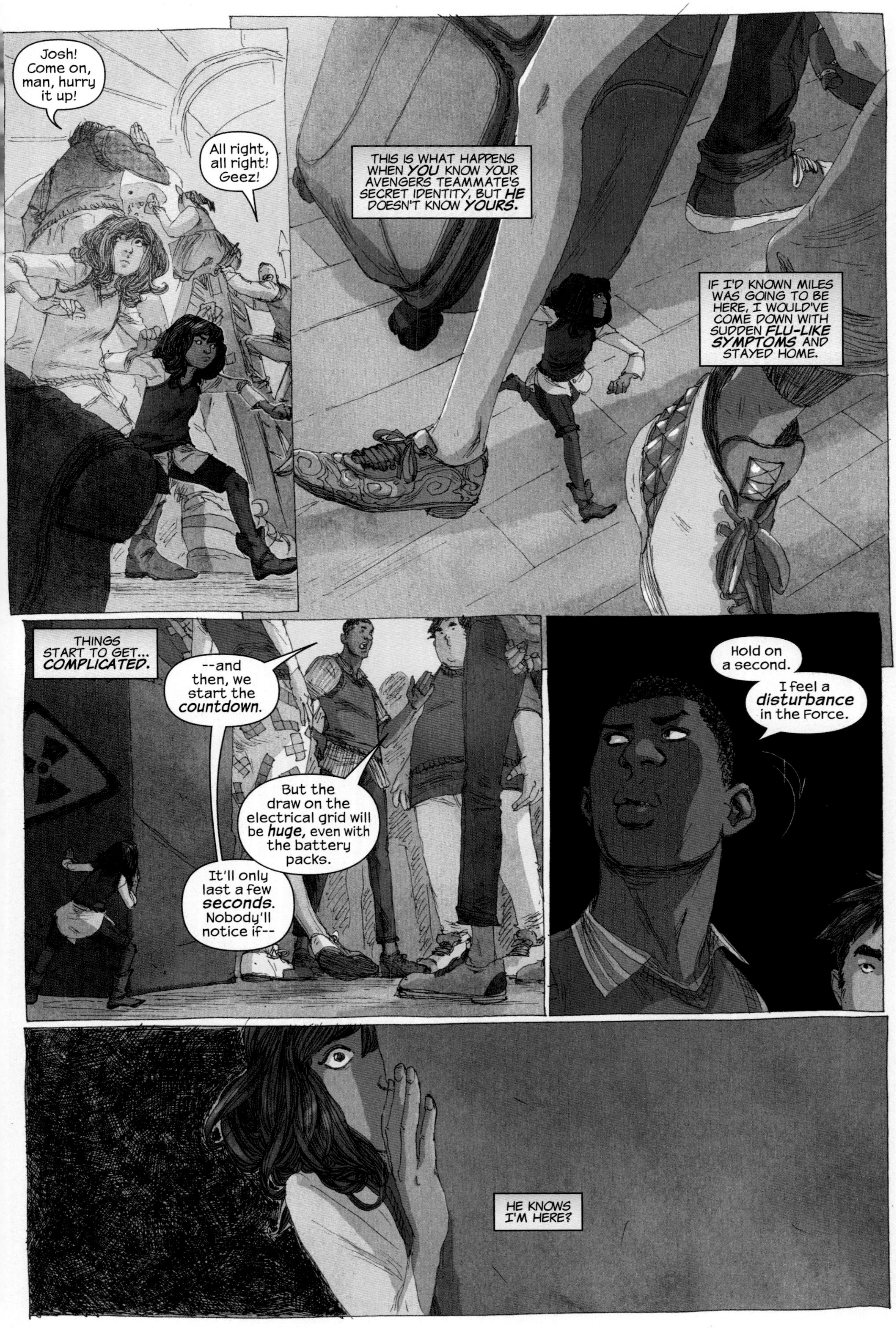
Josh! Come on, man, hurry it up!
All right, all right! Geez!
THIS IS WHAT HAPPENS WHEN YOU KNOW YOUR AVENGERS TEAMMATE'S SECRET IDENTITY, BUT HE DOESN'T KNOW YOURS.
IF I'D KNOWN MILES WAS GOING TO BE HERE, I WOULD'VE COME DOWN WITH SUDDEN FLU-LIKE SYMPTOMS AND STAYED HOME.
THINGS START TO GET... COMPLICATED.
--and then, we start the countdown.
But the draw on the electrical grid will be huge, even with the battery packs.
It'll only last a few seconds. Nobody'll notice if--
Hold on a second.
I feel a disturbance in the Force.
HE KNOWS I'M HERE?

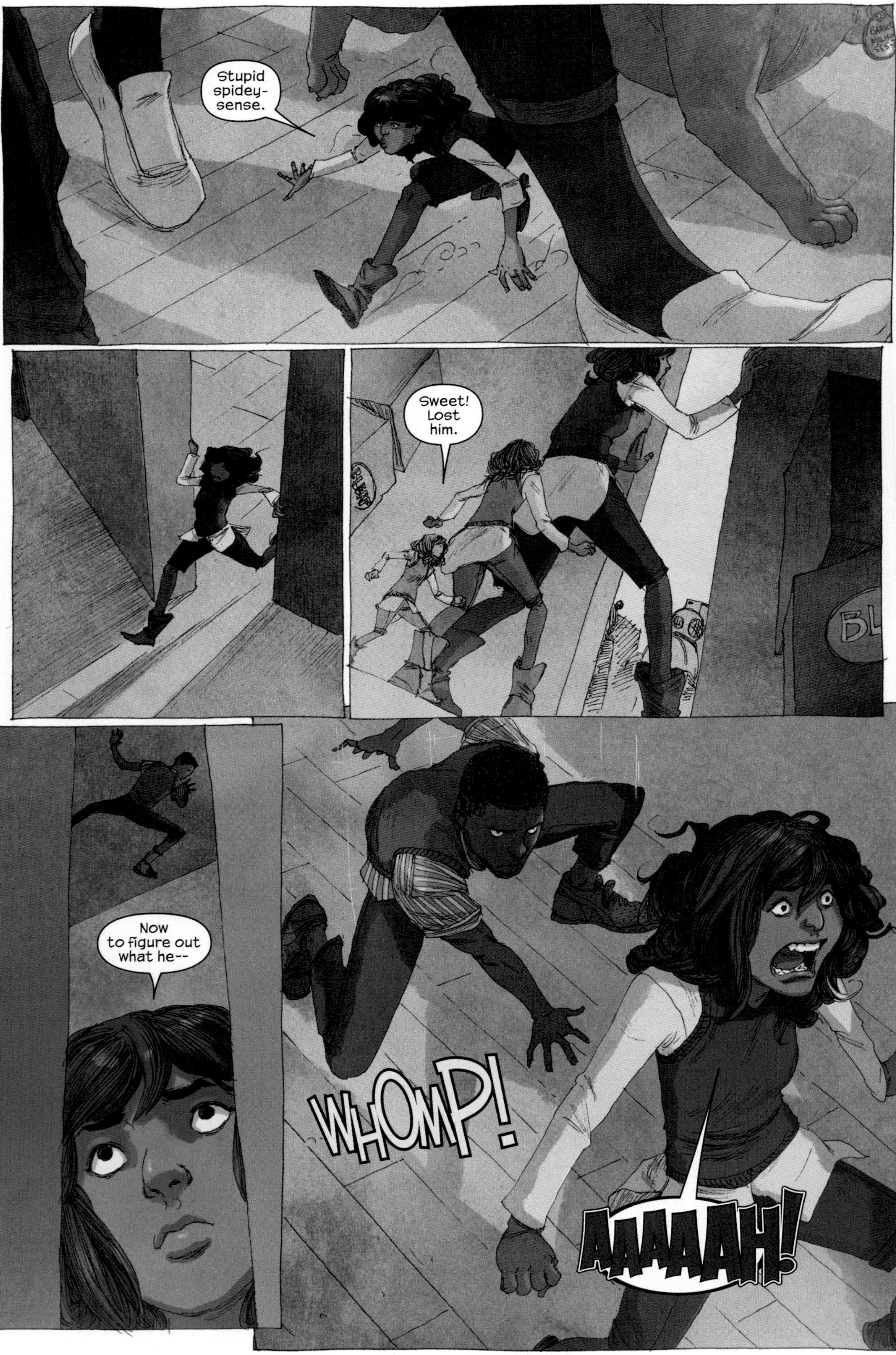
Stupid spidey-sense.
Sweet! Lost him.
Now to figure out what he--
WHOMP!
AAAAAH!

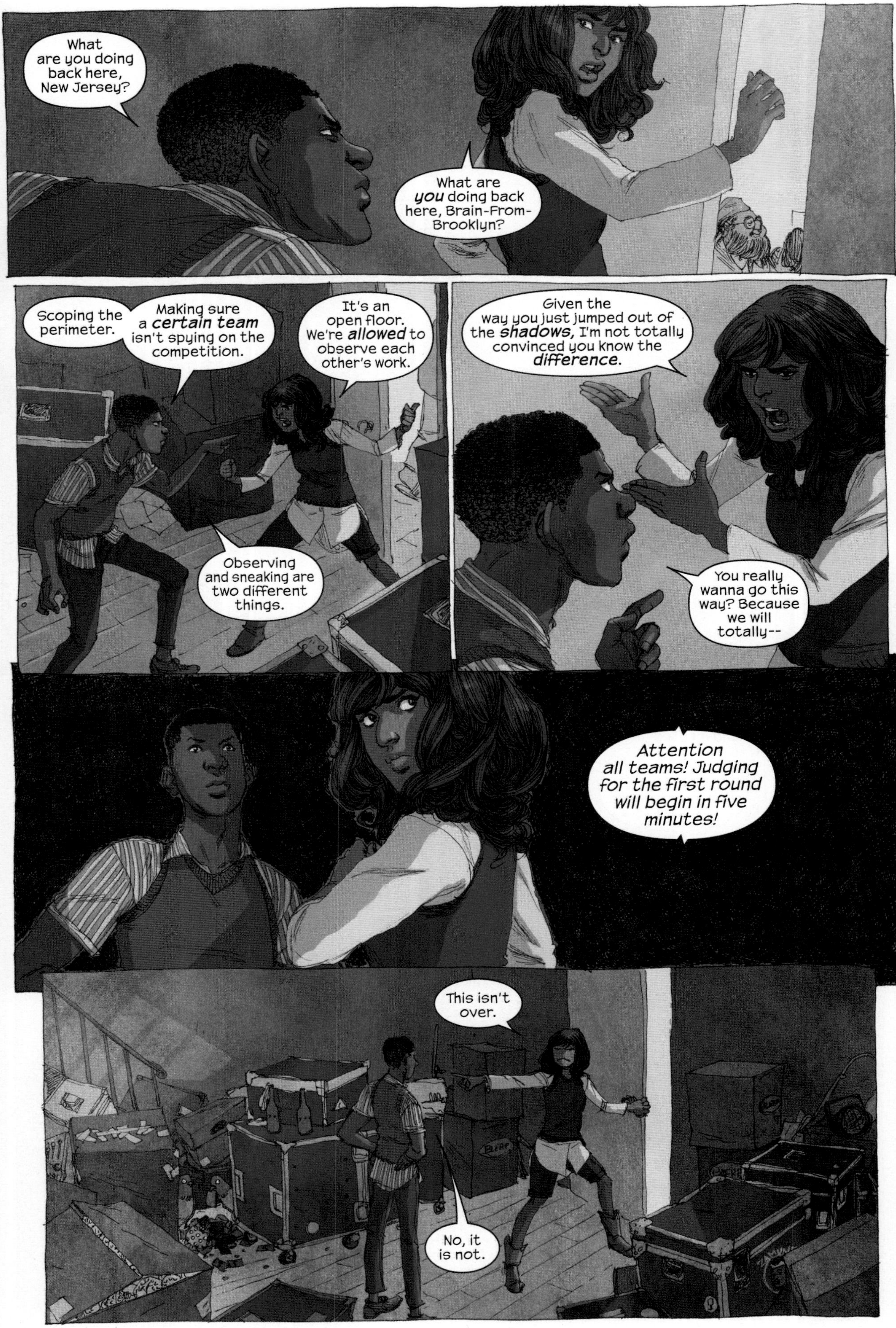
What are you doing back here, New Jersey?
What are *you* doing back here, Brain-From-Brooklyn?
Scoping the perimeter.
Making sure a ***certain team*** isn't spying on the competition.
It's an open floor. We're ***allowed*** to observe each other's work.
Observing and sneaking are two different things.
Given the way you just jumped out of the ***shadows,*** I'm not totally convinced you know the ***difference***.
You really wanna go this way? Because we will totally--
Attention all teams! Judging for the first round will begin in five minutes!
This isn't over.
No, it is not.

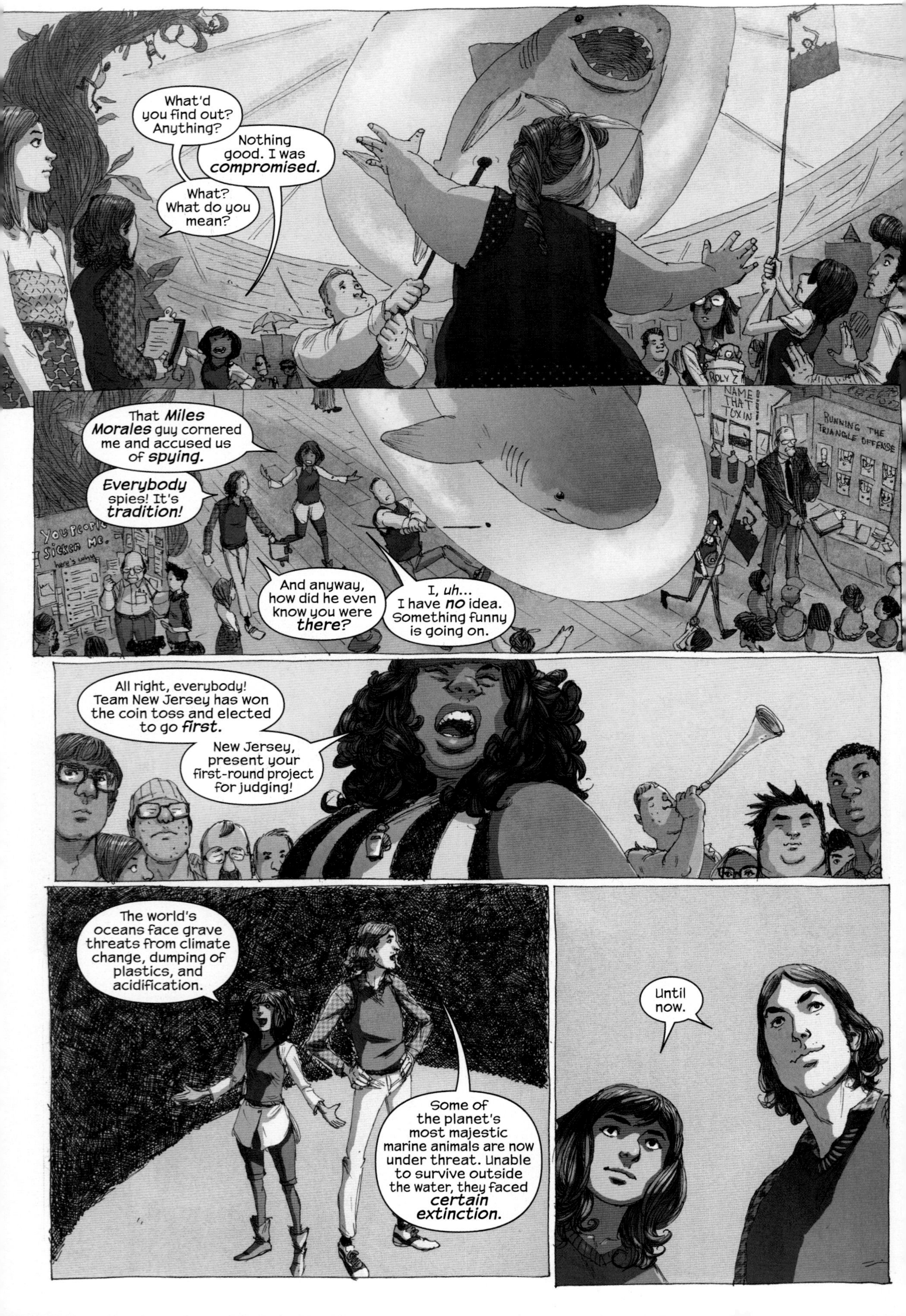
What'd you find out? Anything?
Nothing good. I was *compromised.*
What? What do you mean?
That *Miles Morales* guy cornered me and accused us of *spying.*
NAME THAT TOXIN
RUNNING THE TRIANGLE OFFENSE
You People Sicken Me.
Everybody spies! It's *tradition!*
And anyway, how did he even know you were *there?*
I, *uh*... I have *NO* idea. Something funny is going on.
All right, everybody! Team New Jersey has won the coin toss and elected to go *first.*
New Jersey, present your first-round project for judging!
The world's oceans face grave threats from climate change, dumping of plastics, and acidification.
Some of the planet's most majestic marine animals are now under threat. Unable to survive outside the water, they faced *certain extinction.*
Until now.

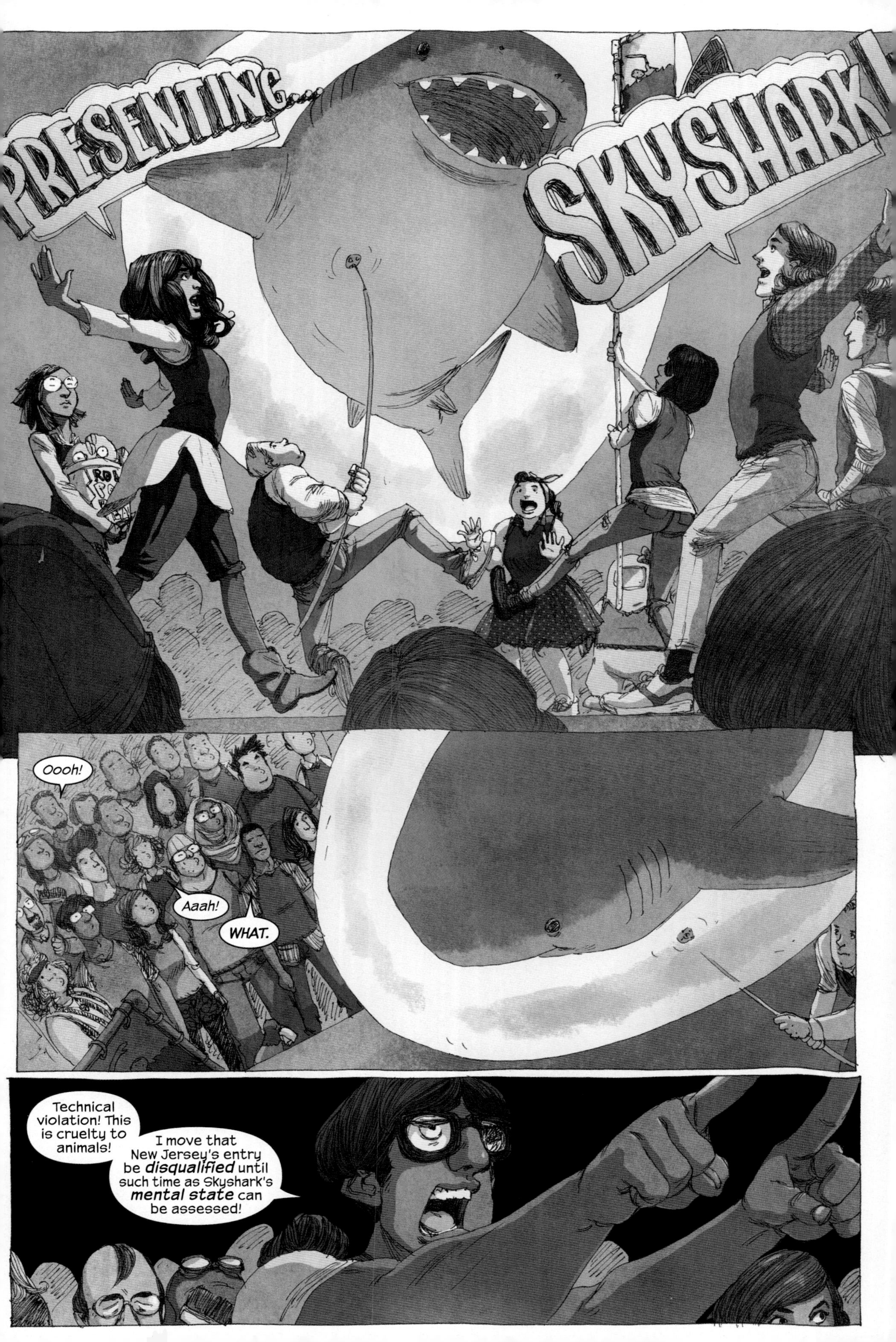
PRESENTING...
SKYSHARK!
Oooh!
Aaah!
WHAT.
Technical violation! This is cruelty to animals!
I move that New Jersey's entry be *disqualified* until such time as Skyshark's *mental state* can be assessed!

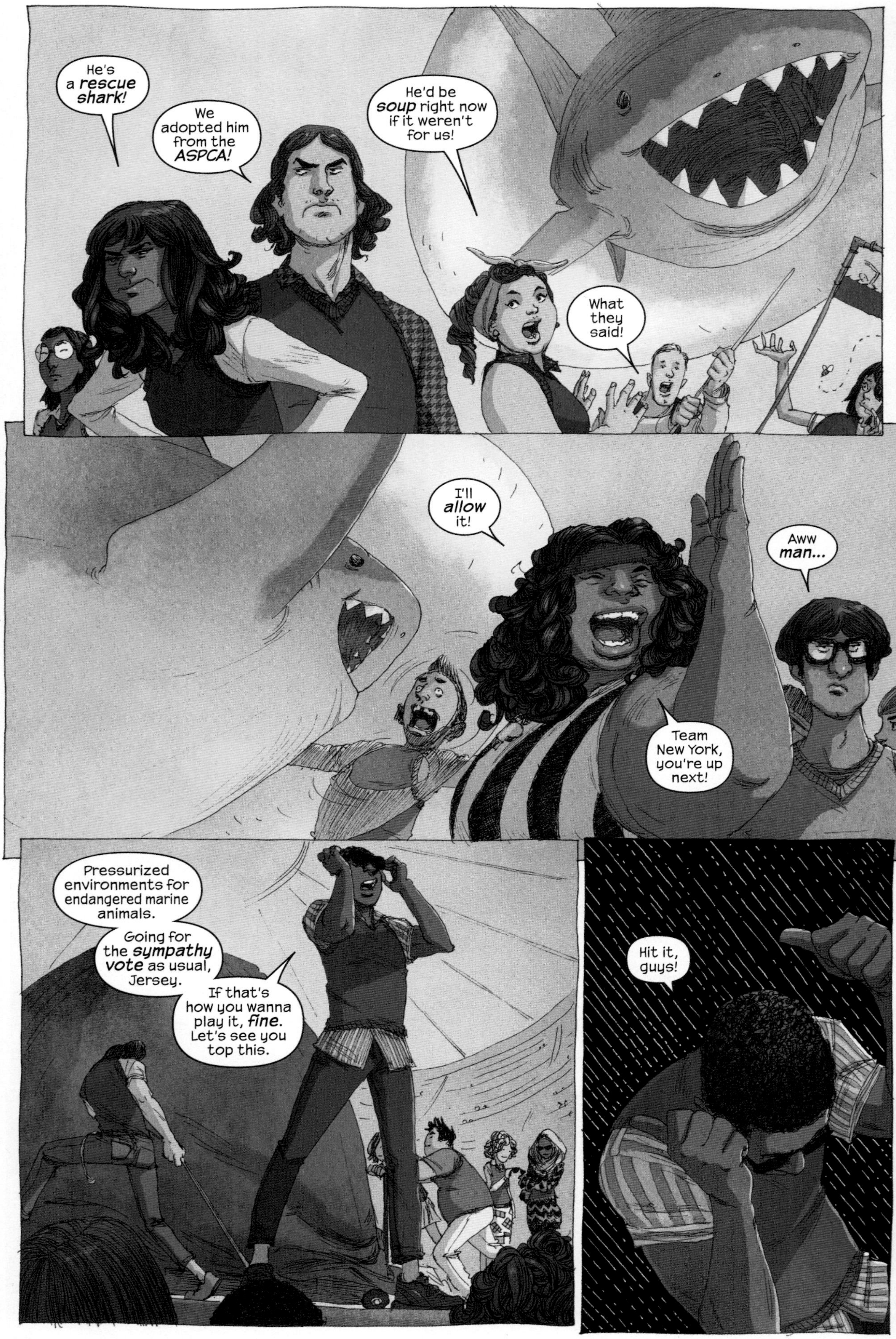
He's a rescue shark!
We adopted him from the ASPCA!
He'd be soup right now if it weren't for us!
What they said!
I'll allow it!
Aww man...
Team New York, you're up next!
Pressurized environments for endangered marine animals.
Going for the sympathy vote as usual, Jersey.
If that's how you wanna play it, fine. Let's see you top this.
Hit it, guys!

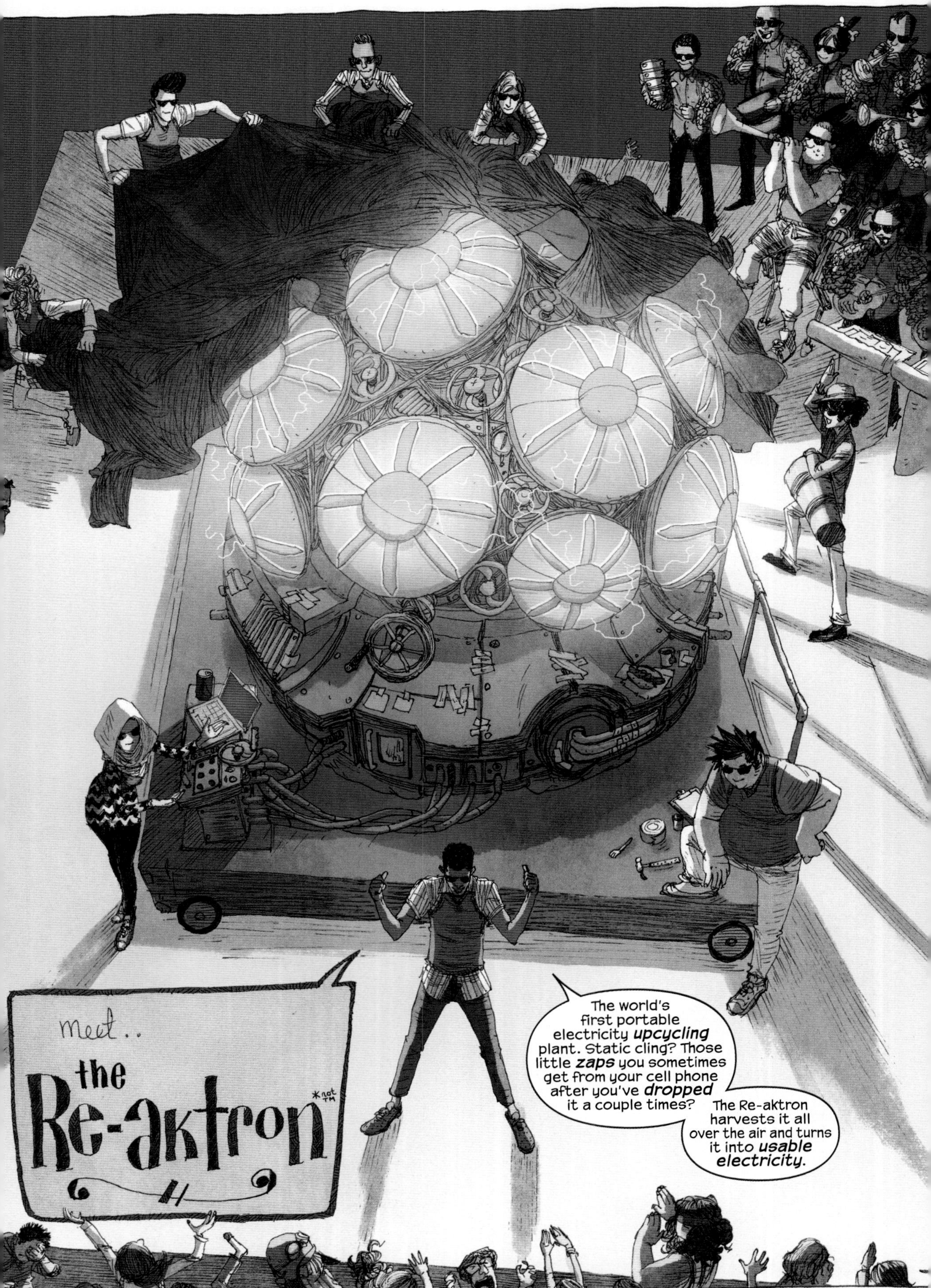
meet..
the Re-aktron *not TM
The world's first portable electricity *upcycling* plant. Static cling? Those little *zaps* you sometimes get from your cell phone after you've *dropped* it a couple times?
The Re-aktron harvests it all over the air and turns it into *usable electricity*.

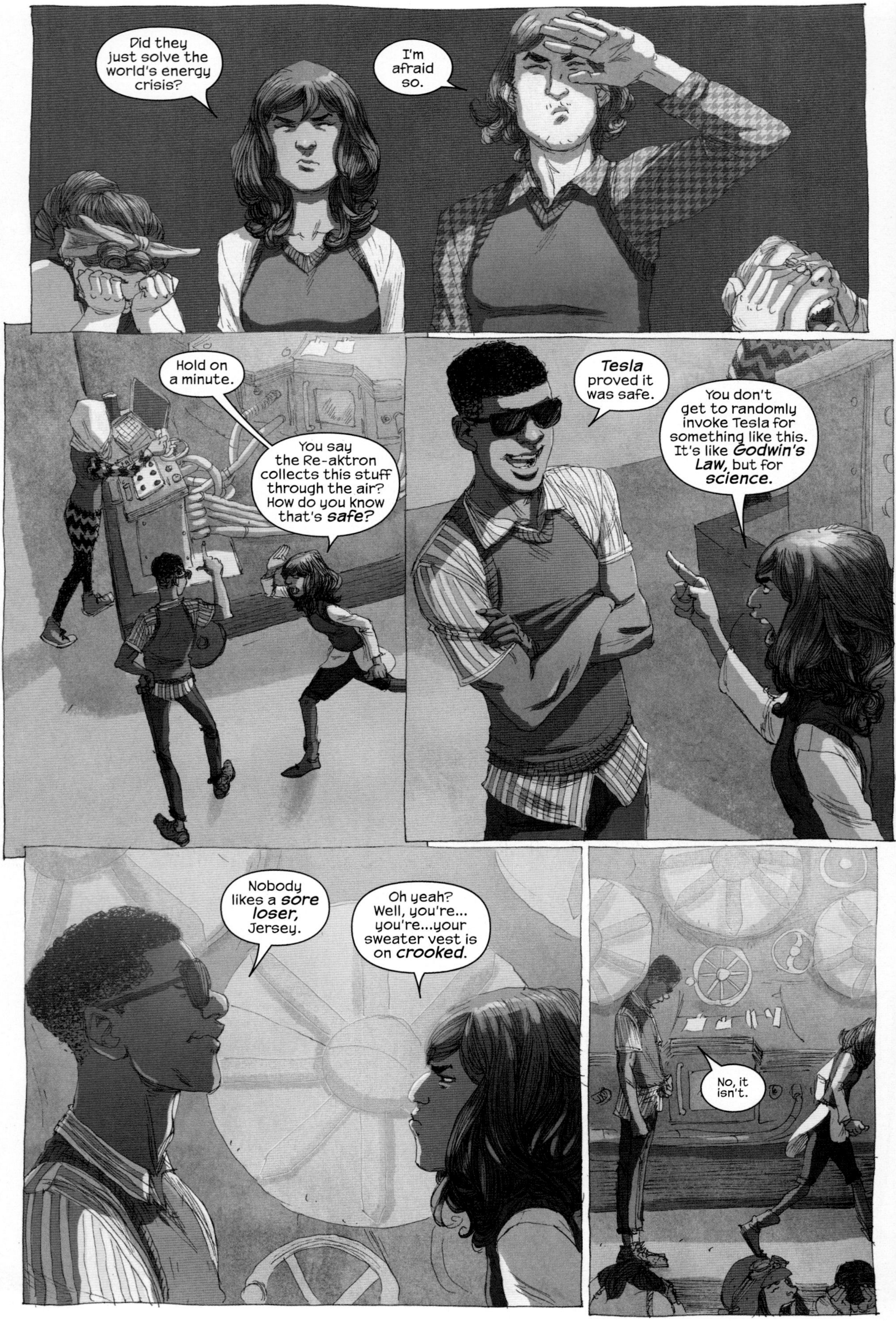
Did they just solve the world's energy crisis?
I'm afraid so.
Hold on a minute.
You say the Re-aktron collects this stuff through the air? How do you know that's *safe?*
Tesla proved it was safe.
You don't get to randomly invoke Tesla for something like this. It's like *Godwin's Law,* but for *science.*
Nobody likes a *sore loser,* Jersey.
Oh yeah? Well, you're... you're...your sweater vest is on *crooked.*
No, it isn't.

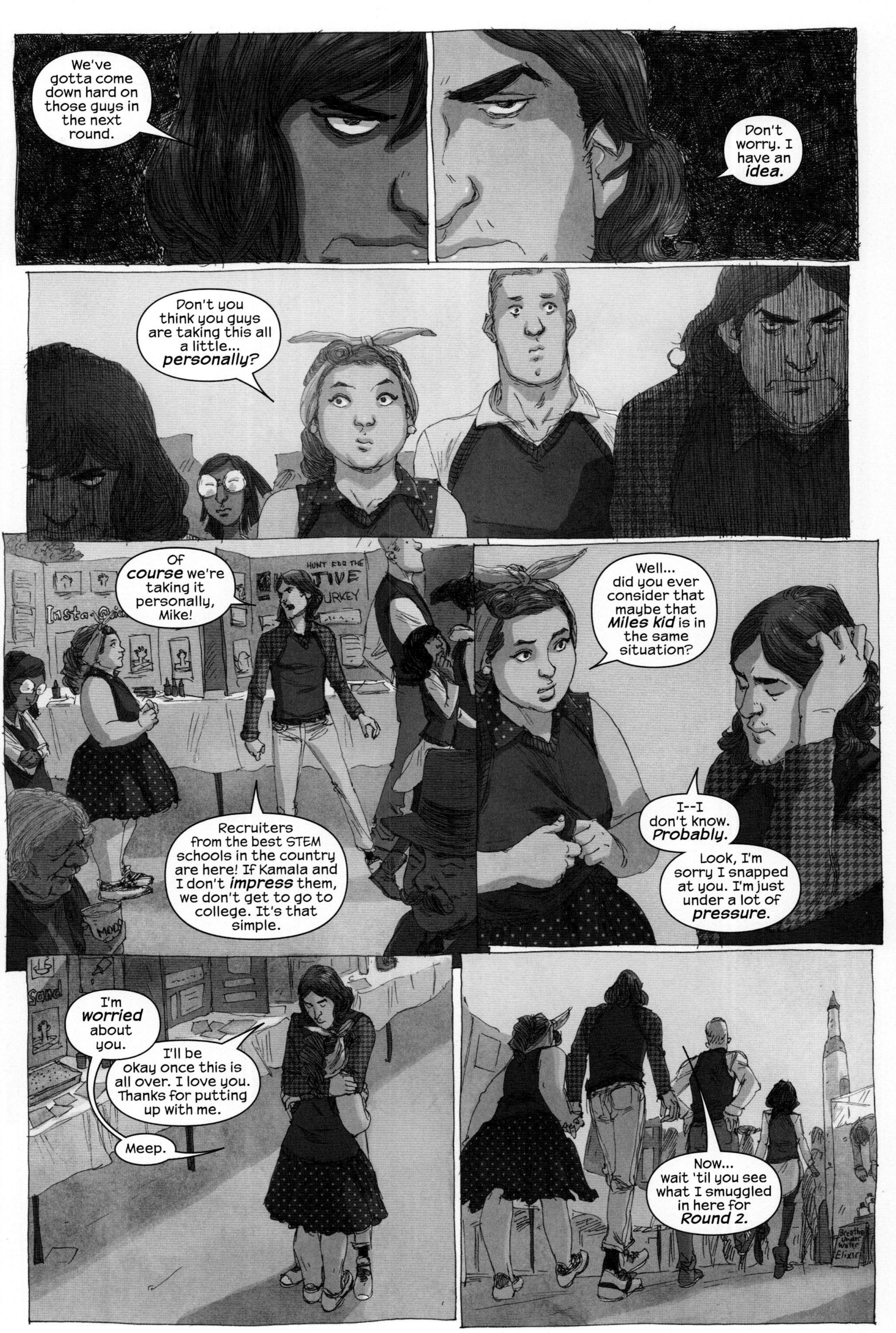
We've gotta come down hard on those guys in the next round.
Don't worry. I have an *idea.*
Don't you think you guys are taking this all a little... *personally?*
Of *course* we're taking it personally, Mike!
HUNT FOR THE ...TIVE ...URKEY
Recruiters from the best STEM schools in the country are here! If Kamala and I don't *impress* them, we don't get to go to college. It's that simple.
Well... did you ever consider that maybe that *Miles kid* is in the same situation?
I--I don't know. *Probably.*
Look, I'm sorry I snapped at you. I'm just under a lot of *pressure.*
I'm *worried* about you.
I'll be okay once this is all over. I love you. Thanks for putting up with me.
Meep.
Now... wait 'til you see what I smuggled in here for *Round 2.*
Breathe Under Water Elixir

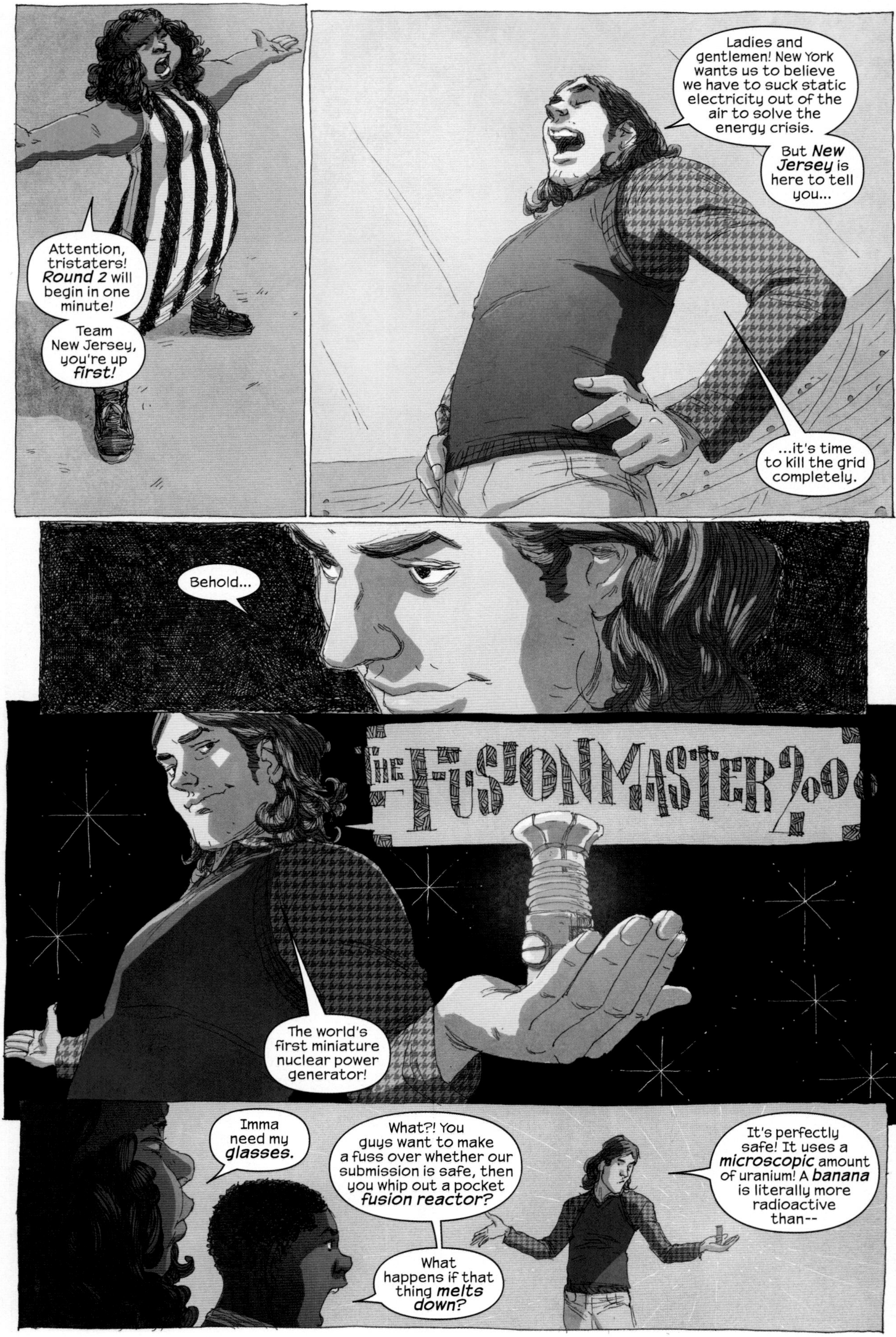
Attention, tristaters! Round 2 will begin in one minute!
Team New Jersey, you're up first!
Ladies and gentlemen! New York wants us to believe we have to suck static electricity out of the air to solve the energy crisis.
But New Jersey is here to tell you...
...it's time to kill the grid completely.
Behold...
THE FUSIONMASTER 2.0
The world's first miniature nuclear power generator!
Imma need my glasses.
What?! You guys want to make a fuss over whether our submission is safe, then you whip out a pocket fusion reactor?
What happens if that thing melts down?
It's perfectly safe! It uses a microscopic amount of uranium! A banana is literally more radioactive than--

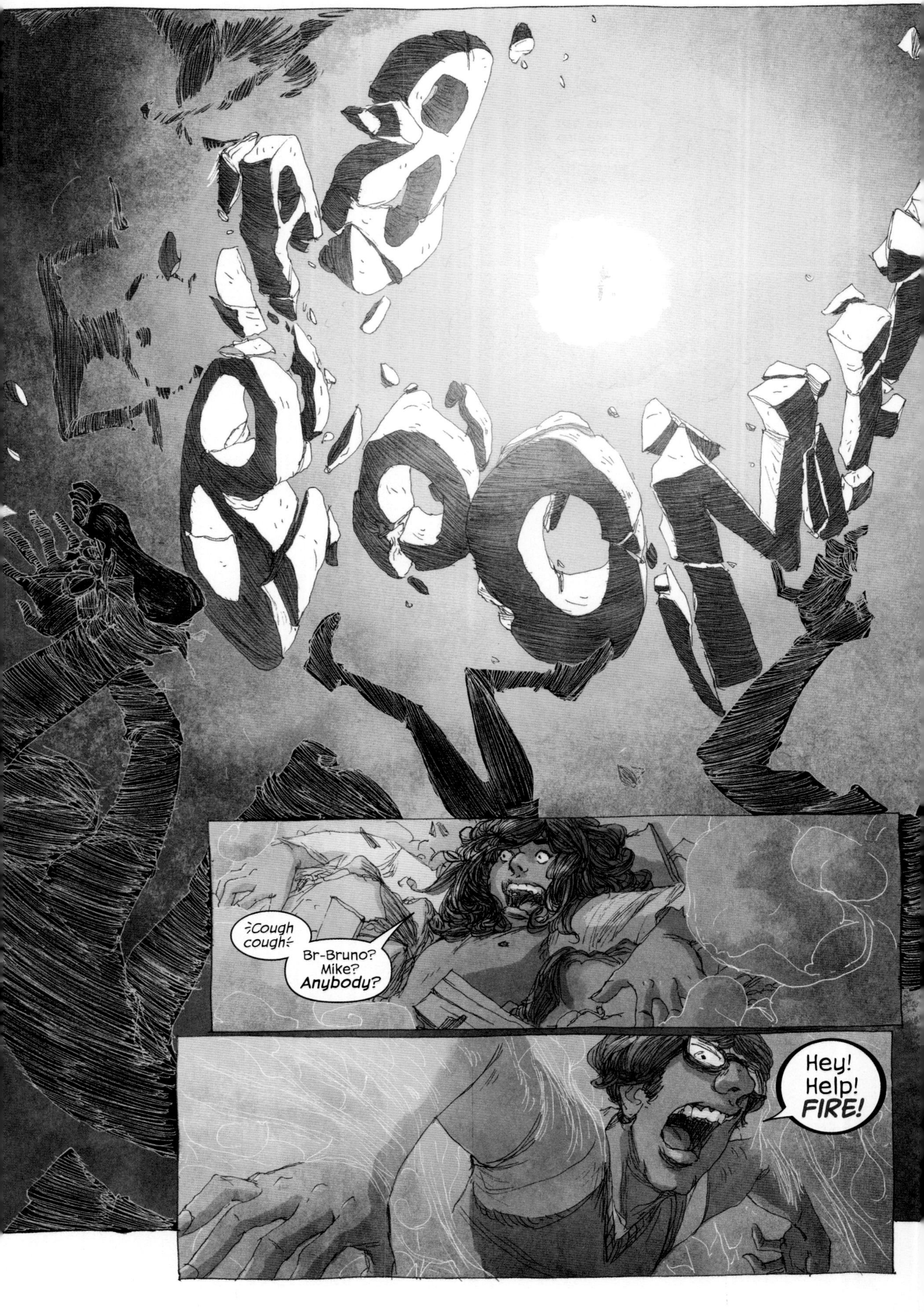

Cough cough
Br-Bruno? Mike? Anybody?
Hey! Help! FIRE!

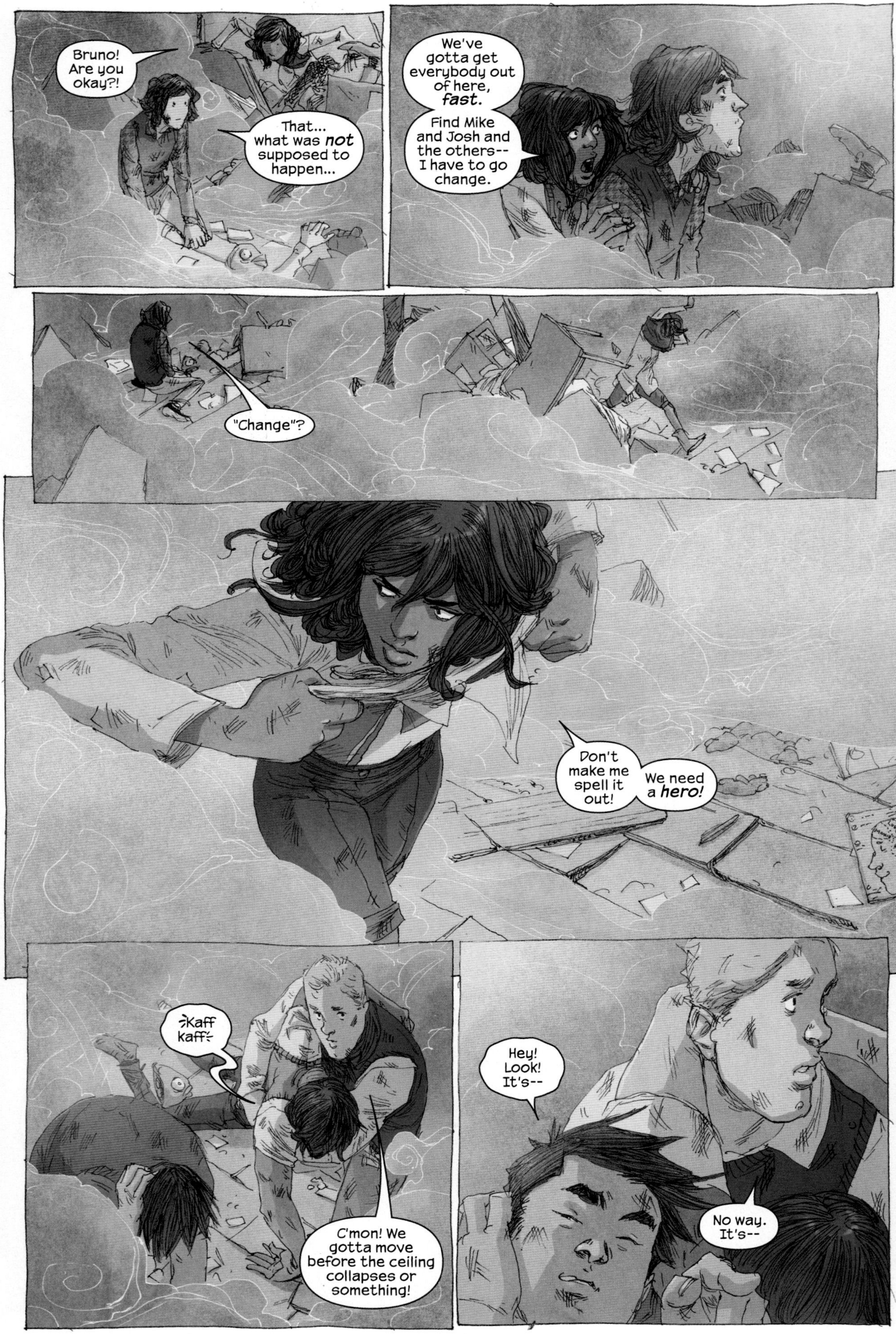
Bruno! Are you okay?!
That... what was *not* supposed to happen...
We've gotta get everybody out of here, ***fast.***
Find Mike and Josh and the others-- I have to go change.
"Change"?
Don't make me spell it out!
We need a ***hero!***
Kaff kaff
C'mon! We gotta move before the ceiling collapses or something!
Hey! Look! It's--
No way. It's--

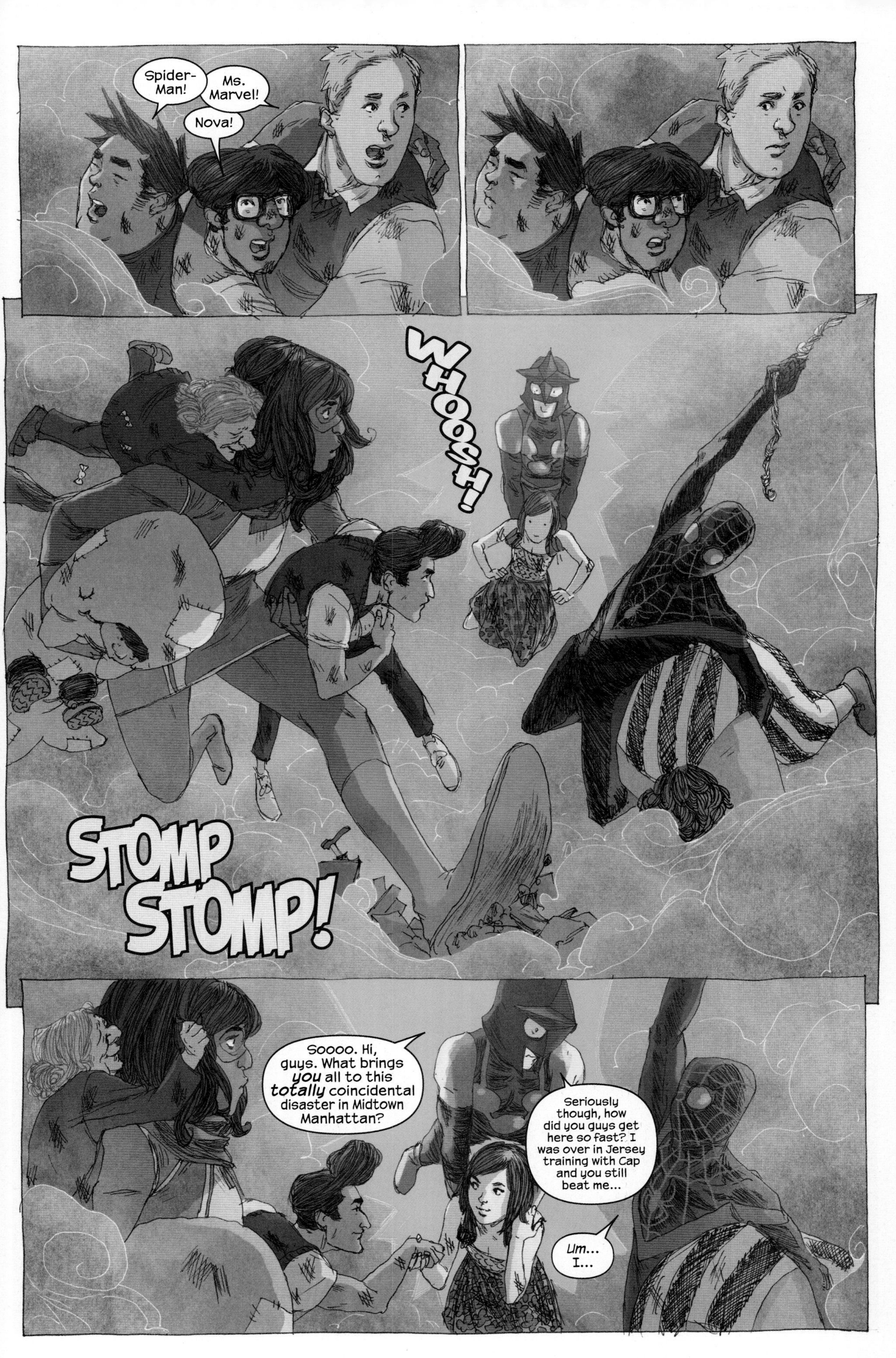
Spider-Man!
Ms. Marvel!
Nova!
WHOOSH!
STOMP STOMP!
Soooo. Hi, guys. What brings *you* all to this *totally* coincidental disaster in Midtown Manhattan?
Seriously though, how did you guys get here so fast? I was over in Jersey training with Cap and you still beat me...
Um... I...

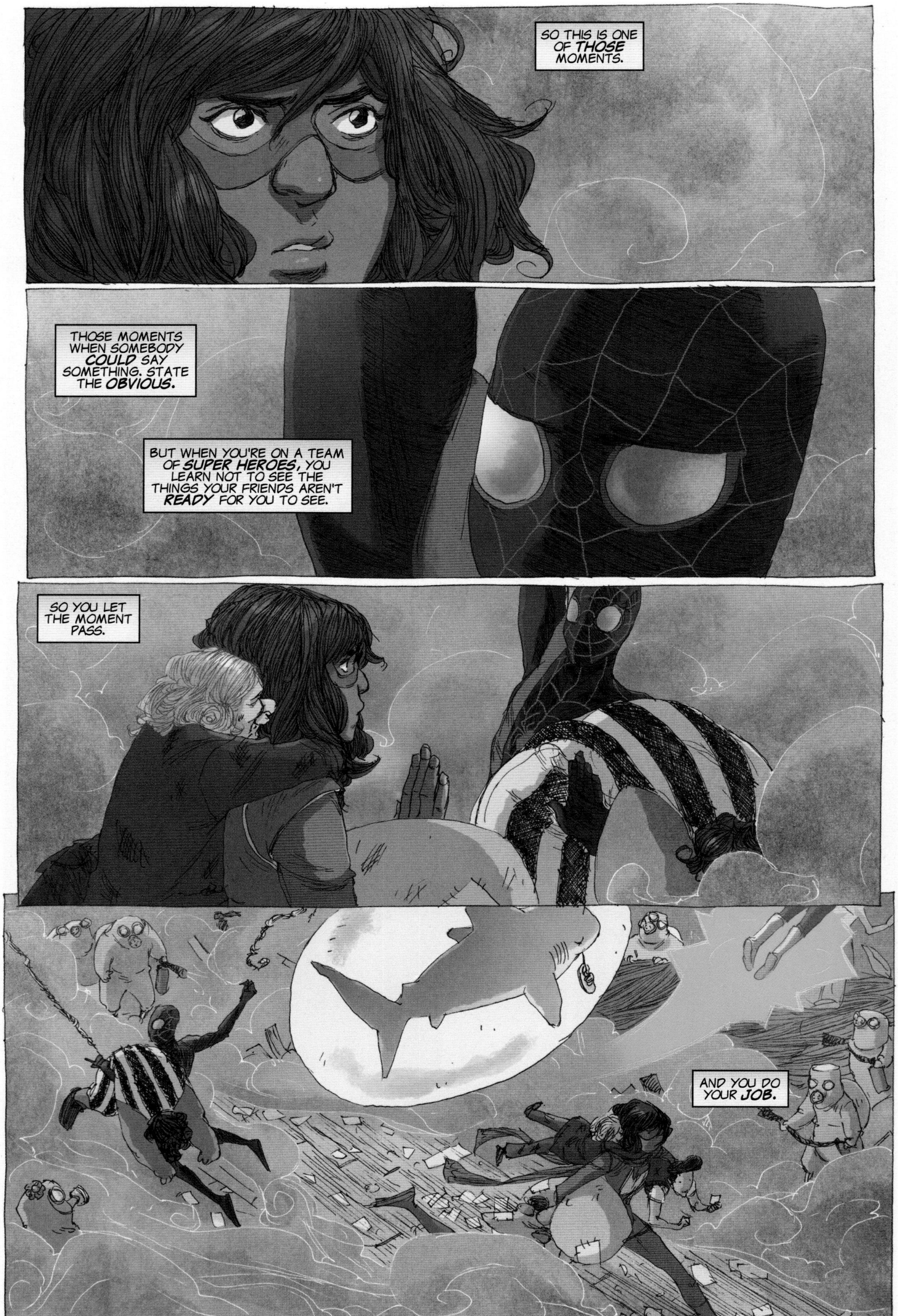
SO THIS IS ONE OF **THOSE** MOMENTS.
THOSE MOMENTS WHEN SOMEBODY **COULD** SAY SOMETHING. STATE THE **OBVIOUS.**
BUT WHEN YOU'RE ON A TEAM OF **SUPER HEROES,** YOU LEARN NOT TO SEE THE THINGS YOUR FRIENDS AREN'T **READY** FOR YOU TO SEE.
SO YOU LET THE MOMENT PASS.
AND YOU DO YOUR **JOB.**

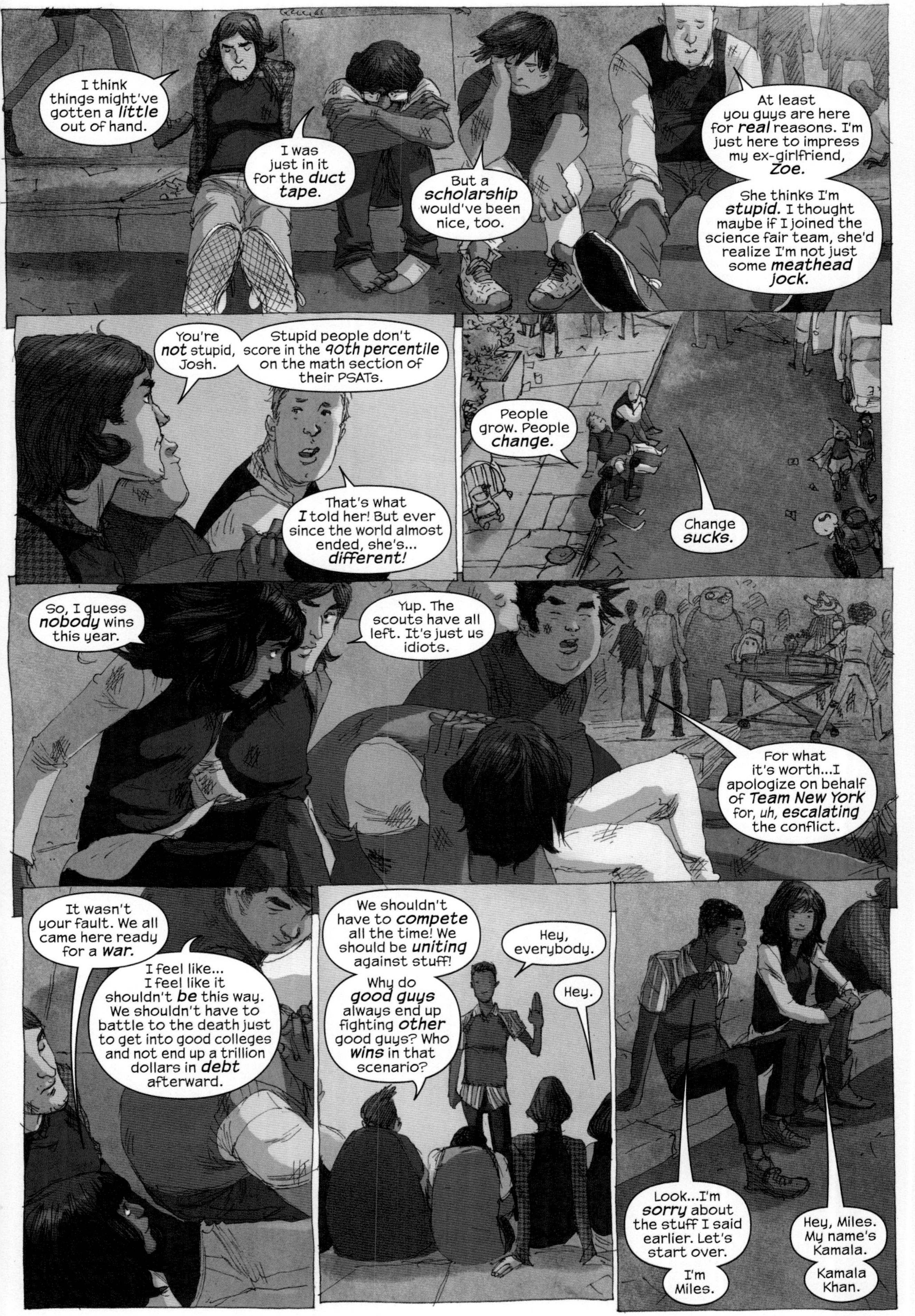
I think things might've gotten a *little* out of hand.
I was just in it for the *duct tape*.
But a *scholarship* would've been nice, too.
At least you guys are here for *real* reasons. I'm just here to impress my ex-girlfriend, *Zoe*.
She thinks I'm *stupid*. I thought maybe if I joined the science fair team, she'd realize I'm not just some *meathead jock*.
You're *not* stupid, Josh.
Stupid people don't score in the *90th percentile* on the math section of their PSATs.
That's what *I* told her! But ever since the world almost ended, she's... *different!*
People grow. People *change*.
Change *sucks*.
So, I guess *nobody* wins this year.
Yup. The scouts have all left. It's just us idiots.
For what it's worth...I apologize on behalf of *Team New York* for, *uh*, *escalating* the conflict.
It wasn't your fault. We all came here ready for a *war*.
I feel like... I feel like it shouldn't *be* this way. We shouldn't have to battle to the death just to get into good colleges and not end up a trillion dollars in *debt* afterward.
We shouldn't have to *compete* all the time! We should be *uniting* against stuff!
Why do *good guys* always end up fighting *other* good guys? Who *wins* in that scenario?
Hey, everybody.
Hey.
Look...I'm *sorry* about the stuff I said earlier. Let's start over.
I'm Miles.
Hey, Miles. My name's Kamala.
Kamala Khan.

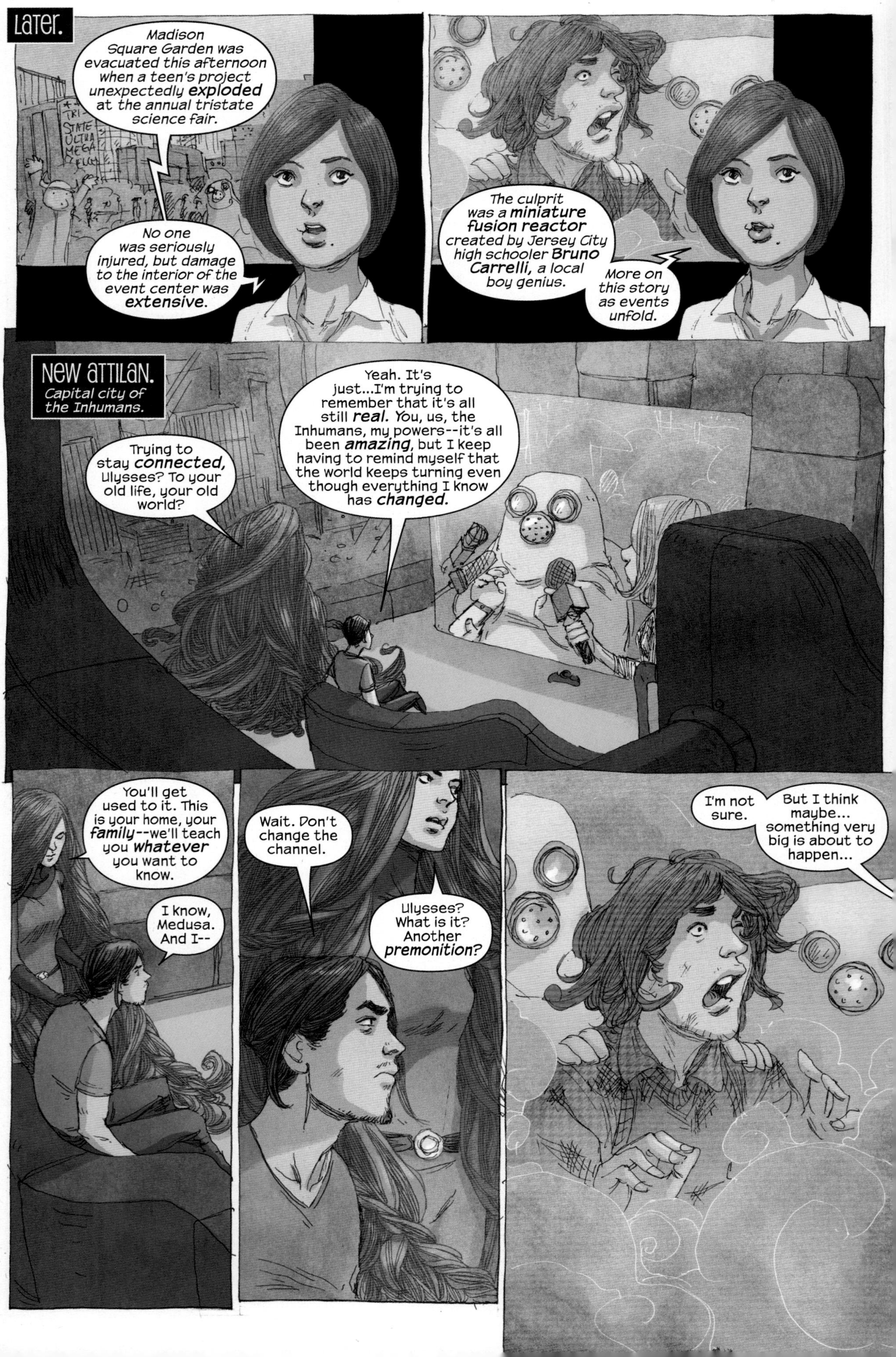

Later.
Madison Square Garden was evacuated this afternoon when a teen's project unexpectedly exploded at the annual tristate science fair.
TRI STATE ULTRA MEGA
No one was seriously injured, but damage to the interior of the event center was extensive.
The culprit was a miniature fusion reactor created by Jersey City high schooler Bruno Carrelli, a local boy genius.
More on this story as events unfold.
New Attilan. Capital city of the Inhumans.
Trying to stay connected, Ulysses? To your old life, your old world?
Yeah. It's just...I'm trying to remember that it's all still real. You, us, the Inhumans, my powers--it's all been amazing, but I keep having to remind myself that the world keeps turning even though everything I know has changed.
You'll get used to it. This is your home, your family--we'll teach you whatever you want to know.
I know, Medusa. And I--
Wait. Don't change the channel.
Ulysses? What is it? Another premonition?
I'm not sure.
But I think maybe... something very big is about to happen...

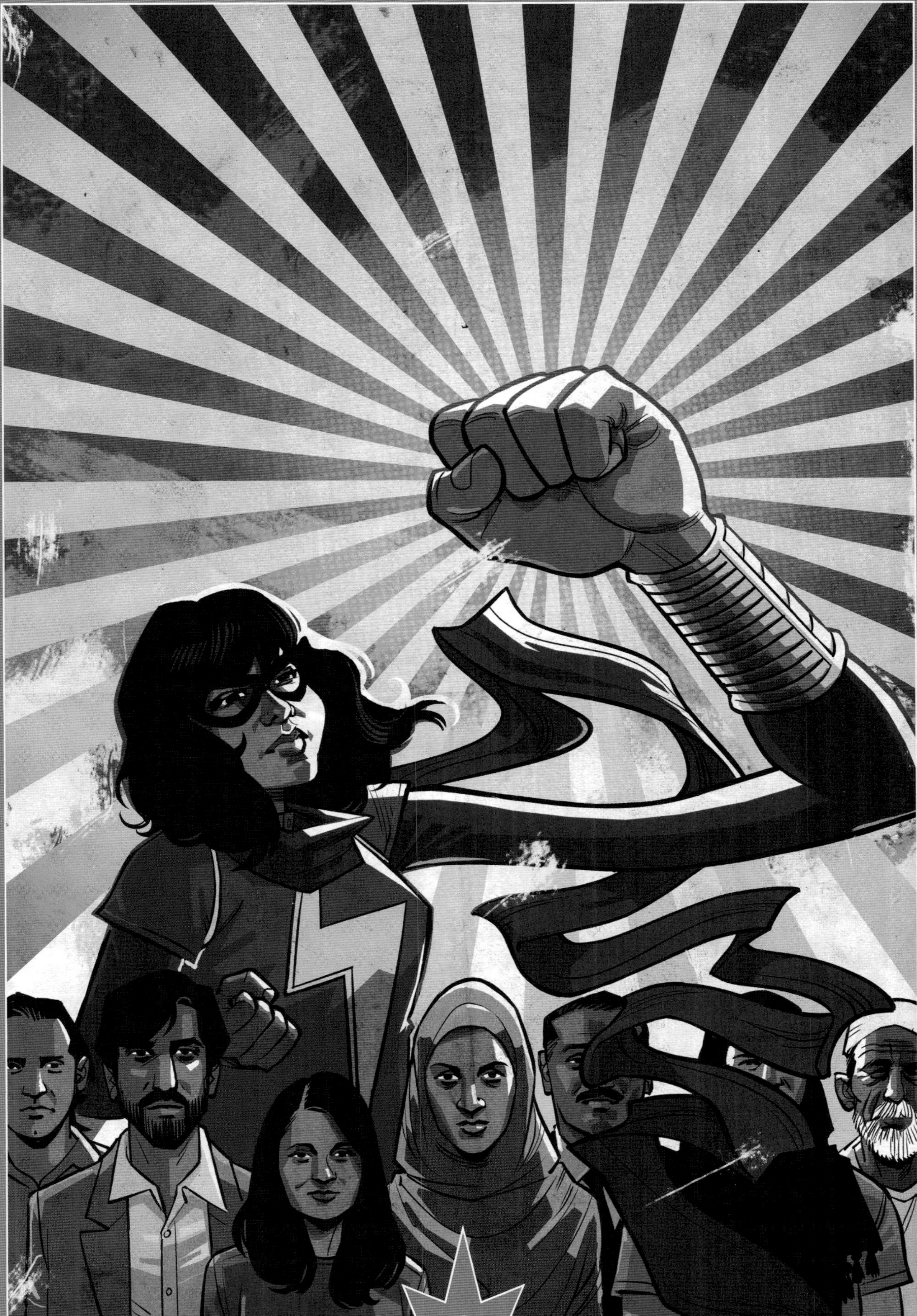
8

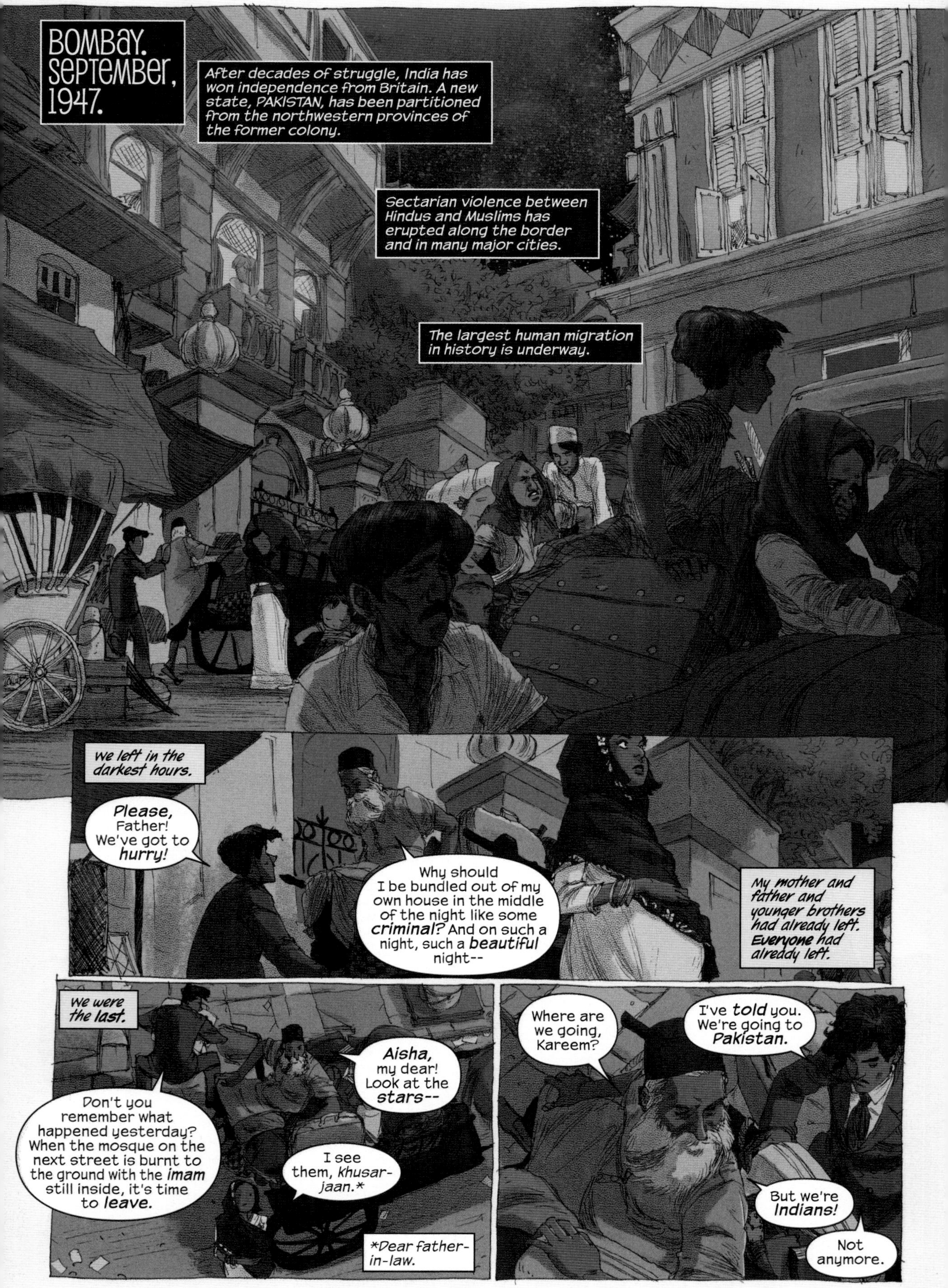

BOMBAY. SEPTEMBER, 1947.
After decades of struggle, India has won independence from Britain. A new state, PAKISTAN, has been partitioned from the northwestern provinces of the former colony.
Sectarian violence between Hindus and Muslims has erupted along the border and in many major cities.
The largest human migration in history is underway.
We left in the darkest hours.
Please, Father! We've got to hurry!
Why should I be bundled out of my own house in the middle of the night like some criminal? And on such a night, such a beautiful night--
My mother and father and younger brothers had already left. Everyone had already left.
We were the last.
Aisha, my dear! Look at the stars--
Don't you remember what happened yesterday? When the mosque on the next street is burnt to the ground with the imam still inside, it's time to leave.
I see them, khusar-jaan.*
*Dear father-in-law.
Where are we going, Kareem?
I've told you. We're going to Pakistan.
But we're Indians!
Not anymore.

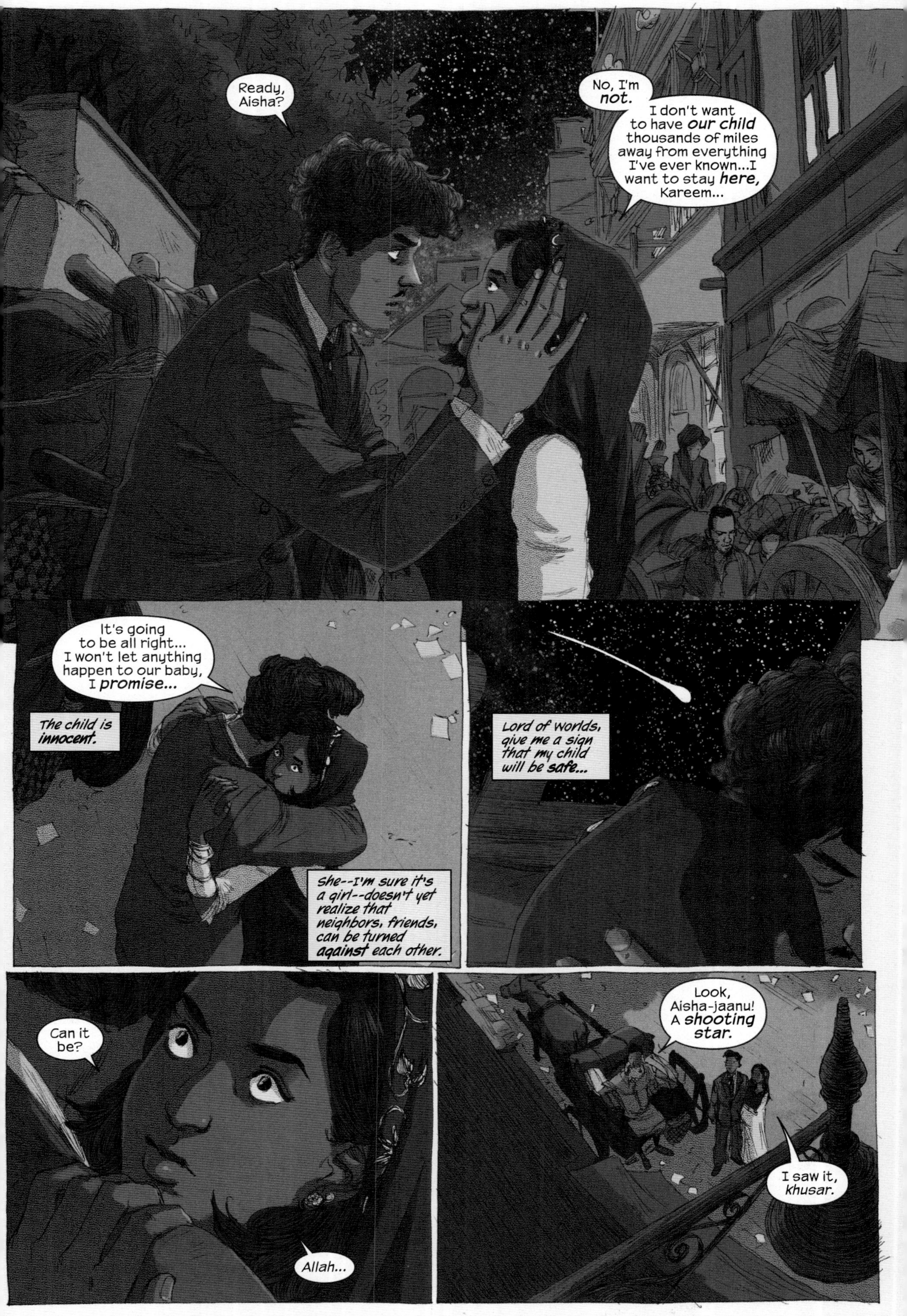

Ready, Aisha?
No, I'm not.
I don't want to have our child thousands of miles away from everything I've ever known...I want to stay here, Kareem...
It's going to be all right... I won't let anything happen to our baby, I promise...
The child is innocent.
She--I'm sure it's a girl--doesn't yet realize that neighbors, friends, can be turned against each other.
Lord of worlds, give me a sign that my child will be safe...
Can it be?
Allah...
Look, Aisha-jaanu! A shooting star.
I saw it, khusar.

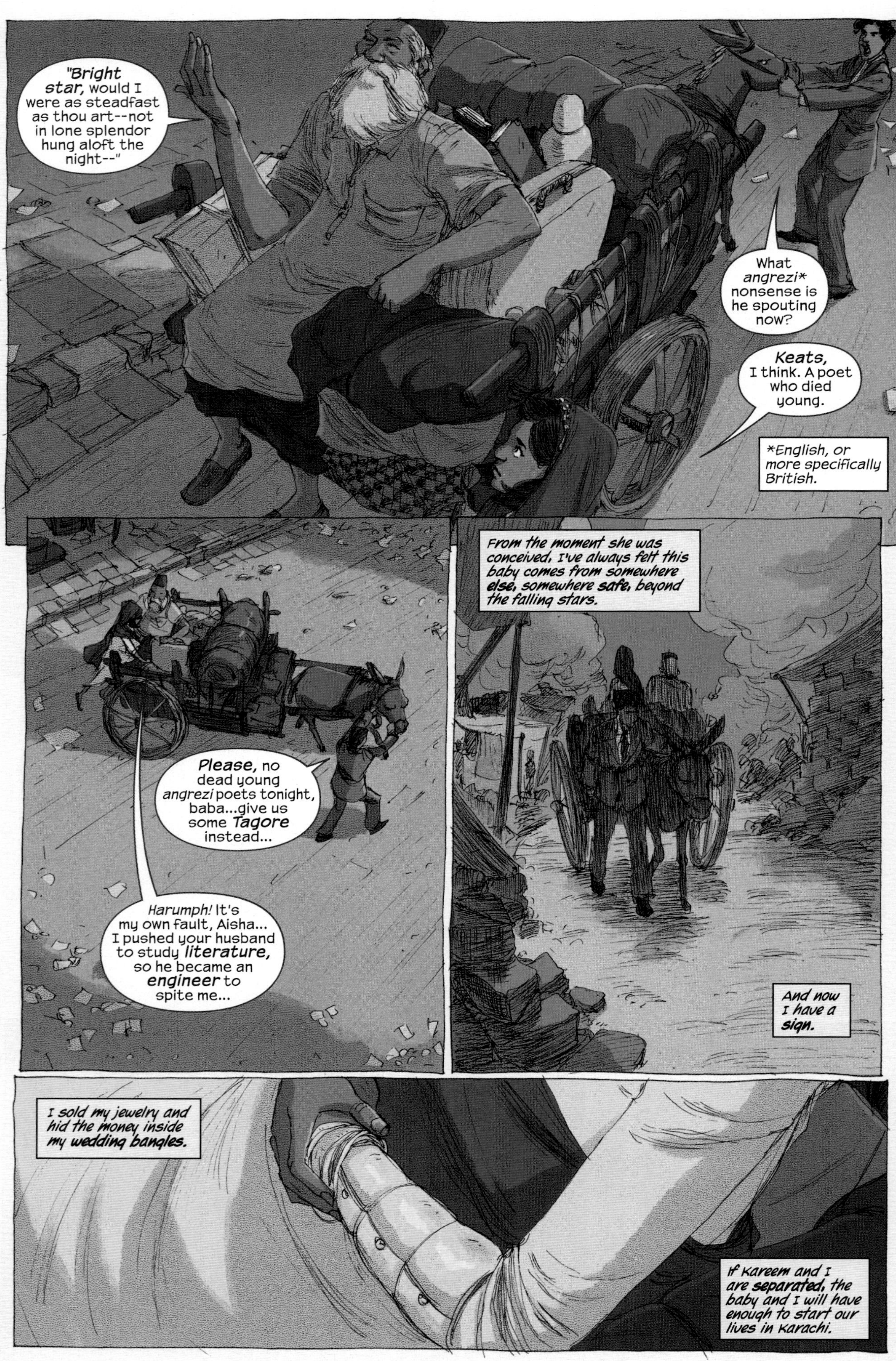
"Bright star, would I were as steadfast as thou art--not in lone splendor hung aloft the night--"
What angrezi* nonsense is he spouting now?
Keats, I think. A poet who died young.
*English, or more specifically British.
Please, no dead young angrezi poets tonight, baba...give us some Tagore instead...
Harumph! It's my own fault, Aisha... I pushed your husband to study literature, so he became an engineer to spite me...
From the moment she was conceived, I've always felt this baby comes from somewhere else, somewhere safe, beyond the falling stars.
And now I have a sign.
I sold my jewelry and hid the money inside my wedding bangles.
If Kareem and I are separated, the baby and I will have enough to start our lives in Karachi.

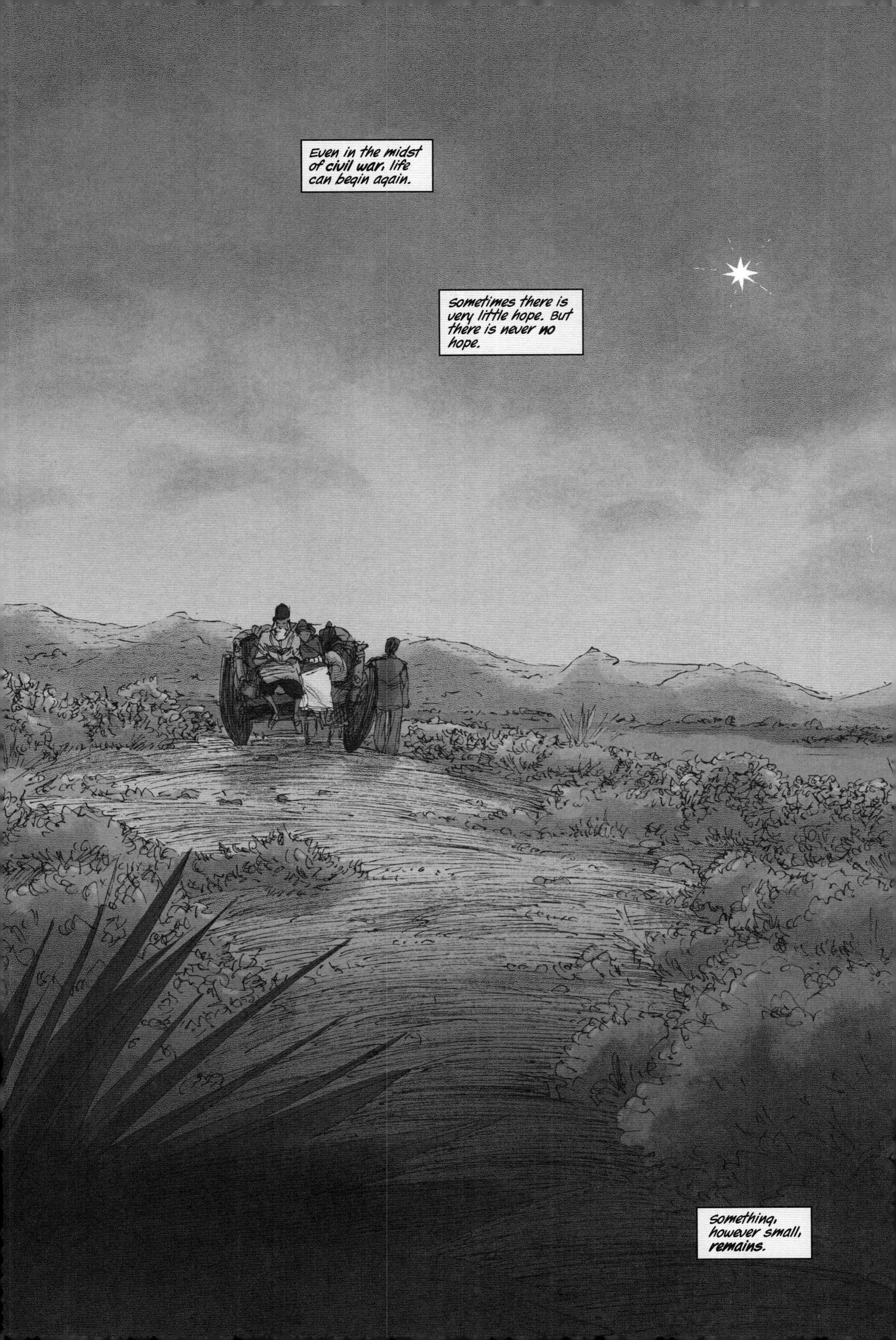
Even in the midst of civil war, life can begin again.
Sometimes there is very little hope. But there is never no hope.
Something, however small, remains.

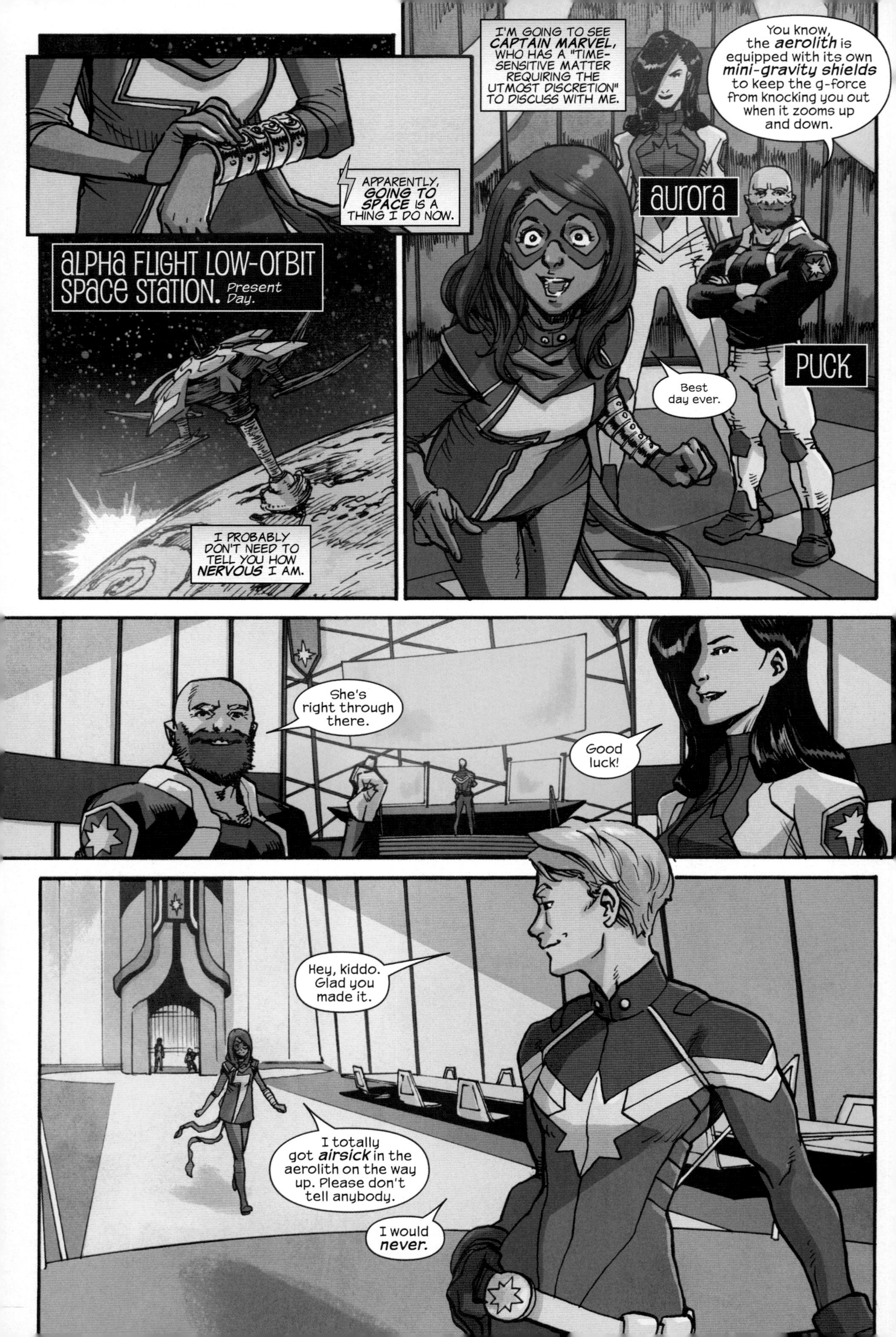
APPARENTLY, GOING TO SPACE IS A THING I DO NOW.
ALPHA FLIGHT LOW-ORBIT SPACE STATION. Present Day.
I PROBABLY DON'T NEED TO TELL YOU HOW NERVOUS I AM.
I'M GOING TO SEE CAPTAIN MARVEL, WHO HAS A "TIME-SENSITIVE MATTER REQUIRING THE UTMOST DISCRETION" TO DISCUSS WITH ME.
You know, the aerolith is equipped with its own mini-gravity shields to keep the g-force from knocking you out when it zooms up and down.
aurora
Best day ever.
PUCK
She's right through there.
Good luck!
Hey, kiddo. Glad you made it.
I totally got airsick in the aerolith on the way up. Please don't tell anybody.
I would never.

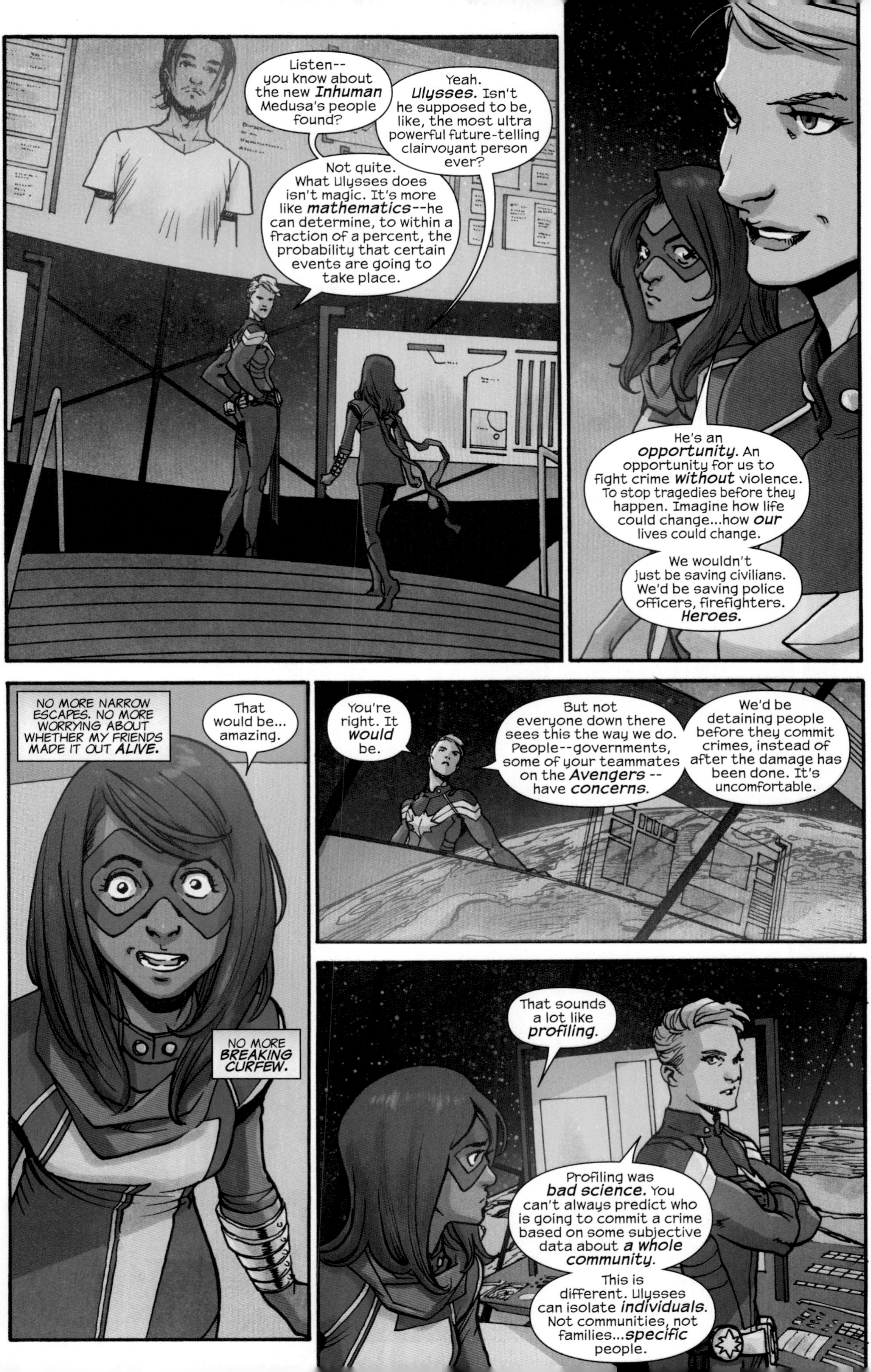
Listen-- you know about the new Inhuman Medusa's people found?
Yeah. Ulysses. Isn't he supposed to be, like, the most ultra powerful future-telling clairvoyant person ever?
Not quite. What Ulysses does isn't magic. It's more like mathematics--he can determine, to within a fraction of a percent, the probability that certain events are going to take place.
He's an opportunity. An opportunity for us to fight crime without violence. To stop tragedies before they happen. Imagine how life could change...how our lives could change.
We wouldn't just be saving civilians. We'd be saving police officers, firefighters. Heroes.
NO MORE NARROW ESCAPES. NO MORE WORRYING ABOUT WHETHER MY FRIENDS MADE IT OUT ALIVE.
That would be... amazing.
NO MORE BREAKING CURFEW.
You're right. It would be.
But not everyone down there sees this the way we do. People--governments, some of your teammates on the Avengers --have concerns.
We'd be detaining people before they commit crimes, instead of after the damage has been done. It's uncomfortable.
That sounds a lot like profiling.
Profiling was bad science. You can't always predict who is going to commit a crime based on some subjective data about a whole community.
This is different. Ulysses can isolate individuals. Not communities, not families...specific people.

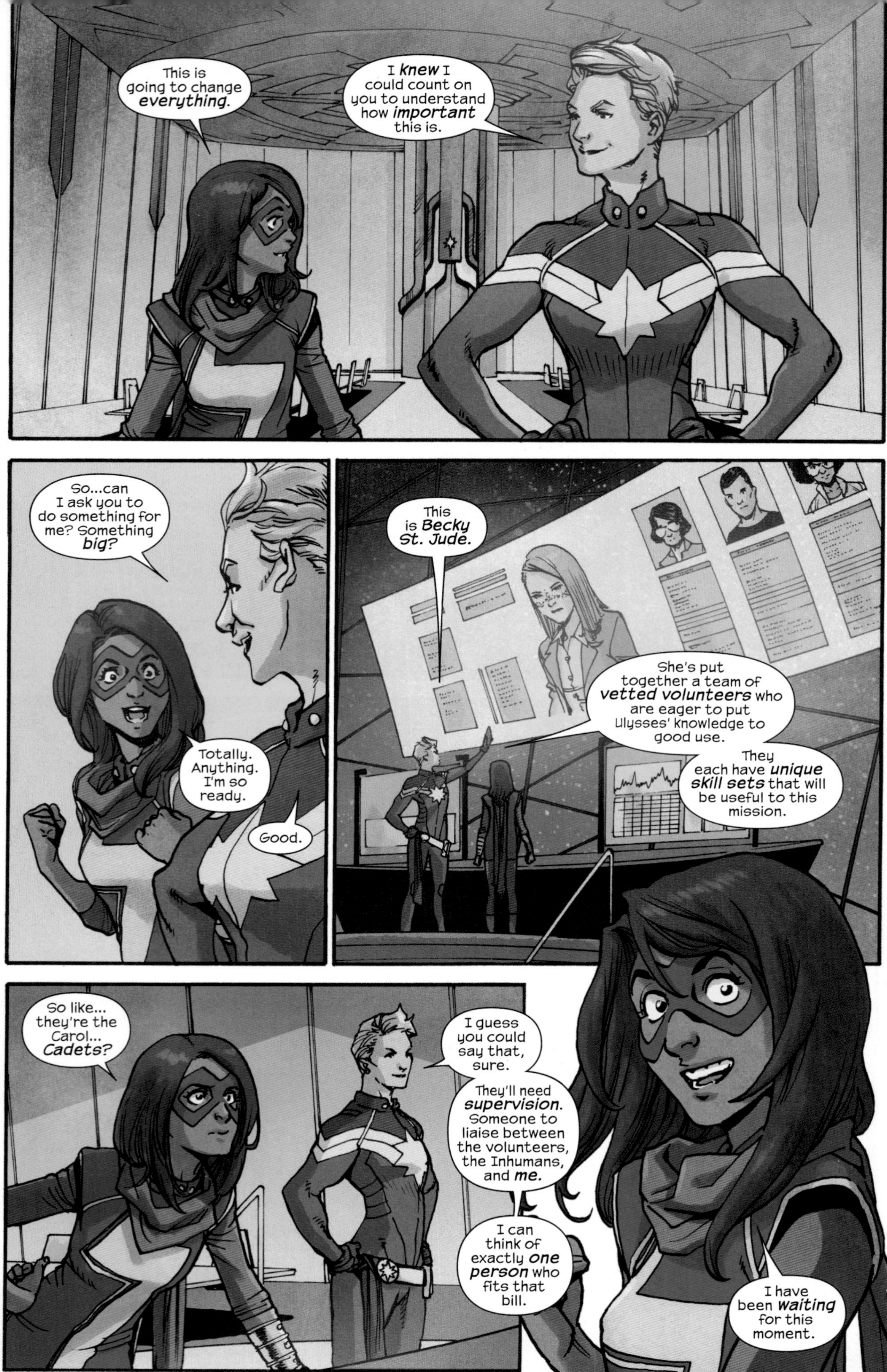
This is going to change *everything*.
I *knew* I could count on you to understand how *important* this is.
So...can I ask you to do something for me? Something *big?*
Totally. Anything. I'm so ready.
Good.
This is *Becky St. Jude.*
She's put together a team of *vetted volunteers* who are eager to put Ulysses' knowledge to good use.
They each have *unique skill sets* that will be useful to this mission.
So like... they're the Carol... *Cadets?*
I guess you could say that, sure.
They'll need *supervision*. Someone to liaise between the volunteers, the Inhumans, and *me.*
I can think of exactly *one person* who fits that bill.
I have been *waiting* for this moment.

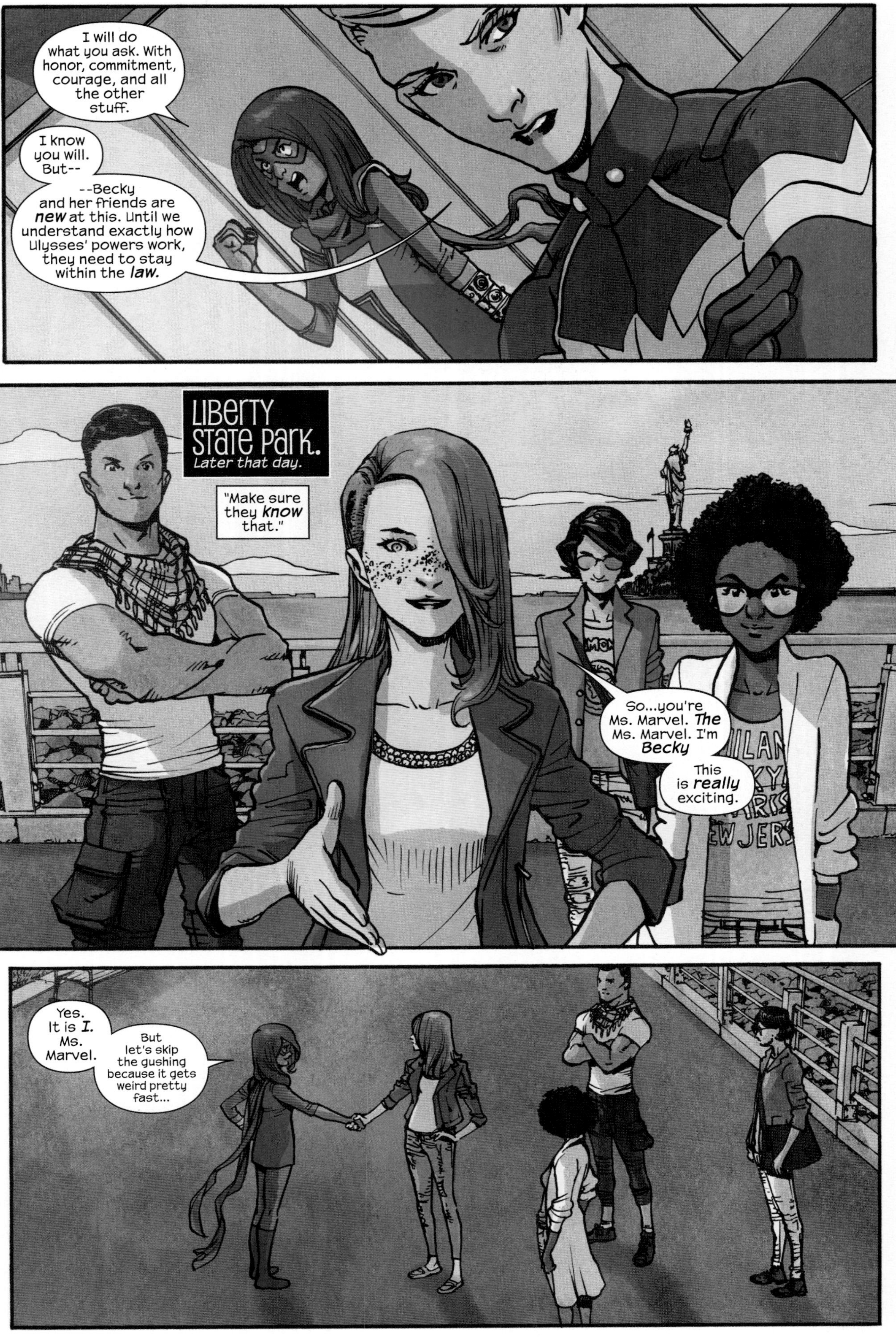
I will do what you ask. With honor, commitment, courage, and all the other stuff.
I know you will. But--
--Becky and her friends are *new* at this. Until we understand exactly how Ulysses' powers work, they need to stay within the *law.*
LIBERTY STATE PARK. *Later that day.*
"Make sure they *know* that."
So...you're Ms. Marvel. *The* Ms. Marvel. I'm *Becky*
This is *really* exciting.
Yes. It is *I.* Ms. Marvel.
But let's skip the gushing because it gets weird pretty fast...

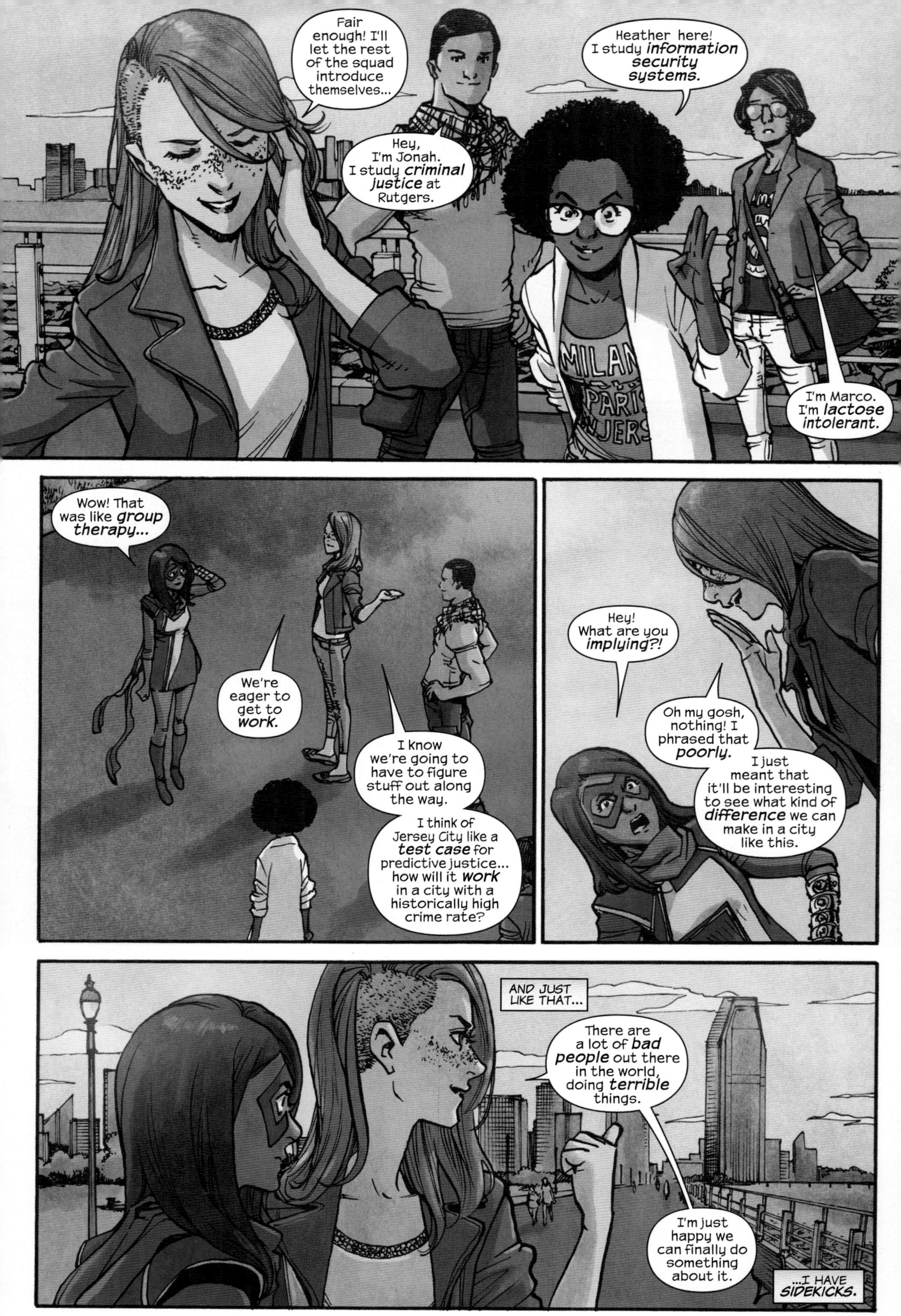
Fair enough! I'll let the rest of the squad introduce themselves...
Hey, I'm Jonah. I study criminal justice at Rutgers.
Heather here! I study information security systems.
I'm Marco. I'm lactose intolerant.
Wow! That was like group therapy...
We're eager to get to work.
I know we're going to have to figure stuff out along the way.
I think of Jersey City like a test case for predictive justice... how will it work in a city with a historically high crime rate?
Hey! What are you implying?!
Oh my gosh, nothing! I phrased that poorly.
I just meant that it'll be interesting to see what kind of difference we can make in a city like this.
AND JUST LIKE THAT...
There are a lot of bad people out there in the world, doing terrible things.
I'm just happy we can finally do something about it.
...I HAVE SIDEKICKS.

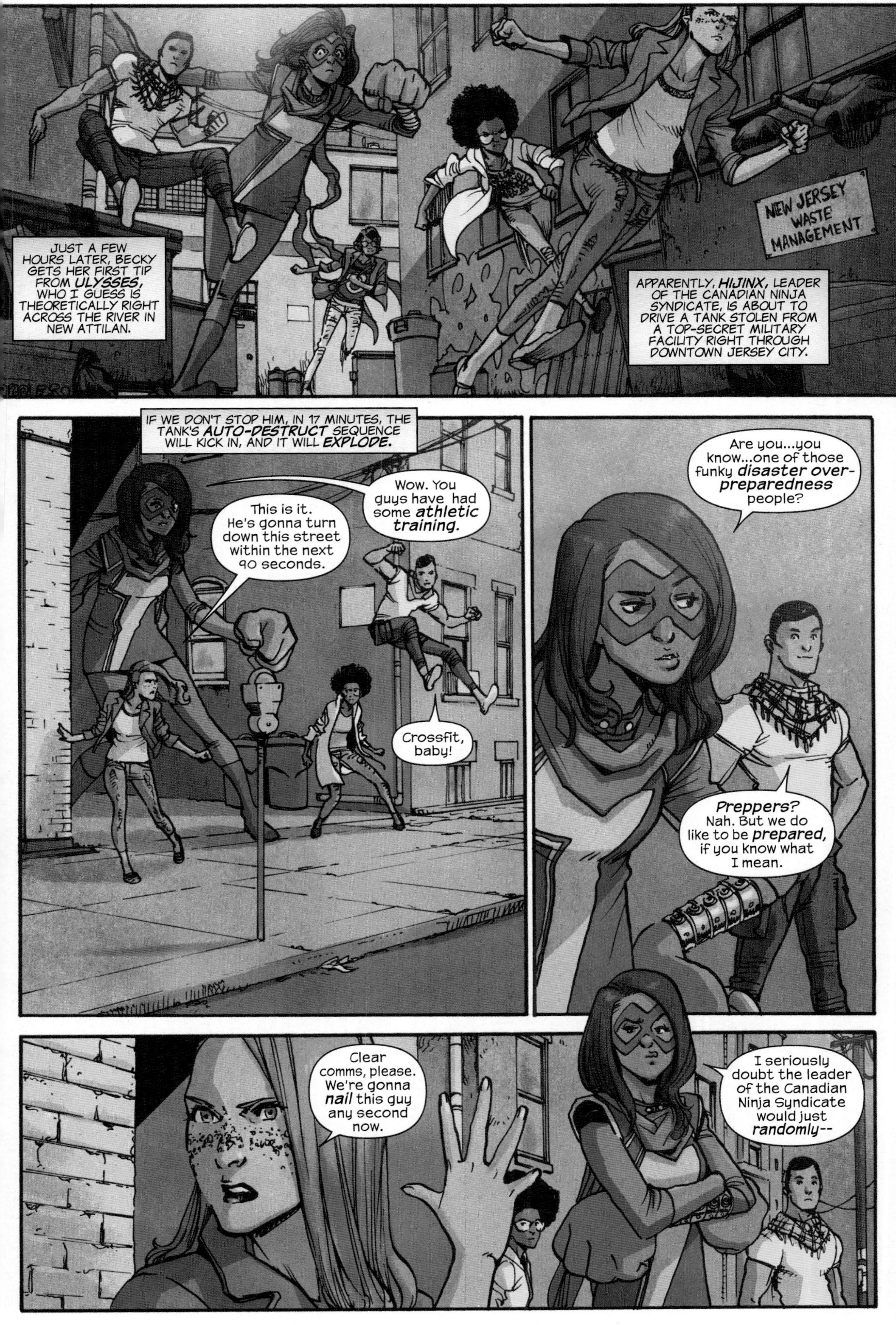
JUST A FEW HOURS LATER, BECKY GETS HER FIRST TIP FROM ULYSSES, WHO I GUESS IS THEORETICALLY RIGHT ACROSS THE RIVER IN NEW ATTILAN.
NEW JERSEY WASTE MANAGEMENT
APPARENTLY, HIJINX, LEADER OF THE CANADIAN NINJA SYNDICATE, IS ABOUT TO DRIVE A TANK STOLEN FROM A TOP-SECRET MILITARY FACILITY RIGHT THROUGH DOWNTOWN JERSEY CITY.
IF WE DON'T STOP HIM, IN 17 MINUTES, THE TANK'S AUTO-DESTRUCT SEQUENCE WILL KICK IN, AND IT WILL EXPLODE.
This is it. He's gonna turn down this street within the next 90 seconds.
Wow. You guys have had some athletic training.
Crossfit, baby!
Are you...you know...one of those funky disaster over-preparedness people?
Preppers? Nah. But we do like to be prepared, if you know what I mean.
Clear comms, please. We're gonna nail this guy any second now.
I seriously doubt the leader of the Canadian Ninja Syndicate would just randomly--

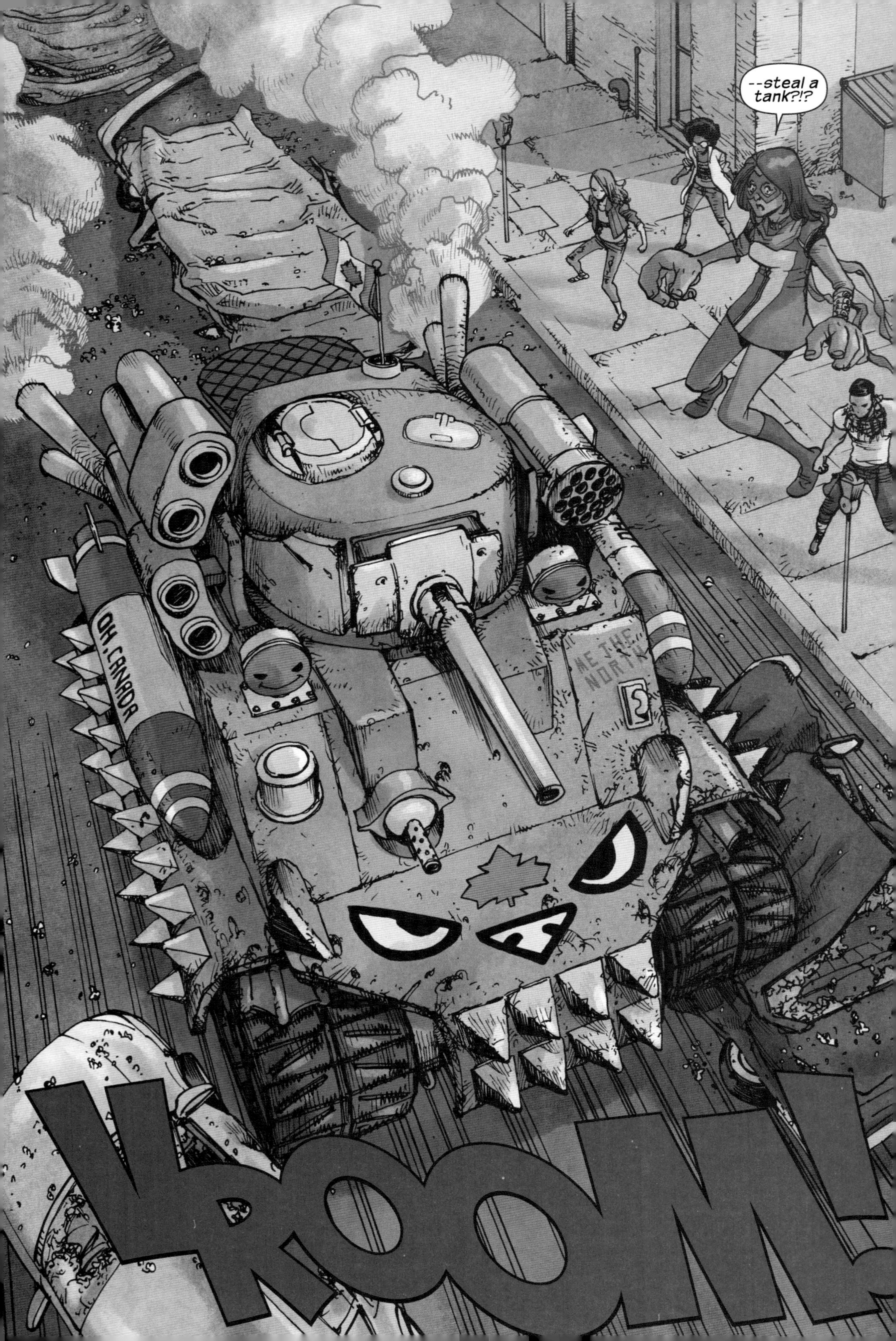
--steal a tank?!?
OH, CANADA
WE THE NORTH
KROOM!

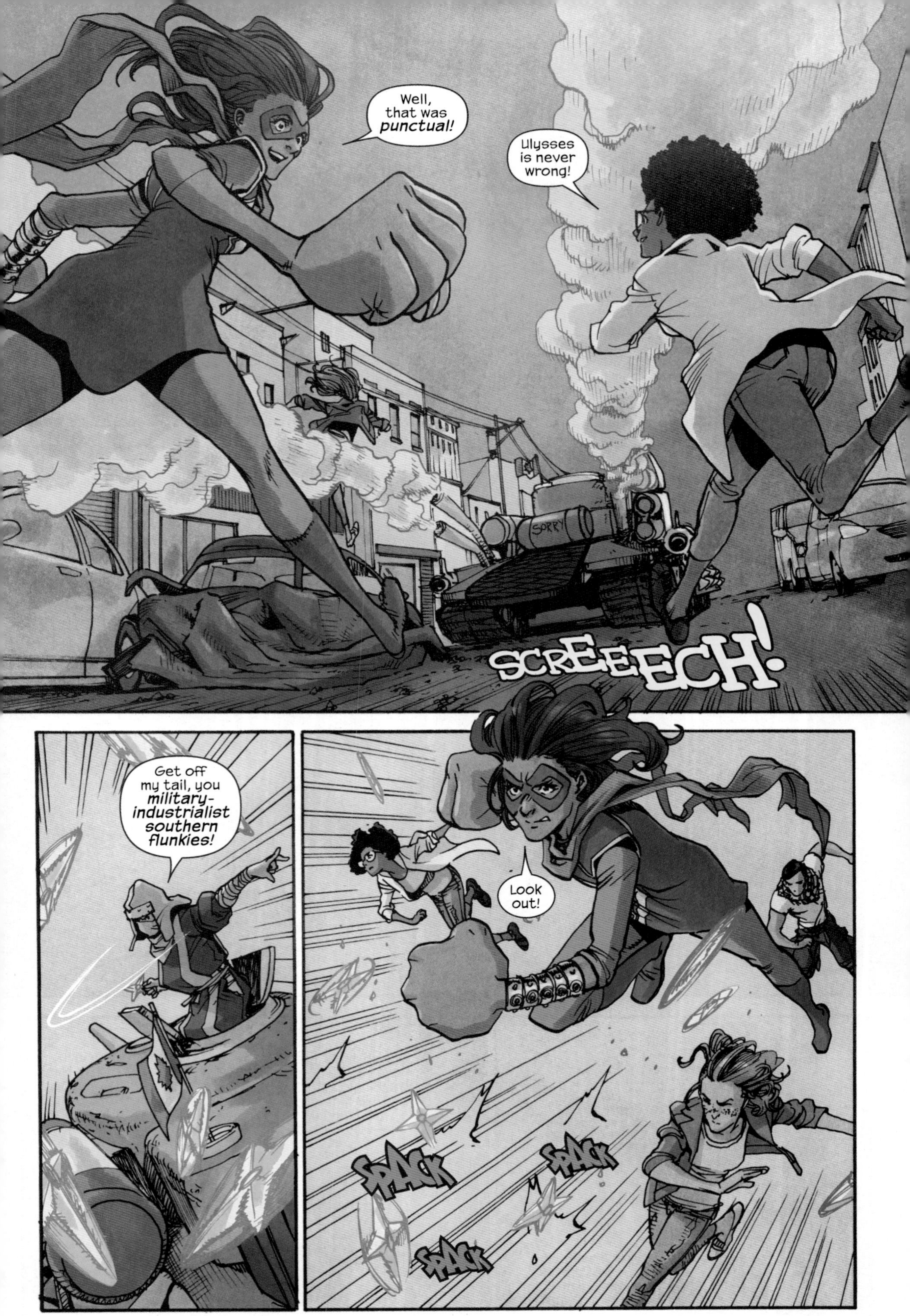

Well, that was punctual!
Ulysses is never wrong!
SORRY
SCREEEECH!
Get off my tail, you military-industrialist southern flunkies!
Look out!
SPACK
SPACK
SPACK

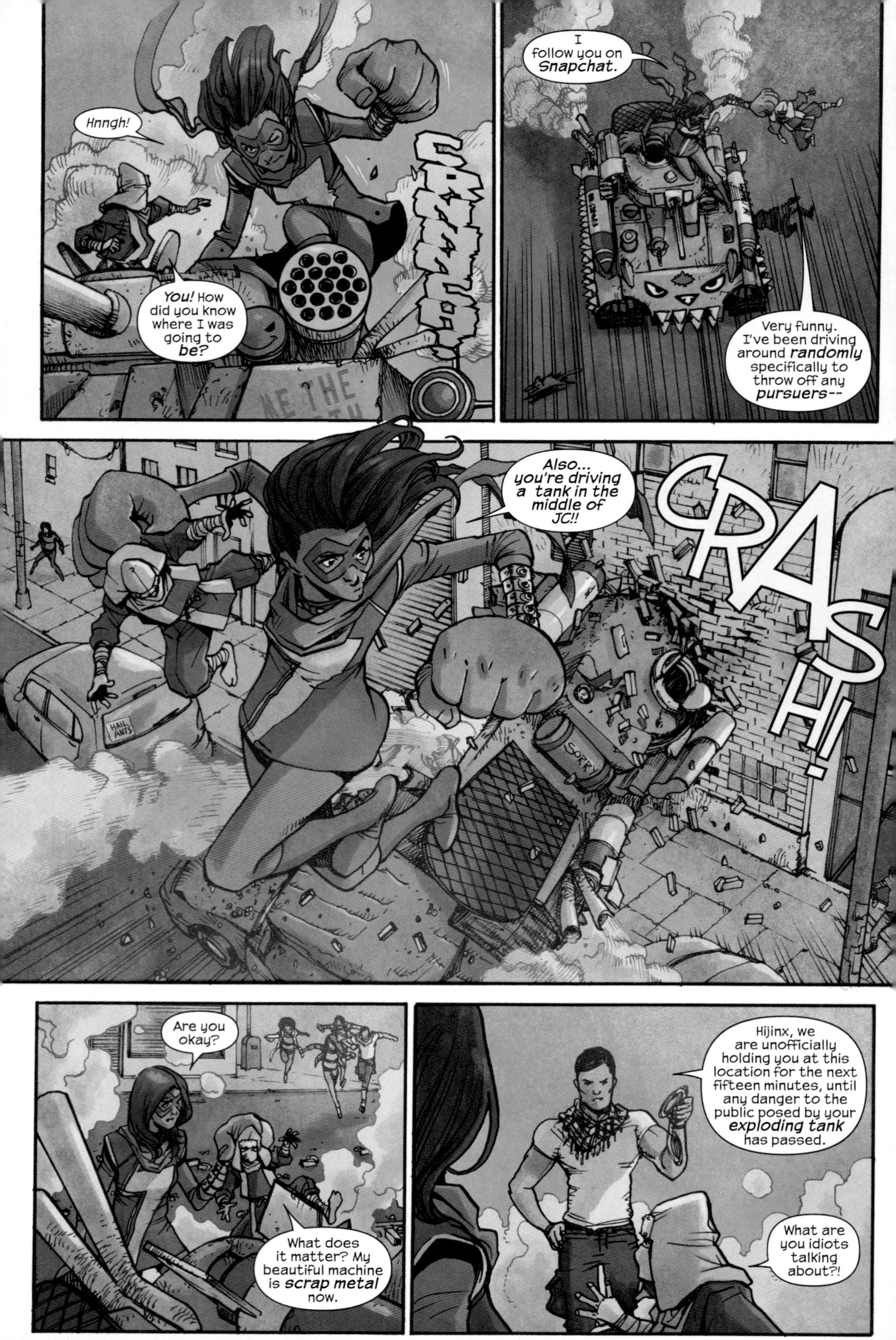
Hnngh!
You! How did you know where I was going to be?
I follow you on Snapchat.
Very funny. I've been driving around randomly specifically to throw off any pursuers--
Also... you're driving a tank in the middle of JC!!
CRASH!
HAIL ANTS
Are you okay?
What does it matter? My beautiful machine is scrap metal now.
Hijinx, we are unofficially holding you at this location for the next fifteen minutes, until any danger to the public posed by your exploding tank has passed.
What are you idiots talking about?!

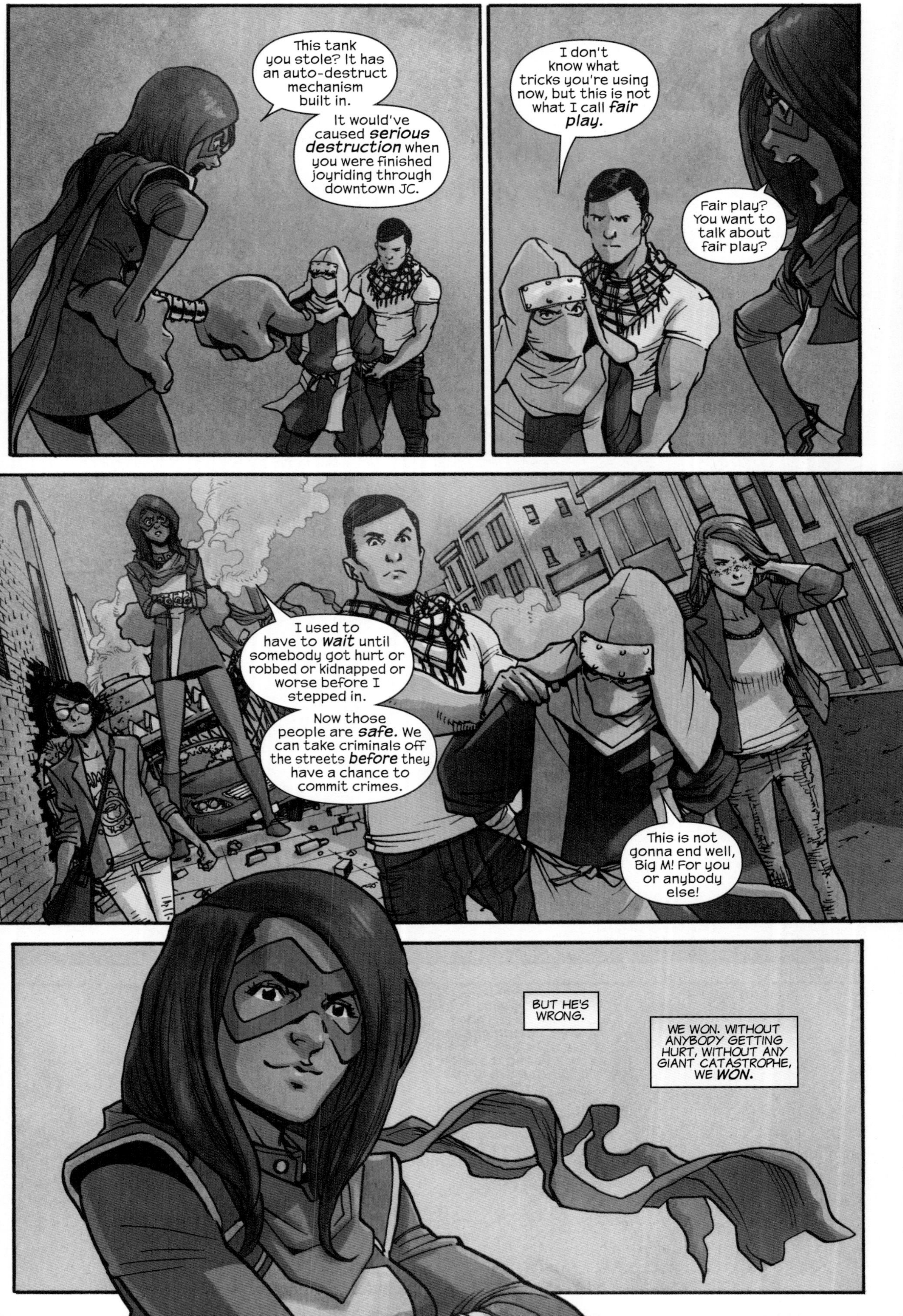
This tank you stole? It has an auto-destruct mechanism built in.
It would've caused *serious destruction* when you were finished joyriding through downtown JC.
I don't know what tricks you're using now, but this is not what I call *fair play.*
Fair play? You want to talk about fair play?
I used to have to *wait* until somebody got hurt or robbed or kidnapped or worse before I stepped in.
Now those people are *safe.* We can take criminals off the streets *before* they have a chance to commit crimes.
This is not gonna end well, Big M! For you or anybody else!
BUT HE'S WRONG.
WE WON. WITHOUT ANYBODY GETTING HURT, WITHOUT ANY GIANT CATASTROPHE, WE *WON.*

Earlier today, the crime lord known only as *Hijinx*, leader of a Toronto-based *smuggling ring*, was apprehended by *Ms. Marvel* and a cadre of *assistants*.

HIJINX

CANADIAN NINJA LEADER APPRE

Though the experimental military equipment stolen by Hijinx was destroyed during a high-speed chase, no one was seriously injured.

Ms. Marvel and her--

This *isn't* gonna end well.

Weird. You're the *second* person who's said that today.

Well it's *true*. If they prosecute this Hijinx guy for something he *might* have done with that tank, we'll have to *redefine* what we call crime.

Tyesha, if he was *planning* to do something terrible with it, isn't it better to get him off the streets *before* he hurts somebody?

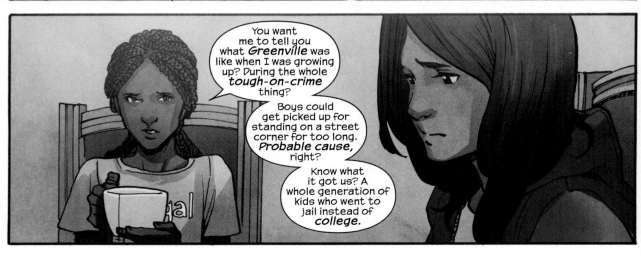

You want me to tell you what *Greenville* was like when I was growing up? During the whole *tough-on-crime* thing?

Boys could get picked up for standing on a street corner for too long. *Probable cause*, right?

Know what it got us? A whole generation of kids who went to jail instead of *college*.

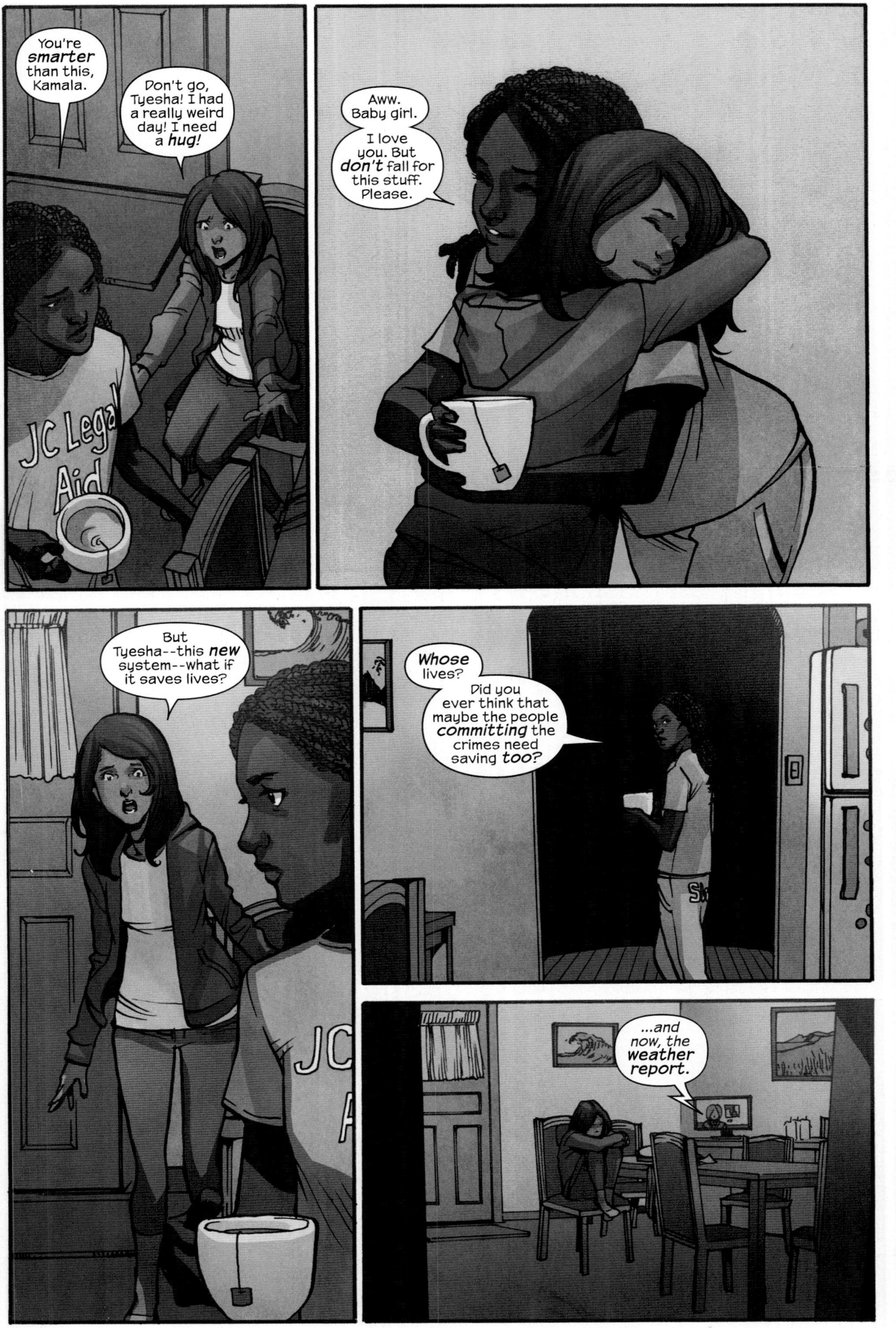

You're *smarter* than this, Kamala.
Don't go, Tyesha! I had a really weird day! I need a *hug!*
JC Legal Aid
Aww. Baby girl.
I love you. But *don't* fall for this stuff. Please.
But Tyesha--this *new* system--what if it saves lives?
JC
Whose lives?
Did you ever think that maybe the people *committing* the crimes need saving *too?*
...and now, the *weather report.*

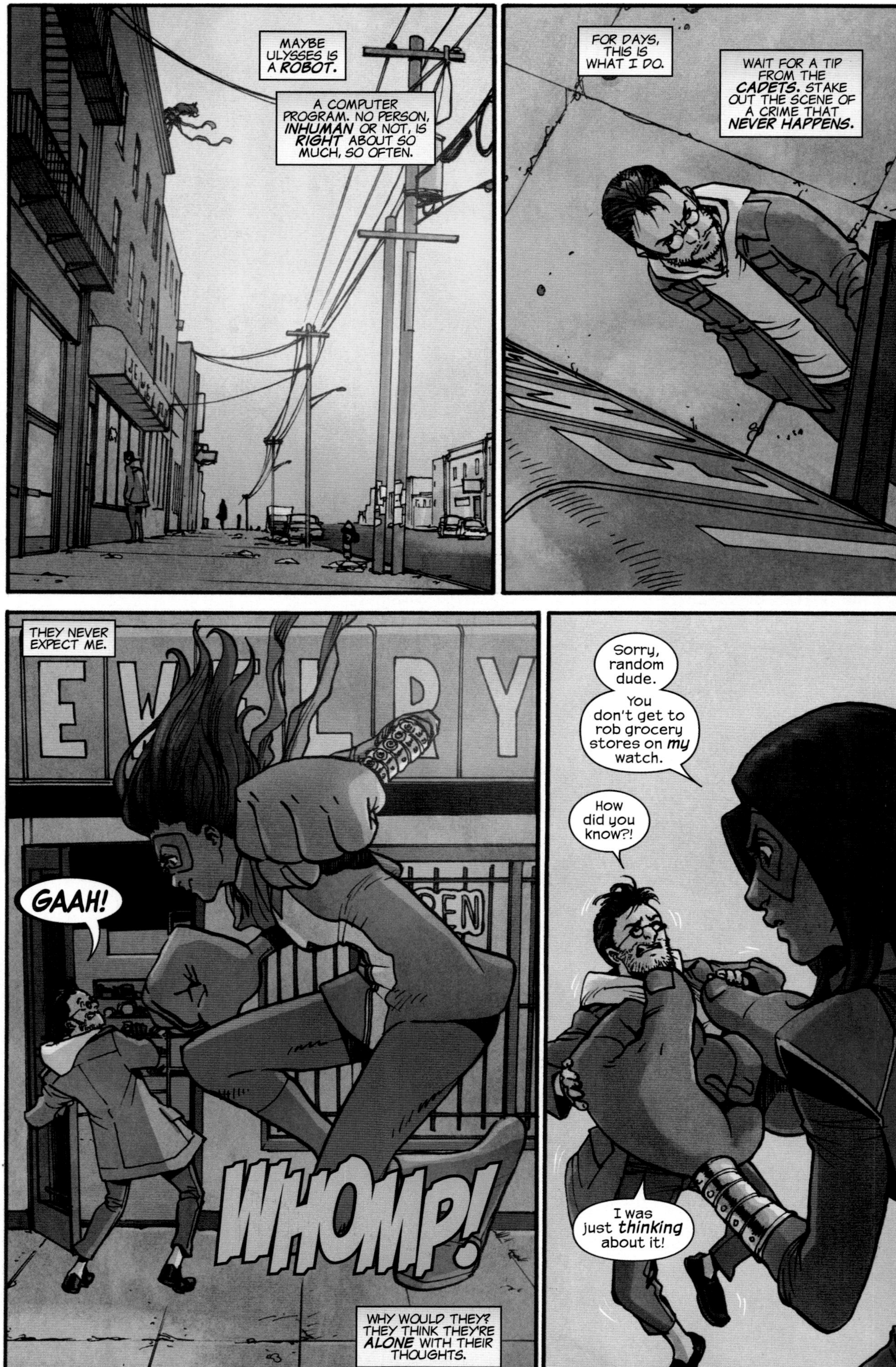
MAYBE ULYSSES IS A ROBOT.
A COMPUTER PROGRAM. NO PERSON, INHUMAN OR NOT, IS RIGHT ABOUT SO MUCH, SO OFTEN.
FOR DAYS, THIS IS WHAT I DO.
WAIT FOR A TIP FROM THE CADETS. STAKE OUT THE SCENE OF A CRIME THAT NEVER HAPPENS.
THEY NEVER EXPECT ME.
GAAH!
WHOMP!
WHY WOULD THEY? THEY THINK THEY'RE ALONE WITH THEIR THOUGHTS.
Sorry, random dude.
You don't get to rob grocery stores on my watch.
How did you know?!
I was just thinking about it!

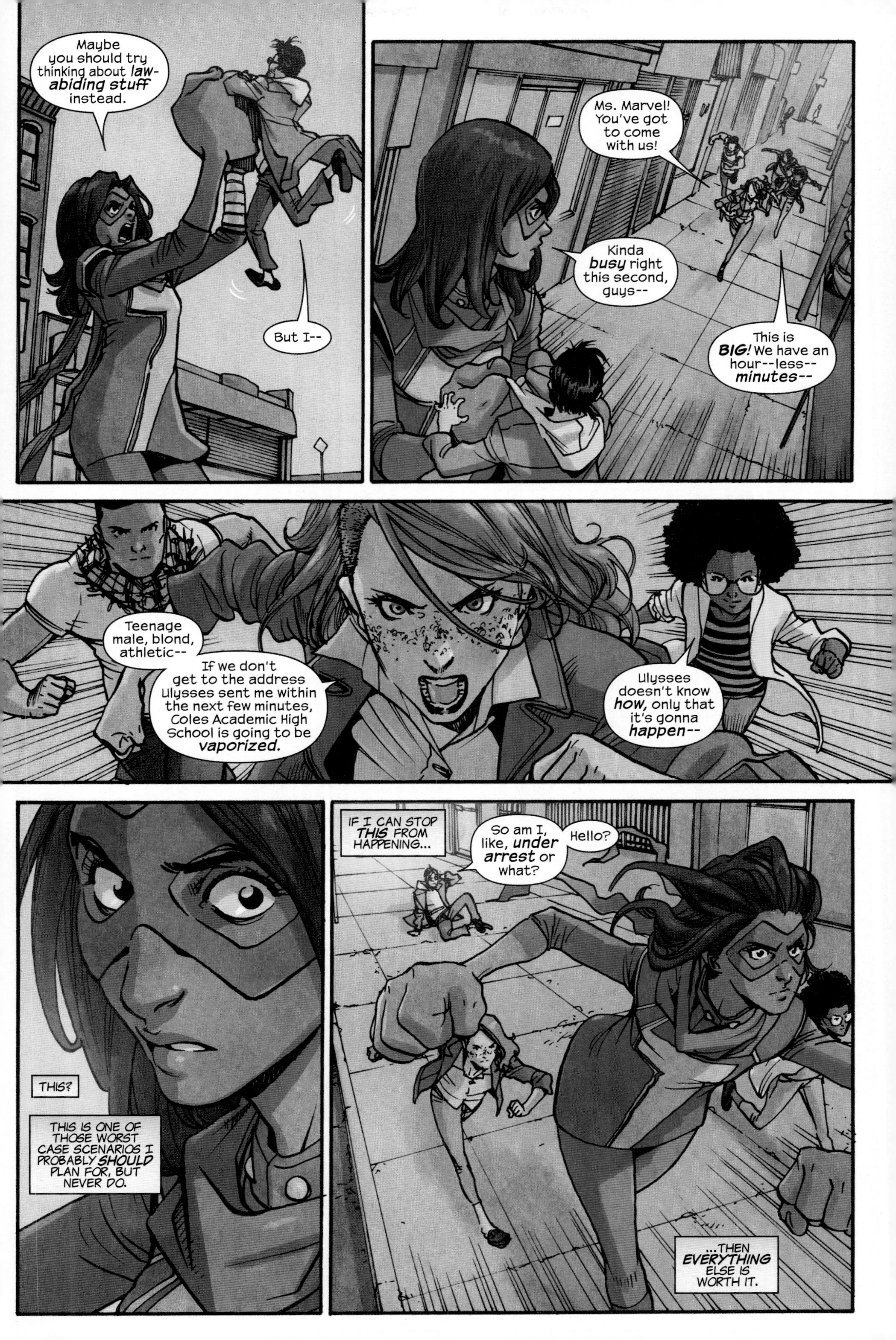
Maybe you should try thinking about *law-abiding stuff* instead.
But I--
Ms. Marvel! You've got to come with us!
Kinda **busy** right this second, guys--
This is **BIG!** We have an hour--less--**minutes**--
Teenage male, blond, athletic--
If we don't get to the address Ulysses sent me within the next few minutes, Coles Academic High School is going to be **vaporized.**
Ulysses doesn't know **how**, only that it's gonna **happen**--
THIS?
THIS IS ONE OF THOSE WORST CASE SCENARIOS I PROBABLY **SHOULD** PLAN FOR, BUT NEVER DO.
IF I CAN STOP **THIS** FROM HAPPENING...
So am I, like, **under arrest** or what?
Hello?
...THEN **EVERYTHING** ELSE IS WORTH IT.

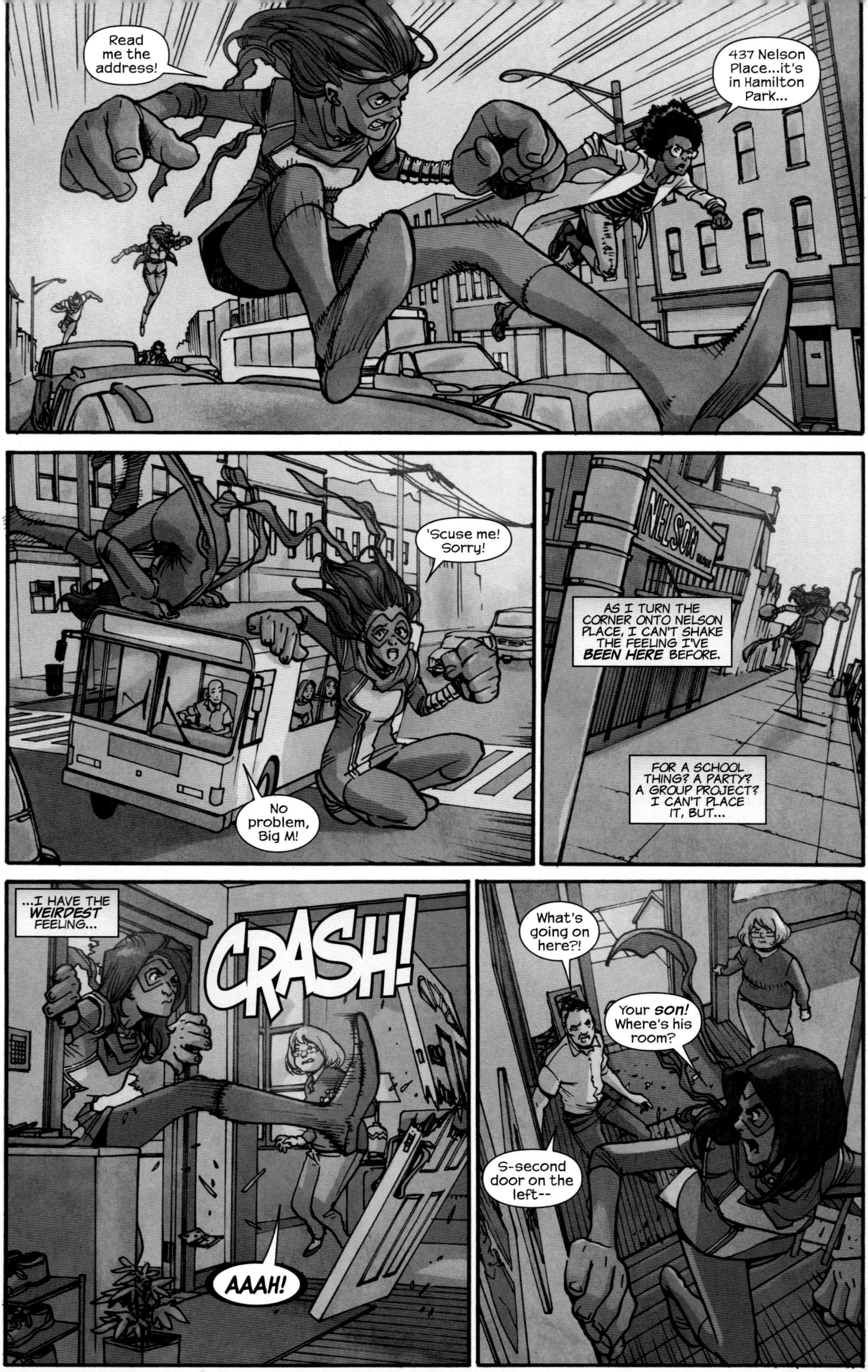

Read me the address!
437 Nelson Place...it's in Hamilton Park...
'Scuse me! Sorry!
No problem, Big M!
NELSON
AS I TURN THE CORNER ONTO NELSON PLACE, I CAN'T SHAKE THE FEELING I'VE *BEEN HERE* BEFORE.
FOR A SCHOOL THING? A PARTY? A GROUP PROJECT? I CAN'T PLACE IT, BUT...
...I HAVE THE *WEIRDEST* FEELING...
CRASH!
AAAH!
What's going on here?!
Your *son!* Where's his room?
S-second door on the left--

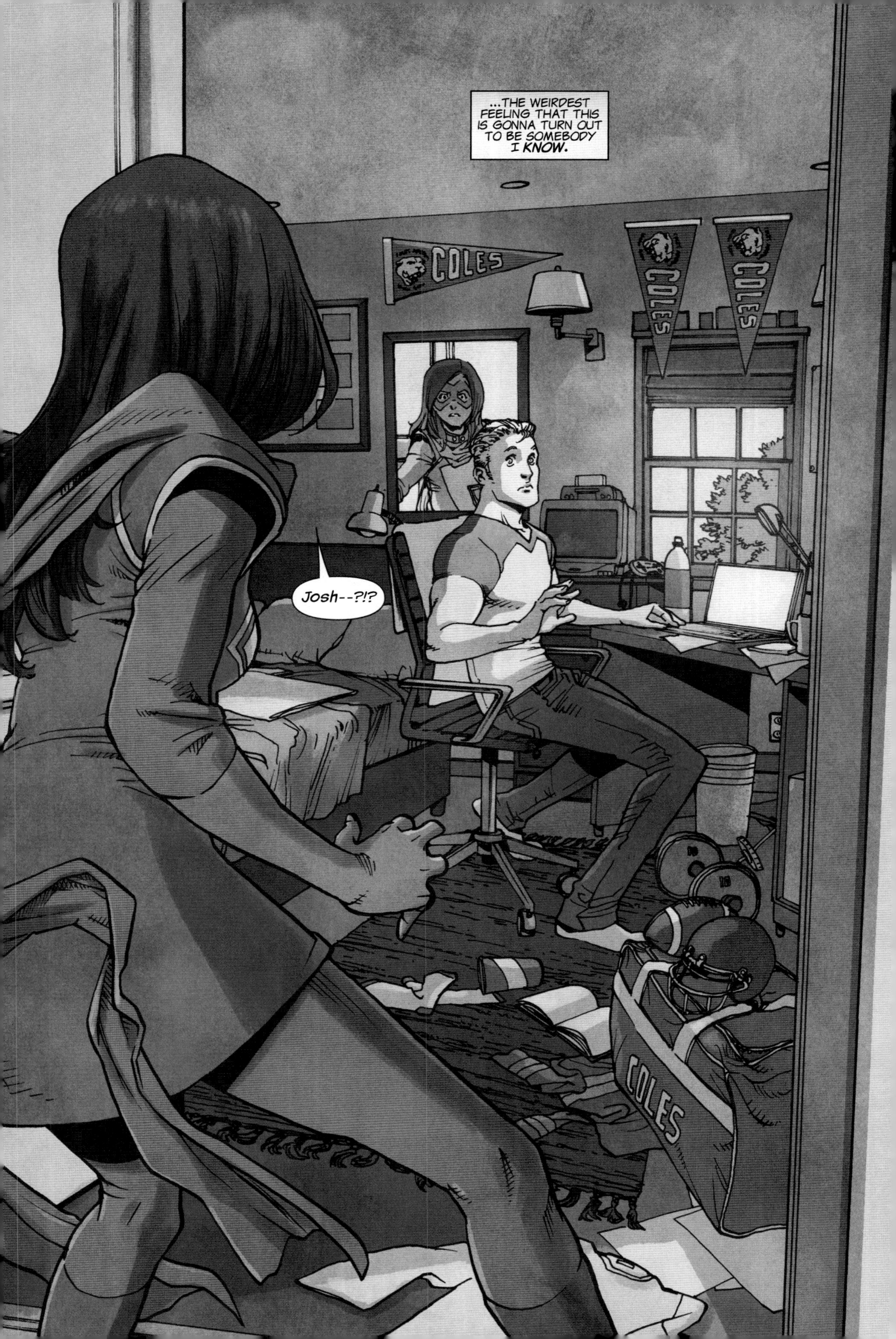
...THE WEIRDEST FEELING THAT THIS IS GONNA TURN OUT TO BE SOMEBODY I KNOW.
COLES
COLES
COLES
Josh--?!?
COLES

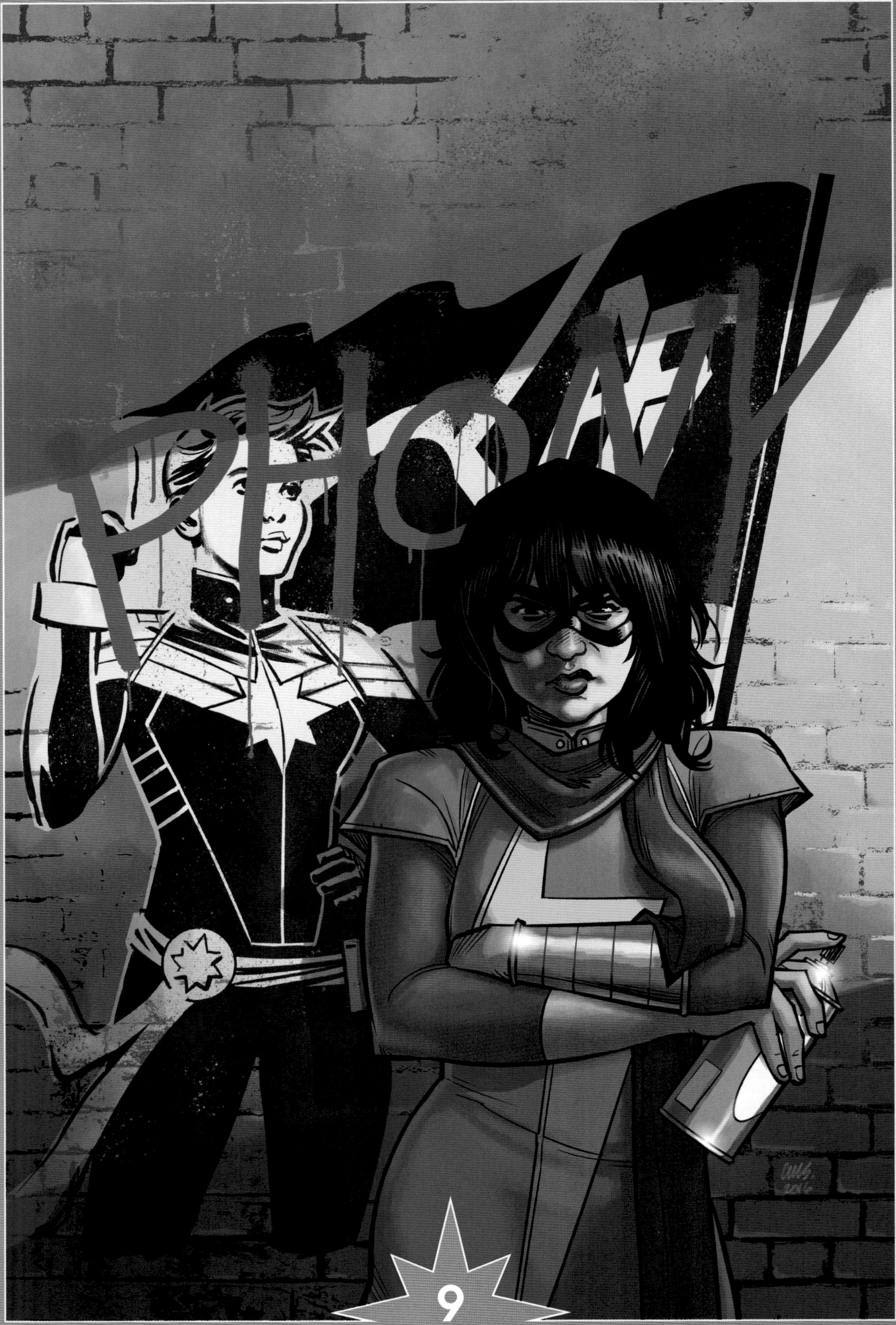
PHONY

9

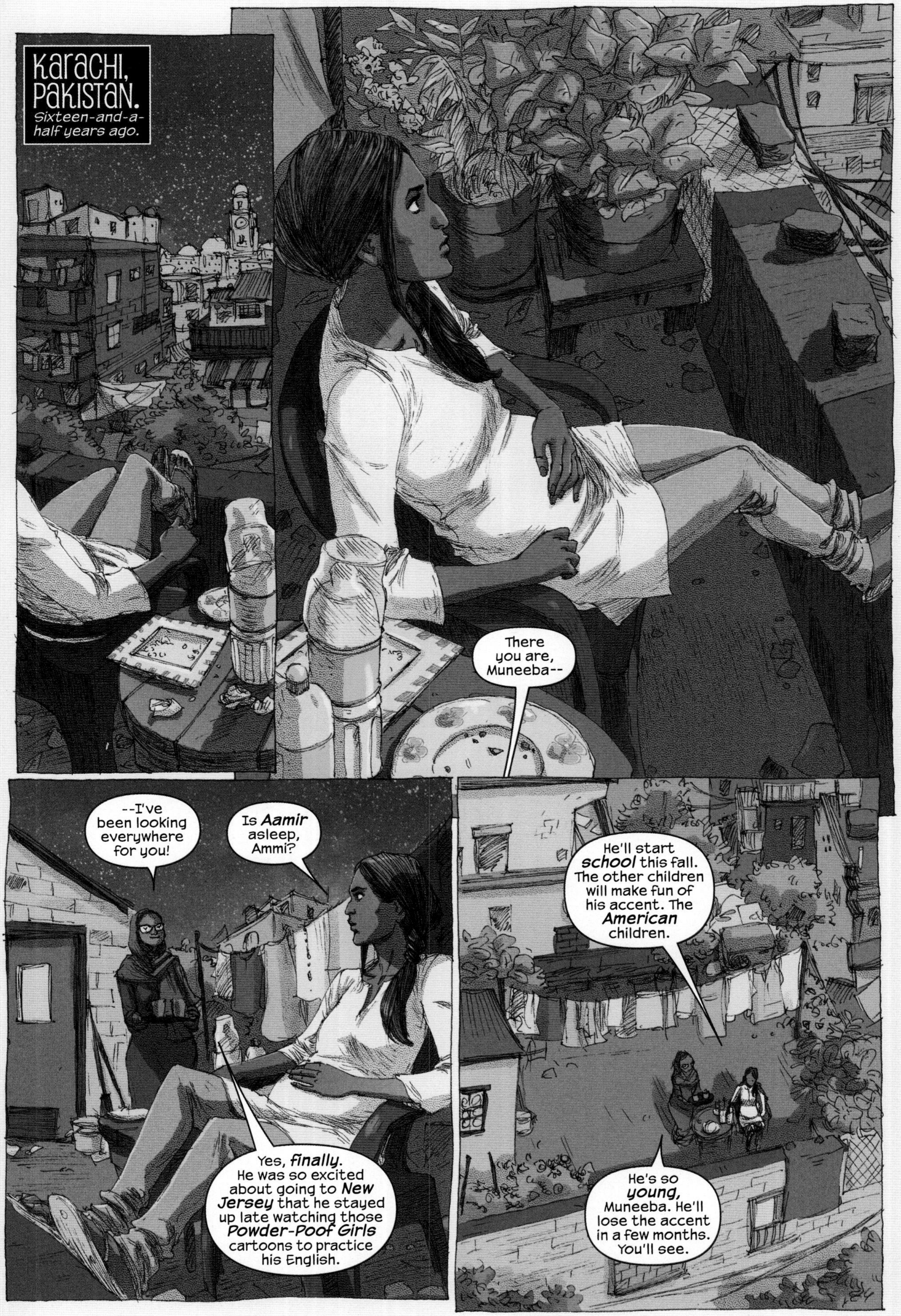
Karachi, Pakistan.
Sixteen-and-a-half years ago.
There you are, Muneeba--
--I've been looking everywhere for you!
Is Aamir asleep, Ammi?
Yes, finally. He was so excited about going to New Jersey that he stayed up late watching those Powder-Poof Girls cartoons to practice his English.
He'll start school this fall. The other children will make fun of his accent. The American children.
He's so young, Muneeba. He'll lose the accent in a few months. You'll see.

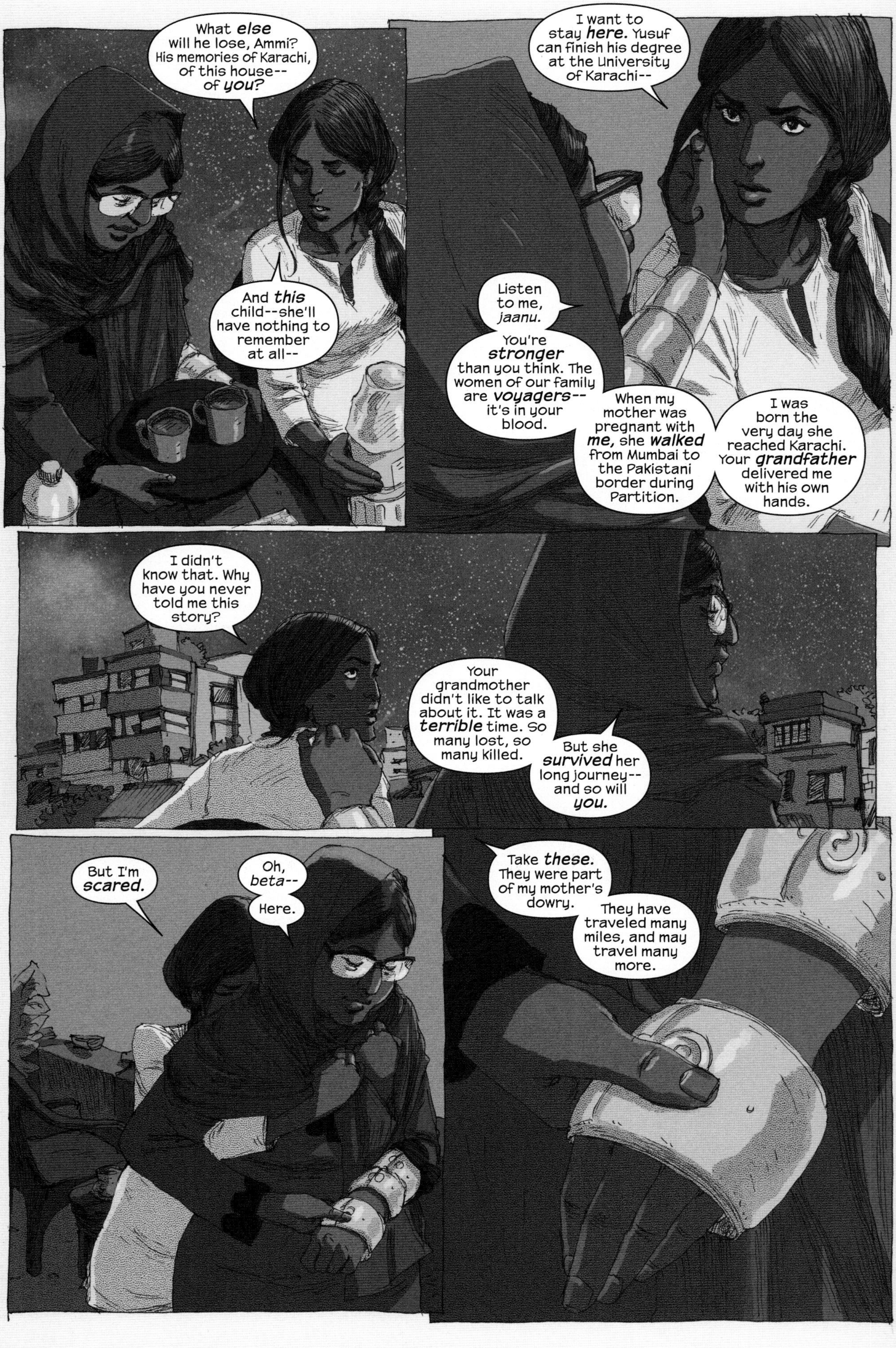
What else will he lose, Ammi? His memories of Karachi, of this house-- of you?
And this child--she'll have nothing to remember at all--
I want to stay here. Yusuf can finish his degree at the University of Karachi--
Listen to me, jaanu.
You're stronger than you think. The women of our family are voyagers-- it's in your blood.
When my mother was pregnant with me, she walked from Mumbai to the Pakistani border during Partition.
I was born the very day she reached Karachi. Your grandfather delivered me with his own hands.
I didn't know that. Why have you never told me this story?
Your grandmother didn't like to talk about it. It was a terrible time. So many lost, so many killed.
But she survived her long journey-- and so will you.
But I'm scared.
Oh, beta--
Here.
Take these. They were part of my mother's dowry.
They have traveled many miles, and may travel many more.

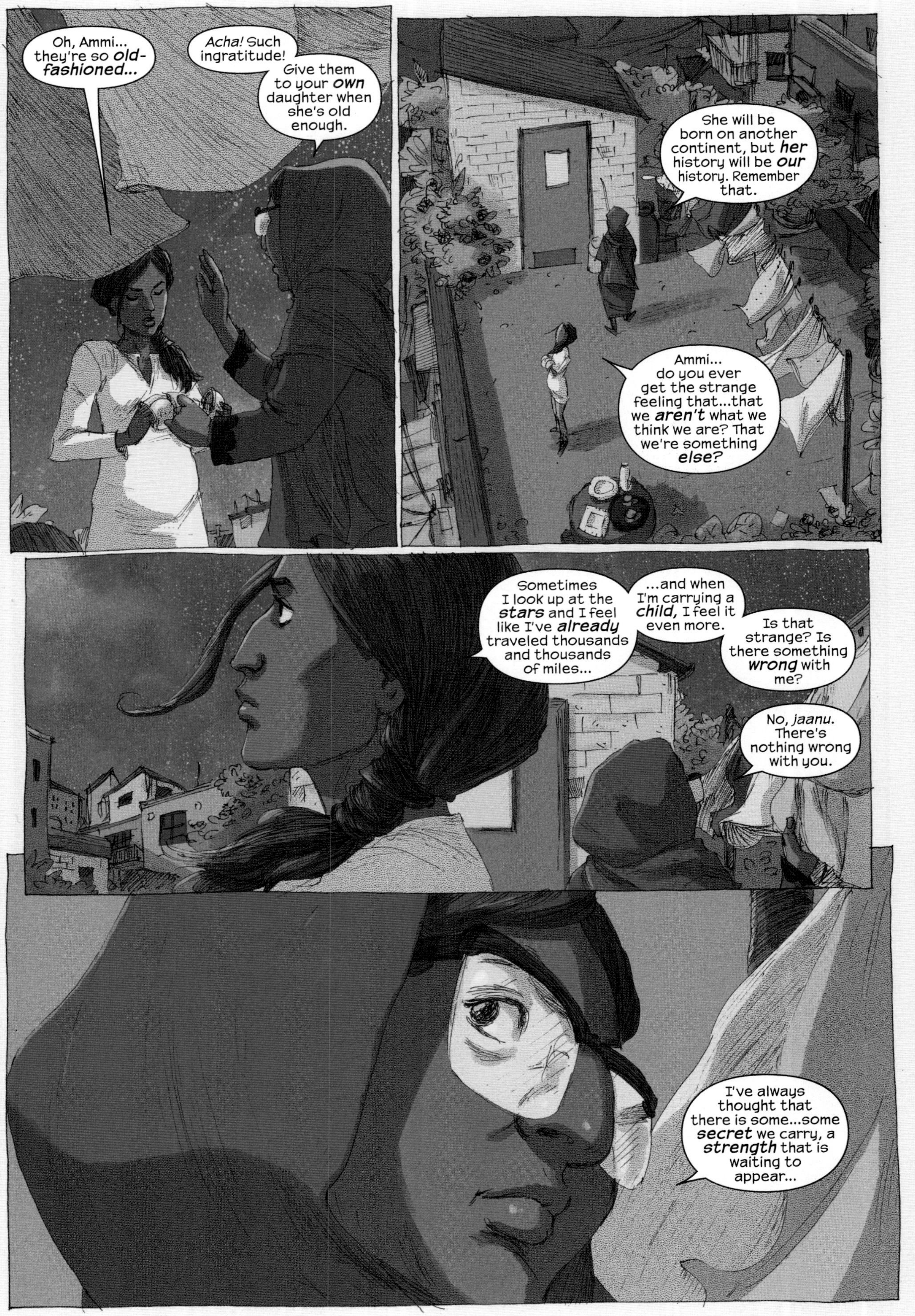

Oh, Ammi... they're so old-fashioned...
Acha! Such ingratitude!
Give them to your own daughter when she's old enough.
She will be born on another continent, but her history will be our history. Remember that.
Ammi... do you ever get the strange feeling that...that we aren't what we think we are? That we're something else?
Sometimes I look up at the stars and I feel like I've already traveled thousands and thousands of miles...
...and when I'm carrying a child, I feel it even more.
Is that strange? Is there something wrong with me?
No, jaanu. There's nothing wrong with you.
I've always thought that there is some...some secret we carry, a strength that is waiting to appear...

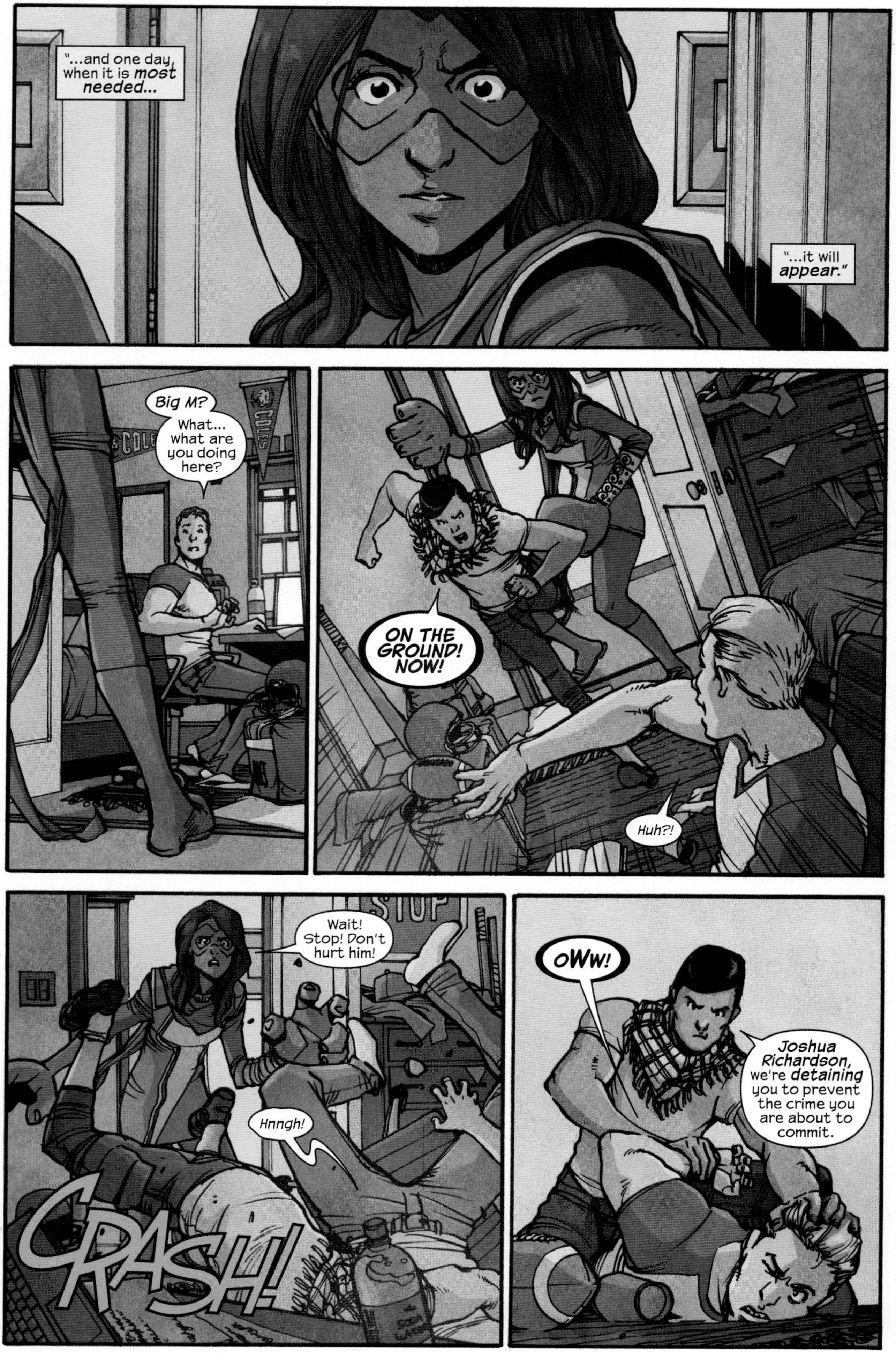
"...and one day, when it is *most* *needed*...
"...it will *appear*."
Big M? What... what are you doing here?
ON THE GROUND! NOW!
Huh?!
Wait! Stop! Don't hurt him!
Hnngh!
CRASH!
OWW!
Joshua Richardson, we're *detaining* you to prevent the crime you are about to commit.

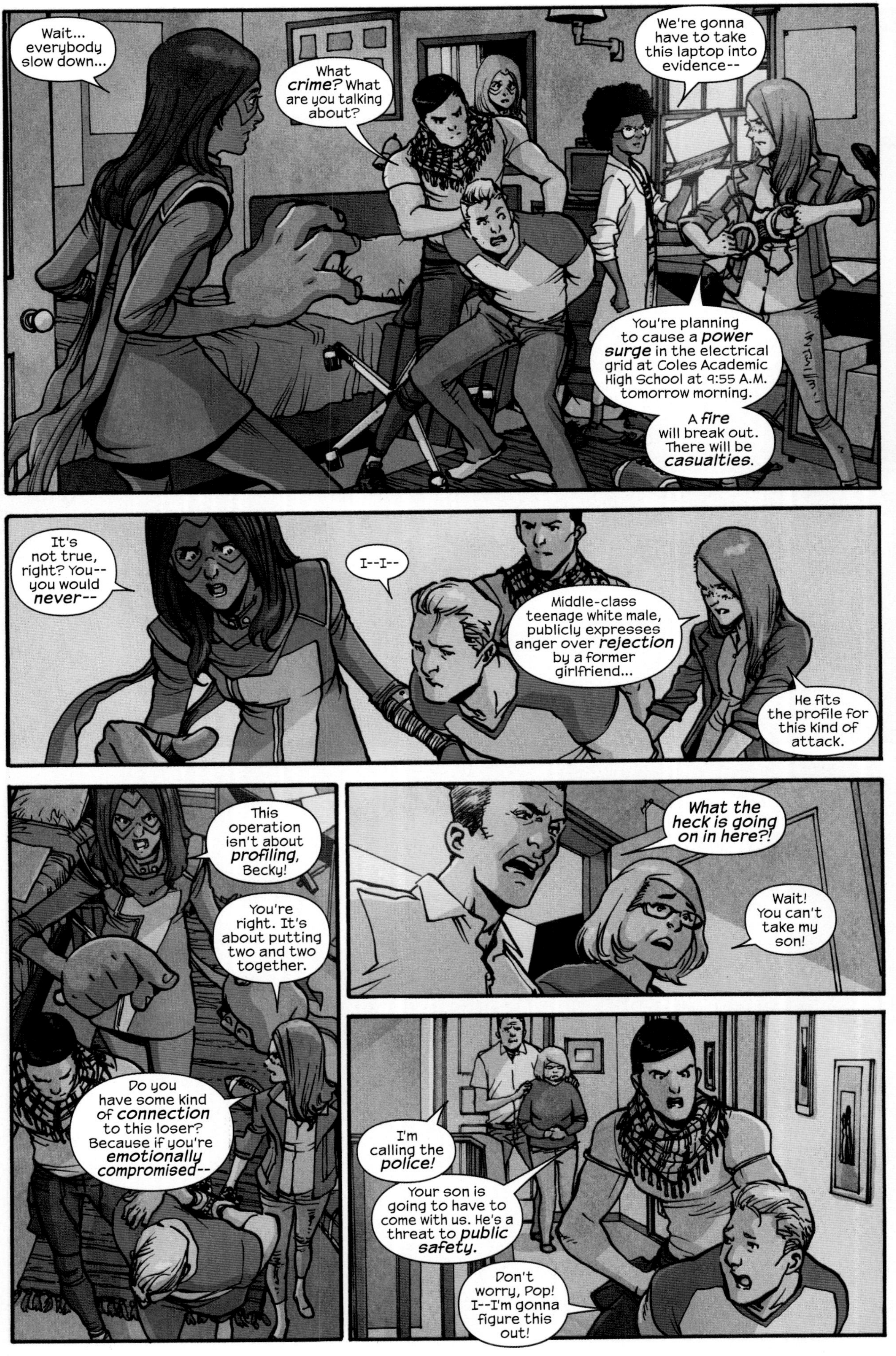
Wait... everybody slow down...
What *crime?* What are you talking about?
We're gonna have to take this laptop into evidence--
You're planning to cause a *power surge* in the electrical grid at Coles Academic High School at 9:55 A.M. tomorrow morning.
A *fire* will break out. There will be *casualties*.
It's not true, right? You-- you would *never*--
I--I--
Middle-class teenage white male, publicly expresses anger over *rejection* by a former girlfriend...
He fits the profile for this kind of attack.
This operation isn't about *profiling*, Becky!
You're right. It's about putting two and two together.
Do you have some kind of *connection* to this loser? Because if you're *emotionally compromised*--
What the heck is going on in here?!
Wait! You can't take my son!
I'm calling the *police!*
Your son is going to have to come with us. He's a threat to *public safety*.
Don't worry, Pop! I--I'm gonna figure this out!

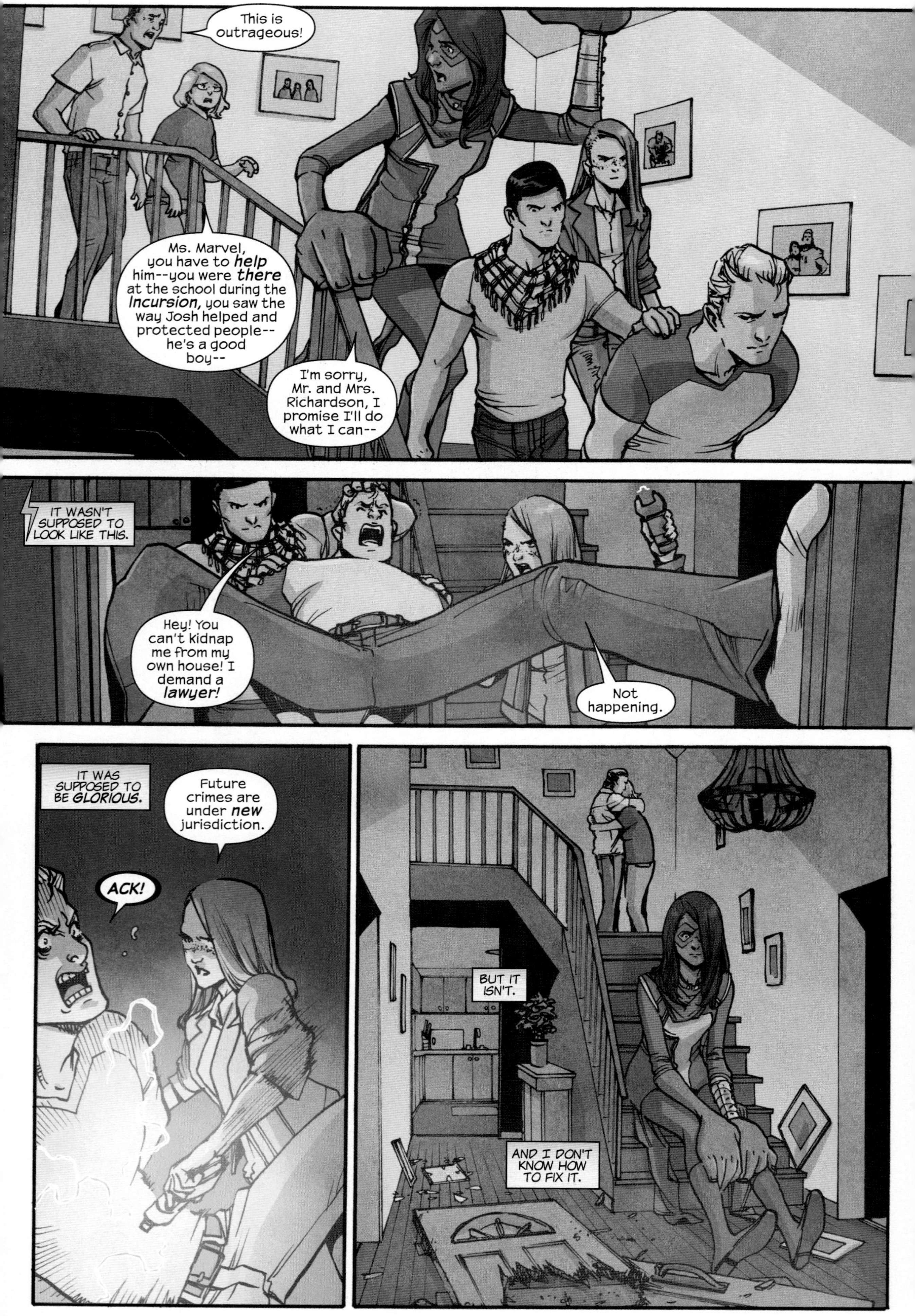
This is outrageous!
Ms. Marvel, you have to *help* him--you were *there* at the school during the *Incursion*, you saw the way Josh helped and protected people--he's a good boy--
I'm sorry, Mr. and Mrs. Richardson, I promise I'll do what I can--
IT WASN'T SUPPOSED TO LOOK LIKE THIS.
Hey! You can't kidnap me from my own house! I demand a *lawyer!*
Not happening.
IT WAS SUPPOSED TO BE *GLORIOUS*.
Future crimes are under *new* jurisdiction.
ACK!
BUT IT ISN'T.
AND I DON'T KNOW HOW TO FIX IT.

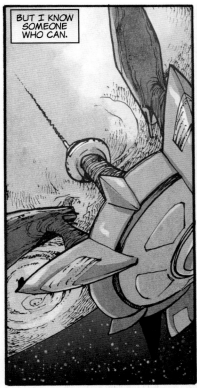

BUT I KNOW SOMEONE WHO CAN.

FSSST!

Captain Marvel, we need to *talk.*

Junior? What're you doing up here?

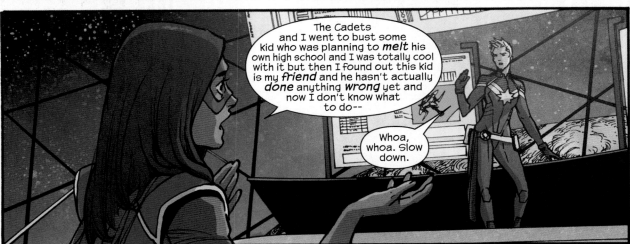

The Cadets and I went to bust some kid who was planning to *melt* his own high school and I was totally cool with it but then I found out this kid is my *friend* and he hasn't actually *done* anything *wrong* yet and now I don't know what to do--

Whoa, whoa. Slow down.

This was *never* going to be easy or simple, kiddo.

And I'm sorry your friend is in trouble, but--

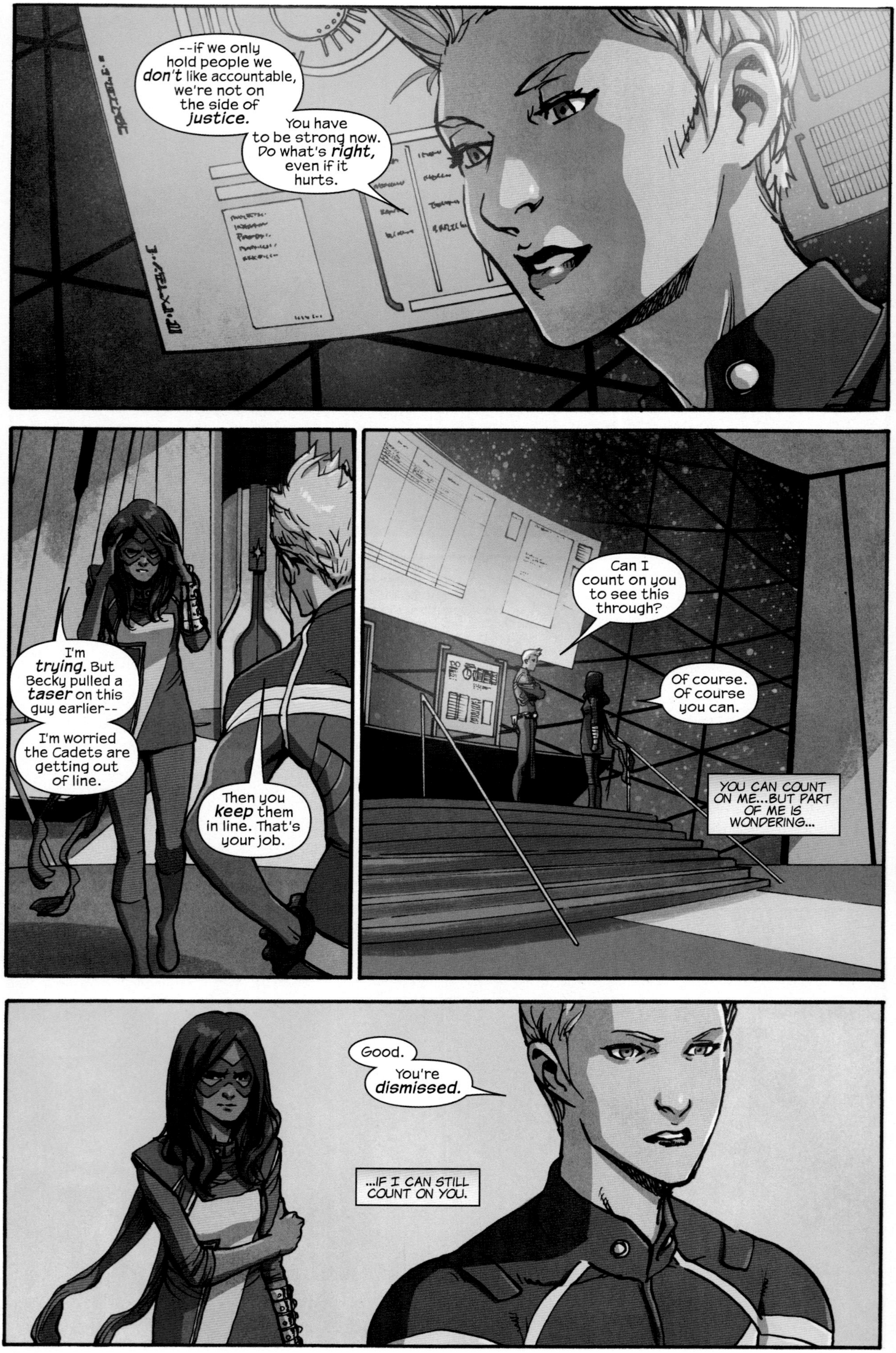
--if we only hold people we don't like accountable, we're not on the side of justice.
You have to be strong now. Do what's right, even if it hurts.
I'm trying. But Becky pulled a taser on this guy earlier--
I'm worried the Cadets are getting out of line.
Then you keep them in line. That's your job.
Can I count on you to see this through?
Of course. Of course you can.
YOU CAN COUNT ON ME...BUT PART OF ME IS WONDERING...
Good.
You're dismissed.
...IF I CAN STILL COUNT ON YOU.

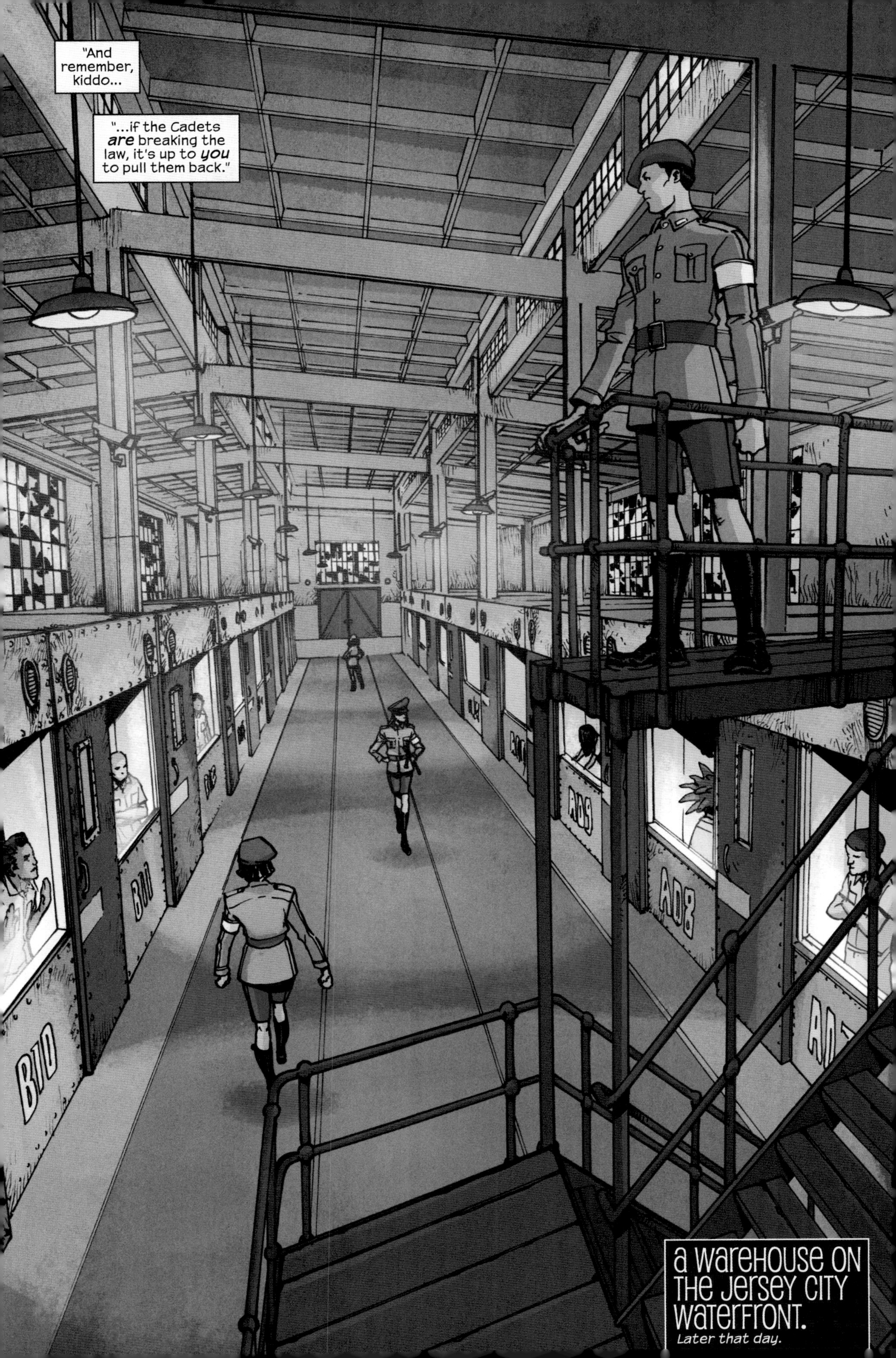
"And remember, kiddo...
"...if the Cadets *are* breaking the law, it's up to *you* to pull them back."
A WAREHOUSE ON THE JERSEY CITY WATERFRONT.
Later that day.

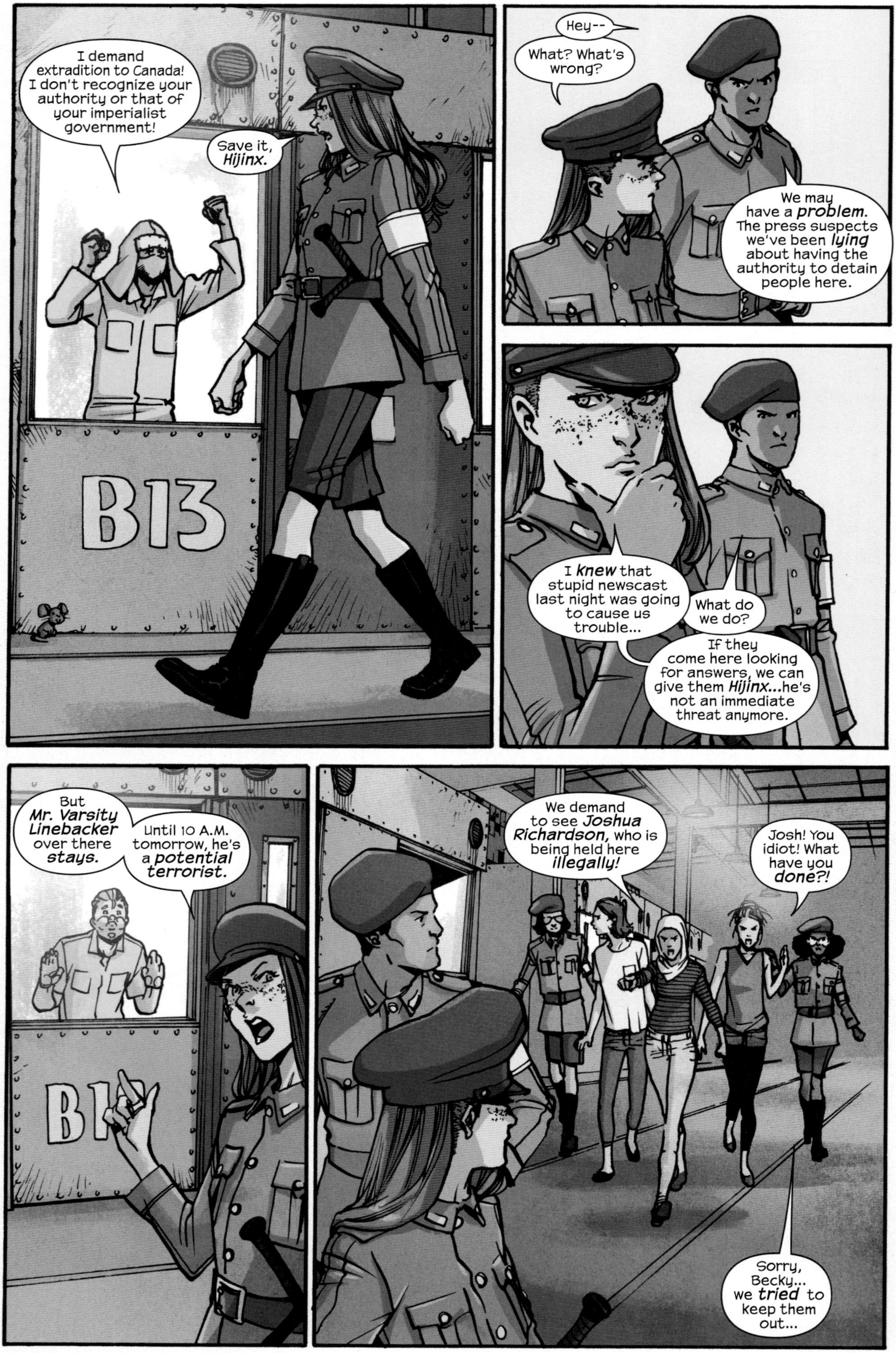
I demand extradition to Canada! I don't recognize your authority or that of your imperialist government!
Save it, *Hijinx.*
B13
Hey--
What? What's wrong?
We may have a ***problem***. The press suspects we've been ***lying*** about having the authority to detain people here.
I ***knew*** that stupid newscast last night was going to cause us trouble...
What do we do?
If they come here looking for answers, we can give them *Hijinx*...he's not an immediate threat anymore.
But *Mr. Varsity Linebacker* over there *stays.*
Until 10 A.M. tomorrow, he's a ***potential terrorist.***
We demand to see *Joshua Richardson,* who is being held here *illegally!*
Josh! You idiot! What have you *done?!*
Sorry, Becky... we ***tried*** to keep them out...

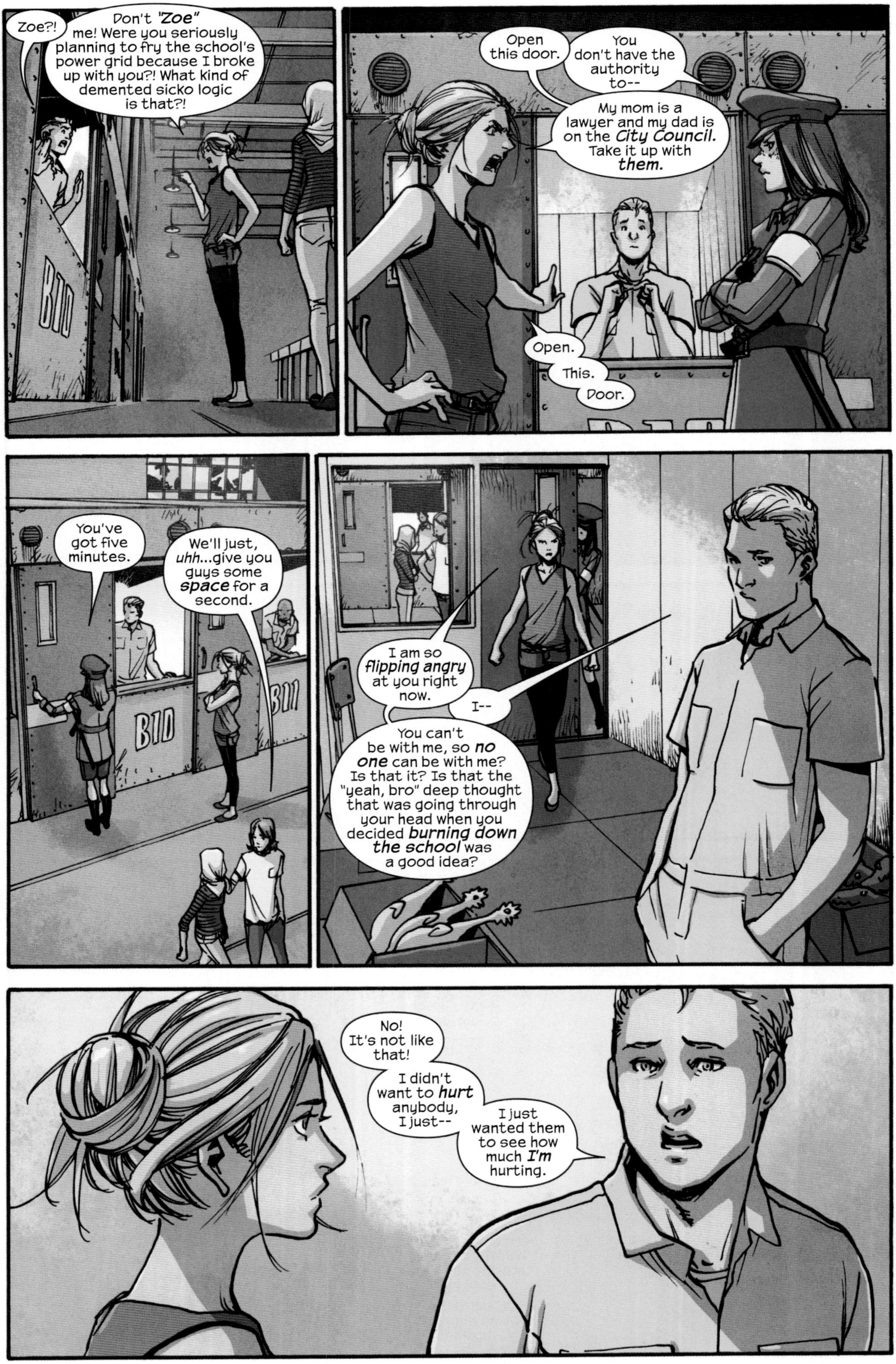
Zoe?!
Don't "Zoe" me! Were you seriously planning to fry the school's power grid because I broke up with you?! What kind of demented sicko logic is that?!
Open this door.
You don't have the authority to--
My mom is a lawyer and my dad is on the City Council. Take it up with them.
Open.
This.
Door.
You've got five minutes.
We'll just, uhh...give you guys some space for a second.
I am so flipping angry at you right now.
I--
You can't be with me, so no one can be with me? Is that it? Is that the "yeah, bro" deep thought that was going through your head when you decided burning down the school was a good idea?
No! It's not like that!
I didn't want to hurt anybody, I just--
I just wanted them to see how much I'm hurting.

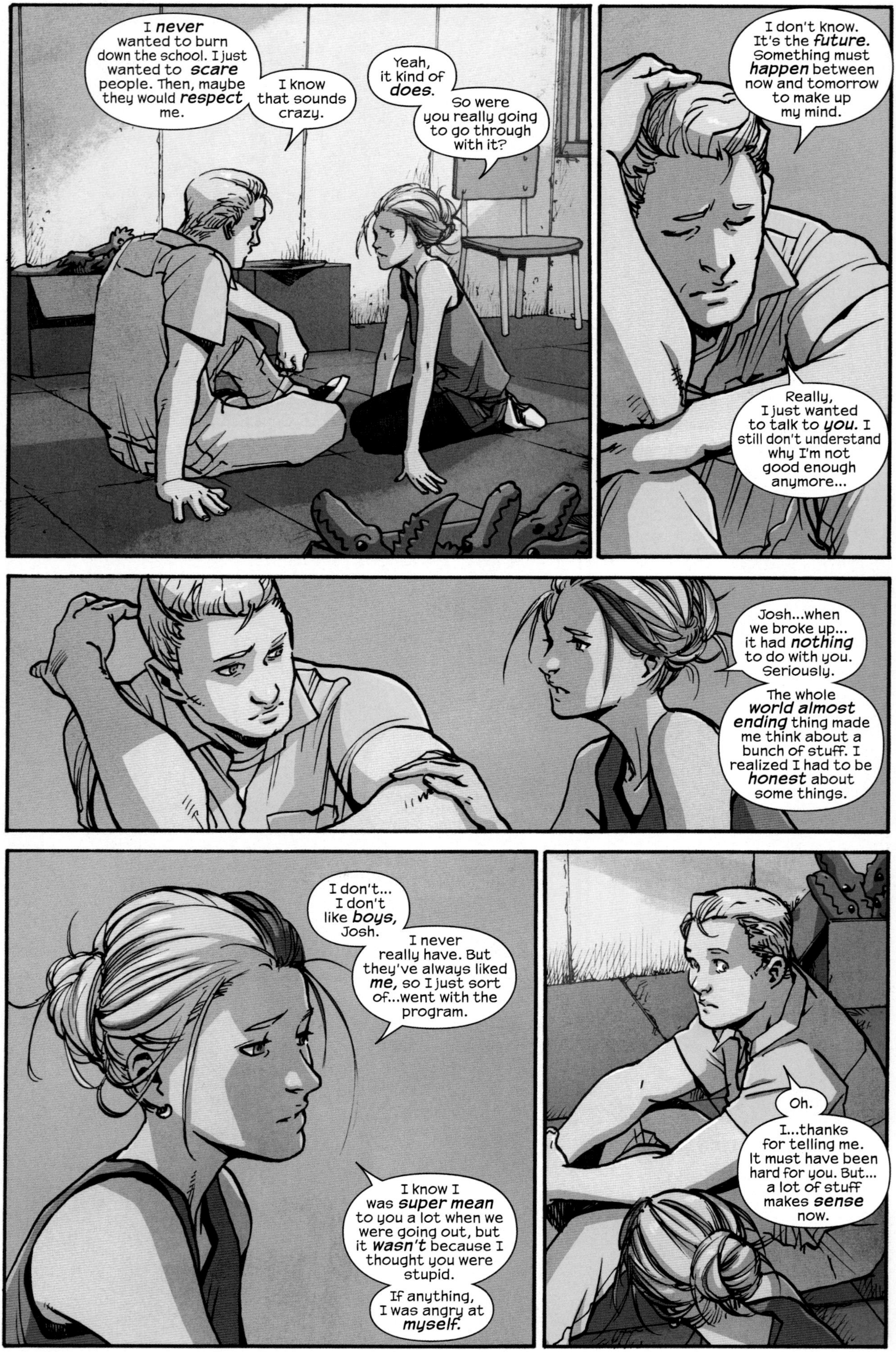
I never wanted to burn down the school. I just wanted to scare people. Then, maybe they would respect me.
I know that sounds crazy.
Yeah, it kind of does.
So were you really going to go through with it?
I don't know. It's the future. Something must happen between now and tomorrow to make up my mind.
Really, I just wanted to talk to you. I still don't understand why I'm not good enough anymore...
Josh...when we broke up... it had nothing to do with you. Seriously.
The whole world almost ending thing made me think about a bunch of stuff. I realized I had to be honest about some things.
I don't... I don't like boys, Josh.
I never really have. But they've always liked me, so I just sort of...went with the program.
I know I was super mean to you a lot when we were going out, but it wasn't because I thought you were stupid.
If anything, I was angry at myself.
Oh.
I...thanks for telling me. It must have been hard for you. But... a lot of stuff makes sense now.

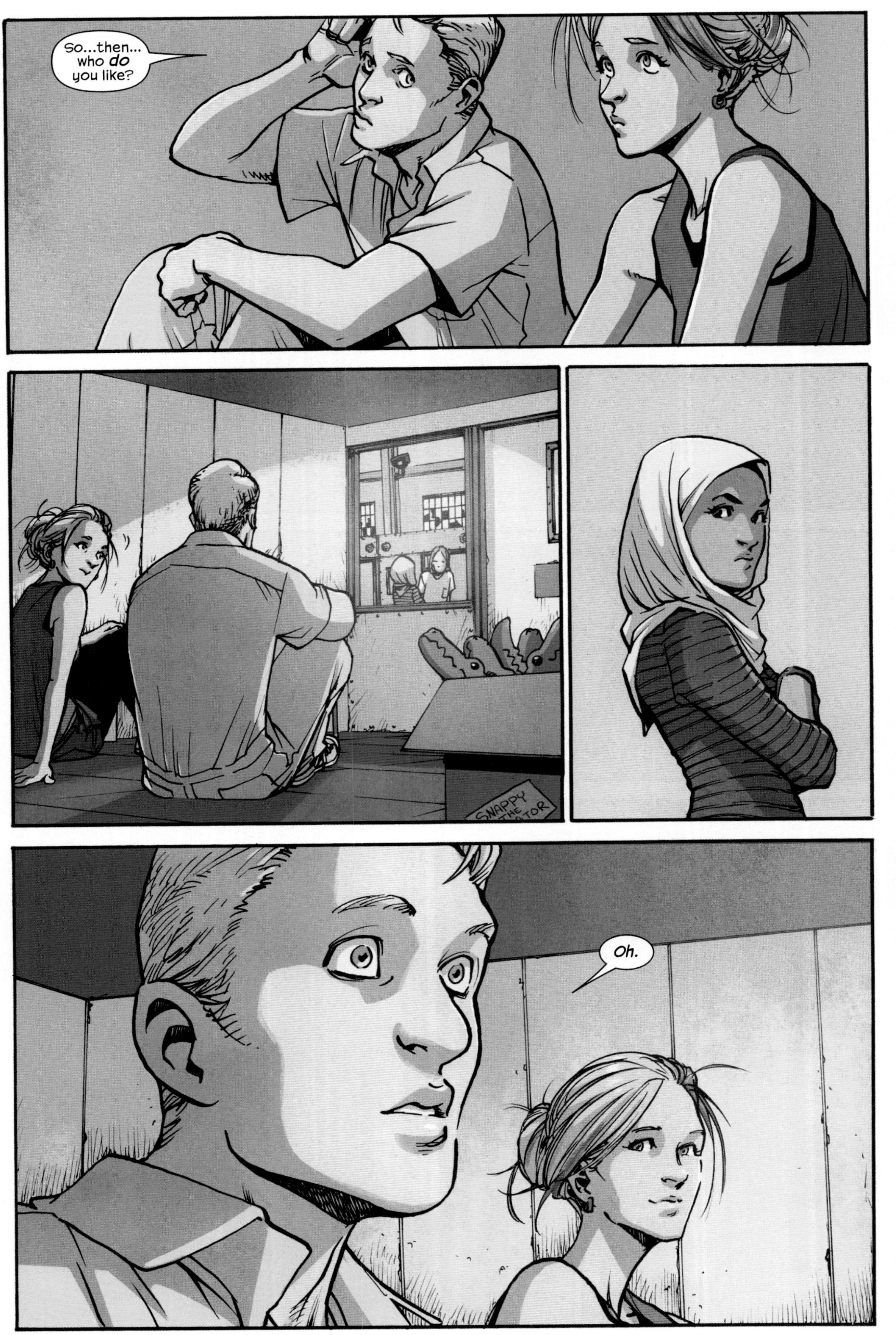
So...then... who *do* you like?
SNAPPY THE GATOR
Oh.

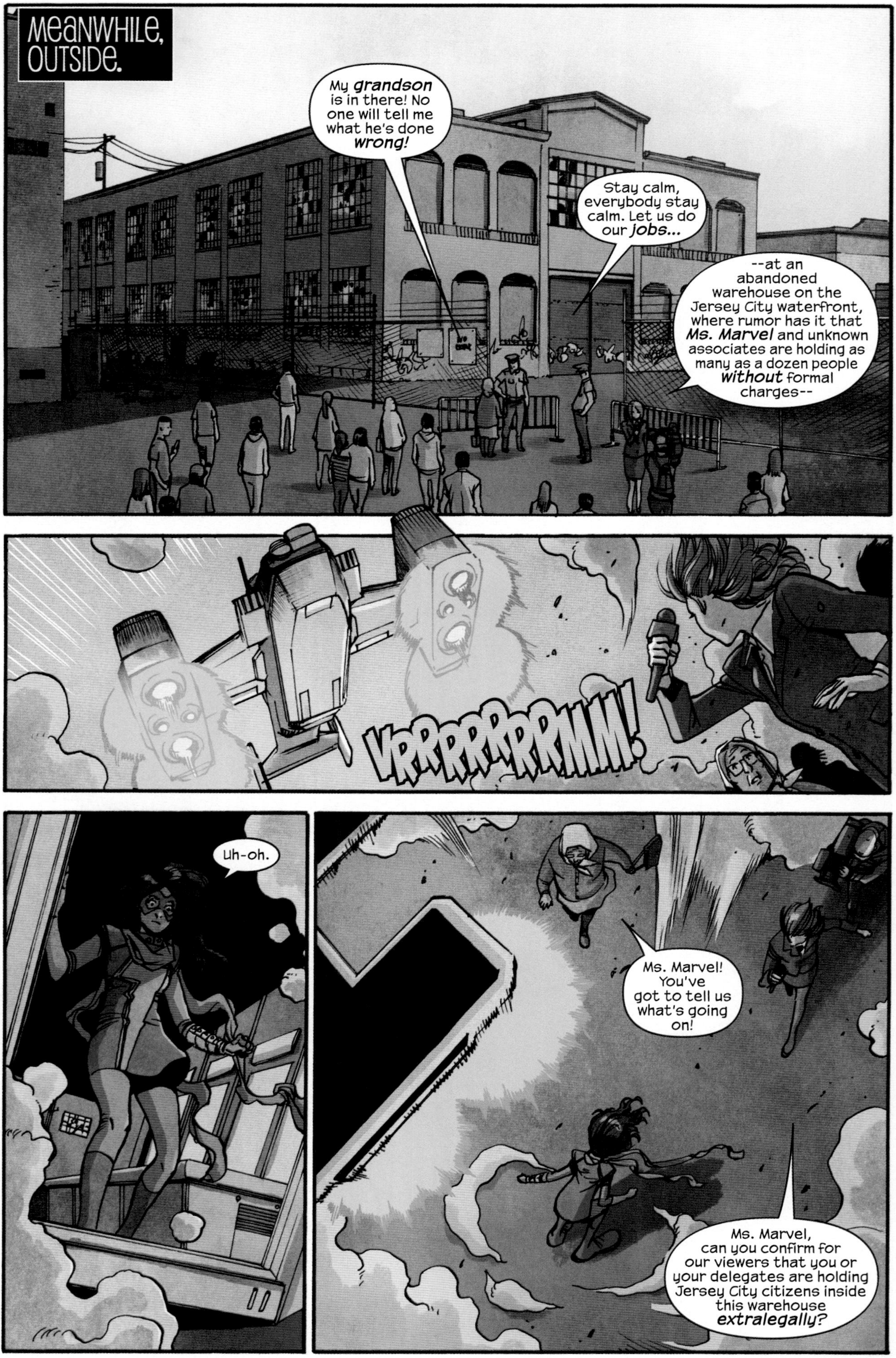

MEANWHILE, OUTSIDE.
My grandson is in there! No one will tell me what he's done wrong!
Stay calm, everybody stay calm. Let us do our jobs...
--at an abandoned warehouse on the Jersey City waterfront, where rumor has it that Ms. Marvel and unknown associates are holding as many as a dozen people without formal charges--
VRRRRRRRMM!
Uh-oh.
Ms. Marvel! You've got to tell us what's going on!
Ms. Marvel, can you confirm for our viewers that you or your delegates are holding Jersey City citizens inside this warehouse extralegally?

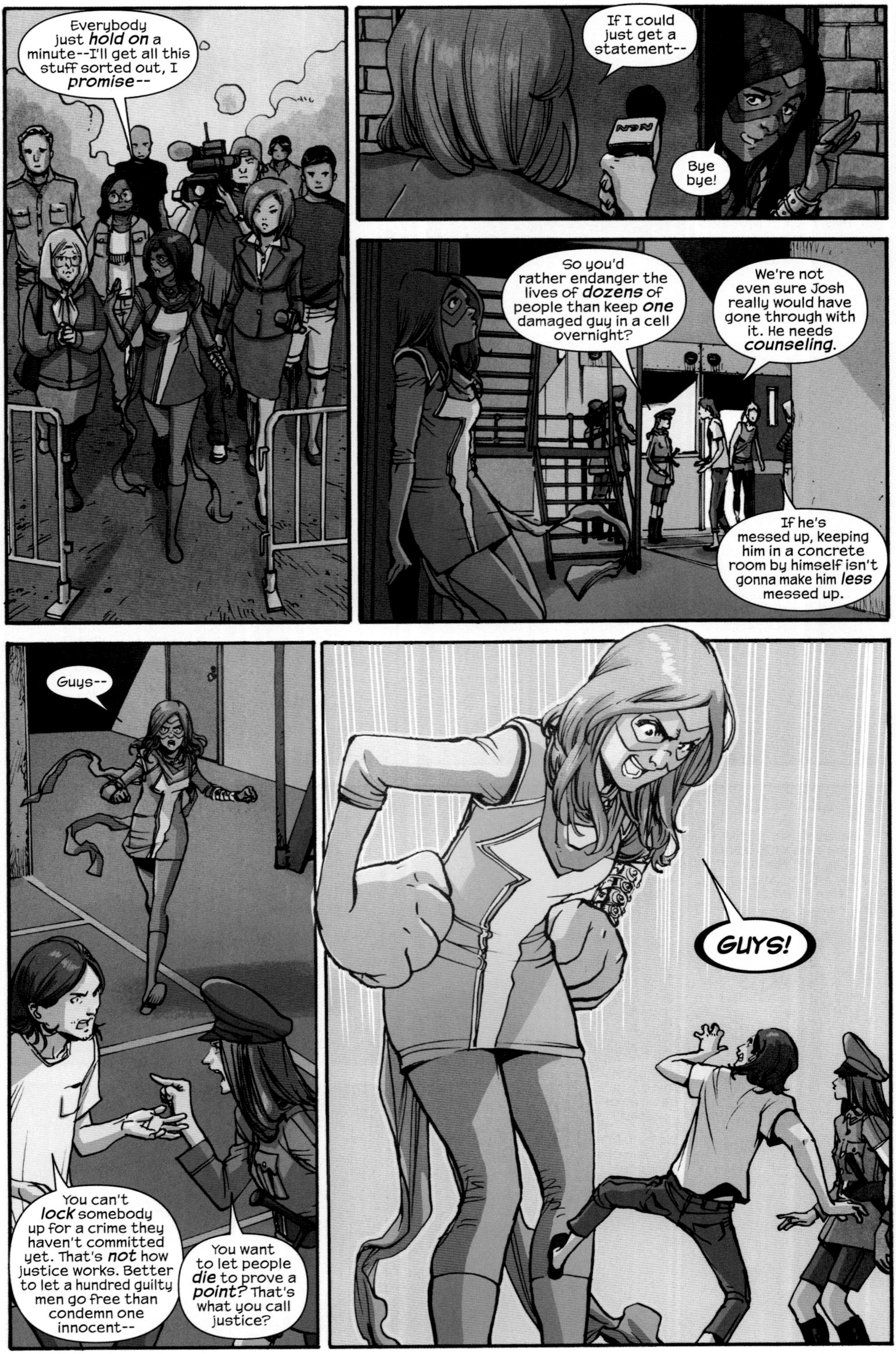
Everybody just hold on a minute--I'll get all this stuff sorted out, I promise--
If I could just get a statement--
Bye bye!
So you'd rather endanger the lives of dozens of people than keep one damaged guy in a cell overnight?
We're not even sure Josh really would have gone through with it. He needs counseling.
If he's messed up, keeping him in a concrete room by himself isn't gonna make him less messed up.
Guys--
You can't lock somebody up for a crime they haven't committed yet. That's not how justice works. Better to let a hundred guilty men go free than condemn one innocent--
You want to let people die to prove a point? That's what you call justice?
GUYS!

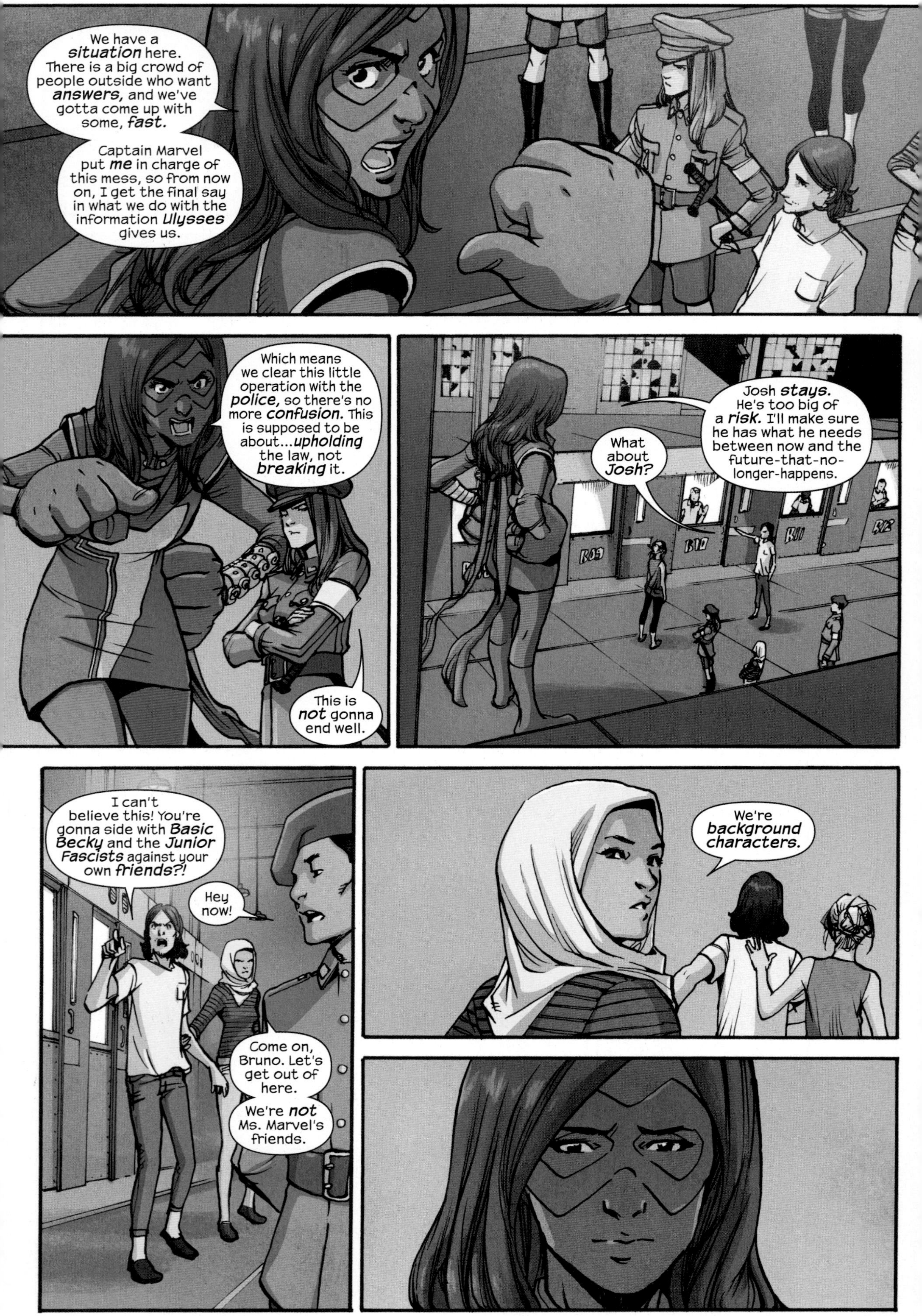
We have a *situation* here. There is a big crowd of people outside who want *answers,* and we've gotta come up with some, *fast.*
Captain Marvel put *me* in charge of this mess, so from now on, I get the final say in what we do with the information *Ulysses* gives us.
Which means we clear this little operation with the *police,* so there's no more *confusion.* This is supposed to be about...*upholding* the law, not *breaking* it.
This is *not* gonna end well.
What about *Josh?*
Josh *stays.* He's too big of a *risk.* I'll make sure he has what he needs between now and the future-that-no-longer-happens.
I can't believe this! You're gonna side with *Basic Becky* and the *Junior Fascists* against your own *friends?!*
Hey now!
Come on, Bruno. Let's get out of here.
We're *not* Ms. Marvel's friends.
We're *background characters.*

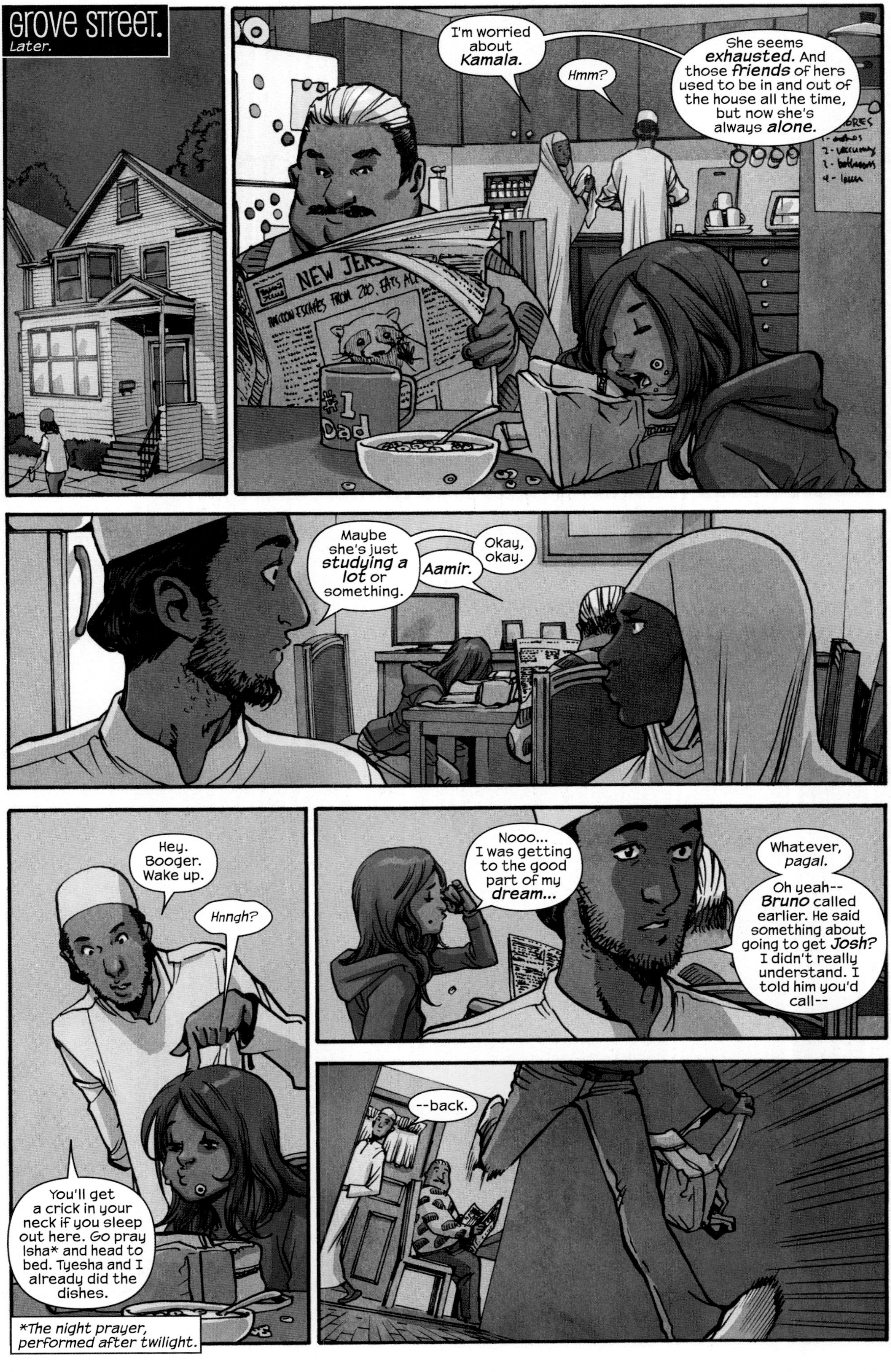
GROVE STREET.
Later.
I'm worried about Kamala.
Hmm?
She seems exhausted. And those friends of hers used to be in and out of the house all the time, but now she's always alone.
NEW JERS
RACCOON ESCAPES FROM ZOO, EATS ALL
#1 Dad
Maybe she's just studying a lot or something.
Aamir.
Okay, okay.
Hey. Booger. Wake up.
Hnngh?
You'll get a crick in your neck if you sleep out here. Go pray Isha* and head to bed. Tyesha and I already did the dishes.
Nooo... I was getting to the good part of my dream...
Whatever, pagal.
Oh yeah-- Bruno called earlier. He said something about going to get Josh? I didn't really understand. I told him you'd call--
--back.
*The night prayer, performed after twilight.

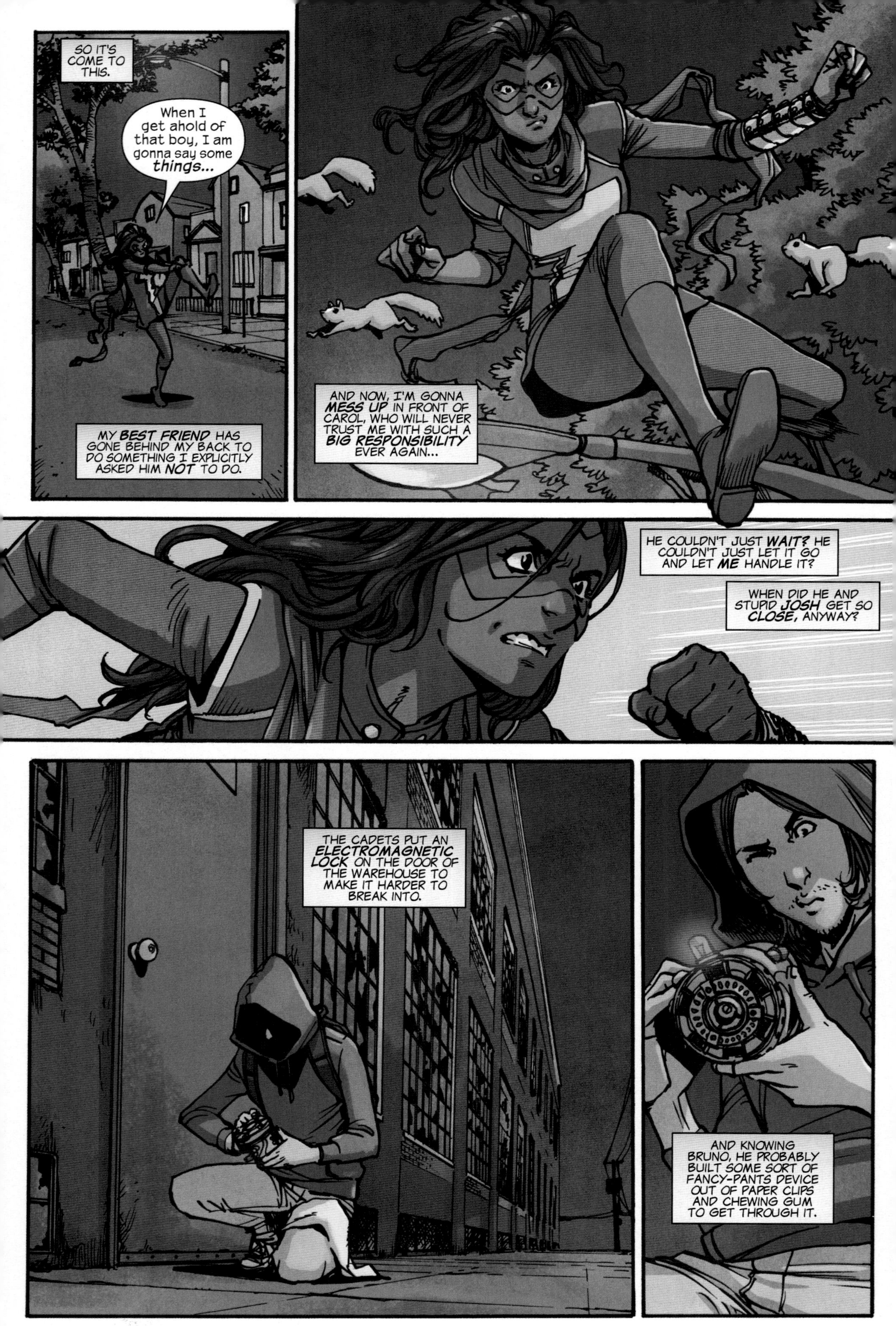

SO IT'S COME TO THIS.
When I get ahold of that boy, I am gonna say some ***things...***
MY **BEST FRIEND** HAS GONE BEHIND MY BACK TO DO SOMETHING I EXPLICITLY ASKED HIM **NOT** TO DO.
AND NOW, I'M GONNA **MESS UP** IN FRONT OF CAROL, WHO WILL NEVER TRUST ME WITH SUCH A **BIG RESPONSIBILITY** EVER AGAIN...
HE COULDN'T JUST **WAIT?** HE COULDN'T JUST LET IT GO AND LET **ME** HANDLE IT?
WHEN DID HE AND STUPID **JOSH** GET SO **CLOSE,** ANYWAY?
THE CADETS PUT AN **ELECTROMAGNETIC LOCK** ON THE DOOR OF THE WAREHOUSE TO MAKE IT HARDER TO BREAK INTO.
AND KNOWING BRUNO, HE PROBABLY BUILT SOME SORT OF FANCY-PANTS DEVICE OUT OF PAPER CLIPS AND CHEWING GUM TO GET THROUGH IT.

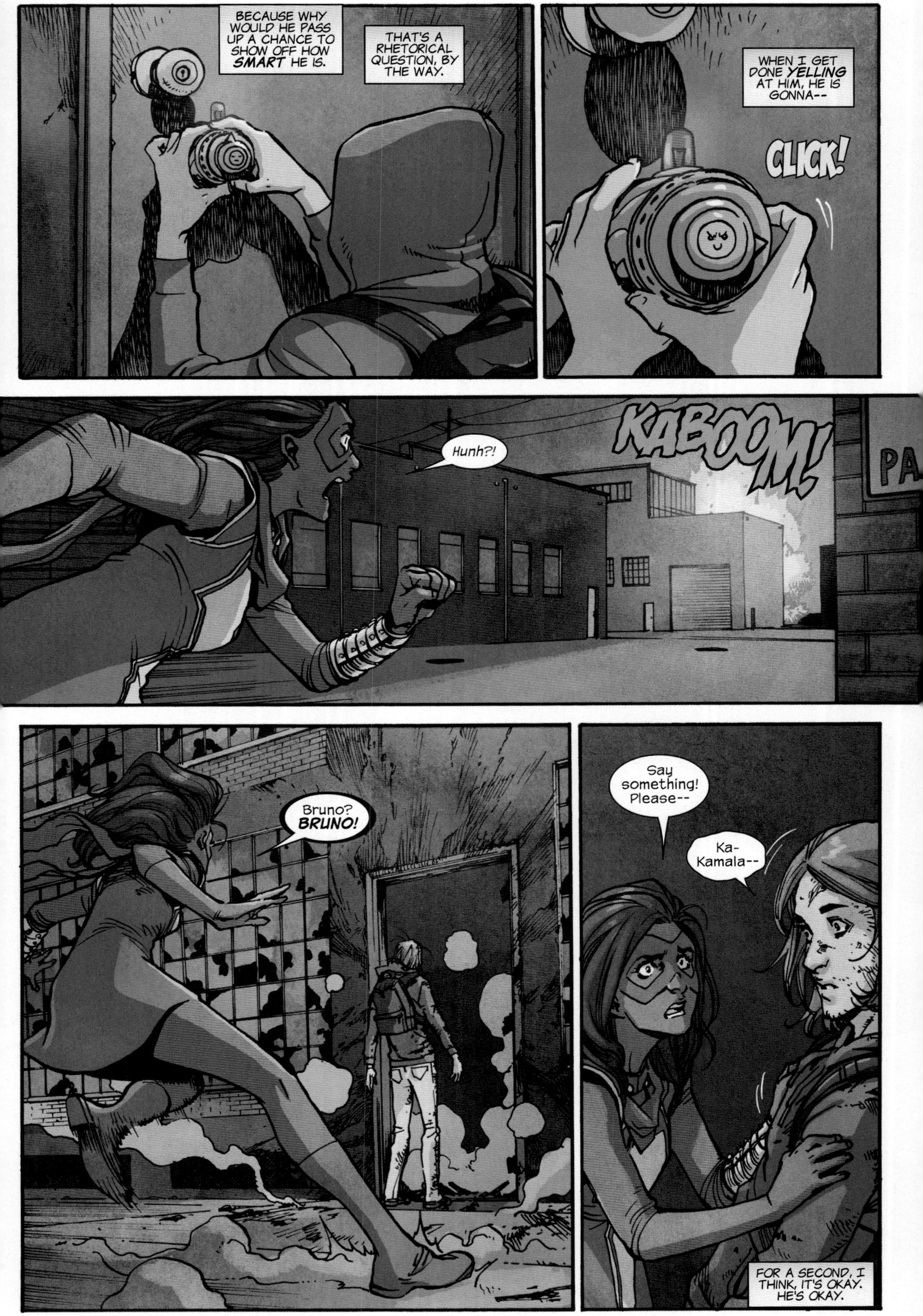
BECAUSE WHY WOULD HE PASS UP A CHANCE TO SHOW OFF HOW **SMART** HE IS.
THAT'S A RHETORICAL QUESTION, BY THE WAY.
WHEN I GET DONE **YELLING** AT HIM, HE IS GONNA--
CLICK!
Hunh?!
KABOOM!
PA
Bruno? **BRUNO!**
Say something! Please--
Ka-Kamala--
FOR A SECOND, I THINK, IT'S OKAY. HE'S OKAY.

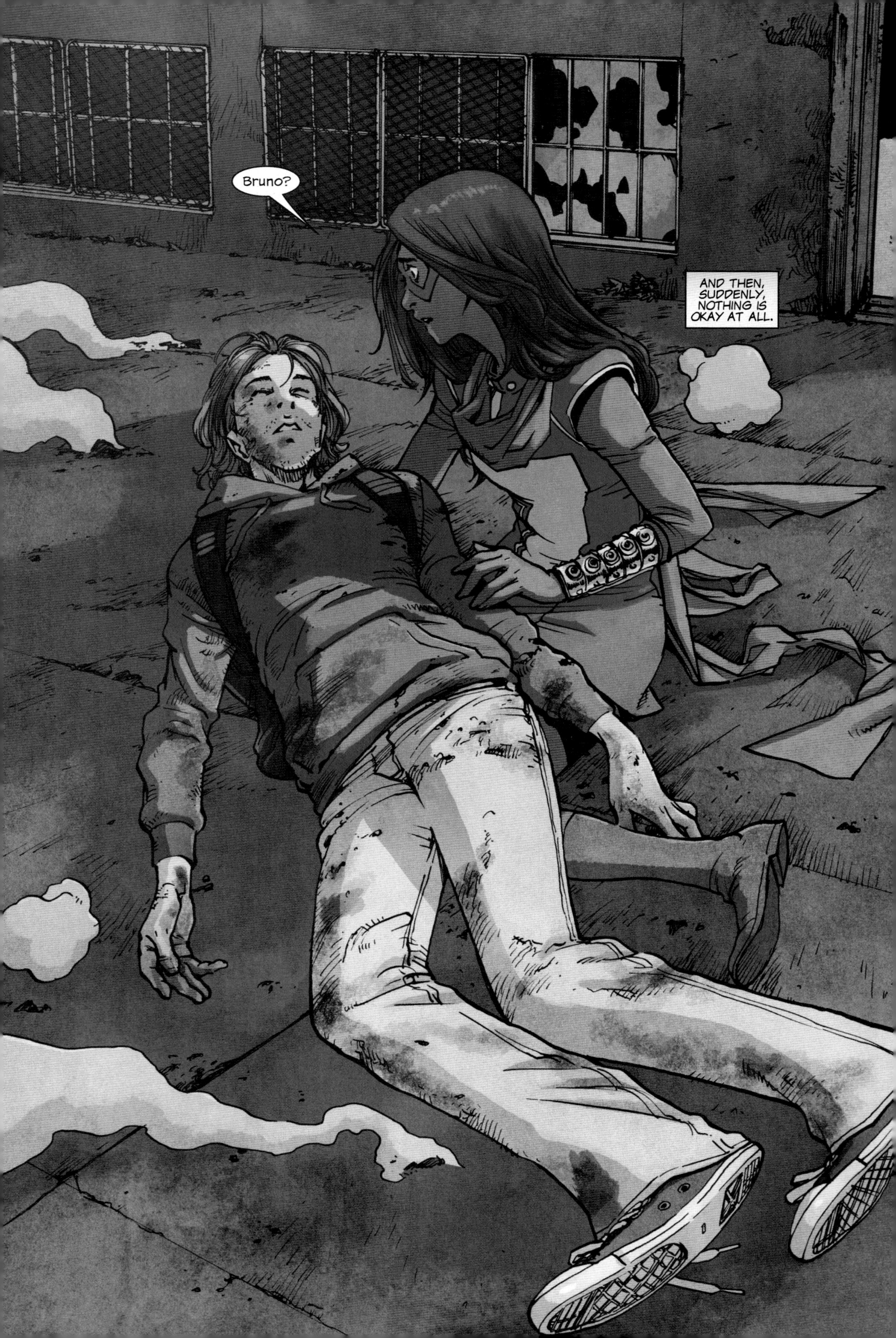

Bruno?
AND THEN, SUDDENLY, NOTHING IS OKAY AT ALL.

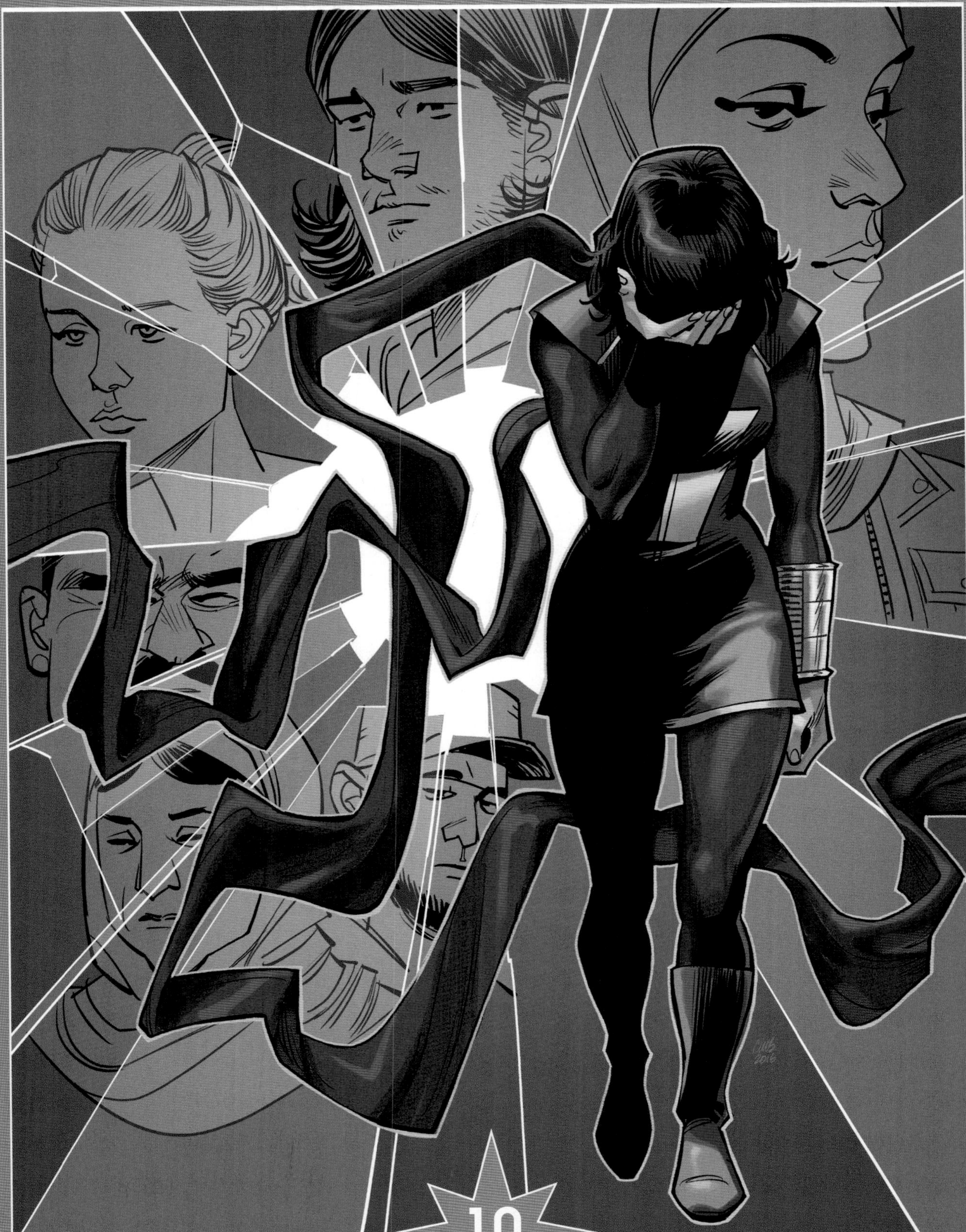
10

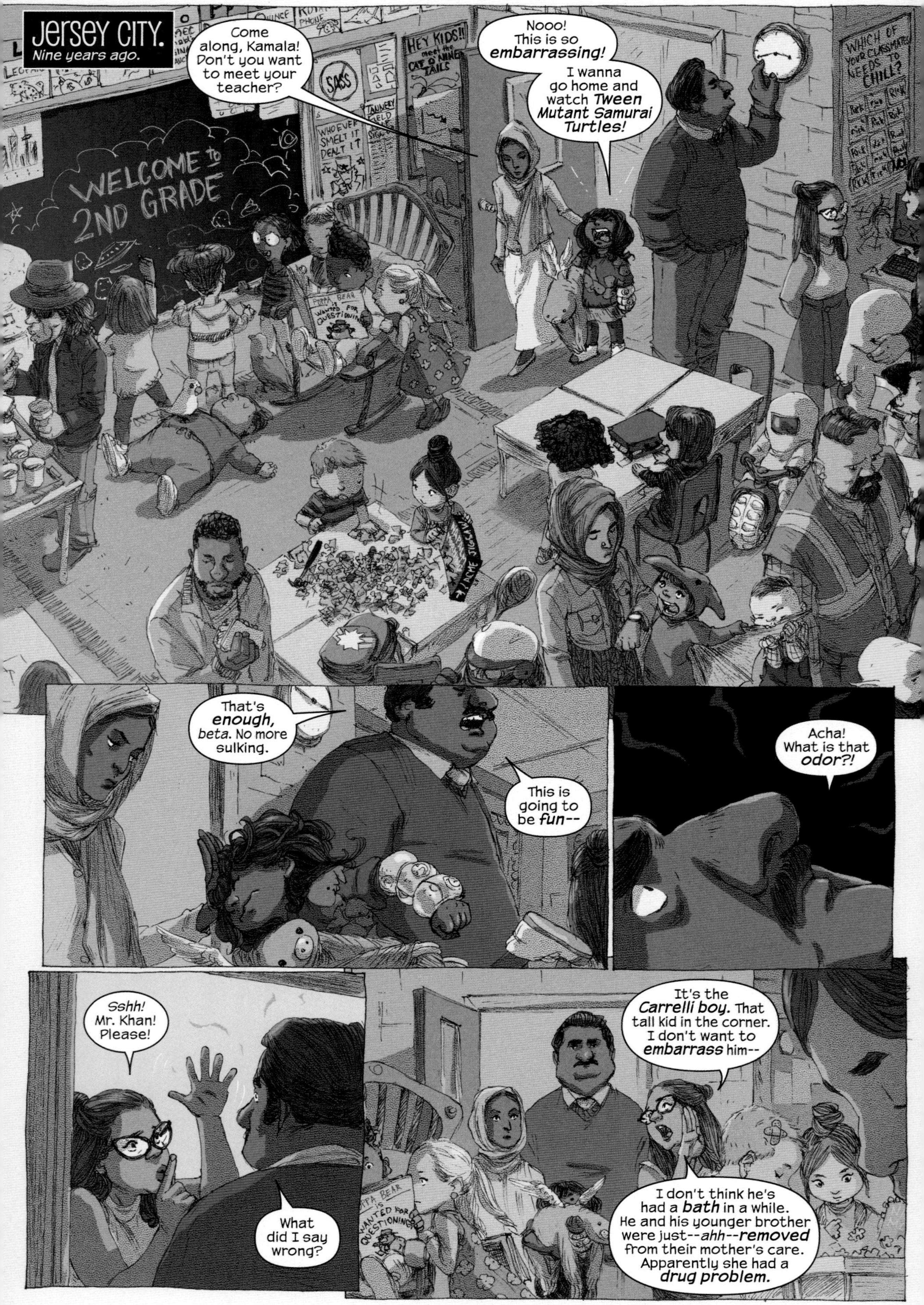

Jersey City.
Nine years ago.
Come along, Kamala! Don't you want to meet your teacher?
Nooo! This is so embarrassing!
I wanna go home and watch Tween Mutant Samurai Turtles!
WELCOME to 2ND GRADE
That's enough, beta. No more sulking.
This is going to be fun--
Acha! What is that odor?!
Sshh! Mr. Khan! Please!
What did I say wrong?
It's the Carrelli boy. That tall kid in the corner. I don't want to embarrass him--
I don't think he's had a bath in a while. He and his younger brother were just--ahh--removed from their mother's care. Apparently she had a drug problem.

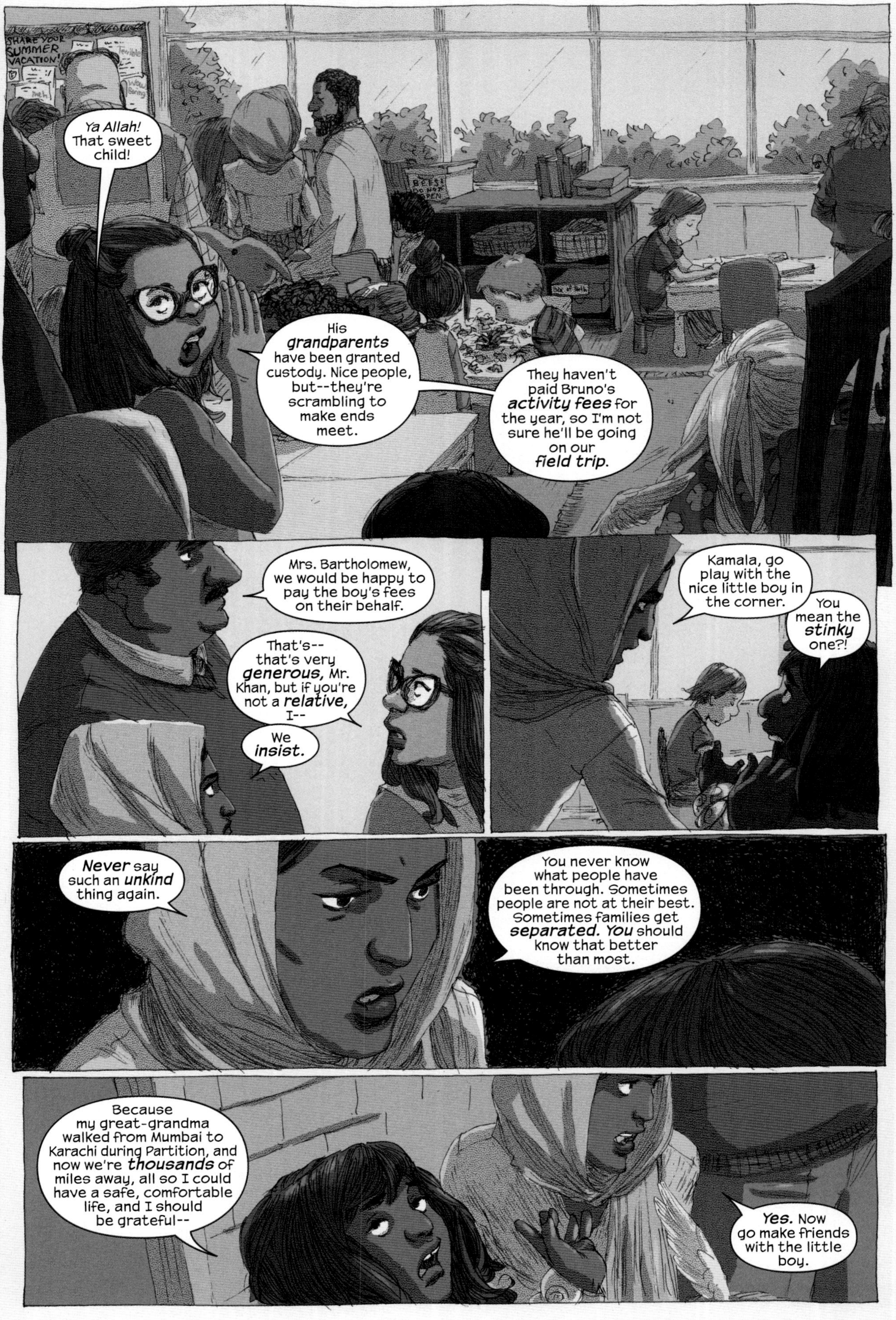
SHARE YOUR SUMMER VACATION!
Ya Allah! That sweet child!
His grandparents have been granted custody. Nice people, but--they're scrambling to make ends meet.
They haven't paid Bruno's activity fees for the year, so I'm not sure he'll be going on our field trip.
Mrs. Bartholomew, we would be happy to pay the boy's fees on their behalf.
That's--that's very generous, Mr. Khan, but if you're not a relative, I--
We insist.
Kamala, go play with the nice little boy in the corner.
You mean the stinky one?!
Never say such an unkind thing again.
You never know what people have been through. Sometimes people are not at their best. Sometimes families get separated. You should know that better than most.
Because my great-grandma walked from Mumbai to Karachi during Partition, and now we're thousands of miles away, all so I could have a safe, comfortable life, and I should be grateful--
Yes. Now go make friends with the little boy.

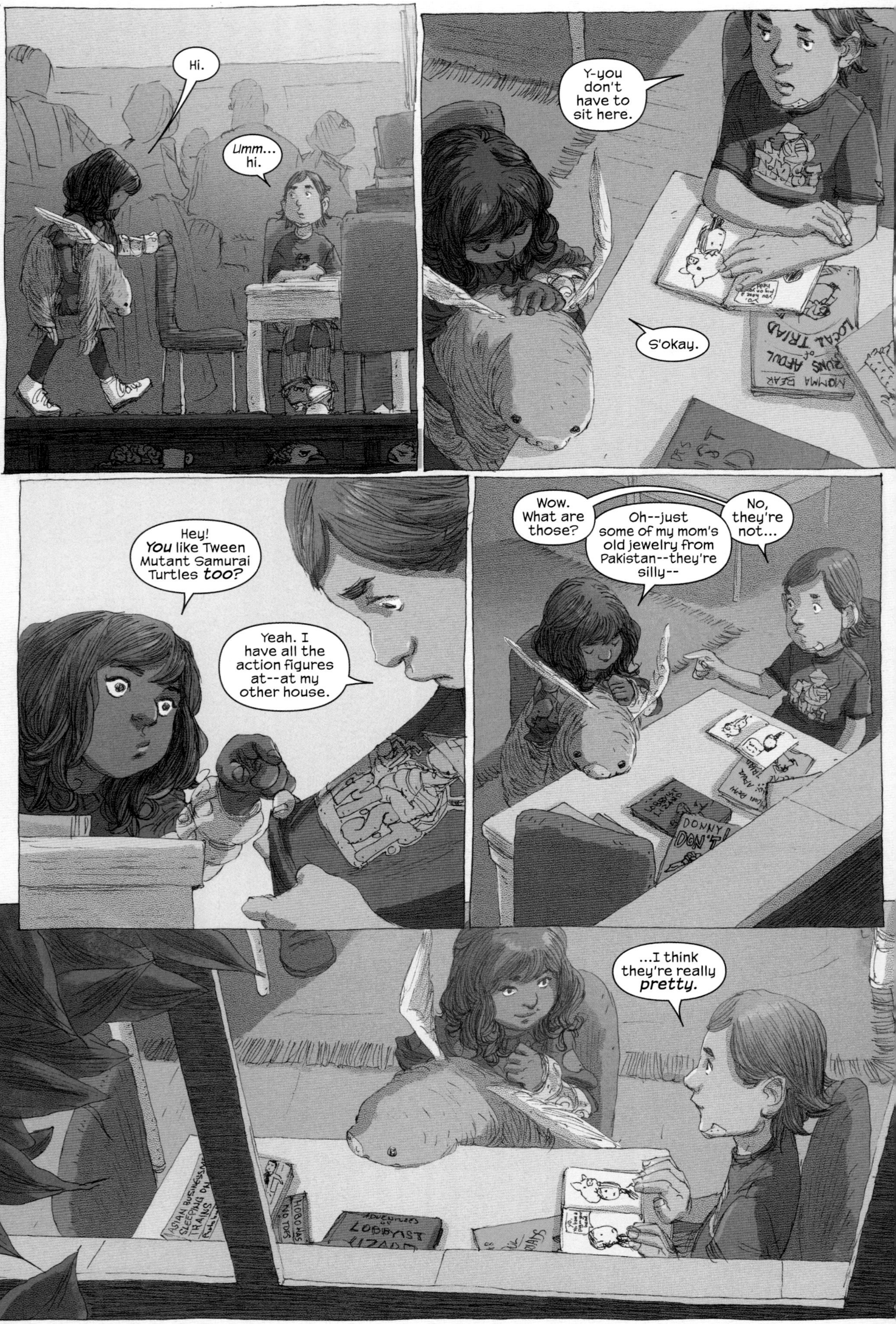
Hi.
Umm... hi.
Y-you don't have to sit here.
S'okay.
Hey! You like Tween Mutant Samurai Turtles too?
Yeah. I have all the action figures at--at my other house.
Wow. What are those?
Oh--just some of my mom's old jewelry from Pakistan--they're silly--
No, they're not...
...I think they're really pretty.

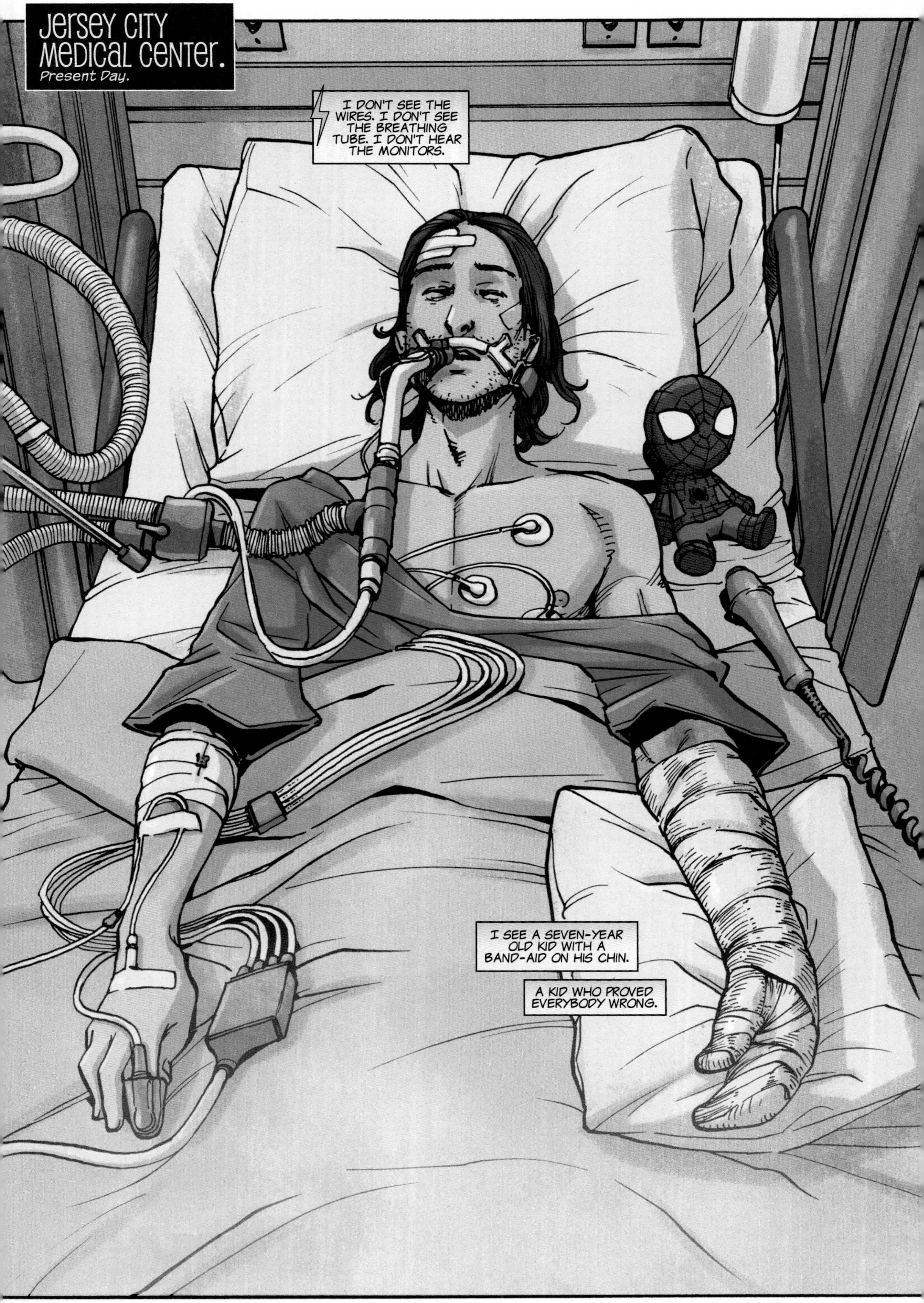
Jersey City Medical Center.
Present Day.
I DON'T SEE THE WIRES. I DON'T SEE THE BREATHING TUBE. I DON'T HEAR THE MONITORS.
I SEE A SEVEN-YEAR OLD KID WITH A BAND-AID ON HIS CHIN.
A KID WHO PROVED EVERYBODY WRONG.

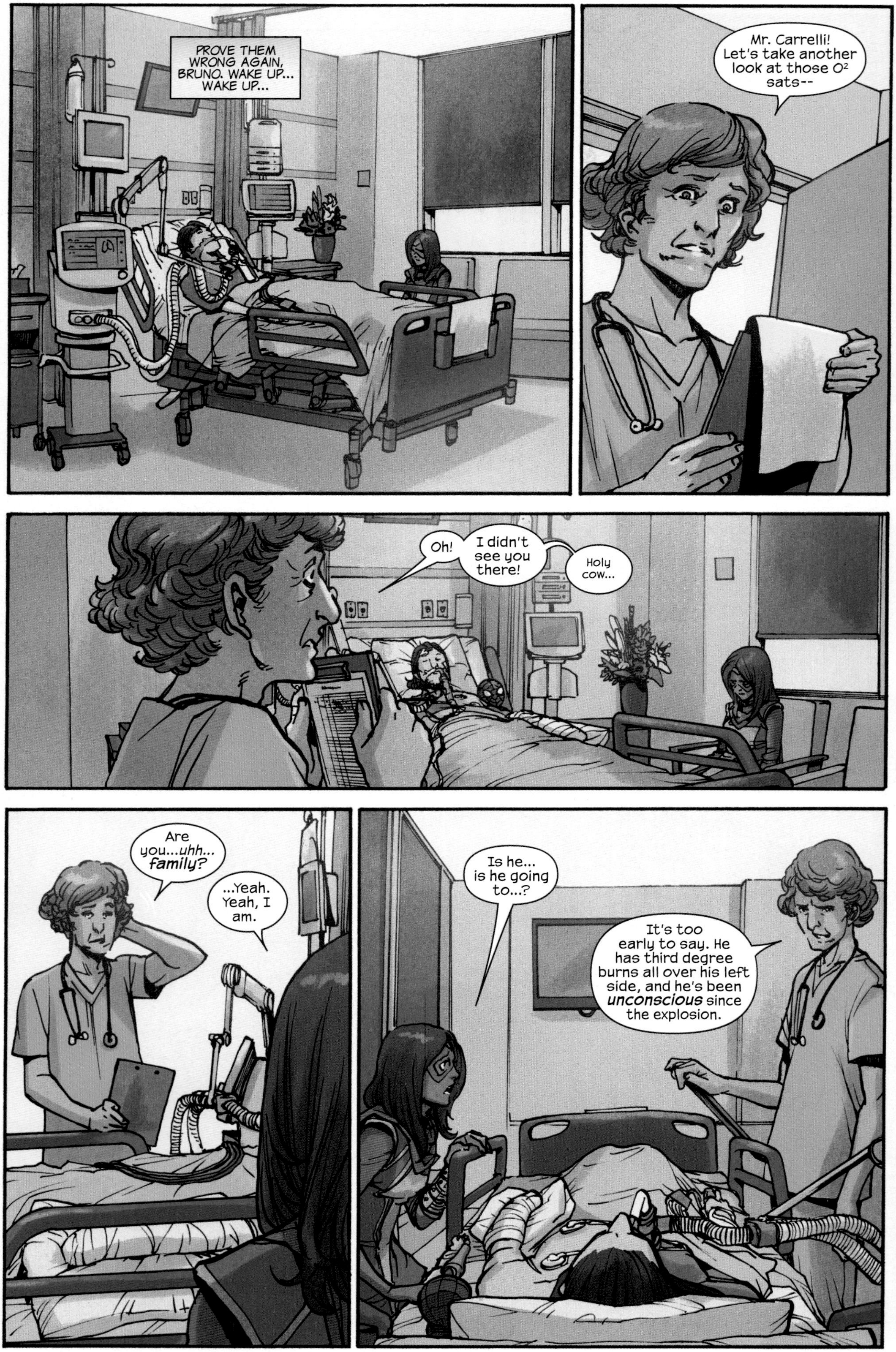
PROVE THEM WRONG AGAIN, BRUNO. WAKE UP... WAKE UP...
Mr. Carrelli! Let's take another look at those O² sats--
Oh!
I didn't see you there!
Holy cow...
Are you...*uhh*... ***family***?
...Yeah. Yeah, I am.
Is he... is he going to...?
It's too early to say. He has third degree burns all over his left side, and he's been ***unconscious*** since the explosion.

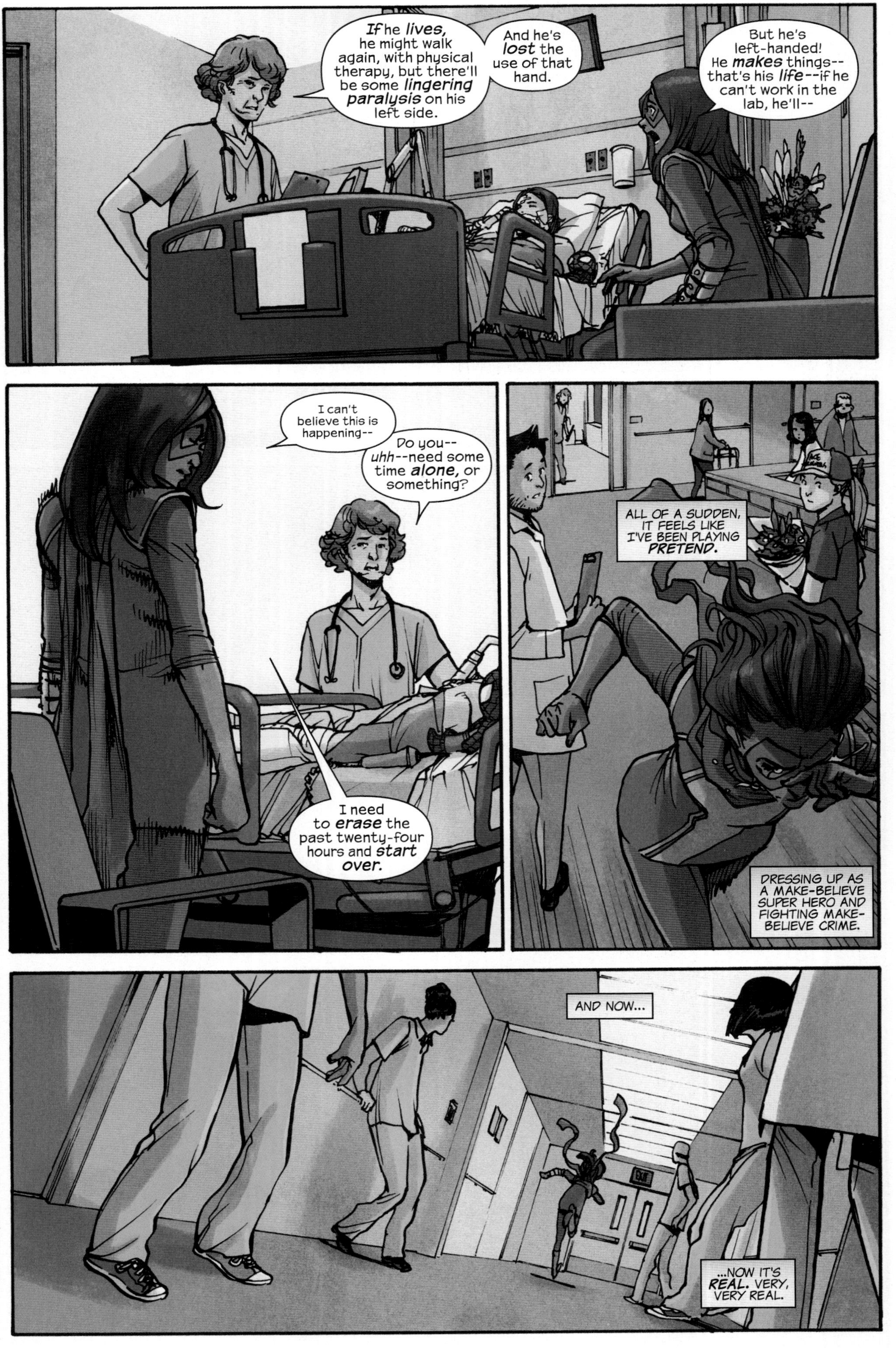

If he lives, he might walk again, with physical therapy, but there'll be some lingering paralysis on his left side.
And he's lost the use of that hand.
But he's left-handed! He makes things-- that's his life--if he can't work in the lab, he'll--
I can't believe this is happening--
Do you-- uhh--need some time alone, or something?
I need to erase the past twenty-four hours and start over.
ALL OF A SUDDEN, IT FEELS LIKE I'VE BEEN PLAYING PRETEND.
DRESSING UP AS A MAKE-BELIEVE SUPER HERO AND FIGHTING MAKE-BELIEVE CRIME.
AND NOW...
...NOW IT'S REAL. VERY, VERY REAL.

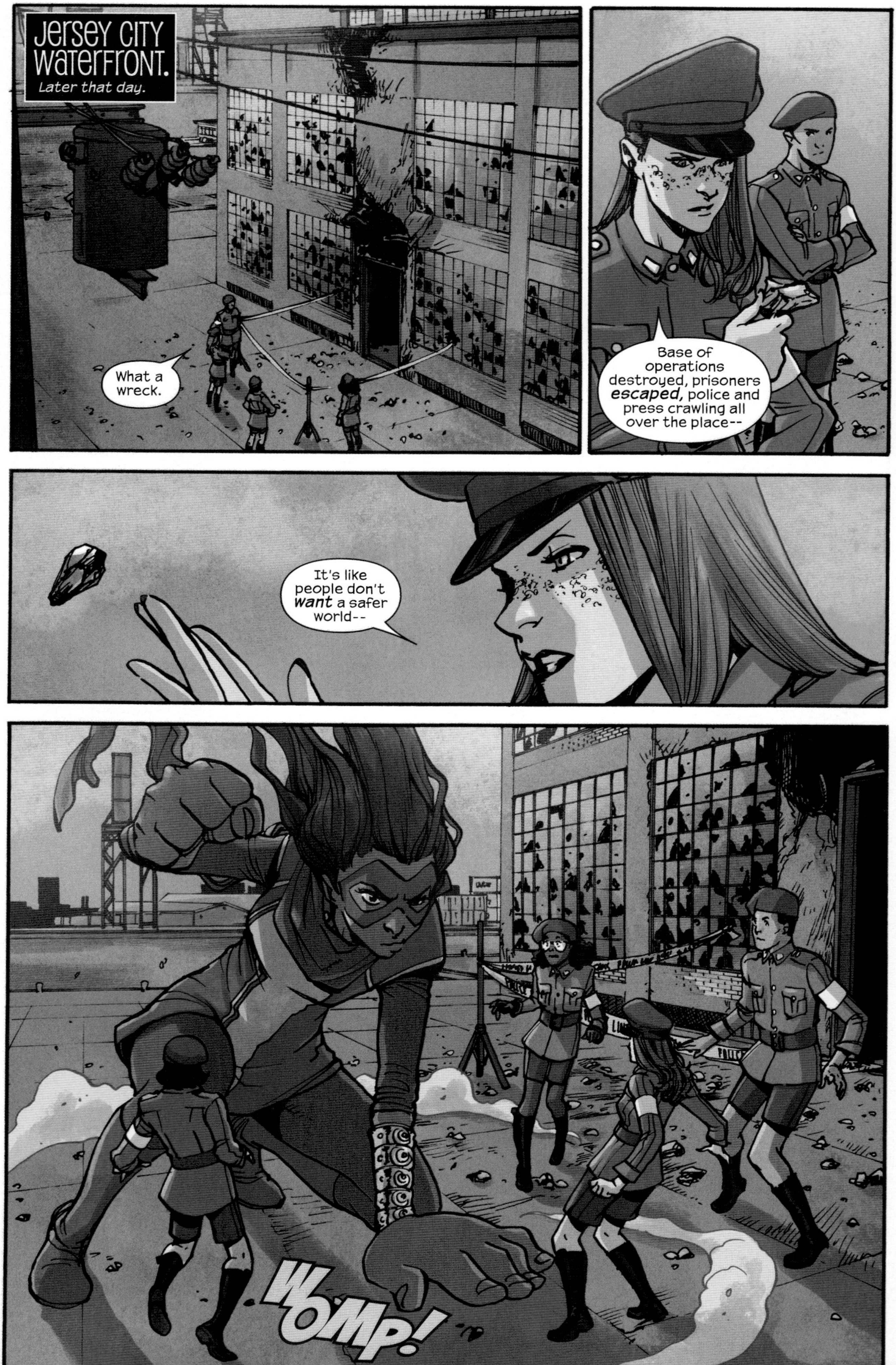
JERSEY CITY WATERFRONT.
Later that day.
What a wreck.
Base of operations destroyed, prisoners escaped, police and press crawling all over the place--
It's like people don't want a safer world--
WOMP!

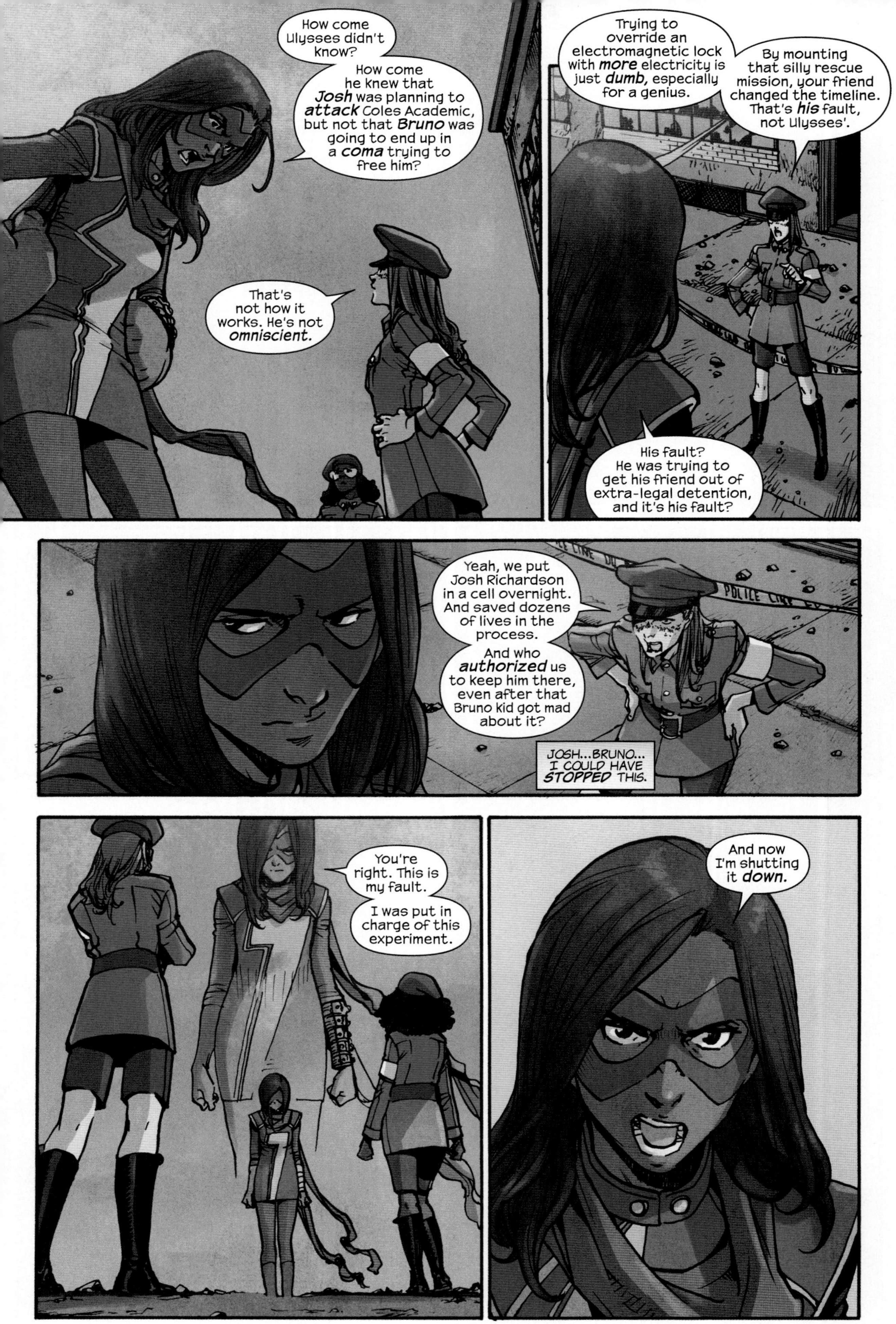

How come Ulysses didn't know?
How come he knew that Josh was planning to attack Coles Academic, but not that Bruno was going to end up in a coma trying to free him?
That's not how it works. He's not omniscient.
Trying to override an electromagnetic lock with more electricity is just dumb, especially for a genius.
By mounting that silly rescue mission, your friend changed the timeline. That's his fault, not Ulysses'.
His fault? He was trying to get his friend out of extra-legal detention, and it's his fault?
Yeah, we put Josh Richardson in a cell overnight. And saved dozens of lives in the process.
And who authorized us to keep him there, even after that Bruno kid got mad about it?
JOSH...BRUNO... I COULD HAVE STOPPED THIS.
You're right. This is my fault.
I was put in charge of this experiment.
And now I'm shutting it down.

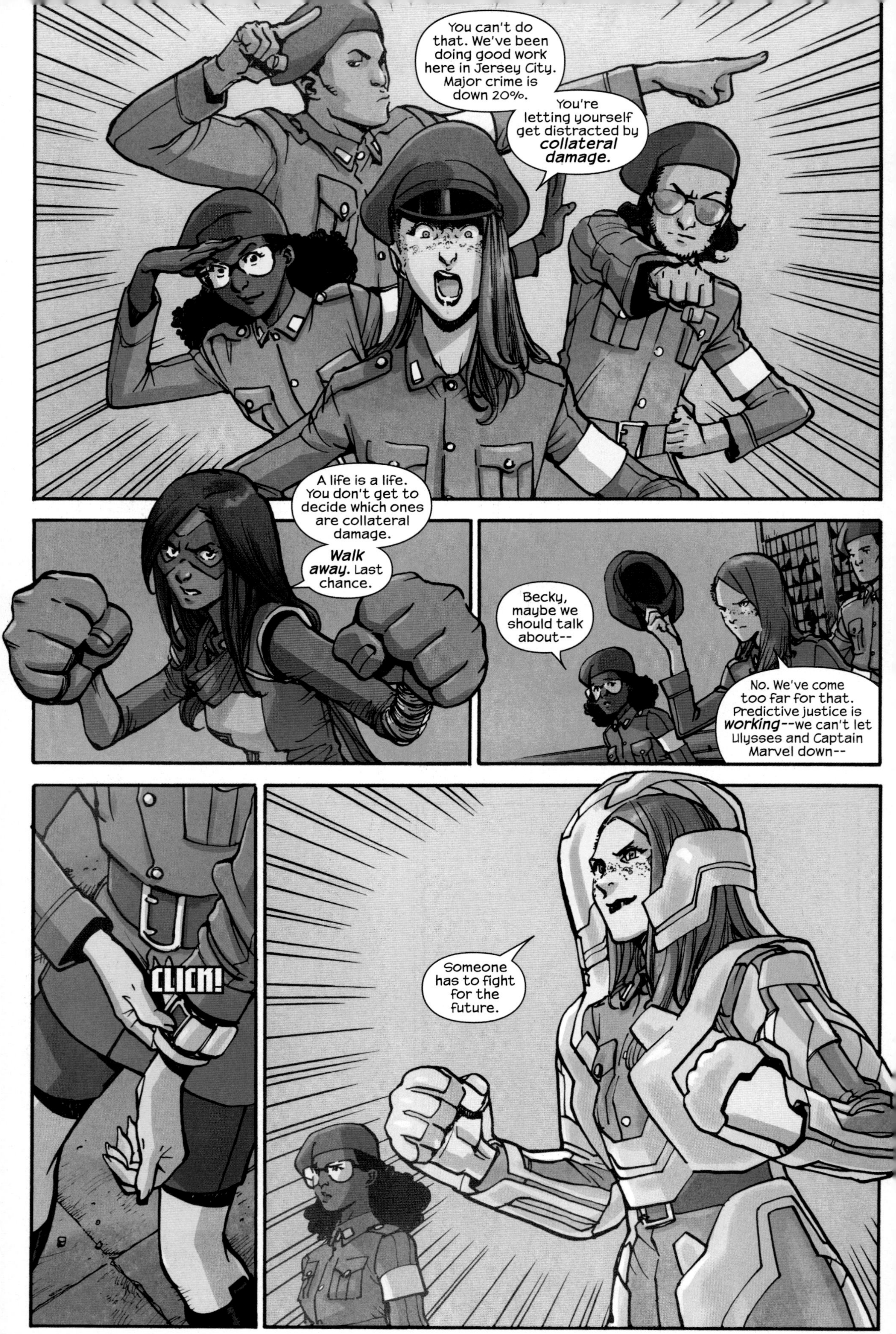

You can't do that. We've been doing good work here in Jersey City. Major crime is down 20%.
You're letting yourself get distracted by *collateral damage.*
A life is a life. You don't get to decide which ones are collateral damage.
Walk away. Last chance.
Becky, maybe we should talk about--
No. We've come too far for that. Predictive justice is *working*--we can't let Ulysses and Captain Marvel down--
CLICK!
Someone has to fight for the future.

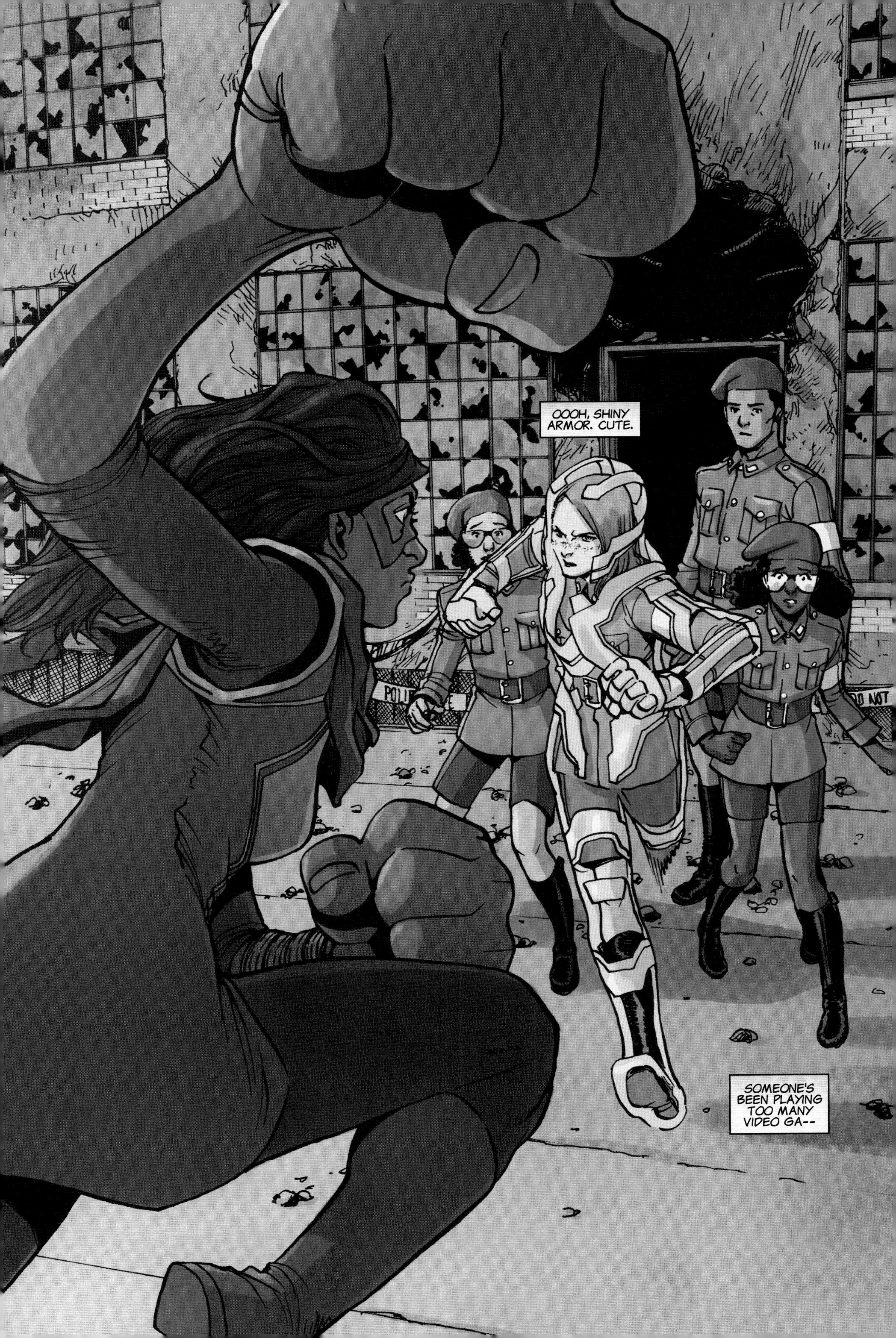
OOOH, SHINY ARMOR. CUTE.
SOMEONE'S BEEN PLAYING TOO MANY VIDEO GA--

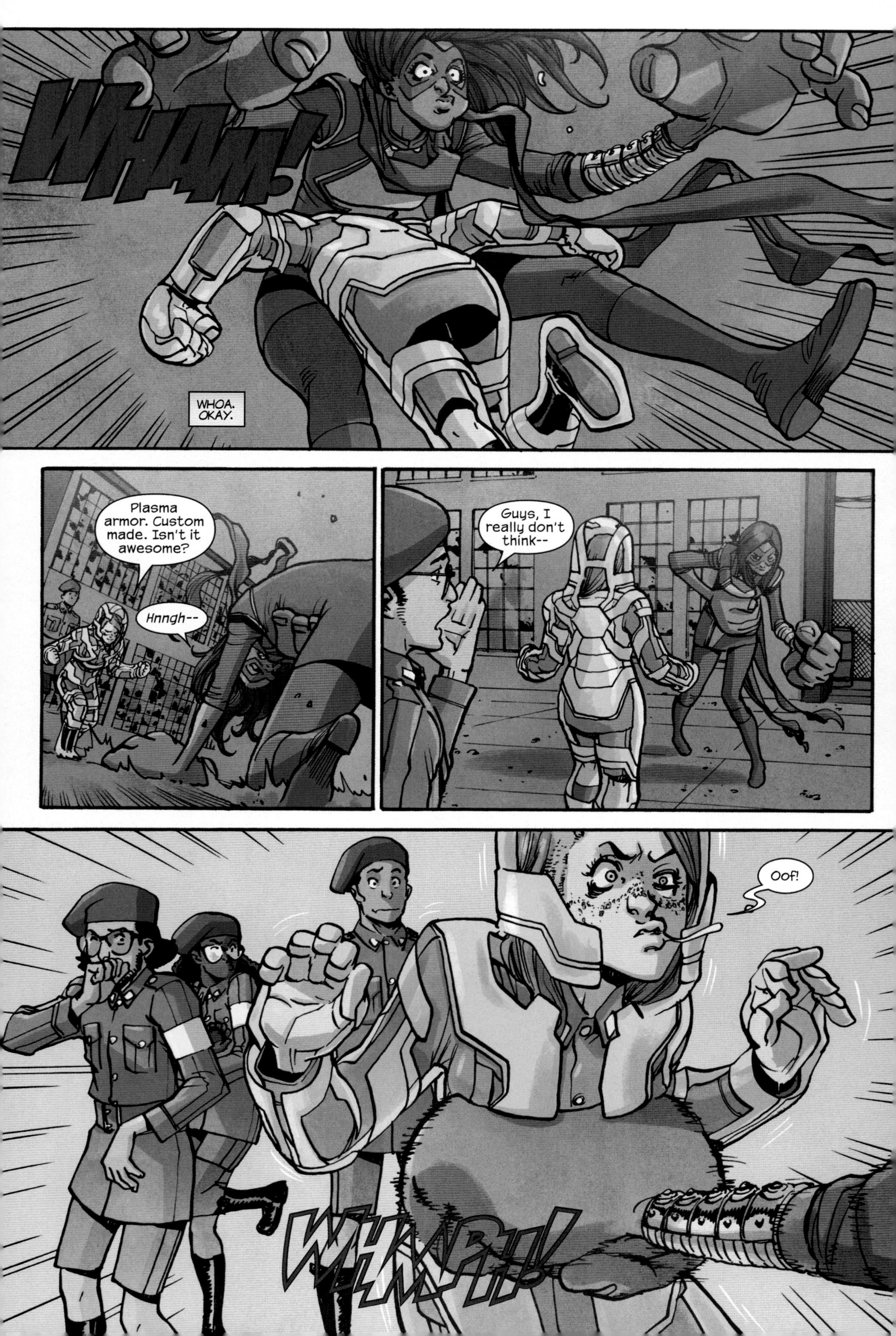
WHAM!
WHOA. OKAY.
Plasma armor. Custom made. Isn't it awesome?
Hnngh--
Guys, I really don't think--
Oof!
WHAPH!

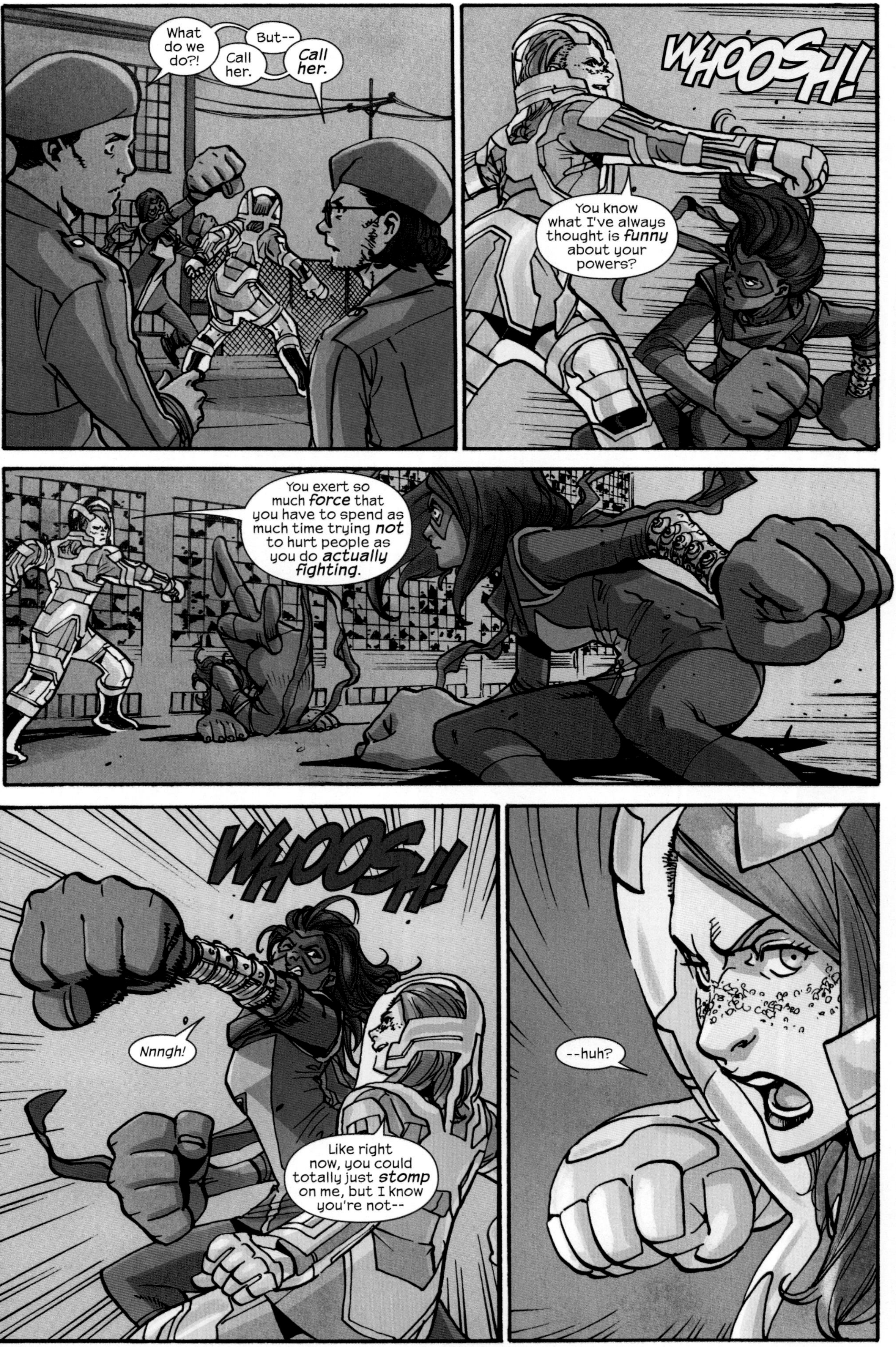
What do we do?!
But--
Call her.
Call her.
WHOOSH!
You know what I've always thought is funny about your powers?
You exert so much force that you have to spend as much time trying not to hurt people as you do actually fighting.
WHOOSH!
Nnngh!
Like right now, you could totally just stomp on me, but I know you're not--
--huh?

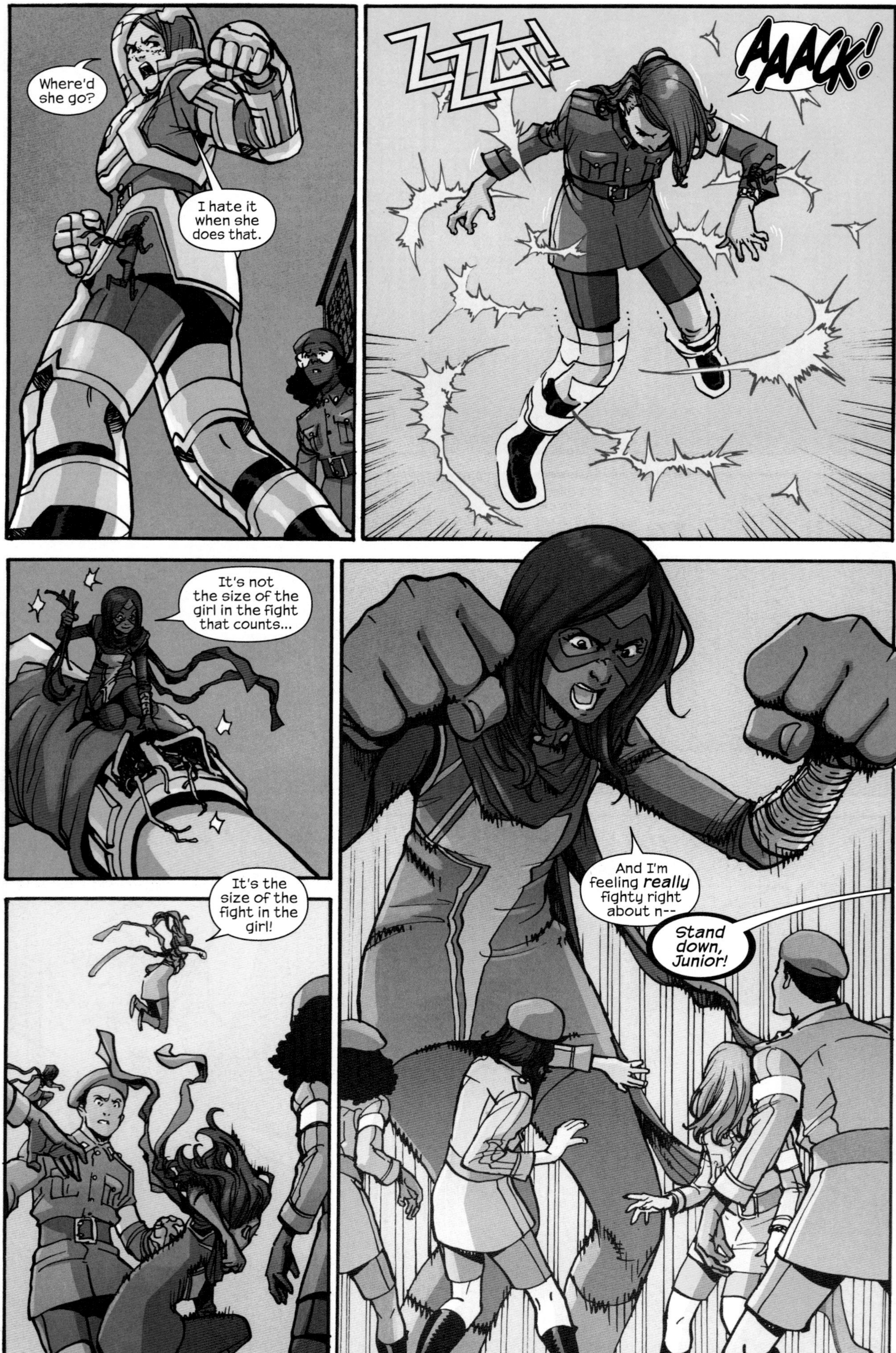
Where'd she go?
I hate it when she does that.
ZZZT!
AAACK!
It's not the size of the girl in the fight that counts...
It's the size of the fight in the girl!
And I'm feeling *really* fighty right about n--
Stand down, Junior!

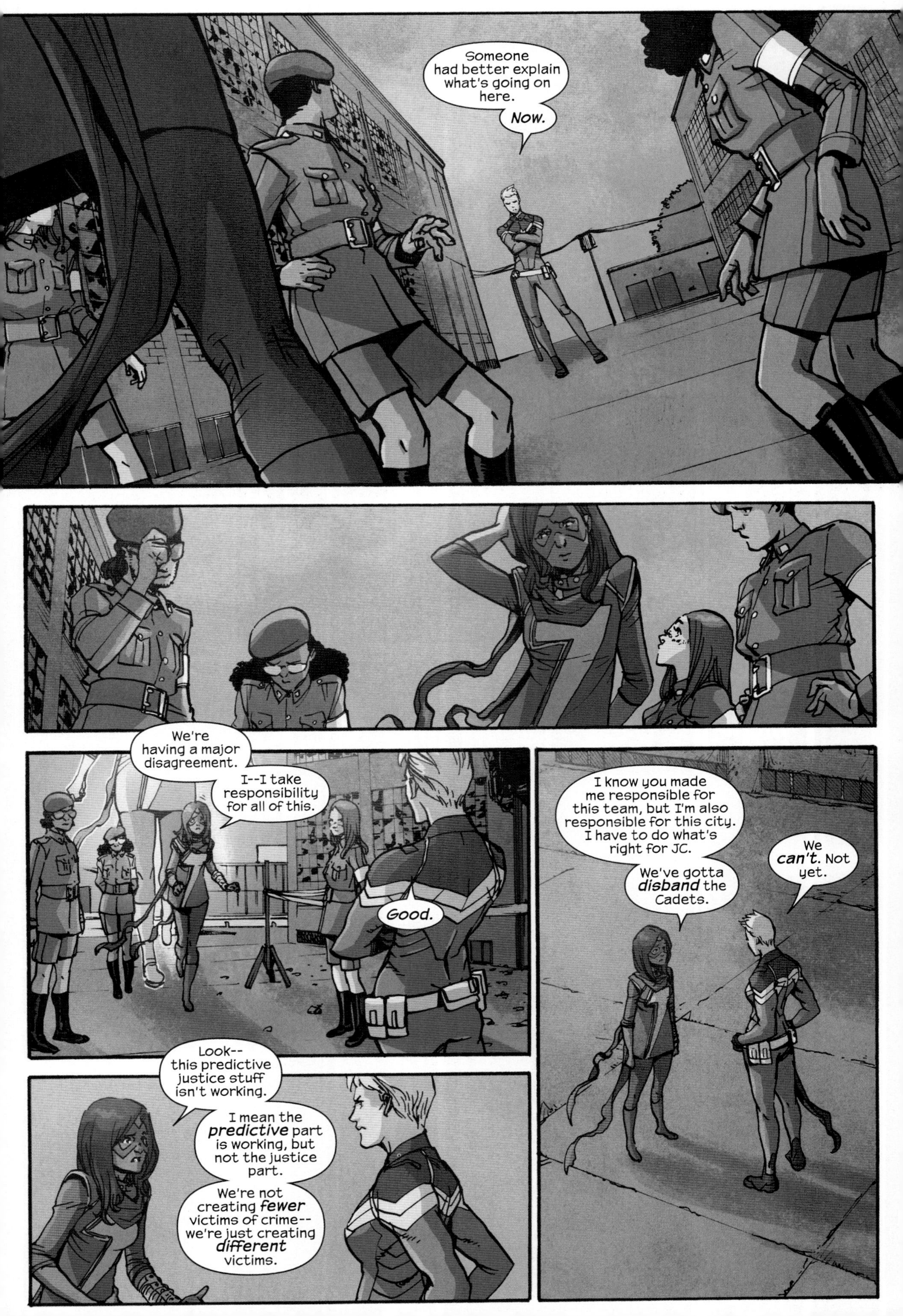
Someone had better explain what's going on here.
Now.
We're having a major disagreement.
I--I take responsibility for all of this.
Good.
Look-- this predictive justice stuff isn't working.
I mean the predictive part is working, but not the justice part.
We're not creating fewer victims of crime-- we're just creating different victims.
I know you made me responsible for this team, but I'm also responsible for this city. I have to do what's right for JC.
We've gotta disband the Cadets.
We can't. Not yet.

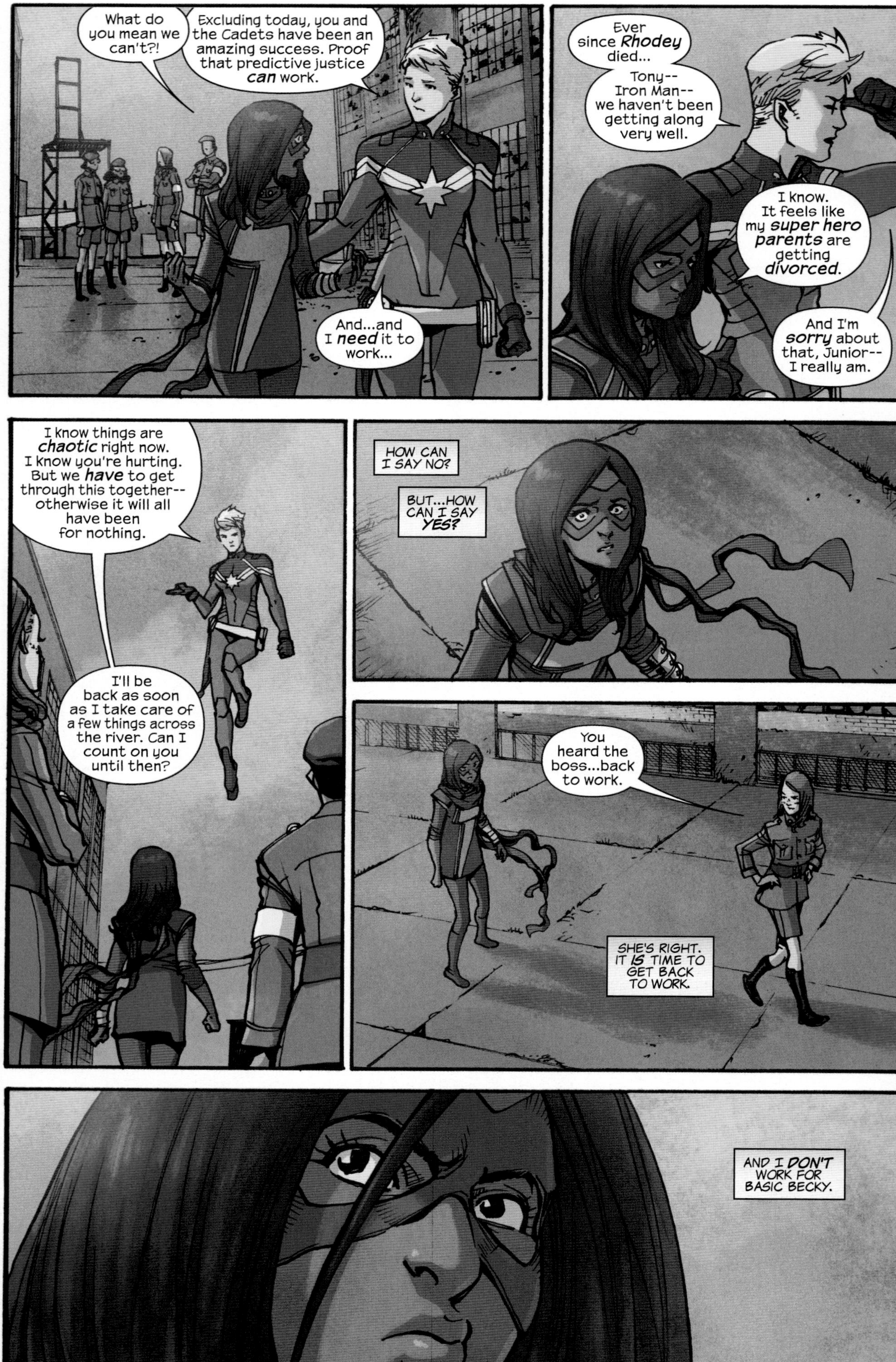

What do you mean we can't?!
Excluding today, you and the Cadets have been an amazing success. Proof that predictive justice can work.
And...and I need it to work...
Ever since Rhodey died...
Tony-- Iron Man-- we haven't been getting along very well.
I know. It feels like my super hero parents are getting divorced.
And I'm sorry about that, Junior-- I really am.
I know things are chaotic right now. I know you're hurting. But we have to get through this together-- otherwise it will all have been for nothing.
I'll be back as soon as I take care of a few things across the river. Can I count on you until then?
HOW CAN I SAY NO?
BUT...HOW CAN I SAY YES?
You heard the boss...back to work.
SHE'S RIGHT. IT IS TIME TO GET BACK TO WORK.
AND I DON'T WORK FOR BASIC BECKY.

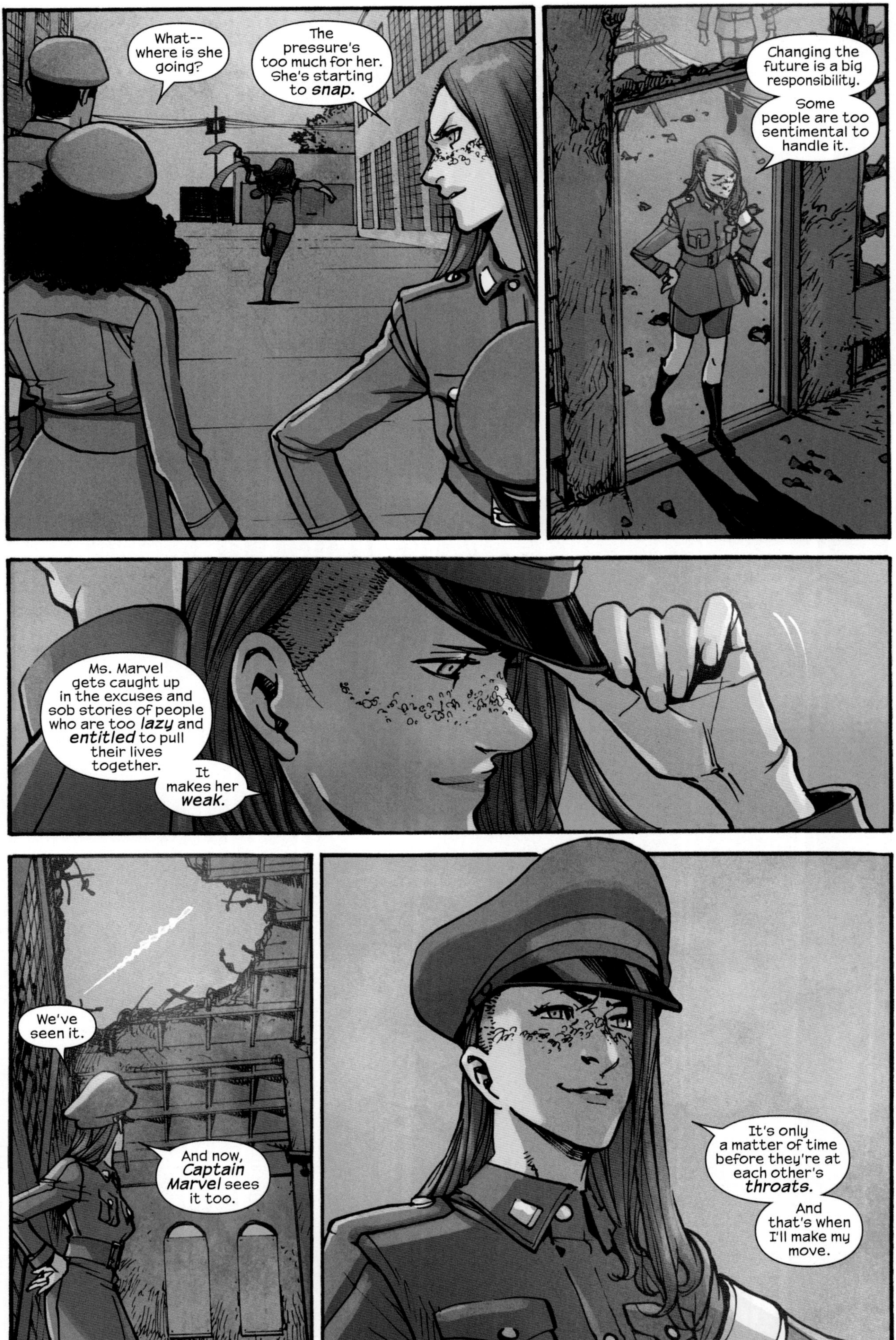
What-- where is she going?
The pressure's too much for her. She's starting to *snap.*
Changing the future is a big responsibility.
Some people are too sentimental to handle it.
Ms. Marvel gets caught up in the excuses and sob stories of people who are too *lazy* and *entitled* to pull their lives together.
It makes her *weak.*
We've seen it.
And now, *Captain Marvel* sees it too.
It's only a matter of time before they're at each other's *throats.*
And that's when I'll make my move.

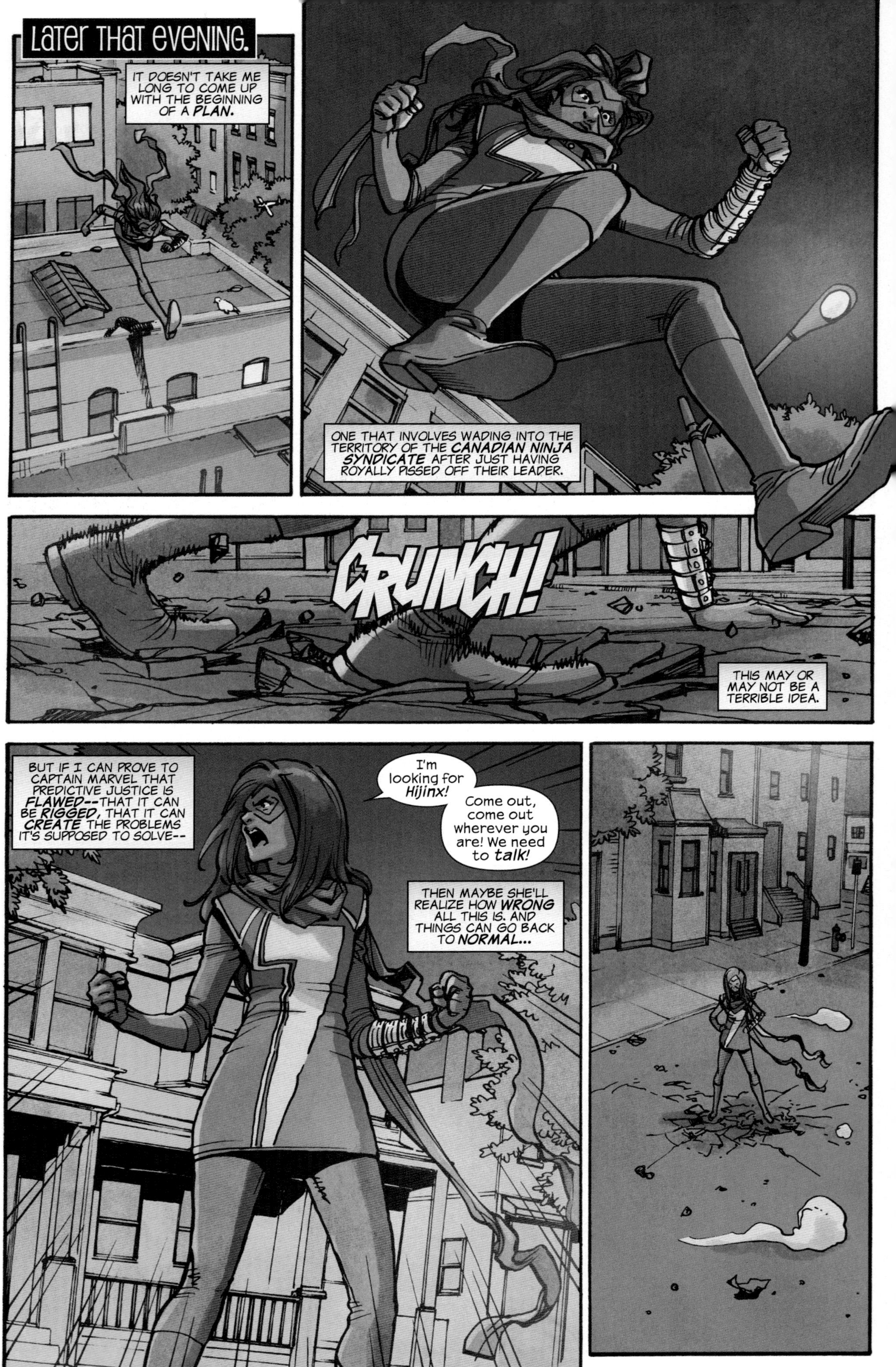
LATER THAT EVENING.
IT DOESN'T TAKE ME LONG TO COME UP WITH THE BEGINNING OF A PLAN.
ONE THAT INVOLVES WADING INTO THE TERRITORY OF THE CANADIAN NINJA SYNDICATE AFTER JUST HAVING ROYALLY PISSED OFF THEIR LEADER.
CRUNCH!
THIS MAY OR MAY NOT BE A TERRIBLE IDEA.
BUT IF I CAN PROVE TO CAPTAIN MARVEL THAT PREDICTIVE JUSTICE IS FLAWED--THAT IT CAN BE RIGGED, THAT IT CAN CREATE THE PROBLEMS IT'S SUPPOSED TO SOLVE--
I'm looking for Hijinx!
Come out, come out wherever you are! We need to talk!
THEN MAYBE SHE'LL REALIZE HOW WRONG ALL THIS IS. AND THINGS CAN GO BACK TO NORMAL...

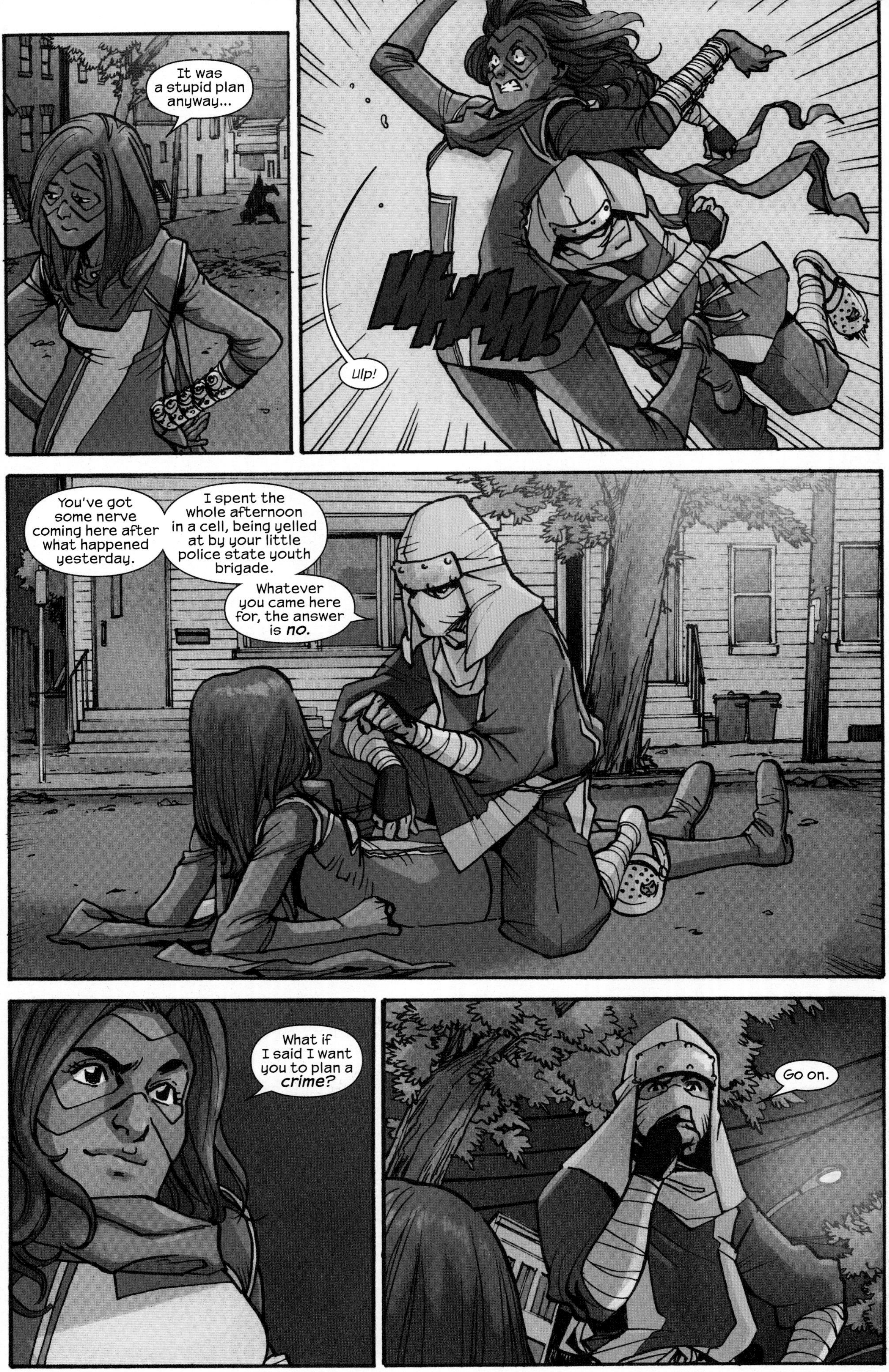
It was a stupid plan anyway...
WHAM!
Ulp!
You've got some nerve coming here after what happened yesterday.
I spent the whole afternoon in a cell, being yelled at by your little police state youth brigade.
Whatever you came here for, the answer is *no.*
What if I said I want you to plan a *crime?*
Go on.

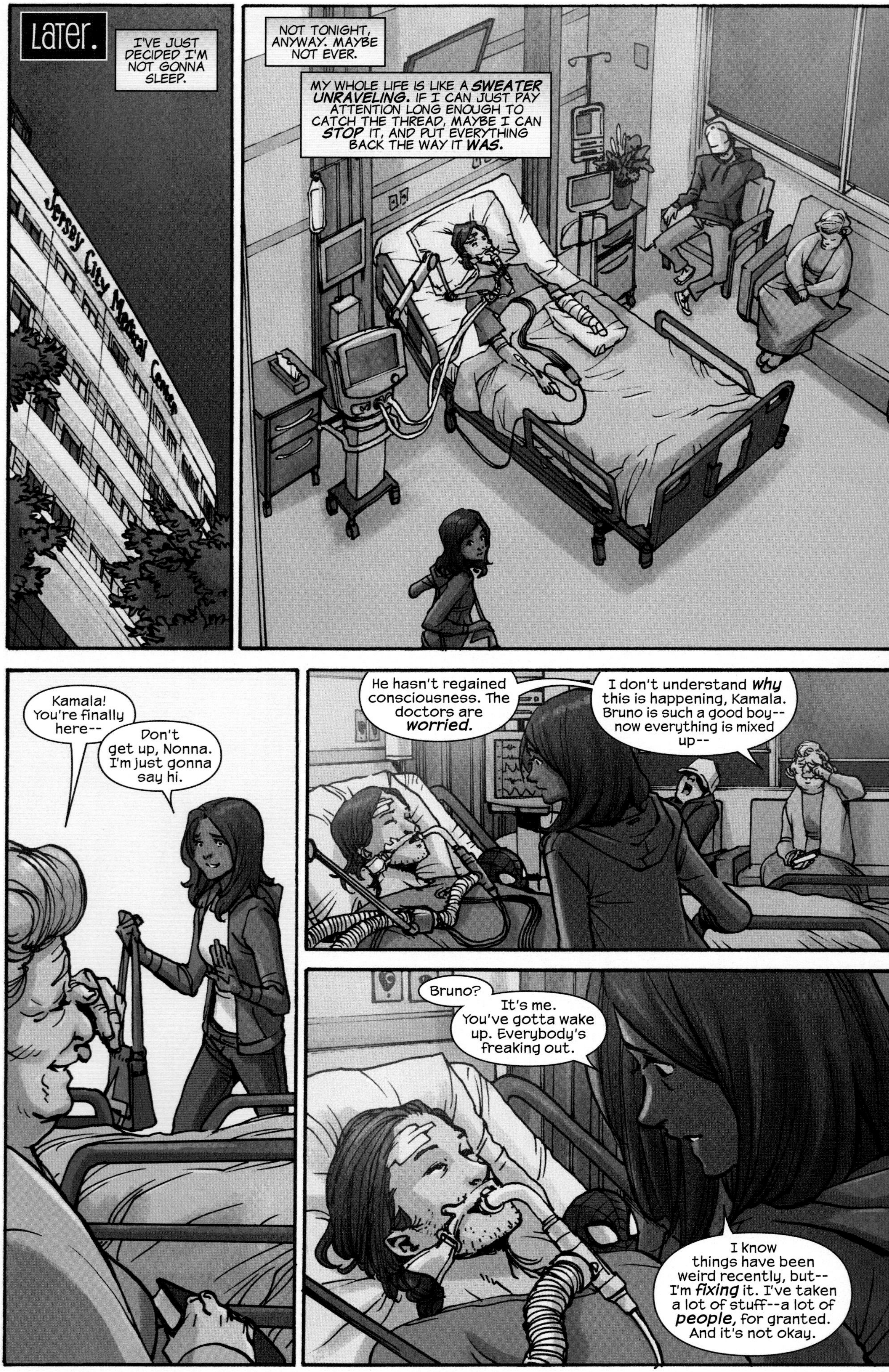
LATER.
I'VE JUST DECIDED I'M NOT GONNA SLEEP.
Jersey City Medical Center
NOT TONIGHT, ANYWAY. MAYBE NOT EVER.
MY WHOLE LIFE IS LIKE A SWEATER UNRAVELING. IF I CAN JUST PAY ATTENTION LONG ENOUGH TO CATCH THE THREAD, MAYBE I CAN STOP IT, AND PUT EVERYTHING BACK THE WAY IT WAS.
Kamala! You're finally here--
Don't get up, Nonna. I'm just gonna say hi.
He hasn't regained consciousness. The doctors are worried.
I don't understand why this is happening, Kamala. Bruno is such a good boy-- now everything is mixed up--
Bruno?
It's me. You've gotta wake up. Everybody's freaking out.
I know things have been weird recently, but-- I'm fixing it. I've taken a lot of stuff--a lot of people, for granted. And it's not okay.

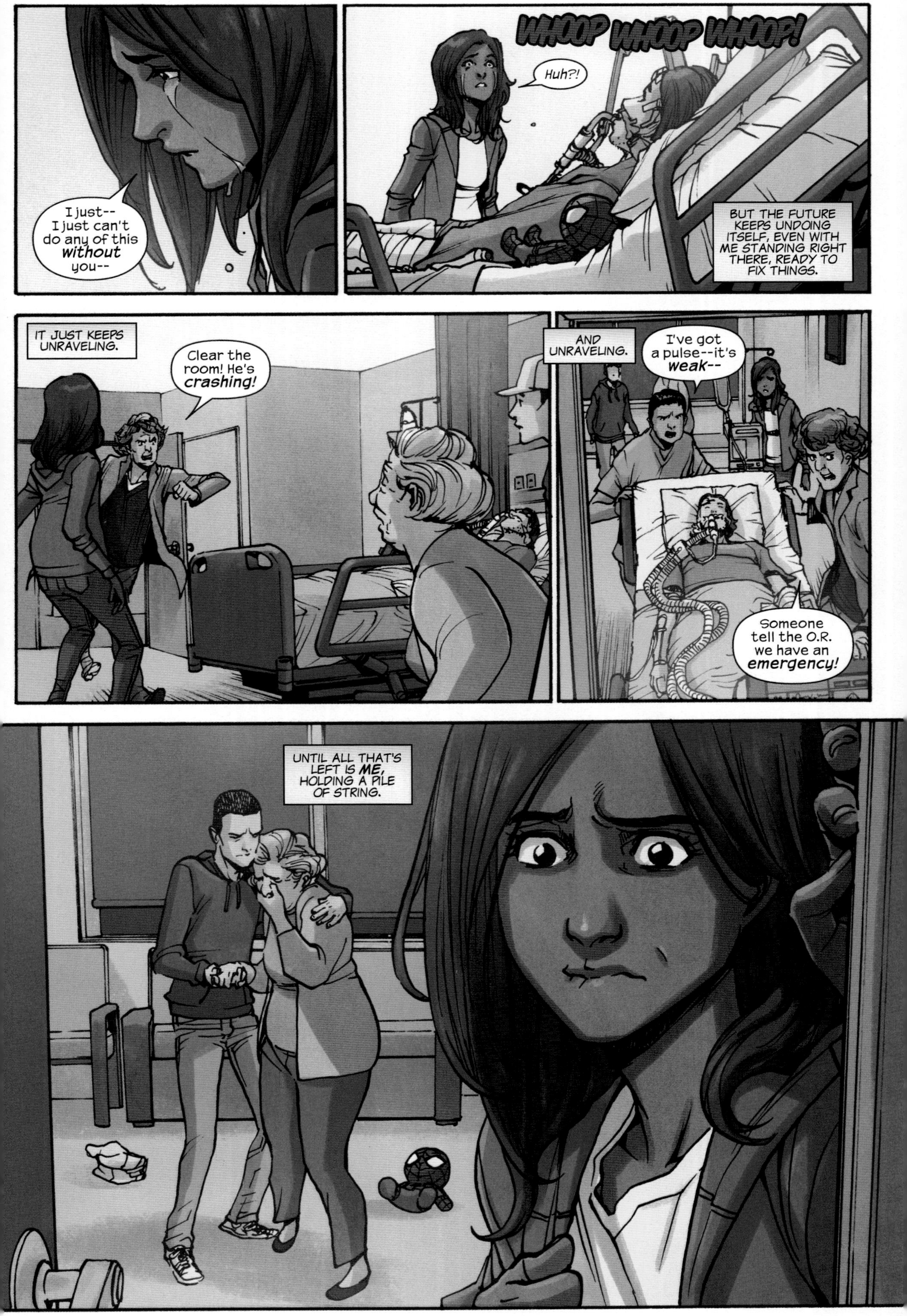
I just--
I just can't do any of this *without* you--
WHOOP WHOOP WHOOP!
Huh?!
BUT THE FUTURE KEEPS UNDOING ITSELF, EVEN WITH ME STANDING RIGHT THERE, READY TO FIX THINGS.
IT JUST KEEPS UNRAVELING.
Clear the room! He's *crashing!*
AND UNRAVELING.
I've got a pulse--it's *weak--*
Someone tell the O.R. we have an *emergency!*
UNTIL ALL THAT'S LEFT IS *ME,* HOLDING A PILE OF STRING.

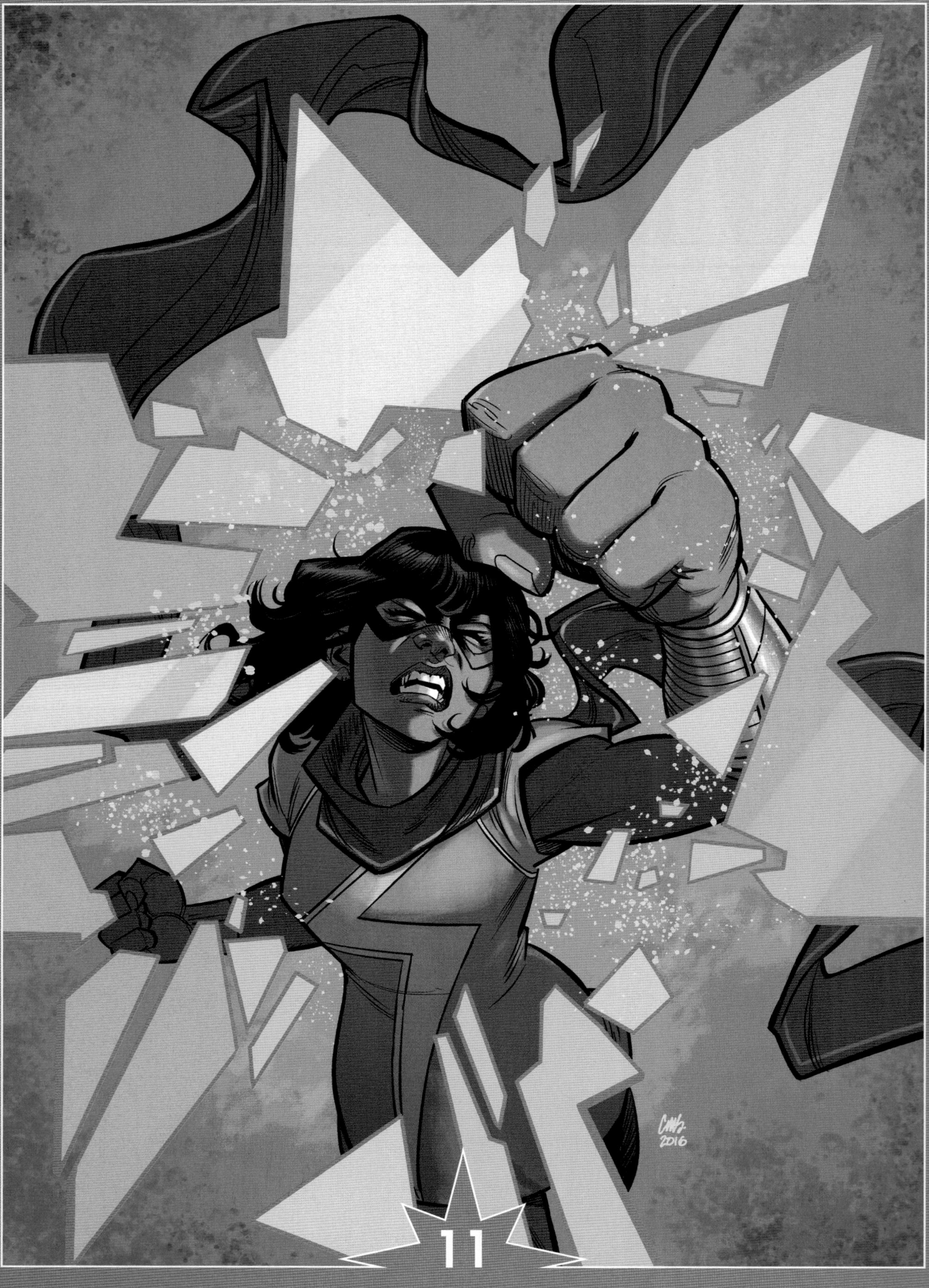
11

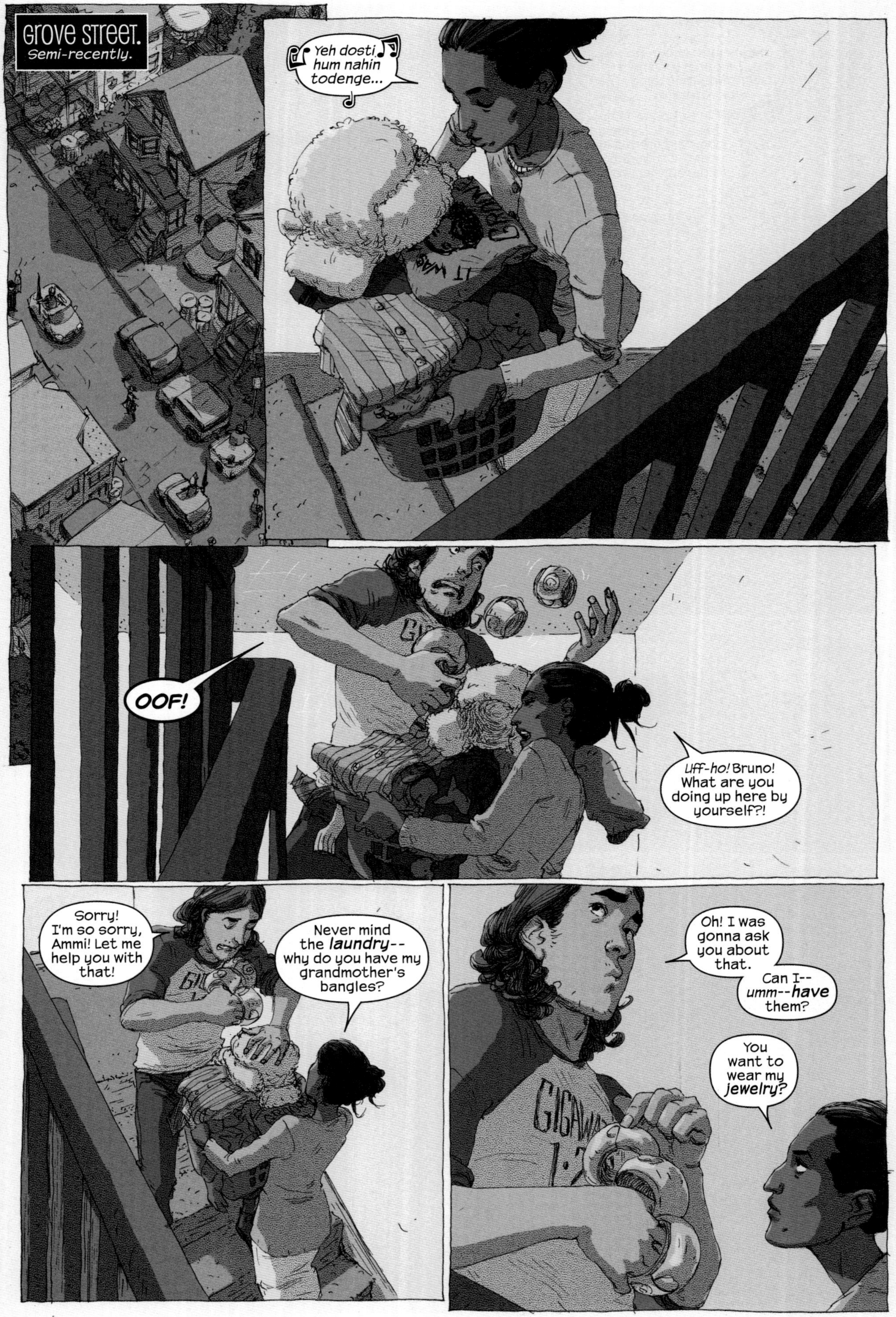
GROVE STREET.
Semi-recently.
Yeh dosti hum nahin todenge...
OOF!
Uff-ho! Bruno! What are you doing up here by yourself?!
Sorry! I'm so sorry, Ammi! Let me help you with that!
Never mind the laundry-- why do you have my grandmother's bangles?
Oh! I was gonna ask you about that.
Can I-- umm--have them?
You want to wear my jewelry?

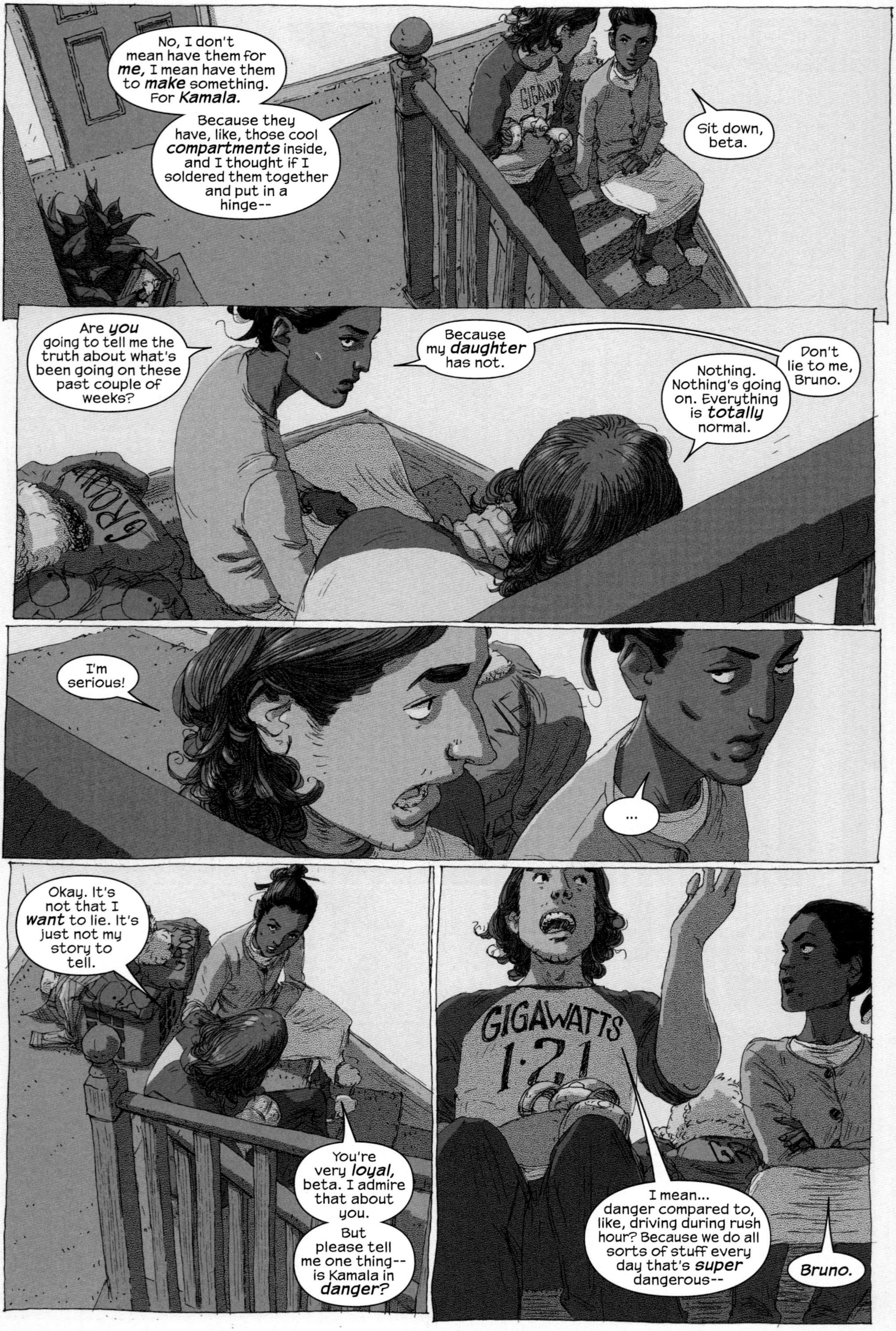
No, I don't mean have them for *me,* I mean have them to *make* something. For *Kamala.*
Because they have, like, those cool *compartments* inside, and I thought if I soldered them together and put in a hinge--
Sit down, beta.
Are *you* going to tell me the truth about what's been going on these past couple of weeks?
Because my *daughter* has not.
Nothing. Nothing's going on. Everything is *totally* normal.
Don't lie to me, Bruno.
I'm serious!
...
Okay. It's not that I *want* to lie. It's just not my story to tell.
You're very *loyal,* beta. I admire that about you.
But please tell me one thing-- is Kamala in *danger?*
GIGAWATTS 1.21
I mean... danger compared to, like, driving during rush hour? Because we do all sorts of stuff every day that's *super* dangerous--
Bruno.

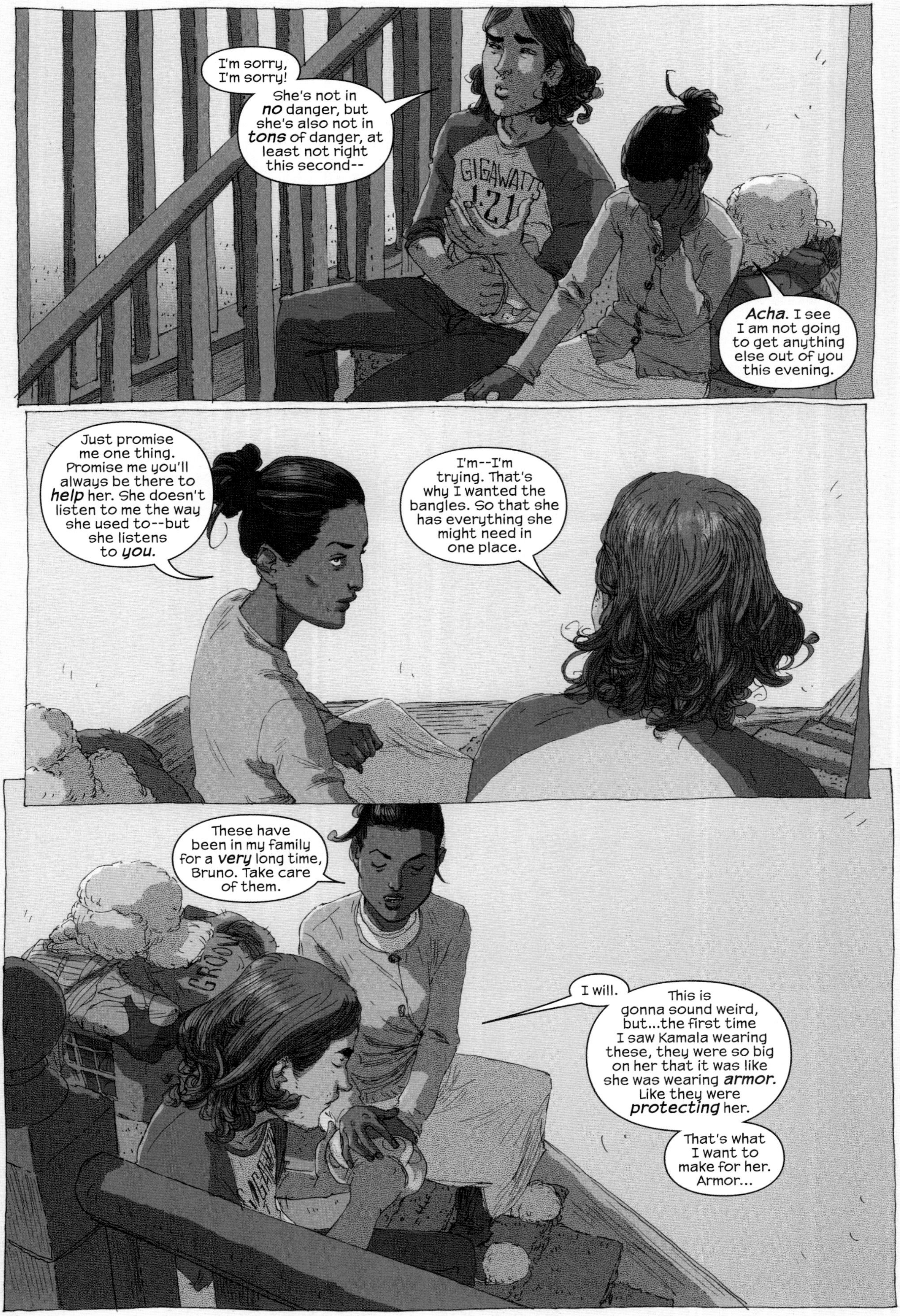
I'm sorry, I'm sorry!
She's not in *no* danger, but she's also not in *tons* of danger, at least not right this second--
Acha. I see I am not going to get anything else out of you this evening.
Just promise me one thing. Promise me you'll always be there to *help* her. She doesn't listen to me the way she used to--but she listens to *you.*
I'm--I'm trying. That's why I wanted the bangles. So that she has everything she might need in one place.
These have been in my family for a *very* long time, Bruno. Take care of them.
I will.
This is gonna sound weird, but...the first time I saw Kamala wearing these, they were so big on her that it was like she was wearing *armor.* Like they were *protecting* her.
That's what I want to make for her. Armor...

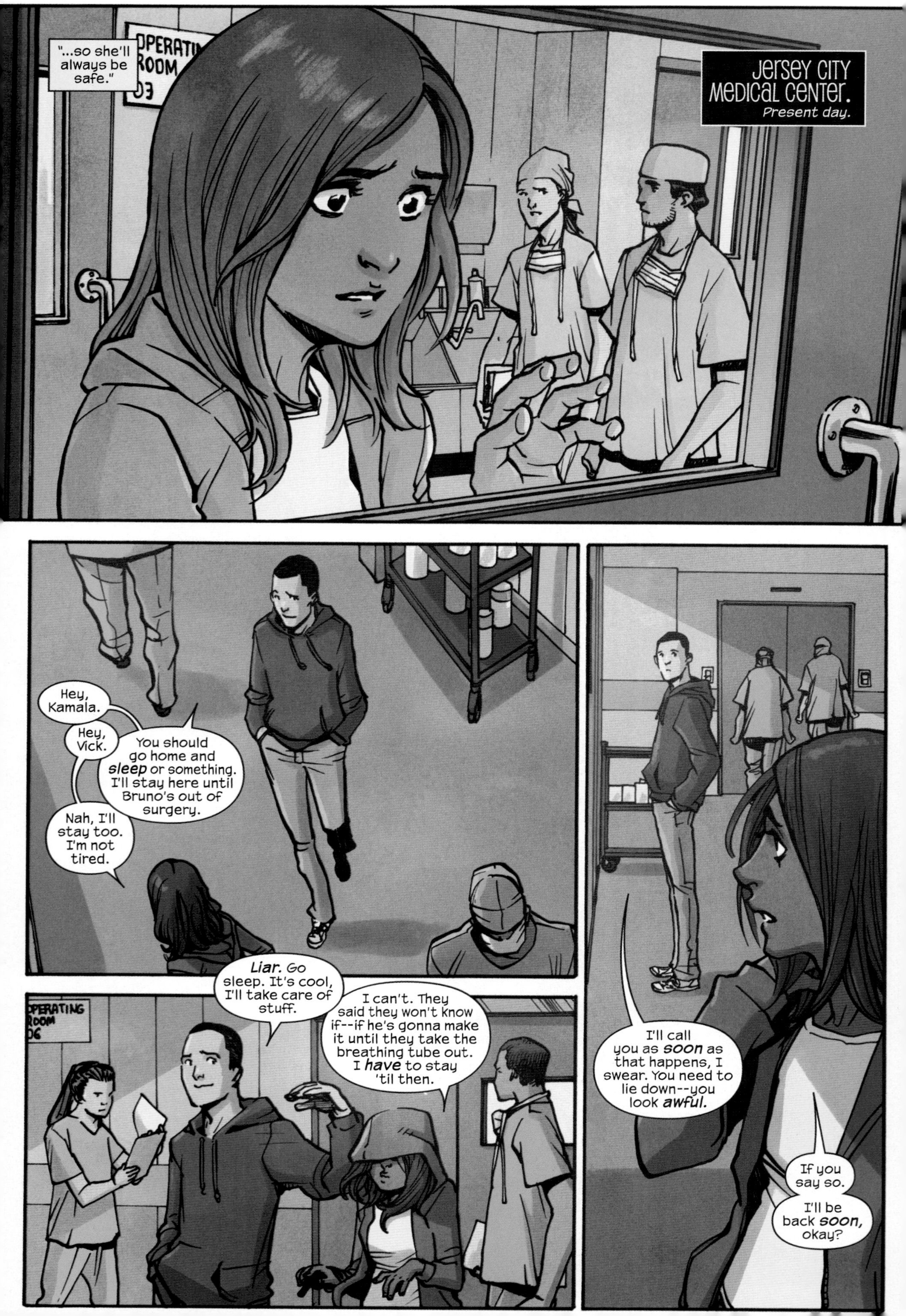

OPERATING ROOM 03
"...so she'll always be safe."
JERSEY CITY MEDICAL CENTER.
Present day.
Hey, Kamala.
Hey, Vick.
You should go home and *sleep* or something. I'll stay here until Bruno's out of surgery.
Nah, I'll stay too. I'm not tired.
Liar. Go sleep. It's cool, I'll take care of stuff.
OPERATING ROOM 06
I can't. They said they won't know if--if he's gonna make it until they take the breathing tube out. I *have* to stay 'til then.
I'll call you as *soon* as that happens, I swear. You need to lie down--you look *awful.*
If you say so.
I'll be back *soon,* okay?

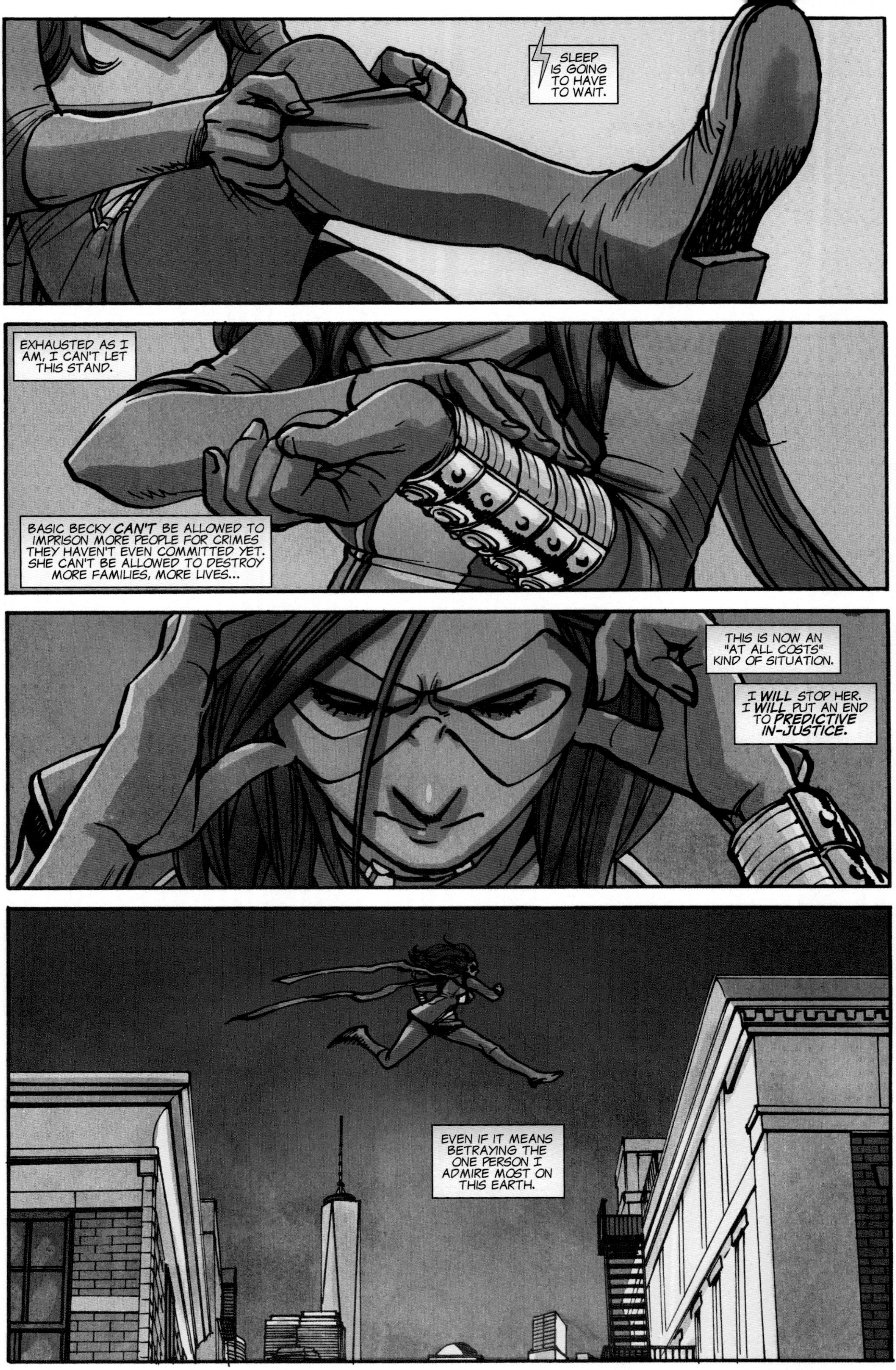
SLEEP IS GOING TO HAVE TO WAIT.
EXHAUSTED AS I AM, I CAN'T LET THIS STAND.
BASIC BECKY **CAN'T** BE ALLOWED TO IMPRISON MORE PEOPLE FOR CRIMES THEY HAVEN'T EVEN COMMITTED YET. SHE CAN'T BE ALLOWED TO DESTROY MORE FAMILIES, MORE LIVES...
THIS IS NOW AN "AT ALL COSTS" KIND OF SITUATION.
I **WILL** STOP HER. I **WILL** PUT AN END TO **PREDICTIVE IN-JUSTICE.**
EVEN IF IT MEANS BETRAYING THE ONE PERSON I ADMIRE MOST ON THIS EARTH.

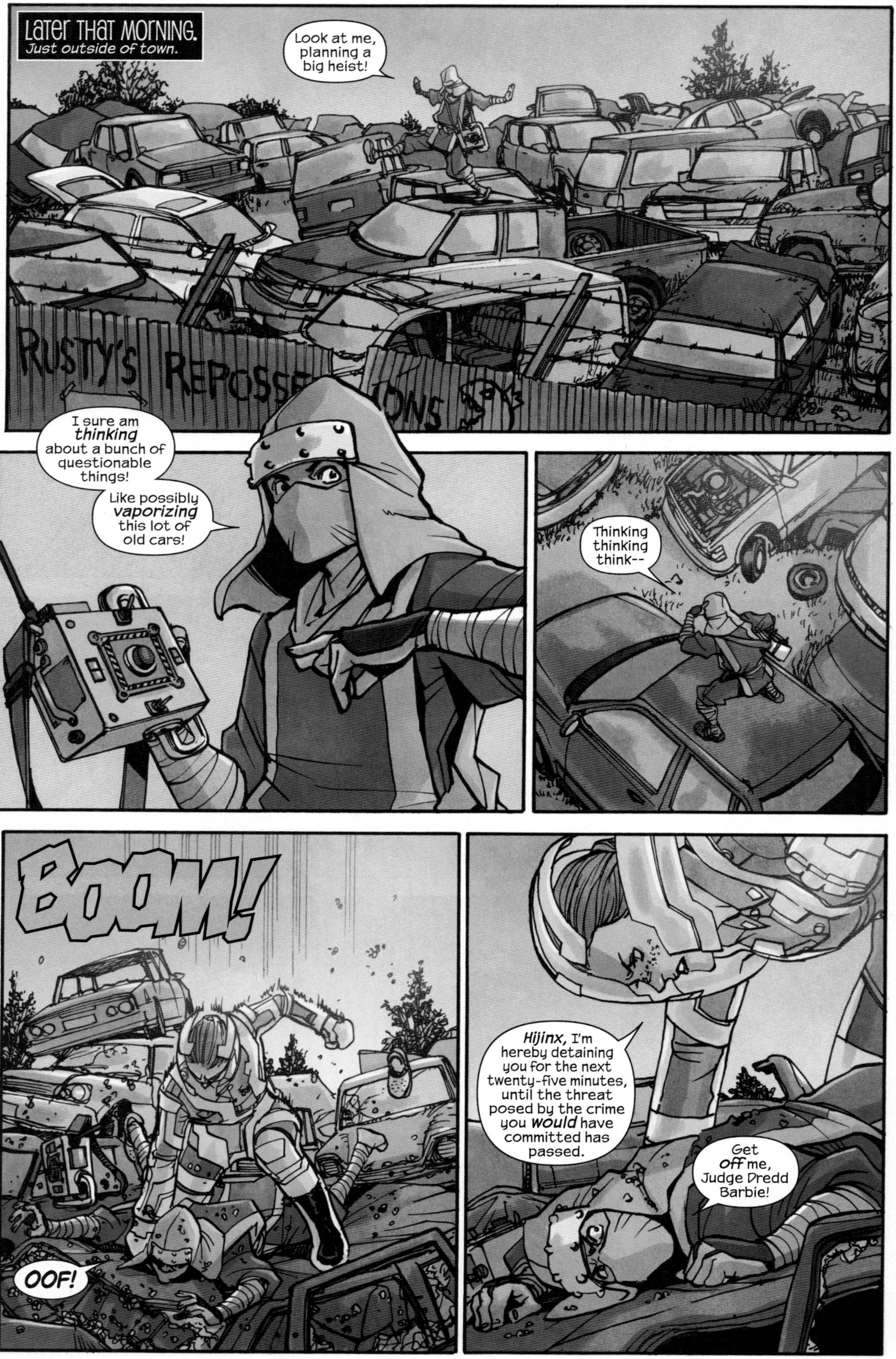

LATER THAT MORNING.
Just outside of town.
Look at me, planning a big heist!
RUSTY'S REPOSSE IONS
I sure am thinking about a bunch of questionable things!
Like possibly vaporizing this lot of old cars!
Thinking thinking think--
BOOM!
OOF!
Hijinx, I'm hereby detaining you for the next twenty-five minutes, until the threat posed by the crime you would have committed has passed.
Get off me, Judge Dredd Barbie!

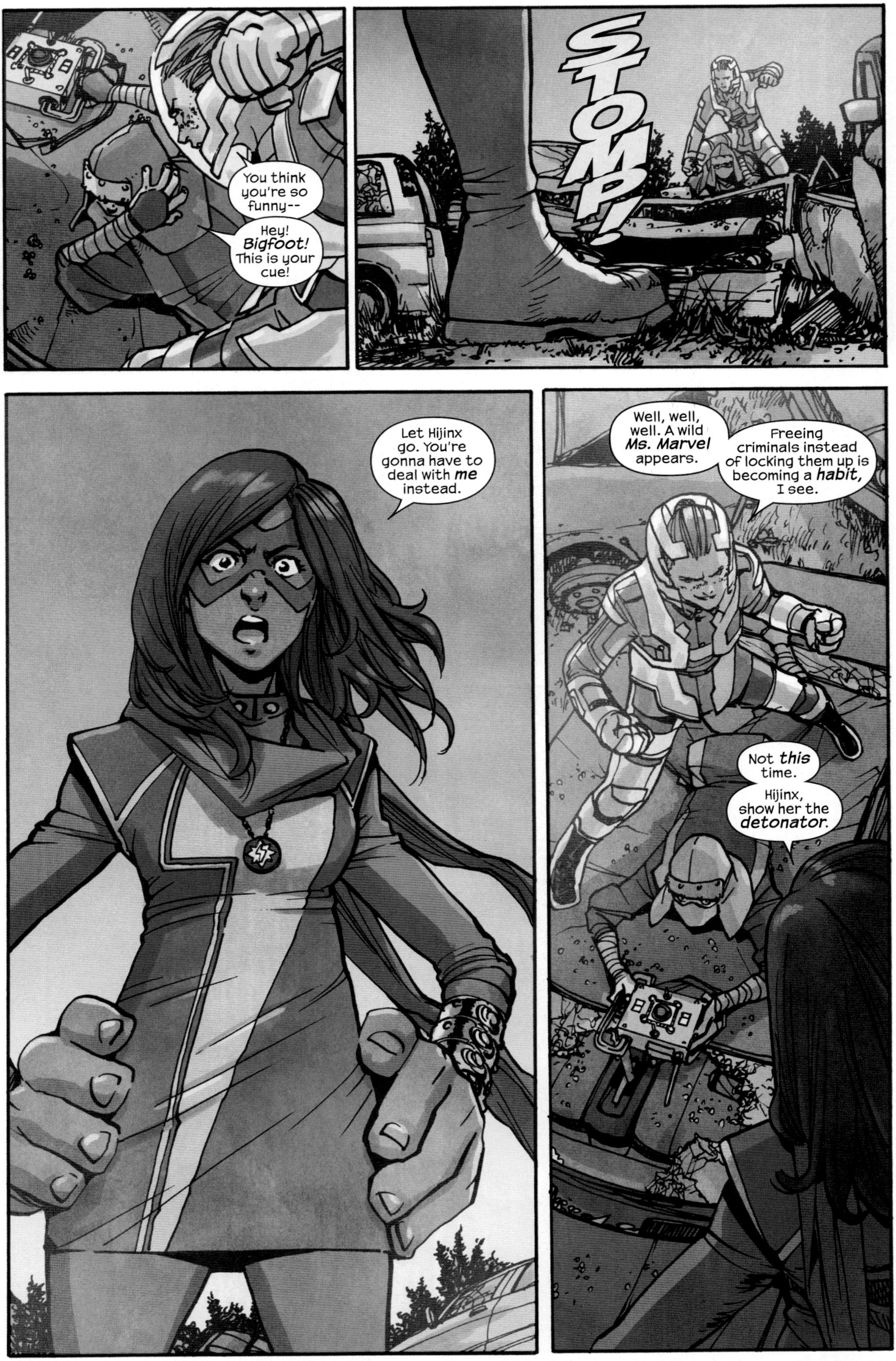
You think you're so funny--
Hey! *Bigfoot!* This is your cue!
STOMP!
Let Hijinx go. You're gonna have to deal with *me* instead.
Well, well, well. A wild *Ms. Marvel* appears.
Freeing criminals instead of locking them up is becoming a *habit,* I see.
Not *this* time.
Hijinx, show her the *detonator*.

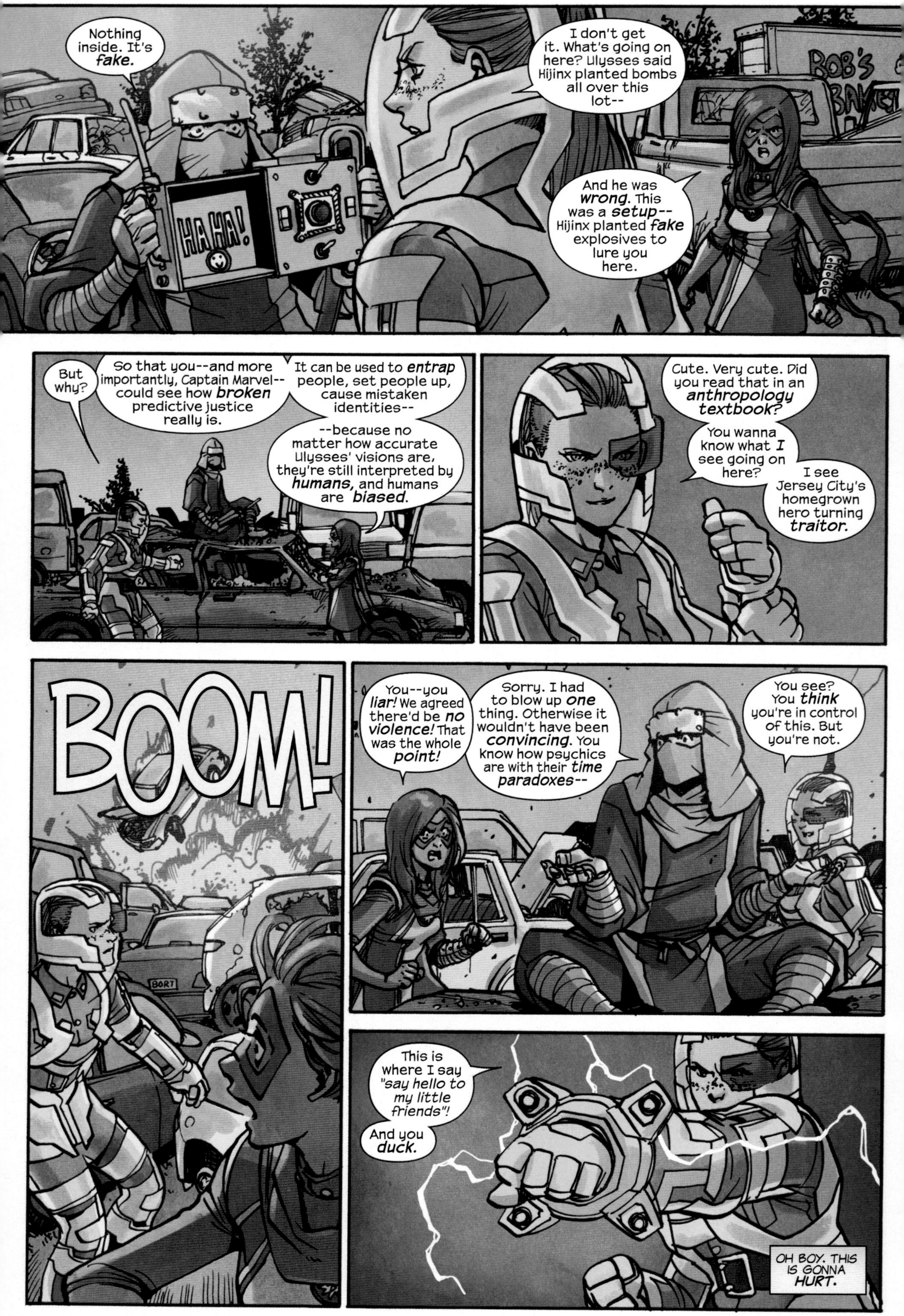

Nothing inside. It's fake.
HAHA!
I don't get it. What's going on here? Ulysses said Hijinx planted bombs all over this lot--
BOB'S
And he was wrong. This was a setup-- Hijinx planted fake explosives to lure you here.
But why?
So that you--and more importantly, Captain Marvel-- could see how broken predictive justice really is.
It can be used to entrap people, set people up, cause mistaken identities--
--because no matter how accurate Ulysses' visions are, they're still interpreted by humans, and humans are biased.
Cute. Very cute. Did you read that in an anthropology textbook?
You wanna know what I see going on here?
I see Jersey City's homegrown hero turning traitor.
BOOM!
You--you liar! We agreed there'd be no violence! That was the whole point!
Sorry. I had to blow up one thing. Otherwise it wouldn't have been convincing. You know how psychics are with their time paradoxes--
You see? You think you're in control of this. But you're not.
This is where I say "say hello to my little friends"!
And you duck.
OH BOY. THIS IS GONNA HURT.

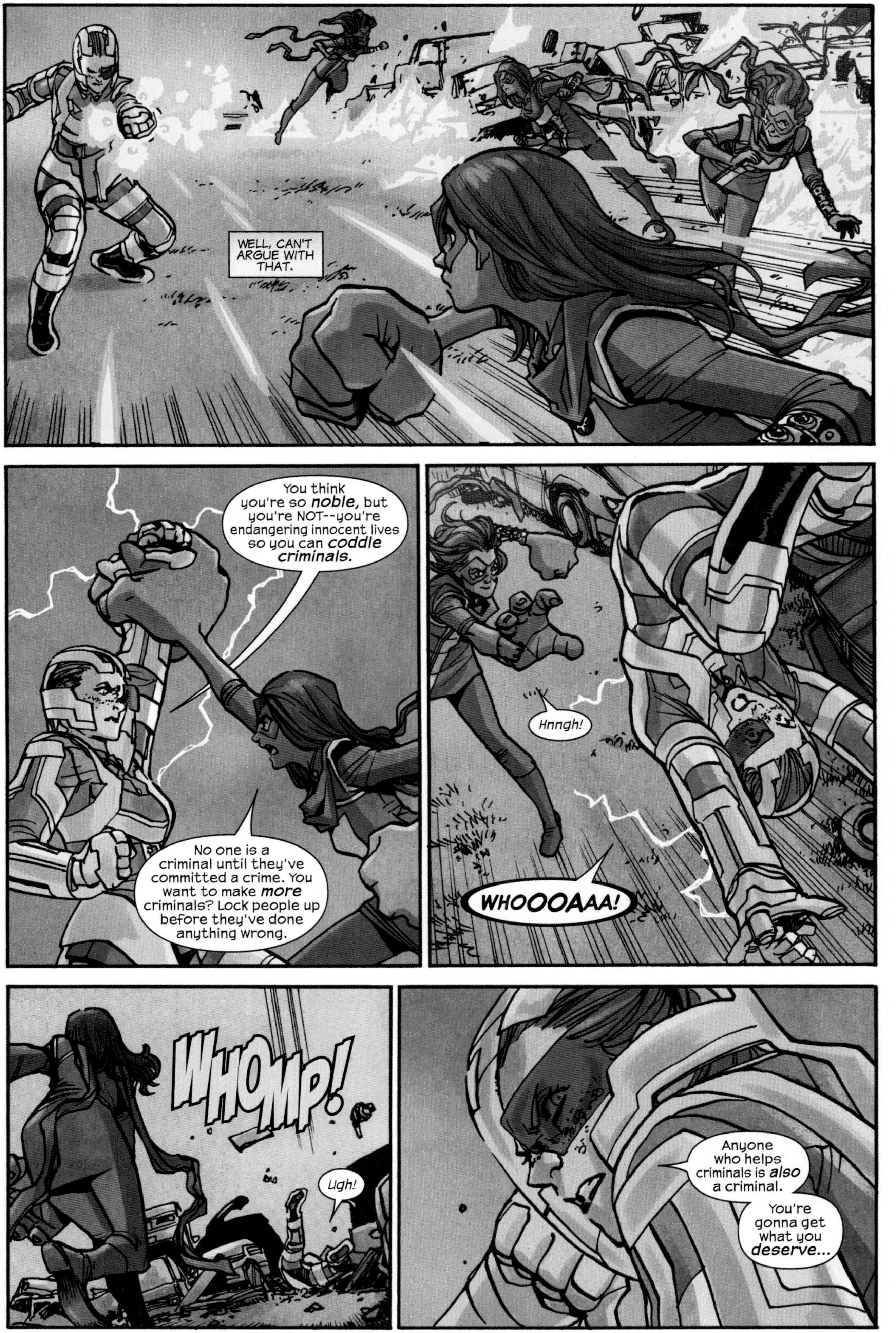

WELL, CAN'T ARGUE WITH THAT.
You think you're so noble, but you're NOT--you're endangering innocent lives so you can coddle criminals.
No one is a criminal until they've committed a crime. You want to make more criminals? Lock people up before they've done anything wrong.
Hnngh!
WHOOOAAA!
WHOMP!
Ugh!
Anyone who helps criminals is also a criminal.
You're gonna get what you deserve...

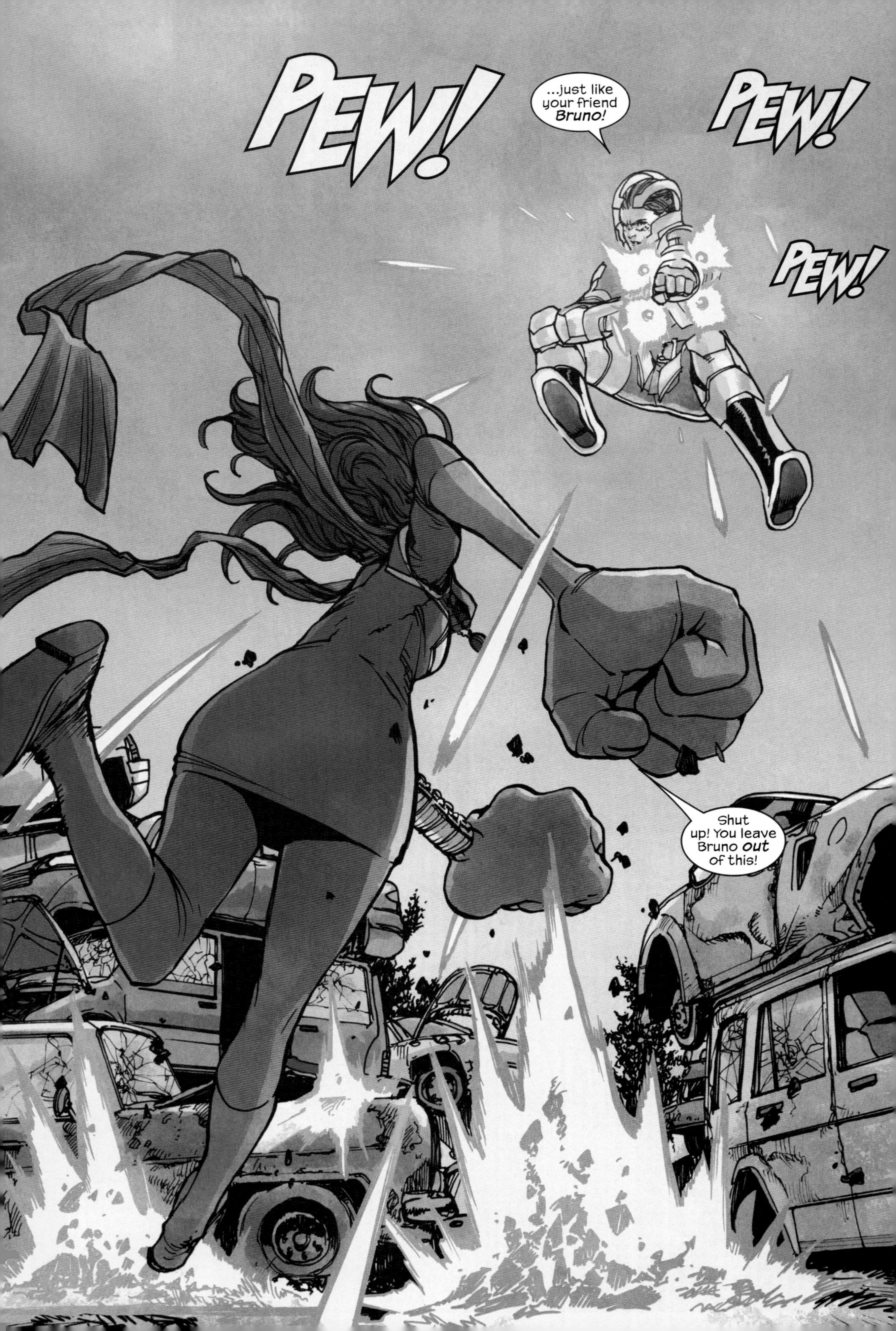
PEW!
...just like your friend Bruno!
PEW!
PEW!
Shut up! You leave Bruno out of this!

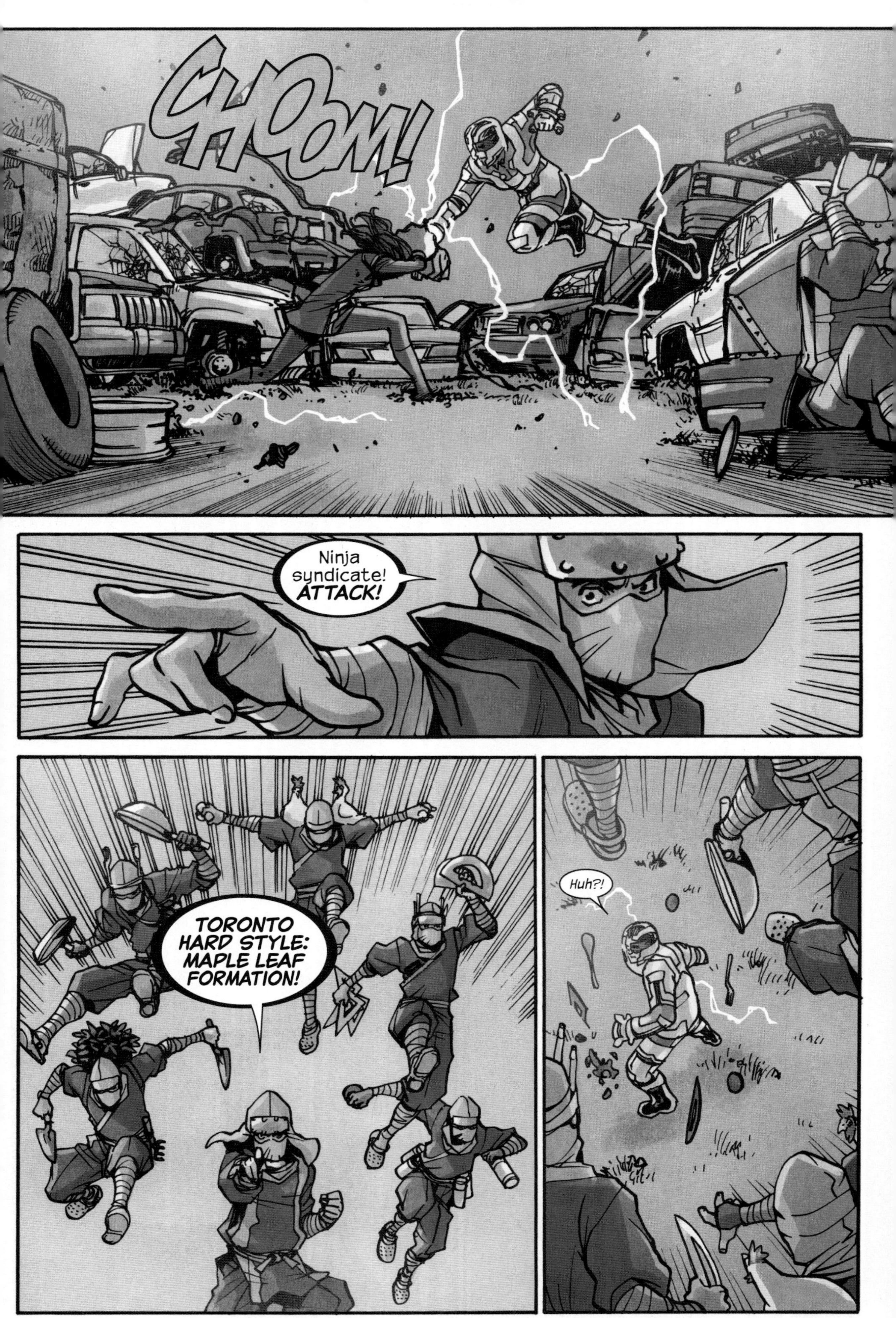
CHOOM!
Ninja syndicate! ATTACK!
TORONTO HARD STYLE: MAPLE LEAF FORMATION!
Huh?!

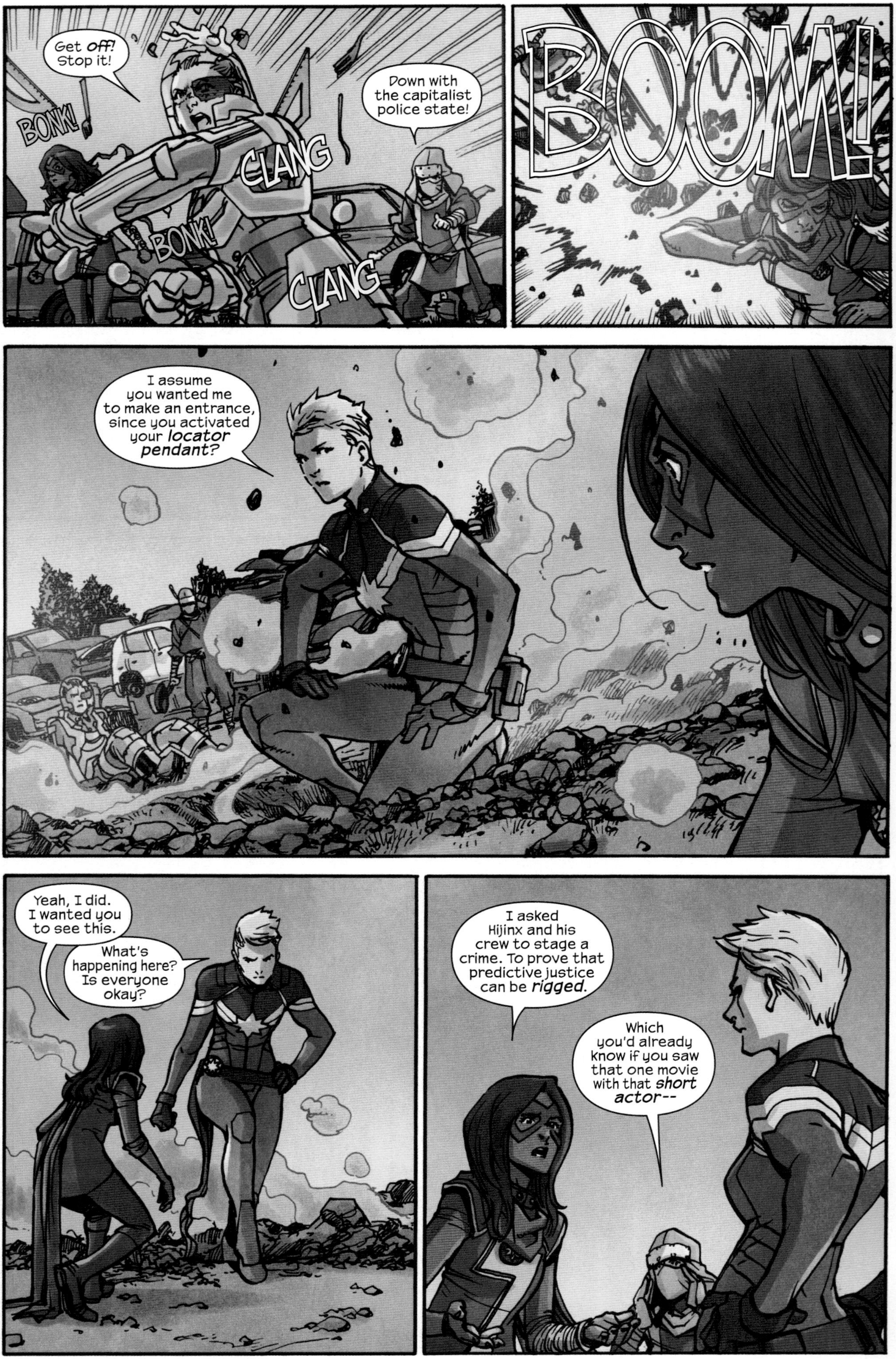
Get off! Stop it!
BONK!
CLANG
BONK!
CLANG
Down with the capitalist police state!
BOOM!
I assume you wanted me to make an entrance, since you activated your locator pendant?
Yeah, I did. I wanted you to see this.
What's happening here? Is everyone okay?
I asked Hijinx and his crew to stage a crime. To prove that predictive justice can be rigged.
Which you'd already know if you saw that one movie with that short actor--

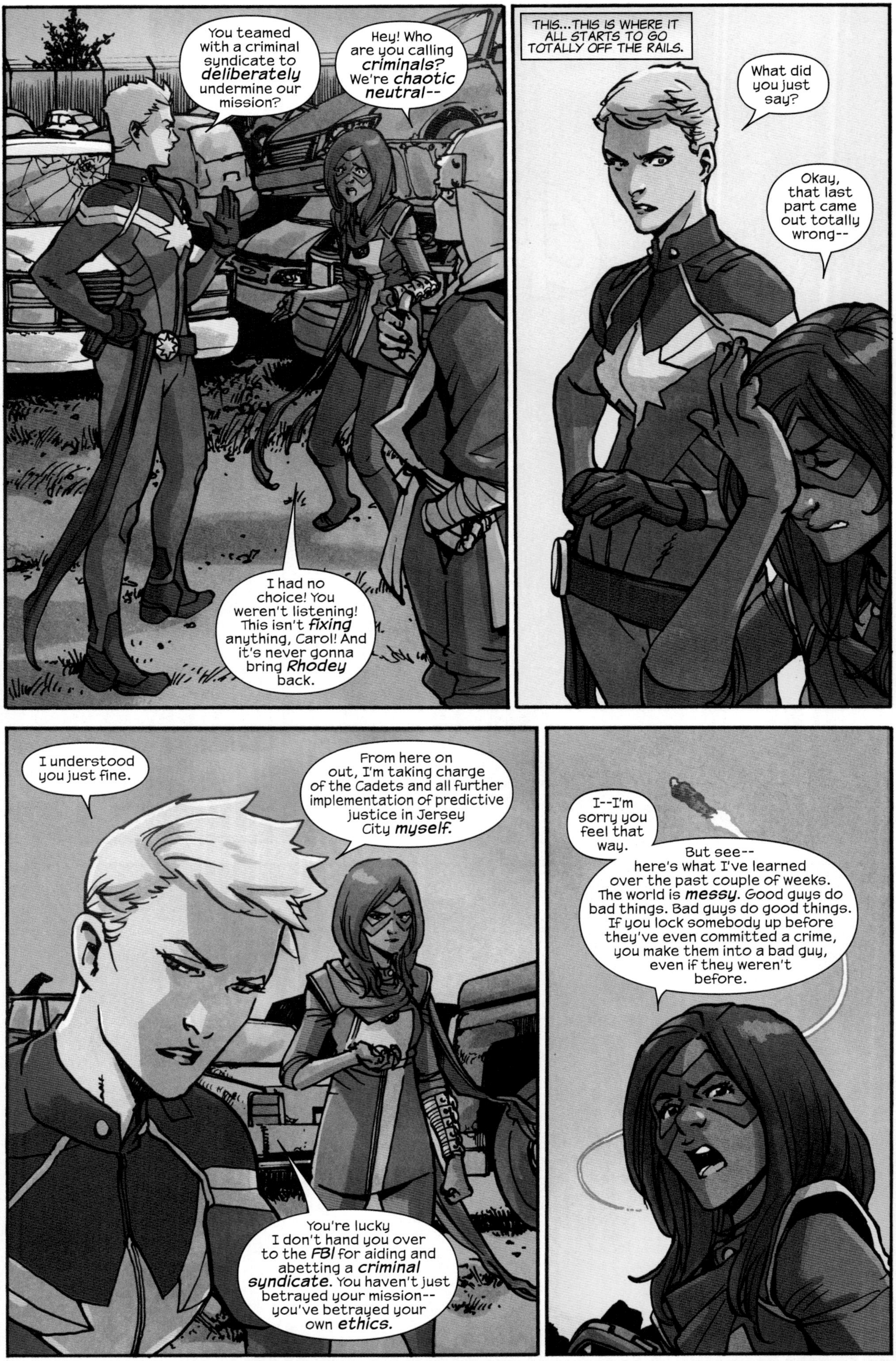
You teamed with a criminal syndicate to *deliberately* undermine our mission?
Hey! Who are you calling *criminals?* We're *chaotic neutral*--
I had no choice! You weren't listening! This isn't *fixing* anything, Carol! And it's never gonna bring *Rhodey* back.
THIS...THIS IS WHERE IT ALL STARTS TO GO TOTALLY OFF THE RAILS.
What did you just say?
Okay, that last part came out totally wrong--
I understood you just fine.
From here on out, I'm taking charge of the Cadets and all further implementation of predictive justice in Jersey City *myself.*
You're lucky I don't hand you over to the *FBI* for aiding and abetting a *criminal syndicate*. You haven't just betrayed your mission--you've betrayed your own *ethics.*
I--I'm sorry you feel that way.
But see--here's what I've learned over the past couple of weeks. The world is *messy*. Good guys do bad things. Bad guys do good things. If you lock somebody up before they've even committed a crime, you make them into a bad guy, even if they weren't before.

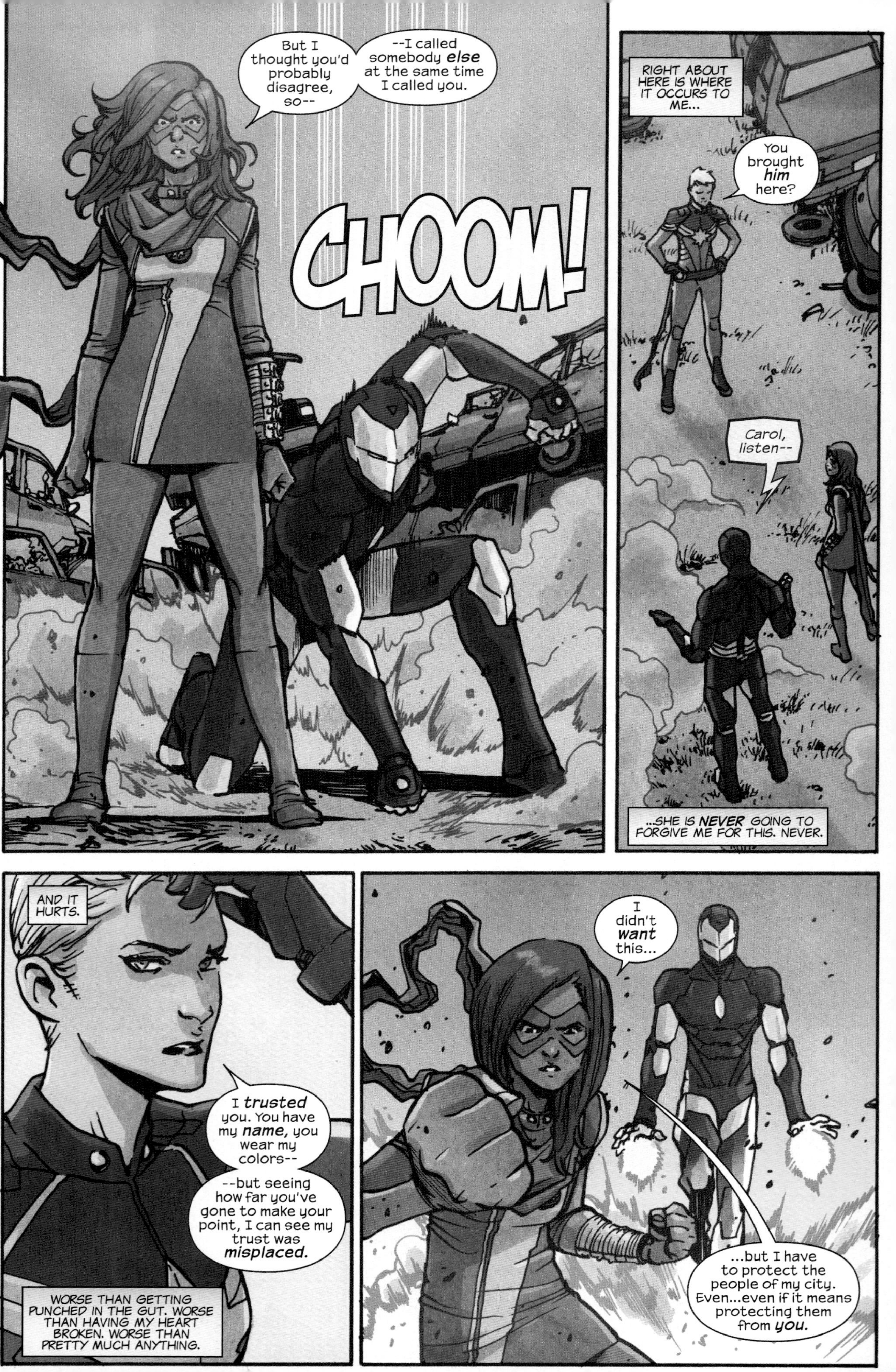

But I thought you'd probably disagree, so--
--I called somebody *else* at the same time I called you.
CHOOM!
RIGHT ABOUT HERE IS WHERE IT OCCURS TO ME...
You brought *him* here?
Carol, listen--
...SHE IS *NEVER* GOING TO FORGIVE ME FOR THIS. NEVER.
AND IT HURTS.
I *trusted* you. You have my *name*, you wear my colors--
--but seeing how far you've gone to make your point, I can see my trust was *misplaced.*
WORSE THAN GETTING PUNCHED IN THE GUT. WORSE THAN HAVING MY HEART BROKEN. WORSE THAN PRETTY MUCH ANYTHING.
I didn't *want* this...
...but I have to protect the people of my city. Even...even if it means protecting them from *you.*

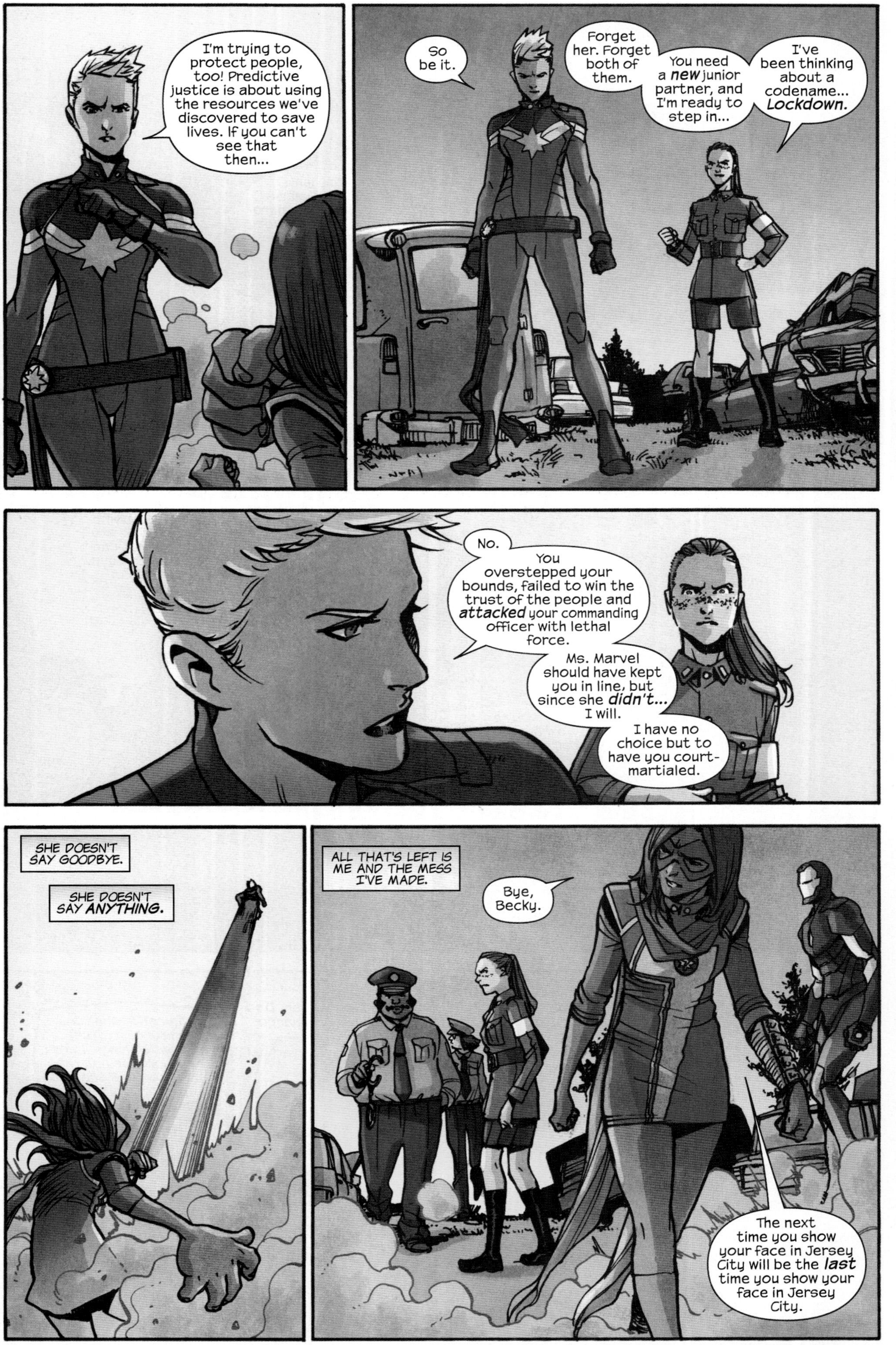
I'm trying to protect people, too! Predictive justice is about using the resources we've discovered to save lives. If you can't see that then...
So be it.
Forget her. Forget both of them.
You need a new junior partner, and I'm ready to step in...
I've been thinking about a codename... Lockdown.
No.
You overstepped your bounds, failed to win the trust of the people and attacked your commanding officer with lethal force.
Ms. Marvel should have kept you in line, but since she didn't... I will.
I have no choice but to have you court-martialed.
SHE DOESN'T SAY GOODBYE.
SHE DOESN'T SAY ANYTHING.
ALL THAT'S LEFT IS ME AND THE MESS I'VE MADE.
Bye, Becky.
The next time you show your face in Jersey City will be the last time you show your face in Jersey City.

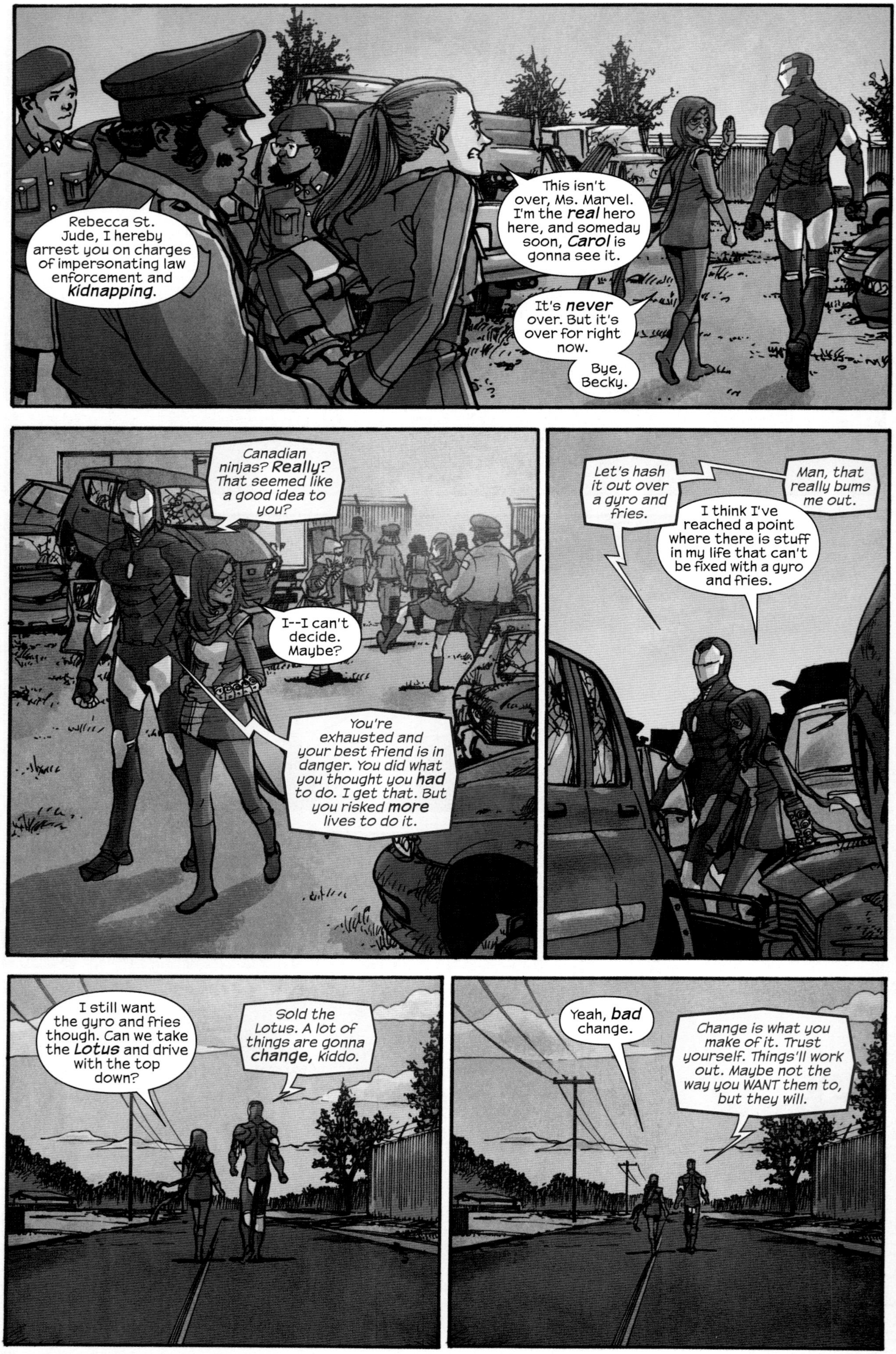
Rebecca St. Jude, I hereby arrest you on charges of impersonating law enforcement and kidnapping.
This isn't over, Ms. Marvel. I'm the real hero here, and someday soon, Carol is gonna see it.
It's never over. But it's over for right now.
Bye, Becky.
Canadian ninjas? Really? That seemed like a good idea to you?
I--I can't decide. Maybe?
You're exhausted and your best friend is in danger. You did what you thought you had to do. I get that. But you risked more lives to do it.
Let's hash it out over a gyro and fries.
I think I've reached a point where there is stuff in my life that can't be fixed with a gyro and fries.
Man, that really bums me out.
I still want the gyro and fries though. Can we take the Lotus and drive with the top down?
Sold the Lotus. A lot of things are gonna change, kiddo.
Yeah, bad change.
Change is what you make of it. Trust yourself. Things'll work out. Maybe not the way you WANT them to, but they will.

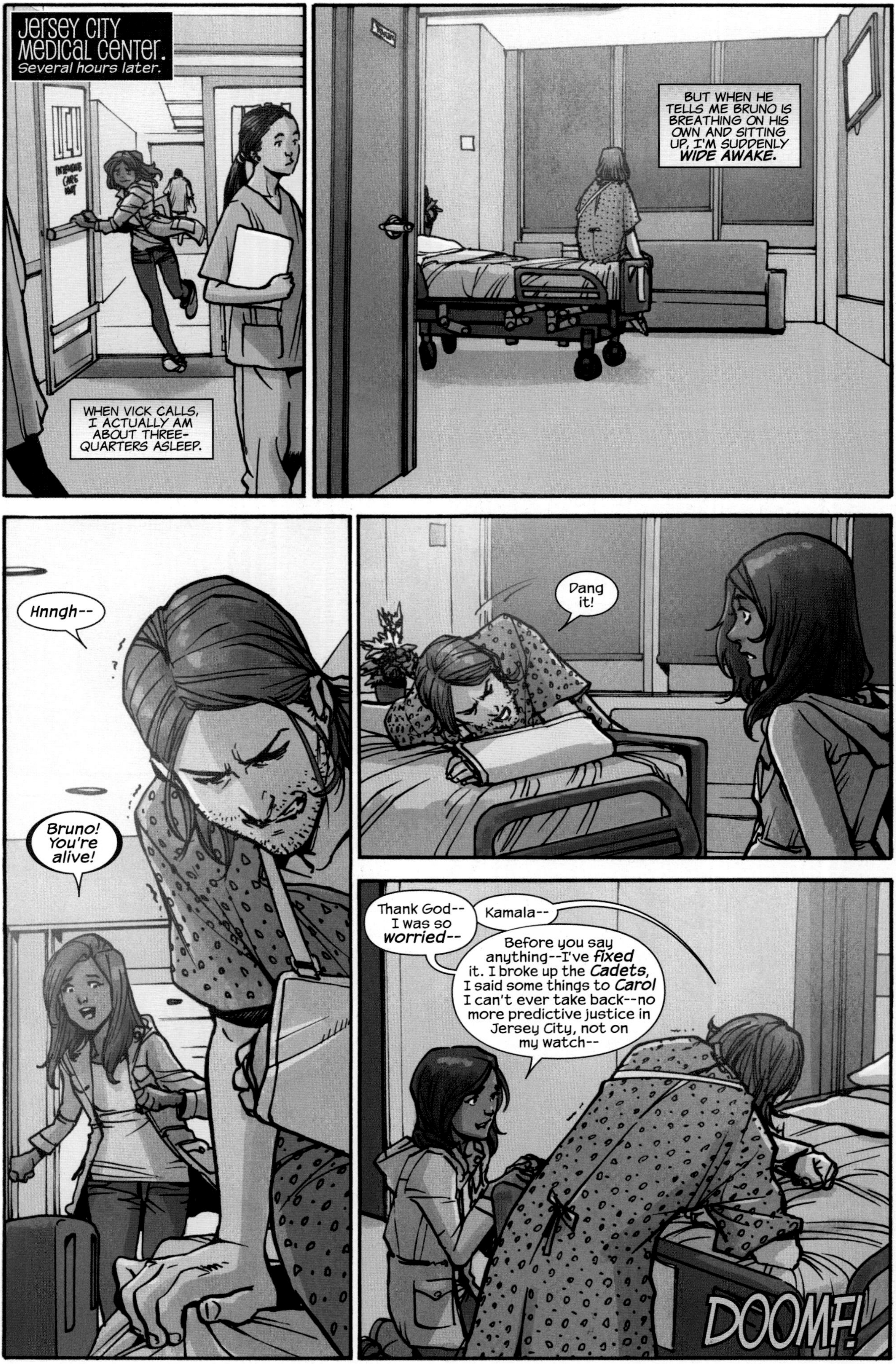
Jersey City Medical Center.
Several hours later.
When Vick calls, I actually am about three-quarters asleep.
But when he tells me Bruno is breathing on his own and sitting up, I'm suddenly wide awake.
Hnngh--
Bruno! You're alive!
Dang it!
Thank God-- I was so worried--
Kamala--
Before you say anything--I've fixed it. I broke up the Cadets, I said some things to Carol I can't ever take back--no more predictive justice in Jersey City, not on my watch--
DOOMF!

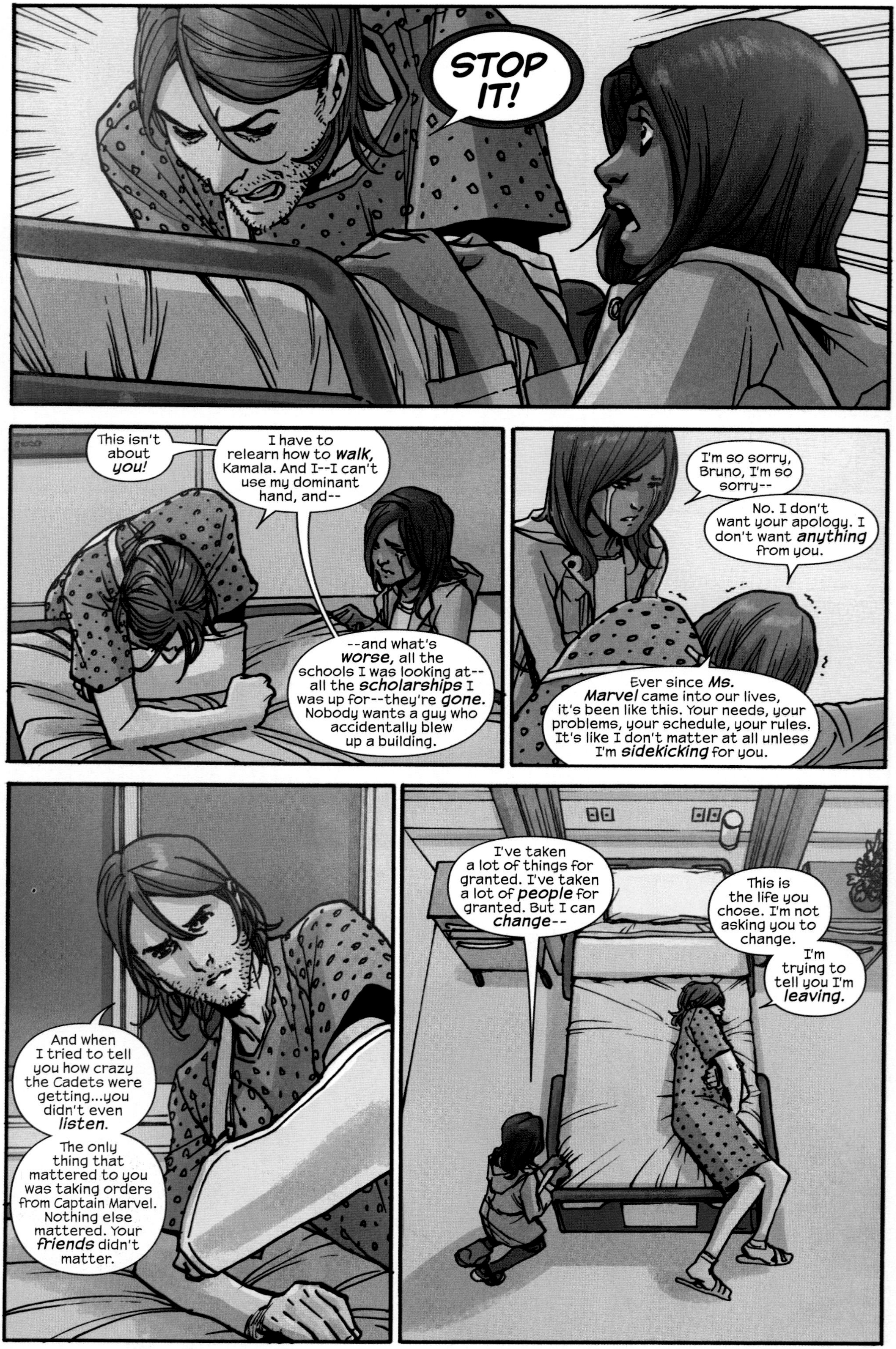
STOP IT!
This isn't about you!
I have to relearn how to walk, Kamala. And I--I can't use my dominant hand, and--
--and what's worse, all the schools I was looking at--all the scholarships I was up for--they're gone. Nobody wants a guy who accidentally blew up a building.
I'm so sorry, Bruno, I'm so sorry--
No. I don't want your apology. I don't want anything from you.
Ever since Ms. Marvel came into our lives, it's been like this. Your needs, your problems, your schedule, your rules. It's like I don't matter at all unless I'm sidekicking for you.
And when I tried to tell you how crazy the Cadets were getting...you didn't even listen.
The only thing that mattered to you was taking orders from Captain Marvel. Nothing else mattered. Your friends didn't matter.
I've taken a lot of things for granted. I've taken a lot of people for granted. But I can change--
This is the life you chose. I'm not asking you to change.
I'm trying to tell you I'm leaving.

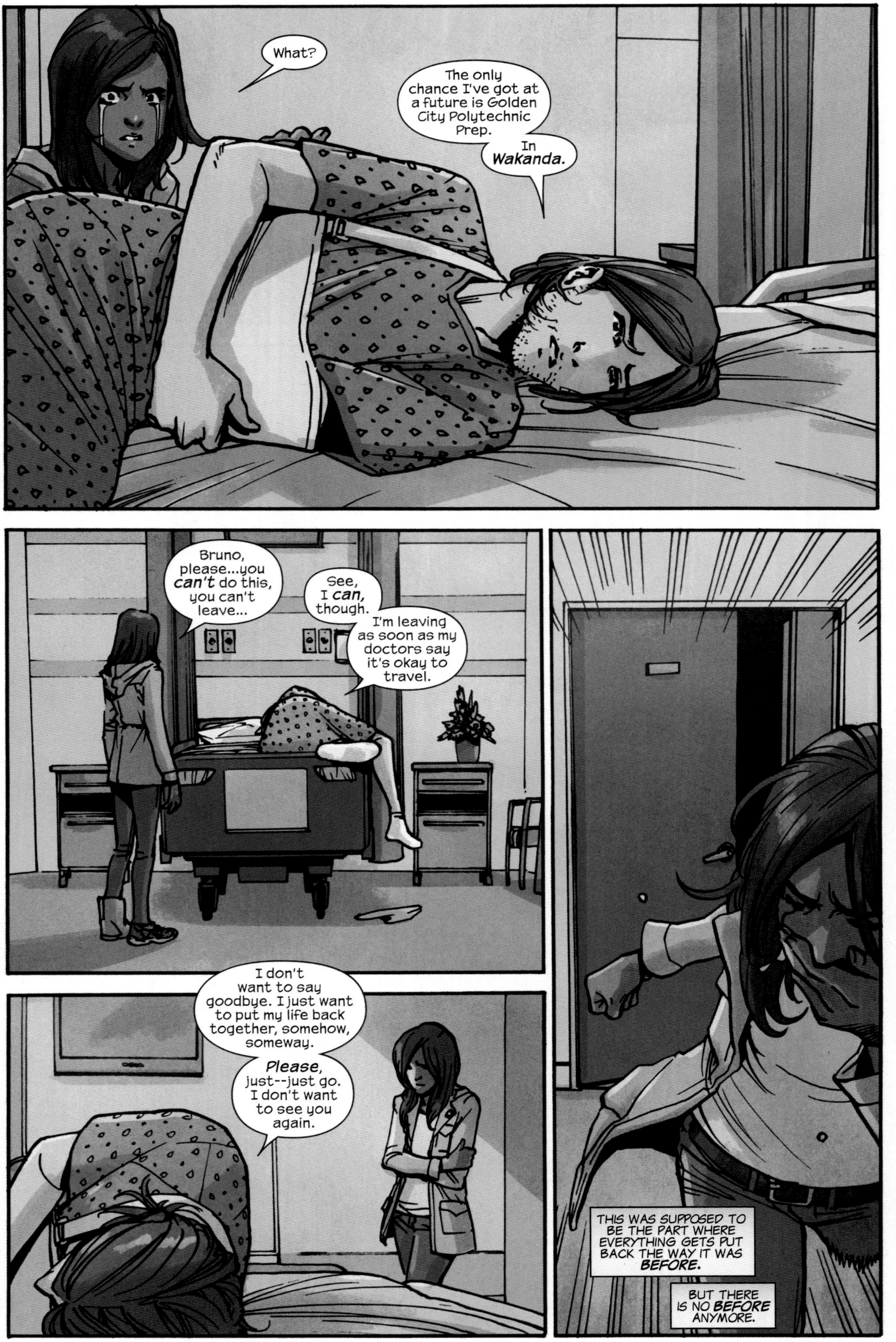
What?
The only chance I've got at a future is Golden City Polytechnic Prep.
In Wakanda.
Bruno, please...you can't do this, you can't leave...
See, I can, though.
I'm leaving as soon as my doctors say it's okay to travel.
I don't want to say goodbye. I just want to put my life back together, somehow, someway.
Please, just--just go. I don't want to see you again.
THIS WAS SUPPOSED TO BE THE PART WHERE EVERYTHING GETS PUT BACK THE WAY IT WAS BEFORE.
BUT THERE IS NO BEFORE ANYMORE.

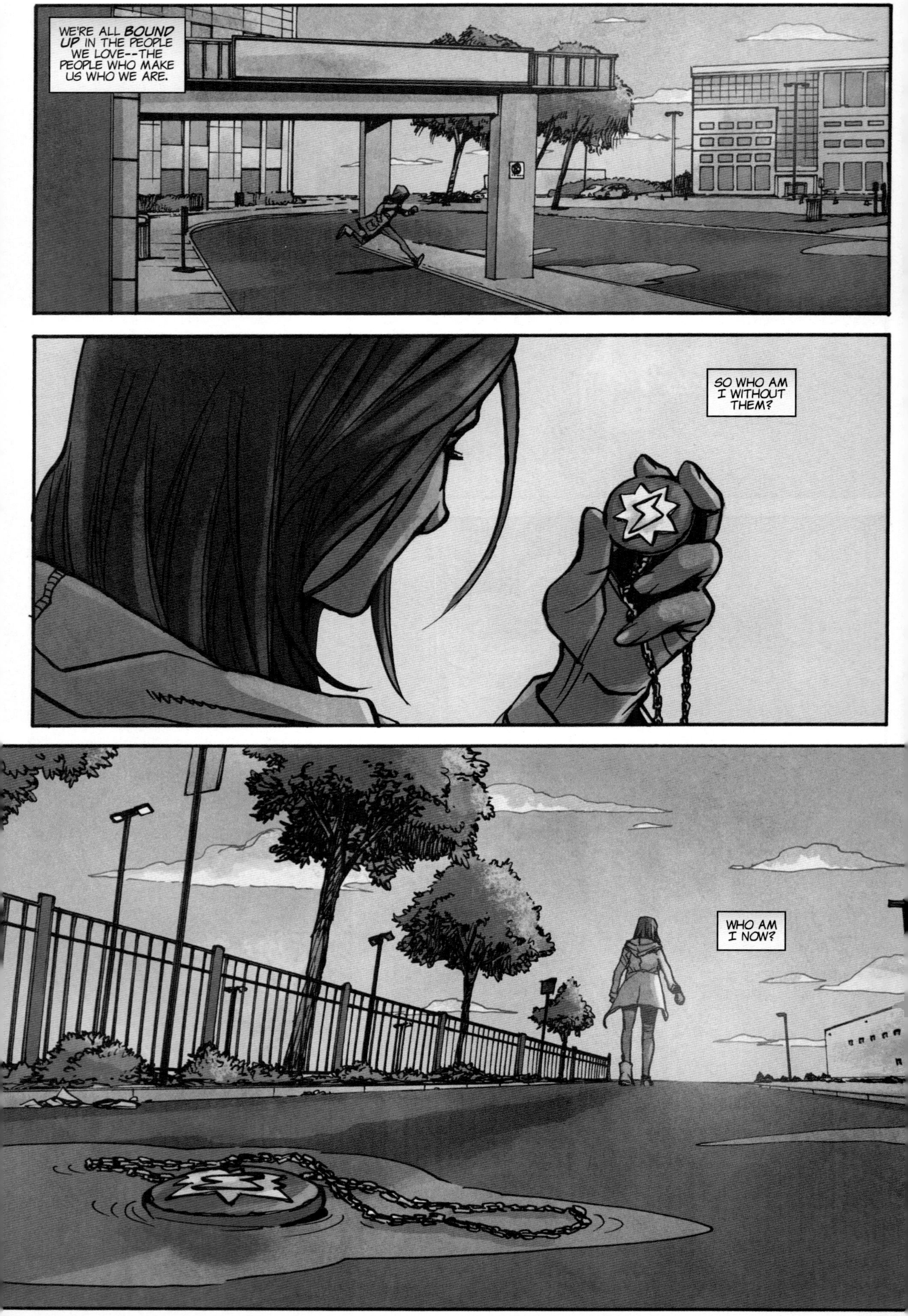
WE'RE ALL BOUND UP IN THE PEOPLE WE LOVE--THE PEOPLE WHO MAKE US WHO WE ARE.
SO WHO AM I WITHOUT THEM?
WHO AM I NOW?

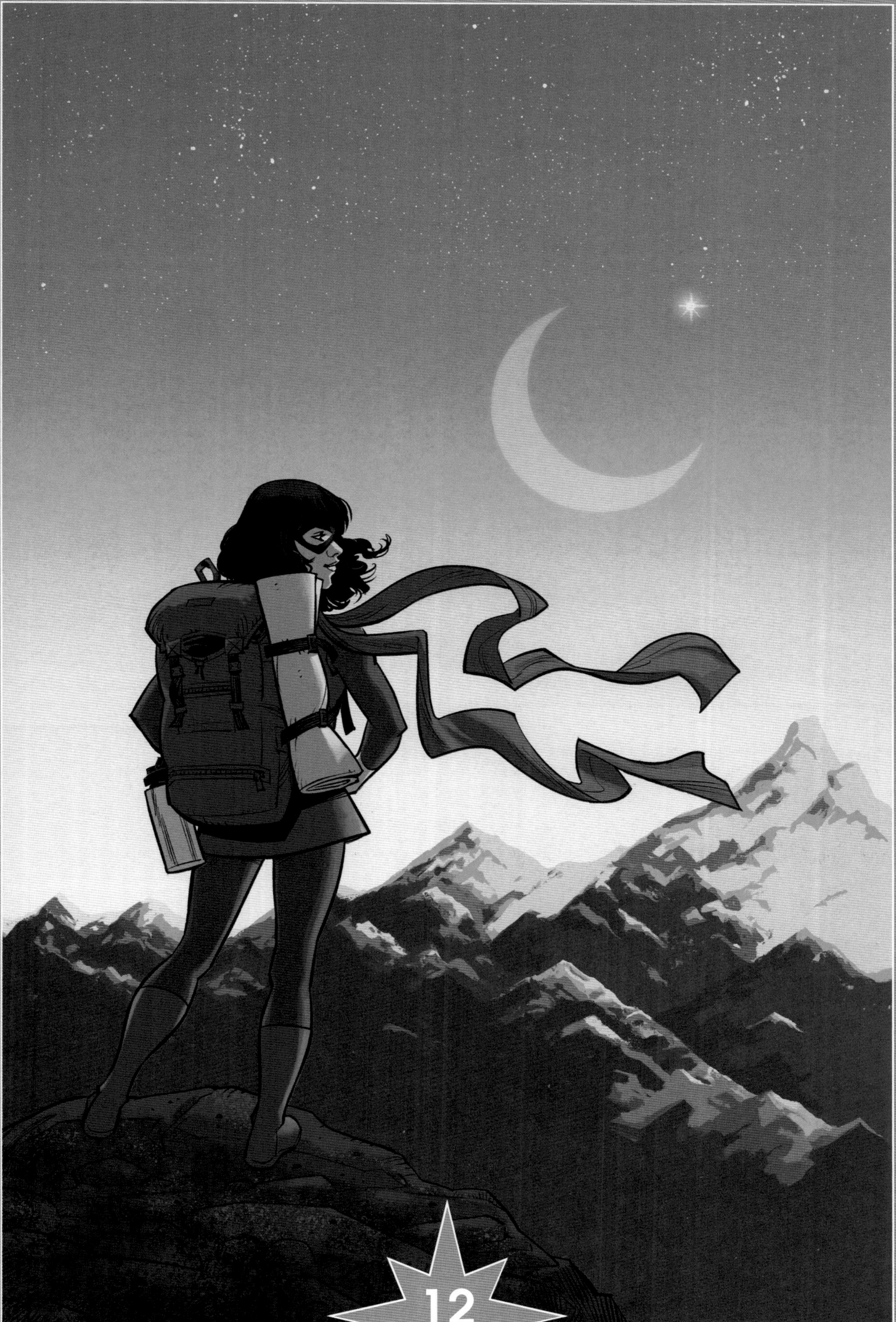
12

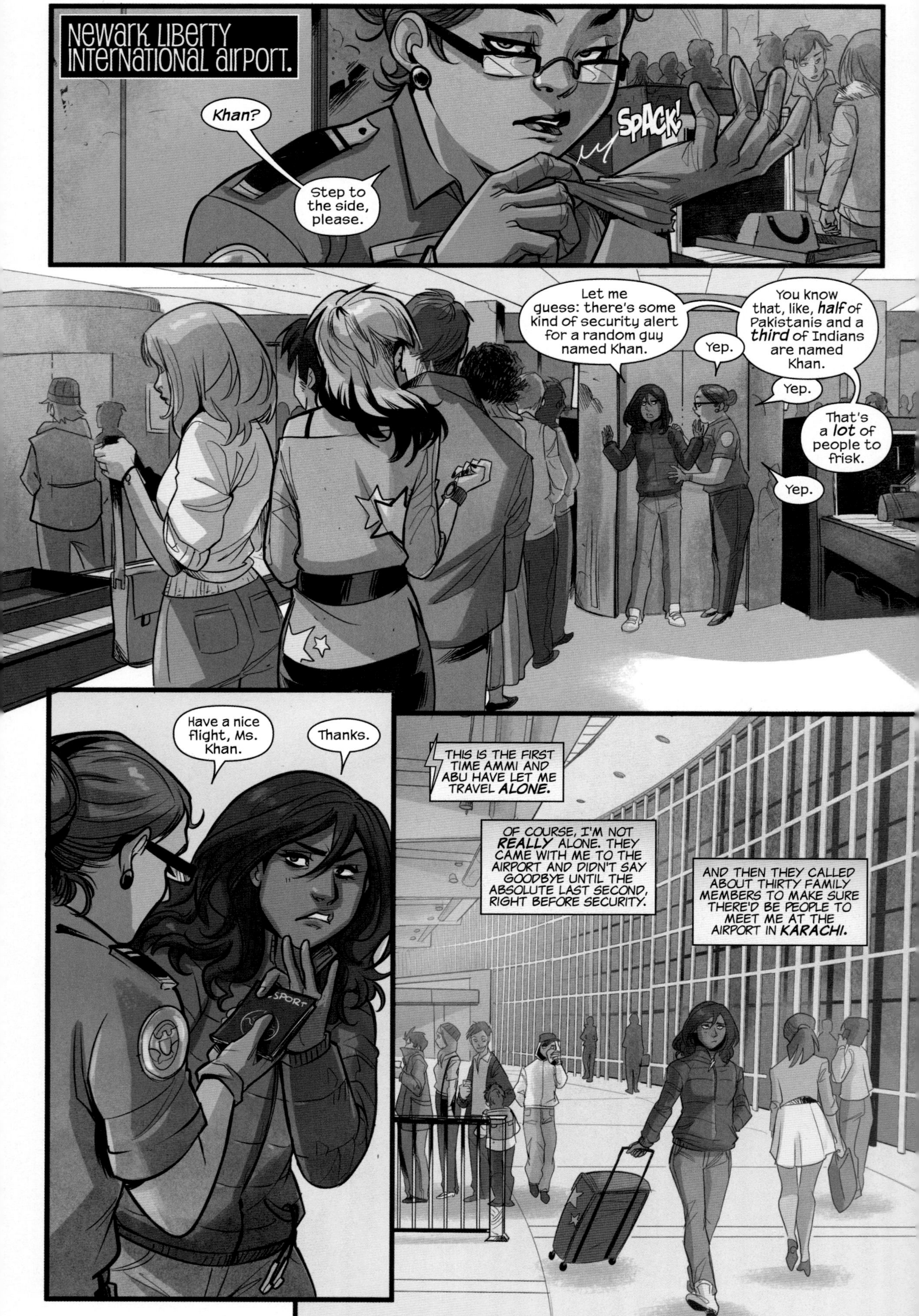

Newark Liberty International airport.
Khan?
Step to the side, please.
SPACK!
Let me guess: there's some kind of security alert for a random guy named Khan.
Yep.
You know that, like, *half* of Pakistanis and a *third* of Indians are named Khan.
Yep.
That's a *lot* of people to frisk.
Yep.
Have a nice flight, Ms. Khan.
Thanks.
THIS IS THE FIRST TIME AMMI AND ABU HAVE LET ME TRAVEL *ALONE*.
OF COURSE, I'M NOT *REALLY* ALONE. THEY CAME WITH ME TO THE AIRPORT AND DIDN'T SAY GOODBYE UNTIL THE ABSOLUTE LAST SECOND, RIGHT BEFORE SECURITY.
AND THEN THEY CALLED ABOUT THIRTY FAMILY MEMBERS TO MAKE SURE THERE'D BE PEOPLE TO MEET ME AT THE AIRPORT IN *KARACHI*.

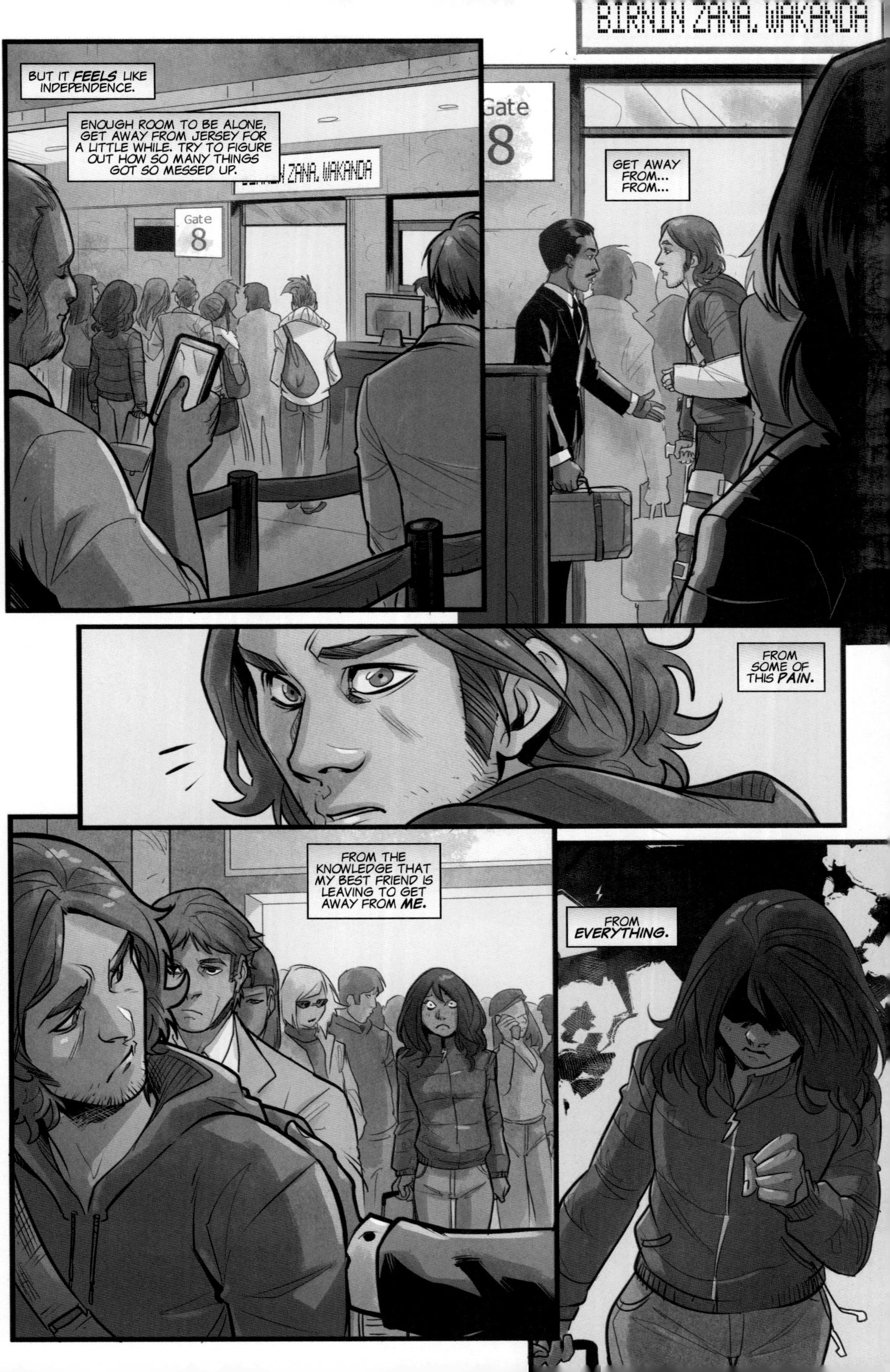
BIRNIN ZANA, WAKANDA
BUT IT FEELS LIKE INDEPENDENCE.
ENOUGH ROOM TO BE ALONE, GET AWAY FROM JERSEY FOR A LITTLE WHILE. TRY TO FIGURE OUT HOW SO MANY THINGS GOT SO MESSED UP.
Gate 8
GET AWAY FROM... FROM...
FROM SOME OF THIS PAIN.
FROM THE KNOWLEDGE THAT MY BEST FRIEND IS LEAVING TO GET AWAY FROM ME.
FROM EVERYTHING.

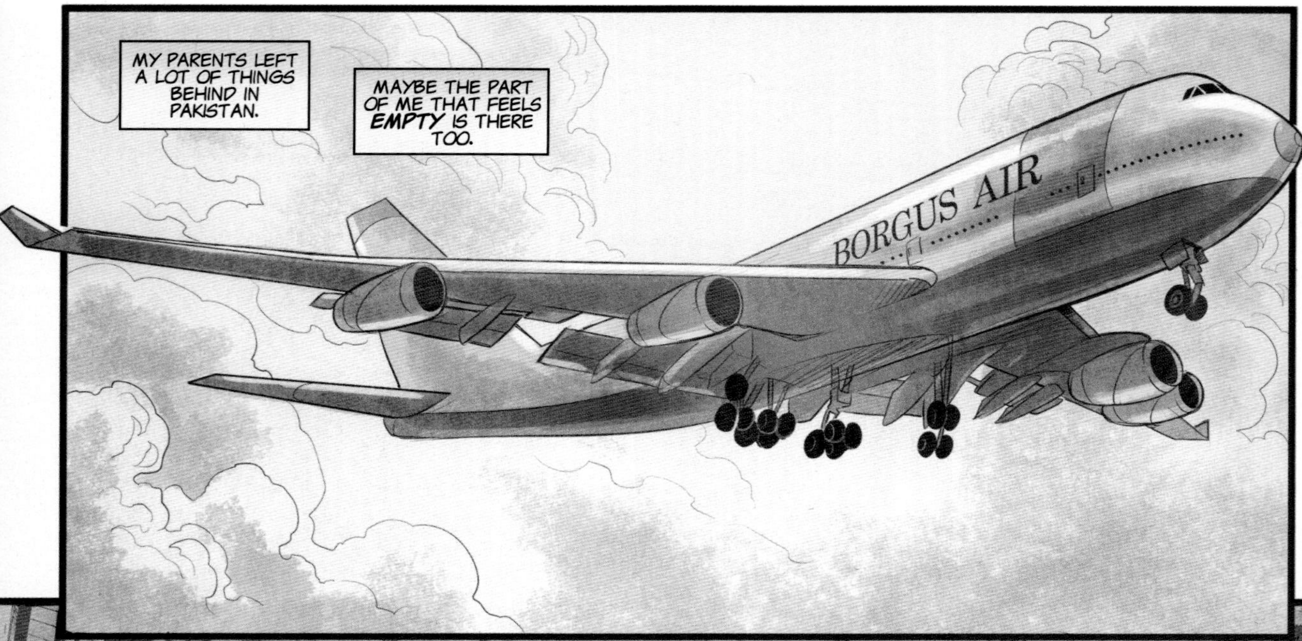
MY PARENTS LEFT A LOT OF THINGS BEHIND IN PAKISTAN.
MAYBE THE PART OF ME THAT FEELS EMPTY IS THERE TOO.
BORGUS AIR

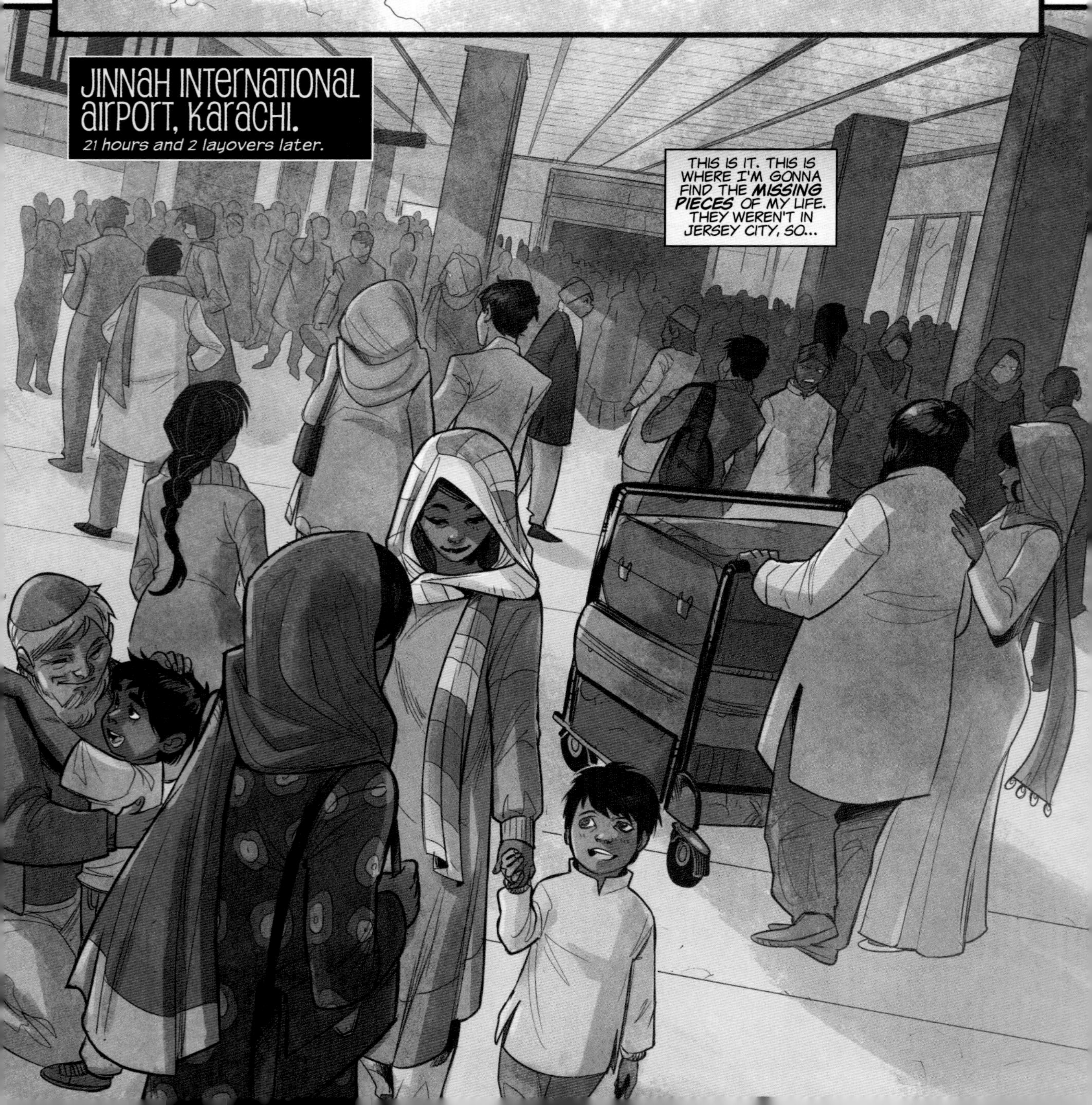
JINNAH INTERNATIONAL AIRPORT, KARACHI.
21 hours and 2 layovers later.
THIS IS IT. THIS IS WHERE I'M GONNA FIND THE MISSING PIECES OF MY LIFE. THEY WEREN'T IN JERSEY CITY, SO...

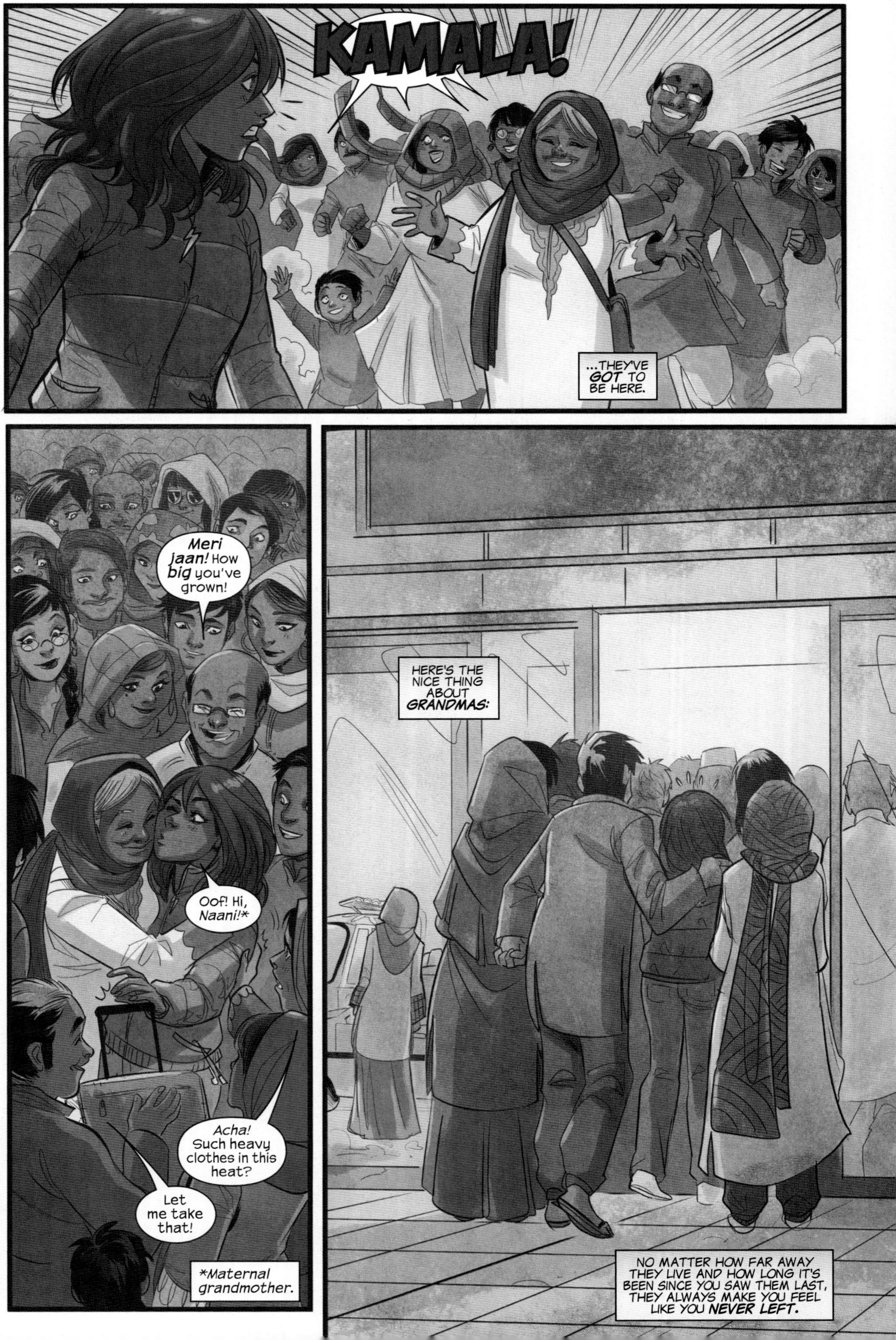
KAMALA!
...THEY'VE GOT TO BE HERE.
Meri jaan! How big you've grown!
Oof! Hi, Naani!*
Acha! Such heavy clothes in this heat?
Let me take that!
*Maternal grandmother.
HERE'S THE NICE THING ABOUT GRANDMAS:
NO MATTER HOW FAR AWAY THEY LIVE AND HOW LONG IT'S BEEN SINCE YOU SAW THEM LAST, THEY ALWAYS MAKE YOU FEEL LIKE YOU NEVER LEFT.

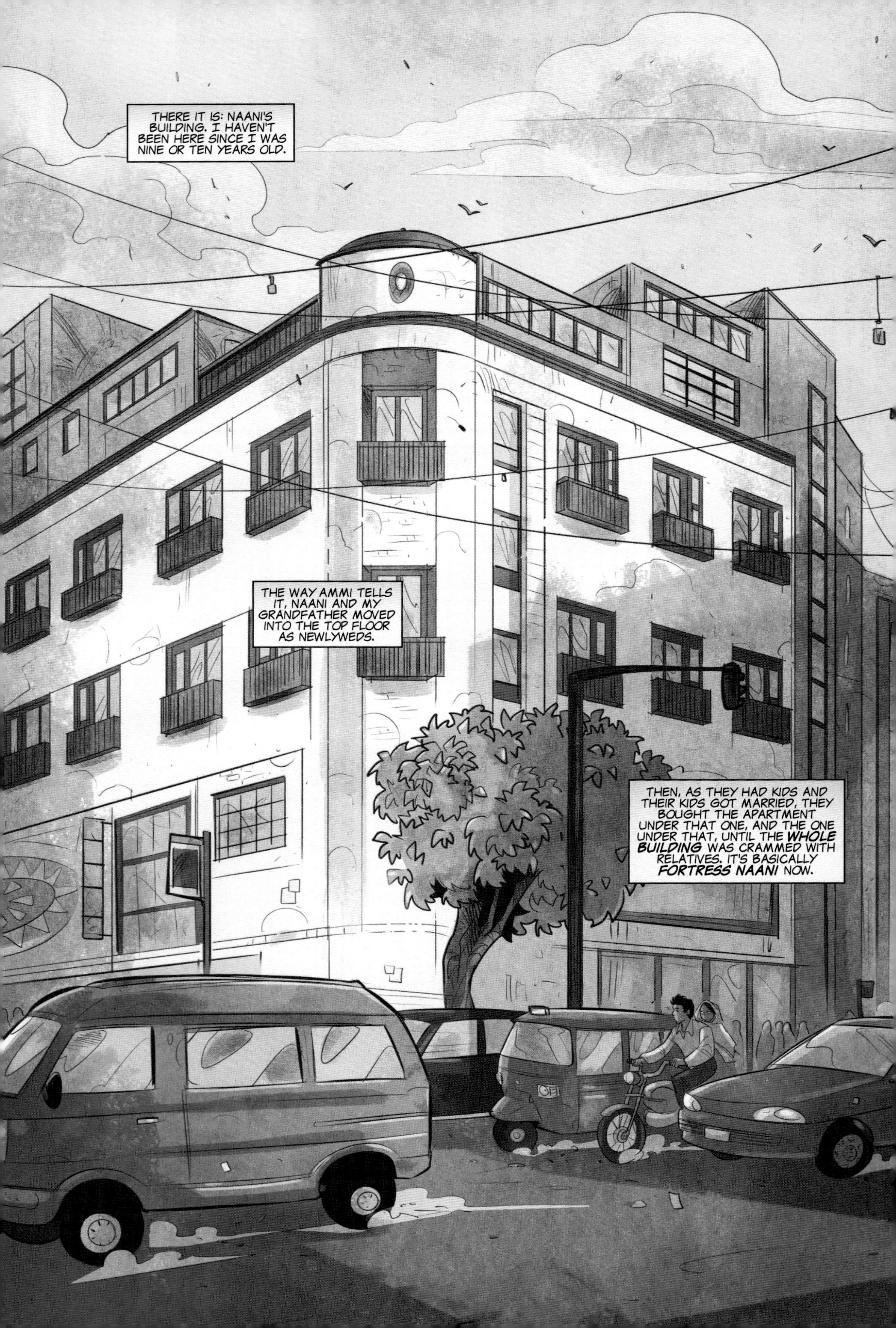
THERE IT IS: NAANI'S BUILDING. I HAVEN'T BEEN HERE SINCE I WAS NINE OR TEN YEARS OLD.
THE WAY AMMI TELLS IT, NAANI AND MY GRANDFATHER MOVED INTO THE TOP FLOOR AS NEWLYWEDS.
THEN, AS THEY HAD KIDS AND THEIR KIDS GOT MARRIED, THEY BOUGHT THE APARTMENT UNDER THAT ONE, AND THE ONE UNDER THAT, UNTIL THE ***WHOLE BUILDING*** WAS CRAMMED WITH RELATIVES. IT'S BASICALLY ***FORTRESS NAANI*** NOW.

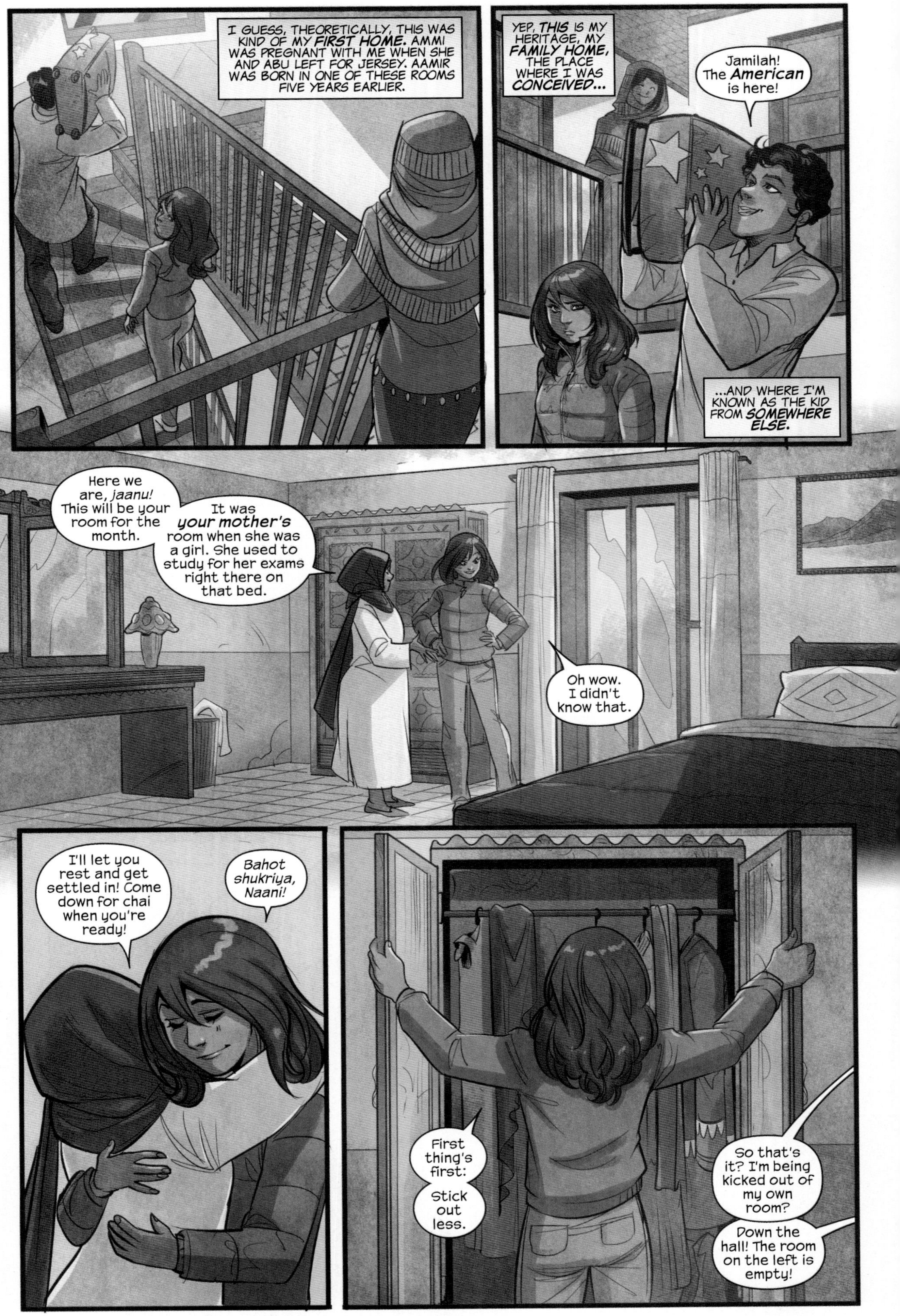
I GUESS, THEORETICALLY, THIS WAS KIND OF MY FIRST HOME. AMMI WAS PREGNANT WITH ME WHEN SHE AND ABU LEFT FOR JERSEY. AAMIR WAS BORN IN ONE OF THESE ROOMS FIVE YEARS EARLIER.
YEP, THIS IS MY HERITAGE, MY FAMILY HOME, THE PLACE WHERE I WAS CONCEIVED...
Jamilah! The American is here!
...AND WHERE I'M KNOWN AS THE KID FROM SOMEWHERE ELSE.
Here we are, jaanu! This will be your room for the month.
It was your mother's room when she was a girl. She used to study for her exams right there on that bed.
Oh wow. I didn't know that.
I'll let you rest and get settled in! Come down for chai when you're ready!
Bahot shukriya, Naani!
First thing's first:
Stick out less.
So that's it? I'm being kicked out of my own room?
Down the hall! The room on the left is empty!

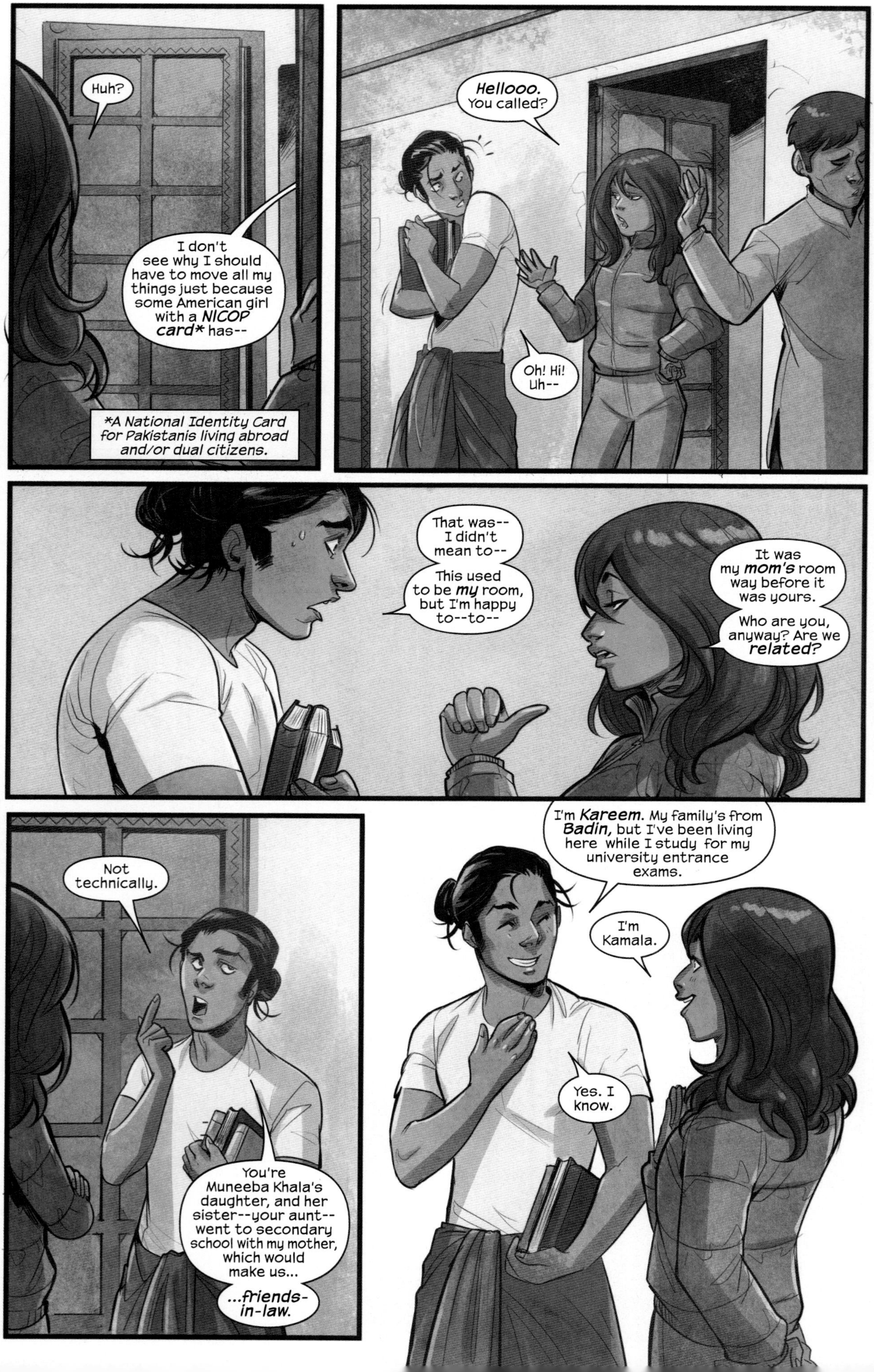
Huh?
I don't see why I should have to move all my things just because some American girl with a NICOP card* has--
*A National Identity Card for Pakistanis living abroad and/or dual citizens.
Hellooo. You called?
Oh! Hi! Uh--
That was-- I didn't mean to--
This used to be my room, but I'm happy to--to--
It was my mom's room way before it was yours.
Who are you, anyway? Are we related?
Not technically.
You're Muneeba Khala's daughter, and her sister--your aunt--went to secondary school with my mother, which would make us...
...friends-in-law.
I'm Kareem. My family's from Badin, but I've been living here while I study for my university entrance exams.
I'm Kamala.
Yes. I know.

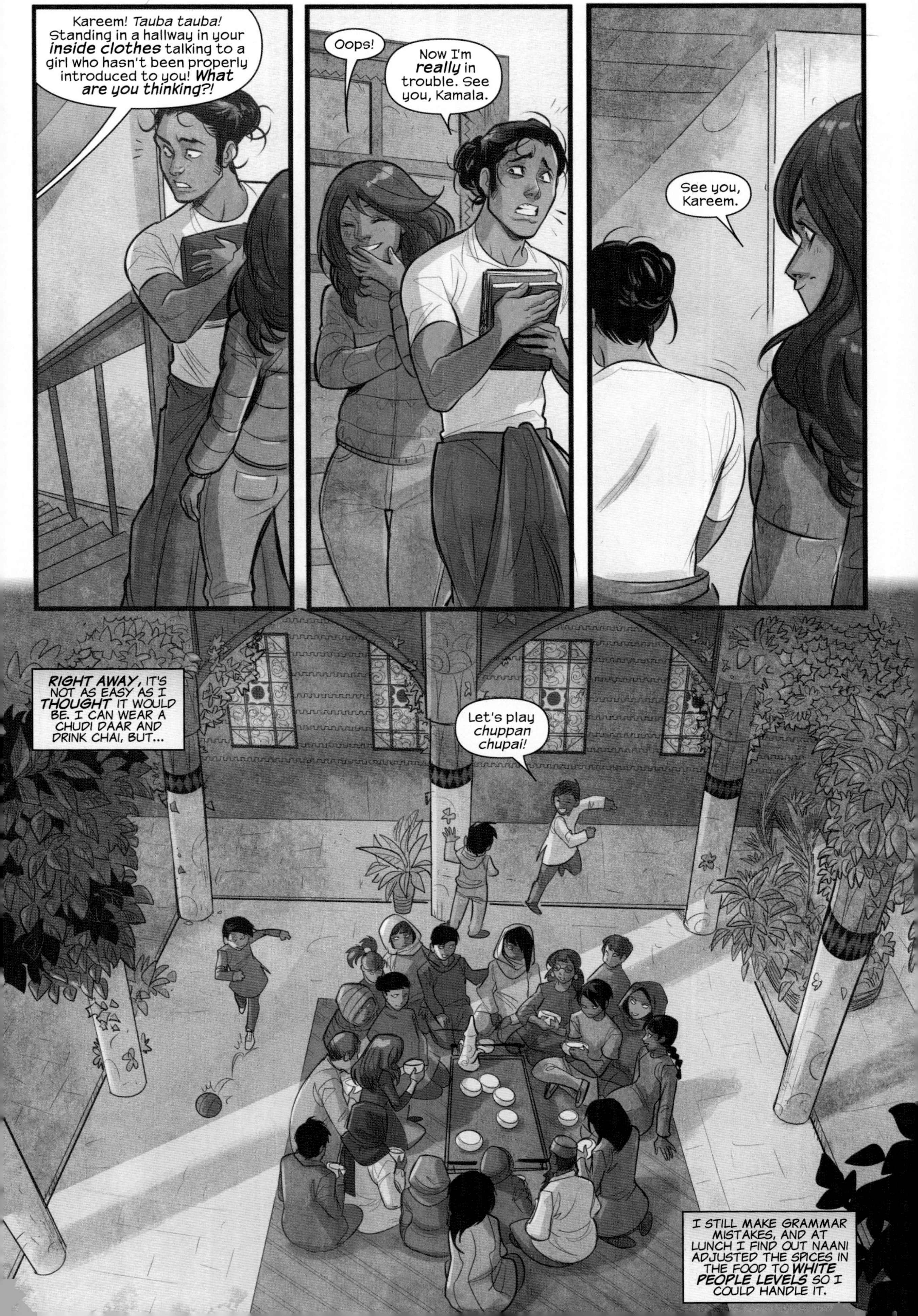

Kareem! *Tauba tauba!* Standing in a hallway in your ***inside clothes*** talking to a girl who hasn't been properly introduced to you! ***What are you thinking?!***
Oops!
Now I'm ***really*** in trouble. See you, Kamala.
See you, Kareem.
RIGHT AWAY, IT'S NOT AS EASY AS I ***THOUGHT*** IT WOULD BE. I CAN WEAR A CHUDI DAAR AND DRINK CHAI, BUT...
Let's play *chuppan chupai!*
I STILL MAKE GRAMMAR MISTAKES, AND AT LUNCH I FIND OUT NAANI ADJUSTED THE SPICES IN THE FOOD TO ***WHITE PEOPLE LEVELS*** SO I COULD HANDLE IT.

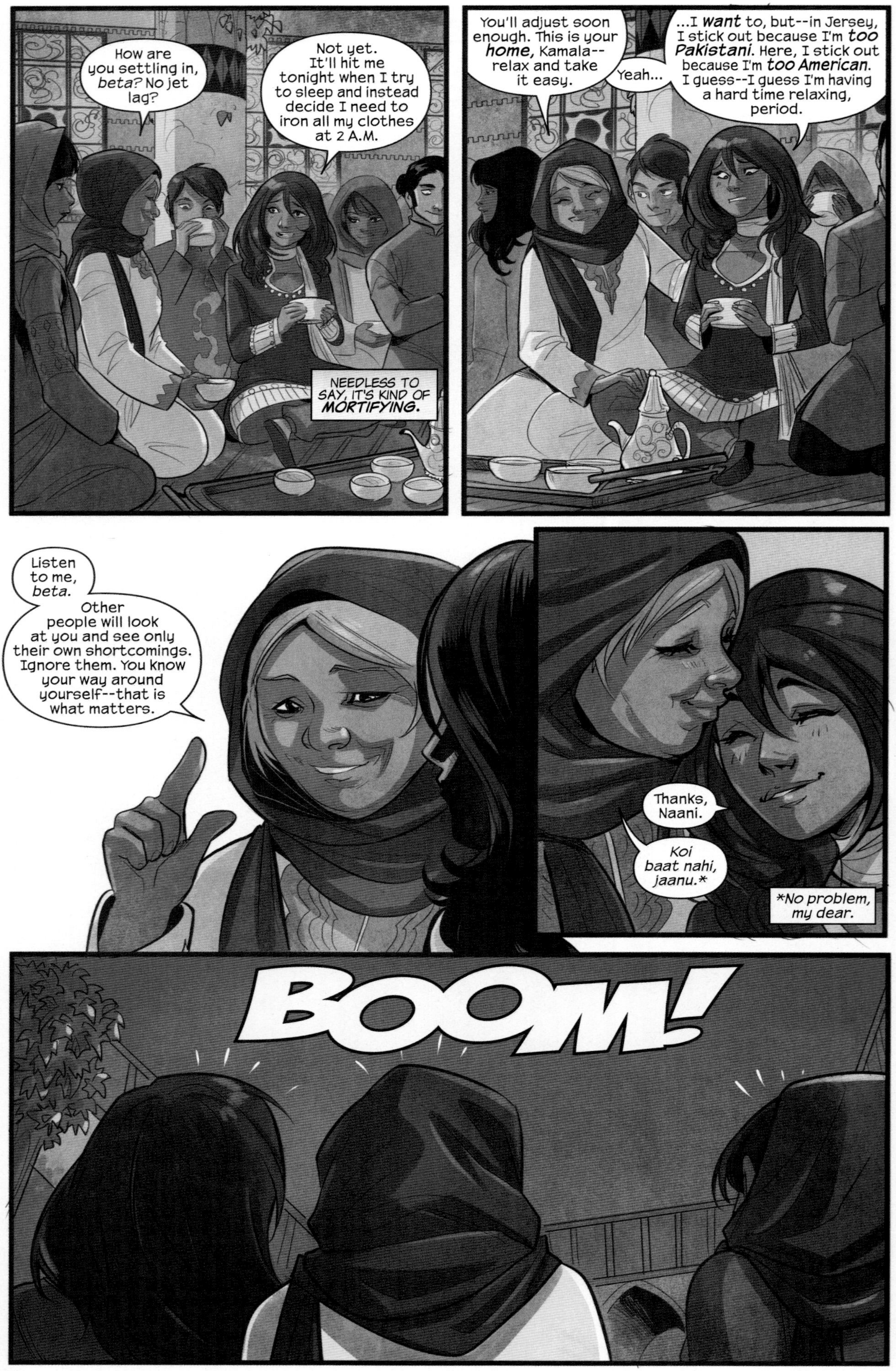

How are you settling in, *beta*? No jet lag?
Not yet. It'll hit me tonight when I try to sleep and instead decide I need to iron all my clothes at 2 A.M.
NEEDLESS TO SAY, IT'S KIND OF ***MORTIFYING.***
You'll adjust soon enough. This is your ***home,*** Kamala--relax and take it easy.
Yeah...
...I ***want*** to, but--in Jersey, I stick out because I'm ***too Pakistani***. Here, I stick out because I'm ***too American***. I guess--I guess I'm having a hard time relaxing, period.
Listen to me, *beta*.
Other people will look at you and see only their own shortcomings. Ignore them. You know your way around yourself--that is what matters.
Thanks, Naani.
*Koi baat nahi, jaanu.**
**No problem, my dear.*
BOOM!

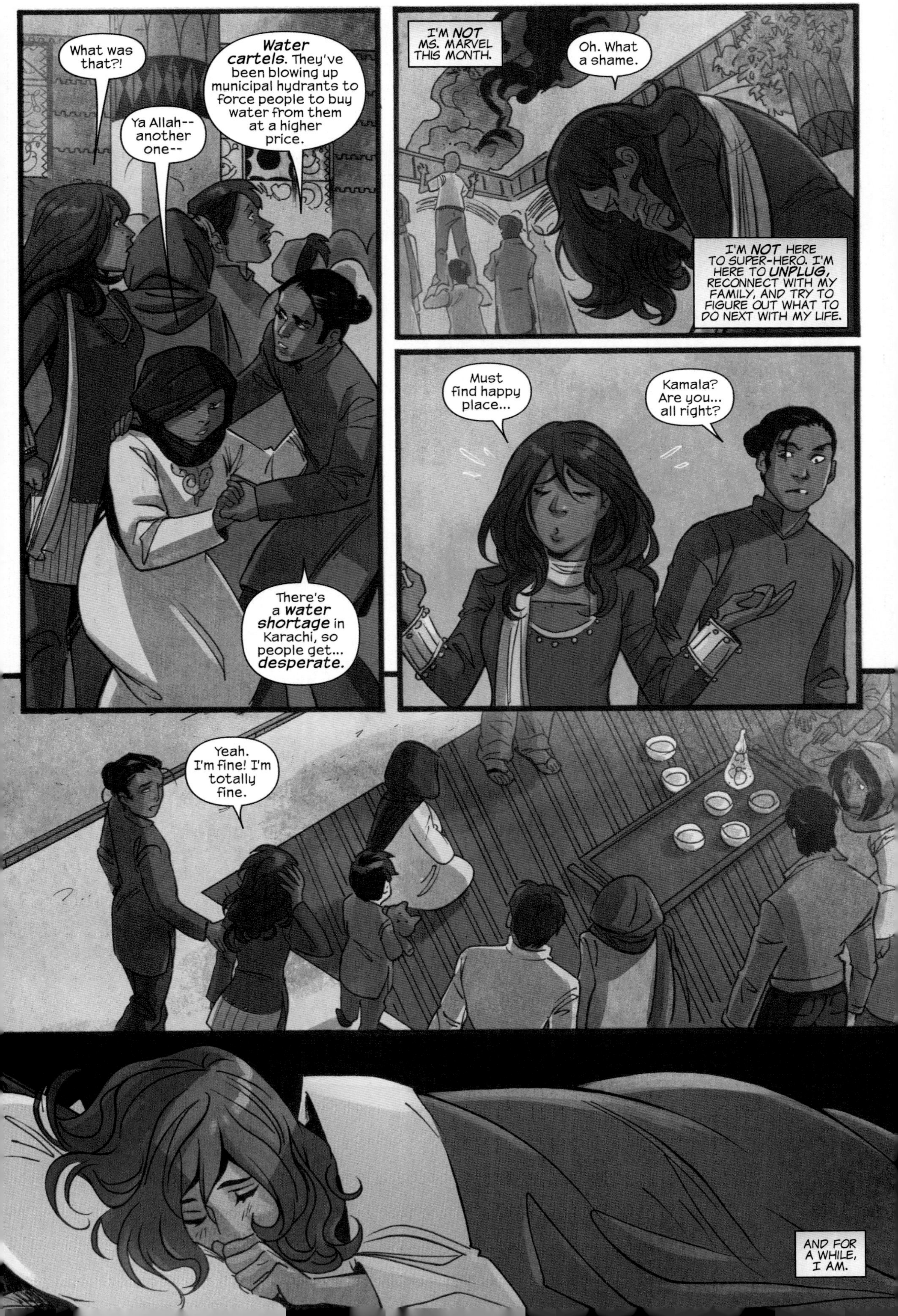
What was that?!
Water cartels. They've been blowing up municipal hydrants to force people to buy water from them at a higher price.
Ya Allah-- another one--
There's a water shortage in Karachi, so people get... desperate.
I'M NOT MS. MARVEL THIS MONTH.
Oh. What a shame.
I'M NOT HERE TO SUPER-HERO. I'M HERE TO UNPLUG, RECONNECT WITH MY FAMILY, AND TRY TO FIGURE OUT WHAT TO DO NEXT WITH MY LIFE.
Must find happy place...
Kamala? Are you... all right?
Yeah. I'm fine! I'm totally fine.
AND FOR A WHILE, I AM.

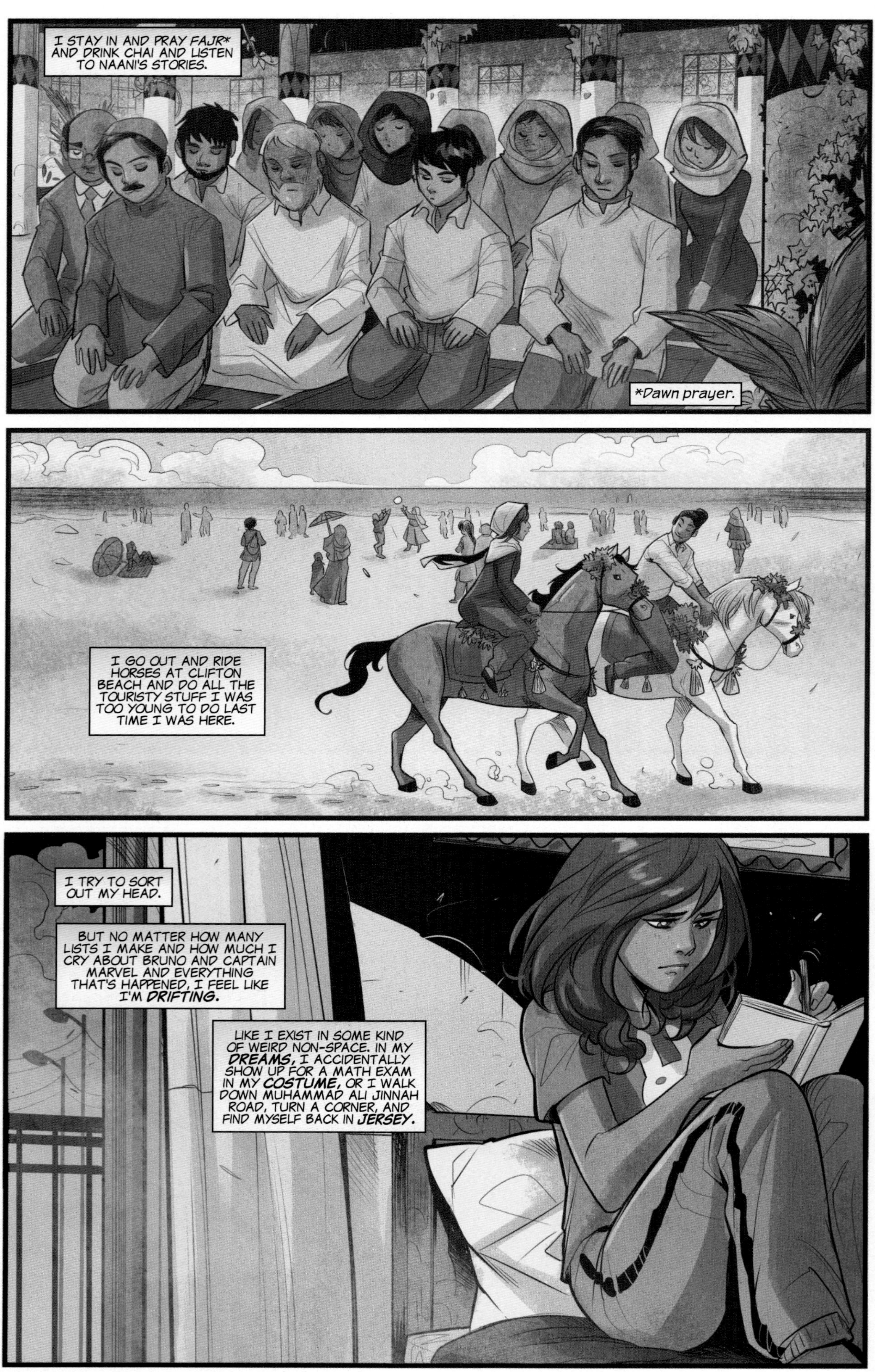
I STAY IN AND PRAY FAJR* AND DRINK CHAI AND LISTEN TO NAANI'S STORIES.
*Dawn prayer.
I GO OUT AND RIDE HORSES AT CLIFTON BEACH AND DO ALL THE TOURISTY STUFF I WAS TOO YOUNG TO DO LAST TIME I WAS HERE.
I TRY TO SORT OUT MY HEAD.
BUT NO MATTER HOW MANY LISTS I MAKE AND HOW MUCH I CRY ABOUT BRUNO AND CAPTAIN MARVEL AND EVERYTHING THAT'S HAPPENED, I FEEL LIKE I'M **DRIFTING.**
LIKE I EXIST IN SOME KIND OF WEIRD NON-SPACE. IN MY **DREAMS,** I ACCIDENTALLY SHOW UP FOR A MATH EXAM IN MY **COSTUME,** OR I WALK DOWN MUHAMMAD ALI JINNAH ROAD, TURN A CORNER, AND FIND MYSELF BACK IN **JERSEY.**

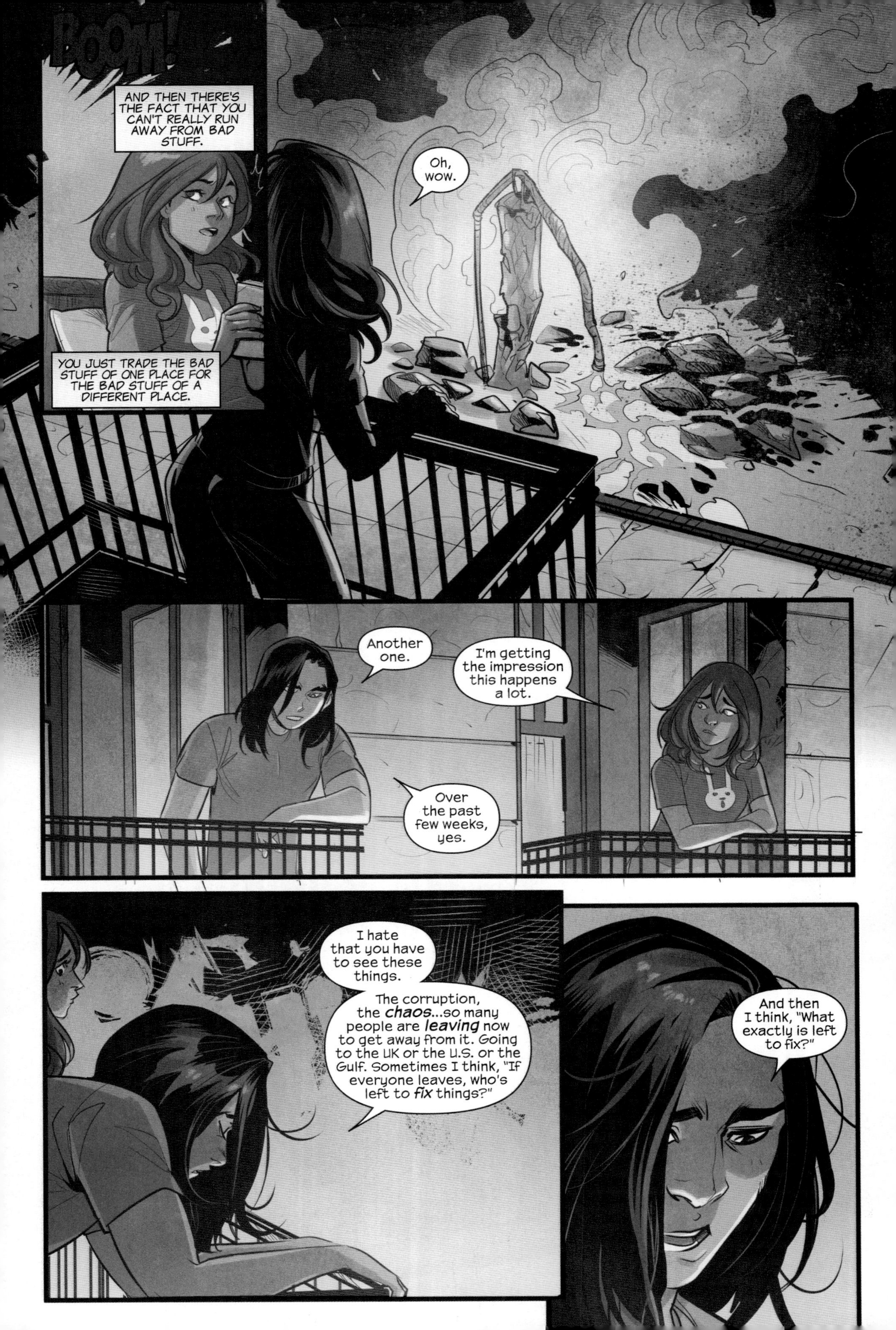
BOOM!
AND THEN THERE'S THE FACT THAT YOU CAN'T REALLY RUN AWAY FROM BAD STUFF.
Oh, wow.
YOU JUST TRADE THE BAD STUFF OF ONE PLACE FOR THE BAD STUFF OF A DIFFERENT PLACE.
Another one.
I'm getting the impression this happens a lot.
Over the past few weeks, yes.
I hate that you have to see these things.
The corruption, the chaos...so many people are leaving now to get away from it. Going to the UK or the U.S. or the Gulf. Sometimes I think, "If everyone leaves, who's left to fix things?"
And then I think, "What exactly is left to fix?"

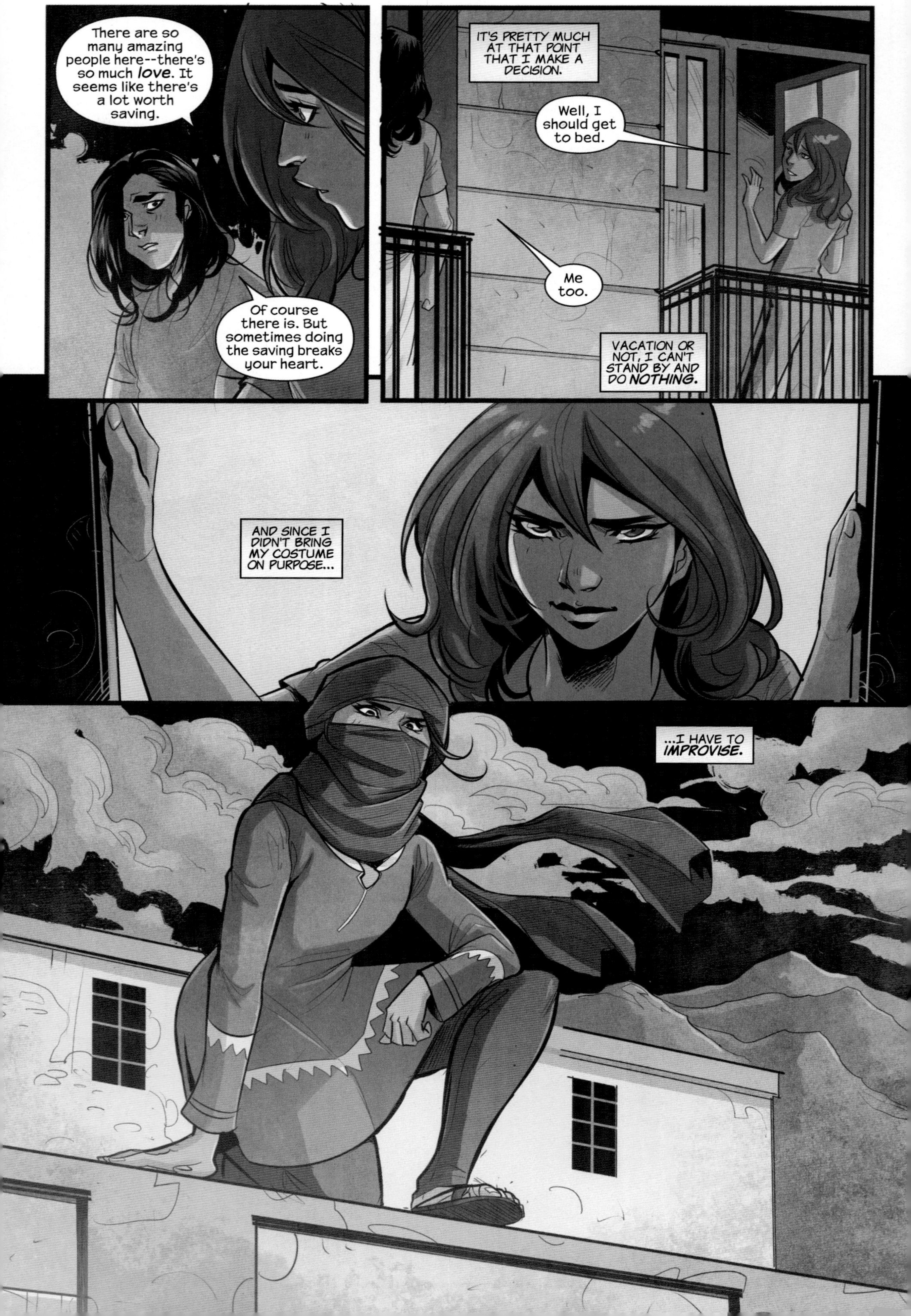
There are so many amazing people here--there's so much *love*. It seems like there's a lot worth saving.
Of course there is. But sometimes doing the saving breaks your heart.
IT'S PRETTY MUCH AT THAT POINT THAT I MAKE A DECISION.
Well, I should get to bed.
Me too.
VACATION OR NOT, I CAN'T STAND BY AND DO **NOTHING.**
AND SINCE I DIDN'T BRING MY COSTUME ON PURPOSE...
...I HAVE TO ***IMPROVISE.***

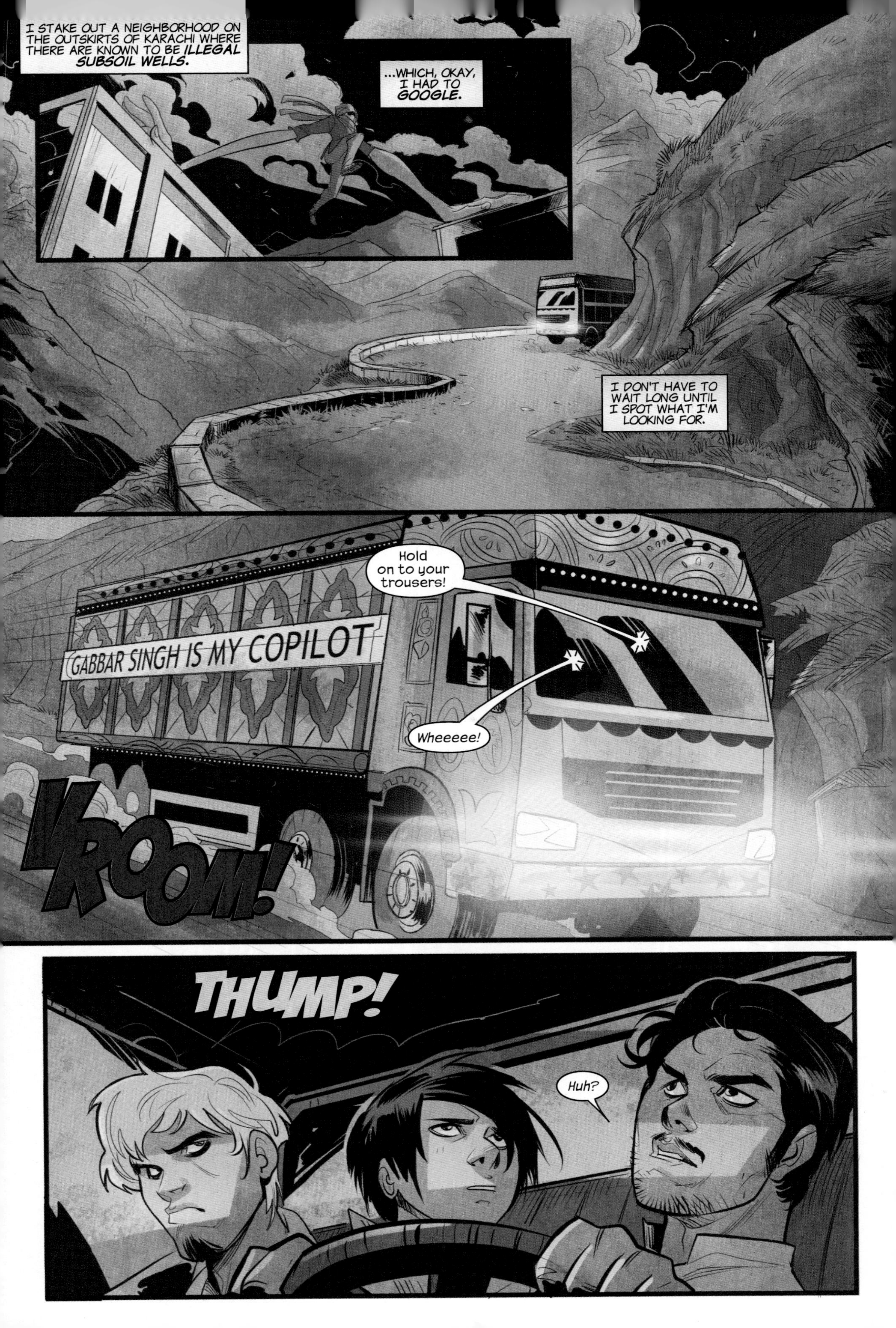
I STAKE OUT A NEIGHBORHOOD ON THE OUTSKIRTS OF KARACHI WHERE THERE ARE KNOWN TO BE ILLEGAL SUBSOIL WELLS.
...WHICH, OKAY, I HAD TO GOOGLE.
I DON'T HAVE TO WAIT LONG UNTIL I SPOT WHAT I'M LOOKING FOR.
GABBAR SINGH IS MY COPILOT
Hold on to your trousers!
Wheeeee!
VROOM!
THUMP!
Huh?

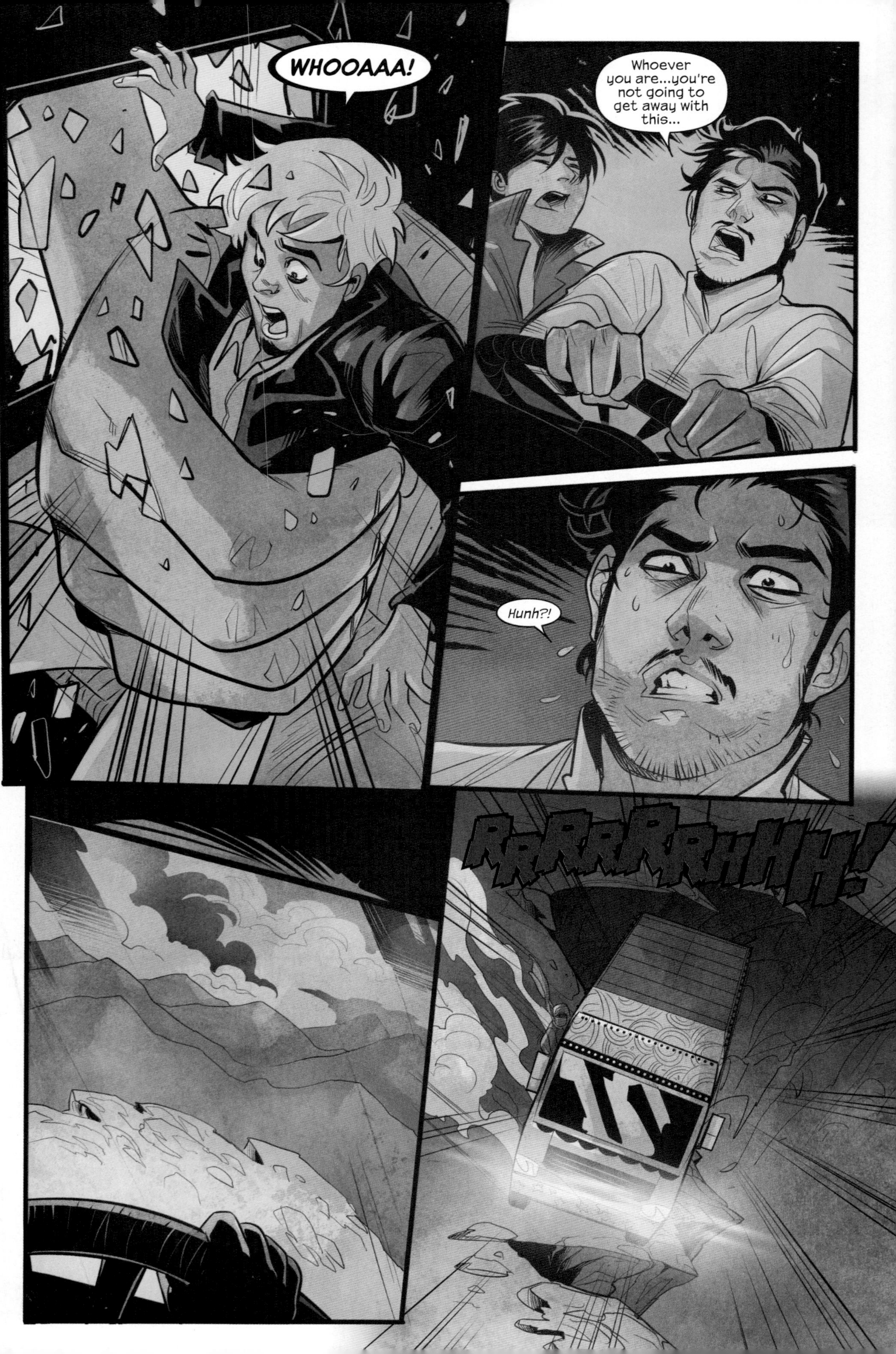
WHOOAAA!
Whoever you are...you're not going to get away with this...
Hunh?!
RRRRRRHHH!

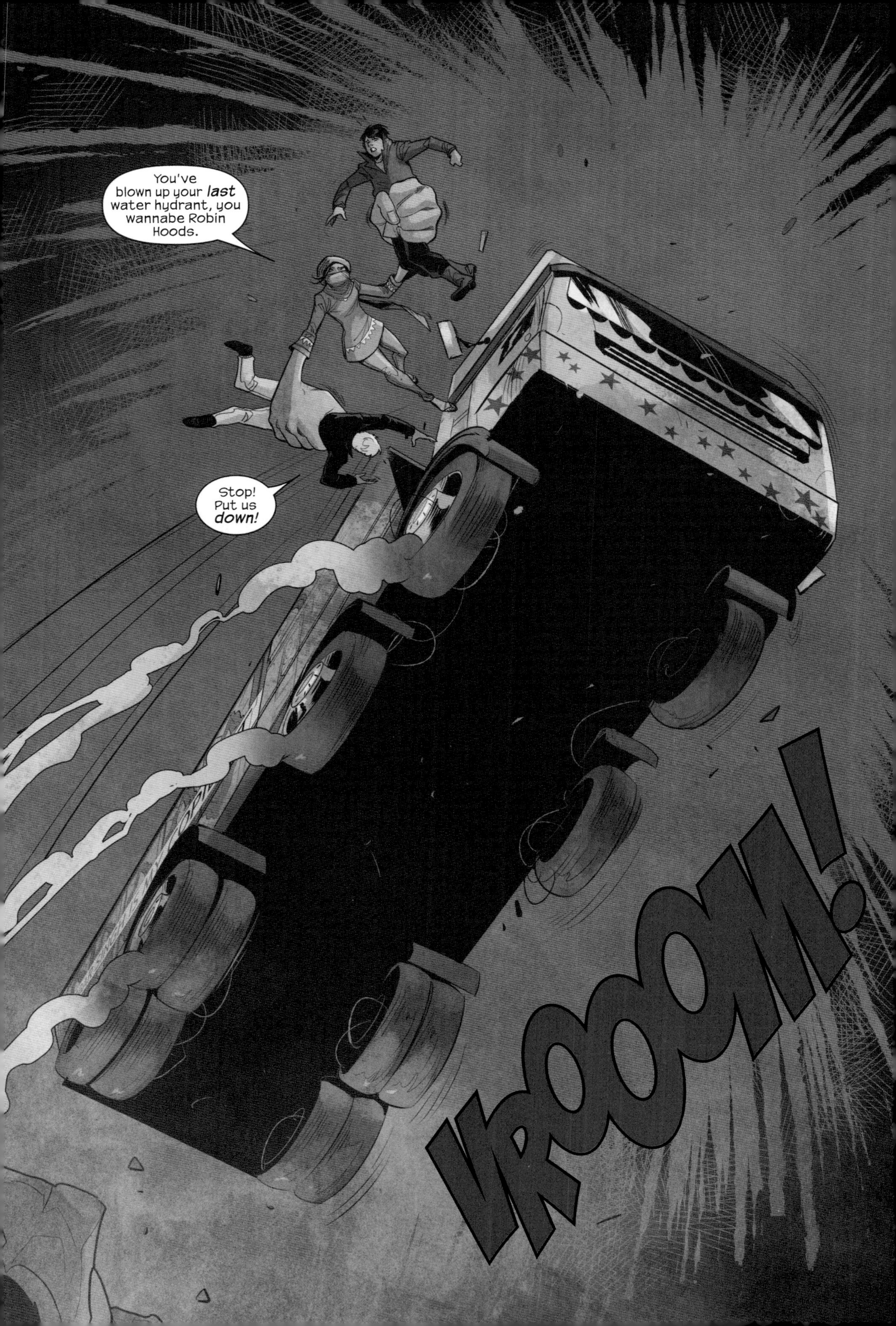
You've blown up your last water hydrant, you wannabe Robin Hoods.
Stop! Put us down!
VROOOM!

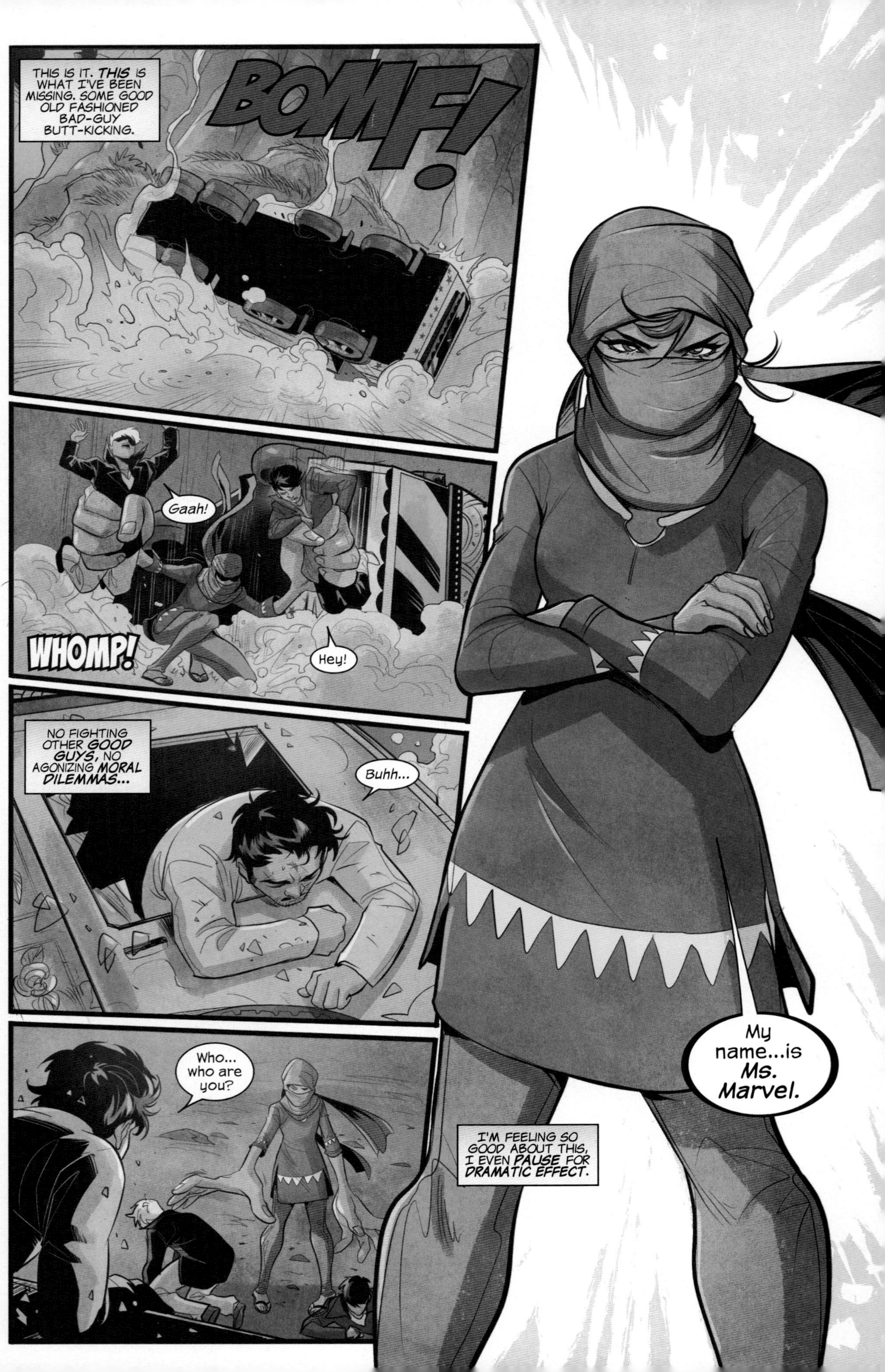
THIS IS IT. THIS IS WHAT I'VE BEEN MISSING. SOME GOOD OLD FASHIONED BAD-GUY BUTT-KICKING.
BOMF!
Gaah!
WHOMP!
Hey!
NO FIGHTING OTHER GOOD GUYS, NO AGONIZING MORAL DILEMMAS...
Buhh...
Who... who are you?
My name...is Ms. Marvel.
I'M FEELING SO GOOD ABOUT THIS, I EVEN PAUSE FOR DRAMATIC EFFECT.

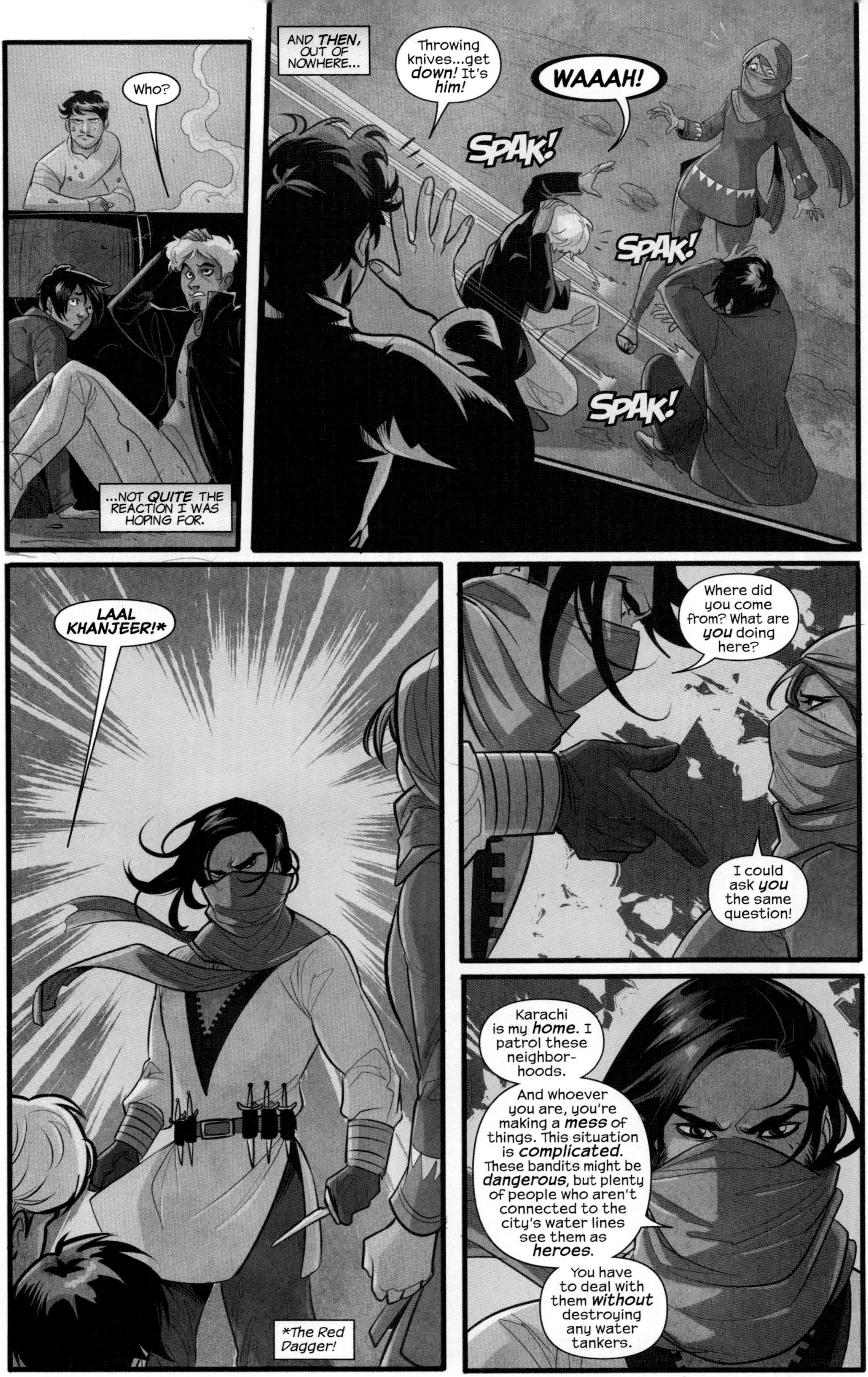
Who?
...NOT QUITE THE REACTION I WAS HOPING FOR.
AND THEN, OUT OF NOWHERE...
Throwing knives...get down! It's him!
WAAAH!
SPAK!
SPAK!
SPAK!
LAAL KHANJEER!*
*The Red Dagger!
Where did you come from? What are you doing here?
I could ask you the same question!
Karachi is my home. I patrol these neighbor-hoods.
And whoever you are, you're making a mess of things. This situation is complicated. These bandits might be dangerous, but plenty of people who aren't connected to the city's water lines see them as heroes.
You have to deal with them without destroying any water tankers.

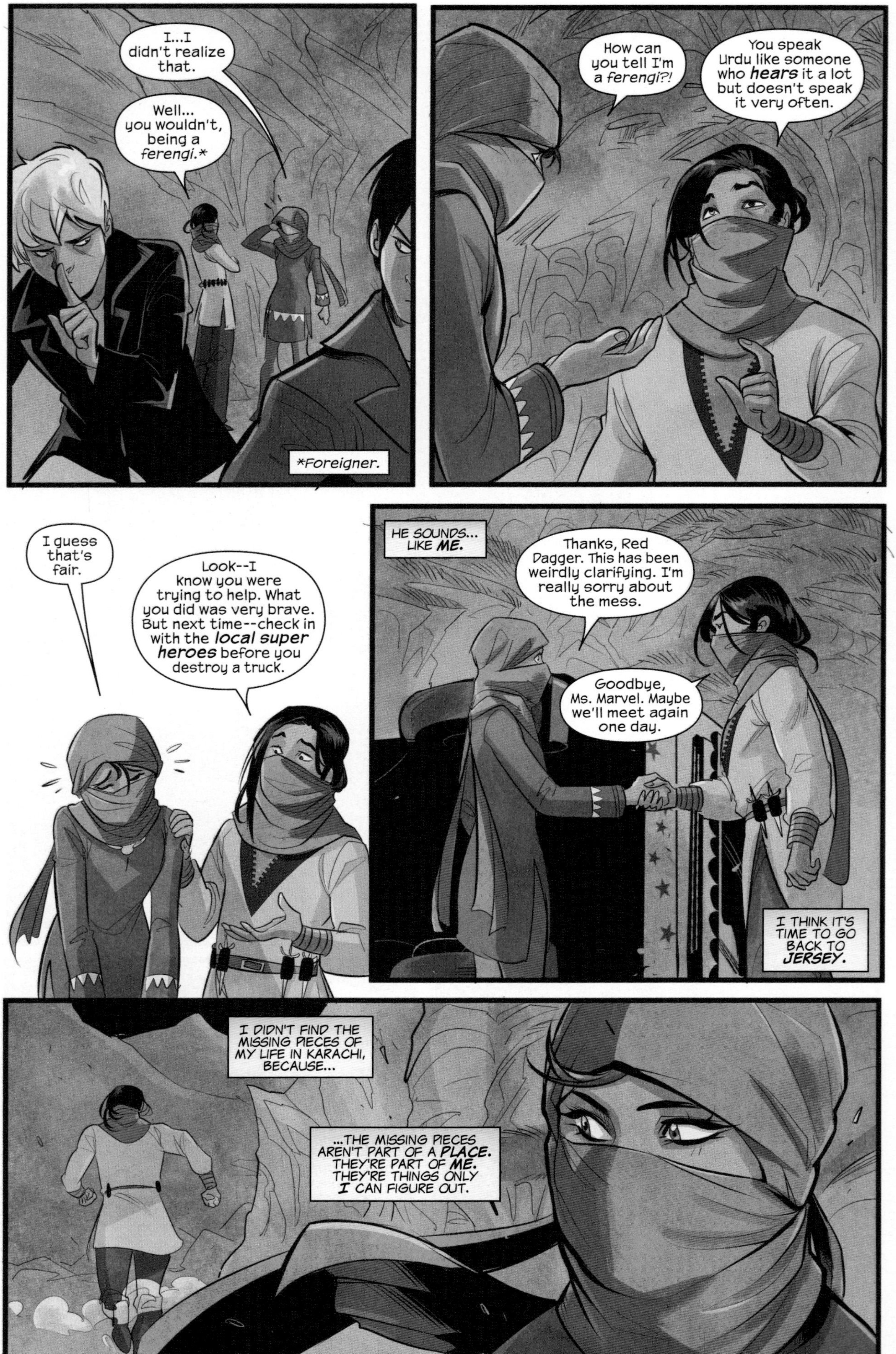

I...I didn't realize that.
Well... you wouldn't, being a *ferengi.**
*Foreigner.
How can you tell I'm a *ferengi*?!
You speak Urdu like someone who **hears** it a lot but doesn't speak it very often.
I guess that's fair.
Look--I know you were trying to help. What you did was very brave. But next time--check in with the ***local super heroes*** before you destroy a truck.
HE SOUNDS... LIKE ***ME.***
Thanks, Red Dagger. This has been weirdly clarifying. I'm really sorry about the mess.
Goodbye, Ms. Marvel. Maybe we'll meet again one day.
I THINK IT'S TIME TO GO BACK TO ***JERSEY.***
I DIDN'T FIND THE MISSING PIECES OF MY LIFE IN KARACHI, BECAUSE...
...THE MISSING PIECES AREN'T PART OF A ***PLACE.*** THEY'RE PART OF ***ME.*** THEY'RE THINGS ONLY ***I*** CAN FIGURE OUT.

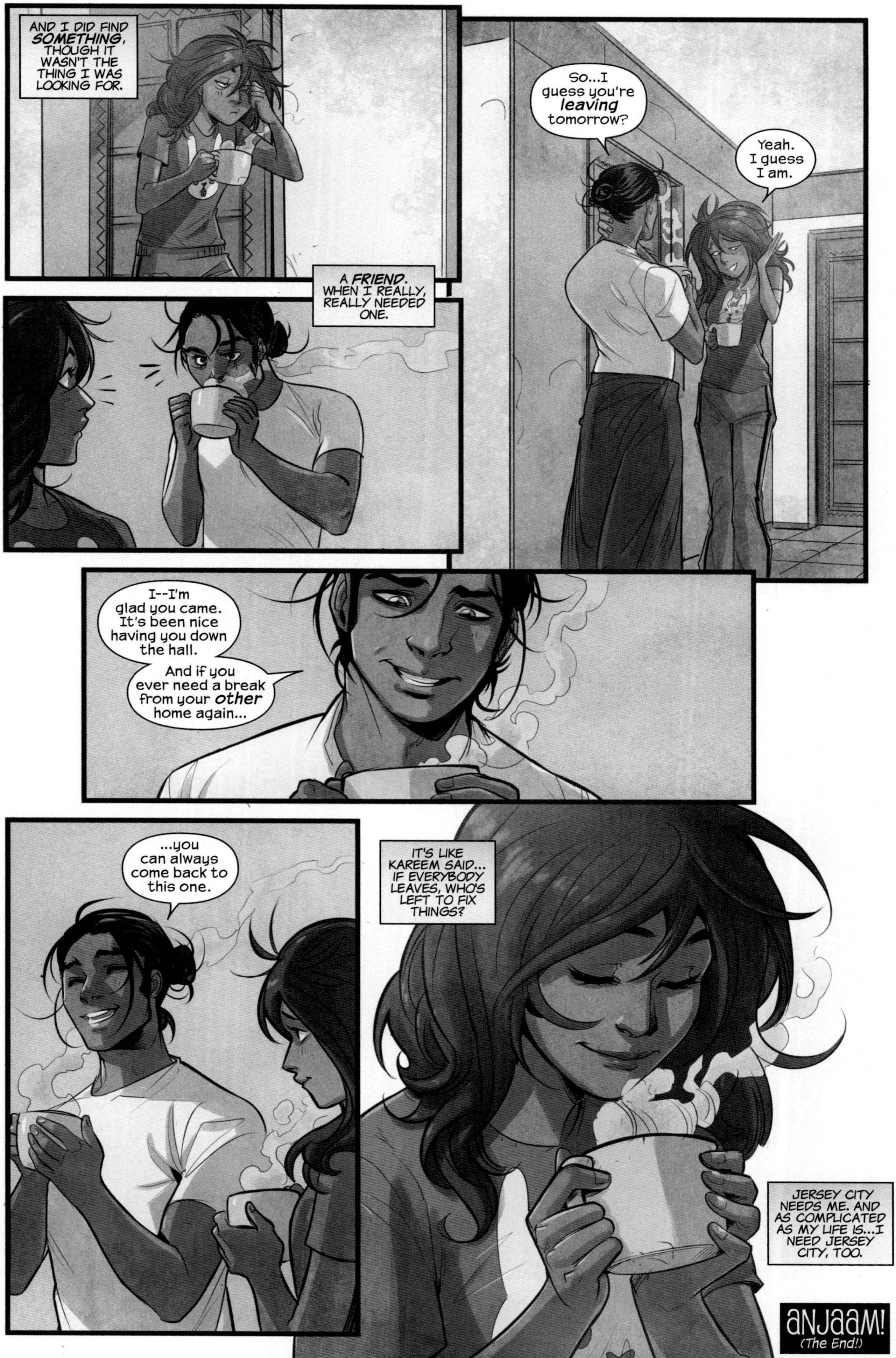
AND I DID FIND SOMETHING, THOUGH IT WASN'T THE THING I WAS LOOKING FOR.
A FRIEND. WHEN I REALLY, REALLY NEEDED ONE.
So...I guess you're leaving tomorrow?
Yeah. I guess I am.
I--I'm glad you came. It's been nice having you down the hall.
And if you ever need a break from your other home again...
...you can always come back to this one.
IT'S LIKE KAREEM SAID... IF EVERYBODY LEAVES, WHO'S LEFT TO FIX THINGS?
JERSEY CITY NEEDS ME. AND AS COMPLICATED AS MY LIFE IS...I NEED JERSEY CITY, TOO.
anjaam!
(The End!)

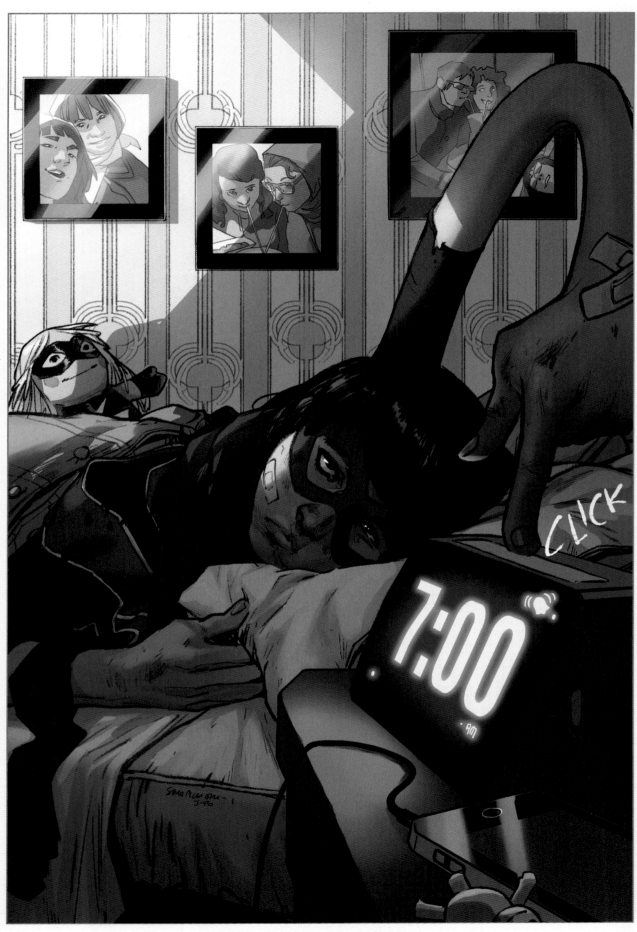

MS. MARVEL #1 VARIANT
BY SARA PICHELLI & JUSTIN PONSOR

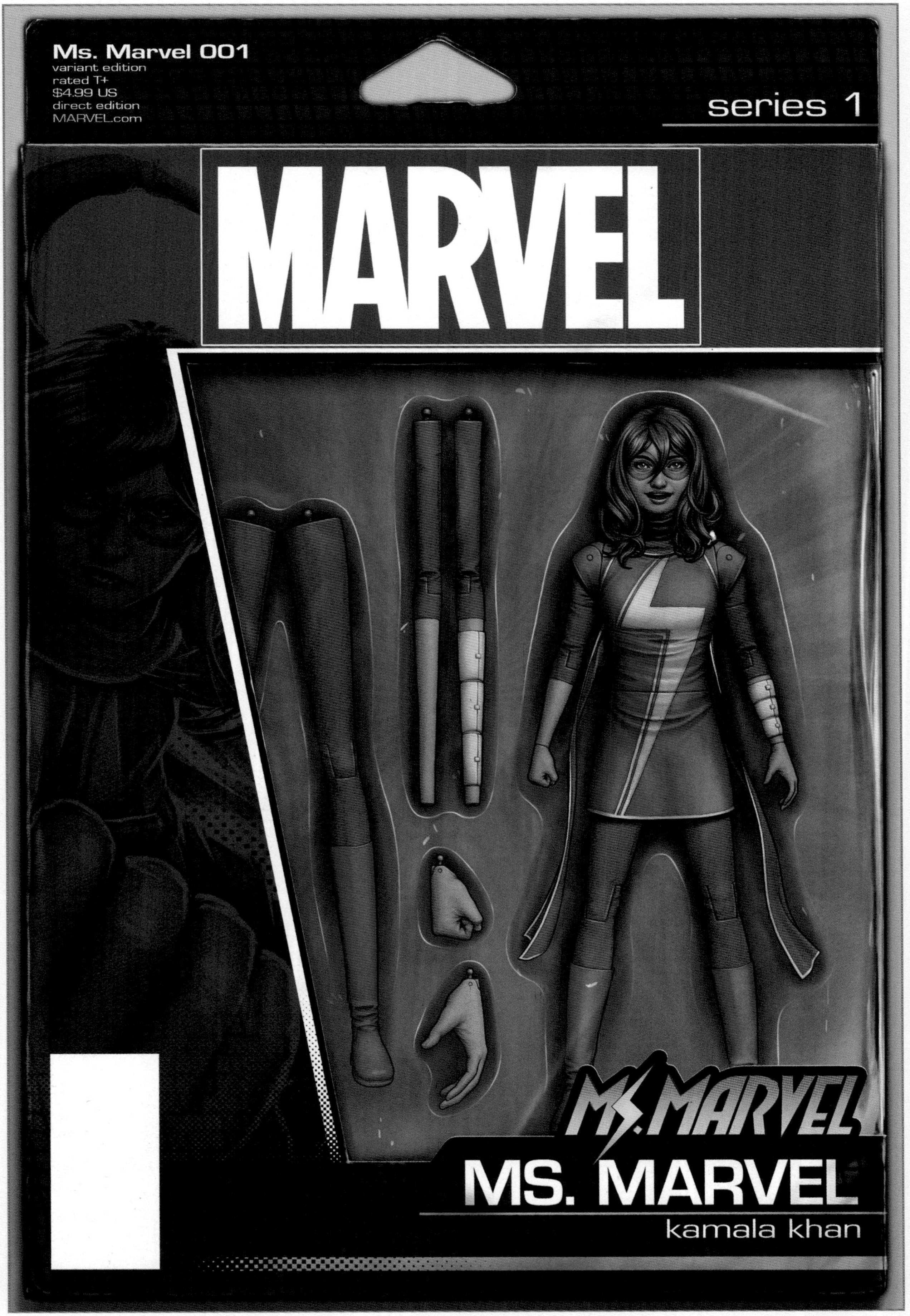
Ms. Marvel 001
variant edition
rated T+
$4.99 US
direct edition
MARVEL.com
series 1
MARVEL
MS. MARVEL
MS. MARVEL
kamala khan

MS. MARVEL #1 ACTION FIGURE VARIANT
BY JOHN TYLER CHRISTOPHER

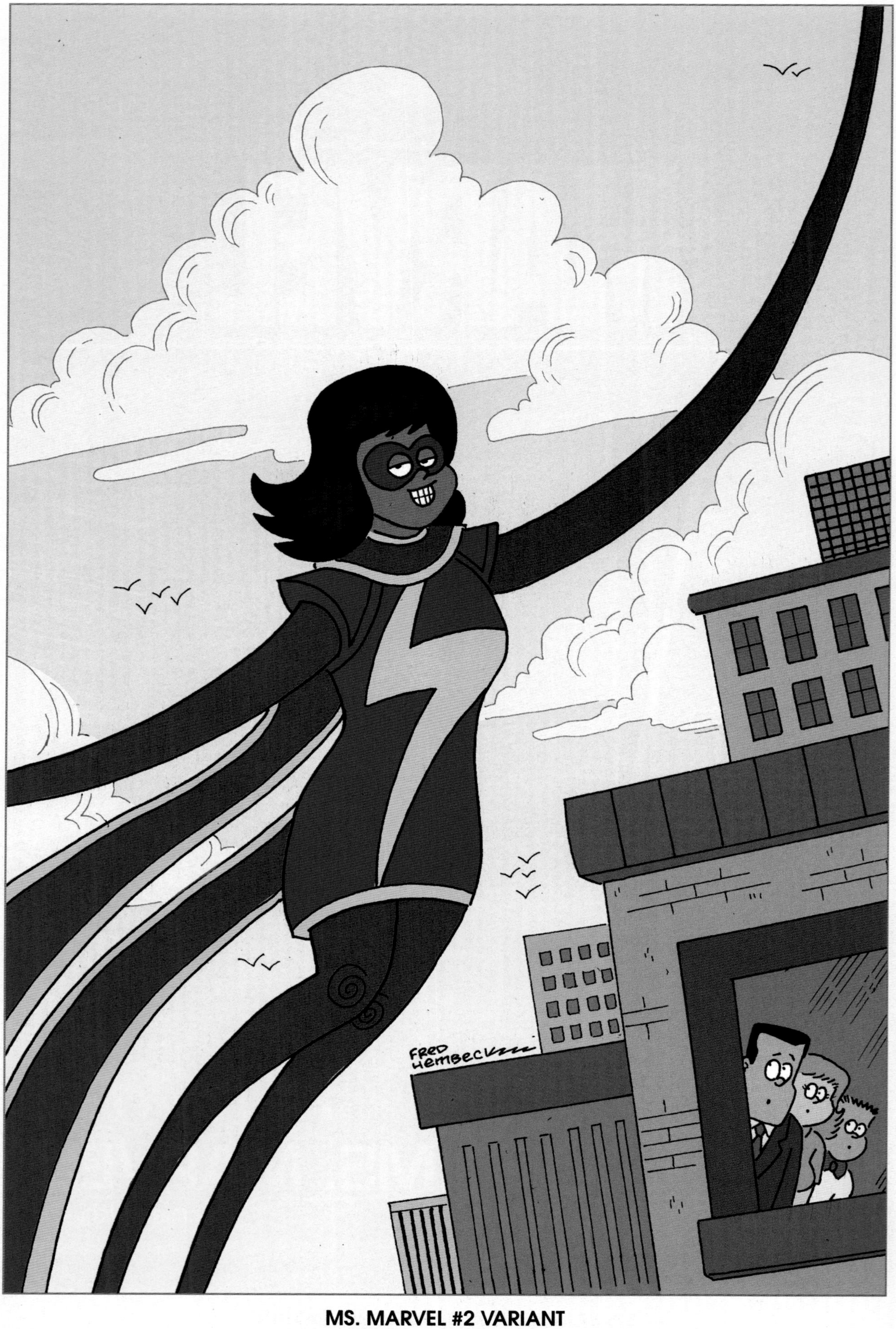
FRED HEMBECK

MS. MARVEL #2 VARIANT
BY FRED HEMBECK & RACHELLE ROSENBERG

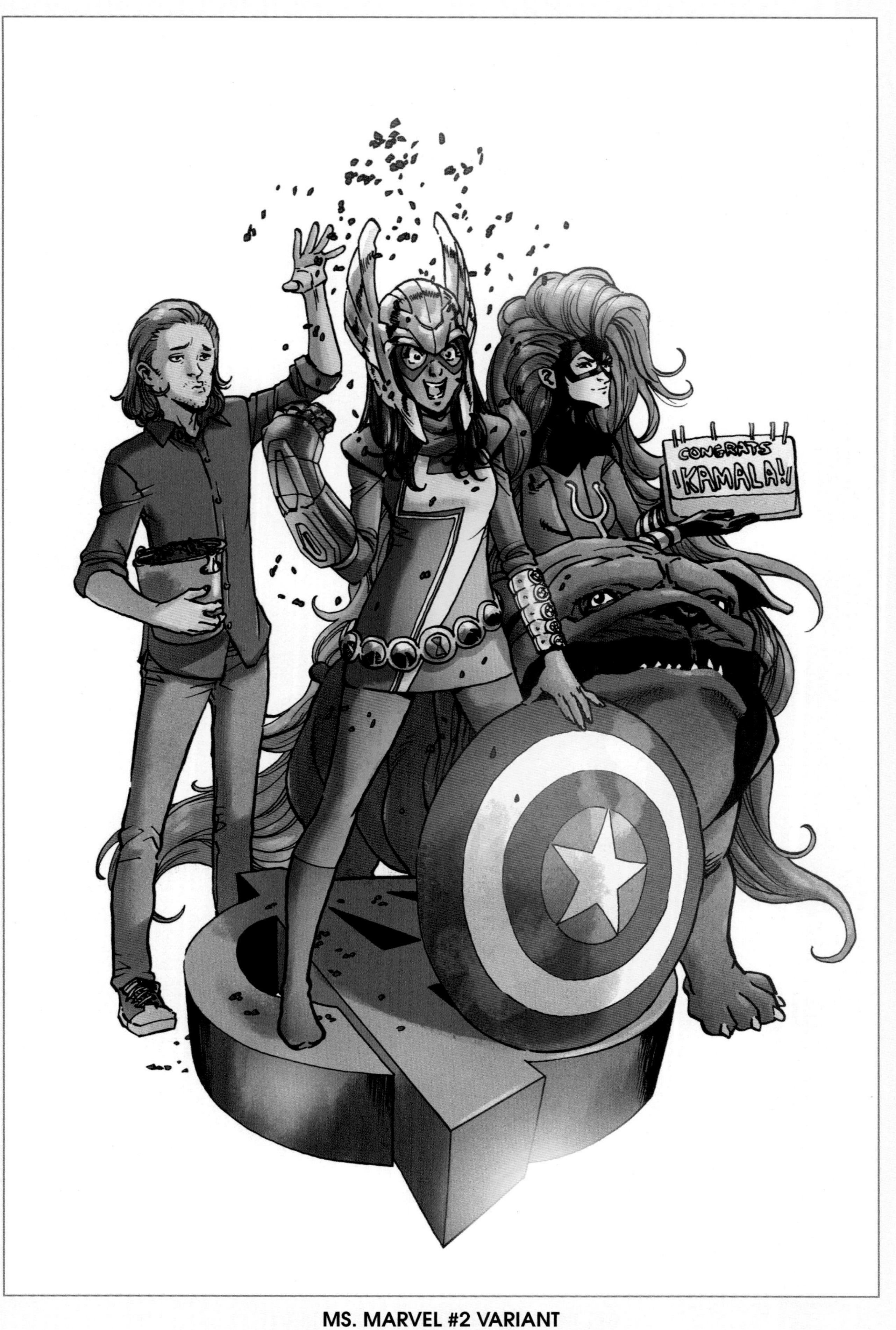
CONGRATS
¡KAMALA!¡

MS. MARVEL #2 VARIANT
BY TAKESHI MIYAZAWA & IAN HERRING

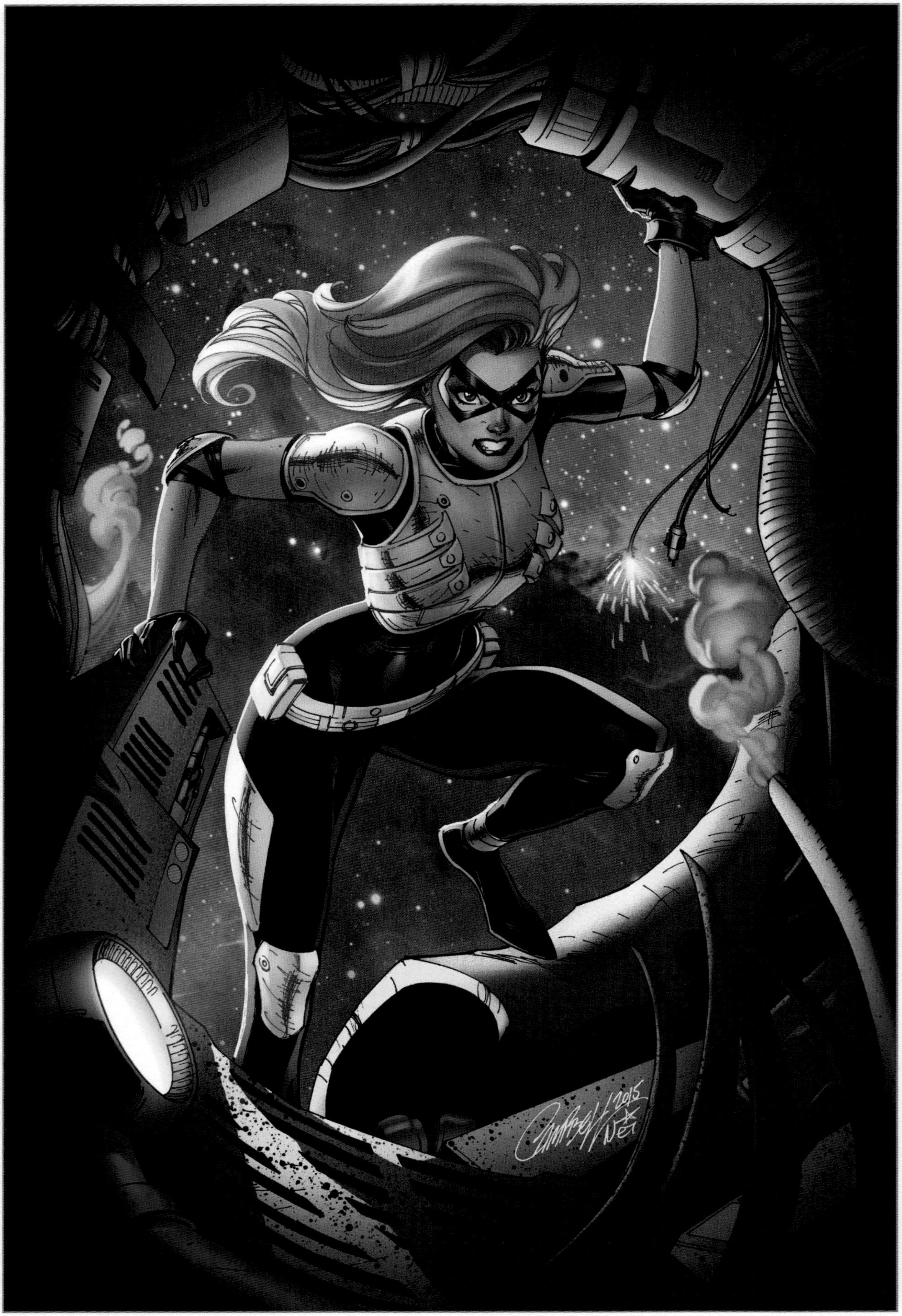

MS. MARVEL #2 MARVEL '92 VARIANT
BY J. SCOTT CAMPBELL & NEI RUFFINO

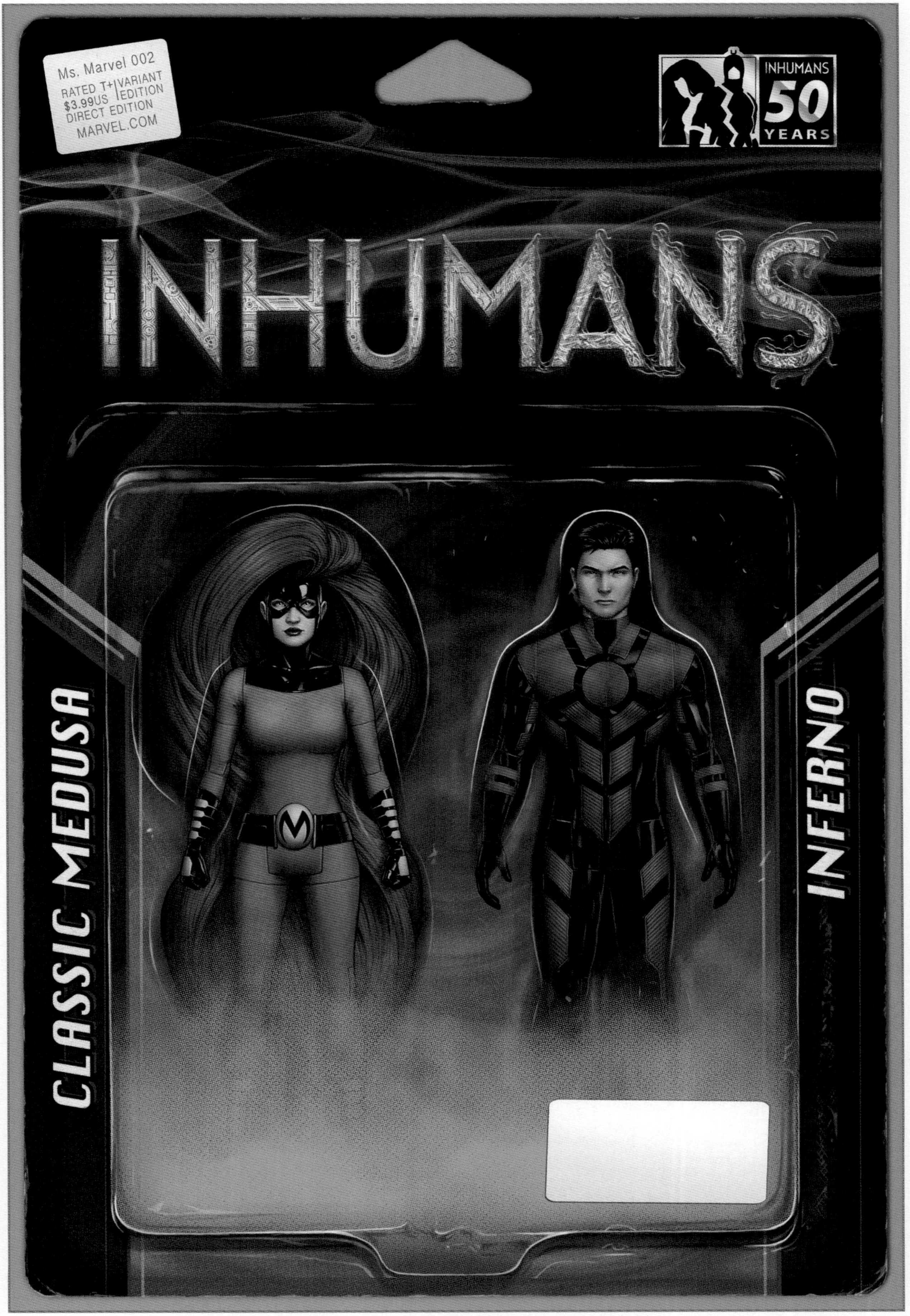
Ms. Marvel 002
RATED T+ VARIANT EDITION
$3.99US
DIRECT EDITION
MARVEL.COM
INHUMANS 50 YEARS
INHUMANS
CLASSIC MEDUSA
INFERNO

MS. MARVEL #2 ACTION FIGURE VARIANT
BY JOHN TYLER CHRISTOPHER

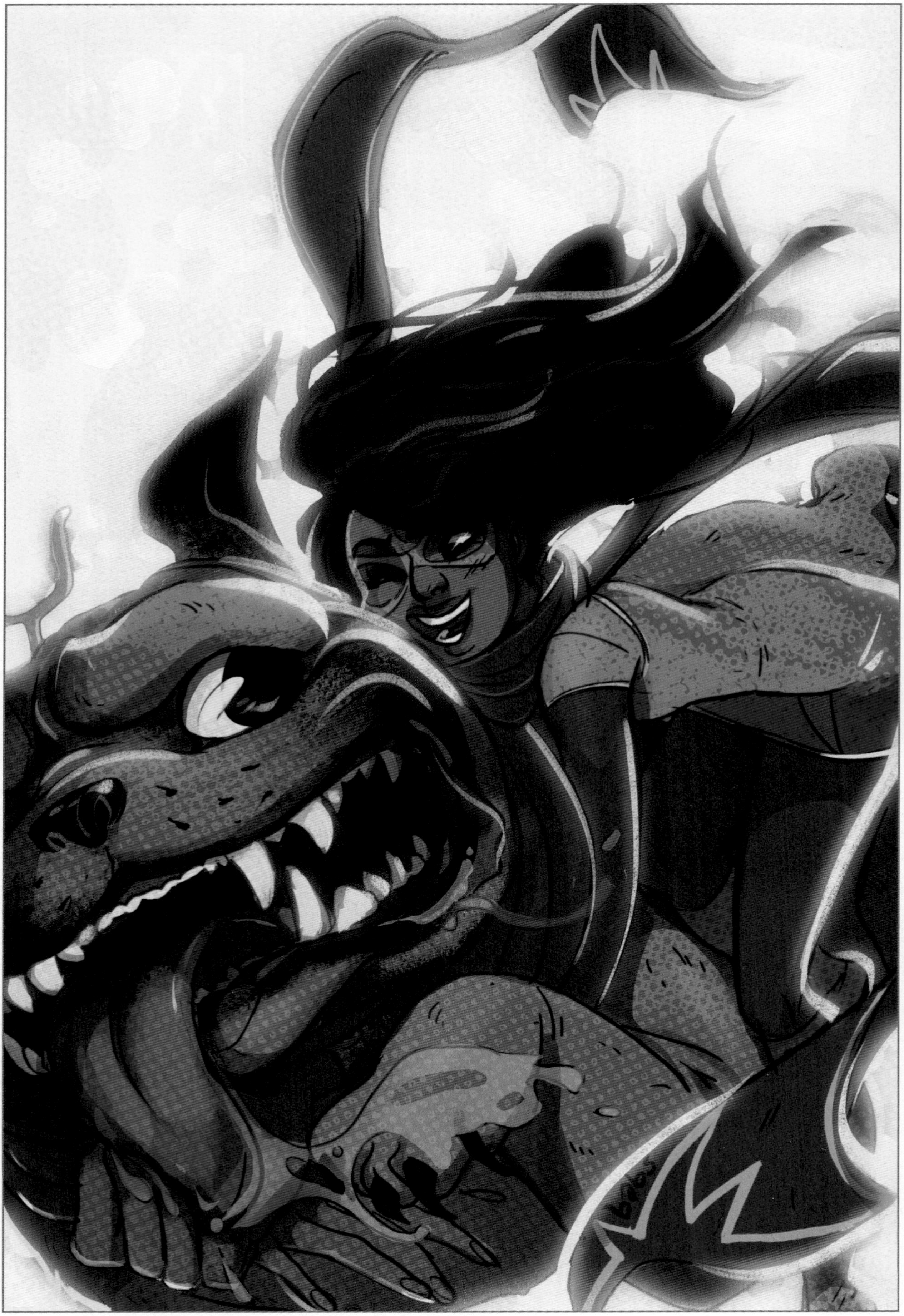

MS. MARVEL #3 VARIANT
BY BABS TARR

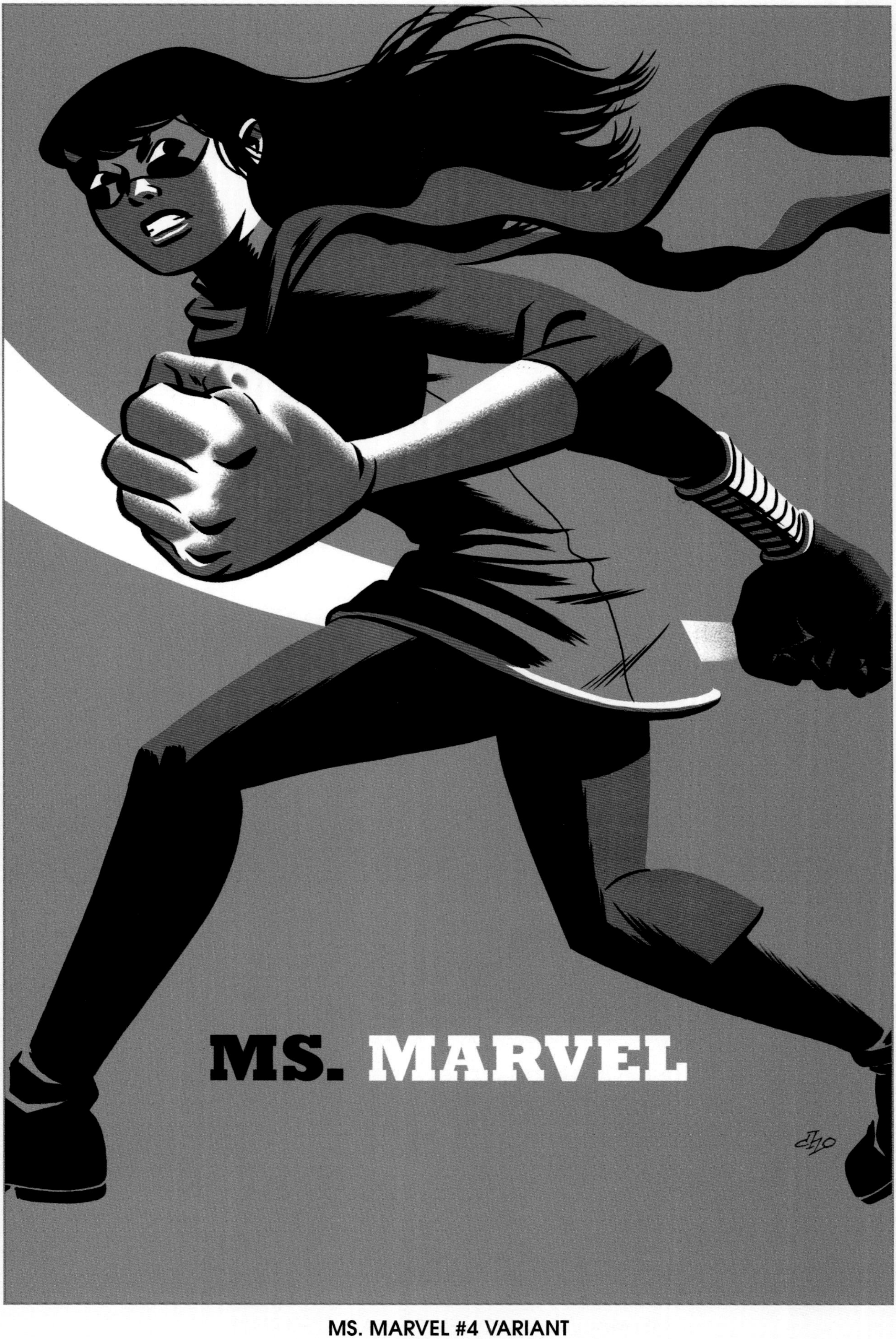
MS. MARVEL
CHO

MS. MARVEL #4 VARIANT
BY MICHAEL CHO

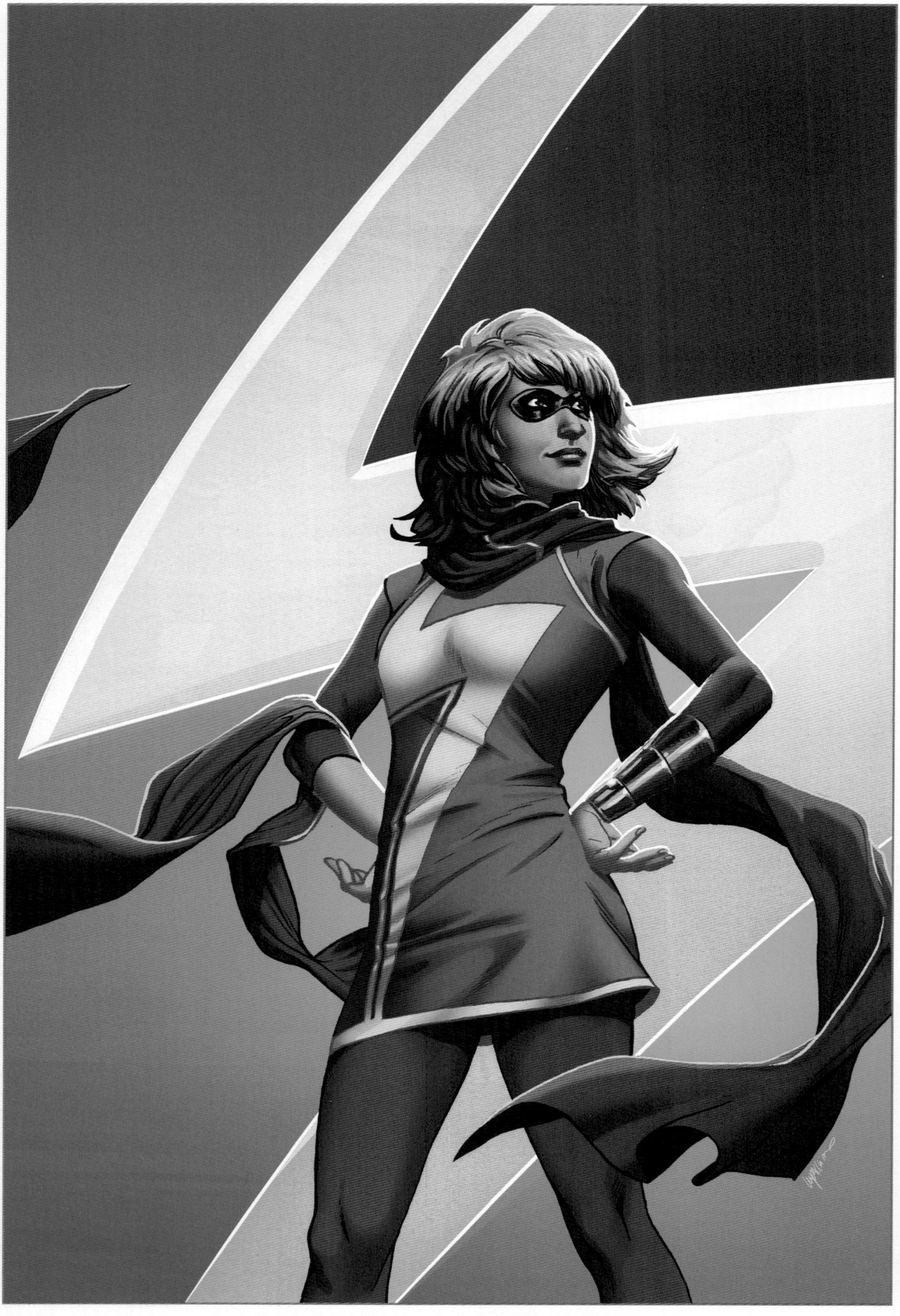

MS. MARVEL #5 WOMEN OF MARVEL VARIANT
BY EMA LUPACCHINO & GURU-eFX

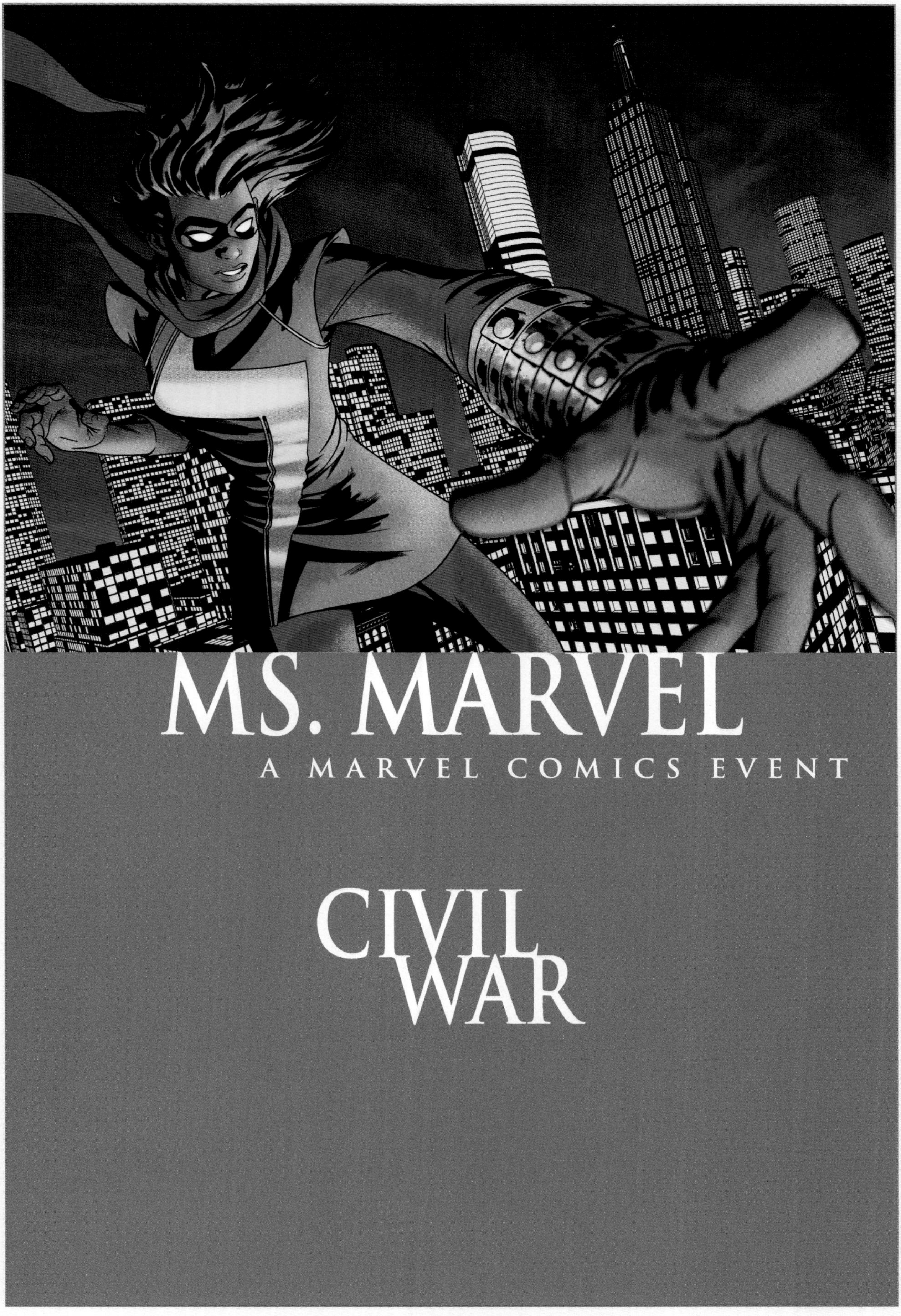
MS. MARVEL
A MARVEL COMICS EVENT
CIVIL WAR

MS. MARVEL #6 CIVIL WAR VARIANT
BY MIKE McKONE

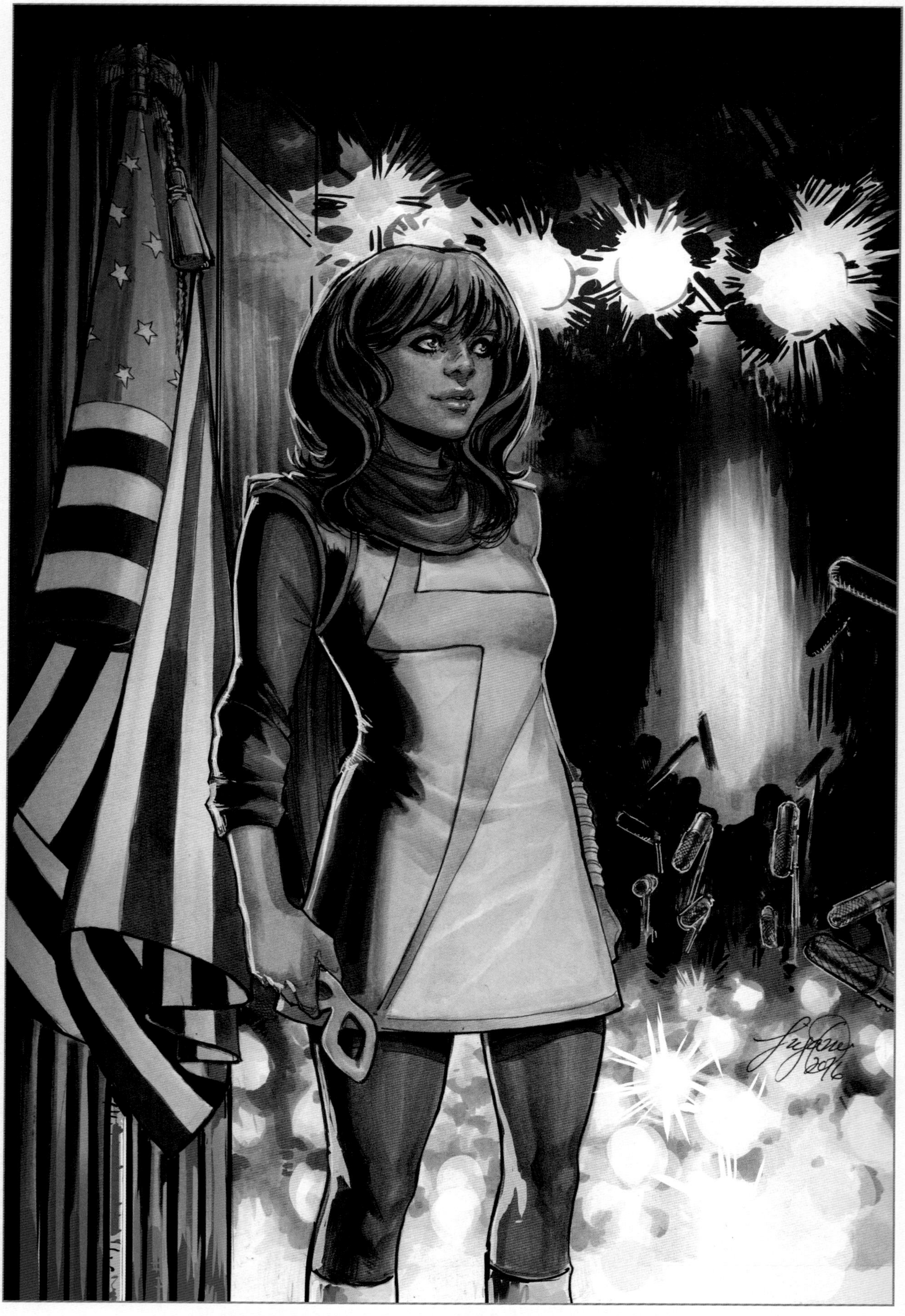

MS. MARVEL #8 CIVIL WAR REENACTMENT VARIANT
BY SIYA OUM

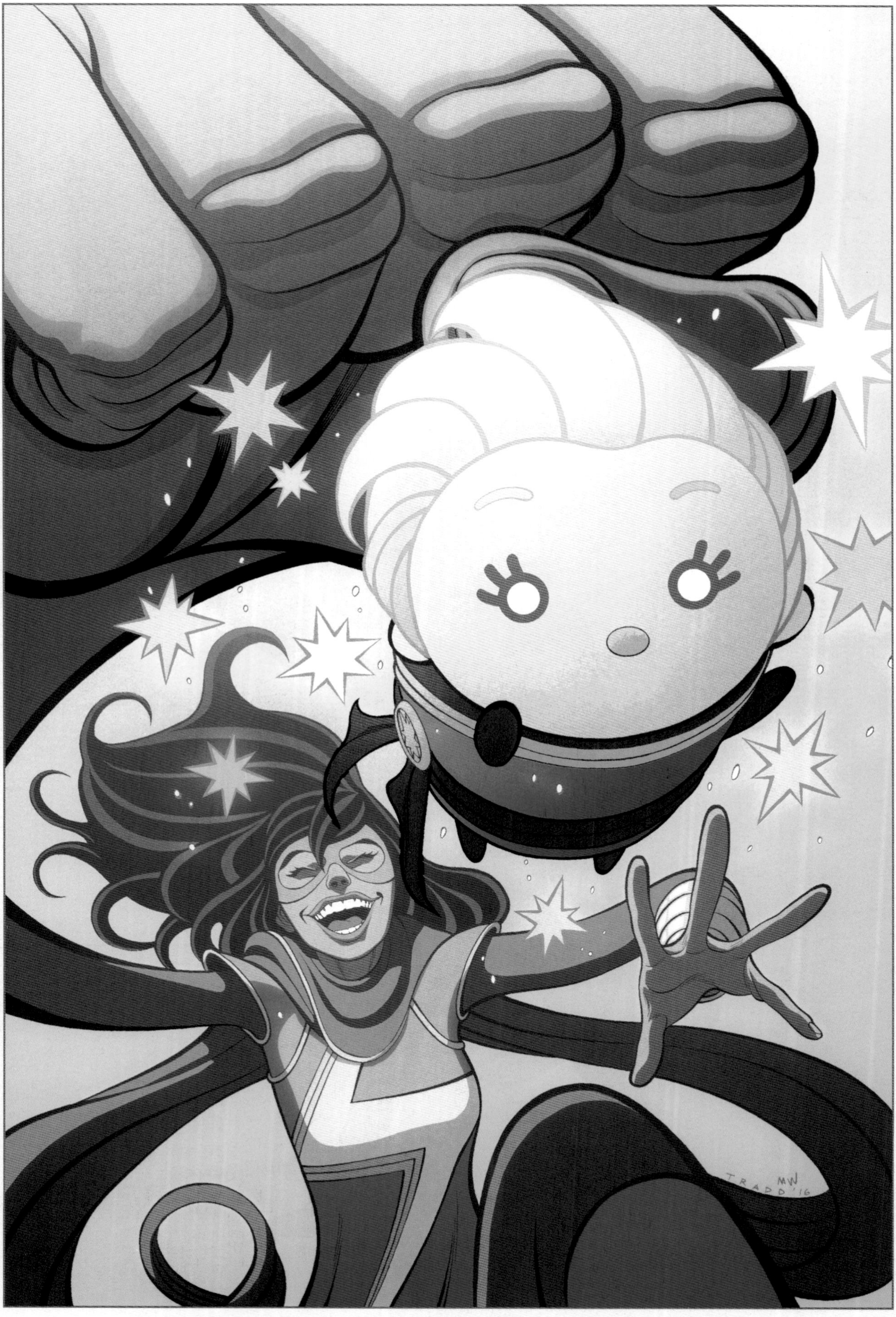
MW
TRADD '16

MS. MARVEL #10 MARVEL TSUM TSUM TAKEOVER VARIANT
BY TRADD MOORE & MATTHEW WILSON

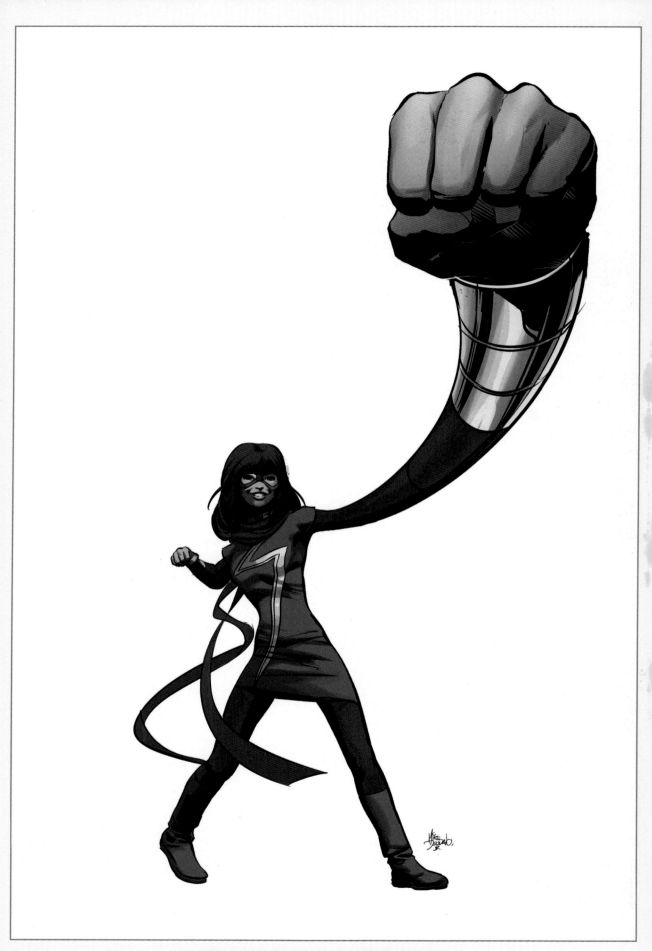

MS. MARVEL #12 TEASER VARIANT
BY MIKE DEODATO & FRANK MARTIN

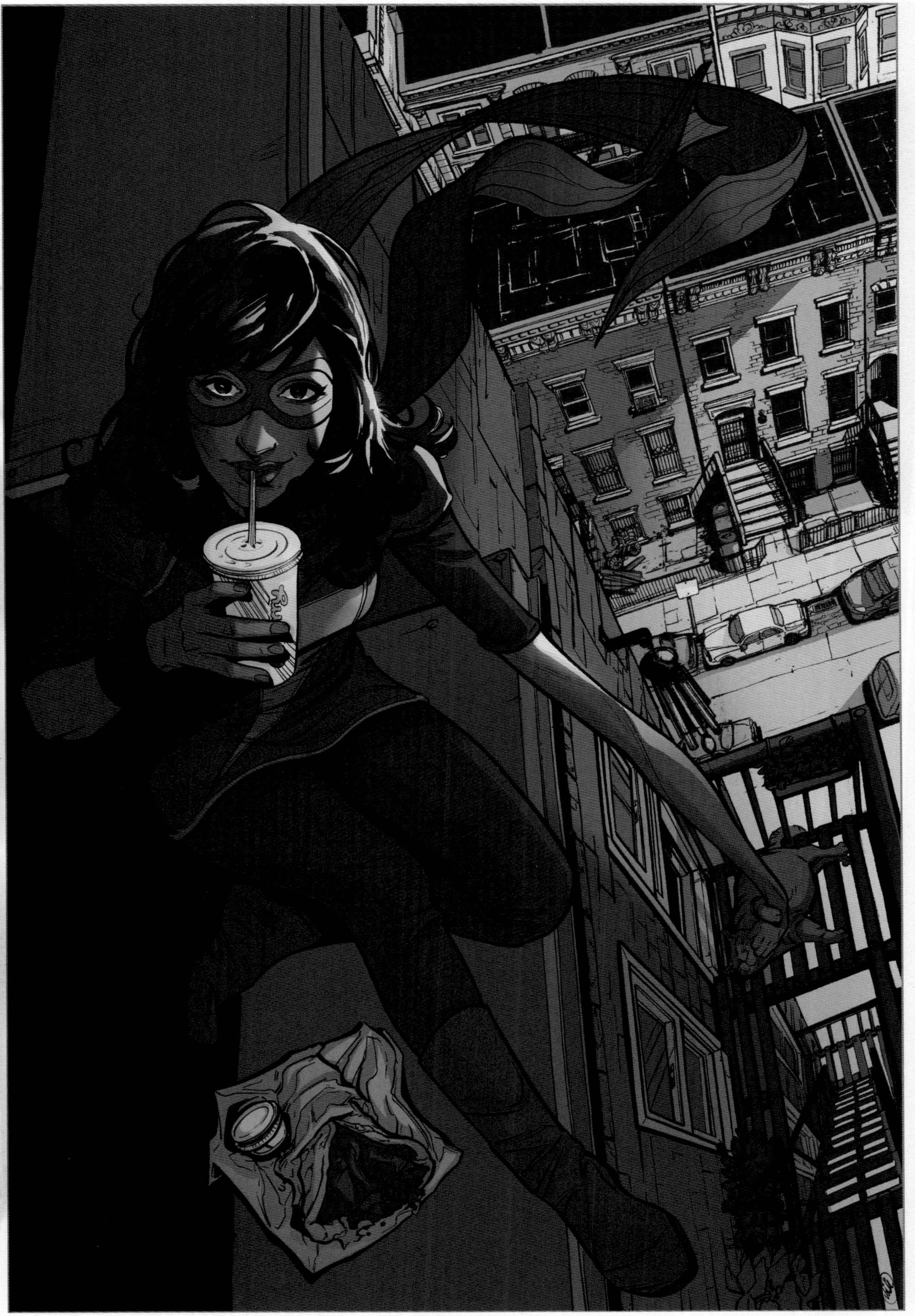

MS. MARVEL #12 VARIANT
BY JOËLLE JONES & RACHELLE ROSENBERG

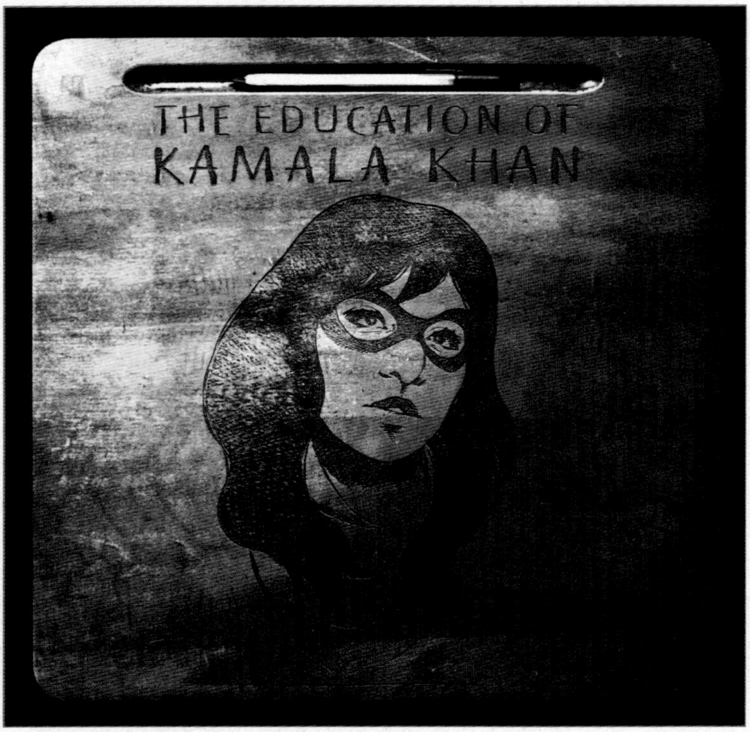
THE EDUCATION OF
KAMALA KHAN

MS. MARVEL #1 HIP-HOP VARIANT
BY JENNY FRISON

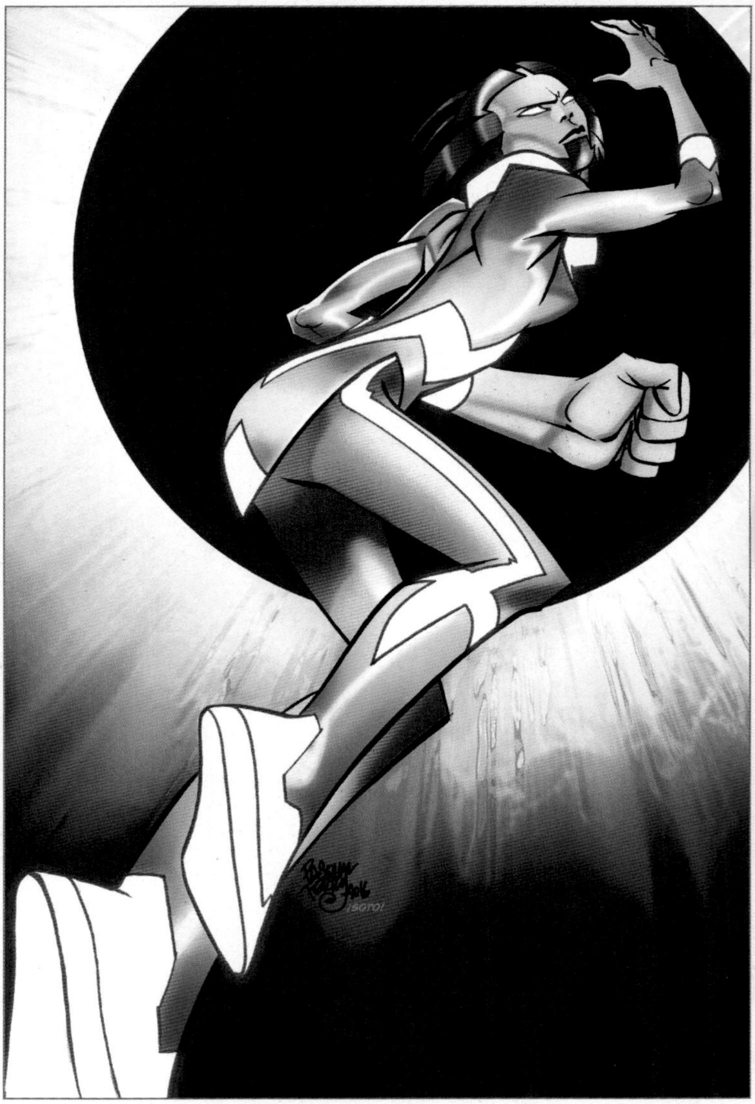

MS. MARVEL #7
AGE OF APOCALYPSE VARIANT
BY PASQUAL FERRY
& CHRIS SOTOMAYOR